ENCYCLOPEDIA OF
SOCIETY AND CULTURE

IN THE
ANCIENT
WORLD

■ VOLUME IV ■

(sacred sites to writing)

PETER BOGUCKI, Editor in Chief

☑®Facts On File
An imprint of Infobase Publishing

Encyclopedia of Society and Culture in the Ancient World

Facts On File, Inc.
An imprint of Infobase Publishing
132 West 31st Street
New York NY 10001

Library of Congress Cataloging-in-Publication Data
Encyclopedia of society and culture in the ancient world / Peter Bogucki, editor in chief
p. cm.
Includes bibliographical references and index.
ISBN 978-0-8160-6941-5 (acid-free paper)
1. Civilization, Ancient—Encyclopedias. I. Bogucki, Peter I.
CB311.E533 2007
930.103—dc22   2007000533

Facts On File books are available at special discounts when purchased in bulk quantities for businesses, associations, institutions, or sales promotions. Please call our Special Sales Department in New York at (212) 967-8800 or (800) 322-8755.

You can find Facts On File on the World Wide Web at http://www.factsonfile.com

Text design by James Scotto-Lavino
Cover design by Takeshi Takahashi

Printed in the United States of America

VB Hermitage 10 9 8 7 6 5 4 3 2 1

This book is printed on acid-free paper.

Contents

Advisers and Contributors

EDITOR IN CHIEF
Peter Bogucki
Associate Dean for Undergraduate Affairs,
School of Engineering and Applied Science
Princeton University

ADVISORY BOARD
Lisa R. Brody
Assistant Professor of Art
Queens College, City University of New York

R. Hunt Davis
Professor Emeritus of History and African Studies
University of Florida

Leo Depuydt
Associate Professor of Egyptology
Brown University

Paul R. Goldin
Associate Professor of East Asian Languages
and Civilizations
University of Pennsylvania

Eloise Quiñones Keber
Professor of Art History
Baruch College, City University of New York

Amelie Kuhrt
Professor of Ancient Near Eastern History
University College, London

Daniel Potts
Edwin Cuthbert Hall Professor of
Middle Eastern Archaeology
University of Sydney

CONTRIBUTORS
Saheed Aderinto is a Ph.D. student at the Department of History, University of Texas at Austin. Some of his most recent publications include "Prostitution and Urban Social Relations" and "Policing Urban Prostitution: Prostitutes, Crime, Law and Reformers in Colonial Nigeria" in *Nigeria's Urban History: Past and Present* (2006) and "Discrimination in an Urban Setting: The Experience of Ijebu Settlers in Colonial Ibadan, 1893–1960" in *Inter-group Relations in Nigeria during the 19th & 20th Centuries* (2006). His writings have also appeared in *IFRA Special Research Issue, Ethnic and Third World Review of Books, African and Asian Studies Journal*, and *The Encyclopedia of Prostitution and Sex Work* (2006).

Olutayo Charles Adesina, Ph.D., teaches at the Department of History, University of Ibadan, Nigeria. He is the author of "The Underground Foreign Exchange Market in Ibadan during Devaluation" in *Money Struggles and City Life: Devaluation in Ibadan and Other Urban Centres in Southern Nigeria, 1986–96* (2002) and "Teaching History in Twentieth Century Nigeria: The Challenges of Change" in *History in Africa: A Journal of Method*, vol. 33 (2006).

David Otieno Akombo, Ph.D., teaches music education and world music at Wabash College of Indiana. He is the author of *Music and Healing across Cultures* (2006).

Francis Allard, Ph.D., teaches in the Department of Anthropology at Indiana University of Pennsylvania. His research interests include the archaeology of early China and Mongolia. He has contributed articles to *Archaeology of Asia* (2005) and *Beyond the Steppe and the Sown: Proceedings of the 2002 University of Chicago Conference on Eurasian Archaeology* (2006).

Miguel Arisa is finishing his doctoral studies in art history at the Graduate Center, City University of New York. He teaches at Technical Career Institutes and is a regular lecturer at the

Cloisters and a docent at the Metropolitan Museum of Art, New York.

Mariam F. Ayad, Ph.D., teaches graduate-level classes on Egyptian language and literature at the University of Memphis, where she is the assistant director of its Institute of Egyptian Art and Archaeology. Her main research interests focus on the role of women in ancient Egyptian temple ritual and the selection and transmission of funerary texts in post–New Kingdom Egypt. Her book on the God's Wife of Amun is under contract with Routledge.

Heather D. Baker, D.Phil., is a researcher at the University of Vienna, Austria, specializing in Babylonian history, society, and culture. She has published widely on Babylonian and Assyrian history and is writing a book to be titled *The Urban Landscape of First Millennium BC Babylonia*.

Robin Barrow, Ph.D., FRSC, is professor of philosophy of education at Simon Fraser University, Canada. His most recent books include *Plato* (2007) and *An Introduction to Moral Philosophy and Moral Education* (2007). He is the author of *Athenian Democracy* (2001) and *Greek and Roman Education* (1996).

László Bartosiewicz, Ph.D., D.sc., teaches archaeozoology at the Loránd Eötvös University in Budapest (Hungary) and the University of Edinburgh (United Kingdom). He is the author of *Animals in the Urban Landscape in the Wake of the Middle Ages* (1995) and principal author of *Draught Cattle: Their Osteological Identification and History* (1997) and has published more than 200 scholarly articles.

Kirk H. Beetz, Ph.D., emeritus, has published over two dozen books and more than 900 articles. His books span topics from endangered mammal species to children's literature, including *Exploring C. S. Lewis' "The Chronicles of Narnia"* (2000). His recent writings have focused on the history and culture of ancient Japan.

Craig G. R. Benjamin, Ph.D., teaches world and ancient Eurasian history at Grand Valley State University. He is the coeditor of vols. 2 (1998), 4 (2000), and 6 (2002) in the Brepols Silk Roads Studies series and the author of *The Yuezhi: Origin, Migration and the Conquest of Northern Bactria* (2007).

Uffe Bergeton, Ph.D., is in the Ph.D. program in the Department of Asian Languages and Cultures at the University of Michigan. He is the author of *The Independence of Binding and Intensification* (Ph.D. dissertation, University of Southern California) and various articles on theoretical phonology and syntax.

Amy Hackney Blackwell has degrees in history from Duke University and Vanderbilt University and a J.D. from the University of Virginia. Her books include *Mythology for Dummies* (2002), *LSAT for Dummies* (2004), *The Everything Irish History and Heritage Book* (2004), and *Essential Dictionary of Law* (2004). She has contributed to the *Encyclopedia of World Nations and Cultures* (2006), *Alternative Energy* (2006), and *Chemical Compounds* (2006).

Christopher Blackwell, Ph.D., teaches classics at Furman University. He is the author of *In the Absence of Alexander: Harpalus and the Failure of Macedonian Hegemony* (1999) and various protocols and software applications for building digital libraries, and he serves as technical editor for the Center for Hellenic Studies of Harvard University.

Amy Bogaard, Ph.D., teaches prehistory and archaeobotany at the Department of Archaeology, University of Nottingham, United Kingdom. She is the author of *Neolithic Farming in Central Europe* (2004).

Peter Bogucki, Ph.D., is an archaeologist who is associate dean for undergraduate affairs of the School of Engineering and Applied Science at Princeton University. He has studied prehistoric settlements in Poland and has a particular interest in the spread of farming in Europe. He is the author of *The Origins of Human Society* (1999) and the editor (with Pam J. Crabtree) of *Ancient Europe 8000 B.C.–A.D. 1000: An Encyclopedia of the Barbarian World* (2004).

Larissa Bonfante, Ph.D., professor of classics at New York University, is the author of several books on Etruscan and early Roman culture as well as publications on ancient dress and nudity, including *The World of Roman Costume*, coedited with Judith Sebesta (1994).

Charlotte Booth is a Ph.D. student at the University of Wales, Swansea, and teaches Egyptology for Birkbeck College and other institutions in the United Kingdom. She is the author of *People of Ancient Egypt* (2007), *The Hyksos Period in Egypt* (2005), and *The Role of Foreigners in Ancient Egypt* (2005).

Lisa R. Brody, Ph.D., teaches Greek and Roman art history at Queens College, City University of New York. Her research interests include Greek iconography and cult, ancient lamps and their decoration, children in antiquity, and representation of ethnicity in Greco-Roman art. She compiled the revised edition of David Sacks's *Encyclopedia of the Ancient Greek World* (2005) and is author of *Aphrodisias III: The Aphrodite of Aphrodisias* (2007).

David Brown, Ph.D., is researching the interactions of the pre-Islamic astral sciences of Mesopotamia, Greece, India, Egypt, Iran, the western Semitic world, and China at the Free University of Berlin. He is the author of *Mesopotamian Planetary Astronomy-Astrology* (2000) and *The Interactions of Ancient Astral Science* (forthcoming).

Deborah N. Carlson, Ph.D., teaches in the Nautical Archaeology Program of the Department of Anthropology at Texas A&M University. She also directs the Institute of Nautical Archaeology's shipwreck excavation of a Roman marble carrier off the Aegean coast of Turkey at Kizilburun and is preparing the final publication of the Classical Greek ship excavated by the Institute of Nautical Archaeology at nearby Tektas Burnu.

Jeffrey S. Carnes is associate professor of classics at Syracuse University. He is the author of *The Uses of Aiakos: Pindar and the Aiginetan Imaginary* (forthcoming) as well as articles on Greek lyric poetry, gender studies, literary theory, and Plato.

Julia Marta Clapp is pursuing her doctorate in art history at the Graduate Center, City University of New York. Her research interests include modern and pre-Columbian Latin American art.

Wendy E. Closterman, Ph.D., teaches ancient history and Greek at Bryn Athyn College. Her research focuses on Athenian burial and funerary ritual. She is the author of "Family Members and Citizens: Athenian Identity and the Peribolos Tomb Setting" in *Antigone's Answer: Essays on Death and Burial, Family and State in Classical Athens*, edited by C. Patterson (forthcoming).

Leah A. J. Cohen is an independent writer and editorial consultant with a master's degree in geography from the University of Florida. She specializes in Africa area studies and food security. She was a senior author for the *Encyclopedia of African History and Culture*, volumes 4 and 5 (2005).

John Collis is professor emeritus in the Department of Archaeology, University of Sheffield, where he taught for over 30 years. He has had a major role in the development of university and professional training in archaeology in Britain, and is secretary of the European Association of Archaeologists' Committee on Training and Education. He is author of several books and excavation monographs, including *Digging Up the Past* (2004) and *The Celts: Origins, Myths and Inventions* (2004).

Constance A. Cook, Ph.D., directs the Asian Studies program and teaches Chinese language and literature courses at Lehigh University. She is the author of *Death in Ancient China: The Tale of One Man's Journey* (2006) and coeditor of *Defining Chu: Image and Reality in Ancient China* (1999).

Susan Cooksey, Ph.D., is the curator of African art, Harn Museum of Art, University of Florida.

Justin Corfield, Ph.D., teaches history and international relations at Geelong Grammar School, Australia. He is the co-author of *Historical Dictionary of Cambodia* (2003) and

has written extensively on Asia, Australia, and European colonial history.

James A. Corrick, Ph.D., is a full-time editor and writer with 25 books to his credit. His most recent titles are *The Early Middle Ages* (2006), *The Byzantine Empire* (2006), and *The Renaissance* (2007).

Arden Decker is a Ph.D. candidate in the history of art at the Graduate Center, City University of New York. Her research interests include Mesoamerican art as well as modern and contemporary art of Mexico.

Leo Depuydt, Ph.D., teaches Egyptology at Brown University and is curious about everything relating to ancient Egypt in its Near Eastern and Mediterranean context, especially the area's languages and history. He wrote *Civil Calendar and Lunar Calendar in Ancient Egypt* (1997) and *The Other Mathematics: Language and Logic in Egyptian and in General* (2007).

Haig Der-Houssikian, Ph.D., is professor emeritus (2003), linguistics, at the University of Florida, Gainesville. His research and publication interests are in morphology, Creolization, and sub-Saharan Africa.

Christine End, M.A., works on the Giza Archives Project at the Museum of Fine Arts, Boston. Her main interests of research are Middle Kingdom funerary iconography, material culture, burial practices, and mummification. As a researcher and illustrator, her work has appeared in Egyptological publications and documentaries.

Linda Evans, Ph.D., specializes in ancient Egyptian art at Macquarie University, Sydney, Australia. She recently completed her doctoral dissertation on the representation of animal behavior in Egyptian tomb paintings and has published several papers on the role and depiction of animals in the ancient world. She has also contributed chapters to *Egyptian Art: Principles and Themes in Wall Scenes* (2000), *The Encyclopedia of Animal Behavior* (2004), *Egypt: The Land and Lives of the Pharaohs Revealed* (2005), and *Historica* (2006).

Stephen M. Fabian, Ph.D., is an anthropologist and currently teaches seminars on religion, myth, and ritual at Princeton University. He is the author of *Space-Time of the Bororo of Brazil* (1992), *Clearing Away Clouds: Nine Lessons for Life from the Martial Arts* (1999), and *Patterns in the Sky: An Introduction to Ethnoastronomy* (2001).

Erin Fairburn is a graduate student in the Department of Egyptology and Western Asian Studies at Brown University. She has contributed to *The City and Urban Life* (forthcoming).

Alessia Frassani is a Ph.D. candidate at the Graduate Center of the City University of New York. Her research interests include the art and civilizations of ancient Oaxaca and issues surrounding the cultural interaction between the Old and New Worlds.

Markham J. Geller is professor of Semitic languages at University College London, in the Department of Hebrew and Jewish Studies. He has recently published a text edition of cuneiform medical texts, *Renal and Rectal Disease Texts, Babylonisch-assyrische Medizin* VII (2005).

J. J. George is working on his Ph.D. at the Graduate Center, City University of New York. His research area is pre-Columbian art and architecture.

Wolfram Grajetzki, Ph.D., wrote his dissertation at the Humboldt University of Berlin and has taught Egyptology there. He has excavated in Egypt and Pakistan and was principal archaeologist and author for the online learning project Digital Egypt for Universities (University College London). He is preparing the catalogue of Egyptian coffins in the Fitzwilliam Museum, Cambridge. His publications include *Burial Customs in Ancient Egypt* (2003) and *The Middle Kingdom in Ancient Egypt* (2006).

Lyn Green, Ph.D., has taught at several Canadian universities and for the Royal Ontario Museum. She has contributed to several encyclopedias, including *The Oxford Encyclopedia of Ancient Egypt* (2000) and the *Encyclopedia of the Archaeology of Ancient Egypt* (1999) as well as *The Royal Women of Amarna* (1996). Currently she is devoting her time to her duties as president of the Society for the Study of Egyptian Antiquities, which has over 400 members and subscribers internationally, and to writing.

Angela Herren, Ph.D., teaches pre-Columbian art and architecture as an assistant professor in the Department of Art and Latin American Studies at the University of North Carolina at Charlotte. A specialist on painted manuscripts from central Mexico, she completed a 2005 dissertation entitled "Portraying the Mexica Past: A Comparative Study of Accounts of Origin in Codex Azcatitlan, Codex Boturni, and Codex Aubin."

David B. Hollander, Ph.D., teaches ancient history at Iowa State University. He is the author of *Money in the Late Roman Republic* (2007).

Brooke Holmes, Ph.D., is an assistant professor of classics at the University of North Carolina, Chapel Hill. She is at work on a book about the symptom in early Greek medicine and classical Greek literature.

Michael Allen Holmes is a freelance editor and writer who recently contributed to *Shakespeare for Students*, 2nd edition (2007). He has also written an unpublished novel.

John W. Humphrey, Ph.D., is professor of Greek and Roman studies at the University of Calgary. A veteran of many seasons of archaeological excavation in Turkey and Greece, he is the author of *Greek and Roman Technology: A Sourcebook* (1998, with J. P. Oleson and A. N. Sherwood) and *Ancient Technology* (2006).

Keith Jordan, M.Phil., is a Ph.D. candidate in pre-Columbian art history at the Graduate Center of the City University of New York. He is currently finishing his doctoral dissertation, entitled "Stone Trees Transplanted? Central Mexican Stelae of the Epiclassic and Early Postclassic and the Question of Maya 'Influence.'"

Amr Kamel is an Egyptologist in the Rare Books and Special Collections Library at the American University in Cairo, Egypt.

David Kelly is an instructor of English writing and literature at Oakton Community College in Illinois. He has written over 100 published literary analyses and wrote the instructor's manual for the *Exploring Poetry* computer program. His short fiction has been published in *The Rockford Review, Grub Street,* and *The Iconoclast,* among other places.

Panagiotis I. M. Kousoulis, Ph.D., is a lecturer in Egyptology at the Department of Mediterranean Studies of the University of the Aegean. He is the author of *Moving across Borders: Foreign Relations, Religion and Cultural Interactions in the Ancient Mediterranean* (2007) and *Ancient Egyptian Demonology: Studies on the Boundaries between the Demonic and the Divine in Egyptian Magic* (2007).

Philippa Lang teaches ancient science and related subjects, with research interests in ancient medicine and philosophy, in the Classics Department of Emory University, Atlanta. She is the editor of *Re-Inventions: Essays on Hellenistic and Early Roman Science, Apeiron* special issue vol. 37 (2004).

Russell M. Lawson, Ph.D., is associate professor of history and chair of the Division of General Studies at Bacone College in Oklahoma. He is the author of *Science in the Ancient World* (2004), *The Land between the Rivers: Thomas Nuttall's Ascent of the Arkansas, 1819* (2004), and *Passaconaway's Realm: John Evans and the Exploration of Mount Washington* (2002, 2004).

Anne Mahoney, Ph.D., teaches Greek and Latin linguistics and literature at Tufts University. She is the author of *Plautus: Amphitryo* (2004) and *Roman Sports and Spectacles: A Sourcebook* (2001). She is also the editor of revised editions of *Allen and Greenough's New Latin Grammar* (2001), *Morice's Stories in Attic Greek* (2005), and *Bennett's Essentials* (2007).

Susan Malin-Boyce, Ph.D., serves as deputy director of the Regime Crimes Liaison Office, Mass Graves Investigation

Team, in Baghdad, Iraq. She has contributed to *Ancient Europe 8000 B.C.–A.D. 1000: Encyclopedia of the Barbarian World* (2004) and to publications addressing Early and Late La Tène settlement in Bavaria, Germany.

Renee McGarry is a student in the Ph.D. program in art history at the City University of New York Graduate Center. Her research interests include Aztec sculpture of the natural world and religious manuscripts from the post-Conquest period.

Paul McKechnie, D.Phil., is a senior lecturer in classics and ancient history at the University of Auckland, New Zealand. He is the author of *First Christian Centuries: Perspectives on the Early Church* (2002) and *Outsiders in the Greek Cities in the Fourth Century B.C.* (1989).

John M. McMahon, Ph.D., teaches at Le Moyne College in Syracuse, New York, where he directs the classics program. He is author of *Cave Paralysin: Impotence, Perception and Text in the Satyrica of Petronius* (1998) and numerous articles on the intersection of ancient literature and natural history. His most recent work includes nine entries in the forthcoming *Biographical Encyclopedia of Astronomers* (2006).

Jianjun Mei, Ph.D., teaches the history of science and technology at the University of Science and Technology Beijing. He is the author of *Copper and Bronze Metallurgy in Late Prehistoric Xinjiang: Its Cultural Context and Relationship with Neighbouring Regions* (2000).

James E. Meier, Ph.D., is assistant professor in the Department of Humanities and Social Sciences at Central Florida Community College. He is a contributor to the *Encyclopedia of African History and Culture* (2005).

Francesco Menotti, Ph.D., is a lecturer in European prehistory at the Institute of Prehistory and Archaeological Science, Basel University, Switzerland. He is the author of *Living on the Lake in Prehistoric Europe* (2004).

Melissa Moore Morison is associate professor of classics and classical archaeology at Grand Valley State University. She has extensive experience in archaeological fieldwork in Greece, Turkey, and the United States. Her research interests include Roman provincial archaeology, Greek and Roman pottery, and ceramic technology.

Penny Morrill, Ph.D., teaches pre-Columbian and early colonial Mesoamerican art at Hood College, Frederick, Maryland. She has an essay, "The Queen of Heaven Reigns in New Spain: The Triumph of Eternity in the Casa del Deán Murals," in a Brill anthology, *Woman and Art in Early Modern Latin America* (2006). She has authored several books on modern Mexican silver: *Mexican Silver: 20th Century Hand-wrought Silver Jewelry and Metalwork* (4th ed., 2007), *Silver Masters of Mexico: Héctor Aguilar and the Taller Borda* (1996), and *Maestros de Plata: William Spratling and the Mexican Silver Renaissance*, a catalog for a traveling exhibit (2002–2004).

Julian M. Murchison, Ph.D., teaches in the Department of Sociology and Anthropology at Millsaps College. His work in cultural anthropology examines the intersections of medicine and religion in East Africa. He recently published a chapter examining stories about a cure for HIV/AIDS in *Borders and Healers* (2005).

Caryn E. Neumann, Ph.D., teaches history in Ohio Wesleyan University's Black World Studies Department. She is a former managing editor of the *Journal of Women's History*.

Emily Jane O'Dell, is a Ph.D. candidate at Brown University and has taught at Brown University in both the Department of Egyptology and Ancient Western Asian Studies and the Department of Literary Arts. She has been the chief epigrapher of the Cairo-Brown University Abu Bakr Epigraphic Survey in the western cemetery of the Great Pyramids in Giza, Egypt, for the past five years.

Simon O'Dwyer is founder and researcher for Prehistoric Music Ireland, author of *Prehistoric Music of Ireland* and prehistoricmusic.com, and contributor to *The Encyclopedia of Music in Ireland* and *The Encyclopedia of Ireland*. He has published four papers for the International Study Group on Music Archaeology.

Penelope Ojeda de Huala is a Ph.D. candidate in art history at the Graduate Center of the City University of New York, where she studies pre-Columbian to contemporary art of Latin America. Her research focus is Guatemala and Peru, particularly the enduring thoughts and practices of indigenous cultures as manifested in art.

Michael J. O'Neal, Ph.D., is a writer who lives in Moscow, Idaho. He is a frequent contributor to reference and educational books, including *Lives and Works: Young Adult Authors* (1999), *The Crusades* (2005), and *America in the 1920s* (2006).

Dianne White Oyler, Ph.D., teaches African history at Fayetteville State University. She is the author of *The History of the N'ko Alphabet and Its Role in Mande Transnational Identity: Words as Weapons* (2005) as well as articles in the refereed journals *Research in African Literature, the Mande Studies Journal*, and the *International Journal of African Historical Studies*.

Katie Parla is an art historian and archaeological speleologist working in Rome and Naples as a docent leading didactic seminars of archaeological sites. She consults for the History

Channel and will appear in their 2007 series *Cities of the Underworld* as an expert on underground Rome and Naples.

Marie Passanante is a doctoral candidate in the Department of Egyptology and Ancient Western Asian Studies at Brown University.

William H. Peck teaches at the College for Creative Studies, Detroit, and the University of Michigan, Dearborn. He was for many years the curator of ancient art at the Detroit Institute of Arts and is at present a member of the Brooklyn Museum excavations in Egypt at Karnak. He is the author of *Drawings from Ancient Egypt* (1987) and numerous contributions to reference books and encyclopedias on the ancient world.

David Petechuk is a freelance writer specializing in educational texts focusing on the sciences, literature, and history. The former director of publications for the health sciences at the University of Pittsburgh, he is the author of *The Respiratory System* (2004), *LSD* (2005), and *Health & Medical Issues Today: Organ Transplantation* (2006).

Mark Anthony Phelps is taking a leave after teaching continuously since 1994 (primarily at Drury University, in five different departments) to finish his dissertation at the University of Arkansas entitled "Sewage from the Orontes: Roman Elite Attitudes toward Ecstatic Religion in the 3rd and 4th centuries C.E." This degree in ancient Mediterranean history augments his graduate degrees from Harvard and Johns Hopkins in Hebrew Bible and ancient Near Eastern languages and cultures. His research interests reflected in his writings are widely eclectic, spanning Paleolithic to contemporary society and including the disciplines of archaeology, linguistics, cultural anthropology, physical geography, historical geography, classical history, ancient Near Eastern history, medieval history, modern history, religion, and biblical history.

Jen Piro is a Ph.D. candidate in anthropological archaeology at New York University. Her dissertation research focuses on the development of pastoral economies in Early Bronze Age Transcaucasia.

Karen Radner, Ph.D., is lecturer in ancient Near Eastern history at University College, London. She specializes in the Assyrian Empire and is the author of *Die neuassyrischen Texte aus Tall Seh Hamad* (2002), *Das mittelassyrische Tontafelarchiv von Giricano/Dunnu-sa-Uzibi* (2004) and *Die Macht des Namens: Altorientalische Strategien zur Selbsterhaltung* (2005).

Judith A. Rasson, Ph.D., teaches in the Department of Medieval Studies, Central European University, Budapest (a post-graduate American-accredited university). Her research interests lie in southeastern Europe (especially the countries of the former Yugoslavia) and focus on Neolithic and historic archaeology and ethnographic material culture.

Kelly-Anne Diamond Reed, Ph.D., teaches ancient Egyptian history and archaeology at Villanova University's Department of History. She is investigating early Egyptian funerary rituals and burial customs.

Duane W. Roller is professor of Greek and Latin at Ohio State University. Trained as an archaeologist, he has over 30 years' experience in field archaeology in numerous Mediterranean countries. He is the author of *The Building Program of Herod the Great* (1998), *The World of Juba II and Kleopatra Selene* (2003), and *Through the Pillars of Herakles* (2006) as well as many other publications in history, classics, and archaeology.

Kelley L. Ross, Ph.D., teaches philosophy at Los Angeles Valley College. He specializes in Kantian epistemology, metaphysics, and ethics, with emphasis on members of the Friesian tradition—Jakob Fries, Leonard Nelson, Rudolf Otto, Sir Karl Popper, and others. Since 1996 he has been the publisher and editor of the online philosophy journal *Proceedings of the Friesian School, Fourth Series*.

Edward M. W. A. Rowlands, M.Phil., has research interests in Mycenaean political geography, trade, and religion.

Lucas G. Rubin, Ph.D., develops master of science programs for Columbia University. He was previously administrator of the university's Center for Archaeology, where he managed multiple excavations and projects. His research and scholarship have focused on fires and firefighters in ancient Rome.

Michael M. Sage, Ph.D., teaches classics and ancient history in the Classics Department at the University of Cincinnati. His main areas of study are historiography and military history. He is the author of *Cyprian: A Biography* (1975) and *Warfare in Ancient Greece: A Sourcebook* (1996).

Rick Schulting, Ph.D., is a lecturer in scientific and prehistoric archaeology at the University of Oxford. His current research interests lie in understanding the Mesolithic-Neolithic transition in western Europe, emphasizing the use of radiometric dating and stable isotope analysis, and in skeletal evidence for interpersonal violence in earlier prehistoric Europe.

David R. Sear, a fellow of the Royal Numismatic Society in London and the American Numismatic Society in New York, has authored an extensive range of numismatic books over the past four decades, aimed at collectors and students of ancient Greek, Roman and Byzantine coinage. He has been a resident of Los Angeles for the past 25 years and operates a research service authenticating ancient coinage. His numerous publications include *Roman Coins and Their Values* (1964; rev. ed., 2000–2005), *Byzantine Coins and Their Values* (1974, rev. ed., 1987), *Greek Coins and Their Values* (1978–1979), and *The History and Coinage of the Roman Imperators, 49–27 B.C.* (1998).

Robert Shanafelt, Ph.D., teaches courses in anthropology, religion, and Africana studies at Georgia Southern University. He has published a number of articles on different aspects of life in southern Africa, among them, "Crime, Power, and Policing in South Africa" in *Democratic Policing in Transitional and Developing Countries* (2006).

Alison Sheridan, Ph.D., is head of early prehistory in the National Museums Scotland, Edinburgh, specializing in the British and Irish Neolithic and Bronze Age. Exhibition work includes *Heaven and Hell—and Other Worlds of the Dead* (2000), for which she was lead curator and book editor. Other books include *From Sickles to Circles* (with A. M. Gibson, 2004) and *Vessels for the Ancestors* (with N. M. Sharples, 1992).

Spyros Siropoulos is senior lecturer of Greek philology and history at the Department of Mediterranean Studies, University of the Aegean, Greece. He has published various articles in three books: *Unlike a Woman: Gender and the Social Function of the Athenian Tragedy* (2003), *The Goat's Skin: The Other Side of Alexander the Great's Power* (2003; in Greek with English summary), and *The Things after Alexander: The Centrifugal Potencies of the Hellenistic Kingdoms* (2005, in Greek).

Bradley Skeen, M.A., has taught at the University of Minnesota, Webster University, and Washington University. He is a specialist in magic, religion, and philosophy in late antiquity and has contributed to research in that field in *Die Zeitschrift für Papyrologie und Epigraphik*, among other journals.

Christopher Smith, D.Phil., is professor of ancient history at the University of Saint Andrews in Scotland. He is the author of *Early Rome and Latium: Economy and Society c 100–500 B.C.* (1996) and *The Roman Clan: From Ancient Ideology to Modern Anthropology* (2006) as well as editor of several collections of essays, including *Trade, Traders and the Ancient City* (with Helen Parkins, 1998); *Sicily from Aeneas to Augustus* (with John Serrati, 2000), and *Religion in Archaic and Republican Rome and Italy: Evidence and Experience* (with Edward Bispham, 2000). He is engaged in work on Roman historiography and oratory.

Nancy Shatzman Steinhardt is professor of East Asian art and curator of Chinese art at the University of Pennsylvania. She is author of *Chinese Traditional Architecture* (1984), *Chinese Imperial City Planning* (1990), *Liao Architecture* (1997), and *Chinese Architecture* (2002) and more than 60 scholarly articles.

Tom Streissguth is a freelance author, editor, and journalist who has published more than 70 nonfiction and reference books. His most recent titles include *Clay v. United States, Genghis Khan's Mongol Empire, Library in a Book: Hate Crimes, Eyewitness History: The Roaring Twenties,* and the *Greenhaven Encyclopedia of the Middle Ages.*

Ananda Cohen Suarez is a Ph.D. student at the Graduate Center of the City University of New York, specializing in pre-Columbian and colonial Latin American art history. She is particularly interested in cross-cultural encounters, vernacular religious art, and manuscript production in the early colonial Americas.

Frank J. Swetz, D.Ed., is professor emeritus of mathematics and education, Pennsylvania State University. His research interests focus on cultural and societal impact on mathematics learning and teaching. Among his recent books are *Legacy of the Luoshu: The 4000 Year Search for the Meaning of the Magic Square of Order Three* (2002) and *Teaching Mathematics to Children* (2003).

John Thorburn, Ph.D., is associate professor of classics at Baylor University, where he teaches a variety of subjects dealing with the classical world. He has published on Greek tragedy, Greek comedy, Greek and Roman history, and a variety of ancient subjects. He is the author of *The Alcestis of Euripides* (2002) and the *Facts on File Companion to Classical Drama* (2005).

Alain Touwaide, Ph.D., is a historian of sciences in the Department of Botany of the National Museum of Natural History at the Smithsonian Institution (Washington, D.C.). He has extensively published on the history of medicine in the Mediterranean world from antiquity to the Renaissance. Recently, he coedited the volume *Visualizing Medieval Medicine and Natural History, 1200–1550* (2006).

Francesca C. Tronchin, Ph.D., teaches Greek and Roman art and archaeology at Ohio State University. Her primary area of research is Roman domestic decor and issues of eclecticism in ancient sculptural displays.

David K. Underwood, Ph.D., teaches Western humanities, art history, philosophy, and Latin American studies at the University of South Florida in Tampa and at Saint Petersburg College in Clearwater, Florida. He is the author of two books and several articles and essays on Iberian and Latin American art and architecture.

David Vallilee is an independent scholar.

Frans van Koppen, M.A., teaches Akkadian at the School of Oriental and African Studies, London. He contributed to *The*

Ancient Near East: Historical Sources in Translation (2006) and *The Babylonian World* (forthcoming).

Lawrence Waldron, M.F.A., is an associate professor and doctoral candidate at the City University of New York, specializing in non-Western fields of art history and culture. He has presented and published various articles on the art and culture of the pre-Columbian Caribbean and Southeast Asia.

Ezekiel A. Walker, Ph.D., teaches African and world history at the University of Central Florida. His forthcoming book is entitled *Growth, Crisis and Transformation in the Cocoa-Farming Economy of Southwestern Nigeria* (2007).

Peter S. Wells is professor of anthropology at the University of Minnesota. His publications include *The Barbarians Speak: How the Conquered Peoples Shaped Roman Europe* (1999), *Beyond Celts, Germans and Scythians: Archaeology and Identity in Iron Age Europe* (2001), and *The Battle That Stopped Rome: Emperor Augustus, Arminius, and the Slaughter of the Legions in the Teutoburg Forest* (2003).

Jacqui Wood is an archaeologist and authority on prehistoric cooking and the lifestyles of prehistoric Europeans. She runs her own excavation in Cornwall, England.

Ronald Young, Ph.D., teaches in the Social Sciences Department at Canterbury School in Fort Myers, Florida. His teaching and research interests are in the area of Latin American Studies. In addition to numerous reference articles, he is presently working on a general history of Colombia to be published by Greenwood Press.

Katharina Zinn, M.A., is writing her Ph.D. dissertation on ancient Egyptian libraries and archives at the University of Leipzig, Germany. She works in a project on scarabs in the Fitzwilliam Museum, Cambridge (United Kingdom) and a project on Middle Kingdom Reliefs from Lisht in the Princeton University Art Museum. She has published articles on the organization of collective wisdom as well as multilingualism in ancient Egypt.

List of Illustrations

VOLUME III

List of Maps and Primary Source Documents

Entries S to Z

► sacred sites

INTRODUCTION

Probably the first sacred sites were aspects of the natural world that people identified with the supernatural. Large formations, such as big rock outcrops, mountains, lakes, and rivers, all could serve as impressive sources of spiritual power. Mountains are imposing not only because of their size but also because they seem closer to the sky. Many cultures have placed shrines or altars atop mountains in the belief that people could be better heard by gods when they were nearer the sky than when they were at the bases of mountains. Rock outcrops often have the advantage of having faces on which sacred images could be painted or carved, allowing people to show in their images what is special about the sacred place. Lakes and rivers frequently are associated with the life force, because water is believed to be part of the life force; after all, people quickly die without water. Lakes and rivers were thought to have gods dwelling in them, and many ancient peoples made sacrifices to lakes and rivers in the hope of making the gods there happy or to persuade the gods to help with crops or wars.

A place in a dense forest where light cannot penetrate past the branches and leaves of trees could be construed as a place where forest spirits would gather or dwell. Shrines in such places might not have survived if they were wooden or consisted of no more than the space among the trees, but historical records suggest that ancient cultures in Europe, Africa, Asia, and America had such places, where good and evil spirits were thought to dwell.

Sacred places can be associated with historical events or important people. Where a special person received enlight-

enment about the supernatural or spoke with spirits can become a holy place to which the faithful will make pilgrimages. Shrines could be built to mark locations where a single religious leader received or proclaimed divine knowledge over his or her lifetime, with the shrines marking stations for religious pilgrimages of the followers of the religious leader or of the religion of which the religious leader's revelations became a part. The locations of great battles that were important sites in mythology sometimes were commemorated with altars, shrines, temples, or tombs. There were so many such places that some ancient people wrote tour guides to the sacred sites.

Otherwise ordinary places could be made sacred by people. One way was to deposit a sacred relic, such as a fragment of hair, bones, fingernail clippings, or a personal item worn or used by a sacred or holy person. Great mounds could be built over the relics, or temples could be erected to house them. Another way to make a place sacred was through ritual. Sometimes ancient cities were made sacred and even objects of worship by depositing icons of gods in central temples or through ritual blessings of the cities. Sometimes the ground on which a city was to be built was consecrated through rituals, making the new city a sacred place that was set apart from the ordinary world.

AFRICA
BY ROBERT SHANAFELT

Sacred sites in ancient Africa include special areas of the natural landscape such as mountains, caves, forests, and springs and human constructions such as mounds, tombs, and pyramids. The continent contains some of the oldest sites in the world that seem to have had ritual significance for human beings. By 10,000 years ago religious symbolism was well established in art, body decoration, burial, and monument building. One substance very widely associated with burial was the red pigment ocher. Ocher is further connected with the land and with sacred sites in that it was painted or smeared on rock surfaces or onto artifacts left in the ground. Studies of ancient religions from around the world suggest that this pigment was a common symbol for blood and life.

A substantial number of ancient engravings on stone and paintings on rock walls have been discovered in many regions of Africa, including the region that is now the Sahara. In very early times graphic images of animals and abstract geometric forms made on rock faces probably were meant to establish supernatural connections among people, animals, spirit beings, and the landscape. Southern Africa provides some of the very earliest examples of rock art with undoubted religious connections, dating back to perhaps 30,000 years ago but continuing into the time of European colonialism.

There appears to be a direct relationship between the religion of the so-called Bushmen (the San) and the ancient rock art sites found in southern Africa. For example, some paintings depict ritual dances similar to those still practiced by Bushmen today. The modern-day Tswana also claim an ancient religious connection. According to one oral tradition a set of engraved footprints in southeastern Botswana marks the spot where the first Tswana man emerged from the underworld. In North Africa the Atlas Mountains of Morocco were favored locations for ritual activities. Here rock engravings made between 5,000 and 7,000 years ago depict otherworldly images such as horned women and men with animal heads.

The impressive megaliths (large standing stones) and pyramids that often mark the sacred sites of the ancient world are usually associated with civilizations that had substantial populations and productive farming. While this is also true for the sites in Africa with the largest monuments and pyramids, in some cases pastoralists (groups who herd animals as their principal occupation) or other societies with relatively small populations constructed megaliths. Herders and early farmers in what are today Niger, the Central African Republic, and Chad built stone monuments to cover the graves of their revered leaders. Ritual cattle sacrifices also occurred in many of these locations. Stone circles and other megalithic monuments are especially pronounced in the region around the present-day town of Bouar in the Central African Republic.

Nabta Playa, a site bordering on what is today Libya, Sudan, and Egypt, served as a ceremonial center for pastoral nomads between 6,000 and 7,000 years ago. In addition numerous tombs, the site has five rows of megaliths that radiate out from a center point. It also has an important stone circle. This stone circle is particularly significant because it is one of the earliest examples of an astronomical observatory in the world, predating England's Stonehenge by some 1,000 years. Although it is quite small compared with Stonehenge, being only about 12 feet in diameter, it is still impressive given

Deep gorge in the Atlas Mountains; these mountains were a favored site for ritual activities in ancient times. (© Board of Regents of the University of Wisconsin System)

its early date. It consists of four sets of upright slabs, with one set aligned in a north-south direction and the second set aligned eastward to face the sun as it arises during the summer solstice.

The Egypt-Sudanese border area that in ancient times was known as Upper Nubia is also the location of a mountain called Jebel Barkal that was sacred for both Egyptians and Nubians. This site became especially important during the Twenty-fifth Dynasty (ca. 712–ca. 657 B.C.E.), when Nubian pharaohs ruled all Egypt. Later Nubian pharaohs built pyramids for themselves and their queens and were laid to rest at nearby Meroë. Another example of a sacred mountain in Africa is Makade Egzi in Ethiopia, near the ancient city-state of Axum. Axum itself is famous for impressive stone gravesites and obelisks. In a much earlier time, around 3000 B.C.E., many stone dolmens (upright stones across which lies a stone slab) were erected in what is now the eastern region of the country.

As mentioned earlier, features of the land and the landscape are sacred in many traditional African religions.

Among the hunting-and-gathering peoples who inhabit the forests of central Africa—so-called Pygmy peoples such as the Mbuti of Congo and the Aka of the Central African Republic—the forest is thought to be a divine being or spiritual force. Many peoples of West Africa also consider portions of the forest sacred, while other groups, like the Tswana, consider the homeland of their ancestors to be the most sacred ground. The elders and keepers of traditional knowledge among the Mijikenda of Kenya also work to protect special areas of forests that they associate with their ancestors. Here it is difficult to tease apart today's spiritual inspiration and imagination from the realities of the past. For example, while oral tradition suggests the Mijikenda sacred forests were inhabited by their ancestors for at least the past 10 generations, some archaeologists think they were occupied more recently. On the other hand, other experts think the occupation goes back to antiquity, much further than oral tradition suggests. Similarly, while it is known that people have inhabited the forests of central Africa for thousands of years, it is not known at what point people began to consider the forest itself as sacred.

Finally, it should not be forgotten that both Christianity and Judaism established early roots in North Africa and in Ethiopia. Today a special treasure house near the Church of Saint Mary at Axum is said by many followers of the Ethiopian Orthodox Church to house the Ark of the Covenant, the chest that contains the original Ten Commandments.

EGYPT

BY CHRISTINE END

The ancient Egyptian worldview was embodied in the concept of *maat*, or divine order. Under *maat*, Egypt was at the center of the universe; night, day, and the seasons were perfectly governed, and the cosmos was harmoniously balanced. Appeasing the gods who presided over every aspect of the Egyptian world was necessary to perpetuate *maat*. A goddess, also named Maat, personified the concept. Kings frequently included "beloved of Maat" in their titles to show their devotion, and surviving reliefs show kings offering small Maat figures to a variety of gods. By giving a figure of Maat, the king was ensuring that the deity would uphold *maat* and therefore Egypt's position in the universe.

The king was not the only one to appeal to the gods; offerings were a part of life for the ancient Egyptians. Excavations revealing abundant offerings indicate an especially sacred site. Individuals left gifts at specific locations to venerate a particular god, to ask for help, or to mark a pilgrimage to a revered place. These offerings could have been amulets, statues, mummified animals, notes or spells written on pottery, foodstuffs, offering tables, or poured unguents or pure sand. Some offerings were much larger, such as shrines, stelae, or even temples. These places were considered sacred because of mythological or religious connotations, the presence of exploitable resources (such as water or metal) in the area,

or symbolic natural or man-made landforms. There are many overlaps within these categories. For example, sometimes a temple was built on a natural sacred mound, or a building's design might have imitated a natural sacred land formation.

The Egyptian perception of the sacred often combined the mythological and tangible worlds. Some myths include descriptions of the beginning of the universe. One popular Egyptian creation story begins with chaotic primordial waters, called *nun* (sometimes represented by a god of the same name). *Nun* was the first thing in the universe out of which the primeval mound, or *benben*, emerged. This mound was the first thing the sun's rays fell upon. Bodies or sources of water were sacred because water symbolized mythological creation and also, in the tangible world, was an essential resource, particularly in the desert. The Nile River was the most important body of water; it was the source of agriculture, transportation, and sustenance for Egypt's people and wildlife. This river was so sacred and boat travel was so engrained in the ancient Egyptian consciousness that some royal burials included boats so that the deceased could navigate the waters of the afterlife.

Sacred bodies of water could also be man-made. Artificial lakes were frequently created at temples if a natural water source was not available. The temples of Amon and Mut at Karnak, Hathor at Dendera, Osiris at Abydos, and other temples and temple complexes at Medinet Habu, Armant, and Tanis all incorporated man-made lakes into their environment. These lakes were used for daily washing, ritual libations, watering sacred animals, and sailing sacred barks during festivals. Wells, a natural water source accessed in a man-made fashion, were another way to exploit water. On desert roads or in towns far from lakes or the Nile, wells were of life-sustaining importance.

Water was not the only exploitable natural resource for the Egyptians. Mines and quarries were considered sacred places where the riches of the earth were accessible. Certain gods were associated with particular types of metal or stone. For example, Hathor was deemed the lady of turquoise, and Ra, the sun god, was said to possess bones of silver, skin of gold, and hair of lapis lazuli. Shrines and stelae dedicated to gods were frequently erected at their mine sites.

Man-made mound structures were sometimes incorporated into sacred sites such as tombs, symbolically associating them with creation myths. In ancient Egyptian creation mythology, the primeval mound was the first thing to emerge out of the turbulent waters. Papyrus was the first thing to grow on the newly emerged mound. This mimicked the agricultural cycle of the emergence of fertile silt-covered land after the Nile flood. Therefore, including a mound at a site would connect it with both the tangible and mythological worlds.

A different type of man-made mound is found at Abydos on the west bank of the Nile. Abydos was considered the mythical burial place of Osiris, god of the dead and the afterlife. Pilgrimages to Abydos honoring Osiris began in early dynastic times. A mound created from the accumulation of centuries of small offerings brought to this sacred site is still visible today. Offerings at Abydos also included structures such as temples and cenotaphs.

Temples were extremely sacred places to the Egyptians. Commoners were not permitted inside the boundaries of the temple. Interaction between the common person and the gods occurred only when shrines were carried out of the temple precincts. Important precincts included the temple of Amon and Mut at Karnak, Luxor Temple in the south, the temple of Ptah at Memphis, and the sun temple of Heliopolis in the north. Architectural elements of the Egyptian temple appear to refer back to the primeval mound and the waters of *nun*. The hall that led into the temple contained columns topped with papyrus (representing its growth on the mound) and sometimes lotus, thus creating an artificial marshland. Papyrus and lotus plants additionally symbolized Lower and Upper Egypt, respectively. In the most sacred area at the back of the temple, the ground rose and the star-painted ceiling became lower, leading into the highest, darkest area representing the primeval mound. The temple therefore stood as a mythological microcosm within which the priests ritually duplicated the creation of the universe.

Limestone stela of Heqaib, from Abydos, Egypt (1990–1750 B.C.E.); Abydos was the principal cult center of Osiris and a place of pilgrimage for Egyptians. (© The Trustees of the British Museum)

Natural land formations may have been the sign of a sacred area. Some scholars believe that the choice of the Valley of the Kings for New Kingdom (ca. 1550–1070 B.C.E.) royal burials was made because of a pyramid-shaped hill at the site, echoing the shape of pyramids used for Old Kingdom (2575–2134 B.C.E.) royal burials. If true, this is an example of a natural site chosen for a sacred purpose because it resembled a man-made structure. Further, there is some argument as to whether the pyramid shape itself derives from a natural mound formation or is a logical progression in the evolution of man-made structures. Areas surrounding pyramids were considered sacred places in which to be buried. In the Old Kingdom it appears that the king was thought to be the only one with the ability to rise from the dead, but individuals buried around his tomb might have a chance at the afterlife because of their location near him.

The sun was also revered, inspiring the building of many sacred structures. The Egyptians identified several solar deities, each representing the sun at various times of the day. Solar worship, especially of the sun god Ra, was an important part of Egyptian religious belief from the time of the Old Kingdom. Obelisks and *benben* stones (the predecessor of the obelisk that represented the primeval mound) were erected at several sites sacred to Ra. Additionally, kings deemed themselves *sa Ra*, or "son of the sun."

THE MIDDLE EAST

BY AMY HACKNEY BLACKWELL

The people of Mesopotamia believed that temples functioned as physical homes for their gods and goddesses. Accordingly, Mesopotamians built their temples specifically to accommodate deities and not as a place for worshippers to gather. A temple would contain a statue of the resident god and a repository to store votive offerings given by the faithful. Priests and priestesses lived next to the sanctuary and performed daily rituals, including furnishing large meals for the gods. Workshops for the manufacture of everything from tools to till the deity's fields to pottery to hold the deity's beer were associated with each temple.

Each city had numerous temples dedicated to different gods and goddesses, but typically one deity would function as the city's patron and inhabit the city's largest and richest temple. The city of Babylon was considered sacred to the god Marduk and his son Nabu. Nabu also had a shrine in the neighboring city of Borsippa. Nippur, another Babylonian city, was sacred to the god Enlil. Assur, the capital of Assyria, was the home of the god Assur, the chief god of the Assyrian pantheon and a counterpart of the Babylonian god Marduk. Nineveh was another important Assyrian city; its most important temple was that of the goddess Ishtar. The city of Ur, near the mouth of the Tigris and the Euphrates, was the sacred city of the god Nanna. In some cities a pair of temples housed a divine husband and wife; for example, in Babylon, the temple to Marduk was next to the temple dedicated to his wife, Sarpanitum.

Israel was home to several sacred sites important to Jews and Christians. Jerusalem has been the holy city of the Jews since about 1000 B.C.E. and has been a destination for religious pilgrimages since that time. The Temple Mount was the site of the Jewish temple, the center of organized worship, and the holiest place in Judaism. Two temples succeeded each other there in ancient times. The first one, Solomon's Temple, was built in the 10th century B.C.E. and was destroyed by the Babylonians around 587 B.C.E. The second temple was built in 515 B.C.E. and was destroyed by the Romans in 70 C.E. The Western Wall, or Wailing Wall, is the retaining wall that supports the western side of the Temple Mount. It was built along with the second temple and survived when the Romans destroyed the temple. According to Jewish tradition, the emperor Titus (r. 79–81 C.E.) left it standing to remind the Jews that Rome had conquered them, but the Jews regarded it as a sign of God's promise that they were his chosen people. The wall has been a popular site for prayer since ancient times.

The tomb of the biblical Jewish woman Rachel (wife of Jacob) was traditionally believed to be on the outskirts of Bethlehem. The town of Bethlehem also contained a grotto where the Roman Church father Jerome (ca. 347–419 or 420 C.E.) translated the Bible into Latin—a translation known as the Vulgate—around 400 C.E. Bethlehem's Church of the Nativity was built by the emperor Constantine the Great (r. 306–337 C.E.) in 330 C.E. over a holy cave where Jesus was believed to have been born. Constantine also built the Church of the Holy Sepulchre over the spot in Jerusalem where Jesus was said to have been crucified.

Ancient Persian worshippers of Zarathustra, or Zoroaster, centered their worship on fires. Each home had its own sacred fire at which family members worshipped daily. In the fourth century B.C.E. Persians began building fire temples that became centers of community worship. Cities and towns had their own temples; famous temples were located in the cities of Shiz, Baku, and Kabulistan. Zoroastrians disposed of dead bodies by leaving them on mountaintops inside stone-walled enclosures called towers of silence, where the bodies were eaten by vultures and dried by the sun. This was considered the cleanest way of dealing with the dead because it prevented decaying flesh from polluting the ground.

Many sacred sites were located in Asia Minor. Mount Ararat, in the mountains of Armenia, was a sacred site for millennia. The Asklepion in Pergamum was a hospital built in honor of the god of health, Asklepios; it was famed for a sleeping cure in which the god was supposed to visit patients in their dreams. The Temple of Artemis at Ephesus was one of the Seven Wonders of the Ancient World. Christian sites included the Cave of the Seven Sleepers in Ephesus, a cave in which seven Christian boys pursued by persecuting Romans hid themselves; the soldiers walled them up inside, and they were said to have fallen asleep until the fifth century C.E., when they were released by an earthquake and learned that Christianity was now prevalent.

ASIA AND THE PACIFIC
BY KIRK H. BEETZ

For many in the ancient Asia and Pacific region, unusual or impressive geological features carried spiritual power. For example, in ancient Japan a mountain would have *kami*, a spiritual power, just because it was massive. Mount Fuji, which stands tall over eastern Honshū, was especially sacred not only for its size but also for its individuality, standing separate, as it does, from the main mountain chain of the island.

Ayers Rock in Australia is another example. Called Uluru by the ancient Australians, it fell from the sky during the dreaming time, the era of the Creation. It was also the site of a great battle between the lizard men and the snake men, before human beings appeared. Uluru is impressive: made of sandstone, it stands 1,143 feet high and is a mile and a half long. It seems to glow red as the sun sets. The rock was said to be "owned" by a single person at a time. This person controlled who visited the rock. Many ancient sacred sites in Australia were "owned" by someone. The owner also owned all the stories associated with the sacred place. He or she could tell others the stories, but they were not supposed to repeat the stories unless they themselves became "owners" of the sacred place. This custom continued through the 20th century for Uluru, with owners taking people into special meeting areas, usually just outside caves, to tell them the stories about the sacred site. As is the case with many ancient sacred rocks, Uluru was painted with symbols. Some of them tell the story of Creation. They were painted with ocher shades and blood drawn from the arm of the painter, which emphasized the artist's spiritual connection to the rock and what he was depicting. Caves that were painted often served as places for initiation rites for children moving toward adulthood, where they would learn some of the sacred lore of their people.

The Chinese had many sacred places. During the Shang Dynasty (ca. 1500–1045 B.C.E.) there were many cultures outside the Shang Empire, and they had numerous different beliefs about their sacred places. Most of these beliefs have been lost. One site that was sacred throughout ancient times was Mount Tai Shan. It is about 5,000 feet high, and its summit is a huge crag of rock that seems to thrust out into the sky, giving those who stand on it a breathtaking view of the rocky, lumpy countryside in Shandong Province. The route up to the summit is marked by shrines. A pilgrim in ancient times was expected to leave offerings at each shrine, and even today people leave gifts of fruit and flowers as they scale the mountain. Confucius climbed the mountain and was recorded as saying, "I feel the world is much smaller," as he gazed at the world from the summit. The emperor Liu Ch'e (r. 141–87 B.C.E.) of the Han Dynasty (202 B.C.E.–220 C.E.), climbed Mount Tai Shan to speak with the gods. He made his climb a proper pilgrimage by stopping at every shrine to pray and leave offerings. By his era Mount Tai Shan had become a symbol of Chinese culture, and Liu Ch'e's climbing the mountain displayed his commitment to Chinese civilization as well as his own important place in Chinese religion. He was expected to speak with the gods on behalf of the Chinese.

In addition to building shrines on already-sacred sites, people made some sites sacred through rituals and the building of religious structures. In India people built stupas, originally tombs of dirt piled in the shape of hemispheres. Stupas took on great importance after the death of Siddhartha Gautama (ca. 563–ca. 483 B.C.E.), who was the Buddha. Parts of his body were entombed in several stupas. Emperor Asoka (r. 268–233 B.C.E.) of India had seven of these stupas opened and their contents divided among 84,000 stupas scattered through India. The most important was the Great Stupa in Sanchi, north of the Narmada River in Madhya Pradesh in central India. Over hundreds of years, people added to it, coating it in brick, surrounding it with a wall, and building ornate gates alive with sculptures of gods and goddesses.

A stupa typically had a circular crown projecting around its top. The one for the Great Stupa looks like many fingers thrusting out horizontal to the ground. The crown was called *chatra*, meaning "umbrella." The dome of the stupa was the *garbha*, meaning "womb." *Garbha* referred not to a physical birth but to the Buddha's passing out of the cycle of birth and rebirth into nirvana, a blissful spiritual state in which the soul escapes the pain of life in the physical world. The dome was also sometimes called an *anda*, meaning "egg," because it symbolized the first egg from which the universe emerged.

Hindus used the concept of the *garbha* to create the *garbhagriha*, a shrine where a person might be seen by a god. Hindu shrines and temples often had images of gods inside them, but the Hindus did not believe that the statues were gods, and they did not believe that gods ever actually entered the statues. The statues frequently were placed in a shadowy part of a shrine, because it was intended to set an observer's mind to thinking about the mysteries of spirituality. It was this train of thought that could bring a person into touch with a supernatural being. This encounter with a supernatural being was *darshana*, meaning "viewing."

Sacred sites were also built with the intention of inspiring awe in visitors. In India, during Asoka's reign, people began carving sacred sites into large stones. At first these were just caves where a monk could sit by himself and meditate. Eventually, they became huge temples that are amazing even today. The best may be at Ajanta in western India. From the 100s B.C.E. to the 600s C.E. temples were carved into immense rocky cliffs. Some temples began in natural caves, but others were carved either from the side of a cliff or from the top down into a cliff. Cracks were hammered into the rocks and filled with wood that was then doused with water, which slowly widened the cracks as the wood swelled. Rock masons carved openings into spaces that became rooms and corridors, with columns and statues. The detail work was done by artisans using tools as fine as those of jewelers. Walls were then painted with religious scenes. The central shrines were often in shadows, with openings allowing light to highlight statues representing the Buddha or gods. Both Hindus and Buddhists carved such temples.

EUROPE

BY AMY HACKNEY BLACKWELL

Long before the Celtic peoples arrived, prehistoric Europeans created sacred sites by arranging giant stones, or megaliths, in ways that were to them spiritually significant. These stones remained standing during Celtic times, and the Celts adopted some of them as their own sacred sites. Celts and Germans also found spiritual power in many natural formations, such as groves of trees, mountains, caves, and islands.

Hundreds of megalithic sites remain throughout Europe, from Ireland to the eastern Baltic area, containing stone structures and graves erected between 4500 and 2000 B.C.E. Many megalithic sites were tombs, and human remains have been found in some of them. Others reveal no obvious purpose, consisting only of upright stones arranged in a pattern but without burials. The most accepted explanation is that megaliths had religious or ceremonial significance. Many of them are aligned in such a way that they catch the sun on specific days of the year, which may be evidence that prehistoric peoples used them in sun worship.

There are several common types of megalithic structures. A menhir is a single standing stone. Some standing stones are arranged in circles or rows, called alignments. A dolmen is a tomb made of several large upright stones supporting a flat stone roof, while a passage grave consists of a corridor lined and roofed with large stones leading to a stone burial chamber. Many megalithic tombs were once covered with mounds either of earth or of small stones. The earthen mounds are known as tumuli; the stone mounds are called cairns.

Most surviving megalithic sites are in northwestern France, Britain, and Ireland. The largest known menhir, the so-called *grand menhir brisé* ("great broken stone") in Brittany, France, stood about 67 feet high before it was broken in an earthquake in 1722. Carnac, another site in Brittany, contains over 3,000 standing stones arranged in straight lines, all erected between 4500 and 3300 B.C.E. Carnac also has several tumuli and several dolmens. Gavrinis Island off the coast of Brittany holds a huge megalithic cairn that dates to about 3500 B.C.E. Inside the cairn a passage leads to a grave chamber constructed of large granite stones. The walls of the passage and chamber are elaborately carved with spiral decorations. Ireland is home to several similar tombs, the most famous of which is Newgrange, built about 3200 B.C.E. Newgrange is especially notable for the way the rising sun of the winter solstice shines directly on a design in the main chamber.

Perhaps the most famous sacred site in prehistoric Europe is Stonehenge in England, which was built in several stages between 3100 and 1600 B.C.E. Stonehenge is a complex monument, and the standing stones that are visible today are only the most recent version of it. Moreover, it was at the center of a landscape of monuments that all had some sort of symbolic or sacred purpose. Barrows dot the surrounding countryside, while a roadway lined with ditches and banks leads the way to the nearby river Avon. Debate rages as to Stonehenge's purpose, but it may have had a calendrical or ceremonial function.

Bronze Age rock art chiseled on rocky outcrops in many parts of Scandinavia as well as in the Alps includes images of animals, people, and boats, as well as abstract spirals and suns. These carvings clearly conveyed some sort of spiritual significance. Some of the scenes found in Sweden show rituals and processions.

Celts adopted ancient megalithic sites as their own; historians believe that the Celts created legends of fairies and other supernatural beings to explain the existence of these mysterious structures. The Hill of Tara in County Meath, Ireland, was a particularly sacred site in Celtic times. The Celts believed that the hill had been the capital of the mythical people who lived in Ireland before them. On top of the hill was a fort built during the Iron Age, perhaps around 1000 B.C.E.; this fort contained a standing stone called the Lia Fáil, or Stone of Destiny. Celtic kings were crowned next to the Lia Fáil, which was supposed to shriek out loud if the feet of the rightful king rested on it.

Most ancient Europeans believed that trees had spiritual significance. The Roman historian Tacitus observed that ancient Germanic peoples worshipped sacred groves of trees, especially oak trees. He described a ritual in which Germans performed annual human sacrifices in the sacred groves. In Denmark and Scandinavia people selected particular ash trees as sacred objects. Oddly shaped trees often gained particular spiritual significance and were believed to be the homes of spirits.

Celtic people throughout Europe believed that certain groves of trees were sacred. Forests sacred to the Celts of France included the Forest of Paimpont near Rennes, the grove in the Greek colony of Massilia (modern-day Marseilles), the Augustonemeton in the Auvergne region of central France, the Memetacum in the Artois region of northern France, and the Forest of Huelgoat in Brittany. The Roman historian Pliny mentioned a Spanish people called the Nemetatae, named after a sacred grove in northern Spain. (One Celtic word for a "sacred grove" was *nemeton*.) A Celtic group in Germany called themselves the Nemetes, or "people of the sacred grove." Sacred groves left their mark on some modern place names, such as Nemetostatio in Devon and Vernemetum in Nottinghamshire, England.

Many rivers, wells, springs, bogs, and hot springs were sacred to ancient European peoples. Archaeologists have found religious artifacts at many watery locations, such as the river Shannon in Ireland and the Seine in France. At Flag Fen in England, Bronze Age and Iron Age people deposited hundreds of bronze objects, as well as animal sacrifices, in the bog. Across northern Europe bogs and marshes have yielded thousands of objects that could only have been thrown in deliberately as offerings. The famous Iron Age bog bodies,

Lindow Man (Iron Age, mid-first century C.E.), found in Lindow Moss, Cheshire, England, and thought to have been ritually murdered; Germanic and Celtic human sacrifice took place at the site of peat bogs, where the bodies were then thrown. (© The Trustees of the British Museum)

of which Tollund Man and Grauballe Man in Denmark and Lindow Man in England are but three examples, were probably individuals who were sacrificed ritually (or perhaps executed for crimes) and then cast into the bogs, where the soil's unusual chemistry preserved the bodies remarkably well.

Hot springs were especially attractive to ancient peoples. The natural hot mineral springs at Bath, in southwestern England, were first frequented by hunter-gatherers around 8000 B.C.E. Celts built a shrine to the water goddess Sulis there around 700 B.C.E. This shrine became a major religious center for Celts in the area. Romans took over the shrine around 65 C.E. Although their name for the town was Aquae Sulis (Waters of Sulis), they replaced Sulis with the Roman goddess Minerva as the focus of worship. Among her many other roles, Minerva was the goddess of medicine, and the shrine became a destination for people hoping to regain their health. Over the next four centuries the townspeople improved the facilities, constructing temples and bathhouses. Other well-known sacred hot springs existed (and still exist) at Baden-Baden in Germany, Perrier in France, and Evian-les-Bains on Lake Geneva.

Ancient Europeans often considered mountains sacred. Celts believed that their gods lived on top of high mountains. Islands were also sacred. The island of Anglesey in northern Wales was believed to be the home and power base of Druids. In about 60 C.E. Romans attacked the island, slaughtered the defenders, and burned the Druids' sacred oak groves in an effort to end their power and influence.

GREECE

BY BRADLEY SKEEN

Pausanius, a Greek of the second century C.E., wrote a tourist guide to his homeland. A modern book of this kind might concentrate on art galleries and battlefields, but Pausanius's main interest was in religious practices and religious places. For the Greeks the sacred was the most important part of life and found its expression in the hearts of cities, in villages, in the wild places of the countryside, and beside the hearth of every Greek home.

The earliest Greeks, the Minoan civilization of Crete (2000–1400 B.C.E.), carried out religious rituals in rural places whose nature seemed connected to the divine. Mountaintops were the closest places to the gods of the sky, while caves seemed connected to the deities of the dead who lived under the earth. Other gods were worshipped within sacred enclosures set off around large trees.

Household shrines also existed in Minoan times and continued throughout Greek history. Each house had its own altar dedicated to the family's ancestors and to whatever gods protected the home according to family tradition. Frequently, such shrines had small statues of divine figures. A ceramic tube usually hung on the wall above the shrine; the tube contained a live snake, the *agathos daimon* ("good spirit") that represented the powers watching over the family.

Greece experienced a cultural collapse or dark age (1100–800 B.C.E.) during which many religious traditions were lost. When Greek cities were established or reestablished in the Archaic Age (after 600 B.C.E.), the sacred had to be brought into them (though many rural shrines had kept their sacred character and maintained their rituals even through the time of collapse). The idea of the temple was imported from the older civilization of the Near East. Because of the central importance of religion to the creation and existence of cities, the temples were built in the very hearts of the cities—either on the agora (business district) or the acropolis (fortress), the places that in modern society would be reserved for government or commercial buildings as the most important public structures.

When a temple was built, its sacred precinct was cut off from ordinary space, usually by a wall, and purified through ritual. The space was further sanctified by a foundation deposit of holy objects buried under the floor of the new temple. A sacred zone such as this was created so that sacrifices could be performed within it. This ritual was performed at an altar that stood in the open air and used the facade of the temple as a backdrop. The interior of the temple usually housed a statue of the god but was rarely entered, since the rituals were conducted outside.

When the temple of Athena Pronoia (Athena of Forethought) was begun at Delphi in the eighth century B.C.E., the foundation deposit included not only the bones of sacrificed animals but also a cache of Mycenaean religious statuettes (dating to about 1600–1000 B.C.E.) that had been hoarded and preserved for centuries, ever since the collapse of Mycenaean civilization. In this way the sacredness of the past was used to create a new sacred institution, which was different from what had gone before yet could not be separated from tradition. This is emblematic of what happened all over Greece in the Archaic Age as Greek civilization renewed itself.

A Greek god was always the god of a particular place. Athena, for example, was not simply one goddess but had a different aspect in each cult place. In Athens alone there were temples of Athena Parthenos (Virgin Athena), Athena Nike (Victorious Athena), and Athena Polias (Civic Athena)—to name only the most important—each with its own form of worship, sacred calendar of festivals and sacrifices, and myths.

The Greeks recognized themselves as a people bound together by common culture and language, and especially by common religion, above the level of the city. When the city-states were established in the Archaic Period, national religious institutions also came into existence, what modern scholars call "Panhellenic" shrines. These sacred sites were available to all Greeks (*pan* meaning "all" and *Hellenes* being what the Greeks called themselves) and helped form a Greek identity.

The most important such shrine was Delphi, where a priestess known as the Pythia gave oracles from the god Apollo. In legend Delphi had originally housed a temple of the earth goddess Gaia, but Apollo had slain the dragon (*python*) that guarded it and took the temple for himself. A stone stood near the temple of Apollo, as raised stones did in many Greek sanctuaries. This one was called the *omphalos* ("navel") of the earth because Zeus had released two eagles from the edges of the world at the same time, and this was the spot where they met: the exact center not only of the earth but of the universe. Each Greek city maintained its own treasury at Delphi, which housed the lavish gifts of artworks or precious materials that the city or its citizens might dedicate in thanks to Pythian Apollo.

Greeks had used athletic contests as a form of worshiping the gods since Minoan times. The most famous games were held at another Panhellenic shrine, the temple of Zeus at Olympia (the same Olympic Games that were revived in 1896 C.E. and continue today). These games (beginning in 776 B.C.E., according to tradition) were held once every four years in alternation with others held at Delphi, Nemea, and Corinth. The contests included artistic as well as athletic competitions. Although no cash or prizes other than honor were given, the contestants were not amateurs. Winners usually received valuable rewards from their home cities, and many other contests existed that did award cash prizes, so there was a large corps of professional athletes and performers, some wealthy from this kind of work. The temple at Olympia used a very ancient kind of altar, a simple pile of the ashes of the sacrificed animals that was allowed to build up into a vast mound year after year through the centuries.

View of Mount Olympus, in Attica (Alison Frantz Photographic Collection, American School of Classical Studies at Athens)

Other Panhellenic sites dealt with purely personal concerns that were beyond the scope of civic religion, such as healing and salvation. Epidaurus in the Peloponnesus was the home of the main temple of Asklepios. As a son of Apollo by a mortal woman, Asklepios was technically only a semidivine "hero," but Greeks soon began to worship him as a god. His priests provided the healing of illness, a subject obviously removed from the collective religion of the city. Patients came to the shrine and slept in the courtyard of the temple overnight. The next morning the priests interpreted any dream a patient might have had and devised a treatment for him or her accordingly. Like many temples, this one had a sacred tree nearby from which offerings were hung—in this case figurines of the patients' body parts that the god had healed. The temple of the grain goddess Demeter at Eleusis (outside Athens) offered initiation into mysteries that would secure for the participants a kind of personal salvation that would let them partake of the same kind of blessed existence as heroes after death, rather than the near nonexistence Greek believed to be the common end of humankind.

ROME

by Katie Parla

Defining sacred space in ancient Rome was the responsibility of high authorities—first of kings and then later of priests. Both used ritual interpretations of occurrences in the natural world when creating sacred sites. The myth of the founding of Rome itself by the twins Romulus and Remus describes such an event. Romulus, by interpreting the flight of birds more masterfully than his brother, was able to define the ritual boundary that divided the sacred space of the city from the world beyond. Supposedly he passed this skill and this privilege on to the kings who followed him. Over time, however, the right of establishing sacred areas became the province of priests called augurs (*augures*).

The augurs were one of the main priestly colleges in the augurs Roman state religion. Originally these authorities divined the will of the gods just as Romulus had done, by interpreting the flight of birds. Later in Rome's history they also interpreted a variety of other natural phenomena: thunder, lightning, and different kinds of animal behavior. By reading these signs—or "taking auspices," as it was known—the augurs could determine the boundaries of sacred space. Occasionally the signs came unsolicited—for example, the sudden appearance of an eagle over the Capitoline Hill—but more often they were the result of deliberate ritualistic attempts to communicate with the divine world.

In Rome—and later in the territories Rome controlled—the augurs could define several types of sacred sites. One type was the *templum*, a consecrated space or site where the augurs would take auspices. For the Romans a *templum* could be a building, but it could also be plot of ground or even a fixed place in the heavens where signs from the gods might be read. Hence the word *templum* does not correspond to the modern concept of a temple, though it does have a religious connotation.

The concept of the *templum* was very broad. It covered areas where magistrates could exercise power and therefore included a wide range of government buildings, such as the Curia (Senate house), as well as open spaces of official public assembly on the Roman Forum. The *templum* could also refer to the city as a whole. In this case it was defined by the *pomerium*, a ritual boundary that divided Roman cities from the world beyond. Since the area within the *pomerium* was consecrated space, cremations, burials, military exercises, and other activities deemed inappropriate for a sacred site had to take place beyond it. The authority of a magistrate was no longer valid once he left the sacred space within the *pomerium*, emphasizing the strong bond between Rome's state religion and its political authority.

Another type of sacred site was an *aedes*. This word was applied to any place where a god was believed to dwell, whether an enclosed space or an outdoor area such as a forest, spring, mountain, or lake. An *aedes* did not have to be large or the god a major one. Many Romans kept small altars in their homes to venerate household divinities, and these altars were considered *aedes*. Minor deities, such as the female nature divinities known as nymphs, were believed to inhabit

Roman gold ring bought by a pilgrim and showing the Temple of Aphrodite at Palaepaphos (ca. 150–250 c.e.), made in Cyprus and found near Koskieni, Rhodes (© The Trustees of the British Museum)

countless outdoor settings. For instance, the nymph Albunea was worshipped at a sulfurous spring near Tivoli. The legendary she-wolf that suckled Romulus and Remus as babies was worshipped at a cave on the Palatine Hill. During Rome's republican era (ca. 509–27 b.c.e.) and through much of the existence of the Western Roman Empire (27 b.c.e.–476 c.e.), temples and altars were erected to divinities throughout Roman territory, often replacing the outdoor settings of archaic traditions.

The layout of major religious and ritual sites evolved during the course of Rome's history. The earliest evidence for sacred sites on the Roman Forum and the Palatine and Capitoline Hills are terra-cotta votive offerings left at a sacred place. A dearth of archaeological evidence makes it difficult to determine the precise layout of these places. During the republican and imperial eras proper temples begin to populate cities, frequently replacing older sacred areas. Contacts with Greece, Etruria, and Carthage influenced Roman temple architecture.

The development of religious structures in Rome began in the sixth century b.c.e. with the Temple of Jupiter Optimus Maximus on the Capitoline Hill. According to legend the king Tarquinius Priscus (r. 616–578 b.c.e.) located it on a site deemed appropriate by the augurs. Its style and decoration were heavily influenced by Etruscan architecture, and it in turn influenced early republican temple design. During the mid- to late republic Rome increased its contact with Greece through alliances and conquest and began to assimilate Greek gods into the state religion. Consequently Roman temples emulated Greek architecture.

During the republic private individuals such as victorious generals or politicians commissioned temples. Accordingly, these structures were less majestic in scale than the imperial structures that followed them. During the empire the Roman state and the imperial family commissioned sacred sites in monumental dimensions. The *aedes* of the empire served not just as holy places but also as symbols of Rome's power and the relationship between the gods and the state.

With the growth of Christianity in Rome and its empire new ideas about sacred places and sites emerged. In the fourth century c.e. the importance of Rome's traditional sacred sites diminished as Christianity spread and ultimately replaced the older state religion. To Christians pagan temples were not sacred areas, and with the end of the old religion the *pomerium* was no longer respected, and *templum* and *aedes* were pillaged, turned to other uses, and neglected. For Christians sacred areas included sites of martyrdom and pilgrimage, the locations of holy relics such as saints' bones, and the burial sites of saints and martyrs. During the first to fourth centuries worship, catechism, and baptism took place in small community centers, often apartment buildings or converted villas, rather than in large churches. Even in such rudimentary sanctuaries as these, however, some delineation of sacred and nonsacred space existed. For example, since unbaptized individuals could not enter the places of worship, baptisteries had to be built beyond the consecrated space. During the reign of the emperor Constantine (r. 306–37 C.E.), Christians began erecting the first large sacred buildings of their own, including several on the sites of martyr cults and burials.

THE AMERICAS
BY ALESSIA FRASSANI

Sacred sites in the ancient Americas were connected with the natural world and deeply rooted in the surrounding landscape. Either man-made or natural, sacred sites reflected AmerIndian cosmology that considered natural forces a manifestation of the divine. The ecological and cultural diversity of the American continent created cultural and subsistence systems that were highly integrated and interdependent. Sacred sites reflected this feature of AmerIndian life and usually attracted visitors from vast areas over periods of hundreds or even thousands of years. Sacred sites, from the northern woodlands to the southern Peruvian desert, share similar characteristics, which include orientation to cardinal points of the compass or landscape, giant effigy constructions, nearness to water resources, and economic importance as trade centers of valued and symbolic items. Religion was a pervasive aspect of AmerIndian daily life and could not be separated from economic activities. Religion and ritual, including pilgrimage to distant places, was an important part of the increasing social complexity that was developing during the rise of intensive agriculture in the ancient period.

In North America the earliest sacred sites recovered are related to the cult of the dead. The so-called Mound Builders left impressive man-made constructions throughout the eastern and midwestern woodland region of the present-day United States. These mounds, large and low, sometimes conical in shape, are most commonly found along the meanders of the Ohio, Illinois, and Mississippi river drainages, from the Gulf Coast to the Great Lakes region. These places were used and visited for generations before being eventually abandoned. People made special travels to these places to bury their dead. (No evidence of residential settlements has been found close to these mounds.) Once there, the pilgrims engaged in elaborate funerary rituals that probably lasted for several days. The mounds' closeness to the transportation system of the rivers and their visibility from afar, in an otherwise featureless landscape, made them significant and helped spread the cult of the ancestors over wide areas.

The mounds take different shapes. The Hopewell of south-central Ohio (ca. 200 B.C.E.–400 C.E.) created earthworks in the shape of connected rectangular and circular enclosures. They served as plazas for large public gatherings that were probably ceremonial. The Hopewell followed a tradition and geography of sacred places that had been previously established in the region. Serpent Mound, in Ohio, was long thought to be an Adena culture (1000 B.C.E.–200 C.E.) site because of ancient burials found nearby. Recent excavations, however, proved that the mound was built at least by

the end of the Hopewell culture. The mound takes its name from the serpentine shape that mimics the flow of the nearby river. Burials and other signs of occupation were found close to the mound, but not on it, indicating that Serpent Mound was visited only occasionally. Among the vast quantities of exotic materials found in the burials, a testament to the wide-reaching wealth accumulated by the deceased, are effigy pipes carved in the shape of birds, fish, and mammals. They were used to smoke tobacco, a ceremonial activity that linked the mundane world to the spiritual one. The animals represented may be mythical founders of clans, and the pipes may have been used in rituals to the ancestors during family burial rituals.

In Mesoamerica the earliest sacred sites either mimic or decorate natural features of the landscape, such as mountaintops or caves, where water supply is generated. Concerns for the crops and general well-being were primary motivations for the visit and care of sacred places. The cave of Chalcatzingo in the modern state of Morelos in central Mexico, dates to the Middle Formative Period of Mesoamerica from between 700 and 500 B.C.E. Chalacatzingo carvings are in an Olmec style, the major civilization of early ancient America settled in the Gulf Coast. Whether or not the site was actually built by foreigners, Olmec-related style and symbols at Chalcatzingo reveals cultural interaction between the different areas of Mesoamerica in a period of economic and religious change. The site is located on and around a mountain peak of the same name. The most famous carving depicts in low relief an enthroned character wearing elaborate attire. His headdress is tall, and he is holding a horizontal bar, symbol of authority, in his arms. He is shown in profile inside a cave, from which large volutes, or scroll-shaped forms, are emanating. The cave itself is an animal creature, as the oval eye on top indicates, while the scrolls can be interpreted as signs of water or of speaking. The enthroned character is perhaps an oracle or ruler in charge of bringing water to the region.

Teotihuacán, the most important urban center in Mesoamerica between 50 and 650 C.E., is dominated by the impressive Pyramid of the Sun. Located along the main axis of the city, the pyramid was both a symbolic and material manifestation of the power of the city throughout Middle America. The pyramid duplicates a mountain looming in back of it, called Cerro Gordo. In this way the gigantic monument is connected to its natural surrounding. In 1971 a man-made tunnel leading to a multichambered cave was discovered under the pyramid. Although it is natural, this cave has been remodeled by humans and was visited centuries before the pyramid was built. Water-related rituals took place inside this cave and contributed to making the place sacred enough that eventually the monumental pyramid was built there.

In South America sacred sites played a major role in the cultural, political, and religious unification of the Andean, coastal, and tropical regions. The earliest sacred place of interregional importance is Chavín de Huántar in the northern Andes, Peru. Set between two mountain ranges where two rivers come together, Chavín is strategically located at the gathering point of natural forces and was visited and celebrated in an effort to maintain a prosperous balance of these forces. It was at the center of a pilgrimage network that extended for over 200 miles in every direction. The most sacred and secret place at Chavín is an inner chamber where hides the so-called Lanzón, a vertical stone in the shape of a knife depicting a mythical fanged creature. Archaeologists have found that openings inside the temple were carefully designed to create sound and light effects produced by water and wind.

In the southern desert coast of Peru hundreds of earth drawings, or geoglyphs, have been found, created between 200 B.C.E. and 600 C.E. by the Nazca people. These geoglyphs were created by removing the upper layer of pebbles and revealing the underlying darker stones. Their designs range from straight lines and geometric shapes to animal representations. The giant drawings can been seen only from the air and are located away from residential dwellings. Contemporary inheritors of the Nazca region still walk in processions along straight lines in the desert. Their pilgrimage is meant to symbolically connect water resources from the sea and mountains in this harsh environment, one of the driest places in the world. Drawings of monkeys, fish, and other exotic animals from the ocean and the Amazon forest lead scholars to believe that the Nazca Lines were sacred enclosures celebrating the economic and natural interdependence of the Andean area.

See also ARCHITECTURE; ART; ASTRONOMY; CALENDARS AND CLOCKS; CLIMATE AND GEOGRAPHY; DEATH AND BURIAL PRACTICES; EDUCATION; FESTIVALS; HEALTH AND DISEASE; LANGUAGE; MINING, QUARRYING, AND SALT MAKING; RELIGION AND COSMOLOGY; ROADS AND BRIDGES; SPORTS AND RECREATION; WAR AND CONQUEST.

FURTHER READING

Mary Beard, John North, and Simon Price, *Religions of Rome*, Vol. 1, *A History* (Cambridge, U.K.: Cambridge University Press, 1998).

Jeremy Black and Anthony Green, *Gods, Demons, and Symbols of Ancient Mesopotamia* (Austin: University of Texas Press, 1992).

Jean Bottero, *Religion in Ancient Mesopotamia*, trans. Teresa Lavender Fagan (Chicago: University of Chicago Press, 2001).

Walter Burkert, *Greek Religion: Archaic and Classical,* trans. John Raffan (Oxford, U.K.: Basil Blackwell, 1985).

David Coulson and Alec Campbell, *African Rock Art: Paintings and Engravings on Stone* (New York: Harry N. Abrams, 2001).

Matthew Dillon, *Pilgrims and Pilgrimage in Ancient Greece* (London: Routledge, 1997).

Henri Frankfort, *Ancient Egyptian Religion: An Interpretation* (New York: Dover, 2000).

Manfred Lurker, *The Gods and Symbols of Ancient Egypt* (London: Thames and Hudson, 1995).

Siegfried Morenz, *Egyptian Religion* (Ithaca, N.Y.: Cornell University Press, 1973).

John Pedley, *Sanctuaries and the Sacred in the Ancient Greek World* (Cambridge, U.K.: Cambridge University Press, 2005).

Simon Price and Emily Kearns, eds., *The Oxford Dictionary of Classical Myth and Religion,* 3rd ed. (New York: Oxford University Press, 2003).

Stephen Quirke, *Ancient Egyptian Religion* (London: British Museum Press, 1993).

Chris Scarre, *Exploring Prehistoric Europe* (Oxford, U.K.: Oxford University Press, 1999).

John W. Stamper, *The Architecture of Roman Temples: The Republic to the Middle Empire* (Cambridge, U.K.: Cambridge University Press, 2005).

Lawrence E. Sullivan, ed., *Native Religions and Cultures of Central and South America* (New York: Continuum, 2002).

Richard Townsend, ed., *The Ancient Americas: Art from Sacred Landscapes* (Chicago: Art Institute of Chicago, 1992).

Richard Townsend, ed., *Hero, Hawk, and Open Hand: American Indian Art of the Ancient Midwest and South* (Chicago: Art Institute of Chicago, 2004).

Panos Valavanis, *Games and Sanctuaries in Ancient Greece: Olympia, Delphi, Isthmia, Nemea, Athens,* trans. David Hardy (Los Angeles: Getty, 2004).

Greg Woolf, ed., *Ancient Civilizations: The Illustrated Guide to Belief, Mythology, and Art* (San Diego, Calif.: Thunder Bay Press, 2005).

▶ scandals and corruption

INTRODUCTION

Bribery, corruption, and scandal were as much the part of the ancient world as they are of the 21st century—and of the centuries between. One problem historians have in reconstructing the nature and effects of corruption and scandal is that written records from the ancient world are often incomplete or nonexistent. Without a free press serving as watchdog over the activities of kings and queens, nobles, civil servants, and institutions such as churches, no one chronicled these events objectively. The written record in many cases is limited to royal decrees, letters, legal judgments, and similar documents—all written from the viewpoint of those in power or from the viewpoint of their political opponents. Court historians and similar figures in the employ of rulers were paid to enhance the reputation of their masters, not to expose scandal and corruption. Accounts provided by outsiders and later historians may have been colored by prejudices, oral legend, and incomplete information.

Bribery was undoubtedly commonplace in the ancient world. People struggled to survive and accumulate some measure of wealth that would secure their old age and give them something to leave to their heirs. In empires throughout the world, legions of inspectors, civil servants, tax collectors, surveyors, and other public officials were in positions to accept bribes to allow an illegal activity to go unnoticed, to modify records in someone's favor, to alleviate a tax burden, to extend the boundaries of a person's property, and so on.

Corruption in the ancient world often centered on the ruling classes. A common feature of government in the ancient world was the dynasty, where rulers inherited the position of king, queen, or emperor. Conflict arose, however, when the line of succession was unclear (for example, when a king died without a male heir), when the inheritor of a throne was mentally unbalanced or a minor, or simply when an individual or group wanted to seize the throne and the power that went with it. Sometimes the corruption resulted from power struggles among groups. The ancient Chinese Han Dynasty (202 B.C.E.–220 C.E.), for instance, fell because of corruption and infighting among powerful groups, including the clan to which the Han empress belonged and Confucian scholar-officials at court.

Finally, some ancient rulers themselves were simply corrupt and ruled entirely with a view to enhancing their own power and wealth rather than the welfare of their people. The ancient Roman emperor Nero (37–68 C.E.) is a good example—though much of what is known about Nero's life was written by his political rivals, who characterized him as a tyrant and even as insane. Nonetheless, many historians believe that in the year 64 Nero deliberately set the great fire of Rome that burned on the nights of July 18 and 19, destroying much of the city, because he wanted to rebuild Rome as a monument to his personal greatness. At a time when rulers held absolute power over their subjects, the potential for corruption and tyranny was enormous.

AFRICA

BY KIRK H. BEETZ

Most of ancient Africa was preliterate, and such matters as scandals and corruption are usually transmitted from the past via written records, leaving much of Africa a blank for the subject. Further, most of the writings of the major civilizations of Kush and Axum are in languages that have yet to be translated, leaving just the Kushite texts that were written in ancient Egyptian and the writings of outsiders, mostly Greeks, for records that modern readers consult.

A scandal that is still renowned involved Queen Makeda (r. ca. 1005–ca. 955 B.C.E.) of Axum, a kingdom of Africans and Sabeans, a people who populated the southern Arabian Peninsula. The name Sheba is derived from Sabean, and Makeda was probably the queen of Sheba mentioned in the Old Testament. The details of her meeting with King Solomon have been distorted over the centuries by writers seeking to modify the tale to support their particular social, political, or religious prejudices. In essence, the story says that a merchant named Tamrin from Axum ventured to King Solomon's court in search of trading opportunities and was very impressed by the king's display of wealth. He reported what he saw to Makeda, who chose to see for herself the wonders of Solomon's court. Solomon was enamored of her beauty and tried to seduce her. She refused his advances. Solomon made a bargain with her: They would sleep in separate beds in the

same room, and if Makeda took nothing without his permission, he would leave her alone, but if she did take something, she would have sex with him. He served her very spicy foods that evening, and she awoke very thirsty that night. Finding a glass of water on a table in the middle of the room, she drank from it; in an instant, Solomon was up, pointing out that she had no permission to drink. Her protests that water was common and surely not part of their bargain were to no avail. Makeda returned home and gave birth to Solomon's son.

The scandal endured during the life of Makeda and Solomon's son. When he was grown, the son visited Solomon, bringing a ring that Solomon had given Makeda. Solomon celebrated the arrival of his son and gave the young man the name Menelik. Solomon asked Menelik to stay with him and, as his eldest son, to become the next king. Menelik refused, insisting that he return to his mother to become the next monarch of Axum. Solomon declared that the eldest sons of his ministers were to go with Menelik and serve as his chief advisers. These eldest sons resented this order very much. For revenge, they sneaked into the temple room where the Ark of the Covenant was stored and replaced it with a copy, taking the original with them. It was not until Menelik and his companions reached Egypt that the theft was discovered. Solomon sent an army in pursuit of Menelik, but by the time the army reached Egypt, Menelik and the Ark had left Egypt. The army returned home, saddened by its failure, and Menelik was delighted when he learned of the theft. According to Axumite tradition, the ark has resided in or near Axum ever since.

How much of this entire story is true is open to debate. For instance, Axum's territory included the Sabean region of the southwestern Arabian Peninsula as well as much of eastern Africa, and Solomon's army could have reached the Sabean region without much trouble and could have waged war on the Axumites there, but it did not. Nevertheless, even if only the barest part of the story is true, it would likely have been a big scandal in Axum, where the queen was expected to remain a virgin until marriage. Further, it gave Axumite Christians a national tradition to cling to during the years in which they were cut off from other Christian nations by the pagans and Muslims of the medieval era.

The ancient African civilization of Kush had its own scandal of corruption that reshaped its national traditions: Egypt had long taken children of Kushite nobility and raised them according to Egyptian customs, especially Egyptian religious beliefs, hoping to make the kingdom of Kush a friendly ally. The children were treated like nobility, and they did indeed return home as practitioners of Egyptian religion when they were adults. As a result, when Egypt fell apart in the ninth century B.C.E., the kings and queens of Kush regarded themselves as the saviors of the Egyptian way of life and eventually invaded Egypt, founding the Twenty-fifth Dynasty of Egypt (770–657 B.C.E.).

At that time Napata was the capital of Kush. Jebel Barkal was a sacred hill or bluff on the other side of the Nile from

Napata, where a great religious complex had been built. The chief temple was dedicated to Egypt's chief god, Amun, who was also at that time Kush's chief god. The queens of Kush would go into the depths of the temple of Amun to give birth, implying that Amun was the father of their children, linking themselves with a tradition of Egyptian religion that Amun recognized his children in their wombs. An oracle also resided in the temple. A statue of Amun spoke to people, telling them the god's will. Priests conveyed Amun's words to the outside world. Thus, the priests had great power. Their temples and dwellings at Jebel Barkal were covered in gold, silver, and gems. Hallways were dazzling with their glittering walls and many statues of Egyptian gods. The statue of Amun even foretold when kings were to die. In fact, the priests actually ordered a king to commit suicide, on Amun's orders, and he obeyed.

Then came King Aspelta (r. 593–568 B.C.E.). The outset of his reign must have been very challenging because a revitalized Egypt had sent an army into Kush, and it had sacked Napata in about 593 B.C.E. Then the priests of Amun declared that the god had said Aspelta was to die. Perhaps not as gullible as his predecessors, or perhaps not as faithful, Aspelta not only refused to commit suicide but also conspired with one of his generals to have the buildings and caves of Jebel Barkal seized and the priests killed. Apparently, nearly every priest was killed, helping to end the importance of Jebel Barkal. Perhaps the invasion by Egypt had soured public sentiment against all things Egyptian enough for Aspelta to get away with such sacrilege. He moved his court to Meroë, farther south along the Nile, formerly an Egyptian military outpost but by then a thriving trading center. He and his successors promoted a lion god as their new chief god.

EGYPT

BY AMR KAMEL

Ancient Egypt, like any other place ancient or modern, was not an ideal society. People who engaged in bribery and all manner of crime and corruption existed alongside people who were humble, law-abiding, and religious. The Egyptians attempted to hold their society together using a group of fundamental principles called *maat*, which eventually came to represent the cosmic order as well, since Egyptians believed their land to be the center of the world. Maintaining *maat* was the major duty of Egyptian kings, and it was the subject of many ancient Egyptian teachings. Any abuse of power by an official could be controlled only if there was ethical awareness and a sense of loyalty in the community. When these faltered, officials increasingly took advantage of their positions, especially when the purchase of offices and the abuse of oracles were concerned. These abuses become apparent notably from the Nineteenth Dynasty (ca. 1307–ca. 1196 B.C.E.) forward.

Desiring reform, Horemheb, the last king of the Eighteenth Dynasty (ca. 1550–ca. 1307 B.C.E.), conscientiously enforced *maat*, issuing a royal decree against bribery and corruption that can still be read on the 10th pylon at Karnak. In the decree Horemheb states that corrupt behavior on the part of the authorities represents an offense and warns that these offenses "from today onward" will be punished by such penalties as flogging and cutting off of noses and, in some cases, will require the redress of any damage inflicted on an individual. He advises his newly appointed officers: "Do not compromise yourselves with people! Do not accept rewards from others!"

Nonetheless, such instructions did not guarantee a peaceful life. Ancient Egyptian literature refers from time to time to scandals, corrupt people, and other illegal behavior. The earliest example was mentioned in the biography of Weni, an important Sixth Dynasty (ca. 2323–ca. 2150 B.C.E.) officer. There appears to have been an unsuccessful conspiracy against Pepi I plotted by one of his numerous wives. Weni seems to have been singled out to hear about that confidential matter when he was in the royal women's quarters. From the same Sixth Dynasty period, a scene in the Saqqara mustaba of the vizier Khentika depicts the judgment and corporal punishment of five district governors brought before the vizier and charged with corruption in collecting taxes. All were punished swiftly and harshly.

Egyptian texts do not mention other cases of immoral behavior until late in the New Kingdom, when abundant evidence of corruption appears, possibly because of a deficiency in the administration. The inscription of Mes, engraved in his tomb at Saqqara from the Nineteenth Dynasty, describes a lawsuit about the ownership of some fields inherited by various members of the family to which Mes belonged. The text refers to a certain Khay, who originally was not a family member but who claimed his right based on forged documents that he submitted to the highest law court in Egypt, presided over by the vizier who pronounced his judgment in favor of Khay.

A literary document dating from the late Nineteenth Dynasty describes the career of a corrupt man named Paneb—the foreman of a group of workers at Deir el-Medina—who, with his son Aapehti, committed several crimes. Paneb is accused of having obtained his position by bribing the vizier. Paneb stole some statues from the temple of King Seti I, with the intention of decorating his own tomb. He then went on to murder his adoptive father, Neferhotep. He was arrested and sent for trial before the vizier Amenope. Nonetheless, by the exercise of some influence or chicanery, he was able to secure his acquittal and not only obtained the murdered Neferhotep's position but also eventually had himself buried in a handsome tomb. He and his son made love with five of his colleagues' wives and their daughters. He was also accused failing to pay for clothes that had been made for him and of drunkenness.

In the reign of Ramses III legal documents describe a trial of persons who planned the murder of the king. The principal defendant was the secondary queen Tiy, who apparently wanted the throne for her son Pentewere. The jury was composed of 14 officials, four of whom were convicted of having sexual intercourse with the wives of some of the defendants and were accordingly deprived of their titles and punished with mutilation. In year 17 of the reign of Ramses III a gang was being shortchanged by a greedy official who used undersized measures to distribute rations and then presumably kept the difference for himself. The matter was brought to the attention of Akh-pet, another scribe of the vizier, who checked the grain measure and found that it held 38 *hin* instead of the standard 40 (ca. one-half bushel). Thus the workmen had been receiving 5 percent less than their due.

The famous Tomb Robbery Papyri also describe the looting of graves and temples during the reigns of Ramses IX and XI, sometimes with the complicity of officials who took bribes to keep silent and release those who were under arrest. Another mid-Twentieth Dynasty (1196–1070 B.C.E.) papyrus records charges of large-scale embezzlement and misconduct against personnel of the temple of Khnum at Elephantine, including an unnamed priest. Another papyrus describes the crimes of a certain Djehutihotep, the chief guard of the Karnak temple. Since this was arguably the most sacred public place in Egypt, his crimes provide evidence of the extent of negligence and corruption at the highest levels of the Theban administration.

In the prayers of ordinary Egyptians, preserved in letters and documents from the village housing the workers at Deir el-Medina, there are pleas to the gods for justice after all other doors were closed to them, pleas to hear their petitions, and pleas to ease their suffering from the rapidly increasing corruption in their society. In one prayer, Amun is "the vizier of the poor; he does not accept bribes from the guilty, he does not speak to the one who witnesses, he does not look to (favor) the one who makes promises." In another source, a lady invokes Amun to protect her from gossip and rumors. Although these documents portray the dark side of ancient Egyptian society, there were nonetheless ordinary good people who attempted to bring up their offspring with ethics and good principles.

THE MIDDLE EAST
BY HEATHER D. BAKER

In Mesopotamia political power was concentrated in the hands of the ruler. The surviving sources for the exercise of royal power therefore have to be treated with caution because they almost always originate with the king and his court; independent testimony is rare indeed. The written documentation available about political scandal at the highest level tends to concern episodes when the transition from one ruler to the next was contested or when a king saw fit to condemn the actions of his predecessor or both. In such cases as these the king whose account survives may have been motivated by a desire to enhance his own reputation at the expense of a previous ruler by seeking to question the legitimacy of his reign or his actions while in office.

The circumstances surrounding the death of the Assyrian king Sennacherib (704–681 B.C.E.) reflect one such instance of a troubled succession from one ruler to the next. Many de-

tails of what happened are still unclear, because the cuneiform sources are fragmentary and difficult to interpret. Still, it is clear that there was a plot to murder Sennacherib, who had taken the unusual step of naming his younger son, Esarhaddon, as his successor. Esarhaddon's case may well have been promoted by his mother, Naqia, a powerful woman well versed in palace intrigue. Following the death of his father, while Esarhaddon was in hiding for safety, his older brothers fought among themselves for the throne, but on his return Esarhaddon defeated them in battle. He took the throne and ruled for 11 years (680–669 B.C.E.).

Another political scandal, of a rather curious nature, involves the Babylonian king Nabonidus (r. 556–539 B.C.E.), who left his country to live in apparently self-imposed exile in Taymāʾ (in Saudi Arabia) for 10 years. Although he went to Arabia in the role of military conqueror, this does not explain why he remained there for so many years, leaving his son Belshazzar to rule in Babylonia in his stead. A conventional view holds that the Babylonian priesthood opposed his unorthodox religious beliefs, especially his attempts to promote the moon god Sin at the expense of the head of the Babylonian pantheon, Marduk. Nabonidus's own inscriptions hint at such a background to these events. His successor, Cyrus the Great, the Persian conqueror of Babylonia, certainly portrayed Nabonidus as an oppressive ruler who did not worship Marduk. Cyrus claimed to have been chosen by Marduk and to have restored Babylonian religious life to the peaceful state it had enjoyed before Nabonidus disrupted it.

A more informal insight into the affairs of state can be found in the correspondence kept in the royal archives. Of course, it has to be borne in mind that letters written to the king were intended to promote the cause of the sender by casting him in a favorable light, sometimes at the expense of his rivals. Sometimes the letters contain reports of alleged injustice; one scholar, for instance, writes to the king complaining that a local governor had taken away a field of his. It seems to be expected that the king will intervene personally in cases such as this where officials abused their power.

The sources for information about economic scandal and corruption are of a rather different nature. Some of the Laws of Hammurabi are concerned with the misappropriation of property, both private and institutional, and with fraud. They include, for example, the case of a (female) innkeeper who gives out short measures of beer. They also set out regulations governing the conduct of trading ventures so as to protect the merchants from fraud.

The great palace and temple institutions of the ancient Near East were extremely bureaucratic, and much effort was expended on controlling and recording the movement of goods between different establishments and their responsible officials. Precious items could be stored in sealed containers or rooms. Sealing was the ancient equivalent of a locking mechanism. The official in charge would impress his seal upon a lump of clay applied to the door bolt. When the room needed to be opened, the sealing would be broken one; it contains many documents recording cases brought before the temple authorities. Most involve relatively minor episodes of theft and embezzlement. There was one particularly persistent offender, a man named Gimillu. His career is documented over a period of around 20 years; at first he was in charge of the livestock owed to the temple, and later he was responsible for the income from the temple's agricultural land. Gimillu misappropriated temple property on a large scale; even after being convicted and fined heavily and then trying to abscond, he continued to work for the temple in a responsible position. There does seem to have been a high degree of tolerance toward convicted thieves and fraudsters. From the private sphere in the Neo-Babylonian Period (625–539 B.C.E.) there is a court record concerning attempted extortion by a man who tried to pass off a forged cuneiform tablet. When challenged by the intended victim, he snatched the clay tablet from his victim's hands and tried to destroy it by chewing it. Other records reveal that even though he was found guilty, the villain continued to conduct business. The scribe who wrote the fake tablet was also liable to be punished when caught.

ASIA AND THE PACIFIC
BY KIRK H. BEETZ

Although Confucius (551–479 B.C.E.) believed that China had an ancient past that featured good and just governments, it seems that no ancient Chinese government at any time was free of corruption. Written records for the Shang (1500–1045 B.C.E.) and early Zhou (1045–256 B.C.E.) dynasties are scant, but those that exist suggest that corruption among military leaders and government officials was constant throughout the history of ancient China. One corrupt practice involved the trading of women by powerful men. During the Six Dynasties (220–589 C.E.) women were used as bribes, and if the bribes persuaded generals to switch sides during a war, the fates of millions of people changed based on a man's lust for women. Many military leaders were not susceptible to being bribed with women but could be bribed with gifts of horses or money. Thus, the corruption of some Chinese leaders reduced women to the level of horses, and for the sake of their bribes they betrayed their province or country, their lord or king, and broke their oaths of loyalty. Sometimes tens of thousands of people died when the man who was supposed to protect them changed sides for a bribe and killed them.

Many historians consider the era of Confucius to have been notably corrupt. Most of the people of China were peasants who were forced to work every day in their fields. From the Zhou Dynasty through the end of the ancient era kings occasionally tried to redistribute land to peasants, but members of the nobility would confiscate land or loan peasants money at interest rates that were impossible to repay. They would then take the peasants' lands and force the former owners to work the lands for the profit of the nobles, making the peasants slaves in all but name.

Stone panel from the palace of Sennacherib, Nineveh, northern Iraq, Neo-Assyrian, about 700–695 B.C.E.; this panel shows soldiers of the royal guard; the king's death was thought to have been the result of a plot within the palace to murder him. (© The Trustees of the British Museum)

in front of witnesses. In this way it would be immediately clear if someone had gained unauthorized access. Livestock could be branded in such a way that marked them as temple property, and even the temple dependents who formed part of its workforce could be marked to make it difficult for them to escape.

Thus the institutional administration contained inbuilt deterrents against fraud and theft, but they could not be entirely eliminated. Normally it is difficult to extract information on these subjects from the cuneiform tablets that made up the institutional archives. To shed light on them, documents that tell a story rather than simply recording the transfer of commodities are needed. In records of accounts there are many cases where the figures do not add up, but it is impossible to prove that these represent a deliberate attempt to defraud rather than simply errors on the part of the scribe.

Suitable sources include records of lawsuits and letters containing anecdotal evidence of corruption. Fortunately, some of the surviving archives contain material of this kind. The Eanna temple archive from Neo-Babylonian Uruk is

A government that had intended to end corruption became one of the most corrupt of all. This was the government of the Qin Dynasty (221–207 B.C.E.), which imposed the legalist philosophy of government. Under legalism, every action was either sanctioned or forbidden by law. The idea was to regulate life so that everybody did what they were supposed to do and never did what they were not supposed to do. The laws were so strict and so numerous that people could not help but break a few every day, and punishments were harsh. Even slight offenses could result in a sentence of mutilation and several years of hard labor on the government's construction projects. Emperor Qin Shi Huangdi used the laws to force hundreds of thousands of people to work on the Great Wall and elsewhere, where many died from the harsh conditions.

When the emperor died, his advisers Li Si (ca. 280–208 B.C.E.) and Han Fei Zi (d. 233 B.C.E.) pretended that he was still alive and sent his eldest son a phony message ordering him to commit suicide. Prince Fusu ignored the pleadings of his father's chief general to make sure the order was real before he killed himself, but he committed suicide anyway. Prince Huhai became emperor, controlled by Li Si and Han Fei Zi. The corruption of this period was so severe that the Qin Dynasty was already crumbling when rebels toppled it.

During the Han Dynasty (202 B.C.E.–220 C.E.), Confucian scholars were allowed to try to impose a more benevolent form of government. It proved impossible to stamp out bribery, especially in remote provinces. The court system was corrupted by wealthy criminals who paid poor people to serve their sentences for them. In cities young people sometimes formed gangs and beat, killed, and robbed people. The government tried to eliminate the gangs with diligent police work and informants, but the police were too often bribed. Tax collectors frequently took more than the law allowed and kept it for themselves. The punishment for this practice was death, but it was common enough to help inspire a peasant revolt in 14 C.E.

Throughout the recorded history of India corruption was a problem. Indian literature, folktales, and historical writings from about the first century C.E. onward feature many tales of corrupt practices, and historians have found accounts in records from as early as the 300s C.E. In the court system witnesses often slanted their testimony in court to favor whichever side was paying them. This meant that innocent people were often convicted and punished for crimes. To make matters worse, the convicted criminal's spouse and children were imprisoned as well. They all were bound by the ankles amid filth and beaten and tortured two or three times a day.

Gambling and prostitution were common. Gambling was forbidden by Hindu religious rules of conduct, but it was usually sanctioned and regulated by the government. Gamblers often lost their family's fortune, forcing them to become slaves or to spend their lives trying to pay their debts. Sometimes a gambler made a fortune, which was known as "black" money, as opposed to money earned honestly through government service or a trade.

Prostitutes almost always associated with such criminals as con artists, burglars, and extortionists, so the government often used them as spies on criminals. A prostitute could earn a good name this way because she worked for the secret police, making her work in the public interest. Prostitutes varied from sickly streetwalkers just trying to earn enough for food to women who were well trained from childhood to seduce rich men. The latter group were well educated, had excellent taste, knew what to say on every occasion, and were gifted in all the various sexual acts that would ensnare men. The education of prostitutes was regulated by the national government, and their teachers were often paid by the government because the work of prostitutes was considered a contributing factor in the health of the nation. When beginning their careers in brothels, they were taught to be without pity; their object was to seduce men, discard them, and move on to the next rich man. Occasionally a prostitute became a man's wife, and typically she worked extra hard to be a good wife.

Sex scandals sometimes shaped India's history. For example, there is the legendary account of Amrapali, a famous courtesan in the Licchavi Republic in northern India around 400 B.C.E. She was so successful that she had become the land's leading lady. King Bimbisāra of Magadha, an enemy of the Licchavis, sneaked into their capital of Vaisali and spent a week undetected enjoying the company of Amrapali. Their pride injured, the knights of Licchavi attacked Magadha with great vigor and sparked a war that Magadha won, which helped to propel Magadha toward building an empire that eventually ruled most of India.

Perhaps equally scandalous was the death of Bimbisāra, who was starved by his son Ajatashatru (fl. 300s B.C.E.). This seems to have been common among the monarchs of ancient India. The king was alleged to have chosen to starve himself to death, but usually a scheming son was responsible. When Ajatashatru's old enemy Prasenajit, king of Koshala, was overthrown in his turn by his son, Prasenajit fled to Ajatashatru and then died of exhaustion. This gave Ajatashatru an excuse to avenge Prasenajit, and he attacked Koshala, ending its existence.

Very little is known of scandals and corruption in ancient Japan, but there are hints from Chinese observers. One such was an ambassador, Zhang Zheng, to Queen Himiko's court in the 200s B.C.E. Himiko lived to a great age but apparently died without a successor. Her kingdom was called Yamatai and was composed of about 50 states, each with its own chief. After her death the chiefs selected a man to replace her. According to Zhang Zheng, the king's rule was marred by constant murders and inept government administration. Zhang Zheng claims that after two years he helped engineer the ouster of the king and his replacement by a 12-year-old girl whose name may have been Inoye.

The rest of Asia and the Pacific's cultures probably had their own forms of corruption and scandal, but archaeologists and historians are making slow progress in uncovering evidence for such practices in central Asia, Southeast Asia,

Korea, Australia, and the Pacific Islands, with most records appearing as inscriptions on public monuments such as megaliths and temples—places where the people who erected them were unlikely to confess their misdeeds.

EUROPE

BY BRADLEY SKEEN

The peoples of Europe living outside the Greek and Roman worlds in a region that scholars often call temperate Europe did not leave behind any significant written records. What is known about their public affairs, including what they considered scandalous, comes only from Roman historians. Of these historians, Tacitus (56–117 C.E.) is the most important. Although he wrote during the Pax Romana, the height of the Roman Empire's power and prosperity, he was deeply dissatisfied with the political and social life of the empire. Much of his criticism is indirect, made in connection with Roman policies in temperate Europe. He denounces the decadent and politically and morally ineffectual life of Roman aristocrats by implicitly contrasting that life with his exaggerated account of the virtues of the Germans in his *Germania* (Germany), a work devoted to the national character of the Germanic peoples. In his *Annales* Tacitus openly criticizes the cruelty deemed necessary for maintaining imperial power in his famous aphorism, "They make a deserted land and call it peace!" referring to the Romans' tactic of slaughtering civilians and warriors alike in their campaigns in Europe.

Along with his praise of the Germans, Tacitus regularly describes German kings and chiefs as betraying the cause of German nationalism, which he considers they should have taken up in order to resist the decadent influence of Rome. He presents the local leaders as bribed and bullied by Roman officials and at the same time greedy for Roman luxuries. He sees these weaknesses on the part of German leaders as scandalous. Tacitus develops the scandalous weakness of German leaders as a literary theme to be used in the criticism of his own culture. What he writes cannot be accepted at face value as objective fact or even as a representation of how things might have seemed to the Germans themselves. He never considers alternative interpretations: for example, that the people outside the Roman Empire might have wanted the peace and prosperity that existed inside the empire in order to make their lives better lives. This very desire was certainly present in temperate Europe, as is seen from the works of a later Roman historian, Ammianus Marcellinus (ca. 325–391 C.E.). Ammianus makes it clear that when the German tribes invaded the Roman Empire beginning in the fourth century C.E. (eventually leading to the collapse of the Western Roman Empire), their initial goal was simply to be allowed to live inside the empire to gain protection from Huns and other tribes pressuring them from the East.

Julius Caesar (100–44 B.C.E.), in his account of his conquest of Gaul, establishes the stereotype of the tribal peoples of temperate Europe when he writes that they possess some kind of innate virtue—characterized as manliness—because they live simple lives devoted to subsistence agriculture and warfare. This way of life could be corrupted through luxury by contact with Roman civilization into a morally inferior condition characterized as effeminacy. Tacitus takes up this theme. He treats as a social scandal the fact that the virtuous barbarian Germans should become corrupted like the effeminate civilized Romans, treating both Germans and Romans as stereotypes. For example, while the simple German people in the interior knew nothing of gold and silver, those living along the borders of the Roman Empire had been corrupted by the greed and luxury associated with these metals in the so-called civilized world, and this he considers scandalous.

Similarly Tacitus admires the Germans' idea of the sanctity of marriage, making a contrast with the adultery that he finds distasteful in his own society. On the other hand, Tacitus considers the Germans' love of gambling scandalous. He says that it is not uncommon for a German to become a slave by gambling away his own freedom after he has lost all his possessions. There is no way to verify this, but given the criticism of the Roman love of gambling by contemporary Roman authors, this was probably meant to make the Roman reader think of his own culture. Tacitus seems to move into fantasy at the end of the *Germania*, where he claims that the Germans farthest removed from the Roman world are even worse than Romans and are actually ruled by women, a condition that he says is worse than slavery. This must be a reference to the vast influence and great freedom of aristocratic Roman women in Tacitus's own society and not necessarily a true statement about ancient Europe.

Tacitus lived during an era in which the imperial government had curtailed the political power and even the property and freedom of his own senatorial class. Therefore he considered the greatest good for humanity to be freedom, the very thing that he and those like him had lost. Accordingly, he considered the greatest scandal among the Germans to be their trading of freedom to the Roman government for what

Base-silver radiate of Carausius, with the emperors Diocletian and Maximian, Roman Britain, late third century C.E.; in the years 287–296 C.E. Britain had its own emperor, Carausius, who had been accused of corruption and assumed power to save himself from punishment. (© The Trustees of the British Museum)

he thought to be luxury, which he considered trivial, since he and his class had it in abundance.

The last great chance for German freedom came with Armin (18? B.C.E.–19 C.E.). He was a chief of the German tribe of the Cherusci and served in the Roman army as an auxiliary. He became an important Roman ally and was given the wealth and status of a Roman knight, the second-highest position in Roman society. But he rejected all of this to turn on his Roman overlords and used his position to destroy the Roman army occupying Germany by ambushing them in the Teutoburg Forest (near modern Bremen). He fought other successful campaigns against the Romans also, until they abandoned all hope of conquering Germany as a province. According to Tacitus, Arminius boasted of fighting for the freedom of the German nation rather than for his own fame and power.

Tacitus contrasts Armin with Armin's father-in-law, Segestes, another German prince, who remained loyal to the Romans, claiming that this loyalty was in the Germans' interest since it brought peace and prosperity, if not freedom. Tacitus defames Segestes by pointing out that, acting as a coward, he handed over Armin's wife and son—his own daughter and grandson—to the Romans as hostages. Tacitus also relates how Armin fought against other German chieftains who were attempting to establish a united monarchy over all of Germany for the purpose of becoming a satellite of the Roman Empire and how still others offered to assassinate Armin out of servility to the Romans. Finally, Tacitus gives an account of Armin's death in a battle with other Germans who opposed his plans to become king of a free Germany.

While much of Tacitus's information may be factually correct, his interpretation of those facts served his purpose of criticizing his own culture. His writing tells more about what he considered scandalous in Rome than how the Germans themselves thought about the excesses of their political leaders.

GREECE

BY PAUL MCKECHNIE

The national myth of Greece began with scandal—namely, the corruption behind the Trojan War. Three goddesses, quarrelling over an apple labeled "for the prettiest" that Eris, goddess of discord, had rolled into a party where she was not invited, decided to parade for a beauty contest. Zeus wisely refused to judge, and Hera, Athena, and Aphrodite were forced to select a mortal judge. They chose Troy's king Priam's son Paris, a foolish young man who was alone in the hills keeping his father's flocks.

When they appeared before him, each goddess proposed a bribe. Hera offered to make Paris a great king, Athena promised to make him a celebrated hero, and Aphrodite, goddess of love, pledged to reward him with the most beautiful woman in the world as his wife. Paris accepted the last offer and judged in Aphrodite's favor. The most beautiful woman in the world, Helen, however, was already married to Menelaus, king of Sparta. When Paris visited Sparta on his father's business, Menelaus was out of town; Paris, captivated by Helen, whispered, "Run away with me," in her ear, and she did not hesitate.

Homer's *Iliad*, written in (probably) the eighth century B.C.E., is the tale of the 10-year war fought by Menelaus, his brother Agamemnon, and their Greek army against Troy to get Helen back. There, the personal is the political with no dividing line between politics and war. But Hesiod, another Greek poet, perhaps after 700 B.C.E., refers to a more recognizably "political" scandal in *Works and Days*, his long poem about how to succeed as a farmer. He and his brother, Perses, were supposed to divide the land that their father left them, but (Hesiod claims) Perses took it all—and Hesiod's court case against him went nowhere because of the "bribe-devouring *basileis*" judging it. They expect presents from both sides, he says, but giving a present is no guarantee of a favorable result—though failing to give a present guarantees that you will lose. Reading *Works and Days*, we can hear only Hesiod's side of the story. If Perses could give us his version, we might look at the matter differently.

In his *Histories* the Greek historian Herodotus of the fifth century B.C.E. wrote about many stories of bribery and corruption, both successful and unsuccessful. He insists that the Alcmaeonidae, a noble Athenian family exiled from their home, caused the Spartans to march to Athens in 510 B.C.E. and expel Peisistratus, an Athenian tyrant. The Alcmaeonidae accomplished this by bribing the priestess of Delphi to give oracular answers to the Spartans in which the supposed voice of the god advised them to liberate Athens. The Delphic oracle was so deeply respected that any advice it gave had a good chance of being accepted: It was a matter (the Alcmaeonidae found) of ensuring that the right advice was dispensed.

Less successfully, in 499 B.C.E. Aristagoras of Miletus went to the Spartan king Cleomenes (r. ca. 521–490 B.C.E.) and tried to talk him into supporting the Ionians in their revolt against Darius I (r. 522–486 B.C.E.), king of Persia and their overlord. He showed Cleomenes a map and explained the campaign to him, but foolishly admitted that he was asking the Spartans to travel three months' march away from the sea. Cleomenes told him that this was an unrealistic request; but Aristagoras came back and tried to change his mind with cash, eventually offering 50 talents, which would have been a large sum of money. According to Herodotus, when Cleomenes hesitated, his eight-year-old daughter, Gorgo, said, "Get up and go, father, or the stranger will certainly corrupt you." He took her advice, and the Ionians had to fight without Spartan help.

In other scandalous stories, Herodotus links the political with the personal. Periander, tyrant of Corinth from 627 to 586 B.C.E., once lost something he had borrowed. Hoping to find it, he sent to the oracle of the dead in Thesprotia to ask the ghost of his wife, Melissa, where it was. The ghost told Periander's messengers that she refused to answer because she was cold—clothes had been buried with her at her funeral but not burned. (The idea seems to be that unless they were burned, the clothes could not go to the world of the dead.) The ghost added that Periander would know that she was really Melissa because he had put his loaves in a cold oven. When he heard this, Periander remembered that he had had sex with Melissa's corpse after she was dead. He announced to all the women of Corinth that they should come to the temple of the goddess Hera. They dressed as if it were a festival and turned out, but then Periander's guards stripped them naked, and all their clothes were heaped in a pit and burned. Afterward, Melissa's ghost revealed the information Periander wanted. In Book 5 of Herodotus's *History*, Socles, a Corinthian, tells this story and concludes by saying, "This, then, is the nature of tyranny, and such are its deeds." Corrupt governments treat people the way Periander treated the women of Corinth.

At Athens under the democratic government of the fifth and fourth centuries B.C.E. officials had to report to the boule, or legislative council, at the end of their year in office and have their accounts examined. In general, transparency was expected, but the Greek biographer Plutarch (ca. 46–after 119 C.E.), in his *Life of Pericles*, records how in the early 440s B.C.E. the Athenian statesman Pericles bribed King Pleistoanax (r. 459–409 B.C.E.) of Sparta and his assistant Cleandridas to lead their Spartan army home instead of fighting. When Pericles presented his accounts for the campaign, he listed 10 talents mysteriously as "necessary expenses," and the council passed the accounts without inquiring closely.

In the fourth century B.C.E. the growing power of Macedon placed a strain on Athenian standards of conduct. Demosthenes (384–322 B.C.E.), the leading anti-Macedonian politician at Athens, prosecuted Aeschines in 343 B.C.E. over events in 347 B.C.E., when Aeschines had been part of an embassy sent to King Philip II (r. 359–336 B.C.E.) to administer oaths confirming a peace treaty. Philip cunningly made important gains between when the peace was agreed and when oaths were taken. Demosthenes alleged in his speech "On the False Embassy," in effect, that Aeschines (and other ambassadors) had been bribed to be complicit. Aeschines delivered a counter oration, and the jury acquitted him by a narrow majority. But in 324 B.C.E., when Alexander the Great's treasurer, Harpalus, had run away with 5,000 talents of Alexander's money and come to Athens for protection, Demosthenes was accused by the Athenian orator Hypereides (ca. 390–322 B.C.E.) in his speech "Against Demosthenes" of accepting a 20-talent bribe from Harpalus: Demosthenes was found guilty.

ROME

BY KIRK H. BEETZ

When looking at the great depravity of some Romans, it is worth remembering that Rome did not survive as a culture for over a thousand years because of fools such as Nero (r.

54–68 C.E.); it survived because for hundreds of years it had midlevel civil servants who were dedicated to the welfare of their nation. A multitude of hardworking government employees kept the empire running in spite of the greed, lust, and cruelty of some of its leaders.

The Roman Republic began with a scandal, the rape of Lucretia by Sextus, the son of King Tarquinius Superbus (r. 535–510 B.C.E.). At the time, the Roman army was laying siege to the city of Ardea, and as a game some Roman officers decided they would discover whose wives were the more faithful by paying them a surprise visit in Rome. Of all the wives only Lucretia was doing exactly what she told her husband she had been doing in her letters to him. The officers returned to the siege, but Sextus remained behind and forced himself on Lucretia, who wrote to her husband to tell him. Her husband, Lucius Tarquinius Collatinus, and some of his friends rushed back to Rome where Lucretia explained what had happened, then killed herself. This triggered the rebellion that threw King Tarquinius Superbus out of Rome and began the Roman Republic.

During the centuries after the founding of the Republic, the upper class of Rome, the patricians, who controlled the Senate and were expected to take leadership roles in government, worked hard to maintain their elite status. In the process, some of them engaged in extreme corruption. Magistrates of Italian cities and governors of provinces looted the public treasury. They stole taxes and property and sold free families into slavery for profit. This rapacious corruption reached its peak during the dictatorship of Lucius Cornelius Sulla (r. 81–79 B.C.E.). He was a Roman general who committed a grave breach of public trust by invading the city of Rome with his army.

Sulla had his political opponents murdered and then went on to murder anyone he disliked. He tried to undo reforms that had given power to common people. Among his laws was one that allowed only juries of senators to hear cases of senators accused of crimes. Senators found they could get away with murder, literally, because their fellow senators on the juries were easy to bribe. Among those who profited illegally was the governor of Sicily, Gaius Verres. He and his henchmen stole almost everything that could be moved. It took almost 10 years to bring the Roman legal system back to a condition where a rich criminal such as Verres could be brought to justice. The lawyer and orator Cicero prosecuted him and used the forum of the court to describe the corruption that had infected the Roman government.

The First Triumvirate (r. 60–53 B.C.E.)—Marcus Licinius Crassus, Gnaeus Pompeius Magnus (Pompey), and Gaius Julius Caesar—was formed in part as a way of ending corruption and conflict in government. Crassus died in an eastern military campaign, and Pompey was closely associated with Sulla and some of the corrupt officials who had profited from Sulla's laws. This left Julius Caesar the only leader common people looked to for help. Caesar became dictator in 49 B.C.E. Although he was a tough and sometimes brutal military

THE VILE VERRES

Gaius Verres (ca. 120–43 B.C.E.) belonged to Rome's social elite. He was a political opportunist who supported whatever person had power, first the reformer Gaius Marius and then Marius's enemy Lucius Cornelius Sulla when Sulla invaded the city of Rome. Already Verres was accused of embezzlement, but Sulla protected him. Verres became an assistant to the corrupt governor of Cilicia, Gnaeus Cornelius Dolabella, in 80 B.C.E. In 78 B.C.E. Dolabella was tried and convicted of numerous crimes, but Verres won a pardon for himself, despite having been Dolabella's partner in the crimes, by testifying against Dolabella. He became a government official in the city of Rome, where he used his office to promote the interests of Sulla, who appointed him governor of Sicily in about 73 B.C.E.

During Verres's time in Sicily he made himself not only one of the most corrupt but also one of the most loathed people in Roman history. He organized his administration like a gang of criminals, and there was no limit to his greed and cruelty. He and his henchmen stripped Sicily's temples of their art, especially their statues. Using government authority his gangs broke into private homes and looted them of everything that was valuable. The loss to Sicily was greater than the loss it had experienced in war. Its once-thriving tourist industry collapsed. When people protested, Verres accused them of being traitors and prevented their cases from being sent on to the city of Rome, which was their right under Roman law. He had them tortured and then crucified.

When Verres returned to the city of Rome in 70 B.C.E., Sicilians asked Cicero to prosecute him for his crimes. Cicero chose to use Verres as an example of corruption throughout government, detailing how Verres used his status as a high government official to brutalize and murder hundreds, perhaps thousands, of people. The lawyers for Verres tried to delay the trial, but Cicero pressed forward. In court he delivered a devastating case, and Verres fled into exile even before he was found guilty. In the south of Gaul he led a comfortable life, having kept much of the wealth he had stolen, until Marcus Antonius had him killed in 43 B.C.E.

and many Judaean officials into slavery to finance his army, and he looted Rome's ally Rhodes of almost all its wealth.

Octavian, renamed the emperor Augustus, ruled Rome from 27 B.C.E. to 14 C.E. Augustus's successor, Tiberius (r. 14–37 C.E.), was an outstanding general with a sober temperament. Yet his sober temperament became very dark. He neglected his civic duties and eventually retreated to the island of Capri in 26 C.E., where he indulged in a taste for sex with children. His absence from Rome allowed the leader of the Praetorian Guard, Lucius Aelius Sejanus, to take over much of the Roman government. Sejanus was greedy and ruthless, using the charge of treason as an excuse for murdering anyone who seemed to be between him and something he wanted. Tiberius was told by his sister-in-law Antonia about Sejanus's corruption, and Sejanus and his supporters were executed.

For sheer depravity historians tend to single out two Roman emperors, Caligula (r. 37–41 C.E.) and Nero (r. 54–68 C.E.). Both started out with a great deal of public goodwill. Nero, in particular, had experienced and talented advisers to help him. But Caligula seems to have been criminally insane. His behavior was bizarre, violent, and cruel. He had sex with all three of his sisters, raped a bride on her wedding day, and tortured people. His public acts were weird; he even nominated a horse, Incitatus, for a consulship. He was murdered and quickly replaced by Claudius (r. 41–54 C.E.). The greatest scandal of Claudius's reign was the marriage of his wife, Messalina, to consul-designate Silius while Claudius was away. She and Silius were executed. Claudius himself may have been poisoned by his last wife, Agrippina the Younger, apparently in the hope that she would rule through her son Nero, who instead had her murdered.

Nero castrated a boy and then married him. He fancied himself a singer and stage actor and forced people to watch him for hours as he performed. Pregnant women gave birth in the audience because they were not permitted to leave. After most of Rome went up in flames, Nero began the construction of a large and very expensive palace in Rome, and rumors circulated that he had started the fire and sang and danced while it burned. This story seems to have been untrue; Nero actually seems to have tried to put out the fire. To direct blame away from himself, he blamed the Christians. He took delight in torturing them and had many tied to stakes and ignited to serve as torches during celebrations at his palace or in the amphitheater. Eventually, when Nero was away from Rome, the Senate sentenced him to death, and he committed suicide.

During the 200s and 300s C.E. corruption was most often found in the collection of taxes. Wealthy men would buy a high public office in a province and then divert government funds into their own pockets. Courts were subject to bribery, and serving on juries and taking bribes proved to be very profitable. Emperors tried to put a stop to the corruption of the courts, and Diocletian (r. 284–305 C.E.), in particular, seems to have struck fear into the hearts of many a corrupt court official as well as provincial leaders who were enrich-

leader, he tried to rule with compassion, pardoning many of his enemies. Some of these pardoned enemies murdered him in 44 B.C.E. Among the murderers was Cassius Longinus, who became a symbol of cruel selfishness. During his war against Marcus Antonius and Octavian, he sold four Judaean towns ing themselves at the public's expense. Even so, even after the general public had lost faith in government leaders, there were still the midlevel public servants, organizing tax collecting, maintaining roads, and seeing to it that the poor received food. After the Western Roman Empire collapsed, these public servants continued to work, serving the Germanic tribes that established kingdoms in Europe and North Africa.

THE AMERICAS
BY KIRK H. BEETZ

When people gather to live in groups, there tends to be scandal, and where they have governments, they tend to have corruption. Still, the nature of scandal and corruption in the ancient Americas north of Mexico is a mystery because there are no written records. In general, written records are the best and often the only way to learn the specifics of scandals and corruption. It is likely that well before 5000 B.C.E. North Americans had diversified enough that what constituted scandal in one tribe did not necessarily constitute scandal in another. For example, in some societies a man could have as many wives as he wished. Scandal would attach to him only if he had more wives than he could support. In another society, however, having more than one wife would in itself be scandalous. The ancient civilizations of South America also left virtually no records related to particular scandals or corruption.

When one looks at Mesoamerican cultures (those ancient societies of Central America and Mexico) that did have written records, another problem appears. Modern people may have very different views of what constitutes scandal or corruption than what might have been held by people living in ancient Mesoamerica. For instance, the torture and slaughter of people in religious rituals would horrify many modern people, but to most Maya torture and execution ennobled victims, turning them into honored offerings to the gods that satisfied the gods' needs for human blood for nourishment and thus staved off disasters the gods could cause if they were hungry. A chink in this confidence might be found in the sacrifice of powerless children. Children without families to protect them were commonly made slaves and sacrificed, mostly because they had no one to protest their murders.

A prominent Mesoamerican center was Teotihuacán, a city in Mexico that was not Mayan but through its military power forced many Maya cities to pay tribute to it. Rumors of scandals probably traveled quickly through the city, because most people lived in apartments that each housed three families and the apartments were tightly packed together in a grid pattern. Any scandal would have passed by word of mouth rapidly in such a place where people had little privacy and could be easily overheard. Of scandals and corruption in Teotihuacán there are few details, though an ever-increasing gap between the prosperity of the ruling elite and the common people probably was viewed as a sign of corruption by some commoners.

In Mayan culture every person was supposed to know his or her place and duty in society. Those who did not have places became slaves. The social contract of the Maya meant that even the *k'uhul ajaw*, or "divine king," had duties that he had to perform or risk losing his mandate to rule. He was expected to speak to the gods on behalf of his people. Members of his family were expected to join him in tormenting themselves with thorns. His wife would pull a rope with thorns through a hole in her tongue. She and others would pierce their ears and tongues to spill their blood, and the king and his first son would pierce their penises and draw their blood, all because the Maya believed that royal blood was the most nourishing blood for the gods. Giddy from blood loss and delirious from taking drugs, the king and his family might cross the divide between physical life and the spirit world and seem to speak directly with supernatural beings. If such communicating with the gods failed to alleviate a natural disaster, for instance, a drought that lasted for a few years, people might believe the king no longer had divine authority.

Knowing this can help one understand how scandalized the ancient Maya probably were by events in the late 300s C.E. In cities such as Tikal and Uaxactún, an increase in trade was generating wealth, but the wealth was going primarily to the nobility; this was creating social instability because commoners no longer perceived their leaders as sharing the risks of Mayan life in the way they were supposed to do. To hang on to their authority, the *ahauob*, or "nobility," tried to enhance their prestige by raiding their neighbors and bringing home goods that could be used for the city as a whole. Most important, they brought home captives for sacrifice, with captured nobles being particularly important because their blood was especially desired by hungry gods. Raiding for people to sacrifice had been a part of Mayan life for centuries, but Chak Toh Ich'ak I, known as King Great Jaguar Paw (fl. 376 C.E.), of Tikal changed the rules of warfare. Instead of trying to capture just enemies, he chose all-out killing; he chose conquest.

His brother Siyah K'ak', known as Smoking Frog, led an army to attack Uaxactún. This was no ordinary raiding party: It was a force drawn from Tikal's many communities; it may have been the largest Mayan army up to that time. One problem the Maya may have had with this event was that the king himself apparently stayed home. For the Maya, there could have been few excuses for this. Thus, his position at home would have been weakened. Meanwhile, Smoking Frog led his forces to victory, capturing the city of Uaxactún and seizing the king of the city. The sacrifice of a king was a special event because a king's blood was sacred and therefore most desired by gods. Kings were occasionally captured in battle, but they ruled their cities as divine monarchs; someone from their line was expected to replace them, perhaps paying tribute to the victors. In the case of Tikal and Uaxactún, Smoking Frog's forces exterminated the nobility and the royal line of Uaxactún, leaving the people of Uaxactún with no one to speak to the gods for them. This would have been reprehensible; it would have been the murder of the spirits of an entire people.

The scandal thereafter became even more intense. Smoking Frog made himself king of Uaxactún, without the divine right to do so. When Great Jaguar Paw died, Smoking Frog put someone of his own choosing on Tikal's throne. This was Nun Yax Ayin, known as Curl Snout, who may have been the son of an as yet unidentified brother of Smoking Frog and Great Jaguar Paw. Although Tikal was supposed to be the preeminent city, it was controlled by Smoking Frog from Uaxactún. These events would have created anxiety among the people of Tikal and the lands Tikal controlled because the world order, which was a divine order, had been twisted and overturned by ambi-

tious leaders. It brought forth a new age of Mayan warfare in which total destruction of a rival society was the object.

See also BORDERS AND FRONTIERS; CHILDREN; CRIME AND PUNISHMENT; DEATH AND BURIAL PRACTICES; EMPIRES AND DYNASTIES; FAMILY; FESTIVALS; FOREIGNERS AND BARBARIANS; GENDER STRUCTURES AND ROLES; GOVERNMENT ORGANIZATION; LAWS AND LEGAL CODES; LITERATURE; MIGRATION AND POPULATION MOVEMENTS; NATURAL DISASTERS; RELIGION AND COSMOLOGY; RESISTANCE AND DISSENT; SACRED SITES; SLAVES AND SLAVERY; SOCIAL COLLAPSE AND ABANDONMENT; SOCIAL ORGANIZATION; TRADE AND EXCHANGE; WAR AND CONQUEST; WEIGHTS AND MEASURES.

| Greece | ∽ *Aeschines, excerpt from "On the Embassy"* (343 B.C.E.) ∽ |

[2.1] I beg you, fellow citizens, to hear me with willing and friendly mind, remembering how great is my peril, and how many the charges against which I have to defend myself; remembering also the arts and devices of my accuser, and the cruelty of the man who, speaking to men who are under oath to give equal hearing to both parties, had the effrontery to urge you not to listen to the voice of the defendant and it was not anger that made him say it; for no man who is lying is angry with the victim of his calumny, nor do men who are speaking the truth try to prevent the defendant from obtaining a hearing; for the prosecution does not find justification in the minds of the hearers until the defendant has had opportunity to plead for himself and has proved unable to refute the charges that have been preferred.

[2.3] But Demosthenes, I think, is not fond of fair argument, nor is that the sort of preparation he has made. No, it is your anger that he is determined to call forth. And he has accused me of receiving bribes—he who would be the last man to make such suspicion credible! For the man who seeks to arouse the anger of his hearers over bribery must himself refrain from such conduct.

[2.4] But, fellow citizens, as I have listened to Demosthenes' accusation, the effect upon my own mind has been this: never have I been so apprehensive as on this day, nor ever more angry than now, nor so exceedingly rejoiced. I was frightened, and am still disturbed, lest some of you form a mistaken judgment of me, beguiled by those antitheses of his, conceived in deliberate malice. And I was indignant—fairly

beside myself at the charge, when he accused me of insolence and drunken violence towards a free woman of Olynthus. But I was rejoiced when, as he was dwelling on this charge, you refused to listen to him. This I consider to be the reward that you bestow upon me for a chaste and temperate life.

[2.5] To you I do, indeed, give praise and high esteem for putting your faith in the life of those who are on trial, rather than in the accusations of their enemies; however, I would not myself shrink from defending myself against this charge. For if there is any man among those who are standing outside the bar—and almost the whole city is in the court—or if there is any man of you, the jurors, who is convinced that I have ever perpetrated such an act, not to say towards a free person, but towards any creature, I hold my life as no longer worth the living. And if as my defense proceeds I fail to prove that the accusation is false, and that the man who dared to utter it is an impious slanderer, then, even though it be clear that I am innocent of all the other charges, I declare myself worthy of death. . . .

[2.181] And all the rest of you, toward whom I have conducted myself without offence, in fortune a plain citizen, a decent man like any one of you, and the only man who in the strife of politics has refused to join in conspiracy against you, upon you I call to save me. With all loyalty I have served the city as her ambassador, alone subjected to the clamor of the slanderers, which before now many a man conspicuously brave in war has not had the courage to face; for it is not death that men dread, but a dishonored end. . . .

(continued)

(continues)

[2.183] A word more and I have done. One thing was in my power, fellow citizens: to do you no wrong. But to be free from accusation, that was a thing which depended upon fortune, and fortune cast my lot with a slanderer, a barbarian, who cared not for sacrifices nor libations nor the breaking of bread together; nay, to frighten all who in time to come might oppose him, he has fabricated a false charge against us and come in here. If, therefore, you are willing to save those who have labored together with you for peace and for your security, the common good will find champions in abundance, ready to face danger in your behalf.

[2.184] To endorse my plea I now call Eubulus as a representative of the statesmen and all honorable citizens, and Phocion as a representative of the generals, preeminent also among us all as a man of upright character. From among my friends and associates I call Nausicles, and all the others with whom I have associated and whose pursuits I have shared. My speech is finished. This my body I, and the law, now commit to your hands.

From: Charles Darwin Adams, trans.,
Speeches of Aeschines (Cambridge, Mass.:
Harvard University Press, 1919).

Rome

∽ Appian, "The Civil Wars—On the Gracchi" (from Roman History, before 162 C.E.) ∽

Gaius Gracchus, who had made himself popular as a triumvir, stood for the tribuneship. He was the younger brother of Tiberius Gracchus, the originator of the law. He had kept silent concerning the killing of his brother for some time, but as some of the senate treated him disdainfully, he offered himself as a candidate for the tribuneship, and as soon as he was elected to this high office began to intrigue against the senate. He proposed that a monthly distribution of grain should be made to each citizen at the expense of the state. This had not been the custom prior to this. Thus he put himself at the head of the populace at a bound by one stroke of politics, in which he had the assistance of Fulvius Flaccus. Right after this he was elected tribune for the next year also, for in cases where there were not enough candidates the law permitted the people to fill out the list from those in office.

In this way Gaius Gracchus became tribune a second time. After, so to say, buying the plebs, he began to court the *equites*, who hold the rank midway between the senate and the plebs, by another similar stroke of politics. He handed over the courts of justice, which had become distrusted on account of bribery, from the senators to the equites, upbraiding the senators particularly for the recent instances of Aurelius Cotta, Salinator, and, thirdly, Manius Aquilius (the one that conquered Asia), all shameless bribe-takers, who had been set free by the judges, even though envoys sent to denounce them were still present, going about making disgraceful charges against them. The senate was very much ashamed of such things and agreed to the law and the people passed it. Thus the courts of justice were handed over from the senate to the knights. It is reported that soon after the enactment of this law Gracchus made the remark that he had destroyed the supremacy of the senate once for all, and this remark of his has been corroborated by experience throughout the course of history. The privilege of judging all Romans and Italians, even the senators themselves, in all affairs of property, civil rights and exile, raised the *equites* like governors over them, and placed the senators on the same plane as subjects. As the *equites* also voted to support the power of the tribunes in the *comitia* and received whatever they asked from them in return, they became more and more dangerous opponents to the senators. Thus it soon resulted that the supremacy in the state was reversed, the real mastery going into the hands of the *equites* and only the honor to the senate. The *equites* went so far in using their power over the senators as to openly mock them beyond all reason. They, too, imbibed the habit of bribe-taking and, after once tasting such immense acquisitions, they drained the draft even more shamefully and recklessly than the senators had done. They hired informers against the rich and put an end to prosecutions for bribe-taking entirely, partly by united action and partly by actual violence, so that the pursuit of such investigations was done away with entirely. Thus the judiciary law started another factional contest that lasted for a long time and was fully as harmful as the previous ones.

Gracchus constructed long highways over Italy and thus made an army of contractors and workmen dependent on his favor and rendered them subject to his every wish. He proposed the establishment of a number of colonies. He prompted the Latin allies to clamor for all the privileges of Roman citizenship, for the senate could not becomingly deny them to the kinsmen of the Romans. He attempted to give the right to vote to those allies that were not permitted to take part in Roman elections, so as to have their assistance in the passing of measures that he had in mind. The senate was greatly perturbed at this and commanded the consuls to set forth the following proclamation, "No one that does not have the right to vote shall remain in the city or come within forty stadia of it during the time that the voting is taking place upon these laws." The senate also got Livius Drusus—another tribune—to intercede his veto against the measures brought forward by Gracchus without telling the plebs his reasons for so doing; for a tribune did not have to give his reasons for a veto. In order to curry favor with the plebs they gave Drusus permission to found twelve colonies, and the people were so much taken with this that they began to jeer at the measures that Gracchus proposed.

From: Appian, "Civil Wars," in Oliver J. Thatcher, ed., *The Library of Original Sources*, Vol. 3, *The Roman World* (Milwaukee, Wisc.: University Research Extension Co., 1907).

FURTHER READING

Anthony T. Edwards, *Hesiod's Ascra* (Berkeley and Los Angeles: University of California Press, 2004).

Bettany Hughes, *Helen of Troy: Goddess, Princess, Whore* (New York: Knopf, 2005).

Andrea G. McDowell, *Jurisdiction in the Workmen's Community of Deir el-Medina* (Leiden, Netherlands: NINO, 1991).

Raphael Sealey, *Demosthenes and His Time: A Study in Defeat* (New York: Oxford University Press, 1993).

Pascal Vernus, *Affairs and Scandals in Ancient Egypt*, trans. David Lorton (Ithaca, N.Y., and London: Cornell University Press, 2003).

► # science

INTRODUCTION

In the modern world scientists adhere to the scientific method in pursuing their work. They make hypotheses about problems, test those hypotheses by gathering data under controlled conditions, and then arrive at generalizations that might in time gain the status of scientific laws, such as the law of gravity. Ancient scientists did not approach science in this systematic way and in fact might not have regarded themselves as "scientists" at all. Among ancient peoples, science was associated with magic and religion, two areas of thought that often overlapped. People saw themselves as subject to the will of the gods and to mysterious natural forces. Their only hope for survival was discovering ways of controlling those forces. Knowledge consisted primarily of knowing the will of the gods and possibly making predictions about future events.

Ancient science, then, often overlapped with what the modern world sees as superstition. In many ancient cultures the scientists were often the seers, the diviners, the shamans and priests, who acquired insight into the properties of nature, the movements of heavenly bodies, the functioning of the human system, and the like. Ancient astronomers and healers provide good examples. Both of these classes of scientists were believed to have divine, supernatural knowledge, which they could use for the benefit of people in their communities.

Another distinction between ancient and modern science is that ancient science was almost never theoretical. Ancient people did not have time to pursue purely theoretical knowledge, or scientific knowledge for its own sake. They were too busy with the practical concerns of day-to-day survival. Thus, science tended to be more in the nature of technology, of finding solutions to practical problems. In attacking those problems, they looked around and saw four fundamental elements that affected their lives: earth, fire, air, and water. Science represented an effort to control these four elements. Thus, perhaps the best way to categorize and summarize ancient science is to focus on how they learned to tame these four elements.

The earth was the most stable, tangible reality, so ancient peoples made efforts to achieve some understanding of it and of ways to use it. Stone Age peoples, for example, learned to make weapons, cutting tools, and the like out of the stones on the ground that surrounded them. Their Bronze Age and Iron Age descendants learned to make these weapons and tools out of metal. To do that, they needed to develop ways to find metal ore, mine it, smelt it, purify it, and cast it into the objects they needed. As ancient chemists, they learned ways to harden metals. Copper workers discovered that by combining copper with tin, they could create bronze, a much harder and more useful metal that defined a historical period, the Bronze Age. Later scientists discovered that they could convert iron, an abundant but somewhat soft metal, into hard and durable steel by the addition of carbon.

The earth also provided abundant building materials. The earliest structures were built with logs, reeds, and mud bricks, but in time people learned to quarry stone such as marble, limestone, and sandstone to make buildings. Along the way they discovered principles for engineering these buildings and in some cases developed sophisticated mathematics to help them.

Early farmers became chemists and botanists by learning how to domesticate crops, cultivate them, store them, and convert them into food. Chemistry, for example, enabled them to convert milk from livestock into cheese. Perhaps one of the most successful plant-breeding programs in history was carried out by the ancient Mesoamericans, who domesticated maize (corn) from a wild plant. Other farmers became chemists when they learned that the dung from their domesticated animals or from animals such as bats promoted crop growth or that burning the stubble from last year's crop provided the soil with nutrients that encouraged this year's crop.

This leads to fire, the second element. Ancient civilizations learned to use fire not only for warmth and light but for other purposes as well. Ancient miners, for example, learned to crack stone during the quarrying process by building a fire next to the rock to heat it and then dousing the rock with cold water. The rapid temperature changes cracked the rock, making it easier to mine. They also learned to create blast furnaces that achieved the high temperatures they needed to refine and melt metal ores. Meanwhile, ancient pottery makers were making detailed scientific observations about materials that would work best for clay pots, substances that could be used as dyes for coloring the pots, and ways to fire and glaze the pots to make them more durable. They also learned to make such materials as glass, using silica (sand) and fire, and to use minerals mined from the earth to make decorative objects.

With regard to air, ancient civilizations observed the power in a gust of wind and decided that they could put the air to work. This led to at least two primary developments. One was to attach sails to boats, giving these boats far greater range for purposes of exploring, trading, and conquest. The other was the development of the windmill, allowing ancient farmers to pump water, irrigate land, and thresh grain in far greater amounts and with much greater efficiency. Meanwhile, ancient astronomers were looking into the heavens and observing regularities in the movements of the sun, moon, and stars.

Water posed a particular problem for ancient civilizations, particularly those that settled near rivers. The ancient Egyptians, for example, found their livelihoods tied to the Nile River and the thin strip of fertile soil along its banks. The problem they faced was that the river flooded each year.

When the floodwaters receded, they left behind a great deal of fertile silt. In ensuing dry months, however, the ground dried out, threatening the survival of the crops. Out of necessity, the ancient Egyptians developed skills as hydrologists and engineers. They learned to build systems of dikes, canals, dams, and storage grounds for water, which could then be released when necessary to irrigate crops. In order to become engineers and build these facilities, they had to acquire knowledge in materials science, construction techniques, and the like, all of which required some ability in mathematics and measurement.

The modern world takes for granted an extensive base of information about the physical world and how it works. Ancient civilizations had to discover this information out of nothing. Without their scientific achievements it is unlikely that they would have survived in any appreciable numbers. Had that happened, the world might still be a frightening place of pure mystery and magic.

AFRICA

BY TOM STREISSGUTH

Ancient Africans viewed the natural world and all that occurred within it as expressions of the unseen realm of spirits. Events on earth were predetermined, the result of malevolent or benign forces that acted at whim. Humans could never hope to control the fertility of the soil, the coming of the rains, the occurrence of drought or illness, or the seasonal flood of rivers and lakes. They could only propitiate the spirits of the natural world, look for guidance in signs appearing on the earth and in the heavens, and seek out the environments that were best suited to their own survival. They did not pursue science for its own sake or by the modern method of testing theories in controlled experiments. Ancient chemistry, botany, metallurgy, physics, medicine, astronomy, and so on came in the form of practical knowledge applied to everyday needs: growing food, fighting wars, curing the sick, or relieving the pain of giving birth. Further, there was no sharp line between religious and scientific practices, since a spiritual outlook governed virtually all aspects of life. Generally speaking, any activities that ancient Africans carried out for the purpose of enhancing their livelihood and manipulating their environment should be considered science.

TOOLMAKING: THE FIRST APPLIED SCIENCE

Early human beings needed to master the environment in order to find food, protect themselves from hostile strangers, and hide from dangerous animals. A vital ingredient in these endeavors was the use of tools. The shaping of stone implements, according to archaeologists, first occurred in Africa. At Olduvai Gorge (in present-day Tanzania) primate species probably ancestral to modern humans were using sharp rocks as tools some 2.6 million years ago. They may have created these rudimentary tools simply by cracking brittle stones to produce a sharp edge. Later ancestral species and modern humans found ways to work harder stone into tools through abrasion or flaking. Drilling and incision allowed a still greater variety of tools as well as a means of fashioning decorative necklaces, pendants, bracelets, and rings. Stone axes and spear points were useful for killing game, stone adzes for hollowing out tree trunks to make canoes, and simple stone hoes for turning the soil and clearing brush.

The control of fire brought a revolution in useful technologies, allowing ancient Africans to harden earth for pottery and, later, to fashion metal tools and weapons. Pottery making developed along with settled agricultural societies, which needed storage for food, water, and seed. The first clay pots were made from river mud heated in a fire and decorated with simple geometric forms. Potters experimented with different soils, with controlled heating for firing and curing their vessels, and with various paints and dyes. Without understanding basic chemical principles or the complex effects of heat and light, they found better methods and ingredients through centuries of trial and error.

AGRICULTURE

Ancient Africa grew imported as well as native crops. Archaeologists believe that wheat and barley arrived in Africa from the Near East and were first cultivated in the Ethiopian highlands as well as father north. These crops required intensive labor and close attention to weather, soil, irrigation, and general growing conditions. Seeking to enhance the soil, African farmers mixed it with the ashes of trees cleared and burned to make room for cultivating plants. They turned the soil with hoes to make it easier for roots and stalks to penetrate and found that cattle dung improved its fertility. In hilly regions they terraced land to control drainage and provide a greater area of cultivation. They rotated crops or allowed land to lie fallow in order to renew exhausted soil. All of these innovations came from centuries of observation and experiment.

In the northern half of Africa native crops such as millet, sorghum, and yams were cultivated and propagated. Instead of simply gathering edible plants, African farmers began working in a systematic manner, controlling the environment as best they could and reading the sky for signs of coming weather and for favorable or unfavorable omens. They shared their knowledge and passed it down to younger generations.

Animal husbandry developed as societies living in the Sahara region captured and raised wild cattle, a development that began around the fifth millennium B.C.E. Sheep and goats also flourished in what is now the Sahara, at the time a well-watered region with a moderate climate. Cattle herding spread southward across the Sahara. Cattle were useful as beasts of burden, for their meat and milk, for fertilization of the soil, and as a store of wealth. Herders bred their animals selectively to increase and improve them. They learned to avoid environments where disease-carrying insects such as the tsetse fly threatened deadly epidemics.

METALLURGY

The techniques of working and shaping stone were most useful for hunters in perpetual search of game. As land came under cultivation, African artisans began exploring the more complex science of metallurgy. Iron production in Africa dates to at least the second millennium B.C.E. For example, in what is now Nigeria the Nok civilization began making iron tools and other objects sometime around 500 B.C.E. The new iron implements allowed people to hunt more effectively, cultivate larger areas for crops, protect themselves from animals, and make war on their neighbors.

The craft of metallurgy gave rise to a new class of skilled artisans. Making and working iron were complex, difficult processes that could be mastered only through years of practice. The first step was to smelt the iron—that is, to separate the metal from the rocky ore in which it occurs in nature. This was done by heating the ore in a furnace, where the temperature could be controlled by the introduction of air through vents. Shaft furnaces were developed, which drew air through holes in the base. These furnaces were easier to use than bellows furnaces, in which air is blown over the fire, but they burned more wood fuel (a demand at first easily met in most regions of Africa, but one that often caused serious problems as local iron industries expanded). Metalsmiths learned to separate usable metal from impurities in order to produce a stronger material. The molten iron was consolidated in heavy crucibles and then poured into molds to cool. Once the iron solidified, the smith could craft tools and weapons by forging it—that is, by shaping it with heavy hammers while it was still hot enough to be relatively soft or after reheating it. The secrets of this craft were held closely by the few who could practice it, and who passed on its mysteries to their heirs and apprentices.

Metalworking encouraged long-distance trade, as iron tools and weapons were in high demand throughout the continent. The industry also supported permanent settlement, as groups with knowledge of the process located themselves near useful ore deposits. In many places the hunter-gatherer existence faded into memory, and life became more settled, with larger communities divided into distinct classes defined by their skills and employment. The need to adjust to the environment led to the development of more sophisticated tools. The iron implements used in the tropical parts of Africa, for example, tended to be stronger than the ones developed by people who lived in the desert.

From about 500 B.C.E. iron and copper metallurgy spread throughout sub-Saharan Africa. Copper deposits were discovered and worked in Mauritania and Niger, in the western Sahara region, and in central and southern Africa. Ancient ironworking sites have been found from about 500 B.C.E. in Nigeria as well as in the eastern Lake District, in what are now Rwanda and Tanzania, in Doulo (in modern-day Cameroon), and in the Termit Mountains region of Niger. In African societies the practice of metallurgy required cooperative effort and expertise that was the privileged knowledge of certain clans, who knew the techniques of locating ore, building smelters, producing charcoal, and maintaining a constant high temperature in a closed furnace. Metal craftsmen trained in the art of iron making eventually mastered other media, such as jewelry making. Some historians believe that in ancient Africa, iron, copper, and bronze were most important in the production of ornaments, and not in the making of tools or weapons.

Historians have noted that Africa did not experience the usual transition from copper and bronze to iron. Copper making usually preceded the iron making in ancient cultures because copper has a lower melting point, making it easier to produce. Iron smelters had to mix burning charcoal and crushed ore in a closed furnace or crucible, steadily raise the temperature of the mixture, separate the metal from the ore, and then hammer their products into shape. As it was harder than copper, bronze, or tin, iron took greater strength and skill to forge into anything useful. Apparently, however, African smiths started working with these two very different materials more or less at the same time.

Further, there is no evidence in Africa for the usual first step in developing metalsmithing techniques—by experimentation in pottery kilns. Finally, no African metalworking sites date from earlier than similar sites in the Near East and Asia Minor, where ironworking technology originated. Together these facts suggest that metal technology probably arrived in Africa over a short period of time from outside the continent. African iron smelters may have learned metalworking from contact with the Near East, which spread new implements and the methods for making them into Africa via Egypt.

The first African iron kingdom was Kush, lying on the southern frontier of Egypt in what is now northern Sudan. This civilization was based on ironworking technology that was spreading from the Nile Valley and the Sahara to West Africa, the Sahel region south of the Sahara, and then to the Bantu populations of southern and southeastern Africa. The effect of the new technology in Kush and elsewhere was profound. Iron tools were better at clearing forests and cultivating the soil. Iron axes, machetes, and hoes increased the food supply, allowing communities to stay in one place longer and grow in population. Iron also made larger areas of the continent habitable, as people moving into a new region could cultivate more land and more effectively hunt. Iron weapons were important catalysts of urbanization; they also strengthened armies in wartime. Iron, copper, and gold produced in surplus were traded over long distances, allowing societies that mastered metallurgy to enrich themselves and, as a result, develop a merchant class and a wealthy aristocracy.

The iron industry of the capital city of Meroë allowed the Kushite civilization to flourish—and it may also have led to its downfall. To fire the charcoal furnaces, iron makers had to cut a tremendous amount of wood. The resulting loss of forests led to severe soil erosion and loss of soil fertility in the lands around Meroë, reducing the supply of locally grown food and requiring more and more food to be imported. The

cost impoverished the city and affected other forms of trade. In about 350 B.C.E. Meroë collapsed, its industries shutting down and its people scattering.

MEDICINE AND SPIRITUAL HEALING

In ancient Africa there was no sharp separation of religion, custom, and science. This can be clearly seen in the field of medicine. Although there is very little written evidence of ancient medical practices in sub-Saharan Africa, historians can surmise some general aspects of ancient doctoring through time-honored traditions that have survived into modern times.

Ancient Africans believed (and many people in present-day Africa still believe) in three different worlds: the worlds of the living, the dead, and the generation unborn. Ancestors, gods, goddesses, and other invisible entities resided in the world of the dead. Also in the world of the dead were spirits that brought bad omens, disease, and misfortune. In order to avoid such problems, the ancestors or gods who brought them had to be consulted to discover the underlying cause, which could be man-made or supernatural.

Man-made medical problems, for example, are those arising from such causes as poor hygiene or a lackadaisical attitude toward one's physical well-being. Some medical conditions, however, such as madness, infertility, or protracted sickness, demand more serious metaphysical understanding. They may result, it is thought, from malevolent humans who are capable of transforming themselves into a different spiritual realm for the purpose of doing mischief. Witches, for example, are human beings with the power of entering the spiritual realm. To counter this kind of problem, the doctor consults a deity that is associated with beneficial and restorative outcomes. In all instances remedies for spiritual anomalies and medical problems involve communication with the spirits by the doctor, who may also be a diviner (a person who has supernatural powers to discover hidden knowledge). Sacrifices are usually needed to appease the entities, return the sick to normal health, and beg for forgiveness.

A spiritual or medical problem can often result from disrespect to the deity. One of the numerous methods of enforcing laws in Africa is through oracular intervention. For example, a person who kills game in a sacred forest might develop a swollen belly until he or she confesses the offense. Remedies are procured through appeasements to the gods or through banishment from the community. In ancient times offenders might even be sacrificed to the affronted deity.

In sum, scientific understanding in traditional Africa is closely tied to spiritual insight and is the concern of doctors, shamans, and priests who are trained in an esoteric body of knowledge. The African priest was, and still is, responsible for conducting the spiritual affairs of the community in accordance with long-established customs. Most important, the priest ensures that the gods do not get angry with the people of the community. The best means of avoiding the wrath of the gods is by making sure that all the rules and regulations of the community are adhered to. Whenever there are problems that might lead to a serious crisis, the gods communicate with the priest, who in turn works with the rulers and the entire community to ensure that the danger—a poor harvest, famine, or a short rainy season—is averted. Spiritual cleaning is needed to appease the gods and put things on the desired track.

ASTRONOMY AND DIVINATION

Astronomy was the most esoteric science known in ancient Africa. The appearance and movements of the stars, planets, and moon posed a difficult question to ancient observers. In attempting to explain their observations, African astronomers relied on religious traditions and their knowledge of the spirit world. They also devised pragmatic systems in order to make something useful of the mysterious celestial events. In some ancient societies the time and position of sunrise and sunset were gauged to plan journeys and decide the activities required for each day. The appearance of certain stars, particularly Sirius, the brightest star in the night sky, delineated the annual calendar of river flood and proper dates for planting and harvesting. The moon, the Milky Way, the constellation Orion, and the bright planet Venus also played important roles in astronomical science.

Archaeologists have excavated several sites in Africa that may have served as observatories or celestial calendars. Stones placed artificially in a row or circular arrangement may have marked the position of heavenly bodies at certain times of year. Such arrangements have been discovered in Zimbabwe, the Central African Republic, Sudan, Kenya, and the western African nations of Togo and Benin. For example, in what is now Kenya a stone circle known to archaeologists as Namoratunga II was laid out by ancestors of the Borana people. This site is an early calendar that fixed the dates of the year by measuring the positions of seven different stars and the moon.

One of the most famous ancient objects possibly relating to astronomy is the Ishango bone, found in what is today Zaire and dated to about 20,000 B.C.E. The bone (a baboon's femur) has markings that may indicate the 28-day cycle of the moon. Some experts have seen in the pattern of marks a counting system or some kind of mathematical table. Without a written record, however, the specific uses and purposes of this object and of such astronomical sites as Namoratunga II remain unknown.

Ancient societies commonly took celestial phenomena into consideration for important undertakings, such as wedding ceremonies, going into battle, migration to a new region, and building their homes. In Togo and Benin the people known as Tamalimba built their houses so that they were aligned with the sun at the time of the equinoxes. The pyramids of Meroë, the capital of the Kushite kingdom, are aligned to face Sirius as it rises on the eastern horizon. Contemporary Africans still hold to many of these traditions. Sirius, Orion, and the star cluster known as the Pleiades guide coastal navigators in eastern and western Africa. The Dogon of Mali consider Sirius and a small companion star, known to them as Po Tolo, as celestial anchors, keeping all other heavenly bodies in their proper courses and guiding events and important decisions on earth.

The appearance of heavenly bodies was interpreted both as a guide to present events and as a portent of the future. Like medicine, divination was a skill reserved to those with specialized knowledge, whose secrets were carefully kept. The purpose of this craft was to access information not available through empirical means. Divination allowed people to understand problems or prepare for imminent danger. Diviners were, and are, consulted before naming a baby, before undertaking a journey, in preparation for war, and to judge the worth of a potential spouse.

The origin of African divination systems is shrouded in mystery. In modern times they fall into two broad categories: the tool system and the medium system. In the latter a human being serves as a medium who interprets coded information accessed through an earthly entity—typically, messages from dead ancestors who communicate through selected individuals. This type of divination is popular among the Shona of modern Zimbabwe. In the tool system a diviner makes use of tools such as palm-nut shells, stones, or animals. The Banen and Mambila of modern Cameroon use spiders and land crabs as tools of divination.

The Ifa system, as one example, is a well-studied system that survives among the Yoruba of Nigeria. The priest of Ifa divination is called *babalawo* (father of secrets). To become a *babalawo*, an apprentice required several years of training and the study of an enormous body of literature, the *odu*, which consists of 256 parts further subdivided into verses called *ese*. There are about 800 *ese* in each *odu*. A person becomes a *babalawo* after going through all the initiation ceremonies and mastering enough verses needed for communication with Orunmila, the deity associated with divination.

Among the Yoruba and other African cultures evidence of ancient divination science exists only in the form of modern practices that echo those of the past. In a continent where archaeological evidence is often scanty, this is the best resource historians have for reconstructing the knowledge systems of societies that have long been extinct.

EGYPT

BY LEO DEPUYDT AND TOM STREISSGUTH

Among the ancient societies of the Mediterranean region, Egypt was home to esoteric and practical knowledge that placed it in a realm apart from all others. Egypt was the center of advanced medicine, mathematics, and astronomy. Moreover, Egyptian engineering technology—embodied by towering monuments, pyramids, palaces, and public works—had no rival in the ancient world. The ancient knowledge of Egypt, however, was hidden in hieroglyphics, a system of picture writing that fell into disuse in the time of the Roman Empire. Until the 19th century the tablets, papyri, and inscriptions of ancient Egypt were undeciphered, and Egypt's medicine, astronomy, and technology were lost to the world.

By the time of the pharaohs the Egyptians were making various household utensils, building clay vessels on a wheel, forging bronze weapons, weaving cotton, and controlling the flood of the Nile to the fields that bordered the river. Most importantly for scientific knowledge, the predynastic Egyptians developed a system of writing and record keeping.

Absent, however, was a tradition of experimentation, theory, and proof by empirical observation. Egyptian science was hidden knowledge, revealed to a select few among the priestly caste, who placed their skill and research at the service of the pharaohs. Their patron god was Thoth, the deity of knowledge and wisdom, represented by the figure of a human bearing the head of an ibis. The knowledge of Thoth was set down by scribes on papyrus rolls that were privileged reading for the few. In a broad sense, nearly every ancient Egyptian text exhibits some aspect, however minimal, of scientific thought. There were mathematical texts and medical texts, as well as astronomical texts and texts related to the reckoning of time and the calendar. Other genres include classifications of reality (as in *onomastika,* or name books) and explanations of dreams as well as texts on geography, botany, chemistry, metrology, mineralogy, pharmacology, philosophy, physics, and technology.

MEDICINE

Works of medicine and mathematics show that these were the most advanced scientific endeavors in ancient Egypt. Only one cluster of sources rivals mathematical texts in size, the medical texts. These include the Edwin Smith Papyrus, the Ebers Papyrus, and the Kahun Papyrus. Within these documents are spells and incantations, diagnoses of various diseases, and anatomy. The Kahun Papyrus focuses on the reproductive system, the mechanisms of conception and pregnancy, and the complications of birth.

The various papyri reveal that medical science in ancient Egypt was bound closely to religious belief and ritual. All in all, Egyptian medicine is perhaps better known as systematic observation of disease and anatomy rather than medicine. For the Egyptians, disease was the manifestation of evil and malevolent spirits, and curing disease was the work of priests skilled in the use of incantation, ritual, talismans, and spells. Along with this magical approach came practical knowledge closer to the modern conception of medical science.

Without the benefits of sanitation and the knowledge of bacteria, viruses, and the nature of contagious illness, the Egyptian physician had a limited arsenal with which to treat a host of mysterious ailments. Egypt was home to endemic malaria, tuberculosis, measles, smallpox, cholera, and bubonic plague; waterborne illnesses included schistosomiasis (an infection of the blood caused by a parasite). Eye diseases, including trachoma, were common, as were malnutrition; neural diseases like epilepsy; hazards of the natural world such as snakebite, insect stings, and poisonous fish and vegetation; and digestive ailments caused by poor food preservation.

Ancient Egyptians classified afflictions and had an intimate knowledge of organs and their function. The practice of mummification contributed greatly to that knowledge. The first mummies were created naturally, by preservation of the human body by the dry heat of the Egyptian desert. The preservation of natural mummies led the ancient Egyptians to the conclusion that artificial mummification could render a body impervious to the forces of time and decay. The process of mummifying a body took as long as 70 days, with each step a ritual presided over by priests trained and expert in the art. The brain, lungs, pancreas, liver, spleen, heart, and intestines were removed with various instruments, and the body was placed on a bed of natron, a mineral salt that dried the skin and tissue. Once the body was dried, the priests

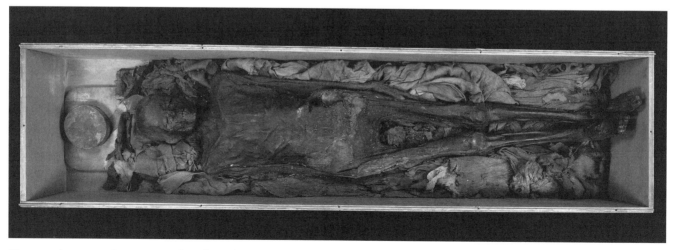

Unwrapped mummy of a woman, perhaps from Thebes, Egypt, Late Period, after 600 B.C.E.; the process of mummification contributed to the Egyptians' knowledge of anatomy and disease. (© The Trustees of the British Museum)

anointed it with oil and spices and then wrapped it in linen bandages. Amulets, talismans, precious stones, and other objects were placed within the bandages as they were wound about the body.

Mummification was not the sole privilege of Egyptian royalty. Members of the wealthy aristocracy also were afforded this practice, as were favored pets and sacred animals, such as cats. Some historians consider mummification as forming the ancient origins of medical science, because the elaborate process allowed Egyptian priests to make a careful study of the symptoms of disease and the causes of physical death.

Egyptian physicians developed skills in surgery, setting broken bones, treating burns and wounds, dentistry, and preparing medications from vegetable plants, herbs, and minerals. Treatments included honey to dress wounds and soothe pain; aloe vera for burns and headache; and frankincense, dill, camphor, mustard seed, onions, garlic, sandalwood, sesame, thyme, and poppy seeds for various ailments and symptoms. An ancient Egyptian prescription could comprise several of these ingredients as well as much more repulsive substances meant to drive away evil spirits: the blood or fat of lizards and snakes, ground pig's teeth, rotten meat or other food, and boiled beetles or rhinoceros horn.

Medical science in ancient Egypt was also preventive in nature. Ritual bathing and purification played a key role in the prevention of disease, and dream interpretation was used to diagnose the causes of illness. The ancient Greeks considered Egypt the home of the medical arts. It was common for Greek scholars and physicians to make pilgrimages to the Nile Valley to study and learn from Egyptian priests and shamans.

METALLURGY AND CHEMISTRY

The Greeks and the people of the Near East took much of their knowledge of metallurgy and chemistry from the Egyptians, who were already systematically mining copper in the Predynastic Period, which ended in the late fourth millennium B.C.E. In the Eastern Desert between the Nile Valley and the Red Sea, copper ores were dug from the earth, refined into base metal, and formed into tools and weapons—a business carried on exclusively under the control of the state. Later the Egyptians learned to combine copper and tin to make bronze and developed uses for lead, cobalt, and galena.

Around 800 B.C.E. Egyptian smiths learned methods of smelting iron, which may have first been mined from meteorites. The "metal of heaven," as it was known, was rare and valuable, and its handling was restricted to the priestly caste and privileged artisans working for the state. By the middle of the seventh century B.C.E. these smiths had learned new ways of hardening iron to make tools more durable and to lend weapons a sharper edge.

Gold mining was another monopoly of the state. Gold (nub) gave its name to an entire region, Nubia, which was renowned for its valuable deposits. The precious metal was extracted from gold-bearing ore as well as river sands. The

Egyptians developed an efficient method of washing this "gold of the river" by placing the ore in bags of fleece and running water through it, thereby removing the soil and dross and leaving behind small gold fragments and nuggets.

The Egyptians also developed an early glassmaking technology in which glass threads were wound around a core of hardened clay. When the clay was burned away, glass jars and bottles were left behind. Glassmaking employed soda, lime, and lead in various combinations and was the subject of constant experimentation and refinement, with the goal to create larger and more transparent pieces. The Egyptians developed an extensive industry around the use of various paints and dyes to create imitation pearls and precious gems from glass. Egypt's glassmaking technology was exported to the Near East and later to ancient Greece and Rome.

MATHEMATICS

Of the two kinds of ancient scientific texts, mathematical texts are more compatible with modern standards of science. (Accomplishments in medicine possible before the discovery of bacteria were, after all, very limited.) The earliest evidence of hieroglyphic mathematics dates to the first half of the second millennium B.C.E. A similar but more sophisticated development in mathematics occurred around the same time in cuneiform sources from Mesopotamia. Near Eastern mathematics then stagnated until the Greek miracle of the later first millennium B.C.E. Two factors put Egypt at the forefront of this resumed growth. First, Alexander's conquest in the fourth century B.C.E. made Greek into an Egyptian language, Egypt's preferred vehicle of intellectual discourse. Second, royal philanthropy transformed Alexandria into the world center for the study of mathematics for several centuries.

Much knowledge of Egyptian mathematics is contained in the Rhind Mathematical Papyrus, a document dating from around 1600 B.C.E. and which contains tables of fractions; formulas for addition, subtraction, multiplication, and division; a table of prime numbers; and a method for solving linear equations. In ancient Egypt mathematics was a practical and not a "pure" theoretical science. Egyptian numbers and calculation developed with the need for precise measurement in construction; surveying land boundaries; building canals and roads; and performing government functions such as calculating taxes and measuring inventories of grain, gold, and other public goods. The numbering systems allowed merchants to trade and exchange goods of various weights and volumes and enabled the state to calculate the size of granaries used for storing corn. The Egyptians developed an advanced system of geometry, a key element in positioning and constructing pyramids and royal tombs and in building various public structures: monuments, sphinxes, obelisks, lighthouses, and gardens.

Egyptian mathematics attained great precision and sophistication. Its number system was decimal, without a zero or a place value system, such as the one in which the first 5 in 55 means 50 and the second 5 means just 5. The Egyptians were the first to develop a base-10 numbering system, which allowed the use of unit fractions and binary fractions. Square roots were in use by about 2000 B.C.E., at which time the Egyptians were also calculating and using the value of pi, the ratio of the diameter of a circle to its circumference. Egyptian mathematicians created tables of addition and subtraction, solved algebraic problems, and developed a precise system of weights and measures.

The Egyptians also studied the aerodynamics of sails and the phenomenon of draft employed by a curving sail. Some historians speculate that the Egyptians used kites and sails to raise obelisks and other monuments.

ASTRONOMY

The gods of ancient Egypt were present in all creation and in visible form. They were present in the stars and the prominent constellations, a fact that bound astronomical knowledge with the practices and rituals of religion. Osiris was visible in the constellation Orion, for example, and the goddess Nut could be seen in the Milky Way. To the Egyptians, the sky was a great roof, supported by immense pillars at the four corners of the world, which corresponded to the four cardinal points of the compass. The sun made a daily course around the earth in a celestial boat, doing constant battle with Set, the god of darkness and night. This striving forced the sun to move from north to south in the course of the year; at the time of the summer solstice, the sun reached its furthest point north. The earth itself was a flat rectangle, extending north to south and having its center in the valley of the Nile, which arose in a great river that lay at the southern boundary of the world.

Egyptian astronomers were priests as well as scholars, for whom a close knowledge of the heavens was most useful in its application to agriculture. The annual rising of Sirius before the sun at the summer solstice, for example, presaged the flooding of the Nile, the event that renewed the fertility of the Nile Valley. The prediction of this event every year lent the priestly caste its aura of mysterious power and esoteric knowledge. It also provided a natural starting point for the annual calendar of days, weeks, and months.

The Egyptian methods of mapping and measuring the heavens gave the world one important basis for its advanced time measurement systems. Egyptian astronomers divided the heavens into 36 decans, with each group of stars covering 10 degrees of the sky. Each of these groups rose at dawn for a period of 10 days, which formed a basis for the Egyptian calendar of 12 months of 30 days, each composed of three 10-day weeks. Egyptian astronomers further divided the year into three seasons—the season of the flood, the season of planting, and the season of harvest—with each season four months in length. The system of months left an extra five days each year that were set aside for feasting and a rest from labor. These intercalary days (inserted between others) were associated with a legend of the god Thoth, who allowed the goddess Nut an extra five days to give birth to her children.

The actual solar year, being slightly longer than 365 days, caused the months and seasons to gradually go out of phase. The result was a long period known as the sothic cycle, in which the seasons returned to their original positions in the calendar every 1,460 years. Later astronomers of Alexandria created a new calendar in which an extra day was added every fourth year, a system adopted by the Romans and which gave rise to the modern leap year. The system of decans and constellations also led to the division of night and day into 12 equal parts, which in turn led to the 24-hour day now used throughout the world. The Egyptians also considered the position of the stars and constellations in raising the pyramids. The faces of these monuments are very carefully aligned. Most face the rising sun at the summer solstice; others are aligned with important stars or the points of the compass. The north face of the Great Pyramid at Giza, for example, lies almost precisely at a right angle to true north. Some have seen in the arrangement of the three pyramids at Giza an imitation of the stars in the belt of the constellation of Orion. The alignment of foundations and walls with the cardinal points of the compass was done with the help of an instrument known as a *merkhet*, a sighting tool made from the central rib of a palm leaf, a string, and a weight, which gives a precise vertical line and allows the user to make a determination of true north and set the north–south axis.

TECHNOLOGY

The Egyptians invented several devices to aid construction of their palaces, monuments, and pyramids. The ramp, an inclined plane that allows large blocks to be raised using less force, and the lever, which uses a fulcrum point to multiply lifting force, were both applied to moving and positioning heavy objects, such as the immense blocks of stone laid for the pyramids. The Egyptians invented papyrus as a writing medium, developed long-distance ships, and adopted the wheel and chariot—originally inventions of the Mesopotamians. Egyptian farmers developed sophisticated irrigation systems, including canals, dikes, and reservoirs to bring water to their fields in times of drought or low rainfall.

Weaving and dyeing technology also made important advances in ancient Egypt. The Egyptians developed new methods of weaving and dyeing cotton and invented the royal purple dye adopted by ancient Greece and Rome. They learned to manufacture pigments and dyes from minerals like cobalt (for blue), iron oxide (for red), azurite or copper carbonate (light blue), malachite (green), and charcoal or charred bone (black).

The perception is widespread that Egyptian science was less sophisticated than its Babylonian and Greek equivalents. Hieroglyphic mathematics and astronomy never reached the level of sophistication of Babylonian or Greek astronomy. But this fact needs to be put in a proper historical perspective. It would be false to conclude that Egypt somehow disappointed or did not perform to expectation. Historically, thinking progressed more or less along parallel lines in Egypt and other advanced early civilizations. A significant increase in sophistication occurred sometime after 500 B.C.E. By then, however, the great epochs of hieroglyphic Egyptian civilization had ended.

Around 525 B.C.E. Persia conquered Egypt. The Persian Empire's intellectual capital, Babylon, lay outside Egypt. In 332 B.C.E. Alexander of Macedonia followed the Persians into Egypt and put a permanent end to the pharaonic dynasties. A Greek presence had been in Egypt since the seventh century B.C.E., but with the coming of Alexander began the Greek Ptolemaic Dynasty, which ruled Egypt until the Romans arrived in the first century B.C.E. Alexander's general Ptolemy made his capital at Alexandria, a city founded by Alexander, who kept a company of philosophers and scientists with him for the purpose of spreading Greek learning and civilization to the barbarous parts of the world he conquered. Ptolemy built the greatest library of the ancient world at Alexandria, which flourished as a center of learning. The Museum, or Temple of the Muses, which housed the library, was a precursor to the modern university, with lecture halls, laboratories, experimental gardens for the study of botany, a zoological collection, and departments of medicine, astronomy, literature, and mathematics. For several centuries Alexandria and its Museum attracted the most brilliant astronomers and mathematicians of the ancient world. The work of the Alexandrian scientists remained dominant even after the fall of the Roman Empire in the fifth century and until new systems of thought were developed in the 17th century by Galileo, Copernicus, and Isaac Newton.

The activity at Alexandria is Egyptian, even if research was conducted in Greek. Claudius Ptolemy, antiquity's greatest astronomer (second century C.E.), was an Egyptian who wrote in Greek and had a Latin-Macedonian name. Egyptian developments in science and medicine, therefore, were not minor but were made obscure by the medium of hieroglyphic writing. For much of the period in which the hieroglyphic script was dominant, Egyptian learning did not significantly lag behind that of any other nation.

THE MIDDLE EAST
BY MICHAEL J. O'NEAL

The Sumerians, Akkadians, Assyrians, and Babylonians did not think in terms of scientific laws, and nothing like the modern scientific method of inquiry existed, with its emphasis on formulating hypotheses and testing them to arrive at general principles about the physical world. They did, however, develop mathematical reasoning to a high level of sophistication, enabling them to calculate everything from the area of a field to the amount of seed required to be sown in order to achieve a predicted yield. Mathematics in turn fed into architectural design, astronomical reckoning, time keeping, and all manner of economic control over seed, yields, rations, and productivity. There was no self-conscious discussion of science per se, but it is clear that the ancient Mesopotamians

were fully capable of thinking and calculating in a rigorous, predictable, and, above all, accurate manner.

MATHEMATICS
The ancient Mesopotamians developed a sophisticated system of mathematics. Early on they learned that they needed a precise system of measurement. Arable land had to be measured accurately so that the requisite amount of seed and irrigation water could be calculated to make the land deliver a high yield. Irregularly shaped plots of land were divided into triangles and rectangles, and area was calculated by summing the areas of the parts. Volumetric calculations were also necessary. In constructing a wall or digging a pit, the need to calculate volumes of earth, the numbers of bricks required, and the amount of labor to be hired and for how long were all important to the planning of a project. The amount of food rations (barley, beer, salt, oil, fish, and so forth) had to be calculated as well. The best surviving records come from what historians call the Old Babylonian Period, dating roughly from about 2000 to 1600 B.C.E.

The mathematical system of the Babylonians (and the Sumerians before them) was a sexagesimal system, meaning that it was based on the number 60 rather than on the number 10. Any metrological system contains within it units of measure with fixed conversion factors. Thus, for example, a foot consists of 12 inches, a mile of 5,280 feet, and so on. The sexagesimal system of the Sumerians and Babylonians evolved out of their conversion factors. In the late third millennium B.C.E. a final step took place, that of place holding. In the modern numerical system, the value of the digit 3 varies depending on its place. By itself it stands for 3, but in the numeral 30 it represents three 10s, in 300 it represents three 100, and so on. The Babylonians developed a similar system. Now they needed only two symbols, one for the digit and one for its place. A vertical wedge was the "base unit." A corner wedge, derived from the small circle, had a value of 10 vertical wedges. A further vertical wedge was worth six corner wedges, and so on. These symbols could be repeated as often as necessary to arrive at such figures as 1, 60, 360, 3,600, and the like. From there it is easy to see the roots of many peculiarities of modern measurement systems. There are 360 degrees in a circle, 12 inches in a foot (for 12 is a factor of 60), three feet in a yard (for three is also a factor of 60), and the like.

Several hundred clay tablets exist in two forms: table tablets and problem texts. The table tablets could be considered an extension of the interest in listing discussed earlier. The tablets have a simple structure and show the two-symbol system of counting, along with the place-holding system. There are no subtraction or addition tables, but there are numerous tables for multiplication. These tables list multiples of one number, called the principal number (p). Thus, there were calculations for $1p$, $2p$, and so on. The tables calculate up to $20p$ and then skip to $30p$, $40p$, and $50p$. For a number such as 53, for example, the results for $50p$ and $3p$ were added. Some of these tables also provide the square of the principal number.

The Babylonians had no division tables, but they did make extensive use of reciprocal tables. (A reciprocal is simply 1 divided by the number in question, so that the reciprocal of 60 is 1/60.) Thus, instead of dividing, they multiplied by a reciprocal. To aid them in this task, they created extensive reciprocal tables. There are hundreds of these tables, along with tables for squares, square roots, and cubes, many of them compiled by students. Finally, there are coefficient lists, which list conversion factors used in geometry (for example, the ratio of a diagonal to a square's side) and weights and measures problems.

In addition to these tables are so-called problem texts, that is, exercises used in schools. Some of the tablets that record these texts contain a number of problems on a single topic; others contain problems related to different topics. They have given historians insight into the kinds of problems examined in schools. Nearly all of the problems ask students to come up with a number, never with any kind of proof. Thus, they are "algebraic" problems, in contrast to the "geometric" problems that ancient Greek students studied. (In algebra the goal is to arrive at a correct answer, expressed as a number; in geometry the goal is often to prove, for example, that the angles of a triangle add up to 360 degrees). Interestingly, modern mathematicians have taken a more extensive interest in Babylonian mathematics because of its emphasis on algorithms, or following a process to arrive at an answer.

Most such problems were what modern students know as "story problems," that is, problems couched in everyday terms by calling for calculations of things in the real world: the length of a canal or broken reeds, the weight of a quantity of stones, or the number of bricks used in a building. Many of the problems are complex, requiring students to use not just single equations but more complex linear and quadratic equations. Some of the texts record the procedures students would follow to solve the problem, but none state general principles. Instead, the emphasis seems to have been on working problems as examples often enough so that the student could then work a new problem with different values. In many cases, all the problems in a group have the same answer, suggesting that the group of exercises was designed to teach a process of computation rather than to arrive at a correct answer.

Although the Babylonians did not have an organized system of geometry—they did not compute angles, for instance—many of the problems have geometric implications, and many contain drawings of squares, rectangles, circles, and triangles. Some problems required the student to compute such quantities as lengths of diagonals or sides or to calculate volume or area. Bricks and calculating a quantity of bricks seem to have been a preoccupation with Babylonian math teachers.

For reasons that historians do not fully understand, the mathematical record of the Old Babylonians comes to an abrupt halt after about 1600 B.C.E. What follows is a thou-sand-year gap in the record. After this millennium the record resumes, and historians have records of continued interest in mathematics in the Mesopotamian region.

ASTRONOMY

During the first millennium B.C.E. the Babylonians compiled columnar lists of stars, with the columns listing the stars and their positions in relation to the positions of other stars. So great became the interest in observation of the stars that temples became astronomical observatories. It should be noted that at the same time, the Assyrians of the Near East also gave great importance to astronomy, and Assyria's capital, Kalhu (modern Nimrud), was a center of astronomical observation and study. In both Babylon and Assyria, lists of such events as eclipses were meticulously kept after about 800 B.C.E.—so accurately that future eclipses could be and were predicted.

Again, the Babylonians lacked a system, an underlying theory to explain and systematize the phenomena they observed in the heavens. Only after about the sixth century B.C.E. did they begin to organize their knowledge into a system. They did so only because they began working alongside Greek astronomers, who seemed, in common with the ancient Greeks, generally to have been better equipped to think systematically. Many of the famous Babylonian astronomers from this period even took Greek names. Naburimanni, who lived around 500 B.C.E., became called Naburianos, and the later astronomers Kidinnu and Belussur became, respectively, Cidenas and Berossus.

Babylonian astronomical observation was not, however, a "scientific" endeavor in the sense of an activity intended to develop an understanding of the atmosphere or the planets and the stars. Rather, the purpose of astronomical observation was completely different than it is today. It was employed in divination, akin to modern and medieval astrology. Celestial divination was used to foretell the fate not of individuals but of kings and the state. The decision to launch a military campaign, like almost all major decisions, was almost always preceded by celestial or some other form of divination.

MEDICINE

Much of the interest in the natural sciences among the ancient Mesopotamians focused on medicine and healing, an early effort to exert some human control over inexplicable forces. In the ancient Akkadian language, the word for *doctor* is literally translated as "fluids expert." Over millennia doctors in the region accumulated a vast store of information having to do with drugs, salves, and other medicines either taken orally or applied to the body. Most of these drugs consisted either of minerals or plant extracts, including spices.

The practice of medicine was closely interwoven with magic and the science of omens. The application of drugs was typically accompanied by prayers and incantations. The goal was to strengthen the patient's will to recover. Interestingly, modern medicine has come to recognize that a patient's frame of mind can play an important role in recovery; modern scientists have begun investigating the power of prayer and religious faith in the healing process, believing that they can boost the patient's morale and promote healing. The ancient Mesopotamians, too, were interested in the psychosomatic properties of the healing arts—that is, the relationship between psychology and medicine.

From a modern standpoint, the fundamental flaw in Mesopotamian medicine was that practitioners were unable to formulate laws based on some overall theory of how the human body worked, in contrast to, for example, the ancient Greeks. Most of the medical literature that survives consists of what modern researchers would call case studies. That is, the texts record the particular cases of individual doctors, without any attempt made to impose some systematic organization on them. Other medical texts consist of letters, those written by both doctors and patients, along with questions that patients put to the doctors. From these texts, historians have even learned the names of some ancient doctors, such as Urad-Nanâ, the court physician at the city of Nineveh sometime around 680 B.C.E.

Most of these early texts contain only minimal efforts at diagnosis, with only cursory descriptions of patients' symptoms. Much of the emphasis is on diagnostic omens, along with indications of whether a particular illness can be healed or whether it is likely to result in death. If a disease was diagnosed as fatal, the texts often note that "the hand of" a particular demon was on the patient. Because some demons were more powerful than others, the demon specified represented a kind of prognosis for how long the patient might hope to survive. Similarly, when the prognosis was good, "the hand of" a particular god was on the patient. These kinds of statements, then, indicate the nature of the rituals that were to be carried out in connection with a patient's treatment. Somewhat later texts contain more exhaustive lists of symptoms and possible treatments, including lengthy courses of medicinal treatments with plants or minerals. Some of these later medical texts also include efforts by practitioners to summarize findings contained in earlier texts, allowing them to follow treatment plans from previous generations.

Again, this process of preserving records represents a form of scientific thinking. Scientists are members of a community of other scientists. They publish and share their findings, and other scientists can replicate their work and either confirm or deny the conclusions. That the Babylonians preserved medical records suggests an effort to forge a community of physicians who could draw on one another's work.

PERSIAN SCIENCE

Science in ancient Persia owed a great deal to Mesopotamia, and during the first millennium B.C.E., following the Persian conquest of Mesopotamia, much Babylonian mathematical, astronomical, astrological, and calendric lore certainly passed into Persian awareness and diffused, via the Persian Empire, as far east as India. Much scientific activity took place during the Sasanian Period beginning

in 224 C.E. In 271 the Sasanian king Shāpūr I (r. 241–272 C.E.) founded a learned academy at Gundeshapur, in what is today Khūzestān, the southwestern province of Iran. Gundeshapur became the empire's intellectual center. The academy was home to the world's first teaching hospital and included a library and a university. Two important contributions of Persian science include the discovery of alcohol and the development of a more sophisticated windmill than the Babylonians had developed.

One intriguing aspect of Persian science was the discovery of the principles of electromagnetism and possibly the world's first electric battery. Housed in a museum in Iraq is a 5-inch-tall clay jar that was discovered outside Baghdad, Iraq's capital city, in 1938. The jar contains a copper cylinder encased in an iron rod. Further, the jar itself shows evidence of corrosion, possibly by an acidic agent such as vinegar or wine. Since then, about a dozen similar jars have been found. While it is unlikely that the Persians understood the principles of electromagnetism, it is a common occurrence in science for something to be invented before scientists understand the underlying principles. What is known is that modern attempts to reproduce these ancient batteries have been successful in creating a current of 0.8 to 2 volts; batteries like these arranged in a series could have produced more voltage.

The basic principle that the Persians seem to have stumbled on is that an electric current is produced from two metals with different electric potentials, with some sort of an agent—an electrolyte—that carries electrons from one to the other, producing current. Wine and even grape juice can function as an electrolyte. It is quite possible that the discovery was made as a result of experiments by ancient alchemists, in both Mesopotamia and Persia. These alchemists, the forerunners of modern chemists, often worked with base metals such as lead, trying to turn them into gold. Alchemists, in their efforts to discover the chemical principles of the natural world, can be thought of as the world's first experimental scientists.

Historians have offered a number of explanations about the purpose of these batteries. One purpose may have been medicinal. Low-voltage electric currents can sometimes ease pain, a principle the Chinese use in the ancient art of acupuncture for healing. Another purpose might have been electroplating. To cover a base metal, such as lead, with a precious metal, such as gold or silver, ancient craftsmen typically had to pound the precious metal into a thin layer and then mix it with mercury to paste it onto the base metal. Electroplating is a much more efficient method for depositing a thin and even layer of one metal onto another.

Other historians have suggested that the batteries may have been used for religious purposes. The battery could have been held inside a metal idol so that a person who touched the idol received a slight electric shock and could see a blue spark. It has been speculated that ancient priests could have asked followers questions; if the follower gave the "wrong" answer, he or she would receive a slight shock from the idol, convincing the person of the idol's power.

ASIA AND THE PACIFIC
by Tom Streissguth

The earliest scientists in Asia, as elsewhere, were farmers, miners, and smiths. The need to supply large communities with food gave rise to settled agriculture as well as the science of botany. Early Asian farmers cultivated rice, wheat, and barley, experimenting with those strains that could be easily grown, managed, and harvested. They domesticated fruit trees and collected wild plants they knew to have useful medicinal properties. Botanical knowledge came about through long periods of questioning, observing, and experimenting. In ancient China farmers developed new techniques of agriculture using the same methods. They learned to plant in rows, irrigate their fields, and build crop terraces on hillsides. Observation of the skies and measurement of the year and the seasons—the earliest scientific astronomy—gave them a method of timing their planting and harvesting.

The Chinese also undertook the world's first geological research. They collected and classified various kinds of rocks and came up with theories as to how the rocks were made. They investigated the properties of soil and climate that allowed crops to flourish in certain regions. They speculated that the earth and the mountains were in constant motion and that the weathering of rock and soil erosion lay at the origins of natural features such as valleys and mountains.

Throughout Asia the growth of farming allowed settlements to gather and store surplus food. This gave rise to a class of artisans who made weapons, tools, utensils, jewelry, and furniture. Mining and smelting metal ores that came from underneath the ground began the science of metallurgy. By observing the properties of ores and heating them in combination, metalsmiths created bronze, an alloy of copper and tin, as well as iron and steel. Bronze making arose independently in China and Southeast Asia, where hunter-gatherers in what is now Thailand were smelting copper and tin and making bronze goods as early as 2000 b.c.e.

ASIAN COSMOLOGIES

Pure science, or theoretical science, arose from observation of the natural world. Scientific understanding varied with the language, religion, and culture of the observers. During the Vedic Period (1500–600 b.c.e.) of India, for example, powerful deities were understood to reign over the earth, the heavens, and all manifestations of life. Brahma was the creator god who dreamed the world into being. Agni was the god of fire and Varuna the god of the sky. Surya was the sun and Mitra the moon. The ancient religious text known as the Rig-Veda, which dates to at least 1000 b.c.e., laid the groundwork for Indian science and mathematics through their ideas about the origin and nature of the universe and of all matter.

In China the philosophy of Dao ("the Way") came to dominant the thinking of sages and scientists. Dao was the basic working principle of the universe, expressed through the concept of yin and yang, the balance of opposites. Yang was the expression of action, dominance, creativity, light, and the sun; yin was the moon and night, the completion of action, and the female characteristics of reticence and submission. Imbalance of yin and yang brought about sickness, poverty, and war; when the two forces were in harmony, peace and health reigned, with yin and yang in an uneasy and always temporary agreement.

In the Chinese view, the yin-yang balance was but one aspect of energy and matter (qi), which also manifested in wuxing, or the five elements of metal, wood, water, earth, and fire. The wuxing acted on one another in many ways: water overcame fire, for example, while wood restrained earth and generated fire. Fire symbolized upward movement, while water always ran downhill. Together these properties and their interactions gave the Chinese a comprehensive explanation of the infinitely varied phenomena of the natural world.

SCIENCE IN ANCIENT CHINA

During China's Han Dynasty, which began in 202 b.c.e., these various ideas and the schools of thought they had engendered, were melded into a single philosophical doctrine, known to historians as the Han synthesis. Chinese scientists of this period attempted to explain all natural phenomena—observations of astronomy, the human body, geology, botany, chemistry and alchemy, physics, biological processes, the weather, mathematics—in terms of the balance of opposing and complementary elements.

The Chinese had already been actively observing the natural world for millennia. Prehistoric Chinese accurately recorded the length of the year, at 365.25 days, as is recorded on inscribed bones. They also estimated the length of the lunar month to 29.53 days; this calculation gave rise to an accurate lunar calendar beginning at the winter solstice. (By order of the emperor's astronomers, a month was inserted at the appropriate time to keep this calendar aligned with the seasons.) A lunar calendar is still in use in determining festival days in China and throughout Asia.

Under the Chinese emperors, astronomers and all other scientists were part of the imperial household. They worked at the behest of the emperor to lend the ruler greater knowledge and glory and to strengthen his claim as the link between the earth and the unseen world. Astronomical observatories, first built during the Neolithic Age, were common structures in China by 1000 b.c.e. They were used to record the motion of the moon, planets, and comets against the apparently fixed stars and constellations. Chinese astronomers also observed sunspots, which are sometimes large enough to be visible to the naked eye, and began recording them in detail in the "imperial histories." They recorded the appearance of comets (including the appearance of Halley's comet in 240 b.c.e.). In the fourth century b.c.e. the astronomer Gan De created a comprehensive star catalogue, plotting the position of more than 1,000 stars. A tradition also records that Gan De made the first observation of Ganymede, a moon of Jupiter, without a telescope or artificial optics of any kind.

EARTH SCIENCE

Geology and metallurgy made important advances in the early Chinese dynasties. Geologists carefully recorded their discoveries while keeping the practical application of their knowledge foremost. For example, they constantly compared rocks and soils above the ground with those found beneath it. The Chinese discovered, for example, that the presence of hematite, or metallic stones, above ground indicates the existence of underground veins of iron ore and that the reddish mineral cinnabar is a good indicator of gold or mercury deposits. These observations led to classification systems for minerals, one of which is found in the *Shan hai jing* (The Book of Mountains), a work of the fifth century B.C.E. This book classified rocks according to their hardness, color, and shape, and guided metalsmiths in collecting mineral ores and smelting them into useful finished metals.

Ancient Chinese iron miners discovered magnetite, a rock with magnetic properties. This discovery led to the navigational compass, one of the most important technological breakthroughs in history. The Chinese built south-pointing compasses to guide themselves over land and sea. The pointers on these devices were commonly spoons or representations of animals such as frogs. Later the spoons were replaced by needles, which allowed the compass or pointer much greater accuracy.

The Chinese were also expert in the science of meteorology. They were setting down weather records by the second millennium B.C.E. and making daily calculations of temperature, rainfall amounts, and wind speed and direction. This diligent record keeping brought them knowledge of the earth's hydrologic cycle of precipitation and evaporation, which manifests in wind, clouds, and storms to keep the earth watered and fertile.

APPLIED SCIENCE

In all scientific endeavors of ancient China, theory and observation had practical uses. While observing the sun, an unknown Chinese inventor realized that the sun's position can be measured by the length of its shadow. He then created the gnomon, a simple vertical pole placed upright to cast the sun's shadow. The shadow shrinks to its smallest length at the summer solstice and to its greatest length at the winter solstice. Thus, using the gnomon, the Chinese measured the length of the year and marked the beginning of the seasons. The taller the gnomon, the more accurate the measurement; to raise large gnomons, the Chinese constructed massive brick structures, many of which still stand. The scientist Zu Gengzhi took the gnomon a step further by adding a horizontal measuring scale and making the device small and light enough to be carried.

Other Chinese breakthroughs include the making of cast iron and the forging of harder, more durable steel by blowing oxygen onto the cast iron and causing its carbon content to drop. This process relies on another ancient Chinese invention, the double-action piston bellows, which forces air continuously into a forge or oven. Chinese inventors also came up with gimbals—small iron rings that support an object and allow that object to remain upright no matter how the rings around it are turned. The gimbal became an important component of marine compasses, which must function accurately aboard ships in constant motion, and the gyroscope, which was invented by the second century B.C.E. The Chinese also invented, in the ancient period, umbrellas, stirrups, porcelain, hot-air balloons, iron plows, kites, and paper. Chain pumps, which allow users to raise water from a canal or ditch into a field of crops, are still in use in rural China. The south-pointing carriage was used for navigation on land. The device supported the figure of a man, pointing toward the horizon; no matter which way the carriage was turned, the figure always pointed south. A complex series of gears governed the transfer of motion from the wheels to the figure.

One of the marvels of early Chinese science and engineering was the curious object known as the spouting bowl. This large, precisely cast bronze bowl was filled with water. When the bowl was carefully rubbed at the handles, the water within the bowl began to spout and the entire bowl began to hum. The steady rubbing created a certain wavelength and frequency in the water's motion that caused a standing wave—one that moves up and down, not sideways.

One of the most important scientific quests of ancient China was the search for an elixir of life. Chinese alchemists sought to create gold and silver from baser elements and experimented with the properties of semiprecious stones such as jade. One could be made immortal, it was believed, if one ingested an eternal substance, such as gold, which does not rust or burn.

Chinese alchemists undertook long and complex experiments, always basing their work on the five elements and the concept of yin and yang. They heated and mixed chemicals derived from rocks, soil, and earth, as well as bones, teeth, and hair. They dissolved them in water, vinegar, mercury, and saltpeter. They studied the changes in the color and appearance of the elements, noting that different metals have different melting points and give off different colors when put in the fire. Alchemists also studied the effect of these substances on the body when applied to the skin or when taken in through drinking or eating them. Early chemical experimentation was held to be a great secret in ancient China and forbidden to common workers and peasants. Chemists, astronomers, geologists, and other scientists worked diligently for the emperor and were kept within the palace quarters and the imperial capital, where they were closely watched.

One of the most important scientists of ancient China was Zhang Heng, a scholar of the Han dynasty, who was born in 78 C.E. He served the dynasty as imperial historian and studied astronomy, geography, and the physics of earthquakes. A brilliant mapmaker, he created detailed renderings of the empire while relying on the magnetic compass, which had allowed greater accuracy in maps and navigational charts. As tools for military campaigns, these maps were of vital importance to the emperor, who kept them a closely guarded state secret.

By recording the locations and dates of earthquakes, Zhang also took a scientific approach to understanding this dangerous natural phenomenon. His ingenious seismograph, known as the earth motion instrument, was a large bronze bowl that held thin copper rods placed horizontally across its mouth. The rods were attached to dragon's heads, positioned at the edge of the bowl at the eight major points of the compass. The dragon's heads held small copper balls and lay directly above small bronze frogs, cast with their mouths open and directed upward. A tremor or earthquake caused the ball to fall from the mouth of the dragon closest to the tremor into the frog's mouth, causing a small warning bell to ring. The device was activated by the wave motion of earth tremors, which move at great speed through the earth's crust. In 138 C.E. the instrument successfully recorded an earthquake 310 miles west of the Han capital.

As an astronomer, Zhang correctly surmised that eclipses were caused by the shadow of the moon passing over the earth. The ability to predict eclipses was sought after by the emperors, who thus gave themselves the aura of seers and prophets who lived closer to the gods. Zhang also constructed a model of the universe, showing the changing positions of the stars. In the field of mathematics he calculated the value of pi (the ratio of the circumference of a circle to its diameter) to 3.162, the most precise calculation of this number up to that time.

MATHEMATICS IN ANCIENT CHINA

Many historians also claim China as birthplace of the decimal system, in which place values are used to express single digits, 10s, 100s, and so on. The earliest Chinese counting systems used a system of rods placed in small boxes; the rods represented certain values depending on their position. No rods meant a value of zero, a concept that was vital to mathematical calculations and which originated in China (though its representation by a symbol came later and may have actually been invented in Southeast Asia.) Later this physical system of representing numbers developed into the abacus—a small, portable counting device that is still in use throughout China and the rest of Asia.

The Chinese also invented the concept of negative numbers, which in their counting system were represented by black rods (as opposed to red, used for positive numbers). The Chinese were the first to use decimal fractions and algebraic calculations for geometrical relationships. By the fifth century C.E. Chinese mathematicians had calculated the value of pi to 10 decimal places, putting them far ahead of Greek mathematicians working out the same value at that time.

The philosopher Mo Zi, who lived in the fifth century, applied himself to important questions in mathematics as well as physics, including the nature of light and matter. His followers, known as Mohists, lived in small communities and devoted themselves to scientific experiment and theorizing. They studied the force of gravity, the laws of motion, the nature of space and time, the use of fulcrums, and the equilibrium of objects floating in water. One of their inventions was a room-sized camera that projected an image through a small hole bored into a wall facing the sun. Mohists also carefully studied shadows cast by animals and natural objects, and the reflections in convex and concave mirrors. They were the first in the world to use experiments to draw conclusions about the nature of light waves. Their ideas were compiled in a book known as the *Mo jing* (The Mohist Canon), a work that has been closely studied by Chinese scientists since the 18th century.

SCIENCE IN INDIA

The civilization of the Indus River valley, in what is now northwestern India and Pakistan, developed while the first large cities were also growing in Mesopotamia (along the Tigris and Euphrates rivers in what is now Iraq) and the Yellow River valley of China. The early cities of India developed a precise system of measurement and made several breakthroughs in technology and engineering. Indus Valley cities, including Harappa and Mohenjo Daro, had drainage and sewer systems, indoor toilets, and paved roads. Chemists applied their knowledge to the craft of smelting molten metal ores to create steel and other useful products. Indus Valley steel was in wide use throughout Asia, the Middle East, and Europe by the first millennium B.C.E.

In later Vedic (or classical) times, Indian philosophers divided the natural world into five elements: earth, fire, air, water, and ether (or space). According to this philosophy, the first four elements are made of invisible small particles, the smallest of which was called *parmanu*. Each element has a corresponding sense in the human being: touch, sight, sound, taste, and smell. Everything on earth was created by chance combinations of the five elements, while the earth itself is a large round object under the control of the sun. The sun, in fact, controls all the planets that wander through the sky against the background of the fixed stars. The earth is divided into seven large islands, all surrounded by oceans of water.

The ancient texts known as the Upanishads delve into the essential nature, or *svabhāva*, of the elements and all objects in nature. These objects are subject to the workings of chance, or random occurrence, known as *yadrccha*. The philosopher Kaṭāda, writing in the sixth century B.C.E., is given credit by some historians as the first creator of the atomic theory—the idea that all matter is composed of invisible, and indivisible, atoms—in his work known as the *Vaiśe Ṣikasūtra of Kaṇāda* (which precedes a similar theory of the Greek philosopher Democritus). Kaṇāda claimed that matter can never be created or destroyed; atoms combine to form particles, which in turn make up all objects in the universe.

The school known as the Jainists came up with some startling ideas about the nature of matter. They theorized that atoms might have a positive and negative charge, a phenomenon that has been proved by modern particle physics. The Jainists also believed that atomic particles had a property of "spin," or intrinsic motion. This is a central idea in quantum mechanics that was further developed by Western scientists in the 20th century.

INDIAN ASTRONOMY AND MATHEMATICS

The ancient Indians were skilled observers of the skies. Texts known as the *Siddhāntas* covered mathematics and astronomy. The authors tackled the problems of planetary motion, the force of gravity, and the position of the sun relative to the earth and planets. Indian mathematics was the most advanced of the ancient world. India developed the set of numerals that now prevail in calculations all over the world, including the Western world. These numbers date back to the earliest civilizations of the Indus River valley. They were employed in a system of weights and measures used by farmers and builders. The Vedic literature of ancient India contains calculations of the proper placement of sacred fires and the sizes and dimensions of sacrificial altars. The writers of these texts worked out the nature of square roots and the concept that became known as the Pythagorean theorem on the area of a right triangle, long before the Greek mathematician Pythagoras existed.

The ancient Indians used and understood addition, subtraction, multiplication, division, algebra, trigonometry, and logarithms. They worked out a basic form of calculus—the science of measuring and representing variable quantities in the natural world. The leading astronomer and mathematician of ancient India, Āryabhaṭa, collected all this knowledge in the *Āryabhaṭa*, a text explaining how to calculate square and cube roots as well as volume and area. Attempting to come up with unified mathematical models of planetary motion, Āryabhaṭa concluded that the apparent motion of the stars and planets is caused by the rotation of the earth and its movement around the sun. Āryabhaṭa understood that the other planets orbit the sun, they orbit in elliptical rather than circular paths, and lunar eclipses are caused by the shadow of the moon. He came closest of all ancient astronomers to understanding the true nature of the earth, sun, moon, and solar system.

Another important field of research in ancient India was the science of linguistics—the study of languages, vocabulary, and grammar. The religious texts of the Vedic Period advanced the idea of tenses, verbs, and noun cases and the concept of the two basic meanings of words: that expressed by the speaker and that perceived by the listener. The linguist Pāṇini, who lived in the early fifth century B.C.E., analyzed the elements of Sanskrit, the language used in religious texts of the Indian subcontinent, and detailed its working in 3,959 rules, which are still studied in modern times. His theories were further developed by Bhartrihari, a linguist of the fifth

century C.E. These two experts laid an important foundation for modern linguistics, which originated with studies in Sanskrit in the 18th century.

EUROPE

BY MICHAEL J. O'NEAL

The concept of *science* as a field of formal scholarly inquiry and organized thought has arisen only in recent centuries, so to speak of science in ancient Europe is not entirely accurate. Modern scientists pursue their research using the scientific method. They assume cause-and-effect relationships between natural occurrences. They make hypotheses about problems, test them by gathering data under controlled conditions, and then make generalizations about cause and effect that might in time gain the status of scientific laws. When the topic of science in the ancient world is discussed, what is generally meant is evidence for a system of observation of the physical world and the evidence for some forms of calculations. The challenge in ancient Europe is that there are no texts, so scholars have relatively few primary sources they can study to learn about ancient European science. In large part they have had to rely on the writings of Greek and Roman historians, who recorded what they observed about scientific practices in their northern colonies and client regions. Their observations, though, were made in late antiquity, so little is known about European scientific practice in earlier ages, such as the Bronze Age.

Ancient Europeans lived in a world in which they were subject to mysterious natural forces: the weather, disease, earthquakes, floods, and the like. Thus, one motivation for making observations about the physical world was to discover ways of controlling those forces, control that could be accomplished by trying to know the gods' will and make predictions about the future. Diviners, seers, shamans, and priests studied the attributes of nature—the movement of heavenly bodies, or the magical properties of plants—to learn how to exert some control over the natural world. These people were believed to have divine, supernatural knowledge, which they could use for the benefit of their communities.

Another way of considering ancient European science is to see it as the sort of science employed in engineering and medicine, where observations about the physical world are used to develop skills in various technologies, including, for example, agriculture, metalworking, and medicine. In the 21st century this is called *applied science*. Agriculture arrived in Europe about 9,000 years ago from the Near East, and over the next 4,000 years agricultural communities were established throughout the Continent. Early European farming communities planted wheat and barley as their main crops and raised cattle, sheep, goats, and pigs.

Clearly, these agriculturalists needed to make observations about the physical world and to develop innovative ways of raising crops that had been brought from the Near East into the European environment. They made observations about the weather and soil conditions. They experimented with fertilizers and various types of crops, primarily grains such as barley and wheat. Early European farmers understood the differing properties of flint and other types of stone and used the ones that best suited their needs. They developed methods for storing their crops. Techniques for making pottery were continually refined using higher and higher firing temperatures. They learned that allowing fields to remain fallow for a period of time increased future yields. Herders learned to breed varieties of cattle that originated in the Near East but had to adapt to the colder climate of Europe. Animals like cattle that had previously been used primarily for their meat were harnessed for power to pull wagons and plows. Early Europeans learned that enzymes mixed with milk produce cheese and that reducing the moisture content of meat, fish, fruits, and vegetables by drying them is a way to preserve them. They also learned to make underground grain silos that kept grain from rotting and succumbing to pests by denying oxygen to the grain. All these activities presume some basic scientific knowledge about how the world works, about the properties of matter, about measurement and engineering, and the like. All of them presume, too, a process of trial and error over time, as agriculturalists tried crops and farming methods, passing along what they learned to their descendants.

Aiding the development of agriculture was the development of metalworking. Like most of the world's cultures, ancient European culture evolved from the Stone Age, when tools were crafted of stone, to the discovery of metals. The first metal widely used in tool making was copper. The Bronze Age began at different times in different regions when it was discovered that mixing tin with copper resulted in bronze, a much more durable metal than copper. At some point during the fifth millennium B.C.E. it was observed that certain ores contained copper, which could be smelted and collected and then pounded into simple forms. Over time, the technology for working copper improved to the point where it could be cast into more complicated shapes. Around 3000 B.C.E. in southeastern Europe, ancient chemists discovered that adding about 10 percent tin to a mixture of copper would produce an entirely new metal, bronze, which revolutionized metallurgy. Again these discoveries and innovations were the product of systematic observations that bordered on what might be considered science.

By about 1100 B.C.E. ancient Europeans entered the Iron Age, having discovered both that the ground in much of Europe was rich in iron ore and how to use that ore. Among the ancient Celts two primary cultures emerged around ironworking. The first was the Hallstatt culture, named after a town near Salzburg, Austria, where extensive mining operations were conducted beginning in about 1000 B.C.E. About 500 years later, the La Tène culture developed in modern-day Switzerland. These cultures produced an enormous amount of iron, and archaeologists have discovered numerous Iron Age artifacts from this region. These developments indicate that there were scientific advances in mining, separating metal from ore, controlling temperatures in furnaces, and turning iron into useful products. Eventually ironworkers became chemists of sorts when they discovered that mixing carbon with iron produced much harder steel.

The development of iron led not only to better weapons—the Europeans carried the art of sword making to new heights—but also to better farming tools such as plows and harrows. Similarly, the Europeans were adept at building carriages and wagons and learned to cover wooden wheels with a metal band, or tire, that made the wheels more durable.

Medicine and healing were other forms of applied science. These activities were often associated with magic and with the ability of some people to understand the will of the gods. The Druids, the priestly class of the ancient Celts, gained wisdom about the healing power of plants. This wisdom was accumulated over long stretches of time by trial and error, as well as by making detailed observations about the effects of substances on the human body. Examples include willow tree bark, which contains a substance that is chemically similar to the active ingredient in aspirin. Celery and parsley were also thought to have healing powers. These substances were probably gathered according to a strict schedule based on the phases of the moon, in the belief that all the powers of nature worked hand in hand. In many senses ancient healers worked like experimental scientists, observing symptoms, trying herbal treatments, and seeing what seemed to help.

The ancient Europeans showed some skill in surgery. Near Munich, Germany, for instance, archaeologists discovered the tomb of a so-called warrior-surgeon that dates to about the third or second century B.C.E. and contained a number of medical and surgical implements: probes, retractors, and a trepanation saw, used for cutting holes in the skull. Trepanation was widely used to treat head injuries and psychological disorders, and healers used both saws and drills to make their holes. A large number of skulls have been found with neat holes drilled or cut into them. While many people died during this type of surgery, many others did not, for the holes in some skulls show evidence of healing. Earlier skeletal remains of two people found in Moravia, a region in the modern-day Czech Republic, show that surgeons operated successfully on them. In one case they removed a portion of bone, and in the other case they amputated a limb. In both cases the surgery took place sometime around 5500 B.C.E. The skeletal remains show that the patients healed and survived for several years following the surgery.

Little is known about the mathematical inquiries of the ancient Europeans. What is known has been discovered from practical applications. For instance, the circular stone megalithic monuments of the British Isles, including not only Stonehenge but also the megaliths at Avebury and other sites, suggest that their builders may have had some understanding of pi, the Greek letter that represents the relationship between the radius of a circle and its circumference. The geometric layout of these sites also suggests that their builders may have grasped the principle of the Pythagorean theorem before Pythagoras, the Greek mathematician usually credited with discovering the relationship between the squares of a triangle's sides and that of its hypotenuse. Clearly, the ancient megalith builders understood principles of measurement and engineering. Measurement was also vital to European farmers, who had to devise ways to measure agricultural output and fields.

Extending back to the Neolithic Period the ancient Europeans were keen observers of the skies. A bronze disk with gold inlays found at Nebra in central Germany and dated to about 1600 B.C.E. is a controversial find owing to the circumstances of its discovery, but it is interpreted as bearing a depiction of the star cluster known as the Pleiades. By the time of the Roman Empire, Roman historians were praising the Celts for their astronomical skill. The writer Martial (ca. 40–103 C.E.), for example, noted that the Celts believed that the world was round, not flat. The Celts devised an astronomical calendar as far back as 1100 B.C.E., and for many years the ancient Greeks debated the question of whether the Celts borrowed their astronomical skills from the Greeks or the Greeks borrowed them from the Celts. In either case the Celts kept meticulous records of astronomical events and were even able to predict many regularly recurring events. A good example is provided by the tides and their relationship with the phases of the moon. A primary motivation was not simple human curiosity but the desire to understand the will of the gods, including the later Christian God, and to exert some measure of control over natural forces.

GREECE

BY PHILIPPA LANG

In ancient Greece before the sixth century B.C.E. people could roughly predict the movements of the stars and constellations throughout the year, relate the movements to seasonal change, and use the stars to navigate their boats and ships. They had the technology to make metals and other materials, such as pottery, both for practical use and pure decoration. They used plants and foodstuffs for medicine, and they had stories that explained the world around them and its origins, usually in terms of gods. The sea god Poseidon was the cause of earthquakes, and thunder came from Zeus. None of this is what is now called science. No word for science existed in ancient Greece, and the category of science, its methods, aims, and content, is a modern construction that does not transfer back to the distant past.

From the sixth century B.C.E. onward, however, some Greeks developed ways of thinking about the world and efforts at controlling it that were similar enough to the modern concept of science that the term can be used. Ancient science can be defined as attempts to explain, understand, predict, and sometimes control the natural world. But it is important to realize that the ancient Greeks did not think of themselves as doing science, and they had no agreed-upon scientific method.

In the sixth century B.C.E. a small group of people now known as the pre-Socratics developed several theories about the origins of the universe and its fundamental components. These theories survive only as fragmentary summaries and quotations in later writers, so not very much is known about them. They did not agree with one another, but what they had in common was the belief that the universe had a consistent and ordered nature that could be understood and explained by human reason. The Greek word for nature is *physis*, which is where the modern word *physics* comes from. The theories explain natural phenomena without involving traditional gods or other supernatural forces, though they may describe natural forces in terms of the gods or they may view the whole of ordered nature as itself divine. This new approach is now often called *naturalistic* or *natural philosophy*. Thales, the earliest pre-Socratic, suggested that the world floated on water and that earthquakes were caused by waves, not by Poseidon. Xenophanes looked at fossils of fish and argued that they showed parts of the earth had long ago been under water.

Most pre-Socratics also argued that the world and everything in it was made out of the combination of a very few elements, or sometimes that it was only one element in many different forms. Such basic elements were usually earth, air, fire, and water, but there were also other views. Democritus theorized that the basic units of matter were tiny unbreakable shapes called *atoms* that fell through a void. When they collided and stuck together, they made larger objects of many different kinds.

Another common pre-Socratic theme was a concern with what counts as truth and what kinds of evidence are reliable. This concern is called *epistemology*, the study of theories about knowledge, truth, and reliability, and it is closely related to science. But pre-Socratics were not scientists. Later Greek thought called them *philosophers*, which means "those who love knowledge." Pre-Socratic inquiries made little to no use of experiment and appealed selectively to everyday observations. They agreed neither on most theories nor on how to evaluate them and decide which is better, or more nearly true. They were often as interested in ethics and politics as in scientific topics. Most pre-Socratics were charismatic individualists with radical and highly speculative views, rather than scientists in any modern sense. For example, Empedocles was a wonder-worker who claimed to be able to control the weather and cure the sick.

ARISTOTLE

The philosopher Aristotle (fourth century B.C.E.) was the first person to do something very similar to science as it is understood now. He argued that the causes of things were within the natural world and could be explained by a careful investigation of nature. He systematically collected information on living creatures and classified them by types and characteristics, trying to grasp how things worked and why. He dissected many animals; made first-hand observations of insects, fish, mammals, and birds; and asked experts and specialists such as fishermen and beekeepers for information. His books *History of Animals* and *Parts of Animals* describe more than 500 species of living creatures, and his account of the dogfish was not equaled until the 19th century.

Aristotle's aim was not just to record details for their own sake but also to gather and use reliable data to arrive at theories about how and why things worked. An important guiding principle for him was the concept of teleology, which assumes that everything in nature is the way it is for a reason, except for unavoidable side effects. Aristotle said that "nature did nothing in vain." So when Aristotle looked, for example, at a heart, he assumed that the heart did something useful for the organism and did it well, and he tried to work out what that purpose might be and how the heart accomplished it. This can be a useful principle of discovery in biology, but it also meant that Aristotle and his followers rarely accepted that anything could happen just by chance, without a final purpose.

Aristotelian physics, though incorrect, was extremely influential. While Aristotle did a lot of sustained and organized investigation into nature, like most other Greek thinkers he rarely carried out experiments. Experiment was rare in the ancient world and did not usually have much authority, and the notion of test by falsification of a predicted hypothesis (the modern scientific method) was never suggested. After the ancient period a later thinker John Philoponus (sixth century C.E.) is said to have done experiments disproving Aristotle's claim that heavier objects fall faster than lighter ones, but no one took much notice until Galileo finally disproved Aristotle some 2,000 years later, in the 16th century.

Despite the lack of experiment, the concept of proof was very important in ancient science and philosophy. Aristotle developed the first explicit system of logic, in which, if the starting points are true, the proof is so constructed and worked out that the conclusion must also be correct. It is an important idea and works well in mathematics, but it is much more difficult, as Aristotle recognized, to apply to biology and other real-world situations that have many complicated variables.

THE LYCEUM

Aristotle set up a like-minded group of thinkers and learners, a school (the Lyceum or the Peripatetic), and many of his followers did similar research. Theophrastus (371–287 B.C.E.), the head of the Lyceum after Aristotle's death, investigated and collected data on plants and stones and wrote books about fire and weather. Strato (d. 269 B.C.E.), who was the leader of the Lyceum after Theophrastus, was interested in basic matter and problems such as how people could hear through solid walls. Little of Strato's work survives, but he seems to have argued that there were tiny pockets of void (empty space) within matter that explained how sound traveled through solids. Strato's theories had practical applications in the work of the mechanists.

The kind of science done by the ancient philosophers and other thinkers was an intellectual project largely restricted to the social and literate elite. Philosophers often justified what they did as the highest form of human endeavor, the acquisition of knowledge for its own sake and not for gain or use, practiced by people who did not need to work. But there were tensions. A comedy of the fifth century B.C.E., *The Clouds*, by Aristophanes, satirizes this kind of thought as ivory tower navel-gazing.

SPECIALIST THINKERS

For Aristotle, scientific understanding of the natural world, natural philosophy, or natural history was part of a broader project to understand and thus to be able to manage human life and ethics in its entirety, from poetry to theology and from politics (Aristotle defined humans as political animals) to the nature of friendship, and he was as interested in rhetoric as in logic. Thus philosophy is not the same as science, even for Aristotle, the most scientific philosopher of the ancient world.

But there were contemporaries of Aristotle who specialized in certain areas of intellectual and scientific enquiry. Mathematics was a developing field. Greek mathematics is primarily geometrical rather than arithmetical (algebra had not been invented). Although many theorems were known to other older civilizations, such as the Babylonian and Egyptian, a distinctive Greek addition, perhaps influenced by philosophy's concern with standards for truth and certainty, was a concern to prove a general theorem would be true for all possible values.

Well-known mathematicians of this era include Theodorus and Theaetetus, both of whom have roles in one of Plato's fictional philosophical dialogues on the nature of knowledge. The Pythagorean philosopher and mathematician Archytas, in the early fifth century B.C.E., viewed mathematics as essential to understanding reality. Archytas developed many solutions and proofs, including the solution to the problem of doubling the cube, and provided a mathematical account of musical scales. There was increasing agreement on methodology, terminology, and what counted as a proof. By around 300 B.C.E., the mathematician Euclid could write a book called *Elements* (of Mathematics) that laid out all known mathematics as a set of demonstrated proofs from which, beginning at the most basic hypotheses and definitions, increasingly complex theorems could be reliably derived. Mathematics had become an ideal of intellectual inquiry, the successful pursuit and discovery of knowledge for the sake of knowledge. It was also vital in several other kinds of investigation, especially astronomy and mechanics.

ASTRONOMY

Naturalistic theories about the universe and its origins, called *cosmology* and *cosmogony*, respectively, had been a major theme of pre-Socratic thought. Anaximander, for example, said that the world was a cylinder, with humans living on one of the flat ends, surrounded by a thick mist that obscured the spheres of fire that enclosed the mist. People could glimpse the enclosing fire through pinpoint holes in the mist, holes that were perceived as the sun, moon, and stars.

Astronomical observations of the movement of the stars and their relationship to seasons were much older, because they were crucial to a largely agricultural society. Official calendars followed the phases of the moon, but over many years such calendars become out of phase with the solar year, until an event originally placed in the spring took place when the leaves were falling.

In the fifth century B.C.E. Meton, probably working partly from Babylonian written observations of the movements of the heavens (going back much further than those of the Greeks), worked out a 19-year lunisolar calendar that would have kept the moon and the sun in step over a 19-year period to a precise degree of accuracy. The Athenian state did not adopt this as the official calendar. The results of specialist intellectual inquiry were not always viewed as socially useful or as an improvement on tradition.

In astronomy itself, however, observations were becoming fuller and more detailed, including Callippus's work (fourth century B.C.E.) on the exact dates of the summer and winter solstices and the realization that the year's four seasons are not of equal length. These observations were incorporated into attempts to produce models of the cosmos that would account for such phenomena as the movements of the sun, the lunar cycle, and the movements of the so-called wandering stars—the planets. (*Planet* is Greek for "wanderer.")

The traditional story is that Plato challenged astronomers and mathematicians to come up with such a model and that in response Eudoxus developed his theory of concentric spheres. In this theory the sun, moon, and five planets are fixed to 27 spheres around the common center of the stationary earth, and these spheres revolve on different axes of rotation and at different speeds. The theory was elaborated by Callippus, mechanized by Aristotle (by which time it had 76 spheres), and eventually abandoned in the second century B.C.E. when the mathematician-astronomers Apollonius of Perga and Hipparchus invented models of epicyclic and eccentric rotation. Their model was further refined into the Ptolemaic universe worked out by the astronomer Claudius Ptolemaeus (Ptolemy) in the second century C.E., a system that survived until Copernicus.

The aim of all such models seems at least partly to have been "to save the phenomena"—that is, to discover a working mathematical model of the heavens that allowed observations to be accepted and not explained away as optical illusions or untrue in some other way. Some of these models may have been largely exercises in mathematical ingenuity, but many astronomers were certainly interested in trying to discover how the universe actually worked. In the third century B.C.E. Aristarchus of Samos proposed a heliocentric cosmos, but only one person supported the idea, and later astronomers such as Claudius Ptolemaeus attacked it on the grounds that

it was not supported by observation or by current (Aristotelian) theories of physics.

Astronomy was an enterprise that required considerable mathematical knowledge, beyond that even of most philosophers, although most people probably had a very basic form of astronomical knowledge. Specialized and difficult though mathematics was, it did have practical applications in the everyday world in meteorology, geography, and especially astrology.

METEOROLOGY

The Greeks traditionally associated changes in the weather with changes in the sky. Storms, for example, were more frequent around the time of the equinoxes. The sun, moon, stars, and planets were thought to be much closer to the earth than they actually are, and so their movements were thought to affect the air around the earth and thus the weather. As astronomy's observations and models became increasingly detailed and precise, predictions of the weather also grew much more elaborate. In the third century B.C.E. the poet Aratus of Soli recast a famous astronomical book by Eudoxus about the movements of the stars and related weather patterns into poetry. It was extremely popular among the literate population of the ancient Greek and Roman world.

GEOGRAPHY

The early Greeks believed that the lands around the Mediterranean Sea were surrounded by a huge ocean. Going far enough east, west, north, or south would take a person to the edge of the world. Slowly, traders and other travelers brought back information about foreign lands, and the world the Greeks knew about got bigger.

By the fourth century B.C.E. many intellectuals had realized the world must be a sphere. Aristotle pointed out that someone watching a ship sailing away sees the front end of it disappear first. In the third century B.C.E. Eratosthenes calculated the circumference of the earth, possibly to within about 311 miles. (The exact length of the unit of measurement he used is not known.) Although only a few experts and, to a smaller extent, educated laymen, traders, and the military needed to know much about astronomical geography, those who did were slowly building up a three-dimensional picture of the Northern Hemisphere.

ASTROLOGY

Before the Greeks, Babylonian priests watched the sky for omens, and their long-term observations provided vital astronomical data for the Greeks. The data enabled astronomers to predict the future movements of the stars based on past patterns. Although the details are unclear, sometime between the third and first centuries B.C.E. this ability to predict movements developed among the Greek population of Egypt into an astrological system, a synthesis of Greek thought with Babylonian omen-based astronomy and some small Egyptian influence. An important part of this astrological system was the notion of a horoscope, in which the positions of the heavenly bodies at the moment of a person's birth determined that person's future; thus astronomy was crucial. There are surviving Greek horoscopes from the first century B.C.E. Astrology quickly became extremely popular, though not everyone was convinced and those who were held many different views as to how it worked. Astrology relied on the astronomical and mathematical knowledge of a very small group of experts, and thus made mathematics relevant to the lives of many people in society other than the literate, intellectual elite.

MECHANICS

Mathematics, with an understanding of certain physical principles, was also crucial to the emerging discipline of mechanics. From very early times in Greek society there had been craftsmen and engineers who could build a ship, a fountain, or a defensive wall. This kind of specialist expertise, which could be written down but was usually passed on in oral and practical lessons from teacher to apprentice, is called a *techne*, usually translated as "art" or "craft." The word *technology* is derived from it.

Some arts, such as architecture, required mathematical knowledge. The physics of motion, materials, and machines was also a topic of interest to some philosophers and other intellectuals. Aristotle's school, the Lyceum, produced a treatise called *Mechanical Problems* that discussed the workings of common machines such as pulleys and windlasses, not to mention the physics of the knee joint.

Theories were developed about the behavior of air and liquids under pressure, or pneumatics and hydraulics. Pneumatics, hydraulics, and other applications of physics resulted in the production of machines made by a specialized group of intellectual inventors, the mechanists. Many of the mechanists' devices involved steam power. Ctesibius of Alexandria, working in the third century B.C.E. invented, among other things, a water organ and statues and doors that moved automatically. These kinds of toys and spectacular set pieces did not usually have any practical purpose. The ancient world had very little industry in the modern sense. They were perhaps made to display cleverness and to surprise and entertain a client base, an audience of the social elite, or anyone else who saw the mechanists' products.

But there were important practical roles for mechanists as developers of improved military technology, defensive structures, and civic buildings. The mechanist Philon of Byzantium, in the second century B.C.E., described how the Greek kings of Egypt, the Ptolemies, funded engineer-mechanists to conduct a series of experiments that would result in building the most effective kind of catapult. The lighthouse of Alexandria was also an example of the mechanists' practical technology.

Mechanics was heavily utilized by governments and had considerable social importance. Many relatively well-off individuals used architects and engineers to construct private buildings and machines for them. But the fact that mechanics and engineering were largely practical and that practitioners were professionals who got funding and payment—and probably also because manual labor was involved—meant that many of the elite regarded the discipline of mechanics as inferior to mathematics and natural philosophy. The ancient Greek intellectual ideal was to study the nature of the universe for the sake of knowledge alone.

Many mechanists argued against this downgrading of their expertise, and some experts managed to become famous both for their mathematical ability and their useful machines. Archimedes (287–212/211 B.C.E.), known for having allegedly shouted "Eureka" (I've found it!) in the bath on discovering the law of buoyancy, was well known both as a highly theoretical mathematician and the inventor of many practical machines. The Archimedean screw, named after and probably invented by him, made it much easier to lift water from the ground and was widely used for centuries in agriculture. During the siege of his city, Syracuse, by the Romans, Archimedes is said to have constructed many innovative war machines, such as a claw that pulled ships out of the water. It is unclear how reliable these reports are in their details, but certainly Archimedes was believed to have been important to the defense of Syracuse.

MEDICINE

Traditional healing in Greece consisted of a combination of the use of plants and foodstuffs as drugs, surgical procedures that were traumatic in themselves, and the use of incantations. This combined approach to medicine became a *techne*, an art, though people might also take care of themselves by self-medicating, appealing to the gods and participating in healing cults, or going to experts such as drug collectors (root cutters), purifiers, and magicians.

In the fifth and fourth centuries B.C.E. many practitioners of medicine adopted a more exclusively naturalistic approach, which both influenced and was influenced by contemporary developments in philosophy. In this naturalistic concept of medicine, physicians developed theories about the nature of the human body as a biological animal and treated illness on the basis of this understanding. The texts of the so-called Hippocratic Corpus were written by an unknown number of anonymous authors during this period. They were later collected together under the name of the famous physician Hippocrates of Cos (fifth century B.C.E.), though it is not known whether Hippocrates actually wrote any of them.

Some of these Hippocratic texts explicitly assert a naturalistic approach and describe theories of physiology and pathology; others are more practically oriented but assume a naturalistic view. The theories described in these works differ, but they often involve one or more substances in the body called *humors*, such as phlegm, bile, and blood, which need to be in balance for health. Physicians demonstrated their authority and expertise by being able to predict the course of a disease and, if it did not seem likely to be fatal, by intervening with advice on diet and activity and sometimes with more drastic remedies such as purgative drugs or bloodletting, all with the aim of rebalancing the humors. They also practiced traumatic surgery and cauterization of wounds. Diet and exercise (together known as *regimen*) were also widely prescribed as preventive measures.

Anatomy in the Hippocratic corpus is very speculative and often inaccurate. Aristotle carried out animal dissections in the fourth century B.C.E. In Alexandria during the third century the physicians Herophilus and Erasistratus performed human dissection and even, according to a later but almost certainly reliable report, human vivisection, or operation on living beings. This greatly improved anatomical knowledge, including discovery of the heart valves, the ovaries and Fallopian tubes, the structure of the eye, the difference between motor and sensory nerves, and many other findings. But physicians still disagreed widely on how to interpret their findings. Herophilus seems to have held a largely traditional theory of humoral imbalance. Erasistratus developed a radical new theory, influenced by contemporary developments in mechanics, of the heart as a pump and the mechanical movement of fluids around the body according to pressure and vacuum. He argued that the arteries contained only air, while veins contained only blood.

Possibly because even systematic investigation of human anatomy had produced neither agreement on theory nor improvements in clinical treatment, some doctors rejected theory altogether as useless. They called themselves *empiricists* and said that doctors should merely remember that certain remedies had in the past been associated with recovery from certain symptoms, without speculating about causes and effects.

Medicine consisted of a specialized and practical expertise carried out by professionals, usually for a fee. As such, some philosophers criticized it as being limited in scope and as having less intellectual status than philosophy. In response, some physicians claimed that medicine was an exemplary form of knowledge and very difficult to master. Other doctors argued that medicine should not be too theoretical but should be based on practical experience and paying attention to the individual case.

Some contemporary dramas and epitaphs for the dead attacked doctors as incompetent. Certainly their rate of success was not high, though probably not noticeably worse than other kinds of healers. The Hippocratic text *Epidemics* seems to imply that physicians treated all social classes, including the very poor, but it is difficult to assess whether doctors were called in for routine illness or only when the situation became obviously serious.

Medicine, in the sense of a naturalistic or scientific medicine exclusive of other forms of healing such as religion or magic, had several roles in society. First, as a practical system of knowledge like that of a craft, it was widely used but perhaps little trusted. Second, as an intellectual enterprise, it tried to investigate and understand the human being as a biological animal, using methods of observation, dissection, and occasionally experiment and reasoning from the data thus produced. This role was strongly associated with literacy, high social status, and natural philosophy, and there was some conflict between philosophy and medicine over their relative intellectual merits.

ROME

BY PHILIPPA LANG

The word *science* is derived from the Latin verb *scio*, which means "to know" and in particular "to know by finding out," though it is not simply equivalent to what we mean by science today. We can roughly define science in ancient Roman as any investigation or understanding of the material and natural world that proceeds by carefully reasoned argument on the basis of empirical data and assumes that the world will be consistent and ordered. If a stone always rises for a little way and then falls back to earth, the presumption of natural philosophy, or science, is that the stone will always behave in the same way and for the same reasons and that we can work out why it does so.

Science in Roman society and culture was derived to a large extent from science and philosophy in Greek culture. Many of the Roman aristocratic elite during the late Republic (second to first centuries B.C.E.) and then in the Roman Empire of the following centuries translated and discussed Greek philosophy and science, while many Greeks in the Roman Empire also continued to investigate and argue about the way in which things worked. In fact, many leading figures in the fields of science during the Roman Empire were of Greek descent and culture, but they resided in places under Roman control and worked for Roman emperors.

These kinds of investigations were strongly associated with the upper classes, who had the education, time, and inclination to pursue scientific and philosophical knowledge either for its own sake or as part of a general understanding of the world. At this time the major Greek philosophies of the Hellenistic Period (323–31 B.C.E.) each offered a comprehensive understanding of the world and humankind's place in it, though none of them agreed with each other. Many Roman aristocrats and intellectuals aligned themselves with one of these philosophies and contributed to them, and their ethics and theology were interdependent with their natural philosophy—their theories of biology, physiology, psychology, and what we would call physics and chemistry.

At the same time, areas of science with important technological and practical applications were used by both Roman individuals and the Roman government. These included civil, personal, and military engineering and surveying, from architecture to ballistics. Medicine was also very important. Roman and Italian culture incorporated a large amount of traditional medicine in which foods and plants were administered for illness, often accompanied by incantations, magical rituals, and appeals to the gods and other supernatural powers. Contacts with Greek culture, however, introduced the professional phy-

Bust of Pseudo-Seneca, before 1626, by Peter Paul Rubens; this drawing is of a Roman portrait bust thought to be the Roman Stoic philosopher Seneca, who wrote several scientific treatises. (Copyright the Metropolitan Museum of Art)

man audience and some Roman practitioners. The Roman politician and philosopher Seneca (4? B.C.E.–65 C.E.), tutor to the future emperor Nero (r. 54–68 C.E.), wrote many works related to his Stoic philosophy, including *Natural Questions*, which explains and discusses such scientific problems as the causes of rainbows and comets.

SOCIAL AND INTELLECTUAL STATUS

There was to some extent, as in Greek society, a social divide between those working on science and philosophy as a matter of intellectual interest and personal development and those who practiced scientific specialties as a profession, for which they received payment. This was closely related to a common attitude, at least among the first kind of intellectuals, that scientific inquiries were greater if they did not involve actual physical materials or things. "Pure" mathematics, for example, was thought to be superior to applied math. This idea was held partly because the notion of the general proof—one that applies to a class of objects and can be logically proved in the abstract rather than having been tested only for specific, concrete examples—was central to the development of Greek geometry and became an ideal for all intellectual enterprises. Thus, Pythagoras's theorem is expressed thus: "The square of the hypotenuse is equal to the sum of the squares on the other two sides." It is not stated as the numerical formula $5^2 = 3^2 + 4^2$, and so on for every actual set of triangle lengths actually tested.

There was also a common assumption that abstract reasoning was more reliable than sense perception and observable data, even though the former obviously must rely to some extent on the latter. The result is that "practical" or productive forms of knowledge, including some applied science, were seen as less true and certain than more abstract inquiries, as well as being usually practiced by people of less wealth and social status.

However, many people actually working in such fields as engineering and medicine strongly resisted that their subjects were evaluated at this lower status. The Roman Empire Greek mechanist Hero of Alexandria claimed—possibly as a joke—that mechanics was actually better at producing the philosophical ideal of a tranquil life lived without fear or worry than philosophy was because a city with good mechanists and ballistics engineers would never be attacked. The Greek physician Galen (129–ca. 99 C.E.), who was the personal physician of the Roman emperor Marcus Aurelius (r. 161–80 C.E.), tried to work out a set of logical and mathematical rules for medicine, such as a theorem for the length of time it took for a wound to heal based on its size and shape.

Many such practitioners, certainly those at the top of their fields, were literate and well-educated men who argued that their discipline was just as reliable and worthwhile as philosophy or pure mathematics. The dividing line was far from absolute. Many elite lay Romans read works on medicine and mechanics, even if they did not regard them as suitable subjects for a gentleman to practice.

sician and methods of surgery, cauterization, and sometimes strong drugs. The first Greek doctor in Rome was nicknamed "the butcher" because of his use of such methods, and some Romans, like Pliny the Elder (23–79 C.E.), criticized medicine as un-Roman. Nonetheless, Greek medicine became popular, and doctors in Rome and throughout the empire were usually Greek.

In general, Roman reactions to Greek ideas, including much of Greek science, were complicated. Many traditional Romans thought that the influence of Greek culture might weaken Roman society through its focus on inessential speculation and ways of life, unlike the conventional Roman emphasis on farming, the army, and the duties of political office. Many elite Romans, however, could speak Greek and were interested in such ideas, and they adapted or developed them, writing epic poetry, history, and drama of their own—all forms of literature that the Greeks had invented. Similarly, Greek works on science and philosophy found an elite Ro-

PHILOSOPHY SCHOOLS

Scientific theories formed an extensive and integral part of several philosophical schools of the Roman age. In this context, a school was a group of like-minded people who learned from each other, sometimes at a shared physical location. No qualifications or formal educational process was implied by the term. These groups had formed in Greece in the third century B.C.E., though their arguments continued to develop. Two important schools were the Stoics and the Epicureans. They had systematic—though completely different—theories about such things as the basic materials of the universe, the physiology of sense perception, and the workings of body and mind. They offered a naturalistic understanding of every kind of phenomenon, from lightning to the way mirrors work to the development of human society. These theories were compatible with, and used to supply evidence for, the Stoics' and Epicureans' theories on ethics, epistemology (the study of nature and the grounds of knowledge), and theology. The Stoics, for instance, considered God to be a material substance present throughout the actual world. Everything that happened was according to God's plan via a mechanistic, completely determined, causal chain. The Epicureans, on the other hand, maintained that the gods were perfect beings made like everything else of constituent particles and void, and they were completely irrelevant to human affairs. For both groups, science was not separable from other areas of human understanding.

A third group, the Skeptics, was not committed to any theory at all because their epistemological position was that there was no definite, clear instance of incontrovertible knowledge about anything and there was no definite proof that any theory was more true than any other. These radical Skeptics in philosophy, and their medical equivalent, the empiricist physicians, criticized the theories and beliefs of everyone else. This meant that people who believed that some theories were true had to improve their arguments against the Skeptics' attacks. It can be argued that skepticism was overall not helpful to philosophy and science because it focused attention away from the actual content of scientific theories and instead highlighted underlying epistemological positions. All theories, whether they were well supported by the evidence or not, were equally vulnerable to skeptical attack because 100 percent certainty was the only standard for truth they would allow.

The scientific theories of the philosophical schools were not often updated. This is primarily because their main aim was to offer the best understanding of the world as a means of achieving what they called *ataraxia*, or a life without disturbance, fear, and worry. They competed with each other as to which of them offered the most convincing way of achieving this state of being, so the philosophical schools had no incentive to revise their basic principles or their scientific theories and tended to be conservative.

MEDICAL SECTS

Professional physicians in ancient Roman society—most of them Greeks—were divided into three broad methodological categories: the Empiricists; the so-called Rationalists or Dogmatists; and, from about the first century C.E., the Methodists. These groups were called the medical schools or sects.

The Empiricists emerged in the third century B.C.E. as a group of doctors who shared a common epistemology and methodology. They seem to have been popular among patients, including high-status ones such as kings. Their position was in many ways similar to that of the skeptical philosophers. The Empiricists said that there was no point in investigating the body with the aim of deducing theories about physiology or illness because no such theory could be proved true beyond any doubt and so might be false. They also said that this kind of theoretical knowledge was unnecessary for good medical practice. Empiricist doctors relied on their own experience of treating diseases (*autopsia*) and the recorded or reported experience of other people (*historia*). They associated certain symptoms with particular successful treatments and when they saw the symptoms again, they were reminded to use the same treatments. But they did not draw any conclusions from this about the nature of the disease or why the treatment seemed to work. Empiricists rejected dissection as useless and maintained that observation of internal organs exposed by accident when someone was wounded was enough to learn basic anatomy for the purposes of surgery.

Methodism may go back to the physiological theory and treatments of Asclepiades, a famous Greek doctor who lived in the Roman province of Bithynia in the first century B.C.E. and taught himself medicine as a second career after having been an orator. Asclepiades developed a theory in which he determined that pores in the body are sometimes blocked by some kind of corpuscle (thought of as a minute particle) and that this is what makes people ill. But Methodists themselves did not think that this information was relevant to being a good doctor. According to the Methodists, all diseases shared one of three common features: the patient was too constricted, too lax, or a mixture of the two. They believed that treatment should be based on that alone and that patients should be treated "by opposites"; thus, patients who were too constricted should be treated with relaxants. This was the method (*methodos*). Other knowledge acquired through experience, deduction, or dissection may have been possible but was unnecessary for medical practice. Medicine was, therefore, easy to learn—the Methodist founder Thessalus is reported to have said it took only six months. Methodists did not think that dissection was useful, though they may have thought it was interesting. One famous Methodist, Soranus, a Greek physician of second century C.E. who practiced in Rome, is remembered for his work on gynecology, which has survived largely intact.

All physicians who were neither Empiricists nor Methodists contended that reliable knowledge about physiology and illness could be rationally deduced to at least some extent. For this reason they became collectively known as "Rationalists" or "Dogmatists." This very general agreement, however, was their only common factor. There were many subgroups and even individuals within the rationalists who disagreed with each other about theories, methods, and treatments. Most of them would have agreed that dissection was useful, but few physicians seemed to have done any themselves in the Roman period, even on animals. A notable example of a rationalist who performed dissections is Galen, who carried out dissections and vivisections (operations performed on the living) on many animals, including dogs, goats, Barbary apes, and once an elephant. Galen's dissections were often carried out in public settings, where anyone could watch as a kind of popular theater that Galen used to lend dramatic visual support for his claims about physiology.

MEDICAL TRAINING AND TREATMENTS

The usual way to learn medicine was by apprenticeship to a practicing physician. Sons of physicians probably often became doctors themselves as part of a family business. Many elite doctors studied in several places famous as centers of intellectual medicine, such as Pergamum and Alexandria. They may also have been educated in philosophy more generally, as Galen was. It was possible to teach oneself by reading works on medicine, as Asclepiades is said to have done. There were no examinations or legal qualifications to take, so anyone who wanted to set up as a doctor could do so. However, whether people came to a particular doctor depended on his reputation and what they knew about him, and in the early stages of a practice it would have helped to have learned from a locally known doctor or a famous physician elsewhere. Doctors were usually men, though it is possible that female midwives, some of whom were literate and trained in medical methods, treated female patients for a broader range of problems than those associated with childbirth.

In ancient Rome a very common medical treatment was the prescription of a combination of diet and lifestyle recommendations, such as exercise and baths, known as a *regimen*. For illness, drugs could be prescribed. In the Roman period these became increasingly complicated. Drugs that contained only one or two ingredients were called simples, but many drugs were made of numerous ingredients, sometimes more than 100, and such a medicine was called a *polypharmacy*. Women might use contraceptives, abortifacients (a drug that causes abortion), and drugs to bring on menstruation. There were many kinds of surgical operations, both for trauma and internal conditions, including an operation to remove cataracts from the eye. Since there were no anesthetics, several assistants were needed to hold conscious patients still for operations.

The combination of mathematics and astrology produced *iatromathematics* (medical astrology). The movements of the stars were thought to affect the course of a disease and the times and ways in which a physician could most effectively intervene. Medical astrology was popular and accepted by many physicians, but not all.

MATHEMATICS

The administration of the Roman Empire required a great deal of organization, much of which depended upon some degree of mathematical knowledge. Arithmetical expertise was needed by the government and army officials and secretaries who dealt with taxes on land, trade, and goods; public expenditure and accounting; army provisions and the payment of soldiers; the regular census of the population; and many other aspects of a large empire. Many traders and other businessmen also needed to be able to manage numbers quickly and reliably or to employ people who could. Bronze abaci were widely used in this period.

Geometry was also vital for the taxation and management of land. Architects and engineers used geometrical theorems in major civic projects like Rome's sophisticated water supply of aqueducts, fountains, sewers, public baths, and private houses; in private enterprise such as the building of luxury villas; and in the military. The Roman architect Vitruvius of the first century B.C.E. describes how to build a water system for a city, as well as many other machines.

The Roman army employed surveyors for mapping military terrain as well as for constructing and attacking siege defenses and fortifications. One example of such a fortification is Hadrian's Wall in Great Britain, a stone-and-turf wall that ran for 73 miles across the width of the country at a height of almost 20 feet and with regular forts. Roman roads tended to be very straight, and roads within the empire might be tunneled straight through a mountain. Surveyors used mathematical techniques and simple instruments like the *dioptra*, or sighting rod, to keep the construction on track.

ASTRONOMY AND CALENDARS

By the Roman period the movements of the stars were well understood. The traditional Roman calendar had 12 months and a year consisted of 355 days. To keep the calendar year in approximate agreement with the solar year, which is longer than 355 days, the state priests in charge of the calendar had to add a month every other year. In the first century B.C.E. the calendar was not properly managed, so in 45 B.C.E. Julius Caesar replaced the old system with a solar calendar on the advice of a Greek astronomer, Sosigenes of Alexandria. This system was slightly altered again by Pope Gregory XIII in 1582, and the Gregorian calendar is the one we still use today.

The Julian calendar reform shows that technical expertise in astronomy belonged largely to the Greek tradition of mathematical astronomy. Although many elite Romans took a lay interest in the stars, they were not concerned with exactitude. The main source for astronomical theory was the Hellenistic Period poem of Aratus of Soli (ca. 315–ca. 240 B.C.E.) on stars and weather titled *Phaenomena* (Appearances). This work had been adapted into verse from a much older astronomical text, which by the time of the Roman Empire was, in fact, rather out of date.

Caesar consulted foreign experts and then used the results to organize the way in which the Roman Empire counted time. (Local cities and regions would have simultaneously often used older methods as well.) Mathematical astronomy thus had an enormous impact on the Roman world because

Roman government perceived it as reliable and useful. It remained, however, the specialty of a few experts, usually those of Greek descent and culture, often from the Greek populations and settlements of Asia Minor, Syria, and Egypt.

The ancient Romans also used armillary spheres, an astronomical device that had moving parts and modeled the movements of the heavenly bodies. Some scholars have suggested that Nero's Golden House contained one. An armillary sphere is depicted in a wall painting of a luxury villa from the Stabiae (modern-day Castellammare di Stabia) region of Italy. The Roman elite liked to own gadgets and to demonstrate an awareness of contemporary intellectual endeavor, but they did not build their own.

GEOGRAPHY AND ASTRONOMY

Ptolemy, a Greek astronomer of the second century C.E. who worked in Alexandria, is known for his theory on the motions of the stars and planets, which built upon earlier Greek astronomy and became the accepted model of how the cosmos worked until the discoveries of Nicolaus Copernicus and Johannes Kepler in the 16th and 17th centuries, respectively. Ptolemy's *Geography* gives the latitudes and longitudes of over 8,000 places on the earth, just as astronomers located the stars in the heavens through their celestial coordinates, though not all of his information was accurate. He also developed a mathematical way to project the three-dimensional world onto a two-dimensional surface such as a map.

Maps existed in ancient Rome but were probably not often used by ordinary individuals for the purpose of finding their way about. More common were "itineraries," which listed the times it would take to travel between two places. Geographical knowledge of the Northern Hemisphere in the Roman period was quite detailed and extensive, especially of the lands of the empire and, to a lesser extent, of the trade routes to India and China. There was a strong link between geographical knowledge and imperial power, both ideological and practical. To know a terrain well was to have some control over it, especially from a military point of view. To be able to display maps, such as the map of the empire that the Roman general Agrippa (63?–12 B.C.E.) had carved in marble, showed the general population the size and importance of the empire and demonstrated the competence of the empire's leaders. Individuals may have known much less about the world beyond the places that concerned them directly.

ASTRONOMY AND ASTROLOGY

Astrology was almost indistinguishable from astronomy in the ancient world since its development in Ptolemaic Egypt over the third to first centuries B.C.E. Many astronomers believed that the stars and planets influenced human lives. The astronomer Ptolemy wrote *Tetrabiblos* (Four Books) as a scientific account of astrology. He thought that the heavenly bodies shaped earthly environments and so affected the character of people according to what time of the year they were born. Although not every event in a person's life was

entirely determined in this way, a good astrologer could estimate the probability of certain events. For instance, a very confident, adventurous person was more likely to die at sea. Other astrologers and intellectuals had different accounts of how astrology worked or how rigidly deterministic it was. Some viewed it as a matter of theology, contending that the movements of the stars were messages from the gods.

There were also skeptics, especially among intellectuals such as the philosopher Favorinus (fl. second century C.E.), who attacked inconsistencies in astrological theories, asking why twins did not always have the same fate and pointing out that many astrological predictions did not come true. The Roman philosopher and statesmen Cicero (106–43 B.C.E.) gave similar arguments in his dialogue *De divinatione* (On Divination), which discusses methods of predicting the future through the observation of signs. It was, however, always possible to explain a false prediction by saying that the astrologer was incompetent or that astrology, like medicine, is difficult and that using it cannot always be done with perfect success. Some astrological predictions could be self-fulfilling, or identified in retrospect. The horoscope of the emperor Augustus (r. 27 B.C.E.–14 C.E.), drawn up after he had become ruler of Rome, unsurprisingly predicted a remarkable career. Augustus put his sign of Capricorn on some of his coinage.

Astrology could also be politically dangerous. Predictions that the emperor would die could easily be connected to assassination attempts. In 11 C.E. Augustus made it illegal to make a prediction about anyone's death. Astrology was also seen as in origin a foreign expertise, connected to Greece, Egypt, and Babylonia. Astrologers were usually called Chaldeans, which was the name of the Babylonian order of priests who watched the sky for omens. Both astrology and magic were at times banned in Rome.

Nonetheless, astrology rapidly became extremely popular in Roman society. In his poems the Roman satirist Juvenal (ca. 55–ca. 127 C.E.) mocks many of its adherents, especially women and the lower classes. Most astrologers were not, in fact, astronomers. By the early second century C.E., however, there was sufficient data to compose planetary tables in which the relevant information could simply be read off for any year and time.

Astronomy and astrology had a close relationship. Astronomy remained a demanding and specialized form of mathematics. Astrology, on the other hand, was widespread and practiced both by professionals and by individuals who wanted to predict their own future. Astrology was, however, ultimately dependent on astronomy and using astronomy's reputation for precise mathematical certainty for its own advantage. Astronomy, meanwhile, could explain its relevance to human life through the predictions of astrology.

SCIENCE IN THE LATE EMPIRE

The late empire included many notable mathematicians, such as Pappus of Alexandria, Theon of Alexandria, and Eutocius, as well as medical writers, such as Oribasius and Paul of Aegina. However, intellectual activity in such subjects increasingly centered on the explication of earlier works, and little new research was done. Philosophy flourished for a while in the form of the Neoplatonism and also as Christian theology, but neither of these doctrines emphasized the investigation of the natural world. Non-Christian philosophy was increasingly linked to magic and to evil, and Christian understanding of the world located authority in sacred texts rather than in inquiry and experiment and the pagan works of the past. Saint Augustine, considered a brilliant theologian of the fourth and fifth centuries C.E., did not believe that the world was round, a fact well known to Greek and Roman intellectuals since the fourth century B.C.E. Many pagan works of science and philosophy were translated into Arabic and survived in the Islamic tradition. The Western world became reacquainted with them after the Middle Ages.

THE AMERICAS

BY MICHAEL J. O'NEAL

Although the chronology and routes by which the Americas were populated are still debated, one version envisions people spilling over the Bering land bridge into Alaska beginning some 30,000 years ago. Migrating steadily southward to form communities throughout North, Central, and South America, they had to become astute observers of nature. For thousands of years they had to adapt to new and sometimes changing climates, new flora and fauna, new food supplies, and new landscapes and terrains. Some settled in the wet regions of the Pacific Northwest, some in the dry regions of Central America, some in the flat plains of the American Midwest, some in the mountainous regions of South America. Some coped with tropical heat and others with arctic cold. In time they adapted so successfully that they were able to build some of the greatest civilizations of the ancient world.

COSMOLOGY AND SCIENCE

The way the aboriginal peoples of the Americas looked at their universe can be difficult for the modern world to understand. In modern life a sharp distinction is made between the natural and supernatural worlds. Some people do not believe in a world of the supernatural, but among those who do, the two realms tend to be thought of as separate; the very word *supernatural* suggests that the world of the gods and the spirit exists above ("super") or outside the physical world. This separation, however, would have been unthinkable to ancient Americans. Every aspect of their lives had religious significance. They saw the universe as composed of spiritual and divine forces that affected them every moment of their lives.

At the center of this view of the world was a cosmos that ancient Americans saw as a hierarchy of spheres or planes. Some of them were superior to the world of the earth; others were inferior. One example is provided by the Nahua people of central Mexico, precursors to the Aztec, also a Nahua people. The Nahua believed that above the earthly level were

numerous other spheres, variously nine, 11, 12, or 13, with 13 being the most common. This belief influenced the calendar, which was composed of 13 periods, somewhat inaccurately called "months," each in honor of the divinity that ruled each sphere. The highest divinity was referred to as Ometeotl, which translates roughly as the "god of duality." Ometeotl was responsible for what the Nahua saw as the duality of the universe: positive and negative, male and female, the spirit and the physical worlds. Artworks depicting Ometeotl are few. Modern researchers working in sophisticated laboratories with the most advanced equipment might regard this duality as myth, not science. To the Nahua, however, it was science. Their belief was based on observations of the world they lived in and explained the origins and development of their universe and humankind.

Because they were keen observers and experimenters, like many other ancient civilizations, the ancient Americans can be regarded as scientists in fields like agriculture, architecture, engineering, construction, metallurgy, and mathematics. Ancient American peoples, for example, made early observations in the fields of astronomy, biology, chemistry, geology, and physics. As astronomers they learned about the movements of heavenly objects and used those observations to create calendars and to predict changes in the seasons. They observed the "hole" in the Big Dipper long before European astronomers did. In fact, so keen was the interest of the ancient Americans in astronomy that priests and astronomers were often one and the same. Because science throughout much of the ancient world was associated with magic and with understanding the power and will of the gods, the earliest scientists were shamans, priests, and others who claimed knowledge of the divine and could read it in the heavens.

As geologists, early Americans knew long before the Europeans did that the world was round. This knowledge was reflected in their myths about the origins and creation of the world. (In this context, a myth is not something that is untrue; rather, it is a narrative that conveys a fundamental truth about the nature of the universe and humans' place in it.) For example, the ancient Lakota nation of North America saw the world's four original beings—Inyan (rock), Maka (the earth), Taku Skan Skan (the sky), and Wi (the sun)—as round, because in the cosmology of the Lakota roundness was the most sacred shape.

As chemists, early Americans often turned their attention to their food supply. They learned, for example, how to deal with stored corn that had become lignified, or hardened. They learned that if they applied alkaline substances (that is, substances that are bases rather than acids) to the corn, they could break down the hardened outer layer and soften the kernel inside. In this way they could return dried corn to an edible state, and the alkaline substance, usually lime water, added valuable calcium to their diet. Sometimes they left the corn in its hardened state to make popcorn.

Even in physics the early Americans made astute observations. During lightning storms, for example, they learned to throw pieces of cedarwood onto a bonfire to ward off the lightning. Even though they could not have fully understood the physical laws that explained why this was successful, successful it was. When cedar burns, it emits a negative electrical charge that repels the negative electrical charge in the atmosphere that produces lightning.

As biologists, the ancient Americans also recognized the principle modern scientists refer to as biodiversity—the notion that there is value in maintaining diverse genetic strains of plants and animals. Doing so allows species to adapt more successfully to changes in conditions. Thus, for example, they developed a bean that sprouted in underground storage chambers; their purpose was to develop a plant they could use in winter religious ceremonies. The bean, it turned out, was resistant to a common pest that attacked bean crops. Thus the new bean became a reliable source of food when pest outbreaks occurred. In cultivating various crops, the ancient Americans appear to have valued diversity in strains of the crop and did not try to breed that diversity out.

Maize

The ancient Mesoamericans (that is, the people who inhabited modern-day Mexico and parts of Central America; from the prefix *meso-*, meaning "middle") carried out one of the most successful plant-breeding programs in the history of the world with the development of maize, known to most North Americans as corn. Maize became an important staple crop among early Americans, contributing to immense population growth and cultural development in regions throughout North and South America

Maize, however, does not reproduce wildly and could not grow without human cultivation. Early Americans bred maize out of a wild plant called teosinte over a period of many years, though whether their success was an event or a process cannot really be known. Teosinte can be found in small patches at higher elevations west of the Sierra Madre in western Mexico. Historians estimate that it was domesticated into maize sometime between 4000 and 3000 B.C.E. Using sophisticated tools they can even locate where it was domesticated: in the drainage areas of the Balsas River in Michoacan, in western Mexico. Its origins lay with small hunter-gatherer bands that had migrated throughout the region, following the changes in the seasons to find deer, antelope, rabbits, and plant foods like nuts and berries. Archaeological evidence, found primarily in excavated caves in Puebla, shows that these early Mesoamericans were experimenting with meals and grains.

Maize was not the first cereal grain the early Mesoamericans domesticated. The first was a grain related to modern-day millet. But by about 2700 B.C.E., historians believe, people in the region were subsisting in part on a type of maize with very small ears and just six to nine kernels per ear. The process of domesticating maize continued over the next 2,000 years, and by about 1400 B.C.E. maize cultivation had spread throughout Mexico, along with methods for grinding and cooking the dough in the form of round, flat cakes. By that time maize had become the staple crop of the Mesoamericans, and the development of Mesoamerican culture, including the invention of irrigation and the emergence of pottery and weaving, corresponded with the spread of maize as a reliable food source.

The development of maize is intimately bound up with Mesoamerican cosmology and creation myths. (Cosmology is the branch of philosophy that deals with the origins, structure, and purpose of the universe.) In these myths the world originated at a time when maize was trapped inside mountains and boulders, where it was inaccessible to humans. Small animals such as foxes could get to the maize, but humans were able to get to it only as a result of divine intervention. Both the Maya and the Aztec envisioned the process of creation as one of the gods progressively providing humans with better and better food. In the earliest stages of humankind, humans ate only fruits and acorns. In the next stage pine nuts were a primary food, followed by a third stage dominated by millet. In the fourth stage of human development, people ate the grains of the teosinte. The Mayan version of the story relates that they were attracted to the teosinte plant because they had observed grains in the dung of wildcats that had eaten the plant. Finally, in the fifth stage the gods gave Mesoamericans maize, the perfect food. Even early Mesoamerican mythology incorporated a kind of anthropology and recognized that over time the conditions of their lives improved.

Maize, put differently, was divinity itself. It meant life, so it was closely associated with fertility and regeneration. The rain that nourished it, which came from the heavens, enabled people to share in the fundamental life spark of the divine. So important to the ancient Americans was maize and maize cultivation that the plant was central to their everyday thought and activity.

Mayan Mathematics

The ancient Maya occupied the Yucatán Peninsula in modern-day Mexico, Belize, Guatemala, and sections of Honduras and El Salvador. The Maya began to inhabit the region in roughly 2000 B.C.E., reached the peak of their influence in the early centuries of the Common Era, and began to decline in the ninth century C.E. In studying Mayan history and culture, historians refer to the classic period, extending from about 250 to 900 C.E., as the period of the Maya's greatest achievements. While much of what historians know about them dates to that period, they also know that classic Mayan culture was built on the achievements of their ancestors dating back many hundreds of years before then.

In the 16th century Spanish explorers landed on the Yucatán Peninsula and eventually overran the regions inhabited by the Maya and the Aztec. Unfortunately, the early Spanish explorers and missionaries regarded all manifestations of Mayan religious beliefs as the work of the devil and had them destroyed. These included not only religious artifacts but also written texts on many subjects. Only a handful of these texts survived and are housed in museums in Paris, France; Dresden, Germany; and Madrid, Spain. While these texts, called codexes (or codices), date to the centuries just preceding European contact, they were based on texts originally written in earlier periods, which in turn were based on knowledge that had been acquired for hundreds of years before that.

Historians of science are especially intrigued by the ancient Mayan system of mathematics, which they applied to fields like astronomy and architecture. Much of this system has been preserved in the codices. Mayan mathematics was a vigesimal system, meaning that it was based on the number 20. Such a system probably evolved because ancient people probably first counted with their fingers and toes, and when they reached the number 20 they had to start over with a new set of 20 in much the same way that modern systems of mathematics are based on the number 10 and its multiples.

Thus in Mayan texts the numeral 1 was represented by a thick dot, 2 by two dots, and so on. The numeral 5 was represented by a straight horizontal line, 6 by one dot above a line, 7 by two dots above a line, and so on. The numeral 10 was then represented by two horizontal lines, 11 by a dot above two lines, and so on up to 15, represented by three lines, and so on up to 20, represented by a single dot above a shell representing zero.

The Mayan system, though, had some irregularities that historians of mathematics believe related to the Mayan calendar—or rather, the two Mayan calendars. One was a ritual calendar that consisted of 13 periods, each with 20 days. Historians are unsure why this calendar was structured in this way, but they speculate that each of the 13 periods represented a god and the 20 days represented humans (because of their base 20 system of math). The other calendar was a solar calendar consisting of 360 days, with 18 periods each consisting of 20 days (and the extra five days regarded as unlucky). The two calendars coincided with each other after 18,980 days, equivalent to 52 years or 73 ritual years. The Maya also observed that the planet Venus returned to its original spot after two 52-year cycles, and in fact they held a great celebration after 104 years—that is, after two 52-year solar cycles or one 104-year cycle of Venus.

But how does this explain the irregularity in the counting system? To answer that, it is necessary to recognize that the Maya also counted time as a linear sequence of days. They calculated, for example, that the world was created on a date that coincides with August 12, 3113 B.C.E., and they dated many of their historical monuments in terms of the number of days that had passed since this creation. In the city of Tikal, for example, is a historical marker dating construction of the structure as occurring 1,253,912 days after the world was created. Put differently, rather than counting determining the structure of the calendar, the structure of the calendar determined counting, enabling the Maya to incorporate into their mathematical system their conception of the gods, creation, the movement of heavenly bodies, and the like.

GEOMETRY, ARCHITECTURE, AND ASTRONOMY

Ancient Americans had a sophisticated grasp of geometry, and geometric patterns can be found in a wide range of Native American structures, from major temples to small ceremonial structures. Geometry and architecture intertwined with astronomy as well, with many of these structures mirroring the movement of heavenly bodies, particularly the sun as it changes position in the sky throughout the year. The geometric regularity of these buildings reflects geometric and astronomic understandings that date back at least 2,000 years.

Ancient American geometry in many respects reflected the geometry of the natural world. It included not only simple squares and circles but also arcs, hexagons (six-sided figures), octagons (eight-sided figures), and dodecagons (12-sided figures, as in a clocks). Thus, geometric understanding among the ancient Americans was a process of discovering and unfolding the geometry found in nature, rather than an artificially constructed system of thought. Ancient Americans began with the simple notion that two points could define a line that extended infinitely in either direction. Additionally, either or both of those two points could become the center of a circle, and the line connecting the two points could serve as the radius of a circle. If circles were drawn using each of the two points as the center, the two circles would intersect at two points. In turn, each of those points could serve as the center of yet another circle. If the process is continued, the result is a six-petaled "flower," known among some ancient American cultures as the Flower of Life.

More important, this system of intersecting points can be used to make many other geometric shapes, including perfect triangles, pentagons (five-sided figures) hexagons, octagons, decagons (10-sided figures), dodecagons, and even polygons with 24 and 48 sides. (The word *polygon* refers to any of these enclosed, flat shapes with angles; *poly-*, means "many.") Once these shapes and how to derive them were understood, architects could apply them to the construction of buildings, including temples, homes, and ceremonial structures, with simple tools like string. Each of the points in an octagon, for example, would become the position for a vertical post, which then evolved into more complex architectural designs.

What role, though, did astronomy play in all this? Historians and archaeologists have long noted that many of the structures of ancient America were oriented along north–south and east–west axes. In recent decades, however, many scholars have turned their attention to a subfield called archaeoastronomy—the study of the relationships between building practices and astronomical knowledge. In connection with ancient American structures they have found that many are built with an understanding of the concept of azimuths, particularly the azimuth of the sun at the points of the winter and summer solstice.

An azimuth is an angle measured from a reference point. Perhaps the best way to understand azimuths is to think about satellites in the sky that beam down television signals. When the customer's dish is mounted, it has to be pointed at the satellite; otherwise, it fails to pick up the signal. But satellite dish installers do not have a single, fixed angle at which they mount the dish. This is because while the satellite is in a fixed place relative to the horizon, usually over the equator, homes are located at various points north or south of the equator. For a home near the equator, the satellite dish would have to point upward at a severe angle; for homes in Alaska, the dish would point at a much lower, flatter angle. This angle is the azimuth. Like the azimuths used to point to satellites, the azimuths of the sun at the summer and winter solstices—that is, the dates when the sun is highest in the sky in summer and lowest in the sky in winter—differ depending on latitude.

Evidence shows that many ancient American structures were positioned with their angles lined up with the point in the sky that marked the azimuths of the summer and winter solstices. The purpose in doing so was probably part religious, part practical. From a religious perspective, it reflected the ancient Americans' view that all of creation is unified. From a practical perspective, it enabled ancient Americans to take maximum advantage of light and warmth from the sun.

SOUTH AMERICA: THE SEARCH FOR RESOURCES

The ancient South Americans, particularly the people of Peruvian Andes, made remarkable technical advances in metalwork, agriculture, and energy production, all based on early understanding of science. In the field of metallurgy, archaeologists have discovered that the Peruvians began to exploit deposits of copper beginning sometime around 1400–1100 B.C.E. They created an alloy called tumbaga, which was a mixture of gold and copper, though the ratio of these elements varied widely, from 97 percent copper to 97 percent gold. A chief technical innovation was adding the element mercury, which hardened the metal and made it more durable.

Additionally, the Peruvians found gold and silver resources and developed complex technologies for mining, purifying, smelting, and crafting them into useful and decorative objects. Along the way they found uses for other minerals they mined, including hematite (an iron oxide), limonite (a mineral with various combinations of other minerals, including hematite), and manganese oxide. The many varieties of hematite, including rainbow hematite, kidney ore, martite, bloodstone, iron rose, and paint ore, suggest that depending on the mineral's composition, it had different appearances, making it a versatile mineral for objects with differing aesthetic properties.

With regard to energy, the ancient Americans, like people throughout the world, burned wood, along with dried dung and charcoal. In time, however, they also discovered and mined coal, particularly as some of the forests became depleted. Archaeologists disagree about whether the Peruvians used coal in the metal-smelting process. Some argue that little evidence suggests that they did, but others claim to have found coal ash in ancient Peruvian smelting sites. The Peruvians also found uses for bitumen, a substance that is similar to asphalt or tar and can occur naturally or as a byproduct of a refining process. The Peruvians used this sticky material as a sealant in coffins and as caulking for ships. The effectiveness of that sealant, along with the Peruvians' skill in mummifying bodies, has given modern scientists unique insight into the physical condition of the ancient Peruvians.

The Peruvians learned to make use of guano, or bat dung, on nearby islands as fertilizer. Guano is still used as a fertilizer because it is high in nitrogen, phosphate, and potassium, all substances essential to healthy plant growth and abundant crops. It is believed that the Peruvians used small reed boats to travel to the islands and transport the guano back to the mainland for use on fields. In some places the guano is believed to have been as much as 65 feet thick.

MEDICINE

An important part of the scientific achievements of any civilization is its ability to find treatments for illness and disease. Again, much of what might have been known about medical lore in ancient Mesoamerica has been lost because the invading Spaniards destroyed the manuscripts that recorded their various branches of knowledge. Some of this ancient knowledge was later reconstructed, and modern paleopathologists—those who study disease and illness by examining preserved tissues from ancient times—have been able to add to that knowledge. Generally, medical practitioners in the ancient Americas were shamans. Like the astronomer-shamans discussed earlier, shamans who practiced medicine were believed to have had access to supernatural power and wisdom.

In common with ancient civilizations the world over, the ancient Americans made wide use of herbs and other medicinal plants. One early colonial manuscript catalogues 204 medicinal plants from a wide variety of climate zones. While this manuscript was copied much later, it doubtless reflects insights into medicinal cures that were hundreds, if not thousands, of years old. Modern people who think of themselves as addicted to chocolate might take heart in knowing that ancient healers of Mesoamerica recognized the therapeutic benefits of chocolate and cacao. They used it not only to deliver other medicines but as a medicine in its own right. It was thought to help people gain weight, stimulate the nervous system, and improve digestion and elimination. Ancient Americans also used cacao to treat anemia, poor appetite, gout, kidney stones, fevers, and, in paste form, burns. Interestingly, modern medical researchers have confirmed what the ancient Americans knew. Chocolate has been shown to be an effective cough medicine. More important, consumed in moderation, it is a good source of polyphenols—chemicals that protect the heart.

See also AGRICULTURE; ARCHITECTURE; ASTRONOMY; BUILDING TECHNIQUES AND MATERIALS; CALENDARS AND CLOCKS; CERAMICS AND POTTERY; CITIES; CLIMATE AND GEOGRAPHY; CRAFTS; DEATH AND BURIAL PRACTICES; EDUCATION; EMPIRES AND DYNASTIES; EXPLORATION; GENDER STRUCTURES

AND ROLES; HEALTH AND DISEASE; INVENTIONS; LANGUAGE; LITERATURE; METALLURGY; MIGRATION AND POPULATION MOVEMENTS; MILITARY; MINING, QUARRYING, AND SALT MAKING; NATURAL DISASTERS; NUMBERS AND COUNTING; OCCUPATIONS; RELIGION AND COSMOLOGY; ROADS AND BRIDGES; SACRED SITES; SEAFARING AND NAVIGATION; SETTLEMENT PATTERNS; SHIPS AND SHIPBUILDING; SOCIAL ORGANIZATION; STORAGE AND PRESERVATION; TEXTILES AND NEEDLEWORK; TRADE AND EXCHANGE; WAR AND CONQUEST; WEIGHTS AND MEASURES; WRITING.

Egypt

～ Herodotus, "Mummification," from The Histories (ca. 440 B.C.E.) ～

The mode of embalming, according to the most perfect process, is the following: They take first a crooked piece of iron, and with it draw out the brain through the nostrils, thus getting rid of a portion, while the skull is cleared of the rest by rinsing with drugs; next they make a cut along the flank with a sharp Ethiopian stone, and take out the whole contents of the abdomen, which they then cleanse, washing it thoroughly with palm wine, and again frequently with an infusion of pounded aromatics. After this they fill the cavity with the purest bruised myrrh, with cassia, and every other sort of spicery except frankincense, and sew up the opening. Then the body is placed in natrum for seventy days, and covered entirely over. After the expiration of that space of time, which must not be exceeded, the body is washed, and wrapped round, from head to foot, with bandages of fine linen cloth, smeared over with gum, which is used generally by the Egyptians in the place of glue, and in this state it is given back to the relations, who enclose it in a wooden case which they have had made for the purpose, shaped into the figure of a man. Then fastening the case, they place it in a sepulchral chamber, upright against the wall. Such is the most costly way of embalming the dead.

If persons wish to avoid expense, and choose the second process, the following is the method pursued: Syringes are filled with oil made from the cedar-tree, which is then, without any incision or disemboweling, injected into the abdomen. The passage by which it might be likely to return is stopped, and the body laid in natrum the prescribed number of days. At the end of the time the cedar-oil is allowed to make its escape; and such is its power that it brings with it the whole stomach and intestines in a liquid state. The natrum meanwhile has dissolved the flesh, and so nothing is left of the dead body but the skin and the bones. It is returned in this condition to the relatives, without any further trouble being bestowed upon it.

The third method of embalming, which is practiced in the case of the poorer classes, is to clear out the intestines with a clyster, and let the body lie in natrum the seventy days, after which it is at once given to those who come to fetch it away.

From: Internet History Sourcebooks.
Available online. URL: http://www.
fordham.edu/halsall/.

Greece

～ Archimedes, Letter to Dositheus (ca. 220 B.C.E.) ～

Archimedes to Dositheus, greeting: Formerly I sent to you the studies which I had finished up to that time together with the demonstrations, which were to show that a segment bounded by a straight line and a conic section is four-thirds of the triangle on the same base as the segment and of the same height. Since that time certain propositions as yet undemonstrated have come to my mind, and I have undertaken to work them out. These are: 1. The surface of any sphere is four times the surface of its greatest circle; 2. The surface of any segment of a sphere is equal to the surface of that circle the radius of which equals the straight line drawn from the vertex of the segment to the circumference of the circle which serves as the base of the segment; 3. That a cylinder with a base equal to the great circle of a given sphere, and a height equal to the diameter of the sphere contains half the volume of that sphere and its surface is equal to half the surface of that sphere.

These propositions, of course, were always true of these figures, but they were hidden to the men who studied geometry before my time. Therefore, since I have discovered that these things hold true of these figures I do not fear to place them alongside my own previous results and the most thoroughly established theorems of Eudoxus, such as: any pyramid is equal to one-third of the prism of the same base and height, and any cone is equal to one-third of the cylinder of the same base and height.

First Postulate. Supposed that a fluid is of such a character that when its component parts are undisturbed and in immediate contact the part which is subject to the less pressure is moved by the part which is subject to the greater pressure; and that each part is forced in a perpendicular direction by the part above, if the fluid is compressed.

Proposition 1. If a surface is always cut by a plane passing through a given point, and if the section thus formed is always a circle whose center is the given point, the surface is that of a sphere.

Proposition 2. The surface of any still fluid is always the surface of a sphere whose center is the center of the earth.

Proposition 3. Those solids which are of the same weight as a fluid in proportion to their size, when sunk in that fluid will be submerged in such a way that they neither extend above that fluid nor sink below it.

Proposition 4. A solid which is lighter than a given fluid will not sink below the surface when placed in that fluid, but part of it will extend above the surface.

Proposition 5. A solid lighter than a given fluid will, when placed in that fluid, be so far submerged that the weight of the solid will be equal to the weight of the fluid displaced.

Proposition 6. If a solid lighter than a given fluid be forced into that fluid the solid will be driven upwards again by a force which is equal to the difference between the weight of the fluid and the weight of the amount of fluid displaced.

Second Postulate: If a solid lighter than a given fluid rest in that fluid the weight of the solid to the weight of an equal volume of the fluid will be as the part of the solid which is submerged is to the whole solid.

From: Oliver J. Thatcher, ed., *The Library of Original Sources,* Vol. 3, *The Roman World* (Milwaukee, Wisc.: University Research Extension Co., 1907).

FURTHER READING

Andis Caulins, *Stars, Stones and Scholars: The Decipherment of the Megaliths as an Ancient Survey of the Earth by Astronomy* (Victoria, B.C., Canada: Trafford, 2003).

Marshall Clagett, *Ancient Egyptian Science: A Source Book*, vol. 3, *Ancient Egyptian Mathematics* (Philadelphia: American Philosophical Society, 1999).

Clifford D. Conner, *A People's History of Science: Miners, Midwives, and "Low Mechanicks"* (New York: Nation Books, 2005).

Alan Cromer, *Uncommon Sense: The Heretical Nature of Science* (New York: Oxford University Press, 1993).

Moustafa Gadalla, *Egyptian Cosmology: The Animated Universe* (Greensboro, N.C.: Tehuti Research Foundation, 2001).

D. C. Heggie, *Megalithic Science: Ancient Mathematics and Astronomy in North-West Europe* (London: Thames and Hudson, 1981).

Constance B. Hilliard, ed., *Intellectual Traditions of Pre-Colonial Africa* (Boston: McGraw-Hill, 1998).

Narendra Kumar, *Science in Ancient India* (New Delhi: Anmol Pulications, 2004).

James E. McClellan and Harold Dorn, *Science and Technology in World History: An Introduction*, 2nd ed. (Baltimore: Johns Hopkins University Press, 2006).

Joseph Needham, *Science and Civilisation in China* (New York: Cambridge University Press, 1996–2004).

T. E. Rihll, *Greek Science* (Oxford and New York: Oxford University Press, 1999).

Peter Schmidt, *Iron Technology in East Africa: Symbolism, Science, and Archaeology* (Bloomington: Indiana University Press, 1997).

John Staller, Robert Tykot, and Bruce Benz, *Histories of Maize* (Burlington, Mass.: Academic Press, 2006).

Robert Temple, *The Genius of China: 3,000 Years of Science, Discovery and Invention* (London: Prion Books, 1998).

Dick Teresi, *Lost Discoveries: The Ancient Roots of Modern Science—from the Babylonians to the Maya* (New York: Simon and Schuster, 2002).

Gloria Thomas-Emeagwali, ed., *Science and Technology in African History: With Case Studies from Nigeria, Sierra Leone, Zimbabwe, and Zambia* (Lewiston, N.Y.: Edwin Mellen Press, 1992).

Ivan Van Sertima, ed., *Blacks in Science: Ancient and Modern* (London: Transaction, 1983).

Wolfram von Soden, *The Ancient Orient: An Introduction to the Study of the Ancient Near East*, trans. Donald G. Schley (Grand Rapids, Mich.: Eerdmans, 1994).

Anthony Kennedy Warder, *A Course in Indian Philosophy* (Delhi, India: Motilal Banarsidass Press, 1998).

► seafaring and navigation

INTRODUCTION

Seafaring has always been a dangerous business, and it was no less so in the ancient world. The fact that ancient civilizations took to the sea despite the dangers of storm, shipwreck, and piracy is testimony to their courage and unquenchable desire to explore the world that surrounded them. Ancient seafarers faced a number of obstacles. One was a lack of navigational tools. More modern seafarers had sextants, compasses, chronometers, and other implements that enabled them to fix their position at sea and determine their direction and speed. Ancient civilizations did not have these tools, though one tool, which was found off the coast of a Greek island and dated from about the first century B.C.E., may have been used for navigational purposes. Otherwise, seafarers learned to navigate using the sun and star constellations, water currents, and the movements of birds and marine animals, and they passed their knowledge along orally.

Few ancient seafarers, however, took to the open sea, although ancient whalers and fishermen sometimes traveled far from land in search of their prey. For the most part, ancient seafarers tended to follow coastlines. They could use mountains visible from sea to maintain their course, and by staying close to the land they could find refuge during storms as well as put in for fresh water and provisions. The ancient Greeks and Romans navigated the coastlines of the Mediterranean Sea; seafarers from the Near East and Middle East navigated the Red Sea, the Persian Gulf, and other bodies of water in the region; and the ancient Chinese, with their large fleet of massive ships, explored the coastline of China and the areas around Japan and Korea. Ancient Americans and Asians of the South Pacific, much like the ancient Greeks, took to the sea to hop from island to island.

Another constant danger was storms and shipwrecks. In general, ancient seafarers kept to the land during the spring and autumn, when storms were more prevalent. Nonetheless, many ancient ships were caught in storms at sea and went down, often carrying valuable cargo with them. Because most of these shipwrecks occurred in deep water, and because water is not kind to the wood from which ships were made, relatively few ancient shipwrecks have been located. The lack of harbors was also a problem, but ancient seafarers learned to make use of natural harbors to escape storms when possible.

Ancient ships lacked artificial sources of power, so seafarers relied on river currents, the power of the wind, or the backs and arms of rowers. Sails were typically square, making them useful when the wind was at the ship's back but of little use when a ship was sailing into the wind. Most ancient ships made use of rowers. The so-called triremes, used by the ancient Romans, were ships that were powered by three rows of rowers. Some ships had up to 10 such rows. Rowers were able to power ships when the wind was not favorable or when the ship needed a burst of speed and maneuverability, as during naval battles.

AFRICA

BY MARK ANTHONY PHELPS

People from the western Mediterranean and Atlantic regions were engaged in trade with the Phoenicians, based in modern Syria and Lebanon, since at least the ninth century, despite the claim of classical authors who placed colonization of the Atlantic coast in the 12th century. On or near the Atlantic coast from Morocco to Senegal lie 13 Phoenician or Carthaginian sites. It is generally not possible to attribute colonies to either, as the distinction between the two centers of Semitic seafaring civilization was blurred by ancient authors. Likewise, technology bearing the label "Phoenician" by ancient authors could have denoted Carthaginian developments as well. One will recall that the wars with Carthage are known to the Romans as the Punic Wars, as *Punic* is derived from the Greek word for the Phoenicians. (The English term is likewise derived from the Greek root.)

Colonies served a variety of economic purposes. Primarily they served to protect Phoenician and Carthaginian (the latter are also known as Punic) vessels. This was accomplished by using their own navies as defense against pirates and other potential enemies and providing safe haven for endangered ships. This ensured that Phoenician and Carthaginian ships would have access to the resources of the western Mediterranean and Atlantic to themselves. These ports also were outlets for their own economic production, both from the cities and the hinterlands. The ports provided repairs for ships and resupplied provisions for ships continuing on their circuits.

Navigation in the Mediterranean was a skill acquired by experience. An intimate knowledge of nature was a requisite for sailing in antiquity. Navigation at night, which tended to be rare, was done by fixing points in relation to stars. Ursa Major was known as the "Phoenician star" because it served as their prime orientation point. The sun, by contrast, is a relative guide, moving as the seasons progress.

Understanding winds was important to navigation. The Phoenicians or Carthaginians invented the wind rose, a device to discern the direction of winds. Winds possessed discernable features to the trained observer. By the first century C.E. Greek sailors were aware of eight distinct winds. Winds were valuable for determining direction and predicting coming danger in the form of storms. Storms and unpredictable winds limited most commercial sailing in the Mediterranean to the months between March and October. Warships patrolled all year long.

Birds were of value in determining distance and direction of land. Land-based birds released from a ship would elevate to locate land and head directly toward it. Likewise, an awareness of the flight patterns of flocks of birds could help one discern direction or nearby landfall.

Naturally, the easiest way to navigate distance was to be in sight of land. This was probably the method employed by the Phoenicians and Carthaginians along the Atlantic coast of Africa and nearby islands. For Greek and Roman sailors, handbooks known as *periploi* described landmarks to guide one along a coast. The *periploi* also gave information about the lands, peoples, and resources the sailors might encounter.

The Phoenicians are credited with circumnavigating Africa on an expedition funded by the Egyptian pharaoh Necho II (r. 610–595 B.C.E.), a feat that took three years. Having no ports, the crews had to plant and harvest wheat twice to provide provisions. The report describes the sun changing sides of the ship, confirming that the crew had entered the southern hemisphere. Based on the account of the Carthaginian navigator Hanno (fifth century B.C.E.), some scholars hold that the Carthaginians may have explored the Atlantic coast of Africa as far south as Mount Cameroon, though a majority assume they never ventured south of Senegal.

During the period of Greek colonization from the eighth to the sixth centuries B.C.E. the region known as Libya to the Greeks (northern Africa outside of Egypt) was an ideal place for establishing new centers. The hinterland of the coast in this region possessed a plain useful for agriculture. In addition, the southern Mediterranean shipping route passed close by as ships looking for the African coast after passing Crete would typically sight landfall in this region. Likewise, eastbound ships would head north from this landmark.

Trade on the Indian Ocean is dictated by the monsoons. The northeastern monsoons occur during winter in the northern hemisphere. These winds abate in March and reverse (become southwesterly) in April. The period from mid-May to mid-August is typically too rough for sailing. The equatorial current flows southward after striking the Somali coast, facilitating vessels heading west from the Arabian Peninsula. With the coming of the southwest monsoon, the current strikes farther south, near Cape Delgado in Mozambique. This produces a strong northern current, facilitating the return from the east.

The kingdom of Axum was located in northern Ethiopia and Eritrea. Its port at Adulis, founded in the mid-second century B.C.E. by the Egyptian king Ptolemy III (r. 246–221 B.C.E.), became a major center for exchange of goods between the Roman, Red Sea, South Asian, and sub-Saharan African worlds. Few of its coins are found in the homeland, while most appear in Yemen and in India.

The kings of the Ptolemaic Dynasty sought to circumvent the Seleucid stranglehold on overland trade by exploiting water routes to India. By the end of the era, Ptolemaic weakness and political anarchy had reduced the trips to some 20 a year. Under the Roman emperor Augustus (r. 27 B.C.E.–14 C.E.) that number was elevated to 120 a year. After destroying Carthage in 146 B.C.E. the Romans had assumed control of shipping throughout the entirety of the Mediterranean, including all African ports.

EGYPT

BY AMR KAMEL

Although ancient Egypt was considered a riverine civilization, where everything was associated with the Nile, it was thought also to be a nation of sailors, navigators, and explorers, who were able to navigate and sail up and down the Mediterranean and the Red Sea as early as the Old Kingdom (ca. 2575–ca. 2134 B.C.E.) and perhaps even before. Although no seagoing ship has survived, numerous pieces of textual and pictorial evidence have fortunately been preserved from most of Egyptian history and particularly from the New Kingdom (ca. 1550–ca. 1070 B.C.E.) onward, referring to the activation of an Egyptian maritime network on both seas.

The earliest evidence for Mediterranean seafaring is a short text from the reign of Snefru (r. ca. 2613–2589 B.C.E.), which mentions 40 ships that sailed to the land now known as Lebanon to obtain cedar and other woods. An Egyptian crew on such a voyage almost 50 years later left its name on an inscribed ax head at Byblos (modern Jubayl). However, the earliest detailed portraits of seagoing ships come from decorated blocks in the mortuary temple of the Fifth Dynasty ruler Sahure (r. ca. 2487–2475 B.C.E.) at Abusir, which illustrates 12 ships, with careful attention to construction, rigging, and passengers, including a mixture of Egyptian and Syrian crewmen. In a relief from the time of Unas (r. ?–2345 B.C.E.), two slightly later ships are shown returning from Syria. Such scenes could help modern archaeologists to estimate the actual sizes of these ships; for instance, a cedar ship built in the Fourth Dynasty (ca. 2575–ca. 2465 B.C.E.) was 100 cubits, or 50 yards, long.

As early as the reign of Sahure ships sailed on the Red Sea for Punt, famed for its incense, precious woods, gold, and other raw materials. Punt is most likely located on the Somali coast of East Africa. In the Sixth Dynasty (ca. 2323–ca. 2150 B.C.E.) a helmsman named Khnumhotep left an inscription describing his 11 round-trips to that land. Although no textual or representational evidence exists for seagoing ships in the Middle Kingdom (ca. 2040–ca.1640 B.C.E.), recent excavations have revealed a Red Sea harbor used by Middle Kingdom ships that sailed to Punt and to the turquoise mines of the Sinai Peninsula, at Marsa Gawasis, about 15 miles south of modern-day Safaga and 31 miles north of Quseir. At this site archaeologists have unearthed 12 large stone anchors, fragments of cedar wood imported from Lebanon, and a man-made cave in which ancient Egyptian sailors stored their gear.

In the New Kingdom seafaring seems to have been more common, with refinements in rigging and steering gear traceable through images and models of ships. No physical remains of New Kingdom hulls have been found as yet. The most remarkable report is preserved in both text and images on the walls of the mortuary temple of Hatshepsut (r. 1503–1482 B.C.E.) at Deir el-Bahri. These scenes show five ships with upright bows and curved papyriform sterns, hogging trusses (thick ropes to keep the bow and stern from sagging), and single masts with broad sails, entering and leaving the anchorage at Punt. Only one includes an illustration of beam ends; otherwise, artistic attention was lavished on the rigging. Fifteen oarsmen shown as well on the side facing the viewer would have required about a yard of room each, suggesting that the ships were at least 24 yards long and perhaps three times longer than broad. Apparently, Hatshepsut reactivated Egypt's Red Sea route to Punt, and this extraordinary series of illustrations suggests that she invested heavily this expedition.

Records from the reign of Hatshepsut's successor, Thutmose III (r. 1504–1450 B.C.E.), document the movements of ships in an expedition to Syria-Palestine, and further records describe cedar acquired and goods stored at harbors for Egyptian use. An Amarna tablet refers to a royal ship moored at Tyre (modern-day Sūr), in southern Lebanon. According to cuneiform texts, Egyptian products, notably grain, were transported to Palestine and Anatolia in vessels, but whether Egyptian or local ships were used is still obscure. In the first two years of Ramses II's reign (1304–1237 B.C.E.), Ramses had to conduct a military campaign against sea pirates, known as Shirdana. Several Egyptian seagoing ships participated in the war of Ramses III (r. 1198–1166 B.C.E.) against the Sea Peoples, as is illustrated on the walls of his temple at Medinet Habu.

In the Late Period (ca. 712–332 B.C.E.) as well as in Greco-Roman times, the Egyptians apparently continued investment in seafaring, and they sometimes built special cargo ships. For instance, they transported obelisks from Alexandria to Rome, and textual evidence refers to a seagoing ship built for Caligula (r. 37–41 C.E.). Unfortunately, ancient Egyptian sources do not say much about the life of the sailors, the length of the sailing season, the durability of ships, and their costs. Nonetheless, these sources refer to numerous titles associated with seafaring occupations and activities, held by ancient Egyptians and sometimes by foreigners, especially Syrians, notably in the construction and operation of maritime ships. Among these titles were navigator, sailor, man at the prow, man at the poop, manager of the crew, captain, and commander of the ship. These titles suggest that their holders had a sufficient knowledge of navigational techniques required to make a voyage possible.

These techniques, theoretically at least, developed over years in the form of oral tradition, with no trace in any written records. A few glimpses can be obtained from Egyptian tomb paintings reflecting these skills. To ancient Egyptians, navigation apparently was an art rather than a science, and it was based mainly on determining position and location. They had several methods for determining direction, among them the winds. The ancient Egyptian language reflects the Egyptians' knowledge of the four winds, from north, east, south, and west, and includes terms for favorable winds and headwinds as well. A scene from an early Old Kingdom tomb shows a ship commander teaching the crew how to steer the ship with the wind. The Egyptians sometimes called upon various gods associated with creation of these different winds to aid in the journey, notably Amun, who was believed to drive back the adverse wind. In daytime a gnomon (the pointer of a sundial) also could be used as a tool to indicate northerly direction

in navigation, as shown on a ship model in an Egyptian museum, where it was mounted on the ship's axis.

A scene from a tomb at Thebes suggests that the Egyptians were familiar with using birds in navigation. It shows a Syrian fleet moored at an Egyptian quay (a wharf built parallel to the shoreline) and a bird flying toward the city. In the ancient Near East, land birds that were unable to land on water, such as ravens, crows, doves, and swallows, were carried on board and released when the crew needed to know how to reach the shore. This scene and a few others show that river and seagoing ships had crow's nests with lookouts, who played a role in determining the direction of land lying beyond the horizon.

THE MIDDLE EAST

BY EDWARD M. W. A. ROWLANDS

In ancient times the sailors from the Near East were famous for their seafaring skills. Written evidence suggests that sailors from Mesopotamia were able to navigate great distances, but there is a lack of archaeological evidence available to support their navigation capabilities. Sailors established successful sea routes by following the coastline. They learned the best times for sailing and discovered ways to counter harsh weather conditions. Navigation was improved by the observation of the sun and stars; seafaring was further enhanced with the addition of several rows of oars to increase speed.

There was a great abundance of cedar trees in what is now Lebanon. These trees supplied the local inhabitants with a valuable supply of wood, which was used in the construction of ships. The port of Byblos, close to modern-day Beirut, is thought to have traded considerable amounts of wood to Egypt (under the reign of the pharaoh Sahure) as early as around 2487–2475 B.C.E. The availability of wood to the inhabitants of Byblos, Sidon, and Tyre meant that they had the resources to attempt seafaring very early in their histories. It is from those locations that the Phoenician civilization, well known for its highly developed seamanship, began.

It is difficult to go into great detail about Mesopotamian seafaring owing to a lack of shipwrecks available for study and the poor quality of the surviving representations of ancient ships in the area. Depictions of ships have been found on seals and reliefs, but this evidence is inadequate to paint a complete picture of seafaring. Sumerian texts, however, do refer to Mesopotamian trade with Magan (Oman or Egypt) and Meluhha (a civilization in the Indus River valley or Africa) in the Akkadian Period, the Third Dynasty of Ur, and the Isin-Larsa Period. This activity spans a period from around 2350 B.C.E. to around 1800 B.C.E. It thus appears that from a very early time in Mesopotamian history, seamen from this area were able to navigate their way down the Persian Gulf to locations as distant as Africa and India, implying a considerable degree of navigational skill.

In ancient sea travel following the coast was essential. Staying near the coast made shelter, fresh food, and water supplies available on a daily basis. Following the coastline and keeping in sight of land also helped with navigation. For example, ships trying to find the right direction in the Mediterranean were helped by the many high mountains that are visible from the sea. The Uluburun (late 14th century B.C.E.) and Cape Gelidonya (late 12th century B.C.E.) shipwrecks are both thought to be ships that were following the eastern Mediterranean trade circuits, through which ships would travel from the Levant to Cyprus and on to Rhodes and Crete. These ships would have stayed close to land as much as possible and traveled from port to port.

Before Artabanus's attack on Greece in the early fifth century B.C.E., the Greek historian Herodotus (ca. 484–between 430 and 420 B.C.E.) quotes Artabanus (younger brother of King Darius I) as saying to the king of the Persians that harbors would be needed all along the coast to receive his fleet "and give it protection in the event of storms." The weather plays an important role in seafaring, and ancient sailors tried to avoid sailing in the autumn and winter. By sailing in the spring and summer, sailors hoped to avoid the worst storms. Protection could be achieved by taking cover behind islands or high points of land. In the eastern Mediterranean many such harbors could be found and were exploited, giving ships the best access to land as well as the best shelter from weather conditions.

It was crucial for any ancient vessel to have experienced sailors who could observe changes in the wind, tides, and current. They would have had the expertise to navigate by monitoring changes in the sky. Navigational instruments, such as the compass, would not have been available to them. By day, Near Eastern sailors would have used the direction of the sun to distinguish between east (Asu) and west (Ereb). By night they would have navigated by following star constellations, such as Ursa Major and Ursa Minor. The Phoenicians developed a reputation as excellent celestial navigators, with the North Star, for example, being known to the Greeks as the "Phoenician Star." Such navigational skills allowed the Phoenicians and their successors, the Carthaginians, to travel considerable distances. Herodotus wrote that the pharaoh Necho II (r. 610–595 B.C.E.) manned ships with Phoenicians, and the ships were then able to circumnavigate the whole African continent.

The use of oars gave ships speed and flexibility. Ships could adjust their position using steering oars. Ancient ships used a square sail that was very effective in helping the ship through heavy seas. When there was a lack of wind to move the sails, the oars were used to move a vessel. From the seventh century B.C.E. there was a gradual increase in the number of oars and the manpower used to propel a ship. Warships developed several rows of oars in the aim of outmaneuvering the enemy, which required extensive manpower and coordination. The Hellenistic Period (323–31 B.C.E.) saw an explosion in the number of the rows of oars. This development was seen in the Wars of the Diodochi (322–281 B.C.E.). For example, in the Battle of Salamis in 306 B.C.E., next to the island of Cyprus, ships were in battle with as many as seven rows of oars.

The ancient Near East and Mesopotamia was to be dominated by such peoples as the Assyrians, the Babylonians, the Hittites, the Persians, the Greeks, and the Romans. Nevertheless, the necessity to maneuver a ship with precision and accuracy remained the same. Sailors needed to focus their attention, to maintain the safe navigation of the ship, and to watch out for any possible dangers. Examining changes in the weather and the sea, keeping a close eye for land, and observing the stars and the sun required an understanding and an awareness that were essential throughout the whole of this period.

ASIA AND THE PACIFIC

BY KIRK H. BEETZ

Among the great seafaring feats of ancient times was the migration of people from southeastern Asia to Australia during the last great ice age in about 30,000 B.C.E. At that time the ocean was lower than it is now, and much more land around Australia was exposed. Australia, Tasmania, and New Guinea were all connected by land. The areas where seafarers would have landed are now underwater; consequently, archaeologists have little evidence for how ancient sailors crossed the open sea. Even though there would have been less sea to cross, those sailors still had to cross hundreds of miles of ocean. Archaeologists disagree about whether the sailors used rafts or dugout canoes, with some saying canoes had not yet been invented.

It is possible that people had learned to fish in the ocean and had gained knowledge of the currents for their particular fishing areas, so when winds blew them away, they were able to return home by finding the currents they knew. Some of these fishermen may even have landed on Australia and then returned home and brought their families with them to live in the new land they had discovered. At that time Australia would have been much wetter than it is now, with forests filled with inviting life. These people would have rowed, used currents, and possibly used sails to cross not only to Australia but also to islands between Australia and the Asian mainland.

The most accomplished seafarers of ancient Asia and the Pacific that are presently known about were the Polynesians. Archaeologists disagree considerably over the dates for Polynesian exploration, but by the end of the ancient era they had probably reached Easter Island but had not yet reached many islands such as those of Hawaii in the Pacific. There were about 20,000 unpopulated islands scattered across an enormous expanse of ocean when the Polynesians began their push to explore and settle them beginning in about the third century C.E.

Their process of exploration seems to have been very risky, but it had a high rate of success. They would have outfitted outrigger canoes—boats with floats extended by wooden spars, or poles, from the sides of the craft to prevent the craft from capsizing. Carrying men, women, and probably children, as well as pigs, seeds for planting, and other foods, they would have set sail into open ocean beyond the last island they knew. This practice probably caused many people to be lost at sea, but the Polynesians had great navigational skills to aid them.

Even today, some Polynesians still can read wave patterns to navigate across large expanses of water with no land in sight. Where most people would just see a chaos of waves, Polynesian navigators would recognize patterns in the directions of the waves, their heights, and their speed. They would be able to tell where a boat was by how waves of different types bumped into each other. This knowledge made navigating between known islands mostly science, not luck. Polynesians also used the sun, moon, and stars to help them find their way. The sun and moon told them whether they were going west or east. For these ancient seafarers, this method alone was valuable for exploring because they knew they wanted to go eastward. The stars gave them an idea of how far they had gone in their journeys. To determine their latitudes—how far north or south they were—they chose what they called "on top stars." By keeping under a particular star, they could sail east or west and know how far north or south they were. For example, the star Sirius was over the latitude for Tahiti, and if one were west of Tahiti, then sailing east under Sirius would enable one to find Tahiti. For exploration, knowing the latitudes of the stars enabled sailors to avoid retracing unsuccessful routes and to find home if they had to do so.

For the mainland cultures of ancient Asia, navigators tended to stick close the coastlines. The Chinese tended to emphasize sailing on China's great rivers, and China's navy was intended primarily for warfare inland on rivers. Piracy was a problem along China's eastern coast, which provided many coves and inlets in which pirates could hide, and the navy was expected to patrol the coastline. It is possible that one reason the Chinese sought out the Japanese as allies in the third century C.E. is that they hoped the Japanese would aid them in curbing the activities of pirates in the ocean near Korea and northeastern China. In about the fourth century C.E. Chinese merchants began to venture farther from the coastline, following routes used by Indian traders. Although the Chinese long knew of the tendency of lodestones (magnetite) and magnetized iron to point north and south, they did not employ them in navigation until the medieval era, perhaps the 12th century C.E.

The feats of Indian seafarers were justifiably legendary because these sailors overcame many great hazards as well as their own fears of giant fish, dragons, and other monsters of the deep that could swallow them up. Under Hindu religious law, people were not supposed to sail across the sea. A Brahman who did so could lose his status, becoming an outcast without home or sanctuary. Others could suffer the loss of funeral rites. This practice left Buddhists, outcasts, and those willing to risk the loss of their status in their communities to be sailors.

The most important person on a ship was the pilot, and no ship left port without one. The pilot knew how to read currents, winds, stars, and birds for directing the course of a ship over open water. A pilot actually trained birds to fly in the direction of land but to return to the ship if they did not see land midway in their flight, and several of the birds would be kept in cages on deck for this purpose. Pilots had their own guilds, through which captains could find pilots for their ships and which regulated the work of pilots. Ordinary sailors were expected to show their inferior status at all times, to pilot, captain, and passengers. Living quarters on ships were always cramped and uncomfortable, with the rocking of the ship causing misery for passengers, but apparently those ships that sailed west toward the Near East, Africa, and the Mediterranean were filled with people willing to take the risks of a sea voyage to visit foreign lands. If they made some good trades, they could return home as rich people.

It seems that most Indian ships reached their destinations despite the dangers. When a ship was in trouble, its crew and passengers would pray to the goddess Manimekhala, who drowned sinners but would save others. When a ship sank, those on board had little hope of survival. If they did not drown, sharks and other predators would eat them, sometimes turning the sea red with blood. If a ship were becalmed for days, those on board would draw lots to see who would be put out of the ship on a raft to be abandoned as a sacrifice to bring wind.

EUROPE

BY MICHAEL J. O'NEAL

The oldest-known European boat, hollowed out from a single log, was discovered at Pesse in the Netherlands and dates to about 7000 B.C.E. Many other such prehistoric boats have been found at submerged and waterlogged sites across northern Europe in which wood was preserved. For example, the Hasholme boat, in Yorkshire, England, dates from about 300 B.C.E. It was crafted from the trunk of a single oak tree that was probably more than 800 years old when it was felled. In inland areas such boats were used along streams and across lakes, but in coastal areas people rowed them a short distance out to sea to catch fish and also used them for transportation along the coast and to nearby islands. Scholars have traditionally believed that during this period navigation relied primarily on the observation of landmarks along coasts and that people usually did not venture far out of sight of land. Supporting this assumption is the large number of ancient boats that have been discovered in shallow coastal waters.

In recent years some archaeologists have been rethinking this long-held belief. In 2005, for example, archaeologists discovered flints and other objects on the Mediterranean island of Cyprus that date from about 10,000 B.C.E. Cyprus, however, was not inhabited until about 9000 B.C.E., so the objects had to have been left there by seafarers from the mainland who had ventured out of sight of the Turkish or Syrian coast at least 30 miles away. This find provides evidence of the earliest seafaring in the Mediterranean Sea. Evidence for adventurous seafaring has also been found in northern waters. The first Stone Age settlers to reach Ireland would have required watercraft to cross the Irish Sea, for example; except for the very narrow northern part where Ireland is visible from Scotland under ideal conditions, they would have been out of sight of land for some part of this trip.

In any case, the sea may not have been the obstacle that historians long thought it was. They note that the archaeological record shows remarkable similarity among cultures up and down the Atlantic seaboard and around through the Strait of Gibraltar into the Mediterranean Sea during the Mesolithic Period, or the Middle Stone Age, ranging roughly from 12,000 or 10,000 B.C.E. to at least 7000 B.C.E. and perhaps as late as 3200 B.C.E. (Dates for these broadly defined periods can differ for different geographical regions.) Some believe that these similarities could have come about only if people along the Atlantic coast traveled by sea, carrying artifacts and practices of their culture with them. The cultural connections seen around the coasts of the North Sea and the Baltic Sea could have been possible only thanks to the ability to navigate across open seas.

An increasing number of finds have offered considerable insight into prehistoric European seafaring. By the Bronze Age people in northern Europe were building boats out of planks that were propelled by more than a dozen rowers. The earliest-known plank-built ships date from about 1900 B.C.E., and others have been found dating from perhaps 800 B.C.E. An important recent example is the Dover Boat, found in 1992, which appears to have been used for crossing the English Channel. In addition, a large collection of bronze axes found at the bottom of Langdon Bay, also near Dover, appears to be a cargo load that did not make it all the way across. The chief advantage of these plank boats was that the freeboard, the distance between the waterline and the top of the hull, was higher than those of other boats, making them more stable in ocean swells. Meanwhile, the Iberians (in modern-day Spain and Portugal) and the Irish were building lightly framed boats covered with hides. These types of vessels were probably used for trade, particularly to carry tin to Gaul and Rome.

The ancient Celts, in particular, were seafaring peoples and developed sophisticated boat-building and navigational skills. The Celts were an ethnic group that spread across large portions of Europe and into the British Isles. One Celtic group was the Veneti, who, along with several other nations, inhabited the region of Gaul the Romans called Aremonica. This region included Brittany, a peninsula that juts westward and is surrounded by the English Channel and the Bay of Biscay. Largely surrounded by water, the Veneti developed sophisticated seafaring technology.

The Roman emperor Julius Caesar (r. 49–44 B.C.E.) fought his greatest naval battle against the Veneti in 55 B.C.E. In his account of the battle in his work *Commentarii de bello Gallico,* he described the Celtic fleet as consisting of 220 ships. The ships were tall and graceful—Caesar called them "swan ships"—and each was able to carry 200 men. The ships were powered by leather sails rather than rowed with oars; because the hulls did not need openings for oars, the hulls were far stronger than those of the Romans' ships. These ships were able to navigate the open seas during storms, but because of their broad beams and shallow draft, they were also able to sail in shallow waters and estuaries. Their timbers were made of oak and fastened with iron nails rather than the wooden pegs the Romans used in constructing ships. Adding to the Veneti's advantage was the rocky and tempestuous coastline, which they could navigate better than the Romans could in their oar-powered galleys. Caesar eventually was able to defeat the Veneti by having his sailors use long grappling hooks to shred the ships' sails, leaving the ships dead in the water.

GREECE

BY EDWARD M. W. A. ROWLANDS

Ancient Greek sailors were first able to sail to the islands around them and then later used those islands as stepping-stones to other locations in the Mediterranean and into the Black Sea. They learned how to use the sun and the stars as a means of direction and determined the best times of the year to sail. Seafaring could be tough, but the experience that sailors would acquire, along with the technological improvements to ships, meant that speed and flexibility would increase over time.

In the Late Bronze Age (ca. 1600–1100 B.C.E.) people from Greece were able to travel from island to island in the Aegean. The Minoan and Mycenaean civilizations spread throughout the Aegean from Crete and Greece, respectively. Depictions of ships, for example, have been found on fresco fragments from the island of Thera (now Thíra) that date from around 1600 B.C.E. Islands were used as landing stages and could be accessed in a day's journey. Shelter, fresh water, and food supplies could then be found on land. Navigation was accomplished by keeping in sight of land and following the coast.

Greek ships were constructed so that they could be moved onto dry land upon arrival. This design was to prevent the destruction of the boat by any sea storm. Homer describes boats as being fast and hollow, suggesting that these boats would have been light and easy to move ashore. This practice continued for many centuries. Ships were also moved overland so that sailors could gain access to other branches of the sea. The port of Corinth became very famous for its Diolkos. The Diolkos was a paved road that was used for the transportation of boats on a platform from the Saronic Gulf to the Corinthian bay, which are on either side of the Peloponnese in Greece. This route proved very successful and was used from the seventh century B.C.E. up to the ninth century C.E.

Ancient Greek navigation was based on observation, and it was important for every ship to have experienced sailors.

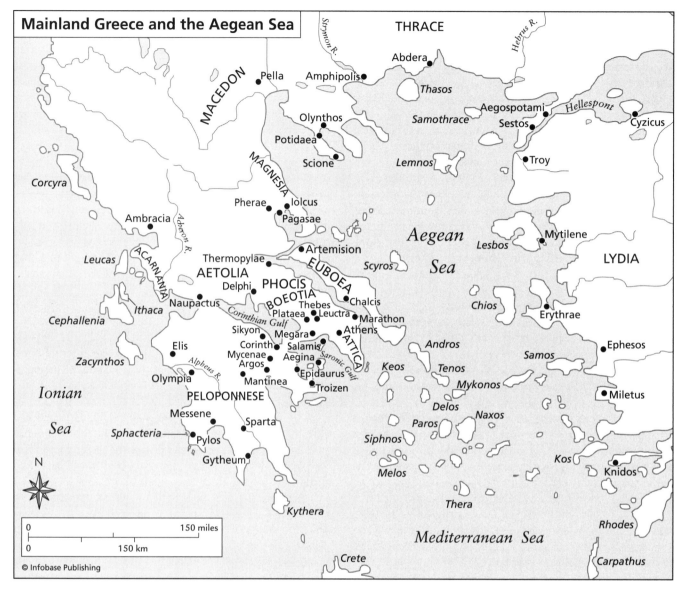

Mainland Greece and the Aegean Sea

Early Greek sailors were able to travel throughout the Aegean Sea and from there eventually to other locations in the Mediterranean and the Black seas.

Having an understanding of wind, currents, and tide was vital to maintain the correct course. For long-distance voyages, the Greeks made use of the sun and the stars. Since no compass, chronometers, sextants, or octants existed, and as it could be difficult to observe landmarks, using the North Star (known to the Greeks as the Phoenician Star) and following the sun were vital in gaining direction. By 600 B.C.E. a philosopher named Thales (ca. 625–ca. 547 B.C.E.) was able to teach sailors how to get to Miletus (on the Aegean coast of modern-day Turkey) by following the Ursa Minor constellation of stars. However, a mechanism found on a wreck off the Greek island of Antikýthēra, dating to the end of the first century B.C.E., may have been used to calculate astronomical positions and could have been used in seafaring.

The weather and the season of the year in which the voyage was to take place were very important factors. Large cargoes were carried by Greek ships all across the Mediterranean, and it would have been wise to avoid the autumn and winter rains and storms. Goods could be lost and crews of men killed, and ship owners would have been well aware of the financial risks. In the spring and summer, as the Greek writer Hesiod (ca. 800 B.C.E.) says, "You are not likely to smash your ship, nor the sea to destroy your crew. . . . At that time the breezes are well defined and the sea harmless."

Seafaring could be a harsh experience for sailors. For hundreds of years little accommodation was given to living space or preparation of food on ancient Greek ships. There was a threat from being attacked by pirates, and iron spearheads found rooted into the hull may suggest that a ship had been attacked. The use of oars provided speed and flexibility. Single steering oars are seen depicted on the frescoes from Thera as early as the 16th century B.C.E. and double steering oars from the sixth century B.C.E. The oars were important to ships in helping them maneuver around islands, keeping close to the coast. Oars were used to propel a ship when there was not enough wind. For vessels such as warships, oars could also provide a valuable means of gaining speed during battle with an enemy. Several rows of oars could be used to give the ship additional pace. According to the Greek historian Thucydides (d. ca. 401 B.C.E.), triremes (ships with three rows of oars) were the invention of boat builders from Corinth around 700 B.C.E. Later the kingdoms of the Hellenistic Period (323–31 B.C.E.) would have tens of rows of oarsmen. These ships required extensive manpower and coordination.

The ancient Greeks would have used a square sail when traveling by sea. A single square sail could be effective in heavy seas. However, it was not very adaptable when the wind was blowing against the course of a ship. The settlement of Troy was situated on the Dardanelles. As it was a protected harbor, it became prosperous, since ships would often stay there while they waited for the direction of the wind to change so that they could move through the Dardanelles and into the Black Sea. Numerous images of square sails on ships have been found. For example, Attic black-figure pottery dating to the mid-sixth century B.C.E. depicts ships with square sails.

Only small amounts of evidence for nautical guides have survived; it may be that sailors passed on their expertise orally. Even as the Roman Empire came to dominate Greece and the Mediterranean, ships still needed to be maneuvered with precision and accuracy. Watching out for changes in the weather and the sea, keeping a close eye for land, and observing the stars and the sun required an understanding and familiarity that were essential throughout the whole of this period. Sailors needed to maintain total concentration to navigate their ships safely and to watch out for any possible dangers.

ROME

BY JAMES A. CORRICK

The fastest method of transporting freight and passengers during the Roman Republic and the Roman Empire was by sea. With the exception of some swift naval vessels, Roman ships averaged 6 knots, a knot being 6,076 feet per hour, and thus they moved along at about 7 miles per hour. A ship, for example, took one to two days to travel from the Roman port of Ostia, at the mouth of the Tiber River, to Massalia (present-day Marseilles in southern France). By land the same journey took weeks. Business travelers, government officials, tourists, and others journeying long distances consequently sought passage via ship.

Despite a healthy passenger trade, no passenger ships existed in the Roman world. Instead, voyagers had to travel on merchant vessels. Nothing except drinking water was provided to passengers, who had to bring their own food, cooking utensils, beds, and servants. Travelers slept on deck with the crew. The crew was generally foreign born, its members most commonly being Greeks or Egyptians because few Romans became sailors. Even on military ships, except for officers, the crew was not Roman. Additionally, it was not unusual for merchant ships to be crewed entirely by slaves, one of whom was the captain.

Without any method of weather prediction, a ship could easily be caught in a sudden storm, and if it could not quickly reach a safe harbor, it might well be sunk or run aground. Because of numerous storms, few ships sailed in the winter months, the summer being considered the best sailing time. Another danger that Roman ships faced was attack by pirates. After seizing a vessel, the attackers either killed the crew and

Altar to the sea god Neptune, an offering from the Roman admiral of the British fleet, second century C.E., from Lympne, Kent, England (© The Trustees of the British Museum)

passengers or, as was more common, sold them into slavery. Indeed, until the middle of the first century B.C.E., pirates were one of the chief sources of slaves for the Roman world. Important captives, particularly high-ranking Roman citizens, were held for ransom. Even Julius Caesar was a captive of pirates. The pirate menace was ended in 67 B.C.E., when the Roman general Pompey swept the Mediterranean free of them. Pirates would not again be a threat until the empire began to lose control of the seaways in the third century C.E.

Navigating a Roman ship was more art than science, since the Romans had no navigational instruments. As a consequence, whenever possible, a ship of the period kept the shore in sight, its crew watching for landmarks to tell them their position. An important aid to navigation was the lighthouse. Most major Mediterranean ports had such structures, the Pharos at Alexandria being the most famous. Lighthouses ranged in height from four to 12 stories and used a mirror of polished bronze to reflect light from a fire. The beacon would warn night-traveling ships of hidden rocks and shallow water or act as a guide into port.

In addition to landmarks and lighthouses, Roman crews often depended on changing water depths to tell them where they were, since specific locations along a coast had known depths. To measure the depth of water, mariners used a lead line. This line was a rope that had a series of knots at spaced intervals and that had a lead or stone weight tied to it. The weighted end of the line was tossed overboard, and when it hit bottom, the number of knots were counted to determine the depth.

Another piece of knowledge useful in Roman navigation was the composition of the sea bottom across which a ship was sailing. That composition could often provide a clue as to a ship's location because certain types of material—gravel, sand, or mud, for instance—were known to be present off certain coastlines. Roman mariners sampled the sea bottom with the lead line, whose weight had a depression filled with tallow, or animal fat, to which sea floor material stuck then to be drawn up to the surface.

The Romans probably had charts and certainly had *periploi*, books containing the distances between various seaports, along with the locations of rivers and freshwater sources. A ship's navigator could calculate his ship's position along its route using the distances given by a *periplus* if he knew how far his vessel had traveled during a day. He made this calculation using dead reckoning. He first had to determine how fast his ship was traveling. The navigator estimated this speed by observing seaweed or driftwood passing by the ship. This observation gave him an approximation of how much distance the ship covered in an hour. Then, at the end of a day's sail, based on his observed speed, the navigator calculated how far the vessel had traveled. He now had a rough idea of where along its route the ship was. The method was imprecise, and often the calculation was far off the mark.

Determining position by dead reckoning also required that the navigator know in which direction his vessel was

headed; otherwise, the craft might be sailing away from its destination. During the day the navigators determined direction by observing the sun. Sailing into it was going west; sailing away from it was going east. Additionally, the navigator knew the ship was going north or south depending on the sun's height above the horizon at noon. The sun would be higher or lower in the sky depending on whether a ship was headed north or south. The height of the sun also depends on the time of year, the sun rising higher in the summer than in the winter, but an experienced navigator took this fact into account. To measure the sun's height, the navigator would hold out a hand and determine how many fingers were needed to span the gap between the sun and the horizon.

At night the navigator established direction using the stars. One star—the polestar, or Polaris—was particularly useful since it marks the position of the North Pole and remains fixed throughout the night. (Other stars appear to revolve around the sky due to the rotation of the earth.) A ship traveling east would have the polestar on its right, and a ship traveling west would have the polestar on its left. A navigator could also obtain a rough idea of a ship's north-south position using the polestar by counting how many fingers were needed to span the gap between Polaris and the northern horizon. The fewer the fingers, the farther south the ship was since in moving south, Polaris drops toward the northern horizon.

THE AMERICAS

BY LAWRENCE WALDRON

Native American hunters have long been credited with possessing the most acute tracking skills. Their ability to observe signs on the earth, in the air, and in the movements of animals and birds has astounded many observers. There is no reason to assume that Native American seafarers were any different. Just as earthbound hunters would observe the movement of celestial bodies to predict changes in weather, animal behavior, and crop growth, so too would Native Americans living on coasts, along rivers, and on arctic ice navigate by observing and predicting their environment.

Native Americans in ancient times were intimately familiar with the courses of key celestial bodies; the different kinds of cloud cover; the varieties of terrestrial, riverine, and marine species; and the flight patterns of birds. They also would have possessed some knowledge of geology, though they would have employed taxonomic classifications and nomenclature very much unlike our own. All these skills would have constituted the Native American navigation kit, necessary knowledge not only for achieving intended destinations and predictable travels but also for preserving self, family, and culture along the course of those travels.

Both on foot and by boat, Native Americans displayed great maneuverability and speed, due largely to their success as navigators, trackers, and aquatic farers. The American continents from Alaska to Argentina appear to have been settled within a thousand years of the first arrival of

Asiatic migrants, testimony to the Native Americans' ability to navigate and negotiate even unknown territories. Once in America, Native Americans greatly diversified their means of water travel and their techniques of navigation as well. From predominantly coastal seafaring, they developed great prowess in the negotiation of rivers, rapids, lakes, and various inland waters unlike anything that would have existed in their Paleolithic Siberian homeland.

Ancient Native Americans took to the water for many reasons, including trade, whaling, and fishing. Ancient whaling could be quite dangerous. Boatmen harpooned the massive animals and attached animal-skin flotation devices to the prey to fatigue it, mark its location, and float its carcass. North American whaling traditions, among Alaskan peoples especially, included journeys in open water far beyond the sight of land. Thus, northern whalers, among the most proficient seamen of all Native Americans, illustrate that Native Americans did not always follow coastlines in their maritime expeditions.

Circum-Caribbean groups such as the Maya and the Arawaks of the Caribbean also made long journeys across open water, culminating in discoveries of the island territories of today's Caribbean. Arawak explorers in the Caribbean some 3,000 to 4,000 years ago encountered Paleo-Indian hunter-gatherers who had arrived thousands of years even before they arrived, bearing out the theory that even the most ancient Native Americans were expert seafarers. In the case of the Maya mariners, the impetus for their travels was largely trade, and Maya objects have been found from the North American Southwest to the Mississippi to the Caribbean islands.

The ancient Americans are known to have exhibited a highly developed directional sense in the building of their monuments and architecture. Palaces, pyramids, and other tombs often opened facing one of the cardinal directions or were aligned to the solstices. Likewise, the celebrated Nazca Lines in Peru demonstrate that ancient Andeans possessed advanced surveying techniques, which they would have also used in their fishing and military expeditions up and down the Peruvian, Ecuadorian, and Bolivian coasts. Both the Nazca and Moche civilizations maintained their empires through the movement of troops, goods, and ultimately their cultural influence by sea.

Their orientation to cardinal points and navigation through the unpredictable marine conditions induced by mist, glacial cycles, and the occasional El Niño effect show a great familiarity with the movement of heavenly bodies and marine currents. There was knowledge of true north and perhaps even magnetic north. The discovery of what is believed to be a 3,000-year-old Olmec compass may confirm that ancient Americans also possessed some tools that helped them approximate the location of cardinal points when celestial bodies could not be seen.

The ancient Americans are not known to have ventured far upon the high seas. They never devised the large ocean-going sailing vessels of their contemporaries in Europe, Africa, Arabia, or Asia. Rather, with their development of a variety of quick-moving and highly maneuverable vessels, from one-man kayaks to massive canoes, they were able to feed communities, stimulate economies, and even build empires.

See also ASTRONOMY; BUILDING TECHNIQUES AND MATERIALS; CLIMATE AND GEOGRAPHY; ECONOMY; EXPLORATION; FOREIGNERS AND BARBARIANS; HUNTING, FISHING, AND GATHERING; INVENTIONS; MONEY AND COINAGE; OCCUPATIONS; RELIGION AND COSMOLOGY; SHIPS AND SHIPBUILDING; SLAVES AND SLAVERY; TRADE AND EXCHANGE; TRANSPORTATION; WAR AND CONQUEST.

FURTHER READING

George Bass, ed., *A History of Seafaring Based on Underwater Archaeology* (London: Thames and Hudson, 1972).

Philip Brooks, Will Fowler, and Simon Adams, *The Illustrated History Encyclopedia: Civilizations, Explorations, and Conquest* (London: Hermes House, 2003).

Lionel Casson, *Ships and Seamanship in the Ancient World* (Princeton, N.J.: Princeton University Press, 1971).

Lionel Casson, *The Ancient Mariners: Seafarers and Sea Fighters of the Mediterranean in Ancient Times*, 2nd ed. (Princeton N.J.: Princeton University Press, 1991).

Barry Cunliffe, *Facing the Ocean: The Atlantic and Its Peoples, 8000 B.C.–A.D. 1500* (London: Oxford University Press, 2001).

Barry Cunliffe, "People of the Sea." *British Archaeology* 63 (February 2002). Available online. URL: http://www.britarch.ac.uk/BA/ba63/feat2.shtml. Downloaded on May 7, 2007.

David Fabre, *Seafaring in Ancient Egypt* (London: Periplus, 2005).

Robert Gardiner, ed., *The Age of the Galley: Mediterranean Oared Vessels since Pre-Classical Times* (London: Conway Maritime Press, 1995).

Emory Dean Keoke and Kay Marie Porterfield, *American Indian Contributions to the World: Trade, Transportation, and Warfare* (New York: Facts On File, 2005).

Fik Meijer, *A History of Seafaring in the Classical World* (New York: St. Martin's Press, 1986).

John S. Morrison and J. F. Coates, *Greek and Roman Oared Warships* (Oxford, U.K.: Oxbow Books, 1996).

Shelley Wachsmann, "Seafaring." In *The Oxford Encyclopedia of Archaeology in the Near East*, vol. 4, ed. Eric M. Meyers (New York: Oxford University, 1997).

► settlement patterns

INTRODUCTION

Before the advent of agriculture, people did not settle in one place for very long. They survived as hunter-gatherers, moving about in search of game animals and edible plants. The basic unit of settlement was the camp, which small numbers of people, usually related by clan ties, used as a base of operations for hunting and gathering. As the seasons changed and food supplies diminished, they moved on to a new camp. Archaeologists learn about prehistoric ways of life by studying stone tools, artifacts, and middens (trash piles) that survive from these ancient settlements.

After the advent of agriculture in roughly 8000 B.C.E. people began to form more permanent settlements. Generally, they favored areas that provided fertile soil, a moderate climate, and water for irrigating crops. Accordingly, settlements in the ancient world were most often formed on the banks of lakes and rivers and along ocean coastlines. Major civilizations such as those of the ancient Mesopotamians and Egyptians grew up along rivers, where fertile soil was left behind after annual flooding. By this time the basic unit of settlement was the village and hamlet, where clusters of houses were built by farmers who tended the land and their herds of livestock. In time, some of these villages grew into towns, which served as administrative centers and places where farmers could sell their crops. Some of these towns evolved into cities, becoming the seats of kings and emperors.

Patterns of settlement could change as a result of changing climatic conditions. As glacial ice receded at the end of the ice age in about 11,000 B.C.E., people moved northward into such regions as Europe, including Scandinavia. Sometimes, though, climatic conditions took a turn for the worse. Parts of ancient Egypt that were (and are) desert were once fertile and green, but climate changes forced people to abandon their settlements to cluster in the fertile Nile River Valley. A similar fate awaited some of the peoples of Mesoamerica, whose fertile land turned into desert, forcing many of them into cities.

Settlement could be influenced by changes in the face of the earth. A good example is provided by Japan, which consists of about 3,000 islands, about 600 of them inhabited. Throughout most of its history, Japan was cut off from Asia and thus remained home to a Stone Age culture long after the rest of Asia had progressed. But Japan was not always an island nation. Sometimes around 30,000 B.C.E. people moved from the Korean Peninsula across a land bridge that connected Japan to Asia; at the same time, many of Japan's islands were connected until rising ocean levels separated them. For thousands of years the Neolithic Jomon culture dominated Japan, but this domination came to an end in about the third century B.C.E. when northern China experienced an extended drought that turned the region into desert. The northern Chinese, in search of more hospitable ground, streamed into Korea, in turn forcing Koreans into Japan. These types of migration patterns, brought about by changing conditions, were commonplace in the ancient world.

AFRICA

BY MICHAEL J. O'NEAL

Settlement patterns in ancient Africa were largely a function of geography and climate. Because Africa is a large continent—about 4,600 miles from east to west and approximately 5,000 miles from north to south—and is bisected by the equa-

tor, it contains a wide range of terrains and climate zones. Much of the continent is covered either by savanna (broad, open plains covered with grasses) or desert. Additionally, the continent includes forested lowlands as well as high mountain peaks, such as Mount Kilimanjaro (in Tanzania) and Mount Kenya. The continent also features five major river systems, including the Nile, the Congo, the Zambezi (where Victoria Falls, the world's largest waterfall, is found), the Volta, and the Niger.

Human history began on the plains of east Africa. During the Stone Age people migrated from these plains to other regions of the continent. They were able to do so because the human species became more intelligent and thus able to develop tools that enabled them to survive in new environments. Central to this history was the search for resources. Among the earliest Africans, the chief resource was food sought by nomadic bands of hunters and gatherers. In time, Africans searched for fertile land where there was sufficient water and a temperate climate for growing crops. Others settled along lakes, rivers, and the coasts, where bodies of water provided fish and seafood. Additionally, this search for resources included materials for building shelters and making household goods and, in time, resources that could be traded for other, scarcer resources provided by people in the ancient Near East, around the Mediterranean Sea, and from other regions within Africa.

The climate zones of Africa had a profound impact on settlement patterns. These climate zones differed by temperature and rainfall. In the lowlands along the equator, rainfall was frequent in lush forests. The heavy forests made farming difficult, and herding was not practicable because of the prevalence of disease in livestock. For this reason, the people who settled in the equatorial regions of Africa relied on hunting and gathering, fishing, and trade and exchange for their livelihood.

Farther from the equator the forests thinned out, and the climate was somewhat drier. To the north and south were the savannas with seasonal rains (rather than the nearly daily rains of the tropical forests), longer dry seasons, and warm days but cool nights. Although the quality of the soil was poorer than in the forest regions, the open land, combined with sufficient rainfall and moderate temperatures, made these regions attractive to farmers and herders. Historically, the savannas were home of Africa's breadbaskets, where people settled to grow fruits, palm oil, peas, yams, sorghum, millet, and other crops. Incidentally, much of the modern Sahara was savanna until about 3000 B.C.E. Climate change at this time forced people to adopt new settlement patterns.

It was in the savannas and the border regions between the savannas and the forests that the major civilizations of ancient Africa emerged—for the simple reason that these regions provided the most resources combined with the most hospitable climate. Historians have identified at least eight such civilizations in a band from east to west. To the east were the ancestral lands of the Bantu-speaking peoples. Next was

Aerial view of the Niger River and surrounding savanna during the rainy season; savanna farming communities were the most common form of settlement in ancient Africa. (© Board of Regents of the University of Wisconsin System)

the region surrounding Lake Chad, the ancestral lands of the modern Kanuri. The lower Niger River region was home to the Nok, a metalworking culture. The middle Niger River region and Volta River valley were the ancestral homelands of the later Akan, Mossi, and Songhai peoples. The upper Niger River provided a home for one branch of the Mande, while the area surrounding Tichît (in modern Mauritania, the likely site of Africa's oldest city) was home to another branch of Mande. The Wolof and Serer (also spelled Sérère and Sereer) settled in the Senegal River valley and along the African coast. Finally, the ancestors of the later Fulani, Taureg, and Berber peoples occupied semiarid regions on the border of the desert. This band of civilizations formed a major east–west trading route.

Farther away from the equator are deserts, including the vast Sahara of northern Africa. Here, people settled primarily around rivers such as the Nile. The Nile River valley was home not only to the ancient Egyptians but also, farther south, to the Nubians and the Kushites. Water was provided entirely by the rivers, which flooded during rainy seasons at their source and then carried silt and water for irrigation to the desert regions. This fertile silt was the lifeblood of agriculture for these cultures. Nomadic herders lived in the deserts, where they could move their livestock about in search of scarce brush.

Finally, the northernmost and southernmost portions of the continent became temperate, with seasonal climates and rainfall similar to those of agricultural regions in the United States and Europe. Here people settled to grow such crops as grapes, olives, and wheat, and to raise livestock, such as cattle and goats. The emergence of agriculture produced major changes in settlement patterns. People had to gather and strike down more or less permanent roots to tend their fields and herds, and they lived their lives according to the rhythm of planting, tending, and harvesting crops. The result was the formation of villages and the allocation of the land that surrounded them. As people gathered in villages, more formal lines of authority had to be developed, typically those surrounding the rights and duties of the lineage or clan. In general, these communities did not form "states." Rather, they remained autonomous (independent), forming alliances and networks as necessary.

Resources had to be managed so that people had equal access to them. Practices surrounding marriage and the raising of children became more formalized. Social and economic patterns changed as people developed new specialties, such as pottery making. Religious practices became more formalized as people worshipped ancestors and gods associated with land, crops, the weather, and so on. African society became more "female" as the emphasis shifted from hunting, the preserve of males, to social and family relationships combined with sedentary gardening and crop raising. New roles developed as people took the lead as heads of clans, as storytellers and historians, as healers and diviners, and the like. Meanwhile, nomadic herders developed their own settlement patterns. While they did not stay in one place, they had to return regularly to places where they could provide shelter and pasturage for their herds. As people produced surpluses of food and other goods, commerce and exchange became more common, with people settling along trade routes and providing services to traders and their caravans. Finally, as communities formed and competed with other populations for resources, conflict and ways of managing it developed. The result of this conflict was often warfare.

EGYPT

BY WOLFRAM GRAJETZKI

In order to understand the location of Egyptian towns and villages, knowledge of the special landscape of Egypt is important. As was true in ancient times, Egypt is dominated by the Nile River and the desert. The Nile, flowing from south to north, was the only regular water source. Fertile land, only a narrow strip along the river, was less than 2 miles wide. There were some oases in the western desert, and in the north the Nile divided into several branches, forming the Nile delta, a broad and highly fertile region. In the west there was also Lake Moeris, connected to the Nile via a branch of the river. The Faiyûm Depression, a region area around this lake, was low and marshy and needed human intervention to convert it into arable land. It was only in the Middle Kingdom (ca. 2040–ca. 1640 B.C.E.) and in the Ptolemaic and Roman periods (304 B.C.E.–395 C.E.) that there were substantial towns and villages in this part of the country. In late summer the Nile rose and flooded most of the fertile land, making transport here only possible by boat. An important point, at least for bigger towns, was the connection to the Nile, either directly or via a canal. In ancient times transport over land was very expensive while water freight was easier to handle.

All settlement types in Egypt adapted to this special environment and the Nile flood. The settlements had to be placed close to the Nile to secure a regular drinking water supply and proper transport, and they had to be built on a place that remained dry throughout the year and was not flooded by the Nile. In general, these are natural "islands" of higher ground within the flood plain. (These hills in the Nile delta are often called after their general appearance "turtlebacks.") The mounds are sometimes not very big, and thus the space for settlements was restricted. If a town grew larger, people might move to another island. In the Nile delta there arose several double cities where the population lived on two or even more of these hills, which were treated in inscriptions as separate towns but were indeed single-population centers.

Desert areas were settled more often in the Greek and Roman periods, when towns and villages were built into the desert around Lake Moeris. Other settlements built at the desert edge often had specific functions, such as workmen villages for quarries or building projects like the tombs in the Valley of the Kings in Thebes. When these building projects were finished, the settlements were abandoned. The biggest building projects in Egypt were the pyramids in the Old Kingdom (ca. 2575–ca. 2134 B.C.E.). For these projects special towns for the workmen and the administration of the building project were erected. While the workmen's places were no longer used after the pyramids were finished, other parts of the settlements could develop into regular towns. Here the cult for the dead king buried in the pyramid was performed, and from this starting point these places became local centers. This is most clearly seen at El-Lahun, the pyramid town of Sesostris II (r. 1897–1878 B.C.E.). El-Lahun flourished as an administrative center for the whole region for the next two centuries. The mortuary temple of Ramses III (12th century B.C.E.), called today Medinet Habu, also became a center that functioned as an important town for 1,500 years. The temple had strong walls, and after the death of the king the local population moved there, perhaps for security reasons.

It is hard to identify the pattern of settlement types in the Nile Valley and the Nile delta, as only a few have been surveyed and a small percentage of the sites have been excavated. In addition, the excavated examples are often exceptional rather than the norm. One such place is the well-researched island of Elephantine. The southernmost settlement of Egypt, Elephantine had special significance as a trading post for Africa and also functioned as a frontier and fortress town.

In Middle Egypt near the modern villages of Qau and El Badâri, a chain of cemeteries was excavated. These cemeteries were placed close to the ancient settlements, and at least for this region it is possible to gain a picture of the distribution of settlements in pharaonic times. The center of this region was the town called in ancient times Tjebu (modern-day Qau el-Qebir). Here was found the biggest cemetery of the region, including the monumental tombs of the local rulers. Tjebu was the center of the local governor with the palace of the local government. It was also the location of an important temple. The temple was closely connected with the administration of local government. Here the taxes of the province were stored and given back to the people when needed.

From ancient texts we know that each province had a main town with a temple of the most important deity of the province. These temples in the local centers not only functioned as religious capitals of a region but were also the contact place between the royal capital of the country and local

(opposite page) Most settlements in ancient Egypt were placed close to the Nile. A high proportion of the population of towns probably lived from agricultural work, taking advantage of the yearly rise and fall of the Nile that left deposits of rich black silt along the riverbanks.

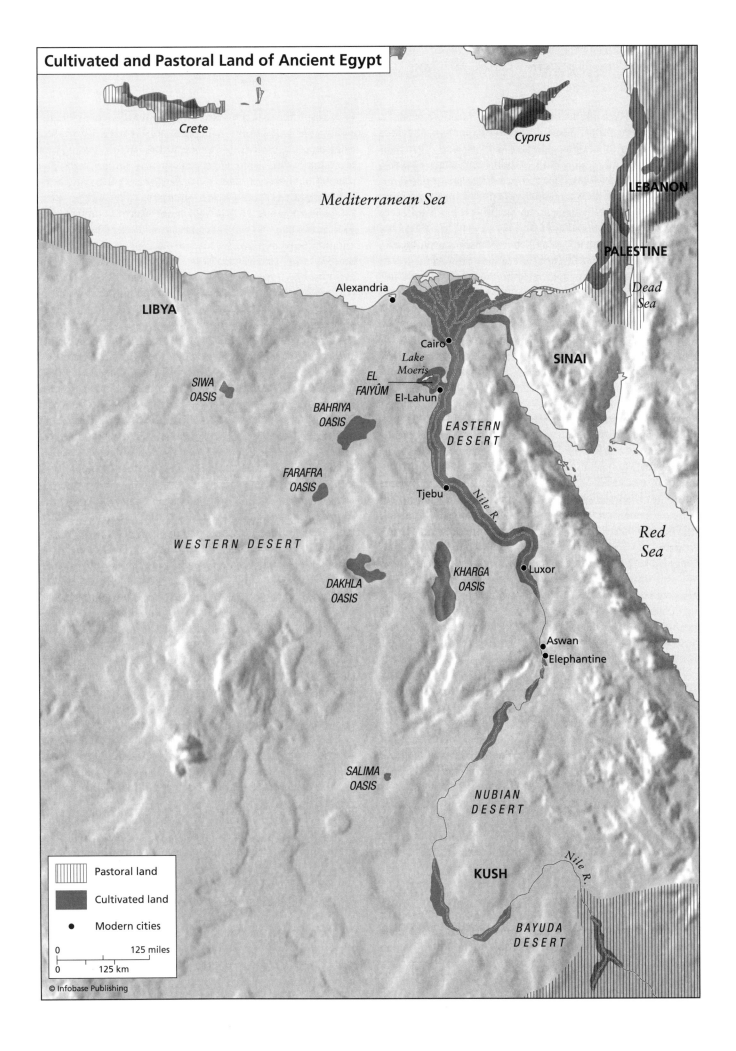

Cultivated and Pastoral Land of Ancient Egypt

Crete

Cyprus

Mediterranean Sea

LEBANON

PALESTINE

Dead Sea

LIBYA

Alexandria

Cairo

SINAI

Lake Moeris

EL FAIYÛM

El-Lahun

EASTERN DESERT

SIWA OASIS

BAHRIYA OASIS

FARAFRA OASIS

Tjebu

Nile R.

Red Sea

WESTERN DESERT

DAKHLA OASIS

KHARGA OASIS

Luxor

Aswan
Elephantine

SALIMA OASIS

NUBIAN DESERT

KUSH

Nile R.

BAYUDA DESERT

	Pastoral land
	Cultivated land
●	Modern cities

0   125 miles
0   125 km

© Infobase Publishing

government. Around these centers, which must have covered the whole Nile Valley, were villages of different sizes, visible from a chain of smaller cemeteries north of Tjebu. In ancient Egyptian times they were rather small; from what is known of the cemeteries we can expect that populations reached not much more than 100 people per village. However, in Greek and Roman times Nile Valley settlements were often quite big, and many of them had the size of small towns. The Egyptian language does not distinguish between town and village in precisely the way that English does. There are several words for settlements, but they may relate to their function and not necessarily to their size.

Not much is known about farmhouses and small agricultural units. In general, we can assume that even in towns and local centers a high proportion of the population lived from agricultural work. From written sources we know that houses or estates existed in the countryside and were involved in food production. Only farmhouses of the Ptolemaic Period (ca. 304–30 B.C.E.) have been excavated showing that they at least were sometimes big buildings.

THE MIDDLE EAST

BY AMY HACKNEY BLACKWELL

When the last ice age ended about 11,000 B.C.E., humans spread through the Middle East. The climate was good, and rainfall was relatively high for the region. As a result, grasslands and forests expanded and provided more food for humans, who quickly inhabited the entire Fertile Crescent, an area stretching from Israel and Lebanon to the Zagros Mountains. These hunter-gatherers sought out regions that included more than one ecological zone so that they could exploit a variety of food sources. They lived in small, highly mobile bands, sheltering in temporary camps that they could easily dismantle when conditions deteriorated.

Starting around 10,000 B.C.E. people began settling in locations for longer periods as they grew dependent on certain types of plant foods. For example, the Natufian people of modern-day Israel lived on acorns and pistachio nuts that grew in a belt in the central part of the region. They built permanent villages with underground storage pits and occupied these settlements for many generations. The people of Abu Hureyra on the Euphrates River in Syria also built a permanent village, hunting and fishing and gathering plant foods from the nearby forests. By about 9500 B.C.E. permanent settlements were common throughout the region.

The first farming settlements appeared around 8000 B.C.E. in the Levantine corridor, a narrow strip about 15 miles wide along the Jordan River from the Damascus Basin to Jericho. This corridor had ample water supplies with a naturally high water table, a rarity in the region. The readily available water meant that people could farm without irrigation. The area also had plentiful sources of wild food, including legumes, nuts, and game. These settlers built villages of mud-brick huts that housed perhaps 100 to 200 residents. As the products of

agriculture furnished more of peoples' diets, settlements became more nearly permanent with farmers were tied to their fields and women tied to their grinding stones. People now lived in the same place for generation after generation. When populations grew, it became harder for people to deal with sudden catastrophes such as droughts.

Because rainfall was low and rivers were the only reliable source of water in the region, settlement patterns in Mesopotamia were dictated by the presence of rivers. All major Mesopotamian cities were built near the banks of either the Tigris or the Euphrates. Some of the earliest-known Mesopotamian cities were Ur, Uruk, and Eridu, built by the Sumerians near the mouth of the combined Tigris and Euphrates sometime between the sixth and the fourth millennia B.C.E. Some archaeologists believe that Eridu was the first city ever built; Sumerian tradition held that Eridu was the first city before the Great Flood to have a king. Southern Mesopotamia was wetter than it is now, and it was conveniently located on trade routes, which made it an attractive location for settlement.

The population of the Mesopotamian river settlements grew quickly. At first the cities were fairly small and surrounded by farming villages, but the climate changed this pattern. Around 3800 B.C.E. the climate grew drier, and the floods that the farmers relied on began arriving later, after harvest. People who had lived in the countryside were unable to farm anymore and abandoned their homes. Some became nomadic herders, wandering with their animals in search of pasture. Others left the outlying villages and moved into the cities in search of food. By 3200 B.C.E. Sumerian civilization had become highly urbanized. Historians estimate that by 2800 B.C.E. some 80 percent of the Sumerian population lived in cities clustered in southern Mesopotamia.

Ur, Eridu, and a group of several other cities within sight of one another were home to thousands of Sumerian farmers who used the rivers' annual floods to irrigate their fields. Small villages extended out from the cities along networks of canals that carried water away from the rivers. Different communities specialized in different products, such as pottery, fishing, or metalwork. Each city had a government that organized irrigation and food distribution and conducted the rituals considered necessary to propitiate the gods. Several land and sea trade routes converged on the area. The cities in the region constantly fought over scarce water and land resources.

People had begun colonizing the upper part of the river during the fifth millennium B.C.E. These cities grew larger during the third millennium B.C.E. and came under the leadership of warlords who competed with one another for water and land. When water was plentiful the settlement pattern resembled that of the early fourth millennium in southern Mesopotamia, with towns spread out from cities, but urbanization proved inevitable there as well. The Akkadian civilization (2350–2100 B.C.E.), for example, arose in the fertile Habur plain south of the Anatolian plateau when, as had happened around 3800 B.C.E., a drought drove people from the countryside into the cities.

While cities were a viable solution to minor drought, major droughts were too much for them. Around 2200 B.C.E. a major drought afflicted all of Mesopotamia. The cities could no longer feed their residents, and the people dispersed, leaving their former homes to sink into ruin. When the rains returned about 1900 B.C.E., the people returned as well, though to different sites; the rivers had changed course, and some of the former city sites were no longer habitable. Cities continued to be the dominant settlement form in the region.

Throughout the Middle East people followed similar patterns, gathering around rare water sources. In the Levant people settled near rivers, lakes, and other sources of water. The Jordan River and the Sea of Galilee were major population centers from early times. The coastline was also valuable to fishermen and sea traders. In Arabia there was so little water that very few people lived there. The ones who did manage to settle there permanently built towns on the coasts of the Persian Gulf and the Red Sea.

In Anatolia most people lived along the Black Sea and Aegean coastlines, which had fertile land and a healthy climate. People had settled the coast of the Black Sea (at that time called the Euxine Sea) by the seventh century B.C.E. When the weather grew warm and wet around 5800 B.C.E. the population on the shores of the sea increased as more farmers took advantage of the fertile soil. Also around 5800 B.C.E. the waters of the sea began rising, and the entire area flooded, forcing residents to abandon their homes and flee to higher ground. Many of them moved into eastern Europe. The central part of the Anatolian peninsula was mountainous and heavily forested, which made living conditions difficult, though some hardy souls lived in caves in the rocks. By the time of the Greek and Roman empires, the western and northern coasts of Anatolia were heavily populated with towns, large cities, and farmsteads.

In Persia the most fertile area was the coastline of the Caspian Sea, which received more rain than any other part of the

Relief fragment showing Assyrian soldiers towing a boat through shallow water (Courtesy of the Oriental Institute of the University of Chicago)

country. Human settlements were concentrated in this region. Settlements also clustered along the trade route that led between India to the east and Mesopotamia to the west. Persian rulers built cities throughout their realm; major cities were Susa, near Babylon, and the Seleucid capital of Persepolis.

ASIA AND THE PACIFIC
BY KIRK H. BEETZ

Most paleontologists believe that early humans spread eastward from Africa along the southern coast of Asia. Many of their settlements would now be underwater. They would have chosen to settle where the fishing was good, spreading inland only where the hunting and gathering were easy and probably not establishing villages inland until population pressures forced them to move. Their villages would have been far apart and their overall population would have been thinly spread over the landscape.

Humans reached the southeastern edge of Asia long before the beginning of the last ice age. From Southeast Asia people moved slowly to outlying islands. In about 30,000 B.C.E. people began to settle Australia, probably inhabiting its northwestern coast, where they could establish fishing villages. They spread slowly through what was then a mostly wet continent, arriving at Tasmania in about 29,000 B.C.E. and reaching the far southern edge of Australia in about 22,000 B.C.E. By 10,000 B.C.E. they were a thinly spread population of about 300,000 people whose villages tended to be near sheltering rocks and forests, where they could escape direct sunlight in what was becoming a mostly dry, hot land.

The earliest-known Indian culture is the Harappan civilization (ca. 2600–ca. 1500 B.C.E.) of the Indus River valley in northwestern India and Pakistan. The first major cities discovered by archaeologists were Harappa and Mohenjo Daro. Both of these cities were near the Indus River, which for a long time had archaeologists believing that the Indus River was the focus of Harappan settlements. Yet the Vedas tell of a major river, the Sarasvati, that was the focus of important events. The Vedas are sacred works of Hindus that were the oral tradition of the Vedic peoples who invaded India in about 1500 B.C.E. and which were written down sometime between the 500s and 300s B.C.E.

It turns out that the Sarasvati had existed but dried up between 2000 and 1000 B.C.E. It was east of the Indus River, and it appears to have had far more Harappan settlements along it than did the Indus. The Harappans were farmers and traders. Most of their population lived near rivers, and they used irrigation canals to water their farmlands. In general, they used every bit of arable land for growing crops and built their homes on land that was more rocky than the land they farmed. Although most of their settlements were along the Indus and Sarasvati rivers, every river in the valley had at least one village along it. They also had many villages in wet lowlands near the Gulf of Kachchh and the Gulf of Khambhat on the coast of the Arabian Sea and at least a few villages well to the east on the Narmada and Tāpi rivers. To further their trade with other cultures, the Harappans established towns far from their river valley: Shortughai in the Hindu Kush mountains to the north and Mundikak, Shahr-e Sokhte, and Bampūr far to the west. Shortughai was in a place to take advantage of trade in lapis lazuli, and the far western settlements may have been for trade with Mesopotamia. The oldest settlement appears to be Mehrgarh near the Bolan Pass west of the Indus River, which was first settled in about 6000 B.C.E.

By about 1500 B.C.E. the Harappan civilization had collapsed, probably because of a combination of natural disasters and invasion by nomadic Aryan groups from central Asia. These groups became the Vedic peoples, and over hundreds of years they migrated through the Indus River valley and southeastward through northern India. They did not immediately settle down into permanent homes but migrated with their cattle. In about 1000 B.C.E. they began to adopt agriculture, and during the 800s B.C.E. small Vedic kingdoms arose, mostly along the Ganges and Yamuna rivers that ran southeastward across northern India. Much of the Ganges flowed through plains that were good for both growing crops and herding cattle.

While the Vedic peoples were slowly expanding southward, they encountered other peoples, often called Dravidians by archaeologists. Many of these people belonged to Stone Age cultures, living in forests as hunter-gatherers. They resisted efforts to settle their territories and continued their ways of life all through the ancient era. Others became farmers. Like the Harappans, they tended to settle along rivers, but in central and southern India rains were so frequent that communities could settle in wet, open lands away from rivers and reasonably hope to receive enough rain to water their crops. When India formed kingdoms, governments tried to take advantage of rains by building dams to create reservoirs, particularly in mountainous highlands. Public works such as dams and irrigation canals allowed people to spread their villages into areas previously unsuited for farming.

Although the Harappans are still mysterious to modern archaeologists, societies in China during the same era are even more perplexing. In much of what is now China, people did not create settlements until modern times, and many in the north still remain nomads, pitching their tents in different places every day. In about 6500 B.C.E. people began farming. By about 5000 B.C.E. there was a fairly cohesive culture farming millet along the lower reaches of the Yellow River, also known as the Huang River. Around the Yellow River and its tributaries was a belt of loess soil, silt blown into layers over many years, and the Yangshao culture of about 5000 B.C.E. spread villages away from rivers into regions where the soil allowed for easy digging. Rice farming was introduced from the south, and the Longshan culture of about 3200 B.C.E. developed to organize people to take advantage of rice's superior yields and nutrition, because rain was less frequent in the Yellow River area and irrigation requiring community cooperation was needed to provide rice with the moisture it needed.

South of the Yellow River was the Yangtze River, where farmers settled along the riverside to grow mostly rice. From about 4500 B.C.E. on the region around the mouth of the Yangtze and a region upstream around the lake Dongting Hu became heavily populated by farmers. The Shang Dynasty (ca. 1500–ca. 1045 B.C.E.) tried to absorb the people of the Yangtze, but it took until the Zhou Dynasty (ca. 1045–256 B.C.E.) for China to conquer the Yangtze settlements, and thereafter the Yangtze farmlands became vital to feeding the empire.

The Zhou, Qin (221–207 B.C.E.), and Han (202 B.C.E.–220 C.E.) dynasties each made the establishment of settlements part of government policy. They made special efforts to settle peasants from central China in the north near the Great Wall to act as deterrents to nomadic raiders, and during the Han Dynasty to help make the Silk Road secure. To absorb conquered lands into the empire, Chinese governments often moved large groups of peasants south or west, going as far south as North Vietnam.

For almost all of the ancient era the majority of people in Korea and Japan settled near ocean shores. Those people who moved inland tended to settle beside lakes or streams. In Japan the mountains were sparsely populated. In Korea invasions and wars influenced some people to move into highlands, where travel was difficult and water sometimes scarce but where the rough territory helped them defend themselves. During the Yayoi Period (300 B.C.E.–300 C.E.) of Japan people often settled near marshes or swamps because they would scatter rice seed in the marshes or swamps and later harvest the new rice. This unsophisticated approach to growing rice was sufficient for Japan's population of about two million people.

Extensive rain forests grew in southeastern Asia. That these lands were populated is known from the records of Chinese and Indian explorers, but little is known of their settlement patterns. The Mekong River attracted many settlements, probably at first because of good fishing and later because rice could be cultivated along it. By about 100 B.C.E. the Mekong Delta in modern southeastern Vietnam was heavily populated, mostly by farmers.

EUROPE

BY JUDITH A. RASSON

The Paleolithic cultural period dates to the geological Pleistocene (the ice ages). Although the climate all over Europe was affected, there were many large ice-free areas. People lived in small groups that moved around throughout the year to hunt and gather wild animals and plants, resulting in a settlement pattern made up of campsites used by different groups at different times. A good campsite needed not only a safe place to set up tents or other shelters but also access to water and food. Some campsites were near sources of stone for tools. People returned to favorable locations year after year, such as Dolní Věstonice in the modern-day Czech Republic, which was on a nonglaciated route between eastern and western Europe.

The shelters that people constructed were only temporary; they took their tents with them when they traveled or built new shelters from brush and tree branches. A conveniently located cave also made a good temporary home that might be revisited every year.

During the Paleolithic everyone lived in groups based on families, and their settlements were similar, though the groups varied in size depending on how much food they had available and what tasks they were carrying out. These tasks and activities mainly had to do with everyday living, such as preparing and cooking food and making tools and clothing. While no group stayed long in any particular place, perhaps once a year different groups gathered for a day or two to renew friendships, find marriage partners, and share information. A few special sites, like the Lascaux Cave complex in France, were not just for the activities of everyday life. At Lascaux and a handful of other places the cave walls were decorated with pictures of animals and other designs. They had social and religious significance.

At the end of the Pleistocene the climate changed, although people remained gatherers and hunters for hundreds more years, adapting to the supply of plants and animals brought by the new warmer climate. Eventually people found out how to domesticate plants and animals to supply their needs for food and other materials, and they developed ceramics, though they still relied on stone for sharp-edged cutting tools. This was the beginning of agriculture, called the Neolithic Period, which began in about 7000 B.C.E. in Greece but not until 2000 B.C.E. in England.

Houses built by Neolithic settlers were made of timber and mud plaster (or the equivalent), more substantial and usually larger than in the Paleolithic. They were occupied for long periods, probably because groups now maintained their own food supplies. Settlements functioned as hubs from which many activities were carried out, such as cultivating fields and herding animals. It is hard to generalize about the locations of Neolithic settlements because their locations were always compromises that made it possible to meet a number of needs, such as access to water, arable land for crops, and grazing land. More people lived in Europe than before, and because their lifeways left more remains than earlier, hundreds of Neolithic settlements are known throughout Europe, for example, Cuiry-lés-Chaudardes in France, Brześć Kujawski in Poland, and Selevac in Serbia. In general, each settlement fulfilled the same social and economic functions as every other settlement, but Neolithic people in many parts of western Europe built special-purpose monuments interpreted as expressions of their supernatural beliefs. Arrangements of large stones called megaliths can be seen at Carnac in Brittany (France). Passage graves were made with stones grouped in various ways with or without soil coverings; the most famous is New Grange in Ireland.

Although settlements were similar, the length of time each was occupied differed. Some settlements were used for long periods throughout the Neolithic, resulting in the accumula-

tion of cultural debris in a large mound (or tell), like Karanovo in Bulgaria. These are more common in eastern and southeastern Europe than in western Europe. Sometimes smaller settlements, occupied for less time, were located surrounding a tell, as at Polgár-Csőszhalom in Hungary. This suggests that the older (tell) settlement had some economic or social function beyond that of the smaller younger settlements.

During the Bronze Age, when metalworking became widespread, some earlier patterns persisted. The basic economic activities of cultivating fields and grazing livestock continued; thus settlement sites were still placed to provide access to the necessary resources. But settlements began to be distinguishable from one another by the number or variety of their differing functions. In western Germany and the Low Countries, for example, there were both single farmsteads and larger villages. As can be seen by their size and internal complexity, some settlements began to benefit from increased trade activity.

In the social system of the Bronze Age (starting as early as 2800 B.C.E., in southeastern Europe) some people earned elite status and political power. Trade intensified, even with far-distant areas, including trade in valuable bronze objects. It was during this period that many settlements throughout Europe began to show signs of defensive fortifications, such as being located on hilltops (sometimes called hill forts) or being surrounded by ditches and wooden palisades. A Bronze Age tell in Hungary has a double ditch and palisade system surrounding it; in Spain, a Bronze Age site with stone walls stands on a high promontory. In Sardinia, in addition to village settlements, Bronze Age people built stone towers called nuraghi.

Later still, iron objects began to be made and used in different parts of Europe—albeit at different times. By the Iron Age (starting around 1000 B.C.E.) iron objects and tools became widely available to most members of society for all aspects of daily life. New technology, such as iron-tipped plows, enabled people to occupy new areas. The Iron Age is associated with increasing social and economic complexity, which was reflected in a hierarchical settlement pattern. Territoriality was evident when some groups began to control important locales, such as river fords or mountain passes. Some villages or farmsteads remained strongly connected to farming and stock raising, whereas others added functions, such as being the residence of a socially elite group. In the Halland area of Sweden agricultural villages are located on well-drained soil, and smaller sites are located adjacent to wet areas, perhaps for special purposes such as hunting. The large site of Slöinge was probably the residence of elite people because the artifacts found there include such unusual items as garnets, amber, gold, silver, and imported glass.

Important settlements were usually protected in some way, often by a ditch, palisade, or rampart, sometimes even by a water barrier such as the crannogs, or artificial islands, constructed in Ireland. In Poland the site of Biskupin is fortified and located on a peninsula in a lake for protection. The Iron

Age settlement of Százhalombatta Földvár in Hungary was protected by both a ditch and an earthen rampart, construction of which was a huge earth-moving project that probably required direction by a respected person of higher social status than most people. Another manifestation of the existence of a social elite was the use of distinctive burial practices. In many areas the elite were buried in specially constructed mounds (sometimes called tumuli). The Iron Age is the first time in European prehistory that something is known about the group names people called themselves. The most famous are the Celts, who were spread from southeastern Europe to the British Isles. Their elite lived in hill forts (often called *oppida*). The settlement of Bibracte, now called Mont Beuvray, in France was surrounded by a wall of timber, stone, and earth, 3 miles long.

GREECE

BY MARK ANTHONY PHELPS

Two geographic factors are paramount in understanding Greece from either a social or an economic context. First, this is an extraordinarily hilly and mountainous land, as over 40 percent of the land is more than 1,600 feet in elevation. The Pindus Mountains extend the length of the region until they submerge into the Aegean Sea, creating most of the islands found there as well as a jagged coast that provides a vast number of protected harbors. Settled life focuses on valleys and a handful of plains scattered throughout the country. Second, no point of the peninsula is more than 38 miles from the sea.

The soil of the region is rocky and often of marginal fertility. Adding to the fragility of the soil is the climate, known as dry summer subtropical. Summer dryness, wind, and heat contribute to crop failure, while winter rains demand modifications of the farmland to enhance drainage and to stop soil erosion. Natural springs and man-made cisterns, necessities for rural life, influence where cities can grow. In ancient times the marginal land that could not lend itself to intensive agriculture was used for pastoralism. After the collapse of the Mycenaean civilization (ca. 1100 B.C.E.), the depopulation of cities may reflect a period of nomadic pastoralism. For the rest of the ancient history of Greece, transhumant pastoralism was the norm.

The hills and mountains of Greece contributed to the political fragmentation that characterizes Greek history. Isolation fosters ethnocentrism, which contributes to the history of independent city-states and continual rivalries. The majority of ancient Greeks were farmers. Wheat was the dominant crop in the plains and valley bottoms, while olives and grapes were typically grown on terraced hillsides.

The model traditionally espoused for ancient farmers is taken from the pattern of farming found in medieval and modern Greece. Historians theorized that farmers lived in villages, leaving in the morning to tend to scattered plots. The distribution of plots was the product of equal devolution of property among sons and the usage of land in dowries.

This dispersion was ultimately advantageous, as land in plots that have some ecological differentiation serves as insurance in the face of droughts, because one piece of land may fare better than others. Further, the village provided protection from raiders. Given the scarcity of water, it was assumed that farmhouses in the countryside would have been impossible to maintain.

However, this model has been successfully challenged by the recent attention to rural archaeology and a closer reading of certain classical texts. The rise of villages and the increase in trade at the beginning of the Iron Age points to a rise in agricultural production. The need for land for intensive farming was a contributing factor to the phenomenon of colonization as Greeks established colonies throughout the Aegean coasts, the Black Sea, Libya, and other scattered centers in Asia Minor and the rest of the eastern Mediterranean.

The image of Odysseus's father Laertes in Homer's *Odyssey* serves as antithetical evidence to the traditional model of ancient Greek farming. In contrast to the notion of living in a village, Laertes resides in a house on his farm with outbuildings constructed on it for storage and drying. He works his farm daily, which must be done if one is growing vines and maintaining orchards. He has a fence and dogs for protection. He labors alongside his slaves, sharing equally in toil. He rarely enters the town, where he owns a lavish house, and he has a profound disdain for urban dwellers. He has a reputation as a warrior.

Archaeological evidence indicates that small-scale irrigation emerged at the time of Homer and Hesiod in the late eighth century B.C.E., providing another argument for the need to have farmers on farms for continual maintenance. In his writings Aristotle (384–322 B.C.E.) asserts that in early days the population of the polis was small, as most were working farms. Surveys in Attica, Boeotia, the Argolis, the Peloponnese, Aegean Islands, Magna Graecia, and the Crimea all support these images where a number of rural structures from these areas have been located.

Ancient Greek farmers would have needed to both protect their land from raiders and hide from invaders. Given that most farms were small, neighbors were not terribly distant. Protection from farming neighbors seems to have been a greater concern than raiders given the attention that Plato assigns to legal codes regulating the relationship between farming neighbors in his work *Laws*. Clearly, settlement in rural areas was dense enough to cause troubles. The largest estates were by no means enormous. The politician and general Alcibiades (fifth century B.C.E.), nephew of Pericles, was fabulously wealthy with an estate of some 80 acres.

The choice for urban settlement was based primarily on access to water, generally springs or (less often) rivers. Sites needed to have an agricultural hinterland to support the urban population that did not farm. This hinterland would have needed a population base to trade its surplus for certain manufactured and imported goods. The two most powerful states during the bulk of the ancient Greek period were the two city-states with the largest agricultural hinterlands, namely, Sparta and Athens. Access to the sea was beneficial for trade but by no means a requisite for cities in classical Greece. These factors account for the resettlement of former urban areas (usually with the same Mycenaean name) during the Iron Age, as Greece has always been a land of limited water and limited agricultural land.

The abundance of harbors and ease of access to the sea for most of the interior fostered a culture of seamanship. This orientation was further driven by the poor mobility between Greek regions and cities owning to the mountainous and hilly terrain. In turn, the period of colonization of distant shores from the eighth through sixth centuries B.C.E. was facilitated by the experience of the Greeks in managing the geographic circumstances of their homeland.

The hills contributed to the isolation and fragmentation of the city-states that emerged in the Iron Age. The rare plains lent themselves to the formation of leagues among the cities and villages ringing them. The members of these leagues would fight among themselves over access to resources, but they formed a united front against outside invaders.

The origin of the institutions of classical Greece can be traced and attributed to the values and experiences of farmers living on this land. The sense of individual worth, egalitarianism, and independence all followed from attitudes expressed by and attributed to farmers. Greek writers took pride in the difficulty of their climate and soil in regard to agricultural production. Such characteristics as courageousness, fierceness, physical strength, and intelligence all sprang from life on farms, according to classical authors.

ROME

BY DAVID B. HOLLANDER

In the Roman world agriculture was the foundation of the economy, and owning land was the basis of social status. Thus both the settlement and use of land were of considerable importance in the development of the empire. Political and military factors influenced where colonies were established, while economic, cultural, climatic, and geographic factors determined the location of farms, villages, and towns and whether they flourished or failed.

A number of different kinds of sources shed light on Roman settlement patterns, each with its drawbacks. Literary sources, such as agricultural manuals and the writings of elite Romans including Cicero and Pliny the Younger, provide some information about the size and location of farms and villas, but these authors rarely discuss the situations and concerns of any but the wealthiest Romans. Survey archaeology, in which a team of archaeologists examines land for surface traces of ancient activity by walking over it, can provide a much fuller picture of settlement patterns. In many parts of the empire one still finds traces of the boundaries established by centuriation, the process Roman surveyors used to mark out land allotments for new settlers. Surveys reveal the

remains of ancient farmhouses and villages as well as those of larger villas. They can also indicate how settlement patterns changed over time. Nevertheless, survey archaeology cannot determine who owned a given structure or how much land was associated with it. Furthermore, it is likely that the dwellings of the poorest farmers left few traces for archaeologists to find. The excavation of the remains of rural structures can suggest how the surrounding land was exploited and the nature of a villa or farm's interaction with the local environment and market. Inscriptions and papyrus manuscripts also sometimes provide information concerning the ownership and use of land.

Several Roman agricultural manuals have survived from antiquity. The earliest, written by Cato the Elder, dates to the second century B.C.E.; Varro wrote another about a century later, and a third was composed in the first century C.E. by Columella. Pliny the Elder, author of 37 volumes on natural history, provides additional information. These writers discuss not only estate management and the cultivation of crops but also the question of where to build a farm. Many factors had to be considered when buying agricultural land. According to Cato, ideally, the climate should be good, and the property should be at the base of a mountain facing south, having access to water and a supply of labor as well as roads, navigable waterways, or a nearby town. Good neighbors and land capable of growing a variety of crops also were considered desirable features. Varro discusses two other important factors related to the establishment of rural estates: health and safety. Proximity to swamps and marshes is undesirable, while, in certain regions, a farmer might have to contend with brigands. Varro stresses the advantages of having property near a town or village, where one could sell produce and purchase necessities.

Small estates on the outskirts of Rome could prove immensely profitable if their production was geared toward the city's insatiable demand for game, fish, and flowers. Wealthy Romans frequently built luxury villas where they might relax or entertain guests. Prior to the eruption of Vesuvius in 79 C.E., the land around the Bay of Naples was a particularly popular location.

Little can be said with certainty about the earliest phase of Roman settlement during the regal period. Tradition held that shepherds and outlaws formed the bulk of the followers of Romulus, Rome's legendary founder. It is likely that pastoral agriculture played a more important role in Rome's first centuries than it did later. Romans of the late Republic believed that their ancestors had worked small plots of land on the outskirts of the city. As the Roman Empire expanded, three important trends emerged: colonization, the designation of conquered land as *ager publicus* (public land), and growth in the size of upper-class estates. Colonies served several functions. The Romans founded some small colonies, such as Antium and Ostia, on the coast to protect against seaborne attacks. Other colonies were essentially garrisons in newly conquered territory.

Colonists, who might be Roman citizens, veterans, or allies, received small plots of land to farm in their new communities. Vast tracts of land were confiscated from Rome's defeated enemies and designated *ager publicus*. Despite the efforts of some Roman lawmakers to limit individual holdings, wealthy Romans came to control much of this land. The rich landowners used slave labor to operate their large estates, which were called *latifundia*. In the 130s and 120s B.C.E. the plebeian tribunes Gaius and Tiberius Gracchus attempted to enforce the limits on holdings of *ager publicus* and distribute the recovered land to less fortunate Romans. They encountered stiff resistance from the Senate; even though both men were ultimately murdered in riots, they did manage to settle thousands of Romans on small plots of Italian land. Such conflicts over land possession and ownership continued into the first century B.C.E. The proscriptions instituted by Sulla in the 80s led to the confiscation of tremendous amounts of land. A number of the Roman general Sulla's associates gained wealth by purchasing confiscated estates. Many landowners continued to rely heavily on slaves to work their estates, as the great slave revolt led by Spartacus suggests. Civil war, debt crises, and the need to find land to reward Roman veterans made the Italian real estate market especially volatile in the final decades of the Republic.

Given the size and varied nature of the Roman Empire, it is difficult to make generalizations about settlement patterns in the Imperial period. Farms of varying sizes, villages, towns, and rural sanctuaries as well as seasonal shelters for farmers and shepherds could be found dotting the landscape. While some individuals amassed large landholdings and debt frequently forced peasants to sell their land, the practices of dividing inherited land among heirs and colonizing conquered regions tended to create new smallholders. Many provinces received groups of Roman colonists, especially in the early empire. Some provincial cities grew substantially under Roman rule due to their status as provincial capitals, their role in the transportation of foodstuffs to Rome, the presence of military units, or the patronage of the emperor. Alexandria, Carthage, and Antioch became particularly important. Other cities and regions suffered from natural disasters, revolts, or proximity to volatile border areas. The relative peace of the first two centuries of the Common Era saw an increase in population and rural settlement in many regions. But beginning in the late second century C.E. plague, civil wars, and Germanic invasions caused a decline in population and rural settlement in some places.

THE AMERICAS

BY J. J. GEORGE

Settlement patterns in the ancient Americas overlap with traditional migration theories on the origin of the first peoples. The traditional theory held that the first Americans crossed Berengia, the Bering Sea land bridge from Siberia to Alaska, around 11,500 years ago. The term *bridge* is somewhat misleading because some models suggest that open land was in excess of 1,000 miles wide, affording ample territory for multiple bands of persons traveling on foot to make their way into the New World. Why did they come? In brief, they came because they were following megafauna, or large animals hunted for food, such as mammoths, mastodons, bison, and giant sloths—the latter as large as 20 feet tall. While Berengia is now under water, save for a scattering of islands, during the period of initial settlement much of the earth's water was locked up in ice sheets that covered much of Canada, dramatically lowering the earth's sea levels and exposing greater expanses of land.

The appearance of the first Americans coincided neatly with evidence indicating that an ice-free corridor had opened between two large Canadian ice sheets referred to as the Laurentide and Cordilleran, allowing these early migrants access to nonglaciated lands in mid-latitude America. These original inhabitants are now called Clovis people, named after the town in New Mexico where their fluted spear points used for hunting mammoth were first found in 1932. Clovis and Clovis-like points are recorded from the late Pleistocene in Alaska to Panama and in California and Nova Scotia. Following this model, the first settlements spread slowly southward, eventually reaching the edge of North America to the east and the southern tip of South America.

However, a well-studied site called Monte Verde in southern Chile, dated to around 12,500 years ago, calls into question the traditional model of a slow and orderly procession southward. The site contains the buried remnants of simple residential structures, stone tools including bifacial projectile points—a stone tool with two sides or faces worked to form an edge for scraping or cutting—and preserved edible and medicinal plants. The question, then, is how did these peoples reach so far south so fast? A competing settlement theory posits a much more rapid southern advance via open coastal routes along the Pacific Coast into Alaska and northwestern Canada and eventually south to Peru and Chile by approximately 12,500 years ago. Any remnant archaeological data that might pinpoint and date coastal settlements are unfortunately lost; as the last ice age receded, rising sea levels worldwide advanced inland, burying the previous coastline and along with it any markers of coastal inhabitation. To date, then, there is agreement only in that the first Americans were *Homo sapiens sapiens*, who were in North and South America by Clovis times, about 11,500 years ago.

Viewed archaeologically, settlement patterns are, like any prehistoric residue, the incomplete and fragmentary markings of something that was once vital and whole, essentially a reconstruction of the physical and material presence of long-disappeared persons. A settlement might be thought of as an archaeologically discernible site, a unit of space that was characterized during some culturally definable period of time by the presence of one or more dwellings or structures. The arrangement of structures on a site with respect to one another forms unit patterns. The arrangement of these patterns, in turn, through a wider segment of space, might be termed a complex pattern. These complex patterns relate to the adjustments of human beings and culture to environment and to organization of society in a broad sense.

Over time a range of settlement types developed, some coalescing into complex settled social units based on agricultural production and others maintaining hunter-gatherer economies. Classifying the variety of settlements presents its own difficulties, with definitions differing by scholar and discipline. In general, however, much of the literature includes the following settlement types: camps, villages, towns, ceremonial centers, village clusters, and, eventually, cities. Generally speaking, these classifications represent advancing complexity based on differing social, economic, and political determinants, and it should be further noted that characteristics are often complementary and overlapping.

The simplest archaeological discernible site, or *camp*, would cover sites with areas between a few hundred square feet and perhaps an acre, where midden (refuse) deposits are thin and impermanent, lightly built shelters were erected without any definite community plan. Camps are most closely affiliated with hunter-gatherer and semisedentary units. Camps persisted in areas such as the eastern United States, Brazil, Central America, Mexico, and the Caribbean from the time of the first human being until at least the historic period, or the period when Europeans first arrived and began recording written history.

A *village* occupies an area of several acres. The number of dwellings might run as high as 30 to 40. The appearance of sturdier structures, which remained in place and were occupied for extended periods of time; deeper refuse deposits; and some level of village planning are in evidence. The spatial and temporal distribution of villages is similar to that of camps, which they began to replace or at least to supplement. It would be common for a village to be politically dominated by a chief with extended kin or clan affiliations. Examples of this type of settlement range from the Tehuacán Valley of Mexico, with pit houses and domesticated plant use in evidence by 3400 B.C.E.; to Hopewell Indian sites in the American Midwest by roughly 200 B.C.E.; to coastal villages in British Columbia and Southeastern Alaska, with evidence of plank houses by 200 B.C.E.; to the burial mounds and earthworks of the Adena people in Ohio, Kentucky, and West Virginia between 1000 B.C.E. and 200 C.E..

Village clusters and *ceremonial centers* are closely related and particularly common, representing a number of neighboring villages so closely related culturally that it is assumed constant contact was common and sociopolitical organization overlapped. It was not uncommon for these affiliated villages to share a ceremonial center. Unlike camps, which lacked complex patterns and seemed not to cluster, religious sites often became linked by larger social and ceremonial considerations and thus could be called a village cluster. Hopewell and Adena temple mound complexes between 1000 B.C.E. and 200 C.E.; Mayan centers in the Central America,

including Cuello in Belize (possibly as early as 2400 B.C.E. until 500 C.E.) and Tikal (250–850 C.E.) in Petén; Guatemala in the second through ninth centuries C.E.; Chavín between 900 and 200 B.C.E.; and Moche from perhaps 1 to 600 C.E. in Peru are all examples of villages or village clusters with a ceremonial center in common.

The key relation in settlement is between settled life, domestication, and population. Greater population density becomes possible with advanced domestication, where people tend to favor plants and produce food in surplus, which is necessary to support larger populations as well as nonagricultural members of society, such the elite, craftsmen, and soldiers. In one sense, towns and cities are simply greater agglomerations of persons gathered in a single area with refined abilities to domesticate and store foodstuffs, such that by the second through eighth centuries of the Common Era a city like Mexico's Teotihuacán, it became possible to support a population estimated at around 125,000.

See also AGRICULTURE; BORDERS AND FRONTIERS; BUILDING TECHNIQUES AND MATERIALS; CITIES; CLIMATE AND GEOGRAPHY; DEATH AND BURIAL PRACTICES; EMPIRES AND DYNASTIES; EXPLORATION; FOREIGNERS AND BARBARIANS; GENDER STRUCTURES AND ROLES; GOVERNMENT ORGANIZATION; HUNTING, FISHING, AND GATHERING; LAWS AND LEGAL CODES; LITERATURE; MIGRATION AND POPULATION MOVEMENTS; NATURAL DISASTERS; NOMADIC AND PASTORAL SOCIETIES; SACRED SITES; SEAFARING AND NAVIGATION; SLAVES AND SLAVERY; SOCIAL COLLAPSE AND ABANDONMENT; SOCIAL ORGANIZATION; TOWNS AND VILLAGES; TRADE AND EXCHANGE; WAR AND CONQUEST.

FURTHER READING

Tim Cornell and John Matthews, *Atlas of the Roman World* (New York: Facts On File, 1982).

Tom Dillehay, *The Settlement of the Americas: A New Prehistory* (New York: Basic Books, 2000).

Gary Feinman, ed., *Settlement Pattern Studies in the Americas: Fifty Years since Virú* (Washington D.C.: Smithsonian Institution Press, 1999).

Daniel J. Gargola, *Lands, Laws, and Gods: Magistrates and Ceremony in the Regulation of Public Lands in Republican Rome* (Chapel Hill and London: University of North Carolina Press, 1995).

Victor Davis Hanson, *The Other Greeks: The Family Farm and the Agrarian Roots of Western Civilization* (Berkeley: University of California Press, 1999).

Oswyn Murray and Simon Price, eds. *The Greek City: From Homer to Alexander* (New York: Oxford University Press, 1990).

David O'Connor, "Urbanism in Bronze Age Egypt and Northeast Afrcia." In *The Archaeology of Africa: Food, Metals, and Towns*, eds. Thurstan Shaw, Paul Sinclair, Bassey Andah, et al. (London: Routledge, 1993).

Evon Z. Vogt and Richard M. Leventhal, eds., *Prehistoric Settlement Patterns: Essays in Honor of Gordon R. Willey* (Albuquerque: University of New Mexico Press, 1983).

Gordon Randolph Willey, *Prehistoric Settlement Patterns in the New World* (Westport. Conn.: Greenwood Publishing Group, Inc., 1981).

► ships and shipbuilding

INTRODUCTION

The archaeological record concerning ships and shipbuilding is thin. Few watercraft from the ancient world have survived, because generally they were made of perishable materials. Some of the earliest were made with such materials as reeds, and ancient kayaks, canoes, and similar small craft were typically covered with animal skins. Later, lumber was used in boat construction, resulting in larger, more durable craft, but over the centuries the wreckages of these ships have largely deteriorated. Still, marine archaeologists have located portions of the wreckages of ships in such areas as the Mediterranean Sea, giving them insight into ancient shipbuilding techniques. The archaeological record also includes artwork that depicts boats and ships, watercraft that were entombed with ancient rulers, and in some cases written descriptions.

Ancient civilizations constructed ships and other types of watercraft to serve a variety of purposes. One, of course, was exploration. As ancient peoples migrated into new regions of the world, they used watercraft to navigate rivers and coastlines, often in search of new food supplies or new places to settle. These craft were powered by oars or, in the case of river barges and rafts, poles. In some parts of the world, this impulse to explore led to the development of larger, more ocean-worthy vessels, along with sails to harness the power of the wind. However, other ancient cultures, such as those of the Americas, were less interested in exploring the world than they were in exploring the region that surrounded them.

Fishing required the use of watercraft. People who lived in coastal communities or along rivers developed a range of watercraft that allowed them to harvest fish, seafood, and in time even whales. These types of watercraft had to be highly maneuverable and able to operate in shallow water. Rafts, canoes, barges, and small boats and ships were used for this purpose.

Trade in the ancient world was often conducted with the help of watercraft. Because large volumes of goods had to be transported and because land routes were both dangerous and difficult, transport by water was often the preferred method. The wreckage of one ship found off the coast of Turkey yielded 20 tons of cargo, an amount of cargo that would have been nearly impossible to transport by land. Similarly, watercraft often were used to transport materials for construction. Many of the stone monuments that survive from the ancient world were built with massive stones quarried in one location and then transported by barges closer to the construction site. In some case, barges were used to ferry goods between islands, such as the many islands of Greece.

Finally, watercraft were used for military conquest. As shipbuilding methods became more advanced and ships be-

came larger, they could be used to transport troops, weapons, and provisions. Additionally, some of the world's great naval battles took place during ancient times. The Chinese, with their immense coastline, led the world in shipbuilding technology during the Qin (221–207 B.C.E.) and Han (202 B.C.E.–220 C.E.) dynasties and built a large fleet of huge warships that came to symbolize China's power and prestige.

AFRICA

BY JUSTIN CORFIELD

Although many ships—Roman, Greek, Persian, and Phoenician—in the ancient world sailed to Africa, the only African state besides Egypt that maintained a large fleet of its own was Carthage. It had not only a massive navy, located in a secret inner harbor at Carthage, but also a sizable merchant navy.

The Carthaginians inherited their naval traditions from the Phoenicians, from whom they trace their civilization. At the height of their power during the First Punic Wars (264–241 B.C.E.), the Carthaginian navy was very large. The Greek historian Appianos (second century C.E.) wrote that the naval harbor at Carthage had the capacity to take 200 ships, and archaeological work at the site confirms this possibility. Because the Carthaginians had bases throughout North Africa and also Sicily, they probably had many more ships. The Greek historian Polybius (ca. 200–ca. 118 B.C.E.) stated that in 256 B.C.E. Carthage was able to put to sea some 350 ships, which would involve a crew of about 150,000: 300 oarsmen and 120 marines on each vessel. Given the number of people used to make the ships, it is evident that Carthage placed a great deal of emphasis on its navy.

The major fighting ship used by the Carthaginians was a quinquereme. There are no archaeological remains of such vessels, but historians believe that they had a large central sail and three rows of oars, with two men pulling each of the top two oars. The Carthaginians also had quadremes and triremes. The trireme had three banks of oars, but the quadreme is thought to have had one row of oars with four men pulling each oar, two rows of oars with two men pulling each oar, or three rows of oars with two men pulling the top oars. All three types of designs might have been used. The ability of the Carthaginians to produce such large numbers of ships was confirmed in 1971 when the hull of a Carthaginian galley was found near the port of Marsala in Sicily. Some of the wood had the marks of shipwrights, proving that they were mass-produced, which would be the only way they could have had such a large fleet.

Many of the Carthaginian sea battles of the First Punic Wars took place around Sicily. The Romans initially copied the design of a Carthaginian ship for their vessels. It must have been an old design because later in the war they captured a faster vessel, which enabled them to build better ships. At the first encounter, at Milazzo in 259 B.C.E., a Carthaginian admiral called Hannibal (not to be confused with the general of the same name who invaded Italy during the Second Punic Wars) attacked the Romans but lost 50 ships.

The admiral narrowly escaped being captured himself and lost his flagship. After they were defeated by the Romans off the coast of Sardinia, the Carthaginians crucified Hannibal as a punishment.

In addition to their navy, Carthaginians also had a large merchant fleet. Their vessels sailed the Mediterranean before the First Punic War and through the wars until just before the outbreak of the Third Punic War in 149 B.C.E. These were the ships involved in trade with Spain and Cornwall, where the Carthaginians and the Phoenicians bought tin. The Roman poet Avienus (fourth century C.E.) makes a reference to a visit of the Carthaginian navigator Himilco (fl. ca. 450 B.C.E.) to Cornwall. Carthaginian ships also sailed down the western coast of Africa. They are believed to have traded with West Africa, although whether they did this directly or through middlemen is not known. According to one theory, the Carthaginian navigator Hanno (fifth century B.C.E.) sailed to modern-day Cameroon.

Apart from the Carthaginians, the Numidians had small trading vessels, but as a client state first of Carthage and then of Rome they had no need for their own fleet. Trading vessels were certainly being built on the western coast of Africa, but most traveled short distances and kept close to the coastline. However, the Norwegian explorer Thor Heyerdahl (1914–2002), in his *Ra* voyages in 1969 and 1970, managed to prove to his skeptics that it was possible to build a vessel that could cross the Atlantic Ocean. Archaeologists have not found the remains of any of the Carthaginian trading vessels, but from descriptions of the goods they carried it would seem that they were similar to the Phoenician merchant ships. These ships relied far more on the use of sails, as the costs of maintaining large numbers of oarsmen, even slaves, would have been too high to justify the gains in speed and the loss of large storage areas for merchandise.

Many small vessels undoubtedly traveled the eastern coast of Africa, including Egyptian ships sailing to Punt, the Egyptian name for a coastal region probably in modern-day Eritrea and Djibouti. Merchants from these and other ships were probably the transmitters of knowledge of metallurgy from Nubia to southern Africa. The dates of the iron objects found in Africa seem to show that the technical advances occurred in coastal areas before permeating inland, which may explain why the Buganda people of modern Uganda learned to utilize iron in comparatively recent times. It is also possible that this trade was carried out not by African ships but by ships from India or elsewhere whose owners plied their wares along the African coast. Items designed by the Chinese and Indians have been found in Madagascar, indicating that this trade did exist from ancient times. In addition, beginning in the second century B.C.E. the use of dhows—sailing vessels with triangular sails—for trade between Africa and southern Arabia started to become important as the exchange of goods between Axum and Arabia significantly increased.

Besides the ships used for navigating in seas and oceans, there was also a need for vessels for crossing rivers and trading along rivers. Rafts would have been used to cover the shorter distances, along with boats made from hollowed logs and small watercraft. Being made entirely of wood, none of these have survived, although some archaeologists have suggested hints of their existence in some of the rock carvings found in the Sahel.

THE *RA* EXPEDITIONS OF THOR HEYERDAHL

The *Ra* expeditions of the Norwegian explorer Thor Heyerdahl, which took place in 1969 and 1970, followed the Norwegian adventurer's success with the *Kon-Tiki* crossing of the Pacific. Heyerdahl intended to demonstrate that it was also possible for people to cross the Atlantic Ocean. He had been interested in connections between the ancient civilizations, and he believed it might have been possible for seacraft to have made the long and hazardous voyages.

For that reason Heyerdahl hired boat builders from Lake Chad, and the boat was constructed out of reeds in Egypt based on designs shown in ancient Egyptian drawings, and then taken to Safi, Morocco. It was accepted that the Egyptians could have sailed along the coastline of North Africa and through the Strait of Gibraltar. Here they might have taken on extra crew or replenished supplies on the boat. Although Heyerdahl's intent was to show that ancient Egyptians could have reached the Americas, the fact that the boat departed from the Atlantic Coast of Morocco also showed that people before even the Carthaginians could have made the journey.

With a seven-man crew, *Ra* sailed on May 25, 1969, but foundered in July after traveling 2,700 miles. It was abandoned after being waterlogged and in danger of sinking. It was a great disappointment for Heyerdahl and the multinational crew, but, undeterred, the team started work on another boat. The second boat, *Ra II*, with almost the same crew, was built by Aymara Indians from Lake Titicaca on the border of Peru and Bolivia. It was then taken to Safi, from where it managed to cross the Atlantic and arrive at Bridgetown, Barbados, in the West Indies in 1970, having completed the crossing in 57 days.

EGYPT

BY ERIN FAIRBURN

Because ancient Egyptian civilization developed in the valley and the delta of the Nile River, it is only natural that watercraft appeared early in Egyptian history. Developed technology in the creation of river craft appeared in the Predynastic

Period (before ca. 3000 B.C.E.), and clear evidence of seacraft is known by the Old Kingdom (ca. 2575–ca. 2134 B.C.E.). Egyptian traditions in boat construction were unique in the ancient world until late in the Dynastic Period, and some techniques have persisted into modern times.

The earliest Egyptian watercraft were developed in response to the need for transport along the Nile and the marshes of the delta, especially during the inundation season, when settlements along the Nile Valley would effectively be turned into islands. These were simple rafts, constructed by tightly binding bundles of papyrus reeds. They were easy to construct, made of readily available material, and required little technology. Longitudinally binding the bundles as tightly as possible made the craft more watertight and reduced the rate at which the reeds would become waterlogged. The binding gave the resultant raft a crescent shape, the front and rear curving upward, with the ends of the bundles splaying outward in the shape of a lotus flower. The appearance of these river craft would be imitated in later Egyptian wooden vessels.

These rafts are probably the types of boats that are depicted on Naqada II (ca. 3500–ca. 3200 B.C.E.) pottery from the late Predynastic Period. Such images show cabin structures and standards on these vessels and seem to indicate that they could carry a fair contingent of rowers. One representation on a Naqada III (ca. 3200–ca. 3000 B.C.E.) jar seems to indicate that sails had been developed by this time and were used on such craft. These simple vessels were used throughout the history of ancient Egypt.

Construction of boats in wood is not known in Egypt prior to the Early Dynastic Period. Native Egyptian woods are of very poor quality and produce only short lengths of timber. However, longer lengths could be produced from timbers imported from the eastern Mediterranean, and it is of note that the apparent advent of wooden boat construction in Egypt coincides with the earliest evidence of imported woods in Egypt. It does seem that Egyptian craftsmen frequently used native and imported woods in combination within a single vessel.

Wooden craft from their inception until the Middle Kingdom (ca. 2040–ca. 1640 B.C.E.) are evidenced archaeologically only from royal funerary contexts, where special pits were excavated in order to inter the boats alongside a king's tomb. This practice began in the First Dynasty (ca. 2920–ca. 2770 B.C.E.), and more than 30 such pits from this time have been identified, at a handful of sites throughout Egypt. Most of the pits' contents were no longer recognizable, but 12 brick structures from the funerary enclosure of the king Khasekhemui (d. ca. 2686 B.C.E.) were discovered in 1991 with their planked boats intact.

Most other known boat pits from the Old and Middle Kingdoms were found at Giza and Dahshûr. From these pits came eight vessels: the famous reconstructed boat of Khufu housed today beside the Great Pyramid in Giza; a second, unexcavated boat from the same pyramid complex; and six boats from the pyramid of Sesostris III (r. 1878–1841? B.C.E.)

at Dahshûr. These vessels give vast insight into the construction of planked vessels in Dynastic Egypt.

Egyptian wooden vessels were created hull first, any framing being installed afterward. Egyptian vessels did not have a keel proper, but they were sometimes built up from a long plank (or a connected series of planks) that was somewhat thicker than the surrounding planks and that may have served as a rudimentary keel. More planks would be placed around this central piece, building up the bottom and sides. These planks were initially attached through a series of mortise-and-tenon joints and then fastened by lashings made through a number of V-shaped cuttings within the thicknesses of the planks. This "sewn" technique persisted through the Ptolemaic Period (304–30 B.C.E.).

Once the hull was complete, crossbeams and other framing elements would be installed, and decking would be laid. Cabin structures could be built on the deck planking. The stem and stern posts were often large and decorative affairs, curving upward to a vertical or bent post with a lotiform (like a lotus petal) finial; as noted earlier, such features mimicked the appearance of reed rafts. The boats would be fitted out with a number of oars and one or two rudder paddles at the stern.

When ships were fitted with sails, they were hung from a bipod (forked) or post mast that was set well forward of the middle of the ship. At first the sails, probably made of linen, appear to have been taller than they were broad, but by the Sixth Dynasty (ca. 2323–ca. 2150 B.C.E.) they were consistently broader than they were tall. The use of a bipod mast was soon abandoned, and the mast itself moved closer to the middle of the ship through time.

Seagoing vessels had additional adaptations. One important addition was the hogging hawser, a rope extending from stem to stern that could be twisted to maintain tension. This line helped maintain hull tension and kept the bow and stern from sagging. Before the New Kingdom (ca. 1550–ca. 1070 B.C.E.) sailing vessels also seem to have had rope netting fitted around the hull above the waterline, which probably served to maintain hull integrity. New Kingdom vessels, however, do not seem to have included this feature. Some of these later vessels do seem to have had a different internal layout that allowed rowers to sit below the hull line.

These seagoing vessels were used by Egyptian kings to conduct trading and military expeditions in the Mediterranean and Red Seas. Egypt is known to have had contacts with the eastern Mediterranean by the First Dynasty and with the Aegean by the late Middle Kingdom and into the Second Intermediate Period (ca. 1640–ca. 1532 B.C.E.). Military campaigns were launched against kingdoms of the Levant as early as the Sixth Dynasty and sporadically throughout the rest of the Dynastic Period. Beginning in the Old Kingdom, trading expeditions were also sent to Punt, a kingdom located on the eastern coast of Africa in the Red Sea region. Hatshepsut (r. 1473–1458 B.C.E.) famously recorded an expedition during her reign on the walls of her mortuary temple at Deir el-Bahri, including wonderful depictions of her ships.

Painted wooden model of a boat, from Meir, Middle Egypt, Twelfth Dynasty, around 1900 B.C.E. (© The Trustees of the British Museum)

One other type of vessel had a vitally important purpose in ancient Egypt and was used throughout the Dynastic Period: the barge. These vessels were similar in construction to seagoing vessels but had no sails and were of potentially massive size. They were used from the earliest times to transport stone for monumental sculpture and construction from quarry sites between modern Cairo and Aswān. These boats had to be tugged upstream or downstream by up to 30 smaller vessels.

Once Egypt fell under foreign rule, first by the Persians and then by the Greeks, Egyptian methods of seagoing vessel construction shifted to those of the greater Mediterranean region. However, river craft design remained essentially the same, as recorded by the Greek historian Herodotus (ca. 484–between 430 and 420 B.C.E.).and the famous Palestrina mosaic of Roman date.

THE MIDDLE EAST

BY EDWARD M. W. A. ROWLANDS

In the ancient world people began to designs ships specifically to carry goods on long journeys. They left the eastern Mediterranean and Persian Gulf to travel great distances. Warship designs were constantly modified to keep up to date with any changes in naval warfare tactics. Various weapons, such as the ram, were developed to fight the enemy, and boats were continually enhanced to increase their speed and defensibility.

In the second millennium B.C.E. merchant ships were broad-beamed craft, which enabled them to have a large cargo space. Square sails were used, and oars were utilized in the absence of wind. Early evidence of these ships comes from the tomb of Kenamun, a mayor of Thebes, in Egypt (ca. 1400 B.C.E.). Ships that are thought to have come from modern-day Syria had dense beams at the front and back ends of the ship. At the front of the ship was a large clay amphora that was probably used to store potable water. On the back end of the boat were two stern oars that would have been used for steering. A wicker fence also stretched across the ship to protect the deck cargo.

By the first millennium B.C.E. merchant ships had adapted to react to any possible enemy attack by placing iron on the bow (front) of the ship. The bodies of these ships were low in height and less rounded than their predecessors. The ships are depicted on pottery beginning in the eighth century B.C.E. For short distances, there is evidence of a small craft that was rowed by one or two men. This ship is represented in the reliefs of the Assyrian king Sargon II (r. 721–705 B.C.E.). The front of the ship, which carried a cargo of timber, is in the shape of a horse's head. The ship's oars would have been used to steer the ship.

There is little archaeological evidence of Mesopotamian ships, owing to the poor quality of surviving representations and a lack of shipwrecks. They certainly once existed, however, as Sumerian texts refer to ships sailing down the Persian Gulf to locations as far away as Africa and India. These texts date from around 2350 to 1800 B.C.E. and suggest that from an early period the Mesopotamians were able to construct ships that traveled great distances. The Persians did not have a standing fleet, since most of their military campaigns were on land in Asia Minor. They relied instead upon their conquered coastal territories to supply them with the ships they needed. They also used sailing ships from the Levant to import wine, oil, metals, and other products into their empire.

In the 11th century B.C.E. a group known as the Sea Peoples caused havoc along the eastern Mediterranean. Areas of the Hittite Empire, Cyprus, and important cities in the Near East such as Ugarit (in modern-day Syria) were laid waste. The Sea Peoples seem to have been defeated by the Egyptians under the reign of Ramses III (r. 1198–1166 B.C.E.). Representations from Medinet Habu in Egypt show the naval battle between the Egyptians and the Sea Peoples. They suggest that naval warfare at first involved mainly hand-to-hand combat, with troops boarding each other's vessels.

Beginning in the late eighth century B.C.E. naval warfare changed with the invention of the ram. Representations of the ram have been found dating from this period in the sculptures of Sennacherib (ca. 681 B.C.E.), who followed Sargon II as king of the Assyrian Empire. This new weapon could cause considerable damage to opposing vessels. The oldest ram that has been discovered was found off the coast of Israel at 'Atlit and dates from the second century B.C.E. The ram was found without any other ship wreckage around it.

Besides the right weaponry, speed was an important factor in naval warfare. The ability to outmaneuver a rival

was vital. Large steering oars on the back of the boat meant that the ship could change direction quickly. Ships were also built very long to counter the effects of a bow wave. This wave was created when ships attempted to sail at high speed. Vessels needed to use a great deal of energy to climb the wave created, which would slow down the ship. Longer, narrower ships could better cut through this wave and so travel more quickly.

On the reliefs of Sennacherib there is early evidence of vessels with a second row of oars, called biremes. This increase in the number of oarsman helped to propel ships at ever-increasing speeds. To maintain the stability of the ship, the platforms where the oarsmen sat were lowered. As a defensive measure, warships often had a balustrade on the top deck that was covered with shields. By the late sixth century B.C.E. ships called triremes had developed a third row of oars. Such ships were used in large numbers at, for example, the battle of Salamis between the Persian and victorious Greek navy in 480 B.C.E.

Beginning in the fourth century B.C.E. changes in design were needed to adapt ships to new changes in battle tactics. Vessels became increasingly used as stages to fire artillery at the enemy. In naval warfare the frequency of troops boarding other ships increased. To counter this, larger and larger ships were constructed. During the period of wars between the rival successors to Alexander the Great (r. 336–323 B.C.E.), called the Diodochi (322–281 B.C.E.), sexiremes, vessels with six sets of oars, were used in the battle of Salamis in 306 B.C.E. After the political unification of the Mediterranean by the Romans the demand decreased for such large war vessels. Triremes were used again, for example, in the Battle of the Hellespont in 324 B.C.E. when Constantine's son Crispus (d. 326 C.E.) defeated the Roman emperor Licinius (r. 308–324 C.E.).

ASIA AND THE PACIFIC

BY JUSTIN CORFIELD

Nautical technology in China was highly developed in the ancient world. The Chinese had vessels for traveling along rivers and navigating the seas. Asians took a number of sea voyages around the Pacific, although details on many of them rely on legends or remain conjecture. With few images surviving of the ships used and no archaeological confirmation, much of the evidence for ships and shipbuilding techniques come from descriptions in chronicles.

It seems probable that vessels were used during the Shang (1500–1045 B.C.E.) and the Zhou (1045–256 B.C.E.) dynasties, but most of the historical records were destroyed during the famous burning of the books by the order of the emperor Zheng (r. 221–210 B.C.E.) in 213 B.C.E., so little information about them survives. The kingdoms of Wu and Yue were known to be important naval powers with significant coastlines, and they often used river-based fleets to attack the inland kingdom of Chu. Their boats would have been constructed entirely from wood, using sails and a rudder for nav-

Terra-cotta model of a merchant ship, Amathus, Cyprus, about 600–500 B.C.E. (© The Trustees of the British Museum)

igation and rowers for military vessels. Given their developed use of siege machinery, it is highly probable that they would have used rams on the front of their ships as was common in Europe during this period. One surviving fifth-century vessel shows the scenes of several battles, including one of a naval battle with oarsmen rowing barges that have mounted platforms with marines engaged in combat. These were made from wood lashed together with rope and, instead of sails, relied entirely on large numbers of oarsmen. While they were easy to maneuver in battle or as river ferries, this design was impractical for ships at sea.

There are many written records from the Han Dynasty; one of them, the *Han shu* (the history of the Han Dynasty), includes detailed accounts of sea voyages to "Tu-yüan" and "I-lu-mo." It took five months to travel from China to the first and another four months to reach the second. It is believed that the first refers to a settlement on the northern coast of Sumatra and the second to Arramaniya, in southern Burma. There are also references to sailing to a place called "Huang-chih," which some scholars surmise is Kanchipuram in south-eastern India. Although no images of the boats survive, they were clearly reliant on the use of sails and rudders. The boats were designed with a hull that was large enough to transport goods and supplies and to shelter the crew in bad weather or at night. Surviving descriptions of voyages at the time make it clear that pirates could be a problem. This would have necessitated building the boats with relatively high sides, not only to protect the merchandise from the sea but also to prevent surprise attacks by people using canoes. Although the story survives only in legend, the attack on the ship carrying Prince Kaudinya of India, the legendary founder of the empire of Funan, when he arrived in coastal Cambodia presents the possibility of surprise attacks.

Ships may indeed have gone farther, judging by the existence of Chinese and Indian goods—or at least Chinese and Indian styles—in Madagascar. Silk from the Han Dynasty was sold to the Romans, though it may have gone by land or through middlemen. There are records of a man who claimed to be a Roman envoy arriving at the Han court in 166 C.E., and two Roman coins have been found in Oc-Eo, a Funanese port in what is now southern Vietnam. That Roman merchants might have sailed to eastern Asia is also surmised from the name the Han used for Rome: "Country West of the Sea." In addition to trade, it seems probable that the Han also used ships for war. Officials had government barges that were rowed along rivers and canals. It is recorded that the general Han Xin was able to cross the Yellow River with rafts that were made from wood and empty, closed pottery vessels used as floats.

Throughout Southeast Asia there would also have been many merchant ships and river vessels. The Funan Empire (first through sixth centuries C.E.) constructed large canals, and they probably used vessels to navigate them, though none have been found. They could have used rafts or simple barges. For their missions to China beginning in 243 C.E. they would have needed vessels capable of navigating the South China Sea, but it is possible that the embassies used Chinese vessels. Mention should also be made of a delegation from the embassy of the Roman emperor Marcus Aurelius (r. 161–180 C.E.) in 166 C.E., which is said to have visited southern China.

In northern Vietnam there are images of ships on the side of several drums that date to 300 B.C.E.; similar drums from the early first century C.E., found in the Sunda Islands, show images of vessels with somebody clearly working a rudder. Carvings on the temple of Borobodur in Java (eighth century C.E.) show the type of vessel that existed at that time.

Canoes with outriggers were used in the Pacific to travel from one island to another, and larger vessels would have been used for making more significant journeys. The presence of people in most of the Pacific Islands, in Australia, and on islands off the coast of Australia during this period is clear evidence of substantial seafaring skills, and the Norwegian explorer Thor Heyerdahl (1914–2002) in the *Kon-Tiki* expedition of 1947 proved that it would have been possible for groups of people to navigate the Pacific. Although there are no historical records detailing these ancient voyages, the aboriginal people of Australia and those of many of the Pacific Islands have preserved legends of sea voyages.

EUROPE

BY MICHAEL J. O'NEAL

The oldest-known European boat, made from a single log, was discovered at Pesse in the Netherlands and dates to about 7000 B.C.E. Numerous other Mesolithic and Neolithic dugout canoes have been found in many parts of Europe, such as the ones at Noyen-sur-Seine in France and Tybrind Vig in Denmark. Dugout canoes were used for fishing in lakes and streams and for transportation on slow-moving rivers and in coastal waters. Paddles found at Tybrind Vig were carved with geometrical designs. Dugout canoes continued to be used in ancient Europe throughout the remainder of prehistoric times. Other early European boats were made of animal hides stretched over frames made of flexible saplings called withies. They were waterproofed with pitch and possibly even butter. Eventually this early form of boat-building technology was overtaken by more sophisticated methods, yet ancient seafarers continued to use skin-covered boats until well into the Common Era. Because these types of boats were made of organic materials, they survive in the archaeological record only when conditions permit their preservation.

During the Bronze Age the inhabitants of northern Europe developed greater skills in shipbuilding, including the construction of boats from planks. Among the first boats that show evidence of advanced shipbuilding technology are the three so-called Ferriby boats, which archaeologists found buried in clay in northeastern England. These boats, built of oak, date to about 1600 B.C.E. While still relatively crude, they show evidence of woodworking skill. The keel was built in two sections joined by a scarf joint, or a joint made by notching the wood so that the pieces overlap, where they can be joined together. Additionally, the keels were grooved to accept vertical planks, and crossbeams were used to strengthen the boat's bottom. The result was a broad, flat-bottomed boat, the largest of which is 5.33 feet wide and 43.5 feet long. This boat illustrates the convergence of two European shipbuilding traditions: One was the "skeleton" structure of hide-covered boats; the other was a tradition of heavy timbered boats. Similar to the Ferriby boats is the boat found at Dover in 1992, a large craft that is estimated to have been rowed by as many as 18 oarsmen during its crossings of the English Channel.

Archaeologists have discovered other wooden boats that date from the second and first millennia B.C.E. Many of these were constructed from a single tree trunk, in effect making them dugout canoes, though they also included transoms (cross pieces, or beams), decks, joinery, and fastenings made with iron and, in some cases, wooden dowels. One of these, called the Brigg raft, was found in Brigg, Lincolnshire, England, and dates to about 600 B.C.E. It is called a raft because only the flat bottom survives. Another, called the Hasholme boat, was discovered in Yorkshire, England, and dates to about 300 B.C.E. This boat and others like it show that their builders lived in a wood-rich environment where trees were cut down to build boats and a good deal of the wood was likely wasted.

The importance of boats in Scandinavia is reflected by their frequent appearance in the rock carvings that cover exposed outcrops in many parts of Sweden and Norway. Long boats constructed by planks carried goods and people across the Baltic Sea and North Sea and among the numerous small islands that line their coasts. The Hjortspring boat, built around 350 B.C.E., was found in a bog in Denmark in 1921. It had probably been used to carry a raiding party, which was then defeated. The victors then dragged the boat to the bog and sank it there as a war sacrifice, along with the weapons and shields of the raiding party. Like the Ferriby and Dover boats from the previous millennium, the Hjortspring boat was built from planks, but its framing system is very sophisticated.

The ancient Celts exhibited relatively advanced shipbuilding capabilities by the first century B.C.E. While the Celts were spread out over large regions of Europe, many groups lived in marine environments, particularly along the Atlantic coast. These ancient mariners faced problems that were much different from those faced by the Romans. While the Romans navigated primarily in the Mediterranean Sea, the northwestern Celts navigated in the more open waters of the eastern Atlantic and Baltic seas. Heavy swells and rocky coastlines required the development of heavy, stable craft that could survive this environment. And unlike the ships of the Romans, these ships could not be powered usefully by rowers.

One group that met the challenges was the Veneti, who lived in Brittany, a peninsula that juts westward into the Atlantic. The Veneti built a large fleet of massive, heavy-bottomed ships with tall masts, sails made of animal hides, and heavy metal cleats to hold the ships together. These ships were highly maneuverable in the ocean. While broad and flat-bottomed, reflecting the tradition of log shipbuilding that was more than 1,000 years old in northwestern Europe, they were also tall and graceful, with high sides that enabled sailors to keep their feet relatively dry. These ships were far more advanced than anything the Romans could throw against them. When the Veneti refused to submit to Roman authority, Julius Caesar (r. 49–44 B.C.E.), before he became the Roman emperor, led a fleet of Roman ships against the Veneti, whose ships he referred to as "swan ships." Caesar initially met with frustration, for his ships were powered by rowers and could not match the nimbler Veneti ships or navigate in the rough waters of the Atlantic. He finally defeated the Veneti in 55 B.C.E. by outfitting his soldiers with long, sharpened grappling hooks, which they used to shred the masts on the Veneti ships. Once the ships were still in the water, Roman soldiers could board them and fight.

In the centuries following Rome's conquest of Europe, Celtic shipbuilding began to show evidence of Roman design. The New Guy's Hospital ship, dating from about the second century C.E., was built with a keel that was similar to Roman keels. The County Hall ship, dating to about the third century C.E., used the mortise-and-tenon joinery common on Roman ships. It had to have been built in the north, though, because it was made of northern oak. The Blackfriars ship, also from the second century, continued the tradition of Celtic shipbuilding but used Roman wood-joinery techniques.

Shipbuilding was not restricted to the seas. River and inland lake societies also built and used ships. Small ships have been discovered in Swiss lakes, and barges were built for transport on the Rhine River. The Romans actually copied certain Celtic shipbuilding methods to design ships with shallow drafts that could navigate the Rhine and other rivers.

GREECE

BY DEBORAH N. CARLSON

The evidence for early seafaring in Greece is indirect and consists of tools of obsidian (a black volcanic glass) and large fish bones excavated in the Franchthi Cave on the Greek mainland and dated to about 9000 B.C.E. Chemical analysis of the obsidian indicates that it can have come only from the Cycladic island of Melos, meaning that it had to have traveled by boat with the earliest seafarers, who were apparently also skilled fishermen, though we have no idea what their vessels looked like. Farther east on the island of Cyprus, stone tools appear suddenly about 8000 B.C.E. in association with the bones of pygmy hippos, pointing again to the presence of ancient mariners.

Travel by sea was a logical development of prehistoric life in the Aegean, which has at its heart a network of small islands known as the Cyclades. In the Early Bronze Age (3000–2000 B.C.E.), a dynamic and artistic culture of stone carvers inhabited several Cycladic islands, including Melos and Syros. The importance of seafaring to the Cycladic way of life is immortalized in miniature model boats of lead and painted depictions of what seem to be long, open galleys. Evidence for the ships themselves has not survived in the archaeological record, but they may have resembled skin boats or dugout canoes.

A Late Bronze Age trading vessel wrecked off the southern coast of Turkey at Uluburun ranks among the most significant finds in the history of archaeology. When it sank around 1300 B.C.E. to a depth of between 140 and 200 feet, the Uluburun ship was carrying a mixed cargo of copper, tin, and glass ingots as well as finished materials, such as glass beads, faience (glazed earthenware) drinking cups, Cypriot pottery, gold and bronze jewelry, and ivory cosmetic boxes. These 20 tons of cargo were sufficiently heavy, and the seabed conditions sufficiently favorable, to preserve intact a small portion of the ship itself, which currently represents the only substantial section of a ship's hull from the Bronze Age Mediterranean.

Study of the hull remains from Uluburun has shown that the ship was constructed in the "shell-first" technique, which was to become the conventional method of Greco-Roman shipbuilding across the Mediterranean for the next two millennia. Unlike the modern approach to building a wooden boat, the ancient shipwright conceived of his vessel from the outside in, first building up a shell of planks connected to one another at their edges with mortises (cavities) and tenons (pieces of wood used to join planks), which were locked in place with wooden pegs. Once the shell was complete, the shipwright made it stronger and stiffer by nailing wooden frames to the planking at regular intervals along the bottom and sides of the hull. The excavation at Uluburun uncovered no indication of a framing system, perhaps suggesting that the Bronze Age shipwright did not feel the need to incorporate frames or that the surviving hull section is simply not large enough for evidence of these timbers to have been preserved.

Roughly a millennium after the Uluburun shipwreck, another small merchant vessel sank in the eastern Mediterranean, this time off the northern coast of Cyprus at Kyrenia. More than 60 percent of the Kyrenia ship's hull was preserved on the seabed, giving archaeologists an opportunity to excavate, raise, conserve, and reassemble over 6,000 pieces of this ancient Greek merchantman. An in-depth study of the Kyrenia ship has made it possible to recreate the construction process: First the keel and posts were erected, and then the hull planking was built up. The floor timbers were fastened to the hull by driving copper nails through wooden treenails, helping to make the vessel watertight. Finally, to protect the wood from the destructive effects of timber-boring worms, the ship's 47-foot-long hull was smeared with gooey, black pitch.

The Kyrenia ship carried a cargo of oil and wine stored in amphoras—two-handled clay jars used for shipping commodities like wine, oil, nuts, fruit, meat, and pine tar. Because many Greek city-states tried to manufacture unique amphora shapes and because these shapes change over time, amphoras are among the most diagnostic and ubiquitous artifacts found on the seafloor. Two other important amphora wrecks from the Greek world illustrate the range in scale of ancient shipping: The modest merchantman excavated at Tektaş Burnu, Turkey, was laden with 213 amphoras, while the shipwreck explored at Alónnisos, Greece, is estimated to have been carrying as many as 4,000 jars.

Pegged mortise-and-tenon joinery was the benchmark of ancient Greek ship construction, but it was not the only method utilized. Excavations of several Archaic (600–480 B.C.E.) wrecks off the coasts of France, Italy, and Turkey reveal the existence of an alternate tradition of sewn or lashed construction. In this method, the planks are still edge-joined according to the shell-first philosophy, but in the place of mortises and tenons the shipwright stitches planks together with plant fibers pulled through angled holes drilled in the plank edges. In one ship from the late fifth century B.C.E., excavated at Ma'agan Mikhael, Israel, both construction techniques (pegged mortise-and-tenon joinery and lashing) were utilized in different parts of the same vessel.

Any study of Greek warships must rely heavily on iconographic and written sources, since the archaeological evidence is effectively nonexistent in that most galleys were likely towed away by the victors or, if badly damaged, floated away in pieces at the surface. The most significant development in Greek naval warfare was the invention of the ram, which probably occurred in the Iron Age (ca. 900 B.C.E.) as suggested by images painted on vases. The ram became the primary offensive weapon of the Greek fleet, and for the next five centuries galleys underwent a rather linear progression, increasing in size and speed with the addition of more and more rowers.

In 480 B.C.E. an allied Greek navy under Athenian leadership won a stunning victory over the Persian king Xerxes at Salamis. The ships taking part in the battle included some older-style pentecontors (50-oared ships), but the majority consisted of larger, faster triremes (warships with three banks of oars), the classic Greek ship of the line. Scholars have long debated how the oarsmen aboard a trireme were arranged— did they sit on three superimposed benches, or were there three men to a bench? The visual evidence, which consists mostly of vase paintings and sculptural reliefs, is plentiful and varied, while the textual evidence includes historical and theatrical works as well as naval inventories from the Athenian port at Piraeus.

Debate about the trireme question, as it is known, will likely continue in earnest until nautical archaeologists can provide more conclusive physical evidence (if it survives) for Greek warships. Until this happens, scholars and naval historians continue to test their hypotheses on full-scale working models, such as the trireme *Olympias*, launched in 1987. The replication of the ancient merchant ship lost at Kyrenia, too, has proved to be an effective tool for understanding the characteristics and capabilities of an ancient sailing ship.

ROME

BY DEBORAH N. CARLSON

During the last three centuries B.C.E. the monarchs of several Greek kingdoms embarked upon a kind of naval arms race dedicated to the construction of enormous oared warships, or galleys, descended from the famed Athenian trireme (a warship with three banks of oars). Various ancient authors describe the thousands of oarsmen required to row these enormous vessels, called polyremes. If the numbers are to be trusted, then these ships must have been outfitted with multiple-rower sweeps, or several rowers pulling each oar on one or two levels. The growth in vessel size brought with it an increase in the number of marines as well as a tactical shift away from ramming and toward the deployment of artillery, such as arrows, grapnel, and missiles, fired from catapults.

According to the historian Polybius (ca. 200– ca. 118 B.C.E.), Rome's entrance into the world of naval warfare occurred rather suddenly, with the emergency construction of a fleet against the Carthaginians in the First Punic War (264–241 B.C.E.). The warships built and employed by the Romans during the Punic Wars were quinqueremes, or "fives," powered by 300 oarsmen and equipped with 120 marines and 50 crewmen. The Romans' early success at sea was due in no small part to their efforts to turn a naval confrontation into a land battle at sea, as exemplified by the *corvus* (Latin for "raven"), a boarding plank outfitted with a large metal tooth, which, when deployed onto the deck of an enemy ship, held fast, locking the two vessels together and allowing Roman marines to board and fight at sea as they did on land.

The large polyremes that had dominated the fleets of Hellenistic Greece gradually became less and less common among Roman commanders, who favored instead a smaller, more maneuverable vessel called a *liburna*. The *liburna* was probably the creation of piratical groups living along the Dalmatian coast of Illyria (modern-day Croatia), for whom speed at sea was a professional necessity. Piracy remained a persistent threat to commercial shipping in the Mediterranean until the campaign of Pompey the Great in 67 B.C.E. The *liburna* played a key role in Octavian's (r. 27 B.C.E.–14 C.E.) historic defeat of the allied fleet of Marc Antony and Cleopatra at Actium, Greece, in September 31 B.C.E. Following his victory at Actium, Octavian erected a commemorative stone monument that had as its centerpiece about 30 bronze rams taken from the captured ships of Antony and Cleopatra.

Although none of the rams has survived, comparison of the sockets in this image with the bronze ram found in isolation off the coast of Israel at 'Atlit suggests that the latter belonged to a vessel about the size of a quinquereme. The Actium monument continued a tradition that dates back to at least the fourth century B.C.E., when the Romans, fighting the Italian Volsci at Antium, captured some enemy ships and displayed the prows along the facade of a low platform in the center of the forum. This speaker's platform, called the rostrum, takes its name from the Latin word for "prow."

Nautical archaeologists have virtually no detailed information about the construction of Roman seagoing warships, since none has yet been found, but they are markedly better informed about the size and construction of Roman merchant vessels, owing to the thorough and meticulous excavation of dozens of ancient shipwrecks. The Roman shipwright followed the same general principles of "shell-first" construction as did his Greek predecessor, first creating a shell of wooden planks fastened together using pegged mortise-and-tenon joinery. Next he nailed large frames (often called floor timbers) inside the hull over the keel and shorter timbers (often called half-frames) along the sides of the hull's interior. Atop the frames the shipwright nailed thin ceiling planking to protect the frames from the weight of the cargo, and outside he coated the ship's planks with pitch or thin sheets of lead to protect the hull from the destructive effects of wood-boring worms. Depictions of sailing ships indicate that most were rigged with a single square sail and occasionally a second smaller sail at the bow and were maneuvered by a pair of steering oars slung on the stern quarters.

Other, less conventional but no less interesting construction techniques existed in various regions of the empire, including the Adriatic, where some shipwrights produced what may be the vessels that the Romans called *naves sutiles*, or "sewn ships." Farther north, archaeological excavations have shown a distinct tradition of assembly characterized by large iron nails, represented in part by the shipwrecks at Blackfriars (England), Zwammerdam (Netherlands), and Mainz (Germany).

The shipwright himself was called either a *faber navalis* or an *architectus navalis*, to judge from various surviving epitaphs and dedicatory inscriptions. In some Roman cities, like Portus at the mouth of the Tiber River, shipwrights organized themselves into *collegia*, or guilds, and excavations at nearby Ostia have uncovered the remains of that local guild's headquarters building. The excavation of Roman harbors on occasion also has yielded the remains of boats and ships abandoned and covered with riverine silt (as at Pisa) or deliberately incorporated into the various concrete structures that constitute the quays and breakwaters (as at Ostia). Careful study of the harbor at Caesarea, Israel, suggests that shipwrights were directly involved with the construction of several concrete-filled wooden caissons (large water-tight chambers) that formed part of a massive breakwater.

Archaeological evidence indicates that most Roman merchant ships transported a wide range of commodities, including wine, oil, garum (fish sauce), fish, nuts, and fruit, in two-handled clay storage jars called amphoras. To date, the largest amphora carriers are represented by the shipwrecks at Madrague de Giens, France, and Albenga, Italy, with thousands of jars amounting to some 400 to 600 tons. The Romans would have classed these vessels as *naves onerariae* (ships of burden), but there also existed a number of specialized ship

Wall painting of Ulysses and the Sirens, Roman, mid-first century C.E., from Pompeii, Italy; the ship, a war galley, is shown in considerable detail. (© The Trustees of the British Museum)

types, such as *naves lapidariae*, or the stone carriers, which transported hundreds of tons of marble and granite from virtually every quarry in the ancient world, to be sculpted into architectural elements (columns, friezes, and monuments), sarcophagi, statuary, and furniture. To gain a better sense of the wide range of vessels that existed in the Roman world, one need only examine the late Roman ship mosaic from Althiburus, Tunisia, or consult the lexicon of ship types assembled by the grammarian and lexicographer Nonius Marcellus in the early fourth century C.E.

By the early seventh century C.E. the shell-first ship construction technique of the Greeks and Romans had changed drastically, as evidenced by the shipwreck excavated at Yassi Ada, Turkey, in the early 1960s. The shallow, widely spaced mortises and loosely fitting, unpegged tenons of this Byzantine cargo vessel no longer contributed the primary source of hull strength; they probably served only to keep the planks aligned long enough for them to be nailed to the ship's frames.

THE AMERICAS

BY LAWRENCE WALDRON

The history of watercraft in the Americas harks back to the very first arrival of people in those continents. As scholars continue to debate whether people during the ice age first arrived from Asia on foot or by boat, it is evident that the original settlers already possessed some knowledge of seafaring. Watercraft and maritime navigation in and around the Ber-

ing Strait in the late ice age would have been used mostly for fishing in coastal waters. Any seafaring skills would have had to adjust to many new environments once people had arrived in the Americas.

Varied American coastal conditions as well as reefs, rivers, rapids, lakes, swamps, and estuaries all presented unique restrictions and opportunities to early American boatmen. Despite the numerous local innovations, ancient American watercraft can be grouped into four major types: skin boats (including kayaks, umiaks, and other bullboats), canoes, rafts, and reed boats. Such watercraft served either as transportation between one seasonal habitat and another or as fishing or whaling vessels. Watercraft were also used in trade expeditions between neighboring groups and between civilizations as far apart as Mexico and Peru.

Coastal and riverine voyages of exploration were made in search of new food sources and trading partners, but it appears that once in the Americas, ancient Indians were never again moved to cross to another continent and so never developed large oceangoing vessels. Many ancient natives turned their attention not to developing sailing ships that might carry seamen beyond the horizon but to pioneering a wide variety of small, highly maneuverable watercraft.

The ancient Indians along the northwestern coast of Canada and the United States developed an unusual kind of boat. In the absence of a steady supply of timber, the obvious choice of wooden boats was not available to far-northern and Arctic Indians. These groups were already adept at making a series of aquatic devices out of sealskin and whale skin, including inflatable flotation devices and wetsuits that remained relatively warm and buoyant in the icy northern waters. Before the Common Era, therefore, the idea of a skin boat had already occurred to them. Made of skin stretched across a frame of wood, these boats proved to be lightweight and easily manageable in water that could sometimes be an obstacle course of floating ice chunks. The Inuit, Aleuts, and other groups call these craft umiaks or kayaks depending on their design.

Seasonal movements enabled ancient northern Indians to maximize their food sources. When it was time to move, they gathered their possessions and piled into large, round skin boats called umiaks. These boats were probably paddled mostly by women, as they were in later times. The male hunters would have traveled alongside the umiaks in smaller boats also made of skin. These smaller, one-person craft were the kind later known as kayaks and were used in both fishing and the hunting of large marine mammals.

Made in a sleek, elongated shape that seemingly sliced through water, kayaks were made of skin stretched over even the top of the boat. Only a small opening was left topside into which the rider could slip his lower body and sit comfortably. In this way the kayak acted like an extension of the boater's body, with only his upper torso visible as he whisked through the water, arms moving the paddle in a circular motion. An ingenious aspect of the craft's design was that it could easily be righted if it was capsized by rough water or large prey. With a skillful turn of his body, the paddler could quickly roll his kayak back into an upright position without even getting his feet wet. The single opening in the top trapped air inside and would not permit water to enter.

While the kayak and umiak are the best known of American Indian skin boats, several other varieties of this technology were used by western Indians as far south as California. The Indian group later called the Gabrielino by European colonists may have used their skin bullboats (a circular vessel much like an umiak) since ancient times. Groups as far inland as Wyoming and the Great Plains also used skin boats, although these were made of the hides of buffalo and other land mammals. The Crow, Omaha, Assiniboin, and Arikara are all known to have used skin boats for inland travel on rivers and lakes.

In wooded areas many of the ancient Americans employed wooden rafts of various kinds for the short transportation of people and heavy goods, often within a single territory. They would have been common in river systems throughout North and South America. The high and often frigid Andes may not have seemed a likely place for residents to develop a strong tradition of rafting, much less boating, but the Andean peoples were daring seafarers and creative builders of rafts and boats.

Some 2,000 years ago early seafarers from the Nazca civilizations employed a kind of inflatable sealskin raft in a number of ways. These inflatable rafts were used not only as vehicles and flotation devices for the fishermen but also as water transports for heavy loads. Nazca and later Moche farmers are known to have acquired tons of guano (bird and bat droppings they used as crop fertilizer) from caves and rocks on the islands off the coast of Peru. Loads of this guano were put in containers and floated back to the mainland on the inflatable sealskin rafts.

Additionally, the Lake Titicaca region between Bolivia and Peru has been inhabited for millennia by groups of natives who employed the use of reed and grass rafts. The Aymara Indians devised a raft, more like a temporary boat in its shape, made entirely of the fibers of *totora* and other kinds of bulrush that grew in the region. The raft of tightly bound reeds was used until it became waterlogged, after which it was discarded. Many centuries later the Inca and various descendants of the Aymara were still making and using the same kind of raft.

The canoe, a boat with two pointed ends, is by far the most common and varied of ancient American watercraft. The majority of canoes, from the northwest coasts of Canada to the islands of the Caribbean, were made of local trees. These canoes varied in design from the plank canoes of California's Channel Islands to the dugout canoes of ancient British Columbia, Florida, Nicaragua, and Venezuela. All canoes, like their kayak counterparts, were propelled by paddles rather than oars so that the boatmen faced the direction they were headed rather than rowing backward as in some Old World boats.

Ancient Indians living in California, such as the Chumash or their ancestors, developed a canoe that at first glance might have resembled a European rowboat in its carvel-planked construction, in which long strips of wood are joined at their edges. Upon closer inspection, however, an ancient observer would notice that the planks were not nailed to the underlying boat frame but rather were cleverly strapped to that frame and to each other with vegetable fibers or strips of leather. To waterproof all the joinery and stitches in this unusual craft, the ancient Californians took advantage of a unique resource: pitch from the La Brea tar pits.

Except for those along the U.S. West Coast, almost all canoes were one variety of dugout or another. The dugout canoe was made by felling a tree of a suitably buoyant species, carving out its shape from the wooden matrix, then hollowing out the hull. The "digging out" from which the design derives it name was usually done with simple stone or bone axes and awls. The shaping of a canoe could take weeks and perhaps even two or three months, especially if any other work was required, such as decorative carving or special treatments of the wood. The types of wood varied with the local habitat, and these different woods might have exerted some influence on the shape of the canoe.

Some canoes, such as the small cedar, poplar, and cypress ones used by the ancient Seminoles, Caddo, and Creek, had a shallow design for skimming across the meniscus of vine-choked swamp or river water. The large, elaborately decorated canoes of early Haida, Kwakiutl, and other Northwest Coast Indians could hold as many as 50 people and were hewn from a variety of large trees, including red cedar, spruce, and birch. These canoes were designed to displace water with their heavy hulls and pointed bows and were used for both river transport and whale hunting. Delaware Indians were known to have used pine for their streamlined dugout canoes, which also glided across the water in the manner of their Seminole counterparts.

Amazonian and Caribbean Indians from the Mesoamerican Maya to the Antillean Taino, like their northern neighbors, fashioned large dugout canoes out of single lengths of trees. Slightly earlier Olmec dugouts were used for inland river travel and for journeys along the coastal waters and swamps of the Olmec heartland in eastern Mexico. Olmec boatmen may have caulked their damaged dugouts with the latex from their Veracruz rubber trees. The Maya of the first millennium B.C.E. diversified into greater coastal travel once they settled the Yucatán. They also built much larger canoes than the earlier Olmec to supply their extended trade expeditions throughout Central America.

Ancient Americans used various different kinds of heat-expansion techniques to alter the shape of their dugout canoes. Amazonian groups expanded the width of their canoes using heat expansion to twice the width of the original tree trunk. They achieved this pot-bellied shape by filling the dugout portion of the canoe with water and heated rocks. The heated water slowly softened the fibers along the grain of the trunk, expanding the hollowed hull. Heat-expansion technology was also used by North American Indians along the Northwest Coast to alter the shape of their canoes. Many Central and North American groups were likewise aware of the use of steam to render wood pliant in the construction of boat frames and hulls. The rounded hull of the vessel not only increased the capacity of the vessel but also added to its stability in rough water.

See also ART; BUILDING TECHNIQUES AND MATERIALS; CLIMATE AND GEOGRAPHY; EMPIRES AND DYNASTIES; EXPLORATION; GENDER STRUCTURES AND ROLES; HUNTING, FISHING, AND GATHERING; INVENTIONS; METALLURGY; MIGRATION AND POPULATION MOVEMENTS; MILITARY; OCCUPATIONS; SEAFARING AND NAVIGATION; TRADE AND EXCHANGE; TRANSPORTATION; WAR AND CONQUEST.

FURTHER READING
George F. Bass, ed., *History of Seafaring: Based on Underwater Archaeology* (New York: Walker, 1972).

Lionel Casson, *Ships and Seamanship in the Ancient World*, 2nd ed. (Baltimore. Md.: Johns Hopkins University Press, 1995).

Basil Greenhill, *Archaeology of the Boat* (Middletown, Conn.: Wesleyan University Press, 1976).

Herodotus, *The Histories*, trans. Robin Waterfield (Oxford, U.K.: Oxford University Press, 1998).

Thor Heyerdahl, *The Ra Expeditions* (London: George Allen and Unwin, 1971).

G. Adrian Horridge, *The Design of Planked Boats of the Moluccas* (Greenwich, U.K.: National Maritime Museum, 1978).

Emory Dean Keoke and Kay Marie Porterfield, *American Indian Contributions to the World* (New York: Checkmark Books, 2003).

Sean McGrail, *Boats of the World: From the Stone Age to Medieval Times* (New York: Oxford University Press, 2002).

Fik Meijer, *A History of Seafaring in the Classical World* (New York: St. Martin's Press, 1986).

John S. Morrison, John F. Coates, and N. Boris Rankov, *The Athenian Trireme*, 2nd ed. (Cambridge, U.K.: Cambridge University Press, 2000).

R. B. Nelson, *Warfleets of Antiquity* (Sussex, U.K.: War Games Research Group, 1973).

J. Richard Steffy, *Wooden Ship Building and the Interpretation of Shipwrecks* (College Station: Texas A&M University Press, 1994).

Jack Weatherford, *Indian Givers: How the Indians of the Americas Transformed the World* (New York: Fawcett Columbine, 1988).

► slaves and slavery

INTRODUCTION
Slavery was a nearly universal practice throughout the ancient world, and some of the world's great civilizations, such as that of ancient Rome, were built on the backs of slaves. Slaves served a variety of functions. Some were domestic slaves,

working in homes, while other worked in fields. Many did the most backbreaking work, including mining, stone quarrying, digging, and construction, though some who were relatively privileged did work that was more administrative.

Slavery took on differing complexions in different parts of the ancient world. In some cases, slaves were pure chattel. They had no rights and could own no property, and their masters had absolute power of life and death over them. A master could arbitrarily kill a slave with no legal consequences in some parts of the world. Sometimes slaves were ritually killed and sacrificed in religious observances, and in ancient Rome they were even trained as gladiators to provide amusement for the upper classes. In other cases, slavery was at least a little bit more bearable. Sometimes people lacked freedom because of the social class—the caste—into which they were born. They might enjoy some legal rights and protections and might even have been able to lift themselves out of servitude. Their masters could not legally abuse them and in fact were sometimes required by law to teach them a trade. Many such slaves, especially those who were literate and showed aptitude, were promoted to responsible positions on estates, in municipalities, and the like. In some cases, child slaves could not legally be required to do adult work.

Slavery was the only option for survival for some people. A person with no prospects in life or who was heavily in debt might have found servitude, with food and a place to live, preferable to imprisonment or a slow death from starvation. Indeed, some people became voluntary slaves as a way of working off debt. In parts of the ancient world slaves were able to own their own property, have their own money, and even themselves own slaves. They could participate in economic activities on their own account, enabling them in time to buy their freedom and attain the rights of full citizenship.

The sources of slaves varied, and slavery was rarely based on racial categories; slaves in ancient Rome, for example, came from all over the known world. Again, some slaves volunteered to become slaves as a way to pay off debt. Others became slaves because they had been convicted of a crime, and slavery was a common form of punishment at a time when there were few prisons. The most common source of slaves was warfare. Wars or raiding parties were launched with the purpose of acquiring slaves, and slaves were part of the normal booty of conquest, seized in the hope that someone would pay a ransom for their return. In many cases, women and children became slaves as a result of conquest. Because conquerors did not want to have to deal with captured soldiers, who might pose a danger to slave owners, they seized family members instead.

AFRICA
BY SAHEED ADERINTO

Slavery was prevalent in ancient Africa. Its history can be traced roughly to the time Africans began to develop villages and towns. The development of a sedentary lifestyle, which paved the way for the emergence of large settlements, has been attributed to the agricultural revolution that took place on the continent some 200,000 years ago. Slavery in ancient Africa is akin to that in other parts of the world: It involved physical, emotional, and psychological containment. By and large, the master of a slave had the power of life and death over the slave. A slave, like chattel, could be sold and bought by someone who occupied a privileged position in the prevailing power configuration.

It is important to differentiate between slavery and other forms of servitude. In Africa pawnship was a form of subordination that differed from slavery. A person could be pawn as a collateral security for debt. People could surrender themselves to pawnship because of the need to raise money for marriage, a funeral, or another purpose that required a lot of money. A pawn was most likely a member of the community where he or she served, but a slave in most cases was brought from another community. While slaves were not likely to be free throughout their lifetime and their masters could enslave their children, a pawn was automatically free after rendering the services equivalent to the debt owned. A master could not exercise any form of control over the relatives of a pawn. A master did not have the power of life and death over a pawn but could kill a slave at will.

The condition of a slave was degrading; a slave could be asked to perform any type of labor, and the most unpalatable works were reserved for slaves. A Yoruba proverb from West Africa that highlights the difference between slavery and pawnship is *Ohun t'o ni oun o so ni d'eru, bio ba so, ni d' iwofa, ki a dupe*, meaning, "If what threatens to make us a slave makes us a pawn, we should be thankful." Only in rare instances did slaves manage to remove the yoke of domination and rise to important positions. Royal slaves in some communities, such as the western Sudanese region of West Africa, were said to have been able to gain freedom, inherit the property of their dead masters, and emerge as prominent members of the place were they had previously served as nonentities. Aside from this exceptional situation, former slaves could not remove the stigma of being formally enslaved.

There were many sources for slaves in ancient Africa. People accused of antisocial behavior, such as murder, thievery, and witchcraft, were sold into slavery. Wars, kidnapping, and raids also produced slaves as part of the booty. There is limited evidence, however, to suggest that wars were fought for the sole purpose of acquiring slaves. Although a trans-Saharan slave trade had already existed, the act of waging wars primarily for the purpose of enslavement came largely through the advent of the trans-Atlantic slave trade, which did not begin until the second decade of the 16th century.

Ancient Africa was predominantly agrarian, and the use of slaves for agricultural purposes was important. Slaves could also be part of tributes that a subordinate state paid to an overlord. Aristocratic families had slaves, and slaves in some palaces were eunuchs (castrated men) who watched over the large harem of royal wives. Others performed domestic functions associated with royalty. A master had control over a slave's sexual relations and reproduction. This implies that a slave could not get married without the knowledge of his or her master. Unsanctioned copulation among slaves carried a serious degree of punishment. A male slave master could use his slaves as concubines, which partly explains why female slaves were more expensive or highly priced than their male counterparts. The offspring produced from such a union became free upon birth, and the status of the mother improved considerably compared with others who did not have children for their masters.

Slaves could serve religious functions. There is much evidence that slaves were killed and used as offerings during periodic sacrifices to the gods. In fact, in most parts of Africa slaves of different ethnic groups were traditionally used to appease the gods and goddess. There is an important connection between this aspect of the religious use of slaves and African belief in life after death. The oral history of people of Africa is replete with references to how slaves were killed and buried with kings and important rulers. According to one belief, dead kings entered another realm, where they lived and communed with the gods and ancestors. In this realm or world they would need the services of domestic servants.

EGYPT

by Mariam F. Ayad

In its most basic definition, slavery implies a loss of freedom, regardless of the degree or nature of this loss. There is little doubt that in ancient Egypt certain groups of people enjoyed less freedom than others. Egyptian slavery, however, was very different from forms of slavery experienced centuries later in Europe and North America. In Egyptian there are no words for *slave* or *slavery*. The word sometimes translated as "slave," *hem*, was also used to indicate "servant." Thus, the Egyptian word for "priest," *hem-netjer* can be translated as either a "god's servant" or a "god's slave." Inherently, the word *hem* did not necessarily indicate servitude. It was used, for example, to refer to the king of Egypt. *Hem-ef*, traditionally translated as "his majesty," may also be rendered as "his incarnation" or "his body."

Meret, a collective noun, is another term that may refer to a group of people without complete freedom, in particular, agricultural workers who could be owned by individuals or temple estates. Mostly found in legal and administrative documents, the term *meret* is closely linked with the transfer of property, especially land and cattle, from one owner to another. Like other kinds of property, people who were considered *meret* could be passed down from father to son as part of an individual's inheritance. *Meret* may have referred to serfs, a special kind of conscripted workforce.

There were several different sources of slaves in ancient Egypt. War and conquest was the principal and oldest way to acquire slaves. Some information about enslaved prisoners of war comes from the tomb biography of Ahmose, son of Ibana, a military officer whose career spanned the reigns of three different kings of the early Eighteenth Dynasty: Ahmose I (r. ca. 1550–1525 B.C.E.), Amenhotep I (r. 1525–1504 B.C.E.), and Thutmose I (r. 1504–ca. 1492 B.C.E.). The inscription indicates that not only were slaves captured at war, but they also were often granted to individuals who exhibited exceptional military prowess. Detailing the conquest of the Hyksos cities of Avaris and Sharuhen, Ahmose indicates that from the former he brought "one man, three women; total, four persons," and "His majesty gave them to [Ahmose] as slaves." Ahmose also was allowed to keep the two women he had captured at Also Sharuhen. Ahmose's valor was recognized by the king and duly rewarded with gold.

While occasionally military officers retained their captives as slaves, such was not always the case. While fighting in Nubia, Ahmose, son of Ibana, captured "two living men" but was rewarded with "two female slaves." On another occasion he brought "two young warriors as captives" but was given "five persons" as a reward. In all four accounts Ahmose's receipt of slaves was part of a greater package that showed the king's appreciation of his military prowess. In addition to slaves, Ahmose was rewarded with gold, parcels of land in his hometown, and a promotion. This and similar texts indicate that prisoners of war were not limited to soldiers from the rival army but also included the inhabitants of the captured towns. The process outlined in Ahmose's biography indicates that Egyptian military personnel were obliged to present their captives to the king, who became the primary owner of these newly acquired slaves. It was the king's prerogative to assign captured prisoners to his officers, the temples, or his own royal household. Occasionally Near Eastern slaves were imported into Egypt.

Certain legal documents dating to the sixth century B.C.E. indicate another source of slavery in ancient Egypt: self-enslavement. To satisfy a debt, not only would a debtor offer all the property he owned, but he also could offer himself, his family, and his children as slaves if the value of his property was insufficient to repay his loan. Legal documents suggest that debts and the inability to repay loans were the primary motives for this type of enslavement. Another source of slaves were the children born to a slave woman. Children inherited their mothers' freedom status and could not become free men or women regardless of the status of the father.

Very little information survives regarding slave trading in ancient Egypt. According to a document dating to the eighth century B.C.E., a special tax was levied on the sale of 32 slaves. In another document 35 slaves were part of a sale involving of some fields. This transaction took place before the council of magistrates (the *qenbet*) and seems to imply that special registers recorded transactions involving the sale of slaves. Royalty and private individuals alike often handed over slaves to the religious establishment to serve at a temple. Bequest, reassignment, acquisition, and the sale of slaves had to be registered with the *qenbet*. The small community

of workmen at Deir el-Medina included several state-owned and a few privately owned slaves.

Egyptian slave owners had several obligations toward their charges, foremost among which was to legally record the acquisition or relinquishment of slaves at the *qenbet*. As soon as a slave was purchased, the owner gave the slave a name and taught him or her a trade. A literate slave could be promoted to the position of estate manager. The owners were also responsible for the slaves' health, making sure they were adequately nourished and well cared for. A letter from the Eighteenth Dynasty indicates that enslaved children could not be given hard labor.

Egyptian slaves could enjoy a measure of freedom and dignity. They could negotiate transactions and own personal property. For example, the Wilbour Papyrus, a document dating to the New Kingdom (ca. 1550–ca. 1070 B.C.E.) on which is recorded the sale of some agricultural land, lists at least 11 slaves (*hem*) as holders of agricultural land. Slaves could also testify at court. Several appear as witnesses in the legal account of the great tomb robberies at the end of the Twentieth Dynasty (ca. 1196–ca. 1070 B.C.E.). In fact, it was the testimony of these slaves that later implicated their master as the main culprit in these tomb robberies. The slaves were not treated any worse than any of the other individuals named in the document: All were made to swear to the truth, and some were beaten to extract confessions.

Although no extant documents record marriage agreements among enslaved men and women, in the New Kingdom freed slaves could marry into high society. In one instance a king's barber gave his niece in marriage to his former slave, indicating that freed slaves could marry members of their former masters' immediate families.

THE MIDDLE EAST
BY FRANS VAN KOPPEN

Slavery in the sense of legal ownership of persons in the manner of chattel was universally accepted in cultures of the ancient Near East, with slaves being extracted from foreign soil but also legally drawn from among the slave owner's fellow citizens. Notions of race or skin color were immaterial for enslavement, and slavery was in effect the most radical form of control over humans alongside other servile conditions that did not constitute full ownership. Slave labor was in demand at wealthy urban households but was economically less important in the ancient Near East than in the Mediterranean world of classical antiquity.

Ancient slavery and the livelihood of slaves have been studied on the basis of literary texts and law codes, including the legal parts of the Old Testament and numerous archival sources in cuneiform script. The terms for slaves in many of the region's languages primarily connote social status and could be used for any socially inferior individual. This ambiguity means that it is sometimes difficult to distinguish slaves from other people who endured exploitation within the framework of social and economic dependency relationships and whose conditions share characteristics with slavery. Some servile conditions could be temporary; for instance, debt bondsmen labored for their creditors as long as the debt was unsettled, or famine refugees voluntarily accepted a servile status in exchange for food and shelter. Other forms of servitude were permanent, such as those of oblates and serfs. Oblates and serfs are modern terms for categories of dependent people who were attached to the temples of the gods and the soil they tilled, respectively. Their status of property was immutable (oblates were actually branded with the god's symbol) and heritable, but their standing also gave them rights that were denied to chattel slaves, such as protection against separation from their families through sale. The distinctive characteristic of slaves is hence their legal status of chattel, which included the owner's right to sell, donate, or devolve them to his heirs but also to liberate them at will.

Slavery was typically a permanent condition; only few people experienced a transition into or out of slavery. The status of slave was heritable, and most slaves were born to unfree mothers whose offspring belonged to their master unless special provisions had been made. Sources for slaves other than biological reproduction were threefold. The first was the capture of foreigners and the purchase of foreign slaves. Second, fellow countrymen could be obtained as slaves as a result of economic failure, with people being sold into slavery by the head of their household or by themselves. Finally, people could be enslaved for their crimes, a punishment that could be imposed by the head of the household (for example, by fathers punishing disobedient adoptive sons) or by the public authorities.

Foreigners were an important component of the slave population since early times: the cuneiform signs for male and female slave, first recorded around 3000 B.C.E., are pictographs combining the sign "foreign land" with the signs "man" and "woman," respectively. Severed from their remote homelands, foreign slaves were considered loyal and more devoted to their masters than domestically created slaves. Many of them had been captured during foreign military campaigns and were brought into the country as the soldiers' share in the booty, where they could, if not redeemed by their families, be sold profitably on the slave market. Supply for these markets was also in the hands of traders, some of whom are known to have specialized in long-distance trade in people. Not every foreigner, however, was prey to slave agents, as subjects of allied sovereigns partook in the state's protection of its citizens against kidnap for the purpose of enslavement.

The state's care at safeguarding its subjects against involuntary enslavement did not mitigate the fall of insolvent people into slavery. Nonpayment of debts brought the human pledge or the defaulting debtor into a servile condition in the household of the creditor. Their condition was, at least in theory, temporal and would be remedied once the debt had been settled; in practice, however, this was often impossible. The transition of debt servitude into slavery can be repre-

sented in legal texts as a voluntary act of sale, with debtors selling their children or themselves to their creditor with the original debt functioning as their purchase price. This way into slavery was often considered a social abuse, and different solutions were proposed to repair this disorder; for example, there existed the biblical rule of releasing debt slaves in the seventh year and the Mesopotamian "clean-slate acts" that canceled consumptive debts and stipulated the repair of their negative consequences, including the release of debt slaves. These measures were largely ideologically motivated and their implementation usually failed to halt a trend of the rural underprivileged toward economic dependency on the rich and powerful.

Although slaves were owned by temples and the palace, most of them were found in urban residences, where many of them, females in particular, were occupied in household tasks. Some slaves had received training in specialist skills and practiced their trade within the master's household or as hired hands for others, but workshops that employed large numbers of slaves seem to have been uncommon, as was the use of slaves in agriculture. Slaves who were particularly trustworthy could be employed as their owners' agents, take up managerial tasks, and have documents drawn up in their own name on behalf of the family business.

Slaves were sometimes distinguished from free citizens by certain marks, such as a distinct hairstyle or a brand with their owner's name or symbol. The risk of slaves absconding was real; their freedom of movement was often controlled with chains and shackles, and they were mostly not allowed to leave the city unattended. Masters could punish their slaves physically, but they usually did not have the legal power to take a slave's life.

As lifelong members of a household, slaves often developed close ties with their owners, although they were never regarded as part of the family. Slaves could be married, even to freeborn persons, and female slaves could become concubines of the master of the house. This relationship could be legally recognized in a polygamous marriage, where the second wife was regarded as a slave of the main wife but a spouse of the man, and her children were considered the free, legitimate issue of their father. Slaves could also be adopted, most often in combination with their emancipation, with a duty to support their former owner in old age. Termination of slavery was an uncommon phenomenon; however, when freedom was granted, it was most frequently bestowed by the owner.

ASIA AND THE PACIFIC
BY KIRK H. BEETZ

When slavery began or whether the practice always existed in Asia is not known. Many anthropologists assume there were slaves of one sort or another throughout Asia and the Pacific, mostly in the form of people belonging to a particular person or to a particular family. So little is known, however, of the ancient cultures south of China and east of India, as well as of Japan, the Philippines, and other island cultures, that it is possible that there were places where slaves were unknown.

In China the earliest details for slavery come late in its history, from the Han Dynasty (202 B.C.E.–220 C.E.). During the Han Dynasty slaves, tradespeople, and merchants were legally nonpersons, ranking lower in importance to peasants, government officials, professional warriors, nobility, and royalty. Writers during the Han Dynasty often noted, however, that slaves lived better than peasants. The generally cruel conditions for peasants during the Shang Dynasty (ca. 1500–ca. 1045 B.C.E.) and the Zhou Dynasty (ca. 1045–256 B.C.E.) have led some historians to refer to ancient China having a "slave economy" similar to that of ancient Rome, but the actual status of peasants probably put them outside the realm of slavery.

Peasants would sometimes borrow money they could not repay, and the lender could take over their land and require that they work it. Nobles and rich merchants could gather land to themselves this way, and the peasants would work for them with little hope of ever owning land again. Emperors occasionally tried redistribute land to the peasants, but the nobility would just start reacquiring the land. Nonetheless, in times of crisis peasants ranked higher in China's priorities than anyone except the nobility and royalty. It seems that the Chinese government, from the era of the Shang on, recognized that peasants were essential to the nation's survival, and governments usually tried to see to it that peasants were cared for.

Slaves primarily served in households. Rarely did slaves work on farms. The proportion of slaves to the general population was always small, perhaps less than 1 percent of the people. The proportion may have seemed higher to people living in cities because most slaves lived in cities or towns, where they served in the households of nobles and wealthy people.

Relatives of convicted criminals were often enslaved by the government. Government-owned slaves worked to haul barges up and down rivers. They cared for the emperor's horses and dogs and worked as gamekeepers in government parks, especially those used by royalty. In the emperor's court they kept track of water clocks and banged drums to mark the hours of the day, they waited on guests and the royal family, and they opened and closed doors for people walking through the palaces. These duties were fulfilled by both men and women.

During hard times peasants sometimes killed their children because they could not feed them, and they sometimes sold their children into slavery in exchange for money. Others sold themselves into slavery to have food to eat or a place to live. Some merchants traded in slaves even though the government disapproved of the practice. A few emperors tried to abolish the slave trade but failed.

Privately owned slaves were house cleaners, cooks, and kitchen staff. Some were used as bodyguards or to guard ancestral cemeteries. Others waited on their masters or mistresses, helping with hairdressing and other cosmetic tasks. Skilled slaves made ceramics and fabrics for sale. Some own-

ers used slaves to form gangs to batter or even kill their enemies, terrorizing a town or city. Both government-owned and privately owned slaves were sometimes given confidential tasks such as bookkeeping and carrying messages.

It was possible for slaves to earn their own money, but in general a slave was a slave for life, without being able to buy freedom. Slaves typically were regarded as lazy and greedy, and many free people resented that slaves were able to earn their own money, especially when ordinary people had to work to survive while slaves had food and housing even when they did no work.

A similar resentment prevailed in India, where slaves were often regarded as lazy and insolent. As sometimes happened in China, people without financial resources would sell themselves into slavery to have food or a place to live. They often received cash from their new owners, and they were allowed to live freely until the money ran out, at which time they had to work for their owners. They lived much like members of the Sudra caste, as laborers and servants. They were rarely Brahmans (members of the highest Hindu caste) because people were expected to give food and other goods to Brahmans without getting anything in return.

Hindu religious law forbade the mistreatment of slaves. An owner was expected to feed slaves well, to provide them with good clothing, and to give them good quarters in which to live. A slave could be beaten in certain cases, but only on the back. A pious owner would treat his or her slaves well. Under law, slaves were allowed to try to escape once; if they were successful, they were allowed to rejoin their caste. The reality of slave life was often very different from what was required by religious law. Slaves were beaten, maimed, and killed. Any slight to their owners could occasion their torture or death, and their lives were constantly beset by terror.

The royal governments often imported slaves. Both men and women imported from Greece served as palace guards. Women often protected the king's harem of concubines, and sometimes the imported female slaves were themselves made concubines. People could become slaves when they were prisoners of war, but they served only one year of involuntary servitude and were then freed. People convicted of crimes could be sentenced to serve as slaves for a certain time, but they were freed when the time ended. Others who lost lawsuits or bets could become slaves, but they were freed if they paid the fine or bet. Still others became slaves to their creditors when they failed to pay their debts, and they were freed if they managed to pay what they owed. Those who sold themselves into slavery had to buy their freedom. In many cases people remained slaves for life, and children born to them were also slaves.

For many slaves life was one of hard labor. They were expected to haul water from a nearby stream or lake regardless of the weather, to carry loads of goods, and to maintain the homes of their owners. Owners often complained of their slaves' laziness, noting that their slaves tended to watch for sundown, when their labors for the day were supposed to end, rather than attending to their chores. Others complained that slaves in cities were not only lazy but arrogant, using much of their time to earn money of their own while having none of the expenses of feeding, housing, or clothing themselves. Even so, household slaves were often treated like part of their owner's family, and when they became too old to work, they were cared for by their owners.

EUROPE

BY AMY HACKNEY BLACKWELL

Slavery was a fact of life throughout the ancient world. Almost every society had some form of servitude in which people exploited the labor of others. Among ancient Europeans slavery existed but not nearly to the extent that it did in the Mediterranean region. European society was not heavily agricultural or urban, so there was not as much need for labor as there was in the Greek and Roman economies. Many thousands of Celts and Germans became the slaves of Greeks and Romans, who used them in a variety of ways.

The Celts, like many ancient peoples, often enslaved the people they conquered when they moved into a new territory. For example, this may have happened in ancient Ireland when the Celts arrived; some historians believe that the Celts enslaved the prehistoric people to build tombs such as Newgrange. The favored slaves were usually women and children, who were more docile than men and better suited for the domestic tasks the Celts needed performed. Celts would use slaves to gather wood, carry water, cook, weave, and perform sexual favors.

It appears that the Gauls, the Celts who lived in France, were using slaves during the eighth and seventh centuries B.C.E. Slaves came from conquered nations in the region. Well-to-do Gauls used women and children as domestic slaves to do basic household chores. Noble families would exchange gifts of slaves as a way of solidifying friendships. Historians believe that Gauls of this period engaged in trade of slaves with the Etruscans in Italy, and some further contend that the Gauls were still engaging in the slave trade with Italy during later Roman times. During the late second and first centuries B.C.E. Gauls are said to have sold their brethren as slaves in exchange for wine. Some 15,000 Gauls may have been enslaved in this way. It is not known whether these slaves were family members of the traders or if they were already slaves of the Gauls.

The Celtic peoples had clear laws about slavery. They divided themselves into several social classes, including nobles, free property owners, and freemen who did not own property. The bottom of the Celtic social ladder was occupied by people who were not free. Some nonfree people were not slaves at all; these individuals did not hold the full rights of the group, but they were still allowed to support themselves by farming on tribal lands. In Ireland, for example, there was a class of nonfree farmers called *fudirs*. These people were not exactly slaves in the modern sense, in that their master could not buy and sell them, but they had almost no legal rights.

They worked the land for their master and were forced to pay rent or tribute every year. This rent supposedly obligated the master to feed and house them. However, their master could throw them off the land at any time and for any reason. When a *fudir* died, the land he occupied did not pass to his children unless the master chose to allow them to stay.

Other individuals were genuine slaves, that is, owned by other people and forced to work without wages. Celtic law set values for slaves; male slaves were considered more valuable than female ones. Celtic slaves were usually Celtic peoples who had lost their liberty through a variety of causes, such as financial misfortune or losing in battle. Sometimes Celts imported slaves from other areas, but usually slaves were local. Occasionally parents sold their children into slavery if they felt they needed the money. Slave traders often raided farms at night to steal children and sell them for slaves. These raiders typically attacked houses on the coast of Roman Britain (modern-day Wales) and carried their slaves over to Ireland. The Irish Saint Patrick (fifth century C.E.) was himself stolen as a boy from his family's estate in Britain and spent several years working as a slave shepherd in Ireland before escaping and taking on a religious vocation. Some sources say that it was a law in Ireland that slaves were freed every seventh year and suggest that Patrick may have been freed under this law instead of escaping.

Both categories of slave were at a severe disadvantage under the Celtic legal system. A person's rank determined the value of his evidence and whether he would be allowed to testify at all. A freeman could testify against a *fudir*, but a

SLAVERY AND DIVINE VISIONS

A youth spent in slavery produced what many consider to be Ireland's greatest saint. Born in Roman Britain (modern-day Wales), Saint Patrick was a teenager when he was stolen from his home and sent to Ireland to work as the slave of a pig farmer. He ate the pigs' food and dressed in whatever rags he could scrounge up. He was always hungry and cold.

In his misery, Patrick prayed to God 100 times a day and 100 times a night. After a few years he began to see visions telling him that he should escape. These visions instructed him to walk to the sea, where he would find a ship waiting to take him away. The visions were persuasive and certainly more attractive than his current life as a slave, so Patrick walked away from his pigs and continued walking to the ocean. Sure enough, there was a ship waiting to take him to Europe. He sailed away and became a priest, but Ireland was deeply ingrained in his soul. He devoted the rest of his life to converting Ireland's people to Christianity.

fudir was not allowed to testify in response. Punishments for slaves who committed crimes were harsher than those meted out to freemen.

The Roman historian Tacitus (ca. 56–ca. 120 C.E.) observed that the Germans kept and used slaves. According to Tacitus, when Germans defeated enemies in battle the losers would go into voluntary slavery, allowing the victors to bind them and sell them. The victors always sold or traded away such slaves because they would have been ashamed to keep them around. German slaves lived in their own households, and their masters treated them as tenants; each slave was required to pay his master a yearly tribute of grain, cattle, or cloth, but otherwise the slaves were free to live as they liked. Slaves did not perform the master's household duties, as Roman slaves did. Tacitus remarked that Germans did not chain or beat their slaves or work them to death. Masters occasionally did kill their slaves in anger; this was apparently acceptable behavior and not considered worthy of punishment.

During the Roman Empire, German society adopted many Roman laws concerning slavery. German slave owners of this time treated their slaves much as Romans did, sometimes paying them and offering them opportunities for social advancement. Slaves were allowed to marry free people, though this meant that the free partner would become a slave. A woman slave owner was not allowed to marry her own slave, and sexual contact with slaves was discouraged. German men, however, had ample sexual contact with their female slaves.

Many ancient Europeans experienced slavery under the more powerful and better organized Greeks and Romans. Some 40,000 Gauls, for example, became slaves of the Romans after Julius Caesar's army won the battle of Alesia in 52 B.C.E. Historians estimate that Caesar may have enslaved half a million Gauls throughout his career. During the early Roman Empire huge numbers of European slaves passed into Roman territory. Romans and Greeks appreciated the exotic appearance of slaves from northern Europe and admired the strength of large German men, who made excellent soldiers and gladiators.

GREECE

BY JEFFREY S. CARNES

For the Greeks, as for most human societies until quite recent times, slavery was an accepted fact of life and, with rare exceptions, it was not subject to analysis or moral criticism. Greece, however, stands out for the degree to which slavery was central to the economy, and every Greek polis had a significant number of slaves, both agricultural and urban.

There existed in Greece both chattel slavery, in which the slave was the legal property of another person, and a number of intermediate forms of servitude, in which a person was forced to labor for another while still remaining technically free; in other words, an individual was not subject to sale. One such form was debt bondage, in which a free person who was unable to pay off a debt came under the power of another until such time as the debt was paid. In practice, interest on a debt could turn this into a form of long-term or permanent servitude, and the creation of a "sharecropper" class in many Greek cities was a key factor in the rise of tyrants and other political reformers. For example, in Athens the lawmaker Solon (ca. 630–ca. 560 B.C.E.) canceled debts to eliminate debt bondage. In Sparta nonchattel slavery took a political form: A permanent noncitizen class—the Helots, literally "the captured ones"—was created as a result of Sparta's conquest of Messene in the 10th through seventh centuries B.C.E. Helots were forced to perform agricultural labor for their Spartan masters (who were themselves forbidden from engaging in such labor), and they were subject to terror at the hands of the Spartans. Helots were not, however, subject to sale or removal; on the contrary, they were bound to the land, and their status was akin to that of serfs.

Chattel slavery dates back to the earliest historical records. Indeed, the initial written records of most societies reveal slavery as an already existing institution. Documents from Mycenae, dating to before 1200 B.C.E., refer to slaves, and Homer's *Iliad*, the earliest work in the Greek literary tradition, begins with a dispute over a slave. The Homeric world shows the Greek attitude toward slavery both explicitly and through its silences: no one questions the morality of slavery, and the lot of slaves is pitied. One of the distinguishing factors of Greek slavery (as opposed to the more familiar model from the pre–Civil War United States) was that anyone could become a slave.

Wars were frequent, and those captured in war were typically ransomed (if their families could afford to pay), kept as slaves by their captors, or sold on the open market. Piracy and brigandage were also common throughout antiquity, and anyone whose fortune was sufficiently bad could wind up a slave. There was some sentiment (particularly from the fourth century B.C.E. onward) that Greeks should not enslave their fellow Greeks, but this was by no means a hard-and-fast rule. By the fourth century B.C.E. it seems that most slaves in Athens were non-Greek, coming instead from a variety of areas, particularly those to the north and east of mainland Greece, including Thrace, Scythia, and Asia Minor. Slaves were not normally permitted to have families, so most of the slave population was purchased rather than homebred, and the slave trade was a thriving one throughout antiquity.

Slaves worked in every sector of the economy, and only a few occupations (such as mining, which was harsh and dangerous work) were viewed as exclusively servile. In Athens state-owned slaves formed the police force and served as clerks in certain courts, but there was no large slave-dominated civil service bureaucracy as there was in Rome. Since Greece was an agricultural society, most slaves worked on farms, but in cities they formed part of the industrial labor force. The largest factory we know of produced shields and employed a labor force of 120 slaves, but many enterprises employed a mix of slave and free labor. Inscriptions for public

Apollo (left), a Scythian slave (middle), and the satyr Marsyas (Alison Frantz Photographic Collection, American School of Classical Studies at Athens)

works projects, which list the status of the laborers, provide ample evidence for this. Household slaves were generally better off than those who worked in the fields, and their duties could include child care and education. The loyal household servant became a common character on the dramatic stage.

Buying a living human being was not very expensive: inscriptional evidence from the late fifth century B.C.E. shows prices below 100 drachmas (perhaps three months' wages for a semiskilled worker), so slave owning was widespread. The slave population in Athens is estimated to have been at a third of the total inhabitants of the city, perhaps 100,000 in the late fifth century B.C.E.; even states with less developed industry must still have had a large percentage of slaves. The absence of large-scale slave revolts is perhaps a consequence of the ethnic diversity of the slave population. Revolts were more likely when large numbers of slaves shared a common language and culture, as the major slave revolts in the Roman world and the Helot rebellions in Sparta made clear. While organized resistance was rare, running away was not: some 20,000 Athenian slaves escaped during the chaos caused by the Spartan capture of Dhekélia. Many of those who escaped

were said to have been skilled craftsmen who would presumably have sought employment elsewhere as freemen. Professional slave catchers were as much a part of the slave economy as were slave traders.

It was possible for Greek slaves to obtain their freedom, though this was not nearly as common as in the Roman world. In some cases slaves were freed in their owners' wills, and in others they were able to purchase their freedom; typically they were denied citizenship and would have a status equivalent to that of other free noncitizens. The case of Pasion, an extremely wealthy freed slave and banker of the fourth century B.C.E. who was granted Athenian citizenship because of his generosity to the city, was exceptional, as was the granting of freedom to slaves who fought on behalf of Athens in the battle of Arginusae.

The intellectual revolution of the late fifth century B.C.E. brought the institution of slavery into question for the first time. Aristotle's defense of slavery can be seen as a response to these issues: He refers to slaves as "animate tools" and argues that some people are by nature suited to slavery, which runs counter to the usual Greek perception that anyone could become a slave. In political theory and popular discourse the concept of slavery was an important one for the definition of citizenship, since the slave was everything the citizen was not: unfree, forced to labor for another, and lacking enforceable rights.

ROME

BY PAUL MCKECHNIE

Most slaves in Rome were foreign in origin, captured in war or bought in slave markets. In the early days it was also possible for a Roman citizen to become a slave; the Twelve Tables (a code of laws of the early Roman Republic, established around 450 B.C.E.) allowed a creditor who was not paid to sell the debtor "beyond the Tiber" as a slave. Within Roman territory it was possible for loan agreements to involve a kind of voluntary mortgage on the debtor's person (*nexum*). A borrower who failed to pay became a debt bondsman but was still a Roman citizen of a sort and not exactly the property of the creditor. The historian Livy (59 B.C.E.–17 C.E.) tells of the abolition of *nexum* in his *Annals of the Roman People*. Livy's account describes public outrage at the sexual abuse of a debt bondsman, whereas the sexual abuse of a slave would not have provoked such outrage. An important disadvantage of the system was that it made Roman debt bondsmen ineligible to fight in the Roman army. The *lex Poetilia Papiria*, a law passed in 326 B.C.E., ended the system of *nexum*.

Slaves, as distinct from debt bondsmen, were the property of their masters and could be bought and sold. In principle, they had no rights at all and could be punished or abused exactly as their masters chose. The emperor Antoninus Pius (r. 138–161 C.E.) changed the law that had given masters the power of life and death over their slaves and introduced the principle that if a master killed his slave without good reason, he would be subject to the same penalty as if he had killed another person's slave; in effect, he could be fined up to the value of the slave.

Slaves were a source of unpaid labor anywhere for the Romans: in homes, in agriculture, and in supporting the army. They were not expected or trusted to fight for Rome. Slaves who survived being captured in war were usually women and children because it was normal for men captured in war to be put to death if there was no one to pay a ransom for them; keeping them alive was a risk their captors would not usually take.

In the third and (especially) the second centuries B.C.E. the Romans' successes in expanding their conquests across the Mediterranean resulted in a great influx of slaves to Italy. The Roman upper classes were able to buy larger estates and work them with slave gangs. The disadvantage was that one had to be a landowner to serve in the army, and as Roman and Italian peasants sold their property to the rich their absence from the military ranks threatened to weaken Rome. Gaius Marius (ca. 157–86 B.C.E.), who was consul seven times between 107 and 86, solved this problem by making it possible for unpropertied Romans to join the army.

Although they could not fight for the army, slaves could be made to fight for sport. Gladiators, who fought in the amphitheaters, were usually either slaves or condemned criminals. Along with his law discouraging killing slaves, Antoninus Pius legislated against sending a slave to the gladiator school without a good reason; making a slave into a gladiator was a punishment virtually equivalent to death.

Life for most slaves was difficult most of the time, but the Roman system of slavery had features that presented opportunities for some slaves. A slave could own no property, but Roman law recognized something called a *peculium*, which was in effect a slave's own money. In a case where, for example, a master went into business with his slave, the fact that some of the capital behind the business was the slave's *peculium* might prevent the master from being liable for all legal claims that might arise against the slave in the course of business. Even though the idea behind a *peculium* was perhaps to protect masters from liability for their slaves' mistakes, in practice a successful slave might manage to use his *peculium* to buy his freedom from his master.

During the Imperial Period (after 31 B.C.E.) the Romans seem to have freed many of their slaves. The emperor Augustus (r. 27 B.C.E.–14 C.E.) was behind the *lex Fufia Caninia* of 2 C.E., a law that limited the number of slaves a master could manumit in his lifetime, and the *lex Aelia Sentia* of 4 C.E., which made 30 the minimum age at which a slave could be manumitted. When the slave of a Roman citizen was manumitted, he became a Roman citizen himself. Slaves had one name, while characteristically Roman citizens had three names: *praenomen* (first name), *nomen gentilicium* (family name), and *cognomen* (last name). A freedman (*libertus* or *libertinus*) had his original name as his *cognomen*, and he took his first two citizen names from his former master. Freedmen had most of the rights of freeborn Roman citizens—for example, the right to vote, to make wills, to marry Roman citizens, and to produce legitimate-citizen children—but they could not hold political office.

Slaves were important at the very heart of the Roman Empire. When the first emperor, Augustus, took over, he used his own slaves and the resources of his own household to administer the empire by, for example, making appointments, keeping accounts, directing the army, keeping records, and managing relations with the Senate and political officeholders.

He and later emperors based bureaus that were virtually government ministries in the palace under the direction of their own freedmen: The *ab epistulis* (minister of the provinces) managed correspondence with Roman governors across the empire; the *a rationibus* (minister of finance) kept the emperor's accounts; and the *a libellis* (minister of justice) processed the petitions that came to the emperor from across the world. As the first and second centuries C.E. went forward, emperors brought in Roman knights instead of freedmen to hold many important posts in the palace, but they were cautious enough to keep the money in the hands of someone they could rely on—one of their own freedmen.

Image of Psyche on a lead coffin lid, Roman; made in Lebanon during the second to third centuries C.E., said to be from Sidon, Lebanon; the lead is thought to be an import from Spain or Sardinia, where there were extensive mines worked by Roman slaves. (© The Trustees of the British Museum)

THE AMERICAS
BY KIRK H. BEETZ

It is not known when slavery began in the Americas. It is possible that the first migrants to the New World already practiced slavery. How ancient Americans north of Mexico practiced slavery is something that anthropologists infer from archaeological information and the practices of Americans when first recorded by Europeans. The earliest peoples to populate the forests and grasslands of North America were nomadic. Their slaves probably would have been people taken captive from other groups during raids that may have been staged for the very purpose of taking slaves. Because there were no beasts of burden native to North America, the captives would have been responsible for carrying goods during migrations.

Some early nomadic people settled and built one village to inhabit during warm months and another for cold months. Others settled year round into permanent villages. Slaves in such villages might have been responsible for mundane chores such as cleaning and cooking. The ancient villagers may have raided other villages or preyed on nomads, taking captives, possibly children. When a village had a shortage of women, girls and young women would sometimes be taken to provide men with mates and to bring in children to repopulate a village that had been decimated by natural disasters or warfare. It is possible that both nomadic peoples and settled peoples had rituals in which slaves could become free members of the nations that held them.

The region for which there is the most information about slavery is Mesoamerica, made up of parts of modern Mexico and Central America. Perhaps the greatest ancient Mesoamerican city was Teotihuacán, in Mexico. Its peak of power was from the first to the seventh century C.E. It was the greatest military power in Mesoamerica during that period, and it forced distant Mayan communities to pay tribute. It seems that the government of Teotihuacán preferred goods such as jade, obsidian, and brightly colored feathers, but sometimes a city did not have enough goods for tribute and sent instead human beings. These slaves were probably used as human sacrifices. The other aspects of slavery in Teotihuacán are unclear, but it is probable that through debt or conviction of a crime, a person could become a slave, and that such a slave might have had the opportunity to earn his or her freedom. In the case of people enslaved because of crimes, their slavery might have been limited to a specified period of service.

The Maya had a long-lived culture, and their practice of slavery almost certainly varied as customs changed over time and from one Mayan city-state to another, but Mayan writings and archaeological evidence allow for some generalizations about how the Maya practiced slavery. Slaves were at the bottom of the social structure. Commoners caught in battle and then enslaved were possibly regarded as almost nonhuman, ranking no higher than animals and perhaps lower than jaguars and other animals associated with Mayan mythology. They existed only to serve their owners, such as the individual warriors who had captured them. During festivals they were often sacrificed. To the Maya these sacrifices, which involved torture, elevated the victims from the status of commoners to temporary gods. If slaves survived long enough, they could earn freedom either through clemency or through good service to their owners.

Nobles captured in battle might also be enslaved. After being tortured, they were usually sacrificed, because their deaths brought prestige to those who captured them, to their cities, and to their kings. Much Mayan warfare was conducted for the purpose of capturing enemy nobility, and warriors who captured nobles often added the nobles' names to their own, enhancing their standing in their community. A captured noble or member of a royal family rarely served long as a slave because sacrificing him or her to a god was valuable in winning the god's favor.

The Maya had an elaborate social structure with a multitude of customs that governed behavior and specified the duties of each member of society. Slavery involved many such customs as well as laws. Children without parents almost always became slaves. People convicted of crimes could become slaves of the people they had victimized. It is possible that people could voluntarily become slaves, perhaps because of burdensome debts or the loss of place in a community. For instance, tradespersons who lost the ability to practice their craft would no longer have a niche to fill in Mayan society.

There is disagreement among archaeologists about how slaves who were not prisoners of war were regarded and treated. These disagreements may stem from variations in Maya culture over hundreds of years. One view is that these slaves were cruelly abused and counted as nothing in Mayan society. They were worked to death, tormented, and sacrificed. They could be killed any time or for any reason by their owners. If someone other than the owner killed a slave, that killer took the place of the slave.

Another view holds that slaves were protected by laws that prohibited an owner from killing a slave anytime the owner wanted to do so. The slaves could hold important positions in households, even becoming the directors of the estates of wealthy people. They could earn their own money, save it, and spend it as they wished. Indeed, the law seems to have specified that a person was a slave only until he paid off a debt he owed someone. Slaves could be as well dressed and well fed as their owners. An owner who did not properly care for a slave could lose the slave, who might be freed, and in extreme cases might find himself the property of his former slave. Thus, slaves were not beaten or otherwise abused. In some cases, if slaves died before their debts were paid, their families would be expected to provide a substitute. How long the substitutes served is unclear; the substitute either served until the debt was paid or was replaced periodically by another member of the family until the debt was paid.

Slavery was practiced in South America, but to what extent has yet to be established. For many South American groups the customs regarding slaves would be much like those of the nomads and villagers of North America. Girls especially were valued, becoming sexual partners of their captors or possibly serving as a sacrifice to the gods. The Moche culture of about 100 to 600 C.E. seems to have practiced slavery. They may have raided other cultures to obtain captives who would be ritually sacrificed. Otherwise, slaves probably became servants in prosperous households.

See also AGRICULTURE; CALENDARS AND CLOCKS; CHILDREN; CRIME AND PUNISHMENT; DEATH AND BURIAL PRACTICES; DRAMA AND THEATER; ECONOMY; EMPLOYMENT AND LABOR; FAMILY; FOREIGNERS AND BARBARIANS; GENDER STRUCTURES AND ROLES; GOVERNMENT ORGANIZATION; LAWS AND LEGAL CODES; LITERATURE; MIGRATION AND POPULATION MOVEMENTS; MILITARY; NOMADIC AND PASTORAL SOCIETIES; OCCUPATIONS; RELIGION AND COSMOLOGY; SETTLEMENT PATTERNS; SOCIAL ORGANIZATION; SPORTS AND RECREATION; TOWNS AND VILLAGES; TRADE AND EXCHANGE; WAR AND CONQUEST.

The Middle East

~ *The Code of the Nesilim, excerpt*
(Hittite, 1650–1500 B.C.E.) ~

1. If anyone slay a man or woman in a quarrel, he shall bring this one. He shall also give four persons, either men or women, he shall let them go to his home.

2. If anyone slay a male or female slave in a quarrel, he shall bring this one and give two persons, either men or women, he shall let them go to his home.

3. If anyone smite a free man or woman and this one die, he shall bring this one and give two persons, he shall let them go to his home.

4. If anyone smite a male or female slave, he shall bring this one also and give one person, he shall let him or her go to his home.

5. If anyone slay a merchant of Hatti, he shall give one and a half pounds of silver, he shall let it go to his home.

6. If anyone blind a free man or knock out his teeth, formerly they would give one pound of silver, now he shall give twenty half-shekels of silver. . . .

8. If anyone blind a male or female slave or knock out their teeth, he shall give ten half-shekels of silver, he shall let it go to his home. . . .

10. If anyone injure a man so that he cause him suffering, he shall take care of him. Yet he shall give him a man in his place, who shall work for him in his house until he recovers. But if he recover, he shall give him six half-shekels of silver. And to the physician this one shall also give the fee. . . .

17. If anyone cause a free woman to miscarry, if it be the tenth month, he shall give ten half-shekels of silver, if it be the fifth month, he shall give five half-shekels of silver.

(continued)

(continues)

18. If anyone cause a female slave to miscarry, if it be the tenth month, he shall give five half-shekels of silver. . . .

20. If any man of Hatti steal a Nesian slave and lead him here to the land of Hatti, and his master discover him, he shall give him twelve half-shekels of silver, he shall let it go to his home.

21. If anyone steal a slave of a Luwian from the land of Luwia, and lead him here to the land of Hatti, and his master discover him, he shall take his slave only. . . .

24. If a male or female slave run away, he at whose hearth his master finds him or her, shall give fifty half-shekels of silver a year. . . .

31. If a free man and a female slave be fond of each other and come together and he take her for his wife and they set up house and get children, and afterward they either become hostile or come to close quarters, and they divide the house between them, the man shall take the children, only one child shall the woman take.

32. If a slave take a woman as his wife, their case is the same. The majority of the children to the wife and one child to the slave.

33. If a slave take a female slave their case is the same. The majority of children to the female slave and one child to the slave.

34. If a slave convey the bride price to a free son and take him as husband for his daughter, nobody dare surrender him to slavery. . . .

36. If a slave convey the bride price to a free son and take him as husband for his daughter, nobody dare surrender him to slavery. . . .

98. If a free man set a house ablaze, he shall build the house, again. And whatever is inside the house, be it a man, an ox, or a sheep that perishes, nothing of these he need compensate.

99. If a slave set a house ablaze, his master shall compensate for him. The nose of the slave and his ears they shall cut off, and give him back to his master. But if he do not compensate, then he shall give up this one. . . .

170. If a free man kill a serpent and speak the name of another, he shall give one pound of silver; if a slave, this one shall die. . . .

173. If anyone oppose the judgment of the king, his house shall become a ruin. If anyone oppose the judgment of a lord, his head shall be cut off. If a slave rise against his master, he shall go into the pit. . . .

191. If a free man picks up now this woman, now that one, now in this country, then in that country, there shall be no punishment if they came together sexually willingly. . . .

194. If a free man pick up female slaves, now one, now another, there is no punishment for intercourse. If brothers sleep with a free woman, together, or one after the other, there is no punishment. If father and son sleep with a female slave or harlot, together, or one after the other, there is no punishment. . . .

From: Oliver J. Thatcher, ed., *The Library of Original Sources*, Vol. 3, *The Roman World* (Milwaukee, Wisc.: University Research Extension Co., 1901).

Asia and the Pacific   ∽ *Kautilya: excerpt from the Arthashastra (ca. 250 B.C.E.)* ∽

BOOK III, CHAPTER 13, RULES REGARDING SLAVES AND LABORERS

The selling or mortgaging by kinsmen of the life of a Shudra who is not a born slave, and has not attained majority, but is an Arya in birth shall be punished with a fine of twelve panas; of a Vaisya, twenty-four panas; of a Kshatriya, thirty-six panas; and of a Brahman, forty-eight panas. . . . Any person who has voluntarily enslaved himself shall, if he runs away, be a slave for life. Similarly any person whose life has been mortgaged by others shall, if he runs away twice, be a slave for life. . . . Deceiving a slave of his money or depriving him of the privileges he can exercise as an Arya, shall be punished with half the fine levied for enslaving the life of an Arya. . . . Employing a slave to carry the dead or to sweep ordure, urine, or the leavings of food; or a female slave to attend on her master while he is bathing naked; or hurting or abusing him or her, or violating the chastity of a female slave shall cause the forfeiture of the value paid for him or her. Violation of the chastity of nurses, female cooks, or female servants of the class of joint cultivators shall at once earn their liberty for them. Violence towards an attendant of high birth shall entitle him to run away. . . . When a man commits or helps another to commit rape with a girl or a female slave pledged to him, he shall not only forfeit the purchase-value, but also pay a certain amount of money to her and a fine of twice the amount of sulka to the government. . . .

From: Kautilya, *Kautilya's Arthashastra*, 2nd ed., trans. R. Shamasastry (Mysore, India: Wesleyan Mission Press, 1923).

Greece

∼ Aristotle, excerpt from "On Slavery" (from The Politics, ca. 330 B.C.E.) ∼

Let us first speak of master and slave, looking to the needs of practical life and also seeking to attain some better theory of their relation than exists at present. . . . Property is a part of the household, and the art of acquiring property is a part of the art of managing the household; for no man can live well, or indeed live at all, unless he be provided with necessaries. And so, in the arrangement of the family, a slave is a living possession, and property a number of such instruments; and the slave is himself an instrument which takes precedence of all other instruments. . . . The master is only the master of the slave; he does not belong to him, whereas the slave is not only the slave of his master, but wholly belongs to him. Hence we see what is the nature and office of a slave; he who is by nature not his own but another's man, is by nature a slave; and he may be said to be another's man who, being a human being, is also a possession. And a possession may be defined as an instrument of action, separable from the possessor.

But is there anyone thus intended by nature to be a slave, and for whom such a condition is expedient and right, or rather is not all slavery a violation of nature? There is no difficulty in answering this question, on grounds both of reason and of fact. For that some should rule and others be ruled is a thing not only necessary, but expedient; from the hour of their birth, some are marked out for subjection, others for rule. . . . Again, the male is by nature superior, and the female inferior; and the one rules, and the other is ruled; this principle, of necessity, extends to all mankind.

Where then there is such a difference as that between soul and body, or between men and animals (as in the case of those whose business is to use their body, and who can do nothing better), the lower sort are by nature slaves, and it is better for them as for all inferiors that they should be under the rule of a master. For he who can be, and therefore is, another's and he who participates in rational principle enough to apprehend, but not to have, such a principle, is a slave by nature. Whereas the lower animals cannot even apprehend a principle; they obey their instincts. And indeed the use made of slaves and of tame animals is not very different; for both with their bodies minister to the needs of life. Nature would like to distinguish between the bodies of freemen and slaves, making the one strong for servile labor, the other upright, and although useless for such services, useful for political life in the arts both of war and peace. But the opposite often happens—that some have the souls and others have the bodies of free men. And doubtless if men differed from one another in the mere forms of their bodies as much as the statues of the gods do from men, all would acknowledge that the inferior class should be slaves of the superior. It is clear, then, that some men are by nature free, and others slaves, and that for these latter slavery is both expedient and right.

There is a slave or slavery by law as well as by nature. The law of which I speak is a sort of convention—the law by which whatever is taken in war is supposed to belong to the victors. But this right many jurists impeach, as they would an orator who brought forward an unconstitutional measure: they detest the notion that, because one man has the power of doing violence and is superior in brute strength, another shall be his slave and subject. Even among philosophers there is a difference of opinion. The origin of the dispute, and what makes the views invade each other's territory, is as follows: in some sense virtue, when furnished with means, has actually the greatest power of exercising force; and as superior power is only found where there

(continued)

(continues)

is superior excellence of some kind, power seems to imply virtue, and the dispute to be simply one about justice (for it is due to one party identifying justice with goodwill while the other identifies it with the mere rule of the stronger). If these views are thus set out separately, the other views have no force or plausibility against the view that the superior in virtue ought to rule, or be master.

Others, clinging, as they think, simply to a principle of justice (for law and custom are a sort of justice), assume that slavery in accordance with the custom of war is justified by law, but at the same moment they deny this. For what if the cause of the war be unjust? And again, no one would ever say he is a slave who is unworthy to be a slave. Were this the case, men of the highest rank would be slaves and the children of slaves if they or their parents chance to have been taken captive and sold. Wherefore Hellenes do not like to call Hellenes slaves, but confine the term to barbarians. Yet, in using this language, they really mean the natural slave of whom we spoke at first; for it must be admitted that some are slaves everywhere, others nowhere. The same principle applies to nobility. Hellenes regard themselves as noble everywhere, and not only in their own country, but they deem the barbarians noble only when at home, thereby implying that there are two sorts of nobility and freedom, the one absolute, the other relative.

From: Aristotle, *The Politics of Aristotle*, trans. Benjamin Jowett (New York: Colonial Press, 1900).

FURTHER READING

H. D. Baker, "Degrees of Freedom: Slavery in Mid-First Millennium B.C. Mesopotamia," *World Archaeology* 33 (2001): 18–26.

Keith R. Bradley, *Slavery and Society at Rome* (New York: Cambridge University Press, 1994).

Daphne Nash Briggs, "Metals, Salt, and Slaves: Economic Links between Gaul and Italy from the Eighth to the Late Sixth Centuries B.C.," *Oxford Journal of Archaeology* 22, no. 3 (2003): 243–259.

Muhammad A. Dandamaev, *Slavery in Babylonia: From Nabopolassar to Alexander the Great (626–331 B.C.),* (DeKalb: Northern Illinois University Press, 1984).

M. I. Finley, ed., *Classical Slavery* (London and Totowa, N.J.: Frank Cass, 1987).

N.R.E. Fisher, *Slavery in Classical Greece* (London: Duckworth, 1993).

Yvon Garlan, *Slavery in Ancient Greece*, trans. Janet Lloyd (Ithaca, N.Y.: Cornell University Press, 1988).

Paul E. Lovejoy, *The Transformations in Slavery: A History of Slavery in Africa* (Cambridge, U.K.: Cambridge University Press, 1983).

R. Westbrook, "Slave and Master in Ancient Near Eastern Law," *Chicago-Kent Law Review* 70 (1995): 1631–1676.

► social collapse and abandonment

INTRODUCTION

Throughout the world archaeologists discover the remains of human settlements that were abandoned at some point in ancient history. These remains include homes, artifacts, middens (that is, trash piles), piles of shells, figurines, household objects, tombs, and public buildings. After studying their discoveries, archaeologists and historians conclude that the people who lived there either abandoned the settlement or died. Even great empires such as the Roman Empire at some point collapsed. While the Romans themselves continued to exist on the Italian peninsula, their empire around the Mediterranean Sea shattered, and the civilizations they had conquered gained their independence from Rome.

Social collapse and the abandonment occurred for various reasons. A common cause was a catastrophic natural disaster, such as an earthquake, volcanic eruption, flood, fire, or tsunami (in coastal regions). Perhaps the most famous example is the eruption of Mount Vesuvius in 79 C.E., a volcano whose ash and lava buried the Roman cities of Pompeii and Herculaneum, entombing people almost literally in their tracks. Natural disasters also include plagues, which often took hold during times of warfare and social unrest. In response, people from the surrounding countryside fled their villages and hamlets to take refuge in nearby cities. The cities, however, were not equipped to handle a large influx of people. Hunger became commonplace, since rural people were no longer producing food. Conditions often became crowded and unsanitary so that disease was easily spread. A plague of this nature killed a quarter of the population of ancient Athens, severely weakening the Greek empire.

Sometimes social collapse and abandonment was a gradual process, often brought about by climatic change. As a region became colder or warmer, rainfall amounts changed dramatically, affecting the flora and fauna of the region. Good examples are provided by parts of Egypt and Mesoamerica, where lush, green areas turned into harsh desert over relatively short periods of time, forcing people to move. Even comparatively minor cooling or warming could play havoc with agriculture, leading to crop failures that forced people to abandon their settlements in search of new farmland. When such changes occurred over a wide region, entire peoples could disappear. Some of these changes were caused by human activity. When farmland was overworked or forests were cleared, the result was soil erosion, flooding, and other disruptions that wiped out communities. Of course, these changes worked in the other direction; as land formerly covered by glaciers warmed and the glaciers receded, new communities of people moved in.

Warfare, too, often led to the collapse of societies. For nearly 3,000 years, Egypt stood at the summit of human civilization. But beginning in the Late Dynastic period Egypt could no longer defend its empire. Successive wars and occupations by the Assyrians, Persians, and finally Greeks led to the end of dynastic rule and the collapse of Egypt as a major world power. The Romans suffered a similar fate when their empire split under the weight of its own sheer size and finally collapsed when it could no longer fend off Germanic peoples from the north.

AFRICA

by Michael J. O'Neal

The peoples of ancient sub-Saharan Africa lived primarily as hunter-gatherers until about the second century B.C.E. Accordingly, they did not form cities or permanent settlements that expanded into empires or dominant civilizations. Housing and other structures were built with temporary material, such as mud and wattle, rather than the stone and brick used by some other cultures. Thus, little can be known in detail about the collapse and abandonment of settlements in the ancient sub-Sahara, although social scientists can make inferences about the processes that led them.

One such process was probably environmental degradation. Although the sub-Sahara was rich in resources that allowed people to subsist and even thrive as hunters and gatherers, it was inevitable that as the population of a given area increased, resources were strained, particularly the food supply. As game animals became scarcer and native plants were exhausted for their food value, communities would simply pick up, abandon the region they inhabited, and move on to a new region, where the process began again.

Similar processes affected the ironworking cultures of the sub-Sahara. This region was unique in that it seems to have skipped the Bronze Age that was so important to the development of other world cultures and passed directly from the Stone Age to the Iron Age. Iron smelting, however, requires high heat in furnaces. The most common fuel used to fire these furnaces was wood—and wood in massive amounts. The result was deforestation in the area immediately surrounding an ironworking community. As time went on, firewood had to be brought to the site from farther and farther away. This deforestation led to soil erosion and the disappearance of game, making it increasingly difficult for surrounding populations to feed themselves.

Another process that led to social collapse and abandonment was climate change. The most noteworthy example in ancient Africa had to do with the Sahara. For thousands of years this vast region has been a harsh, forbidding desert. It was not always this way. Until about 3000 B.C.E. much of the Sahara was fertile grassland that supported populations of people. In the area that is modern-day Mauritania, for example, an early Berber culture called the Bafour survived by farming and grazing herds. Then the climate began to change, the rains disappeared, and the desert grew relentlessly southward (overcultivation and overgrazing of the land may have contributed to its decline). The Bafour had to abandon the region. Many people simply moved to urban centers, including those of Egypt, where they and their descendants forged a new kind of life. Historians believe that the descendants of the Bafour include the Imraguen, who became fishermen on the African coasts; the Toucouleur, who moved to Senegal; and the Wolof peoples, who settled in Gambia, Senegal, and Mauritania. All three of these ethnic groups survive in the 21st century. The process was intensified as the Berber people from the north, themselves facing environmental degradation and political turmoil, expanded southward in the third and fourth centuries C.E., driving out surviving members of the indigenous groups. This example illustrates the complex movement of peoples as they faced crisis, abandoned their communities, and were absorbed into other cultures.

Disease and famine, too, contributed to the collapse of ancient African civilizations. A noteworthy example is the Nok civilization, which emerged in modern-day Nigeria in about 500 B.C.E., survived into the Common Era, and then mysteriously disappeared. The Nok were an advanced civilization best known for ironworking and, especially, terra-cotta sculptures. Historians do not know with any certainty why the Nok simply disappeared, but they speculate that famine or disease led to a sharp decline of the population and the merger of the Nok with the Yoruba people. Famine and disease are mutually reinforcing; food shortages make hungry people more susceptible to disease, and as people die, less and less food can be produced. A civilization weakened in this way could not survive.

Finally, warfare and the desire for empire led to the collapse of African civilizations. A good example is provided by Kush, a region just south of the Egyptian Empire. The Kushites developed a flourishing culture between about 1700 and 1500 B.C.E., primarily because Egypt was under the control of the Hyksos, a Semitic people from Asia. However, when the Egyptians expelled the Hyksos, they set their sights on Kush, wanting control of the region not only as a buffer to protect their southern border but also as a trading colony. Then, in about 1000 B.C.E., the Kushites again asserted their independence, unified their kingdom, moved their capital city upriver (that is, to the south, since the Nile River flows south to north) to Napata, and became a major power in the region. They had access to rich gold mines and grew so strong that they attacked and conquered Egypt for a time.

However, this power was not destined to survive. Kush came under attack from the Assyrians and later the Persians.

When Napata finally fell in the fourth century B.C.E., the Kushites abandoned it and moved their capital farther south, to Meroë. They survived for the next several hundred years as traders. Meanwhile, a new power in the region emerged, the kingdom of Axum, which lay to the Kushites' east. In the second century C.E. Axum conquered Kush, and the Kushite civilization for all intents and purposes disappeared.

Warfare also contributed to the decline and disappearance of the Carthaginian culture along Africa's northern coast. Carthage had been founded in the ninth century B.C.E., and over time it developed into a major trading power, supported by a sophisticated agricultural system. Protecting its large mercantile fleet in the Mediterranean Sea was a massive navy. However, Carthage was a threat to the Roman Empire, and Rome concluded that Carthage had to be subdued. A series of three wars began in 264 B.C.E. Although the outcome of the first war was indecisive, the treaty the two powers signed forced Carthage to pay huge indemnities to Rome, depleting its treasury and beginning the process of collapse. At the end of the third war, in 146 B.C.E., Rome decisively defeated the Carthaginians; sacked the capital city, Carthage; and effectively wiped out Carthaginian culture and society.

EGYPT

by Mariam F. Ayad

The Egypt of the pharaohs lasted more than 3,000 years. The wonderful monuments preserved at Luxor, Saqqara, and other archaeological sites testify to the greatness this civilization enjoyed. Except for those magnificent ruins, however, little remains of this ancient culture.

Egypt's long history is divided into Old, Middle, and New Kingdoms, spanning the period from about 2575 to 1070 B.C.E. These periods of prosperity, expansion, and massive construction projects are interrupted or followed by times of weakened royal authority and even chaos known as the First, Second, and Third Intermediate Periods, respectively. The Second (ca. 1640–ca. 1532 B.C.E.) and Third (ca. 1070–ca. 712 B.C.E.) Intermediate Periods witnessed foreign domination over parts of Egypt; the First Intermediate Period (ca. 2134–ca. 2040 B.C.E.) is unique in that internal rather than external factors seem to have caused the collapse.

The First Intermediate Period survived in literary works long after stability was restored to the land. More than any other period of Egyptian history, it affected the Egyptian collective psyche. For centuries after its end Egyptians viewed it as a time of social collapse in which fundamental notions of justice and social order were overturned. Several literary works, including *The Complaints of Khakheperre-sonb* and *The Admonitions of Ipuwer*, vividly describe the social conditions prevalent during the First Intermediate Period.

In *The Complaints of Khakheperre-sonb* we read of a land destroyed and broken up, where "order is cast out," chaos rules, and the temples are deprived of their regular rations. This text describes a general state of mourning, distress,

inequity, and crime. It paints a picture of reversed social norms wherein the rulers become ruled. *The Admonitions of Ipuwer* describes similar conditions. The author imparts a sense of overarching futility and infertility: "Lo, . . . the women are barren, none conceive." Several passages explicitly refer to bloodshed: "There's blood everywhere. . . . Lo, the river is blood." Others mention that there was "no shortage of dead," that "many dead are buried in the river," and that "the stream [became] the grave, the tomb became stream." *The Admonitions of Ipuwer* has been cited as evidence of an Egyptian civil war.

Another text, known as *Instructions to Merikare*, written sometime in the Middle Kingdom, may also contain references to a civil war, such as in a warning that "troops will fight troops." Traces of the name "Khety" preserved in *Merikare* and written within the royal cartouche (the oval that typically encircles the king's name in ancient Egyptian writings) may indicate that the events referred to took place in the First Intermediate Period, as "Khety" could conceivably be another way to write Akhtoy, a name held by several rulers during that difficult time. Yet another text, known as the *Prophecy of Neferti*, suggests that Egypt's rulers were "many" during this period and that the land was in "turmoil" and "uproar." People "seize[d] weapons of warfare," the son becoming as enemy, "the brother as foe," and "a man slaying his father."

Scattered references in *The Admonitions of Ipuwer* and in the *Prophecy of Neferti* as well as in other texts suggest an extended severe drought. In the *Prophecy of Neferti*, "Dry is the river of Egypt. One crosses the water on foot; . . . The land is bowed down in distress." This text also describes the land as "ruined" and "shrunk," "bare" and "deprived of produce" and "lacking in crops." Indeed, it has been suggested that toward the end of the Sixth Dynasty (ca. 2323–ca. 2150 B.C.E.) a series of low Niles and the ensuing economic decline may have directly contributed to the collapse of centralized power so characteristic of the First Intermediate Period.

Literary and autobiographical texts as well as archaeological evidence indicate that the Second Intermediate Period witnessed a massive wave of Asiatic infiltration into the Nile delta. Whereas early scholars have assumed that an outright invasion resulted in the Hyksos rule in Egypt (*Hyksos* being a Greek version of the Egyptian *heqa khasut*, "rulers of foreign lands"), it is now believed that the Hyksos infiltrated the delta gradually but massively at the end of the Middle Kingdom. What exactly caused this mass immigration is not known, but possibly it resulted from a period of drought in western Asia. The Second Intermediate Period ended with the military expulsion of the Hyksos through campaigns initiated by a series of Theban rulers of the Seventeenth Dynasty (ca. 1640–ca. 1550 B.C.E.), leading eventually to the establishment of the Eighteenth Dynasty (ca. 1550–ca. 1307 B.C.E.) and the New Kingdom.

The Third Intermediate Period shares some similarities with the first two. Like them, it was characterized by much

Sarcophagus of Nectanebo II, the last native ruler of Egypt, from Alexandria, Thirtieth Dynasty, around 343 B.C.E.; Nectanebo's reign was ended by the second Persian occupation of Egypt, and it is said that he fled to Ethiopia. (© The Trustees of the British Museum)

internal conflict and long periods of foreign domination. Competing claims over the Egyptian throne at the beginning of the Twentieth Dynasty (ca. 1196–ca. 1070 B.C.E.) undermined the royal authority, and toward the end of the dynasty a series of weak kings ruled, often only briefly. Inevitably, weakened royal authority led to a drastic rise in the influence and power of prominent figures of the priesthood, who added military titles with civic duties to their priestly roles. One such figure was Herihor, a high priest of the god Amun who assumed royal titles and enclosed his name in the royal cartouche even while Ramses XI, the last pharaoh of the Twentieth Dynasty, still ruled.

With the death of Ramses XI the New Kingdom ended, and an era of "foreign" dominion began. Because of its rulers' foreign names, the Twenty-first Dynasty (ca. 1070–ca. 945 B.C.E.) is often characterized as Libyan. Although Libyan by origin, these rulers had been assimilated into Egyptian society. Some had been members of the Egyptian court or army and had used their positions to gain power. The Twenty-second through Twenty-fourth Dynasties (945–712 B.C.E.) were also Libyan in origin and often contentious, with various dynasts claiming royal titles even though they controlled only small areas. The resulting competition divided Egypt into warring fiefdoms. It may be that the Libyans' decentralized approach to rule was their cultural heritage as people who had led a tribal, nomadic existence. Texts from earlier periods of Egyptian history often mention wars with the "Libyan tribes" along Egypt's western border.

The Libyan period ended in the second half of the eighth century B.C.E. when invaders from Nubia to the south of Egypt took power in Memphis. The Nubians claimed to be restorers of order who wanted to reunify Egypt and purify it of sacrilegious Libyans. In 664 B.C.E. Necho, a ruler from the western delta city of Sais, formed a military alliance with the Assyrians and with their help drove the Nubians out of Egypt. Necho's son Psamtik I (r. 664–610 B.C.E.) became the

first ruler of the Egyptian Twenty-sixth Dynasty, which lasted until the Persian invasion of Egypt in 525 B.C.E.

During the Twenty-sixth Dynasty contacts with other Mediterranean and Near Eastern countries strengthened, and Egypt became increasingly involved in the politics of the region. Egypt was invaded twice by the Persians, in 525 B.C.E. and 343 B.C.E., and then by Alexander the Great's Macedonian troops in 332 B.C.E. After Alexander's death in 323 B.C.E. one of his generals, Ptolemy, declared himself ruler of Egypt. His descendants reigned for almost 300 years, during which Egyptian culture became increasingly Hellenized. After Cleopatra VII's defeat at the battle of Actium in 30 B.C.E., Egypt was annexed to the Roman Empire, and its distinctive pharaonic culture gradually disappeared.

THE MIDDLE EAST

BY FRANS VAN KOPPEN

The ancient Near East offers a historical record of unparalleled length, continuity, and complexity for the development of human society over time. From the beginning of urban culture in late prehistory up to the Middle Ages, this record is replete with evidence for episodes of social collapse after periods of relative stability. These episodes typically involved settlement desertion on a regional scale, changes of subsistence strategies, and political fragmentation. Evidence for these events comes primarily from archaeological surveys using landscape investigation to determine the growth and decline of regional settlement systems. Excavations, climatic data, and ancient texts shed further light on social collapse and help reveal the complex interplay of socioeconomic and environmental factors that lay at the root of it.

Differences in landscape, rainfall, and temperature divide the Near East into distinct environmental zones, each of which accommodated specific forms of human subsistence: sheep and goat herding in the semiarid and mountainous regions, trade and crafts along the interregional routes, dry farming and small-scale cattle herding in the low-rainfall zones, and intensive cereal cultivation in the floodplains, again in combination with herding away from the rivers and fields. Maximum population density occurred near the rivers, and the Mesopotamian floodplains, in particular, exhibited the greatest size and number of settlements throughout the millennia.

Ancient agriculture was, however, always a dangerously fragile system operating under critical social and environmental constraints and therefore susceptible to abrupt fluctuations. Strong central control coincided with agricultural expansion and an increase in settlement, while disruptions of the political order were typically characterized by a reversion to local self-sufficiency and the abandonment of villages and smaller rural towns. In the face of such fluctuations the rural population maintained a spectrum of subsistence options and moved back and forth between village-based farming and other economic strategies such as herding, relocating if necessary to neighboring environmental zones.

A typical cycle of rural settlement and abandonment includes some or all of the following elements: Expansion is instigated by the urban centers, the seats of elite governments and their trappings of symbolic identifications on which regional states are founded. Growing demand in the center stimulates agriculture and settlement of the countryside, including ecologically marginal areas. Maximal growth is contained in order not to cross the threshold of the environmental carrying capacity, but the system at its greatest expansion is vulnerable when this threshold drops—for example, if yields diminish because of minor shifts in rainfall or river levels. Political demands for surplus remain constant, and pressure on the rural producers therefore increases, leaving them no alternative but to grow more on their land, which compounds the problem of diminishing returns by increasing soil poverty and salinity. Once producers start fleeing the oppression of their urban landlords, the agricultural infrastructure can no longer be maintained, and the downward spiral accelerates, ending with the desertion of rural settlements and the decline of the urban political center, usually resulting in dynastic collapse.

Ancient Mesopotamian texts show that sequences of political growth and waning and the associated expansion and contraction of settlement were thought to obey universal cyclical patterns. The Mesopotamian word for "dynasty" designates any temporary term of public duty, and dynastic collapse was considered an inevitable shift in office. Political discontinuity sometimes occurred well before expansion endangered the resilience of the rural economy—for example, when the last indigenous Mesopotamian dynasty fell and the land was integrated in the Persian Empire (535 B.C.E.)—but more often dynastic change took place when the fragility of the rural social and ecological systems had already eroded the state's economic foundations. Under these circumstances even relatively minor external pressure, such as an attack by rival powers, could topple dynasties.

Major cities suffered during phases of settlement reduction and agricultural decline but usually survived. Cities were the custodians of divine worship, high culture, and learning, institutions that were quickly revitalized by new contenders to power who sought to be recognized and took up the traditional seats of rule. Nevertheless the archaeological record contains ample evidence for crises that disrupted a region's urban centers over and beyond its rural settlements. In many cases large cities were permanently abandoned, often with telltale signs of destruction in their final moments. Extreme instances reveal widespread breakdown—for example, the great collapse that occurred around 1200 B.C.E. when the Hittite capital, Hattusha, and the Syrian cities Emar and Ugarit (as well as many centers of Mycenaean Greece and Cyprus) were abandoned, never to be reoccupied. This and similar episodes clearly represent major disruptions in the development of human society. A comparable cycle of urban decay occurred at the transition from the Early to the Middle Bronze Age (ca. 2200–2000 B.C.E.).

Many of the theories proposed to account for collapses of this scale attribute them to external forces. Two factors, in particular, are often brought into the debate: abrupt climatic deterioration, leading to droughts and famines; and foreign invasion. Current consensus is that no single factor was decisive and that combinations of a variety of causes—external as well as internal—could lead to societal breakdown. Economic interdependency through trade networks explains how episodes of collapse could simultaneously affect large areas of the Near East and beyond.

Despite the fragility of the Near Eastern environment, agriculture, and settlement, ancient societies were remarkably successful in preserving their civilizations over time, an endurance that can be credited to the cities and their palace and temple resources. Only when the collapse of a state involved the total destruction of its urban centers—for example, during the fall of Assyria in 614–612 B.C.E.—was it possible to fully eradicate an ancient Near Eastern civilization.

Basalt relief of a gazelle, Neo-Hittite, ninth century B.C.E., from Carchemish, southeastern Anatolia (modern-day Turkey); after the collapse of the Hittite Empire around 1200 B.C.E., Hittite culture survived in places such as Carchemish that had once been under Hittite control. (© The Trustees of the British Museum)

ASIA AND THE PACIFIC

BY FRANCIS ALLARD

Asia and the Pacific region make up a large and culturally diverse area with a history marked by the rise of numerous states and empires, some of which display continuity with present-day nations. Less well known are the many archaeological cultures and polities that emerged as culturally and politically distinct entities but eventually collapsed or underwent transformation. Early instances of social collapse in Asia are evident in various areas and periods and exemplify some of the reasons scholars have proposed for collapsed societies, including environmental disturbances, social upheaval, military defeat, and even peaceful contact with other regions. It is important to note that the nature of the evidence—solely archaeological in the case of prehistoric cultures and archaeological and textual for the more historical polities—affects the type of interpretation proposed, with military conflict more likely to be advanced as the trigger to collapse for polities discussed in written sources. Also worth noting is the likelihood that the various names given by archaeologists to successive periods and cultures may not necessarily reflect dramatic instances of social collapse, concealing instead more gradual, but nevertheless significant social and political transformations.

The prehistory of the Korean peninsula and Japanese archipelago provides evidence of the long-term impact of external forces on local cultures, transformations that witnessed the abandonment of sites and undoubtedly challenged their social and political structures, although the details of such strains are difficult to identify in the archaeological record. In Korea the 6,000 years of the Chulmun (ca. 6000–ca. 1500 B.C.E.) and Mumun (ca. 1500–ca. 300 B.C.E.) periods were characterized by the presence of village life, the use of pottery, and a reliance on the products of fishing, hunting, and gathering. By the third millennium B.C.E. millet cultivation had been introduced from northeast China. Further reflecting the diffusion of ideas, skills, and even materials (for example, bronze daggers, and mirrors) from China, the Mumun Period is marked by intensification of agriculture, megalithic tombs, and greater social and political differentiation.

In Japan the Jōmon Period (13,000–300 B.C.E.) is similarly characterized by villages, pottery, a reliance on wild (nonagricultural) resources, and incipient agriculture. The succeeding Yayoi Period (300 B.C.E.–300 C.E.) points to a significant transformation of Jōmon society as the arrival of immigrants, styles, and ideas from the Korean peninsula was associated with the intensification of wet-rice agriculture, metallurgy, defensible sites, objects imported from the mainland (like mirrors), and an increasingly hierarchical society.

The Neolithic Period of mainland China, typified by the highly distinctive archaeological cultures known as Hongshan (ca. 4500–ca. 3000 B.C.E.) and Liangzhu (ca. 3200–ca. 2100 B.C.E.), provides clearer instances of apparent social and political collapse, though the absence of texts renders interpretations of the archaeological data highly tentative. Centered in northeast China, the Hongshan culture is characterized by what are believed to have been ceremonial centers (including so-called temples and altars), female figurines and statues, and large complex tombs. The grave goods include finely crafted jades (representing birds, clouds, turtles, and "pig dragons") that suggest the presence of elites. It is significant that by the middle of the third millennium B.C.E. these features had disappeared, and the number and size of residential sites had decreased.

Located along the coastal regions of central China, the Liangzhu culture shares with the Hongshan culture the presence of ceremonial centers and wealthy tombs whose exquisite jades (tubes, discs, bracelets, and pendants) point to control of production by an elite. At the end of the period Liangzhu residential sites, which were concentrated on riverbanks, were abandoned. The succeeding Maqiao culture (ca. 2100–ca. 1300 B.C.E.) is marked by a dramatic reduction in the number of sites and an almost complete disappearance of Liangzhu traits.

Explanations proposed to account for the collapse of Hongshan and Liangzhu include climatic change (associated with flooding in the case of Liangzhu) and an inability to manage economic resources efficiently. In addition, the elite of both cultures may have lost the support of their respective populations when workers felt they were not adequately rewarded for their efforts at producing the elite's symbols of power.

Instances of social growth and collapse become easier to chart over the course of the first millennium B.C.E., when increasingly detailed texts become available. This is especially true of the region encompassed by present-day China. During that region's Warring States Period (453–221 B.C.E.) numerous small states (Zhao, Shu, Chu, Yue, Han, Wei, Qi, Song, Lu, Yan, and Qin) emerged and suffered subsequent defeat through military conquest. The Qin Dynasty (221–207 B.C.E.), the eventual victor of this period of instability, was led by China's famous "First Emperor," an autocratic and firm ruler whose harsh treatment of detractors and forced conscription of laborers (used, for example, in the building of the Great Wall) led to popular uprisings and the downfall of the dynasty. The succeeding Han Dynasty (202 B.C.E.–220 C.E.) proved highly successful at expanding China's territory to reach close to its present-day borders, an increase in territory that, like the contemporaneous Roman Empire, led to contact with sometimes powerful foreign cultures. In the end the Han Dynasty would fall victim to internal rebellions and the problem of maintaining control over distant regions of its empire.

Not surprisingly, the territorial expansion of the Han Dynasty in eastern Asia was associated with the collapse of a number of preliterate and culturally distinctive polities, events that the Chinese recorded in their historical texts. Two examples pertaining to the Han's southern periphery illustrate this. First, the Dian culture (third century B.C.E. to first century C.E.), centered in southwestern China's Yunnan Province, is known for its highly distinctive and elaborate material culture, which includes bronze drums and cowry shell containers. Although the Chinese texts relate the defeat of the Dian by Han forces in 109 B.C.E., burial evidence points to the survival of Dian cultural traits for another century following its incorporation into the Han Dynasty. The second example is the Dongson culture, located in present-day North Vietnam and noted for its large bronze drums. The Dongson culture survived through much of the first millennium B.C.E., finally succumbing to the Han in 43 C.E. after an earlier defeat in 111 B.C.E. It is significant that Chinese cultural traits had already infiltrated Dongson culture by the second century B.C.E. The histories of the Dian and Dongson cultures signal the need to distinguish between military defeat and cultural decline in reference to "collapse."

Centered on the Indus Valley of Pakistan and northwestern India and represented by the large sites of Harappa and Mohenjo Daro, the Indus civilization (3000–1600 B.C.E.) provides a dramatic example of a flourishing South Asian

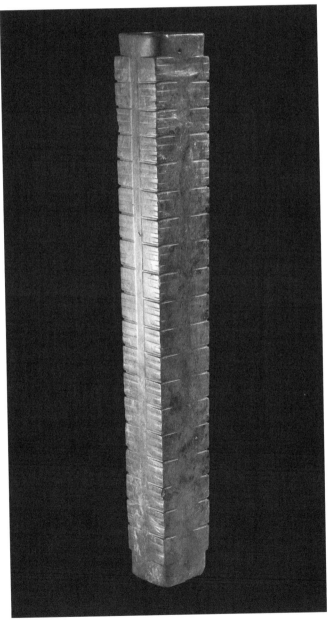

A burial jade carved with faces, from southern China, Neolithic Period, Liangzhu culture, around 2500 B.C.E.; tombs rich with jade objects were characteristic of this culture, whose sites were abandoned in the mid-third millennium B.C.E. (© The Trustees of the British Museum)

culture as well as a fitting illustration of the complexities of societal collapse and transformation. Although the absence of clear textual references to the Indus civilization limits an understanding of its political structure and religious life, it nevertheless displays a range of features common to other civilizations of the ancient world, including urbanism (centers with streets, specialized quarters, amenities, public structures, and populations numbering in the tens of thousands), a writing system (as yet undeciphered), a system of weights and measures, long-distance trade (with Mesopotamia, among other regions), and craft specialization (bead making, metallurgy, shell working, weaving, and the like).

By the beginning of the second millennium B.C.E. it appears that both Harappa and Mohenjo Daro had stopped functioning as urban centers, a change paralleled by a reduction in the number of sites in a large sector of the region encompassed by the mature phase of the Indus civilization. This transition might represent a migration out of this area or a restructuring of the settlement pattern or both. The possible forces behind this change remain open to debate. They include the destruction of the civilization by invading Aryan peoples (mostly rejected, owing to an absence of clear evidence for such destruction at the sites themselves), the drying of the large Ghaggar-Hakra River, the decline of the trade system, and the flooding of a large area resulting from the formation of a natural dam.

Population and urban decline apparently characterized only a portion of the area encompassed by the Indus civilization, with some sectors experiencing continued growth during the second millennium B.C.E. Moreover, certain features of the Indus civilization appear to have been maintained throughout later periods. For example, Hinduism has retained some of the civilization's customs, such as ceremonial bathing, the importance of bulls and elephants, and Yogic positions. This illustration of the maintenance and transformation of cultural features over long periods underscores the need to disentangle the many strands subsumed under the term *societal collapse*.

EUROPE

BY JUSTIN CORFIELD

Throughout Europe traces exist of ancient settlements long ago abandoned. Sometimes the reason for this abandonment is known, but often it is not. Mobile hunter-gatherers lived in a spot for several weeks or months and then moved on, but they often returned to the same locations. Neolithic farmers lived in farmsteads and hamlets for decades. Sometimes they needed to shift their settlement locations owing to changes in their agricultural systems. Some archaeologists have speculated that settlements were abandoned when a lineage died out and no longer had an attachment to a particular location. Resource depletion of the surrounding countryside is another possible reason for abandoning ancient farming settlements. Occasionally warfare and raiding may have driven out the inhabitants of local settlements. Given the relatively simple organization, based on households and hamlets, of societies in Europe before about 2000 B.C.E., it is not really possible to speak of true social collapse on any large scale.

Rural farmsteads were the prevailing settlement form during the Bronze Age (ca. 2800–ca. 700 B.C.E.) and Iron Age (ca. 1000 B.C.E.–ca. 500 C.E.) in most of Europe, though some larger sites arose that could be considered villages. The settlement at Biskupin in Poland, built between 750 and 720 B.C.E., was inhabited by several hundred people but abandoned after several decades. The two major theories have been advanced for the abandonment of Biskupin and similar sites nearby. One is that rising water levels in the lakes that surrounded the peninsulas on which these sites were built forced the residents to leave. The other is that the local population was driven out by marauders, possibly Scythians from lands to the east, since some of the sites show traces of fire and Scythian-type arrowheads have been found in the archaeological deposits.

Farther north there have been studies of Iron Age settlements in Denmark. Some of these settlements may well have been more densely populated in ancient times than today. Many other sites appear to have been abandoned when the food supplies ran out or when the population increased to such a level that a new settlement had to be established.

Inhabitants of Bronze Age and Iron Age Britain and France built numerous hill forts. Very many of them are located in the southeast of England at sites that have never been populated since and that were clearly abandoned in ancient times. Because these settlements had low population densities and good agricultural land, it seems unlikely that they suffered from a lack of food crops. A more probable reason for their abandonment is social collapse following the emergence of a more powerful local group or federation. For example, the Celtic hill fort at Danebury, on the South Downs, England, near the river Test, was built from the sixth century B.C.E. and abandoned around 100 B.C.E. after what appears to have been an enemy attack—there is archaeological evidence that the east gate was burned down, and the remains of bodies were found in channel pits.

On a much larger scale the Roman invasion of Gaul (which consisted essentially of present-day France, Belgium, and Germany and the Netherlands west of the Rhine River) under Julius Caesar in 58–51 B.C.E. brought widespread destruction of villages and towns. Many communities were wiped out. As a large number of those killed were men, many groups lacked the ability to collect the harvests, leading to collapse of their societies, with the result that Gaul remained the most quiescent of Roman provinces until the fall of Rome itself in the fifth century C.E. Similarly, military campaigns in Spain as part of a Roman civil war despoiled some of the country in 46–45 B.C.E. The civil war, which pitted Caesar against other powerful Romans and their armies, led to the destruction, temporarily, of many other cities across Roman-held territory, such as Massilia (modern-day Marseilles, France).

In Germany the Romans managed to seize the lands west of the Rhine, but even in the areas they did not control the Roman legions destroyed much of the infrastructure. In 9 C.E. the campaigns of the Germanic tribal leader Armin ("Arminius" to the Romans) and the Roman commander Varus spread mass destruction, though Armin and his forces all but annihilated three Roman legions at the battle of the Teutoburg Forest. Fighting continued for the next four years and then recurred sporadically from 17 until about 200 C.E.

In eastern Europe fighting between the Romans and such peoples as the Dacians and the Goths and later wars with the Bulgars led to the abandonment of many inland settlements, but a number of coastal ones remained, suggesting that the more isolated places were perhaps harder to defend and the coastal ones more easily reinforced or rebuilt. Certainly in Roman Britain, when the cities of Camulodunum (Colchester), Londinium (London), and Verulamium (Saint Albans) were destroyed during the revolt of the Iceni under Queen Boudicca in 60 C.E., the three cities were easily rebuilt on the same foundations; archaeologists have found a layer of ash in many places representing the destruction. Other cities flourished under the Romans but after the fall of the Western Roman Empire in 476 C.E. never regained their former wealth and size. Although most Roman cities have been built over and massively enlarged in the last 2,000 years, there are still some, such as Cirencester (Roman Corinium) in England, where the old city walls extend well beyond the current size of the town.

GREECE

BY SPYROS S. SIROPOULOS

Greece had never been a rich country. Small-scale agriculture, including the cultivation of olive trees, along with animal keeping and fishing were the basis of its population's nutrition. The scarce natural resources were balanced by a favorable climate that allowed the Greeks to remain outdoors for most of the year to cultivate the earth and to engage in trade and seafaring. To make most of the natural resources, large parts of the country's population did not inhabit the famous civic centers of antiquity but instead lived permanently in the countryside. In a typical city-state the polis, or city, was the decision-making center; a relatively small agricultural area called the *chóra* lay outside the polis and included a number of smaller settlements called *kómai*. A fine balance was formed between the city and the *kómai*: The civic way of life and the stability and growth of the civic community were sustained and secured by the provisions from the agricultural settlements.

This delicate balance could easily be upset in the ancient world. The mass desertion of rural settlements, with all the catastrophic repercussions for neighboring cities, could occur for various reasons, including natural causes, economic or political causes, and war.

Because people depended upon the climate to produce the maximum of the land's potential, any unpredicted natural catastrophe, such as a flood, prolonged draught, fire, or earthquake, could drive the people to abandon the countryside and move to cities to earn a living. Civic communities were not always prepared to handle such events. It was easy for agricultural problems to become social problems if the city could not compensate the devastated farmers or provide alternative ways to incorporate them into the broader social mechanism. In some cases extreme situations called for extreme solutions. The Greek historian Herodotus (ca. 484–ca. 425 B.C.E.) describes the case of the small island of Thíra in the fourth century B.C.E. Unable to provide for the needy farmers or to handle the political and social tension created by the dissatisfied citizens, the state of Thíra sent a large population to colonize another territory. The state released a decree that prohibited the colonists from returning to Thíra before five years had elapsed. In this case the successful colony of Cyrene was founded in northern Africa. Between 750 and 550 B.C.E. colonization became a common way to diffuse internal social tension and to divert the surplus of a city's male population outside the society.

The economic and social organization of the city-states were closely connected to the way a given city handled the economic and political crises that manifested toward the end of the Homeric Period (ca. 1600–ca. 1100 B.C.E.). Rapid population growth and the inability of city governments to redistribute land satisfactorily led to social unrest. Sparta tried to solve this problem by waging war on other regions to gain more land, the Athenians encouraged trade, and most cities turned to colonization. The demand for greater amounts of raw materials or agricultural products and the heavy taxation of farmers often drove farming communities to desperation. In the Hellenistic Period (323–31 B.C.E.) the abandonment of the countryside (a phenomenon the Greeks called *anahorisis*) became an economic and political problem for the Ptolemaic Dynasty of Egypt. The first rulers of this dynasty tried to expand their power by rapidly developing their naval economy; for this they demanded heavy taxes from farmers. Consequently, the farmers deserted the countryside and sought guidance and protection at the local temples, thereby upsetting both the local Greek economy and the intentions of the Ptolemaic kingdom.

War is an obvious reason for the abandonment of rural settlements. Farmers, woodsmen, goatherds, and inhabitants of small fishing villages often were forced to seek protection behind the walls of a nearby city with the advent of war. This was bad for the city in two ways. First, the city was deprived of the replenishment of natural goods upon which the civic population depended for sustenance. This was the intended result of a prolonged siege on a strong, fortified city: to exhaust the resources and compel the citizens to surrender.

Second, other practical problems arose from an unpredicted overpopulation. The Greek historian Thucydides (d. ca. 401 B.C.E.) describes how a plague was added to the problems of the Athenians during the Peloponnesian War (431–404 B.C.E.). Pericles (ca. 495–425 B.C.E.), the leader of the democratic party in Athens at the time, had thought that the famous "long walls," the fortification that connected Athens with Piraeus, would secure the country's population. He also thought that the walls would enable the city to communicate undisturbed with the vital harbor of Piraeus during the siege, thereby replenishing its products and withstanding the Spartans' siege. But Pericles had not provided for proper housing for all of these refugees. In 430 B.C.E. the inevitable pestilence, caused by a lack of elementary hygiene and the concentration of thousands of people, wiped out more than a quarter of the population of Athens. Among the victims of the pestilence were Thucydides' family and Pericles himself.

War puts a stop to the development of a society in more than one way. In the western plain of Boeotia there was a marshy lake called Copais that was a source of illnesses. The Minyae, a native people of the 13th and 14th centuries B.C.E., had tried to drain the lake to provide arable land for the local farmers. This ambitious plan was stopped because of a war with Orchomenus.

Some historians see a definite connection between the collapse of the Mycenaean society around 1100 B.C.E. and the formation of cities. When the Mycenaean civilization, also known as the Palace civilization, collapsed and the Dorians colonized Greece, many important social changes took place. People ceased being dependent upon the prosperity of palaces and stopped living in small settlements around them. This and the repopulation of the countryside led to the formation of the first cities, marking the beginning of a new social and political era for Greece. The interdependence between social order and the agricultural economy of Greece was a defining factor in the development of Greek cities throughout antiquity.

ROME

BY CHRISTOPHER BLACKWELL

The third century C.E. was a time of social crisis for the Roman Empire even as the emperors completed some of the most striking and enduring monuments to Roman greatness. From 193 to 312 C.E. the Column of Marcus Aurelius, the Arch of Septimius Severus, the Baths of Caracella, the Aurelian Walls, and the Basilica of Maxentius were added to the splendor of the city of Rome. Also during this period the death of the emperor Commodus (r. 180–192 C.E.) led to the chaotic "Year of Four Emperors" (193 C.E.), the emperor Severus (r. 193–211 C.E.) died campaigning in Britain, Ardashir I (r. 224–241 C.E.) took the throne of Iran and began a war with Rome that would continue for 400 years, and Rome and its provinces suffered invasions from Goths, Heruli, and other Germanic groups. The entire Mediterranean world suffered from a recession in trade, and prices soared. Despite the Constitutio Antoniniana, or Constitution of Antoninus (r. 211–217 C.E.), issued in 212 C.E.—a law that granted universal citizenship to all free men living under Roman rule—the population of Rome was neither growing nor harmonious;

birthrates declined, and communities were wracked by official and unofficial persecutions of the Christians, a new but growing religious minority.

By 280 C.E. these pressures came close to destroying Rome, but a new and strong emperor, Diocletian (r. 284–305 C.E.), took office in 284. For the 23 years of his reign and the 31 years of his successor, the emperor Constantine (r. 306–337 C.E.), imperial policies both averted immediate collapse and perhaps ensured that it would eventually occur.

Diocletian attempted to take control of the economic crisis by putting strict control on the prices of certain goods, which prompted farmers, artisans, and merchants simply to stop dealing in those goods. When Constantine tried to increase trade and commerce by distributing gold from the Roman temples, inflation increased even more dramatically. Under Diocletian the bureaucracy of the Roman Empire was split in two, east and west, and Constantine reacted to the pressures of foreign invasion by virtually eliminating the authority of the Senate, thereby putting all power into the emperor's hands, and by building up the army. These changes did allow Rome to ward off invasion, but they also had immediate consequences for Roman society.

Diocletian's splitting of the empire doubled the weight of bureaucracy. Always prone to corruption, the now more numerous civil officials became generally more rapacious. Citizens found themselves subject to extortion or required to pay bribes to secure basic services such as protection under the law. In succeeding years, the emperors' various efforts to crack down on corruption only made matters worse. Officials came to realize that they could lose their jobs at any time, and they reacted by trying to amass as much illicit profit from their positions as they could before being caught.

New laws against usury, which began during Constantine's reign, had a similarly paradoxical effect. These laws forbade lending money at exorbitant interest, and they were passed as the result of influence from Roman Christians. But citizens still needed to lend money, and bankers continued to make loans. Under the new laws, however, a lender could not expect the courts to support claims against debtors who defaulted on loans. This increased the risk to the lender, which led creditors to charge ever-higher rates of interest. The common citizens suffered accordingly.

Constantine's efforts to consolidate military power under the emperor and to defeat the invasions of groups from northern Europe, while largely successful, held long-term consequences for Roman society. In Constantine's army increasingly more legions, and eventually all of the most effective legions, were composed of soldiers from the very Germanic peoples that Rome was resisting. These soldiers served and became Roman citizens, some of them reaching high military and civil office, and introduced new cultural elements into Roman society.

The rise of Christianity had other effects on Roman culture. For example, in the middle of the fourth century C.E. the Greek prelate Gregory of Nyssa (ca. 335–ca. 394 C.E.) pub-

Coins from the Hoxne hoard, Roman Britain, buried in the fifth century C.E. and found in Hoxne, Suffolk; the hoard is thought to have been buried for safekeeping during difficult times for the Roman British, who were left without any help from the Roman Empire to defend themselves from the attacks of the barbarians. (© The Trustees of the British Museum)

lished tracts arguing, from a Christian perspective, against the institution of slavery. While enslaved people revolted numerous times and earlier philosophers had argued against the cruel treatment of slaves, Gregory is the earliest example of any writer from the Greco-Roman world suggesting that slavery was, in itself, an evil institution. The economic consequences of a rejection of slavery, by the late Roman Empire, may not have been great, but such a radical rethinking of a universal social institution was destabilizing. Similar Christian arguments against capital punishment and aggressive wars drove wedges between the Christian and non-Christian populations.

As the official institutions of Rome became dominated by Christians and, after Constantine, officially Christian, divisions within the faith continued to disrupt society at all levels. Starting in the fourth century C.E. a series of schisms between Orthodox Christianity (whose definition changed decade by decade) and various alternative sects, branded heretical by defenders of orthodoxy, often brought legislation to a standstill and repeatedly sparked riots in all the major cities of the Roman world. Nestorians, Monophysites, Donatists, Monothelites, and Arians all differed in theology (sometimes only by exceedingly fine points of doctrine), but each claimed to represent true Christianity. Each sect argued, legislated, and fought against the others whenever and wherever they could.

During the fourth and fifth centuries imperial power grew weak and dispersed. The city of Rome itself became less hospitable as the mouth of the river Tiber silted up and became a malarial marsh. The center of political activity in Italy moved to Ravenna and Milan. Constantinople, the splendid new capital, became less involved in affairs to the west and increasingly Greek in its language and customs. New generations of

THE DEATH AND REBIRTH OF THE LATIN LANGUAGE

Augustine of Hippo (354–430 C.E.) and Jerome (ca. 347–419 or 420 C.E.) were the last two masters of the classical Roman literary tradition. Both of these writers, while writing on Christian topics, were steeped in the Latin of Cicero (106–43 B.C.E.), Virgil (70–19 B.C.E.), and other writers of classical Latin. As early as the fifth century C.E., however, the Latin language had begun to split apart. In some quarters people tried to preserve the classical language by continuing to write in an elaborate style; works such as those of Martianus Capella (fourth to fifth century C.E.), a Vandal writing in Carthage around 470, are full of allusions to classical literature. In other quarters, local dialects became more pronounced, beginning as early as the fourth century C.E. Egeria, a woman who made a pilgrimage from Spain to Jerusalem in 384 C.E., left a diary that shows a version of Latin that would have been hard for a classical Roman to understand.

The elaborate system of Latin grammar became simplified, and its verbs became more regular. By the seventh century the language of Italy resembled medieval Italian more than classical Latin. In the eighth century in formerly Roman parts of France, the definite article (the) first appears as lo, la, lis, moving toward modern French's le, la, les.

In the western part of the former empire Latin survived as a tool that allowed scholars and church officials to communicate with each other. As a means for communicating with the common people, it died by the ninth century when, in 813 C.E., a decree from the bishop of Tours forbade sermons in Latin, which the common people could no longer understand.

rulers, while considering themselves Roman, were more likely to be Gothic or Germanic in ethnicity and culture. For ordinary people, the Roman Empire was no longer the organizing institution, upholder of laws, or guarantor of security. Ecclesiastical institutions (churches and monasteries) and ecclesiastical officers (priests, monks, abbots, and bishops) were more likely to take over local government and play central roles in local economies.

So, for example, Apollinaris Sidonius (ca. 430–487 or 488 C.E.), from Lugdunum in Gaul, grew up in an aristocratic Roman family and married a Roman woman whose father, Avitus (r. 455–456 C.E.), would eventually become a Roman emperor. But his political career ended when Avitus was killed and Apollinaris Sidonius became bishop of Auvergne. There he dedicated his life to writing histories of Roman emperors. His numerous letters reveal, however,

that he was not, in fact, preserving a corner of Rome (as he believed) but governing a small, independent fragment of a collapsed empire.

THE AMERICAS

BY KEITH JORDAN

Several episodes of cultural and political change in the ancient Americas fit modern definitions of social collapse—the breaking down of a complex (by modern Western standards) sociopolitical arrangement into what look like simpler or more chaotic systems. We must be careful, however. *Collapse* carries a negative connotation, but ancient peoples may not necessarily have experienced these changes as negative or as forced upon them. Nor can we cling to discredited theories of cultural evolution, claiming that societies develop toward greater complexity (often defined in Western terms) and that a change in the opposite direction constitutes disaster. Finally, since we lack written records for any of these developments in the ancient Americas, our reconstructions from archaeological data are always speculative and tentative and may be invalidated when the next major find is unearthed.

In the North American Midwest the Hopewell culture (200 B.C.E.–400 C.E.)—more accurately described as a ritual and burial complex linked by trade networks—seems to have vanished by 400 C.E. No more Hopewell burial mounds or ceremonial centers were constructed, and the trade networks linking areas as distant as the Rocky Mountains and the Gulf Coast ceased to bring exotic materials to Ohio and Illinois sites. Pottery decoration became less elaborate and objects included in graves simpler and scantier. Societies seem to have become more egalitarian: No longer do burials include a very few with especially rich items, suggesting the existence of an elite.

Some archaeologists once believed that a shift toward cooler weather in the Midwest around 300 C.E. spurred the decline of the Hopewell phenomenon by making it difficult to grow the corn on which the culture supposedly relied for food. However, we now know that Native Americans in the Hopewell areas did not start growing corn on a large scale until five centuries after Hopewell culture disappeared, and there is no firm evidence for the alleged climate shift. On the contrary, in the centuries following the Hopewell "collapse" the peoples of eastern North America became more dependent on corn agriculture, leading to growing populations, bigger settlements, and ultimately the rise of the complex Mississippian cultures (900–1600 C.E.) with their huge towns, massive mounds, and powerful chiefs.

Other proposed reasons for the disappearance of the Hopewell include economic factors. In one theory trade networks collapsed because Native Americans in the southeast started to work local copper deposits instead of relying on copper mined in the Lake Superior region. But the archaeological evidence indicates that Lake Superior copper was mined and widely traded up to the European invasion in the

17th century. Another factor implicated in the Hopewell decline is increased warfare. War does seem to have become more common after roughly 500 C.E., but this may be the result of the increase in population and rise of chiefs with the adoption of corn farming after Hopewell's demise, rather than being the cause of that demise. Some late Hopewell structures once thought to be forts are now regarded as ritual centers. Similarly, although use of the bow and arrow became more common after 500 C.E., we cannot say that its introduction increased warfare and led to the Hopewell decline—the weapon may have been used for centuries before this time. Ultimately the disappearance of the Hopewell culture remains a mystery.

Another mystery confronts us near the Gulf Coast of southern Mexico, where the Olmec political and religious center of San Lorenzo flourished between 1500 and 1200 B.C.E. Its rulers erected monumental images of themselves and conducted trade in exotic materials with other ruling groups across Mesoamerica. Around 1200 B.C.E. the creation of monumental sculpture seems to have ceased, and the palaces of the rulers were abandoned. Although San Lorenzo itself was not abandoned at that time, its influence over the Gulf Coast and other parts of Mesoamerica ended. When the site was excavated in the 1960s, finds of broken statues seemed to suggest destruction by foreign invaders or by a revolution of local farmers against their kings, whose statues they purposely smashed. However, more recent excavations reveal that the broken statues simply represent the recycling of the monuments of previous kings into new ones by artists working for their successors. Recent geological evidence indicates shifts in the courses of the rivers surrounding the site, possibly as a result of silt buildup from erosion after the Olmec cut down forests to clear land for agriculture. These changes may have damaged the local environment and interfered with trade and travel.

Whatever the reason for San Lorenzo's decline, La Venta, to the east, succeeded it as the dominant Olmec center. La Venta flourished from 1200 B.C.E. to around 400 B.C.E.—after which it, too, collapsed and was abandoned. At this same time Olmec civilization itself began to fade, developing into the so-called Epi-Olmec culture (ca. 400 B.C.E.–250 C.E.). Like San Lorenzo's demise, La Venta's may have been related to the silting of adjacent rivers, whether due to natural factors (even a volcanic eruption) or to the effects of agriculture. But that would not explain why the culture itself disappeared or why the population of the eastern half of the Olmec Gulf Coast dropped drastically around the same time. Nor can we say that the Epi-Olmec culture represents a decline. This culture created sophisticated art and played an important role in the development of hieroglyphic writing and the calendar in Mesoamerica, influencing the Maya. It was hardly decadent, as some archaeologists have described it.

A third mystery of social collapse and abandonment exists in South America. Sometime around 2700 B.C.E. inhabitants of the Peruvian coast began building huge ceremonial structures in U-shaped arrangements. They continued this practice for more than 2,000 years. Then, in the early first millennium B.C.E., it came to an end. Few new large coastal cities were built between about 900 B.C.E. and 600 B.C.E., and construction at many existing sites ground to a halt. Large settlements were abandoned, sometimes reoccupied by small groups of squatters who left their rubbish in the deserted temples. Where new construction took place, as on the north-central coast, the old U-shaped pyramid groups were replaced by labyrinthine arrangements of smaller structures, and fortifications became increasingly common. Meanwhile, religious influences from the highland site of Chavín de Huántar made their appearance, supplanting the long-dominant coastal traditions.

The mechanism for these changes remains poorly understood. The religious system that led to the creation of the U-shaped enclosures suddenly lost its influence and prestige, but why is unclear. Invasions from the highlands have been suggested as a cause, but there is no solid evidence for this. Conflict might have broken out between priestly leaders and their followers in the relatively egalitarian coastal cultures—especially if those leaders tried to emulate the new class of hereditary nobles that seems to have arisen in highland cultures at the same time. Finally, there is evidence that an El Niño climatic event in the middle of the first millennium B.C.E. created catastrophic flooding and killed off much of the cool-water marine life on which coastal folk depended for much of their food supply.

See also AGRICULTURE; BORDERS AND FRONTIERS; CITIES; CLIMATE AND GEOGRAPHY; ECONOMY; EMPIRES AND DYNASTIES; EMPLOYMENT AND LABOR; FAMILY; FOOD AND DIET; FOREIGNERS AND BARBARIANS; GOVERNMENT ORGANIZATION; HEALTH AND DISEASE; LANGUAGE; LAWS AND LEGAL CODES; LITERATURE; MIGRATION AND POPULATION MOVEMENTS; MILITARY; MINING, QUARRYING, AND SALT MAKING; NATURAL DISASTERS; NOMADIC AND PASTORAL SOCIETIES; RELIGION AND COSMOLOGY; SETTLEMENT PATTERNS; SLAVES AND SLAVERY; SOCIAL ORGANIZATION; TOWNS AND VILLAGES; TRADE AND EXCHANGE; WAR AND CONQUEST.

FURTHER READING

Robert McC. Adams, "Strategies of Maximization, Stability, and Resilience in Mesopotamian Society, Settlement, and Agriculture," *Proceedings of the American Philosophical Society* 122, no. 5 (1978): 329–335.

Gina Barnes, *China, Korea, and Japan: The Rise of Civilization in East Asia* (New York: Thames and Hudson, 1993).

Carlos E. Cordova, "The Degradation of the Ancient Near Eastern Environment." In *A Companion to the Ancient Near East*, ed. Daniel C. Snell (Oxford, U.K.: Blackwell, 2005).

Roland Enmarch, *The Dialogue of Ipuwer and the Lord of All* (Oxford, U.K.: Griffith Institute/Alden Press, 2005).

K. A. Kitchen, *The Third Intermediate Period in Egypt (1100–650 B.C.),* 2nd ed. (Warminster, U.K.: Aris and Phillips, 1986).

► social organization

INTRODUCTION

The topic of social organization speaks in many ways of why people study ancient history. It speaks of the vast possibilities of the human imagination, revealing that there have been and still are many solutions to the problems human beings have faced over their existence. Some solutions have been successful, helping cultures survive for hundreds or thousands of years, while other solutions have been unsuccessful, resulting in the decline and extinctions of some cultures.

The sheer variety of social organizations is in itself an attraction to modern readers, but there are practical reason for looking at ancient ways societies organized themselves. One reason is highly personal, belonging to each individual student of ancient life: Ancient social organizations can help tell people why they are here and why they are living as they are. Many problems the individual person faces in modern society are not new. For instance, when a modern Western woman wonders why she faces social barriers in the business world, she may wonder about the truth of the common notion that her biology has fated her to a difficult career. She need only study the ways of ancient Sumer to see that a society in which women could have equal opportunities with men is possible, because it has existed. Further, she can discover how civilizations evolved to restrict her opportunities. Knowing why she is where she is can be spiritually liberating—reason enough to study ancient social organizations. Beyond that, there may be clues to why the culture of Mesopotamia changed from one where women were social equals with or even superior to men to one in which women were treated as less than human, as in the Neo-Assyrian culture. From that understanding can come ideas for solutions to her modern difficulties, because she will have learned that society changes and that creative minds can be the agents of change.

When human societies began to form, they were almost certainly kinship groups, composed of parents, their children, siblings, and cousins. Even within such close groups, there had to be rules of conduct. For instance, the young had to learn to be respectful of their elders for the very good reason that they would die without their parents' knowledge of how to survive. The larger social organizations that emerged with larger groups of people probably had that imperative: survival. In ever-larger social groups there are greater opportunities for the young to learn from their elders and a better chance of being cared for if sick or injured. Still, larger social groups mean more chances for conflict among people. Many ancient social organizations were created in part to find ways in which people could conduct their lives without harming or being harmed by others in their groups.

With the development of agriculture, the need for social rules that were organized in a manner that most people could understand became more important. Agriculture gave human beings an enormously greater opportunity to survive childhood by making the food supply more reliable and regular than it had been previously. The chances for survival increased even more if people found ways to manage their harvests so that they could eat well during seasons when food would normally be scarce, and those chances could increase further if they found a way to manage their harvests so that they did not starve during years of drought or other disasters that caused poor harvests. Such management of harvests required progressively more complex rules for storage and distribution of food. Some societies became very successful at management of food supplies. For instance, Egypt's granaries kept its people fed through lean times as well as fat times for thousands of years. Cultures that mismanaged food or kept food supplies to a small minority of elites faced uprisings, as China did, or collapse of their economies, as the ancient Maya did.

It is perhaps part of human nature that people, whatever their stations in their societies, wish to share in the benefits of their cultures. Good clothes, good food, and good schooling seem to be desired in almost any culture, yet rarely are there enough supplies of anything that everyone can share in. To deal with the problem, cultures have devised various solutions. In many cultures outright repression holds society together, with those in charge of the armies controlling the benefits of society. In others, it is religion. In ancient India religious doctrine developed in such detail that every person could know what he of she was supposed to do throughout life. Who shared in which benefits was determined by birth and explained by a doctrine that held that people were born into certain social groups because of the good and evil they had done in previous lives. The hope for a better life lay in fulfilling one's duties in the present life, providing motivation for one to contribute to society in the role allotted. The notion of being able to improve one's life has been a safety valve for many cultures.

When reading about social organization, look for how rigid the organization was as well as for the ways in which it was flexible. This requires thought, because a culture might, in theory, have very strict rules for organization but, like ancient India, be somewhat flexible in how the rules were actually applied. Then, too, look at how much a society allowed for social mobility. Even for someone who had no realistic chance of improving his or her life, just having the possibility for improvement could be a powerful motivator, one that could encourage people to be industrious and faithful to the organization of their society because the organization gave them hope. It can be enlightening to see how cultures with long histories, such as ancient Egypt and China, organized and reorganized themselves to cope with changes in environment, technology, and their neighbors. Perhaps some of what they did still has value for the modern age.

AFRICA

BY LEAH A. J. COHEN

Many factors contributed to the forms of social organization in ancient Africa, including environmental and climatic conditions that affected animal and plant resources as well as social, political, and livelihood characteristics. Common social structures during this ancient period in history grouped people by family, lineage, kinship, clan, and tribe. Later there were social structures based on caste or trade (occupation). The political systems that existed in ancient Africa are often categorized into three distinct forms: stateless societies, centralized city-states, and centralized kingdoms or empires (although not all human groups fit so neatly in these three categories). People in early ancient Africa lived primarily by hunting and gathering or fishing and harvesting of aquatic resources. Changes in the climatic conditions over time led to mass migrations and changes in ways of surviving that resulted in the widespread development of societies based on pastoralism, agriculture, and eventually skilled trades.

NOMADIC HUNTER-GATHERER GROUPS

Around 10,000 years ago (at the start of the Holocene), the climate was becoming increasingly moist as much of Africa entered a humid period that would last until around 4,000 years ago. At least during the early part of this humid phase most human groups in Africa were engaged in nomadic hunting and gathering activities in which they occupied no single location permanently. This ancient wetter African landscape, which included the Sahara, provided ample resources to support this lifestyle. Furthermore, population densities were low, meaning that there was relatively little competition for animal and plant resources.

While the specific characteristics of social structure for hunter-gatherer groups certainly varied based on culture and location, the archaeological record indicates some common structures. Hunter-gatherers were generally organized into small bands. Given the existing archaeological evidence, it is difficult to know the size of these ancient groups; modern hunter-gatherer groups range from 20 to 60 people. Although there was a richer natural resource base, which might have affected the size of these groups, ancient groups would nevertheless have been relatively small because of their need to move from place to place, at least seasonally, to follow the water, plant, and animal resources that sustained them. Physical evidence from burial sites shows a lack of material objects, since the nomadic lifestyle left little time for the accumulation of material wealth. This evidence is interpreted as indicating that there was little social or political stratification within ancient hunter-gatherer groups compared with later, more settled or sedentary agricultural and pastoral groups.

In contrast, burial sites of the elite class in more hierarchical societies, such as ancient Egypt, are bigger, more elaborate, and filled with more nonessential items compared with those of non-elite members of society. Archaeological records also show few differences in size and condition of individual homes in ancient hunter-gatherer sites (unlike more socially hierarchical societies), and this lack of difference indicates little social stratification.

One problem with archaeological evidence is that while it can speak about the material characteristics of ancient hunter-gatherers, material wealth might not be the only basis for social stratification. There might have been ancient hunter-gatherer societies in which social hierarchy was based on hunting skill or the ability to communicate with deceased ancestors rather than on material objects, but these bases for status are more difficult to detect in the archaeological record.

To supplement archaeological evidence, travel records of European, Arab, or Mediterranean explorers and traders have been used to shed light on ancient human groups. However, these records describe the social situations of African groups only after foreigners entered Africa (around the fifth century C.E. for Arabs and the 15th century C.E. for Portuguese), and they were certainly colored by the worldview of the writers. In addition, many assumptions made about social organization of ancient hunter-gatherer groups are based on the study of modern hunter-gatherer groups. If modern groups can be used as a window into the life of ancient hunter-gatherers, a much more complete picture of social organization can be painted. One criticism of this commonly accepted technique of exploring the lives of ancient hunter-gatherers is that many aspects of life for ancient hunter-gatherers—for example, climate and available resources—were too different to make accurate assumptions.

Ethnographic studies of modern hunter-gatherers indicate that labor is divided according to gender and age, a feasible division for ancient hunter-gatherers as well. Based on these studies of modern groups it is thought that women were primarily responsible for gathering the wild roots, tubers, berries, and plants that made up the majority of the daily diet, and men were responsible for hunting to provide meat on a periodic basis. Because women carried young children long distances and breast-fed them for long periods (which often served to limit population growth), there were probably long periods of time between the birth of each child that allowed the women to do the gathering.

Hunter-gatherer bands were composed of several families often related by lineage (descendants of one common ancestor). Lineage systems are a more specific type of kinship group in which individuals and families are organized by bloodlines, often traced back to the group's founding ancestor. Today these lineages are most commonly patrilineal (familial connections and lines of descent recognized through the father's bloodline) or matrilineal (familial connections and lines of descent recognized through the mother's bloodline), although there are rare cases today where social systems recognize both lines of descent. In more hierarchical lineage systems, individuals with closer links to the founding ancestor are often granted more decision-making power. In a lineage system a council of elders is often responsible (to varying degrees) for the group decisions. It is difficult to know what importance lineage had for early hunter-gatherers and how strongly it influenced the system of hierarchy they lived within.

Lineages have often been the basis by which individuals have access to resources and groups. In traditional hunter-gathering bands, lineage determines whether individuals remain with their birth group or migrate to another group. When young men leave their parents' group to find their mates, the culture is called matrilocal; when young women leave their parents' group to live with their mates' band, the culture is referred to as patrilocal. This kind of social organization serves to diversify the gene pool and keep bands small. Bands also might have split in ancient Africa once a critical threshold for population was reached, a threshold possibly created by whether resources were available.

Although lineage is a type of kinship system, not all kinship systems are necessarily based on genetic descent. Hunter-gatherer and later agro-pastoral groups could have also been organized based on more generalized kinship relations not necessarily rooted in blood relations. In some kinship systems, subgroups have differential degrees of influence over the entire society. All societies have underlying kinship groups, but the degree to which they are the basis of organization and structure varies considerably.

Early hunter-gatherer groups often are referred to as acephalous societies, meaning they had no centralized, specialized political leader, such as a chief or a king. Informal leaders might have emerged based on skill and accomplishment, but these leaders are thought to have had little absolute control and to have led more by group support than coercion, force, or intimidation. Decisions might have been made on a consensus basis by all group members or with heads of families having a stronger vote. Consensus-based decision making was possible because of the small size of the groups.

EMERGENCE OF SEDENTARY SOCIETIES

At some point in the ancient period human groups began to experiment with domestication of animals and plants in northern Africa. The exact dates for the origins of farming and herding are not certain, since many of the early steps toward domestication of animals and plants are not detected in the archaeological record. What is detectable in the record is that increased reliance on agriculture led to more sedentary lifestyles, since agriculture requires farmers to remain in one location for at least one crop season. Once humans started manipulating the land, they realized the benefits of staying in one spot and were able to improve their ability to grow the food they needed where they needed it.

One of the earliest examples of sedentary villages is the site of Nabta Playa (western deserts of southern Egypt), some 62 miles west of the Nile River. Nabta Playa is the site of a village with permanent houses from as early as 8,000 years ago that were formally organized around a "street." This village had wells and granaries to store food; although in the beginning the majority of their diet still came from wild animals and plants, evidence of domestic animals appears as early as 7,000 years ago, and agriculture may have been adopted as early as 6,500 years ago. There are some who believe that human groups may have experimented with agro-pastoral activities in the Nile Valley prior to the Holocene.

Although many (but not all) human groups would eventually rely mostly or only on farming or herding, the transition from hunting and gathering to farming and herding was gradual, and there were long periods during which human groups continued to rely on all of these activities simultaneously. Changes in climatic conditions were instrumental in the spread and eventual dominance of herding and farming activities. Around 4,000 years ago the African continent began to dry out, which forced human groups to migrate out of the increasingly dry Sahara region into the Sahel and the oases around rivers and lakes. When people moved out of the desert areas, more and more people were compressed into smaller and smaller areas, which further encouraged development of herding and farming activities as the climate change brought a decrease in wild animals and plants. Adoption of herding and farming moved south and east, eventually reaching southern Africa around 2,000 years ago with the mass migration of the Bantu farmers across the continent that started around 1000 B.C.E. In general, in the densely forested areas of central Africa, hunting and gathering persisted much longer.

This change in livelihood strategies had profound effects on the population and organization of human groups. When human groups became more sedentary and skilled in herding and farming, populations grew even more, and people had the opportunity to accumulate material objects and build permanent structures. The increased importance of a specific area of land led to ownership of property, which in turn led to the development of rules and laws to enforce ownership rights. Over time, increases in population densities and accumulation of material possessions led to labor specialization and more and more complex social organization. Competition for resources, wealth, and social status started to increase in importance and affect social organization through the dictation of alliances based on a variety of relationships, not just family, lineage, and kinship.

Anthropologists, using more modern human groups to draw conclusions about ancient cultures, often apply E. E. Evans-Pritchard's term *segmentary societies* (coined in 1940 for his study of groups in southern Sudan) to ancient agricultural human groups. This term is commonly used to describe societies that are subdivided into groups based on kinship that are relatively equal in status. Segmentary societies are often led by elders, and participation in the collective decisions and activities is accomplished through relationships with these elders.

Another ancient system of governance and stratification was based on the power an individual was granted as a result of the size of the group loyal to him or her (that is, patron-client relationships). Kinship-based societies might have had this type of organization, which brought more (but not necessarily absolute) power over decisions affecting the entire society to individuals who had larger families or more "clients" that pledged loyalty to them.

CENTRALLY ORGANIZED HIERARCHICAL SOCIETIES

The ancient civilization of Nubia in present-day Sudan and part of southern Egypt (also known as Kush during certain periods) formed around 3100 B.C.E. This area came under Egyptian rule between 2000 and 1000 B.C.E. and as such is outside the terms of this discussion, but for much of its history it was autonomous from Egypt. (Nubia even governed Egypt from around 800 to 700 B.C.E.) From about 900 B.C.E. this civilization was based on a divine kingship, which developed from a loosely related collective of locally governed human groups. This might have been partly due to the nature of their livelihoods as nomadic pastoralists and the low population density of the region. Women appear to have had an important role in Nubian culture. Nubian queens were depicted in art as defending the nation's interests, and in religion the cult of the goddess Isis was widespread. The Nubians developed a system of writing and were also known for their skilled warrior bowmen.

The great African kingdom of Axum (present-day Ethiopia, northeastern Africa) emerged as a city-state during the first century C.E. and dominated trade in the Red Sea by around the third century C.E. This state was another centrally organized, hierarchical, sociopolitical system. The king was the leader of the political, military, and religious systems. Axum was founded in the Ethiopian highlands, which at the time was fertile ground where agricultural innovations such as terracing and the ox-drawn plow increased productivity. This civilization developed an indigenous written script, engaged in extensive trade with Arabia, and issued its own coinage. Axum gained control over other lands (including ancient Nubia) and, at the height of the empire, there was a firmly established elite class whose members surrounded themselves with luxury goods from Axum and beyond.

LESS CENTRALLY ORGANIZED AND LESS HIERARCHICAL SOCIETIES

Urban societies that appear from archaeological evidence to have been less centrally governed also existed in Africa. One example is the settlement of Jenne-jeno, which appeared sometime in the third century B.C.E. in Mali (West Africa) near the modern town of Djenné. (It reached its height around 900 C.E. in the medieval period.) Despite the apparent lack of centralized governance and rigid hierarchy, the city grew to be very densely populated with houses situated very close together, and there may have been a centralized marketplace. Households were often organized based on trade (farming, metallurgy, fishing, and ceramics). Other than the location of housing, dedication to a specific craft did not seem to indicate any hierarchical status.

It is thought that many of the pastoralists, agriculturalists, and fishermen in the region around Jenne-jeno had moved from the drying-out Sahara. West African rice became an important agricultural product. Houses were made of mud bricks. Despite numerous human groups in the region and different ethnic backgrounds, centralized, rigid hierarchical political systems did not prevail in the Niger delta. Archaeologists typically look for evidence of monumental architecture as one of the main signs of a political system ruled by one person or a relatively small group of wealthy individuals. Sites in the Niger delta offer no such evidence (with the exception of the wall surrounding the city of Jenne-jeno, which has been interpreted somewhat tentatively as a defensive structure to protect the city from floods).

In other areas of ancient Africa many nomadic and semi-nomadic pastoral groups (for example, some of the Berber—also known as Amazigh—groups) in northern Africa near the Nile delta during the first millennium B.C.E. were organized into segmentary societies characterized by social and political systems that often did not have a specified leader but that placed individuals within a series of progressively larger networks such as family, lineage, clan, and tribe. These networks played a primary governing role only when it was necessary to settle disputes with opposing networks.

The archaeological record is not as complete yet for social organization in ancient southern Africa, but it is known that around 300 to 400 C.E. sedentary groups that relied on agriculture and herding lived in villages. Many of these villages engaged in trade for goods from at least as far away as the eastern Africa coast.

ANCIENT SOCIAL ORGANIZATION IN LIGHT OF MODERN SYSTEMS

The term *chiefdom* is applied to societies in which one individual holds the decision-making power and in which his or her authority is related to his or her relationship to an important ancestor of the group (often the founder); ability to communicate with the ancestors; success in wielding the power and maintaining or improving living standards; or obtaining loyalty in a patron-client relationship through a large following. There were African chiefdoms in western Africa that were connected by a council of chiefs who shared power among many leaders representing their respective chiefdoms. Many of the southern African Bantu societies that were observed by the first European travelers (after 1400 C.E.) were organized into chiefdoms where successive chiefs inherited their position based on their lineage back to previous chiefs. Another feature of these societies was the categorization of clans in which some were less definitively associated with the royal lineage but were recognized as related enough to allow clan members to be part of the higher leadership community. In this way a system of hierarchy was established based on clan membership. However, there is little evidence from ancient times that tells when human groups developed into chiefdoms, what their social and political organization had been prior to that development, or if they had always been organized into chiefdoms.

Colonialists may have created the concept of tribe, which has been applied to African societies from the ancient past (as well as today). A tribe has been defined as a society larger in number than a band (hundreds of individuals) that is composed of subgroups united by associations or social constructs, such as councils of elders who are members of the same age set, secret societies, warrior societies, and religious cults. Tribes often have a lead headman or less commonly headwoman, although this person may not be occupied with the task of leadership full time. The application of *tribe* and other terms to describe the social organization of human groups has often served as the focus of strife and conflict and may not be useful. These terms can hide unifying characteristics between groups and overly accentuate irrelevant differences. So although the perception of Africa as a multitude of competing tribes seems to be one that has stuck to the concept of Africa's ancient history, it is difficult to assess the accuracy of this picture.

The age-set system (known as *gerontocracy*) draws lines of distinction based on gender and age. It is a social, political, and economic system in which elders hold power. Among the modern Masai in East Africa, one age set is responsible for cattle and community safety. The individuals that carry out this service are supervised by the elders, who are male. Individuals move from one age set to another as a group, often in a very ceremonious fashion known to anthropologists as a rite of passage. For many ethnic groups in African history circumcision has been a manifestation of movement from one age set to another. Most commonly, the consensus of the entire age set determined those individuals who would emerge as leaders to act on behalf of the age set. In this system, which was and is widespread in sub-Saharan Africa, age is highly respected. This system balanced a system in which family lineage might concentrate power in a way unrelated to individual skills recognized by the group. Despite the fact that upon European contact with Africa there were many examples of age-set social systems, which may indicate a long history of this type of social organization, it is not known whether this system dominated the social organization of ancient sub-Saharan African human groups or how far back it dates.

EGYPT

by William H. Peck

The social structure in ancient Egypt, like almost every other aspect of Egyptian life, underwent changes over 3,000 years of history. However, the general structure of the society can be visualized as a pyramid, with the ruler at the top supported by progressively larger groups underneath. Directly below the ruler were the royal family and kin and then, in progressively larger groups, the high-level administrators, middle-level functionaries, supervisors of labor and crafts, specialized craftspeople, and finally the peasant class, made up mainly of agricultural workers, who were the base of the pyramid. This multilevel society reflected the complex bureaucracy that had begun to develop in the country as early as the emergence of a unified Egypt and was well established by the beginning of the Old Kingdom (ca. 2575–ca. 2134 B.C.E.)

KING, GOVERNMENT, AND EXTENDED FAMILY TIES

The concept of kingship is central to any discussion of Egyptian society and Egyptian civilization. The king was the absolute monarch, supreme ruler, considered a personification of a god on earth and inheritor of his position by divine right. He was not only chief executive, head of state, and commander of the military but also the chief priest and main intermediary between humankind and the gods. The king was considered responsible for guaranteeing the cosmic order of the universe by his continued attention to the gods. He ensured that the gods were pleased by the uninterrupted sacrifices and offerings made to them and the rites carried out for them in all the temples of the land. In theory, the king led all of the activities in the country, both civil and religious. In actual fact, a large bureaucracy and well-organized civil service shouldered these responsibilities as his appointed representatives. The social structure of the country was dependent on the complexities of the bureaucracy and cannot be examined without reference to the levels of governance.

In the Old Kingdom the upper level of the administration was largely based on close family relationships such that most important posts were occupied by the ruler's closest relatives. As an example, the person responsible for overseeing the construction of the Great Pyramid, King Khufu's burial monument at Giza, was Hemiunu, a cousin or nephew of Khufu. This tradition of family ties was somewhat modified and gradually relaxed as history progressed, but the king's family continued to be appointed to important posts. In the Nineteenth Dynasty (ca. 1307–ca. 1196 B.C.E.), as a further example, sons of Ramses II filled a number of key positions. One was commander in chief of the army, another was high priest of the god Ra at Heliopolis, a third was the overseer of the royal vineyards at Memphis, and a fourth was the administrator of the entire Nile delta region.

On other levels many posts and positions were hereditary, evidenced by fathers and sons who had the same titles and ranks of office. This allowed for considerable continuity and probably increased overall efficiency. The training received by a son who learned his job as an apprentice and assistant to his father was more personalized and specialized than an organized education along academic lines could be. Although family relationships played an important part in the rule and administration of the country, ambition and talent could also be rewarded. From the biographies found on the walls of tombs it is possible to trace the careers of functionaries as they rose through the various levels of the bureaucracy. While these biographies were more in the nature of a tribute or eulogy than a real life story, they did detail important accomplishments and virtually every title that the deceased might have held during his lifetime. They give a good idea of the key events in a person's career and also illustrate how mobile the society might have been.

Although the upper classes were originally created from the family and relatives of the ruler, it was still possible for talent and ambition to be recognized. A prime example of social mobility is illustrated in the career of Senenmut, an official in the reign of Queen Hatshepsut of the Eighteenth Dynasty (ca. 1550–ca. 1307 B.C.E.). His family origins were undistinguished, but Senenmut rose through the ranks from a relatively low position, when he may have been Overseer of the Royal Seals or Overseer of the Audience Chamber, to an appointment as tutor to the queen's only daughter. During the period when Hatshepsut reigned alone, he became the chief Steward of the Temple of the god Amun at Karnak and thus one of the most powerful and influential men of his time. He was also chief adviser to the queen and is credited as being the chief architect of Hatshepsut's mortuary temple at Deir el-Bahri. On the other hand, a reversal of fortune was also possible. In the Middle Kingdom (ca. 2040–ca. 1640 B.C.E.), when the office of nomarch (semi-autonomous provincial ruler) was abolished, those officeholders were demoted and striped of their rank by royal decree.

CLASS STRUCTURE

Within the pyramidal structure of Egyptian society there were essentially two clearly delineated classes for which designations in the Egyptian language have survived. The wealthy and privileged (usually termed "nobility" or "elite" in the modern literature) were the leaders in every aspect of life; the lower class included workers, farm laborers, and servants. From the few examples of communities that have been preserved, it is possible to study the evidence of this division in the arrangement of villages and towns. These arrangements generally reflect the stratification of Egyptian society into two main parts. The archaeological excavation of sites clearly shows class difference, as at el-Lahun, a village built for those constructing a pyramid in the Middle Kingdom, and at Deir el-Medina, the settlement inhabited by the artisans who excavated and decorated the tombs in the Valley of the Kings. At el-Lahun the class distinction is unmistakable because the town was divided in two by a wall that separated the district with the large and lavish villas of the administrators from the much smaller row houses of the workers.

At Tell el-Amarna in Middle Egypt, the capital built by Akhenaton during his religious revolution, about 10 percent of the dwellings are large, many-roomed structures, while the workers' houses are much smaller and simpler. But that does not necessarily mean that all the family activities took place in limited, cramped quarters. In the climate of Egypt it was possible to cook out of doors and sleep on the roof for relief from the heat as well as to sit and congregate in the narrow streets. Although the family was the basic unit of society, interaction with neighbors and community was obviously necessary for day-to-day activities and for the mutual support provided by a community.

The two basic classes, the elite or nobility and the workers or commoners, were sharply divided not only in privileges but also in responsibilities. The nobles were the administrators and governors, the members of the priesthoods, and the officers of the military. These duties brought the usual rewards of material goods, social position, and community respect. The workers were for the most part free laborers, but there is some indication of a serflike arrangement where the workers were tied to the land they cultivated. The class of individuals who were actual slaves generally consisted of enemies captured in battle, convicted criminals, and debtors. Slavery was not so common in Egypt until the New Kingdom (ca. 1550–ca. 1070 B.C.E.) when more foreign conquests made it practical to employ the growing number of captives as slaves. These defeated foreigners were used at the will of the king. Slaves captured in battle could be employed on state projects or awarded to outstanding members of the military as reward for service. The old fiction that the pyramids were built by slave labor generally has been discounted. The workers on the pyramids were essentially field hands employed generally during the period of the annual flooding of the Nile, when they were not needed to sow and reap the crops.

ORGANIZATION OF WORK AND ECONOMY

A system of corvée (or drafting) of workmen for state projects was used throughout Egyptian history. Members of the general population were called to duty for service in the military, for work in mines and quarries, and on state construction projects, such as the building of temples or pyramids. Drafted crews were also used to work on roads, canals, and the complex irrigation systems. This draft was so much a part of Egyptian life that a tradition of substitute figures to be buried with a workman developed for use of the spirit in the afterlife. The *shabiti*, mummy-shaped statuettes equipped with symbolic tools and baskets, were intended to magically answer for the deceased if he was called on to do any kind of draft labor in the next life.

The economy of Egypt was essentially based on agriculture. The largest landholders were the state and the temples, and a system of taxation on these lands, worked by tenants, provided the means to pay the employees of the governmental and religious institutions. All of the land of Egypt was in theory the domain and possession of the king. The system of tenant farming, where free individuals were allowed by contract to work the fields of royal or religious (temple) establishments, was vital to the national economy. In the New Kingdom, as the powers of the temple priesthoods became stronger and the temple holdings larger, tenant farming was one obvious solution to the management of temple estates. Since most of the economy was organized and controlled by the government, the workers in state institutions were dependent on rations provided for them. Many of these employees were also able to supplement their incomes by other activities carried on privately. Members of the upper class enjoyed the privilege at the pleasure of the king of owning property and estates and profiting from the produce of them. It was also possible for free men who were not members of the elite to own land and cultivate crops that could be used to sustain their families or traded for other goods. These landowners had the possibility of moving up in the administrative ranks to offices of responsibility. This was one of the avenues of upward mobility for those not born to rank.

Coinage as it is known today did not exist in ancient Egypt until very late in its history. Weights and measures were standardized, and some metals, such as gold and silver in bars and rings, were used as one medium of exchange. Far more common was a system of barter. The basis of this trade was generally wheat so that workmen who were paid in wheat could make bread from part of it and exchange the rest for other needs. Therefore the chief measure of wealth was land and other possessions rather than some bankable instrument of exchange.

Much of the information about the material display of wealth comes from the tombs. This evidence is either in the form of the actual objects preserved for the use of the spirit in the next life or represented in wall paintings, relief carvings, or models. Lists of estates owned by the deceased with their locations occur as part of the offerings depicted in the tomb. Models of activities to benefit the spirit suggest the wealth necessary to provide the services of the craftspeople depicted in the models. In one case, the grave of a mayor of Thebes, 15 model boats were included, giving some indication that a person of his rank would be well equipped for travel on the Nile. One additional measure of wealth, in life and in the tomb, was the possession of large quantities of cloth. This could be in the form of garments or simple sheets. In the Old Kingdom there are a small number of offering reliefs that include a "linen list" detailing great quantities of linen cloth of different types and quality. In some tombs piles of folded linen have been found, giving added evidence of the use of cloth as an indication of affluence.

Craftsmen—sculptors, painters, and furniture and jewelry makers—were generally in the service of the state or the religious establishment. They enjoyed regular employment and income and were able to pass their craft occupations on to their sons. Where it was possible or desirable, they lived together in a community of others who were similarly employed. Deir el-Medina on the West Bank at Luxor was inhabited by the workers who made and decorated the tombs in the Valley of the Kings. It is the best example of a village especially intended for workers and craftsmen. As such, excavations there have produced a great deal of information about the organization of this specialized labor, the worker's family relationships, and their day-to-day activities.

NUCLEAR FAMILY, WOMEN, AND MARRIAGE

The basic nuclear family was the most important societal unit in ancient Egypt. The ancient Egyptians were especially proud of family and lineage. The family was a close-knit group of father, mother, and children not usually extended to a larger organization such as a clan. Inscriptions on statues of individuals often give parentage and sometimes grandparentage with details about the rank and title of these forebears. However, a modern understanding of the relationship within the family is complicated because the same words in the Egyptian language were used to designate different members of the family. The word for *brother* could also be used to identify the husband, just as *sister* could also designate a wife. *Father* could easily mean a grandfather or an ancestor. Teachers were also sometimes called "father" and coworkers might be termed "brother," not signifying an actual relationship but another close affiliation or other bond. This somewhat ambiguous use of language caused earlier scholars to believe that there was a general tradition of brother-sister marriage in Egypt, but this was not the case and can rarely be proved. This confusion of language still occasionally leads to difficulties in clearly understanding of family structure.

There were exceptions to the general rules against brother-sister marriage, however. Kings sometimes did marry their sisters, and marriage with their daughters is also attested, but this was rare and had to do with providing an heir of royal blood. Likewise, only royalty enjoyed the custom of multiple wives, though commoners could have concubines as well as a wife.

Adulthood was considered to begin for women at the start of menses and for men with circumcision, performed in adolescence. For the most part, daughters lived with the family until marriage, but it was possible for sons to join others of their age group and live outside the family home. Newlywed couples might live for a time with either partner's parents, but generally this was not considered an ideal arrangement. Marriage usually took place when the man had the means to establish his own separate household. Unmarried, divorced, or otherwise single female members of the family, such as widowed mothers, divorced sisters, or maiden aunts, might live with their sons, nephews, or other close male relatives. For reasons not completely clear, two households could be joined so that two families shared living arrangements. This kind of extended family, though it was not the norm, was not unusual.

Since the family was a close-knit group, its members might be held responsible for the actions of one another. This meant that punishment might be applied for a crime committed by one to others or that family members could be held hostage to ensure the loyalty of others. It also meant that heirs could be forced to make good the debts of deceased family members. The obligations of family membership extended not only to resolving the matters of inheritance but also to securing the proper burial rites for the dead. One of the most important obligations an Egyptian had was to provide parents with the guarantees of continued life after death. This included not only the traditional preparation of the corpse (mummification) and the tomb or burial place but also the maintenance of continued rites and offerings for the spirit of the deceased.

Even though the importance of the family in Egyptian society is clear, no evidence for a formal marriage ceremony is known, and there is also no evidence that government records were registered or kept. Marriage can be characterized as a social contract, not a legal one. It is also not clear how matches were arranged or how partners were chosen. Some marriages were arranged by parents, but there is no strong indication that the arrangement could be forced on the participants. Marriage was essentially a private affair, to which the husband and wife both agreed. Both members brought property to the union, and it was possible for the wife to maintain title to her portion. Divorce was possible, and the penalties were carefully spelled out, at least there is evidence that this was regularized in the later centuries of Egyptian history. Even though society in Egypt was clearly male dominated, women held a position unequaled in any other ancient culture. Women could own property and slaves, could manage their own affairs to a certain extent, and were even able to institute legal suits. They could also conduct businesses and engage in trade. The weaving of cloth was just one example of a home-based industry carried out by women for profit. Women also had a part in the temple cults, but those responsibilities were generally limited. There are some records of women with the title "priestess" in the service of a god, but generally the title found is "chantress" or ritual singer, attached to a particular temple.

VOCATIONS, EDUCATION, AND SOCIAL MOBILITY

Craftspeople in Egypt enjoyed occupations that were relatively secure and respected. Since coinage did not exist until late in Egyptian history, they were paid in grain and sometimes cloth or other products that could be used for barter for other necessities. On the level of the trades and crafts there is a clear gender division. Women are seen in representations of spinning and weaving, in the textile crafts. Occasionally they were also employed as potters, but sculptors, painters, carpenters, boatwrights, chariot makers, metalworkers, and jewelers are almost exclusively male.

The priesthood in Egypt was not an exclusive vocation as it is in many other cultures and in modern religious institutions. The position of priest was a rotating one, where an individual would serve for a prescribed length of time, continue to occupy his secular positions, or return to his other duties after his service was finished. Priests could also serve in several different capacities, devoted to different deities, at the same time. It was only with the growth of the power of the priesthoods in the New Kingdom that the temples became important economic powers, owning vast tracts of farmland and collecting the income from estates. With this added influence the higher levels of the clergy became managers similar to the executives of large corporations. The career of Nebwenenef, high priest of the god Amun in the early years of the reign of Ramses illustrates both service in multiple cults and concurrent civil duties. He served as high priest in the cult of the god Anhur and the goddess Hathor, Lady of Dendera, before being appointed to the priesthood of Amun. His several secular titles included "overseer of the Double House of gold and silver" (the treasury) and "chief of all the craftsmen of Thebes." He exemplified the ability of individuals to occupy the top levels of power and influence in Egyptian society in both the religious and governmental spheres.

In a society that had an estimated literacy rate of 1 to 5 percent, the training to acquire the ability to read and write was very important, especially where a premium was put on record keeping. Scribes were vital to every aspect of life, from the simplest duties of letter writing and keeping accounts to the greater responsibilities of serving as administrator, emissary, or ambassador. Scribes were held in high esteem, and the initial training was sought after by bright and able young people. It was mainly the children of the elite who were able to study to be scribes, but there are examples of students from the lower classes finding access to scribal schools. The subject matter was essentially designed to prepare students for practical applications and consisted of the basics of reading, writing, and applied mathematics. The scribes' education took place in the palace or temple precincts, and its method consisted essentially of repetition and rote learning, which included the copying of classic texts. Many of the important literary texts that have been preserved, often in several versions, were copied by apprentice scribes.

There is a preserved document called "The Satire on the Trades," a glorification of the occupation of the scribe, which is written in the form of a father's advice to his son. In it the father describes many of the other occupations, with their obvious drawbacks, in contrast to the life of the scribe. He tells his son that other jobs are dirty or smelly or otherwise undesirable but not the life of the scribe. "You never see a sculptor sent as an emissary, but scribes are always chosen for such tasks"—a typical observation intended to make the young person devote himself to his studies. It is clear that the person with scribal training enjoyed a privileged position.

Most scribes were attached to governmental or temple service, but there is some indication that there was also a class of independent literate individuals whose services were available for hire. However, the importance of keeping accurate state records and managing the system of taxation required large numbers of specialists who were well trained. Tomb paintings and funerary models attest to the varied activities of the scribes, mainly keeping accounts of the produce of the fields for tax purposes. They are almost always depicted in twos and threes at the same work, suggesting a system of careful accounting.

THE SOCIAL ORGANIZATION OF DEATH

The stratification within Egyptian society can be illustrated with a variety of examples. A simple and obvious illustration is the size (or even the existence) of a tomb. Certainly only the well-to-do had the resources to construct or carve out tombs for burial. The very fact that an individual was buried in a tomb automatically demonstrates that he or she had wealth and influence. The ability to plan, commission, and carry out the preparation and decoration of a tomb of any size implies considerable wealth. The quality of the tomb furniture, including the mummy cases and ritual vessels, gives a good indication of disposable capital. Even the differing sizes of private tombs imply differences in rank and status. This evidence serves to correct the notion that everyone in ancient Egypt was mummified at death and accorded a lavish burial. The truth of the matter is quite different. The remains of ordinary people were treated simply. A grave furnished with a few personal possessions was all that the lower classes could expect. The relatively small number of tombs preserved from all periods in proportion to population estimates offers yet another example of the separation between the small upper class and the much larger lower classes.

When the unlimited expenditure used for a royal burial is compared with the simple preparation for a common grave, the disparity between the two major classes in ancient Egypt becomes even clearer. The often-cited example of the material from Tutankhamen's tomb includes one coffin of solid gold that weighed 300 pounds. In contrast, the grave of a workman might have contained a bronze razor or a mirror. It is hardly necessary to add that Tutankhamen was a minor ruler who died young and was buried in a tomb prepared for someone else. It is difficult to imagine what would have accompanied such great kings as Amenhotep III or Ramses II in their burials, a reminder of the pyramidal structure of society in ancient Egypt with the supreme ruler at the apex and a gradual lessening of responsibility and wealth at each wider level below.

THE MIDDLE EAST

BY KIRK H. BEETZ

There are large gaps in modern knowledge of the ancient societies of the Near East, partly because many did not leave relics in durable materials such as stone, partly because on occasion entire peoples were wiped out with few traces of their having existed and partly because much of the modern Near East has been and still is very dangerous for archaeologists, with many important sites having been out of their reach for decades at a time.

ÇATALHÜYÜK

One ancient people whose existence was forgotten for thousands of years lived at Çatalhüyük, in south-central Turkey. The ruins of this large village or small town—its population was perhaps 5,000 to 8,000—lay undiscovered until 1958. The earliest structures so far excavated date to before 7200 B.C.E., predating sites in Mesopotamia that were long thought to be the oldest urban areas in the world. The people at Çatalhüyük seem to have left no written language, so their social organization has to be deduced from physical remains.

Çatalhüyük consisted of mud-brick houses built side by side with no streets or passageways between them, making it look somewhat like a beehive. It had no defensive walls, but attackers would have had to fight house by house to get into and through it. In effect, the houses themselves were walls. They had no doorways and rarely had windows. People moved about by climbing through trapdoors in their ceilings and walking from roof to roof, sometimes using ladders when the roofs were uneven.

Many, perhaps even most houses had shrines in them, suggesting that religious ritual was an important part of everyday life. Some houses were much bigger than others, and the burials that are richest in goods tend to be under the floors of the larger houses, suggesting that some members of society ranked higher than others, perhaps forming a social elite group. The people of Çatalhüyük often buried their dead in their homes, under large platforms on which people could sit. Paintings on walls of headless people being picked at by vultures suggests a custom of leaving corpses out to be cleaned by scavenging birds, but many burials were of completely intact bodies, which seems to contradict the idea that corpses were picked clean before burial. Perhaps there were divergent burial customs; perhaps the paintings have another meaning. The dead were segregated by gender into separate graves, with women typically having the larger coverings and the better burial goods, suggesting that Çatalhüyük had a matriarchal society, meaning a society in which women were dominant over men. Many archaeologists believe that early societies in the region of Turkey were matriarchal.

The dwellings of Çatalhüyük are rich in manufactured products such as ceramic vessels. Excavations have revealed that these objects were created in homes. A section of each house seems to have been designated for craft work. At present, archaeologists suspect that every member of society was expected to know basic crafts such as basket weaving and home building. Çatalhüyük was abandoned sometime around 5600 B.C.E. The cause for its desertion is unknown. Some of the skeletons that have been recovered show signs of a mosquito-carried disease that may have killed many people, but this evidence does not necessarily mean that the settlement was afflicted with an epidemic. Instead, some residents may simply have come from marshlands to the south, where the disease and mosquitoes were more likely to be found.

JERICHO

Among very ancient remains are those of Jericho, in what was later known as Palestine. In about 8000 B.C.E. people built a large stone wall and a 30-foot-tall tower at this location. Archaeologists disagree over what the tower was for, with some insisting it was a watchtower, others supposing it was used for astronomical observations, and still others believing it was a defensive structure intended to protect either stored grain or a spring, or both. The tower has a sophisticated design and is not just a pile of rocks. It had an interior stairway, and its stones were fitted carefully together. The skill shown in the construction suggests that even earlier stone walls and towers must have existed somewhere in the area, since the builders at Jericho clearly were sure of their techniques.

The wall and tower are associated with human skulls that were apparently cleaned and then covered with clay sculptures of human faces, with seashells for their eyes. This treat-

Servants carrying food for the king's tables, palace of Xerxes, Persepolis, Persia (modern-day Iran) (Courtesy of the Oriental Institute of the University of Chicago)

ment may indicate that the builders of the wall and tower worshipped their ancestors and that the skulls represented dead leaders or priests who could be consulted by the living. An alternative possibility is that people thought they could capture and hold prisoner the spirits of the dead, forcing the spirits to do as they were ordered. Some art historians think that the tradition of realistic depictions of human beings found in such places as Egypt and ancient Greece derives from a similar ancient tradition begun in Jericho.

ERIDU

Most archaeologists point to ancient Sumer, in what is now southern Iraq, as the first broadly influential culture of the Near East, starting in the 4000s B.C.E., when city-states arose. The ancient Mesopotamians believed the city of Eridu was the oldest in the world and that it stood on the very spot where the world was created. Ancient Mesopotamian writers claimed that Eridu was founded before 72,000 B.C.E. Although it is not nearly that old, the city does seem to be the oldest yet discovered in the region of the Tigris and Euphrates rivers. At the bottommost layer of Eridu is a small shrine, which may mean that the city was built on a site already considered sacred as well as that the builders were very religious. Eridu was part of

a region archaeologists designate as southern Mesopotamia, the lands approximately south of the Diyala River, a tributary of the Tigris. Northern Mesopotamia, encompassing lands mostly near the north of the Tigris, did not come into cultural prominence until about 1900 B.C.E.

Many archaeologists dispute whether Eridu should be considered a real city, because its population probably did not exceed 9,000. To them Uruk just to the north, which at its peak in about 2700 B.C.E. had a population of at least 50,000, was the first true city. In the 4000s B.C.E., however, Eridu was the by far the largest settlement in a region in which villages of 250 or so people were regarded as notable, and it must have seemed crowded and metropolitan to the people of its era. It also represented a more complex social organization than would have been found in the villages of Mesopotamia. It did not become a capital of an empire or kingdom, and it was not even a great economic power, but it was the focus of religion for the Sumerian culture, and it therefore remained an example for the Sumerian cities that followed.

Many archaeologists have assumed that cities could not have been built without centralized leadership—for example, a king—because of the large public works projects required for building and maintaining an urban center. For the ancient cities of Sumer these projects included streets, irrigation canals, and walls to guard against invading armies, but Eridu and other Sumerian cities until about 3000 B.C.E. probably did not have monarchs. Instead, they developed an institution that was called the *lugal*, which translates as "great man." In a crisis such as a great flood or a war, an assembly of free citizens chose a leading fellow citizen to take charge until the crisis was over. It is possible that at some point crises came so frequently that a *lugal* was able to stay in power permanently.

Some historians call the earliest Sumerian city-states simple democracies because people in them supposedly had equal civil rights. Individual cities varied in how they organized themselves around the concept of free, socially equal citizens, but in general no one person was supposed to be born superior to another. These societies may have been matriarchal in outlook, with female ancestry being more important in identifying a person's heritage than male ancestry and with priestesses dominating religious rituals, but gender rights seem to have been equal in matters of social standing, control of land, marriage, and divorce. Much about the social organization of Eridu's era, about 5000 to 4000 B.C.E., is vague because of the absence of written records.

THE URUK PERIOD

The Uruk Period (ca. 4000–ca. 2900 B.C.E.) is somewhat clearer because written documents exist both from that time and from soon afterward. The period is named for the dominant city of the age, Uruk, known as Erech in the Bible. During this period men and women shared civic duties, with a man called *en* and a woman called *nin* holding chief administrative powers over a bureaucracy, each serving a term of one year. Divisions of labor seem to have been developing between the genders, with women in charge of the textiles industry, which was important to a city's wealth through trade. Wool was the primary material.

Although some archaeologists believe that there was no social differentiation in Uruk, with all free people being equal, there is evidence of an elite group of government workers who organized and directed group activities. Governments combined civil administration and religious practices, making public service an act of faith. Although the *en* and the *nin* supposedly controlled both government activities and religious rites on behalf of the general population, the existence of a permanent bureaucracy indicates that those who knew procedures and rituals well could manipulate the short-term administrators.

Archaeologists sometimes point to physical evidence that Uruk had an egalitarian society, meaning a society in which no one had special privileges by right of birth. They note that the temples and government buildings were open, airy places with numerous large doorways that were open to the outside, so that anyone passing by could see what was taking place inside. This free access implies that the government was open to public scrutiny. Citizens could know all they wanted about government and religious business merely by observing from

a doorway or simply strolling in among the government and religious officials. From this point of view, the *en*, the *nin*, the bureaucrats, and the priests and priestesses were all accessible to any citizen and were accountable to the public for what they did.

The institution of the assembly, even though it lingered for hundreds of years after kings and dynasties appeared, is another indication of egalitarianism. The assembly originally consisted of all free people, probably including women (but excluding slaves). At some point women lost their right to vote in the assembly; exactly when this happened is unknown, and possibly they retained their right to vote in some cities long after they lost it in others. By 3200 B.C.E., however, the egalitarian aspects of Sumerian society had begun to fade. Cities had not only *ens* and *nins* as well as the occasional *lugal* but also governing boards composed of wealthy landowners. Previously burials had shown no difference in status between rich and poor, but this began to change as landowners asserted their economic power to influence society. Even so, an assembly of citizens could overrule the governing board if someone, perhaps an *en* or a *nin*, brought a board decision to a public vote, which was typically held outside in a courtyard or other large, open public space.

DYNASTIC PERIOD

During the Early Dynastic Period (ca. 2900–ca. 2340 B.C.E.) in southern Mesopotamia, permanent kingship developed, but the kings had an uneasy relationship with their subjects, who retained many of the rights they had held during the Uruk Period. Perhaps the most interesting and most unaccountable change during this period was the loss of civil rights for women. They still had some legal protections, but by and large they were owned by the men in their lives, with their wealth always controlled by a male family member.

Social organization was dominated by the *oikos*. Archaeologists use this Greek word, which means "household," to refer to an extended family of close relatives who jointly own land and perhaps workshops. An *oikos* always had a male as its head, whose responsibilities included using family funds to support infirm family members, provide dowries, and pay fines for criminal convictions of relatives; possibly it was also his responsibility to carry out court orders for punishments of family members. One of his most important duties was to find mates for the unmarried men and women of his *oikos*. Marriages were arranged on the basis of wealth, although discrimination based on social class seems to have been rare.

By the time of Babylon's King Hammurabi (r. 1792–1750 B.C.E.) society had divided itself into three groups: the *awilum*, the *mushkenum*, and the *wardum*. The *awilum* were landowners. They had the most political power, and as the centuries passed they came to possess most of a city-state's wealth. They tended to hold the highest posts in government and religion, and they expected the best government jobs to go to their family members. The *mushkenum* were free people but did not own land. They retained the right to assemble in public places, and they could vote during assembly meetings. In most places women were now excluded from these rights. The *wardum* were slaves. They consisted mostly of prisoners of war who were forced to work for the government in public works projects or were sold to private citizens. Sometimes free people were sold into slavery. The head of an *oikos* could sell family members for money; a father could sell his children or his wife or even himself to escape poverty or debts. Slaves had few rights, and everything they made belonged to their owners. In a social practice that continued at least through the Old Babylonian Empire of about 2000 to 1600 B.C.E., members of one of these classes could move to another. A member of the *awilum* could join the *mushkenum* by selling all his land, and a member of the *mushkenum* could become part of the *awilum* by purchasing land. Slaves had to be freed first but then could join either of the classes of free people.

Women held on to one principal source of power, religion. In what was probably a relic tradition of the past, certain rituals had to be performed by women. In a practice that lasted at least through the Old Babylonian Empire, women could join a *gagum*. A *gagum* was a cloister for women whose lives were devoted to the priesthood. In the Uruk Period, if these women gave birth to children it probably would have been seen as a blessing, a sign of their fertility in service to the gods and therefore a good omen for the city. After women had lost most of their civil rights, however, members of a *gagum* were forbidden to have children. In a patriarchal culture, denying them the right to bear children was a means of symbolically taking away their creative power in religious life. A member of a *gagum* who even visited a tavern was put to death because taverns were where people often met to find partners for sexual relations. The women of the cloisters may have had a small victory over their oppressors, however: They were avid writers and many, possibly most, of the writings surviving from the Old Babylonian Empire are theirs and reflect their view of their society.

Sexuality was an important part of civic life in southern Mesopotamia. Every city was believed to be sacred, and the cities themselves were worshipped. One way to increase the health of a city was to have sexual relations in it. This was considered to be a joyful activity, and people were discouraged from having sexual relations in private. Indeed, some ancient writers bemoaned the antisocial behavior of young lovers who had sex in private rather than out in the street as proper people did. On the other hand, childbirth was an occasion for anxiety because only about one in two babies lived long after birth. Women giving birth were subjects for artists, probably because giving birth was an affirmation of life in the city and among its people.

THE HITTITES

Archaeologists disagree greatly about when the Hittites migrated from southern Europe into Anatolia (modern Turkey), dating it to between 2750 B.C.E. and 1700 B.C.E. In any event, by the 1600s B.C.E. the Hittites were expanding their domain, attacking their neighbors and raiding deep into the lands of Babylon. Their kings were remote and usually inaccessible to ordinary people, with a large bureaucracy between them and commoners. The king's palace was its own community within the broad community of the empire, with its own priests, physicians, craftspeople, and animal tenders. Princes lived within the palace's compound but in a house separate from the king's residence.

The apex of society was the king and queen. If the king died, the queen became the ruling monarch. Even while he lived, she exercised considerable control over the government bureaucracy and public ceremonies. Possibly this queenly power was a legacy of earlier matriarchal cultures in the Anatolian region, adopted by the Hittites in order to provide stability for their government: If a king died prematurely, he was succeeded by someone who already had experience of rule. Beneath the monarchs in social standing were nobles and beneath them government officials. Next in line came craftspeople and tradespeople: manufacturers of ceramics, blacksmiths, weavers, carpenters, sculptors, and the like. Farmers ranked below the craftspeople and tradespeople, and below them were slaves.

ARABIA AND ISRAEL

While the Hittites were building their empire in the northwestern Near East, another culture was making itself felt in the south. These were the people of the Arabian Peninsula. By 1154 B.C.E. the Arabs had become a significant distraction to the Kassite Dynasty (ca. 1530–ca. 1155 B.C.E.) of Babylon. The Kassite kings devoted so many resources to coping with the Arabs that the kingdom of Elam was able to invade Babylon and overthrow the Kassites.

The peoples of Arabia were nomads, herders of sheep. They raided their neighbors for food and wealth. Sometime before 1000 B.C.E. one of these groups, known as the Sabeans, settled in the region of modern-day Yemen. (The biblical place-name Sheba is derived from *Sabea*.) The Sabeans were a mercantile people, specializing in being go-betweens for the shipping of goods from Africa and the Near East to southern Asia, especially India, as well as for the return trade. They formed part of the kingdom of Axum, named for its capital city in eastern Africa.

Little is known about the social organization of the Sabeans, partly because their written language has yet to be translated and partly because during the 20th century their buildings and canals in Yemen were dismantled, the stones and bricks being used for modern house building. They had a long tradition of rule by queens and seem to have been a fairly open society for women, allowing them to become merchants as well as members of the ruling elite. Ethiopian oral tradition says that around 955 B.C.E. this legacy was abandoned when Queen Makeda was succeeded by Menelik, her son by King Solomon. Thereafter, so the oral tradition says, only men could rule. Women seem to have been limited to officiating in the worship of female gods.

King Solomon of Israel was probably viewed as something of an upstart at that time. Israel had been a backwater dominated by the Sumerian culture. Israel had a social organization similar to that of southern Mesopotamia. Women were severely limited in what they could do and were probably excluded from most religious rituals. Although Solomon's kingdom had a strong military force, merchants tended to dominate social life. Government officials seem to have been preoccupied by tasks intended to smooth trade within Israel and with other nations. The many wives of Solomon were part of the effort to gain protection for Israeli traders; the wives tended to be political brides, the marriages intended to cement goodwill between Israel and the kings and queens who were their parents. This was a common practice among Near Eastern rulers of the time. Among Israel's commoners polygamy tended to be reserved for political leaders and the rich. Enslaved women were often kept as concubines.

NEO-ASSYRIAN EMPIRE

The culture of the Near East suffered a significant upheaval with the rise of the Neo-Assyrian Empire of 934–612 B.C.E. in northern Mesopotamia. Assyria of the Old Assyrian Period (ca. 1813–ca. 1365 B.C.E.) had been primarily a trading empire with customs derived from Sumer, but the new empire was a military state in which warriors were the elite of society. Women were reduced to the status of nonhumans. They were forced to wear garments that covered them entirely, not for the sake of modesty but to symbolize their utter lack of worth. Further, the garments made clear that the women belonged to certain men, who were the only ones allowed to see them without their coverings. Female babies were often killed at birth because only male babies were valued. A woman's duties consisted of bearing male babies to supply the army and obeying her husband, father, or brothers in all matters. The Neo-Assyrian social practices toward women influenced all of the Near East and much of central Asia, even pervading some Hindu sects in India. The Neo-Assyrians created such loathing among their subject peoples that after their overthrow they were hunted down and killed for another 10 years, until they were exterminated, but the status of women in the Near East never recovered from their suppression under the Neo-Assyrian regime.

PERSIA

During the reign of Cyrus the Great from 559 to 529 B.C.E., Persia (modern-day Iran) conquered much of the Near East. The Persian government typically allowed conquered peoples to continue to live their lives as they had before, provided they paid their taxes and supplied soldiers for the Persian army. Thus, even at this late date, Sumerian customs continued to be practiced in much of the Near East. Most of what is known about Persian social customs comes from Greek writers, who tended to be very biased in their accounts because Greece and Persia were bitter enemies. From these Greek authors comes the image of the decadent oriental potentate, based on their depictions of Persian courts as places of idle luxury and lazy nobility. One Greek historian who provided an alternative view was Herodotus, in the 400s B.C.E. According to him, the Persians were courageous fighters and intelligent statesmen.

The Persian monarch kept himself remote from his subjects, surrounding himself with impressive buildings and elaborate rituals intended to awe outsiders. He employed many artists and craftspeople who decorated his public works. The Persian social order is not clear to modern historians, but it seems that after the king came nobles, who were born to their high status. After them came governors of conquered territories and then officials who ran the day-to-day operations of the government. Among the latter were probably the generals of Persia's large armies. Persian rulers were much occupied with enhancing communications and trade within their empire, which suggests that merchants were important members of society. There were many slaves, mostly prisoners of war.

Greeks already had settled in parts of the Near East near the Mediterranean Sea, and they had made themselves nuisances to the Persians, sparking wars that made Persians and Greeks long-term enemies. From 336 to 323 B.C.E. the Macedonian king Alexander the Great conquered and occupied most of the Near East, bringing Greek culture all the way into India. Out of Alexander's conquests arose the Seleucid Kingdom (ca. 311–ca. 140 B.C.E.). Although they were Greek in outlook, the Seleucid monarchs imitated the trappings of a Persian court.

PARTHIANS

The Parthian Empire began in about 250 B.C.E. in northeastern Iran, and under Mithridates I (r. 174–136 B.C.E.) the Parthians supplanted the Seleucids through most of Mesopotamia. Although the Parthians had migrated into Iran from central Asia and had used Iran as their base for conquering much of the Near East, they made their capital city of Ctesiphon in Mesopotamia, near modern-day Baghdad, and they ruled their empire as if it were a Mesopotamian one. The first Parthian dynasty, the Arsacids, ruled from about 250 B.C.E. until they were overthrown in 226 C.E. by people from western Iran. The newcomers founded the Sassanid Dynasty, which lasted until an invasion by Arabs in the 600s C.E. Although it is sometimes confusingly called the Persian Empire, the Sassanid Dynasty had little in common with the original Persian Empire. Like the Arsacids, the Sassanids ruled as a Mesopotamian culture from Ctesiphon.

The official language of the Parthians was Greek. They derived their laws and social customs from the Near Eastern peoples they conquered, and little is known of their native customs, which had been replaced by those of Mesopotamia. Women had few rights, children were expected to follow the professions of their parents, and local cultures were compelled to provide the Parthian military with troops. The preoccupation of Parthian monarchs was war, and they often fought Greeks and Romans in the west and nomads from central Asia in the east. Despite the emphasis on military conquest, trade was essential to life of the empire, with numerous trade routes extending as far as China and Africa. This activity brought the rise of a merchant class whose members used their wealth to climb the social ladder by buying their way into government. Government officials, like nobles, ranked higher than ordinary members of society.

ASIA AND THE PACIFIC
BY KIRK H. BEETZ

INDIA

The earliest-known civilization in India was that of the Harappans, named by modern archaeologists for a place near one of their major cities. Although the Harappans had a written language, it survives mostly on seals, meaning that it is in fragments, and it has not yet been translated. The ancient Sumerians made only a few written references to the Harappans. Therefore, the social organization of the Harappans must be deduced from their physical remains, which consist of two or three cities and numerous towns and villages scattered throughout the valley of the Indus River, with some farther south and others farther west or north.

Mohenjo Daro seems to be the best preserved of the cities. The city was well planned, with a grid pattern for streets, a well-maintained sewer system, and separate areas for public gatherings and residences. The residential areas are divided distinctly into sections with big houses with brick walls that were laid in decorative, abstract patterns and sections with small houses with little or no fancy brickwork. To some archaeologists, these divisions mean that the Harappans had class distinctions between rich and poor. Archaeologists infer that those with small houses were oppressed by those with big houses. Nevertheless, all residential areas had the same sort of narrow streets and the same high-quality sewers, with manholes giving access to sewer repair workers in all areas. This evidence suggests that while there may have been a difference in wealth among the Harappans, the poorer Harappans had access to civic services equal to richer Harappans. Further, public areas seem to have been accessible to all.

There was a large public swimming pool, perhaps for ritual bathing. There were large buildings that may have been used for worship. Archaeologists have also discovered foundations to a long building, with air ducts to keep its interior dry, which was a huge facility for storing grain. The existence of this structure implies that food was collectively owned by the community, in turn implying that the land on which the grain was grown was collectively owned by the community. From this information, some archaeologists surmise that the Harappans had a social elite who owned all the means of production and that most people were slaves or serfs who worked the land for the benefit of the elite. Other archaeologists think the evidence indicates that the grain was kept in public trust and belonged to all.

Exactly when the Harappan culture began is not known, but it was thriving by 2600 B.C.E. and began to decline between 1900 and 1700 B.C.E.; it was eclipsed by Aryan invaders by 1500 B.C.E. These Aryans were nomadic cattle herders from central Asia who overwhelmed the Harappans, who had already been weakened by natural disasters. The era from about 1500 to about 600 B.C.E. is known as the Vedic because of the Vedas, sacred works of the Hindus that began as an oral tradition telling of the events of the Aryans' migration into northern India.

The Vedic peoples were slow to settle, preferring for hundreds of years to move their herds across the land, especially the grassy plains near the Ganges River, which ran northwest to southeast across northern India. Their culture mingled with the local cultures to become the Brahmanic social order, the basis of Hinduism. Much of the history of India is the story of the Vedic culture spreading ever southward over thousands of years. The Vedic people brought with them the caste system of social organization. A caste was a class based on birth that restricted the professions, civil rights, and marriage possibilities of people born into it. How many castes the Vedic peoples originally had is not known, but by the fourth century B.C.E., when the Vedas were written down, there were four. The top caste was that of the Brahmans, followed by Kshatriyas, Vaishyas, and Shudras. After these came the people without caste.

People born into the Brahman caste were priests and were expected to be spiritual leaders. They could not be punished for many crimes and could not be put to death or physically harmed. Even to annoy a Brahman was a crime. Sometimes, however, even a Brahman could commit a crime so vile that it had to be punished, in which case the knot of hair on the head—which in Brahman tradition was tied at the age of three years old—was cut off. This act made a Brahman a nonperson. It cut off a Brahman from all family and friends and denied a Brahman any social rights.

Many Brahmans lived off donations from members of other castes. It was considered a social obligation for members of lower castes to make gifts to Brahmans. Social customs and religious laws forbade someone to give his family's entire wealth to a Brahman, but Brahmans often received houses, even whole villages, as gifts. Giving gifts to Brahmans was thought to improve a person's karma, the spiritual energy that governed how many times a person would have to be reincarnated before becoming one with the universal spirit. Many Brahmans worked at professions that were supposed to be outside their caste. Brahmanic laws allowed them to take such jobs if they were in distress, a rule that applied to members of other castes as well.

The Kshatriyas were the caste of high government officials and warriors. Kings and nobles belonged to this caste. Such was the power of India's social organization that even at the end of the ancient era, kings were bound by the rules of their caste and usually followed the rules. Not to do so could invalidate their right to rule, but if they followed the rules carefully, no one had the right to depose them. In actual practice, however, kings were often deposed, sometimes by their own sons.

Kshatriyas were supposed to devote themselves to the good of the nation. As warriors, they were expected to serve their king and to strive to increase the power of their king. As government officials, they were supposed to be honest and impartial when making decisions. As court officials, they were expected to be above bribery and other inappropriate influences. Brahmans did not have to pay taxes because they were expected to improve the welfare of the public through their piety, but the Kshatriyas were expected to pay taxes. Their taxes were lower than those of the lower castes, a circumstance that inspired resentment among members of lower castes. Even so, members of the lower castes were expected to be respectful toward Kshatriyas.

The Vaishyas were merchants, moneylenders, and farmers. They were expected to pay extra high taxes because under Brahmanic law it was their duty to support the Brahmans and the Kshatriyas. Even so, some Vaishyas managed to become wealthy. The Vaishyas, Kshatriyas, and Brahmans were all allowed to learn the holy writings of the Vedas, and they were twice-born, meaning that as children they underwent rituals that resulted in a spiritual birth. Shudras were barred from reading most religious works and were not allowed to be spiritually reborn. They could not participate in public religious rituals, only private ones.

Craftspeople, servants, laborers, wage earners, and minor government officials were Shudras. Some historians believe that when the Aryan nomads invaded India, they made the local peoples members of this fourth caste. The Shudras tended to be paid poorly and usually worked for the same employer from one generation to the next. The Shudras were subdivided into three groups: pure, unexcluded, or excluded. The pure Shudras could hope to read minor religious works. The unexcluded and excluded Shudras were treated with disdain. Beneath them were outcastes. Outcastes were expected to do the work that would defile members of the four castes, such as hunting, fishing, butchering live animals, executing human beings, and carrying the dead. They were not allowed to walk on roads but had to walk to the sides of roads. A Brahman could kill an outcaste with little or no penalty.

There were two kinds of outcastes that were treated better. One included people who had detached themselves from society to live as hermits, forsaking most of the pleasures of life. Such people could be respected and could even become considered holy and were often treated well. The other kind consisted of foreigners. Foreigners could be treated well, though their lack of caste meant that they could not be accepted to meals; Brahmans often could not let foreigners into their homes. There was a feast day on which foreigners and Indians were allowed to dine together, and sometimes foreigners were absorbed into castes, with foreign dignitaries joining a high caste.

Women were protected by laws, but those of lower castes could be abused by those of higher castes. A woman's word could not be taken over that of a man of her caste or higher. In matters of law, women were not to be subjected to the same severity of tortures and punishments as men. On the other hand, if they were wives or daughters of a man sent to prison, they were sent to prison as well and suffered as he suffered. A woman's testimony was usually unacceptable in court proceedings. Women often earned their own money, but those who belonged to the Brahman or Kshatriya castes were not supposed to work at menial jobs. Sometimes they had to, and they then usually worked at home weaving cloth, which they could sell to a factory. The workers at the factory were not allowed to look at the women while the transactions took place.

Rebellion against Brahmanic laws came in the form of new, rival religions. One such religion was Buddhism, which began as just a sect within the Brahmanic tradition. Buddhists rejected the caste system, holding as a tenet of their faith that any person could attain enlightenment through good deeds, religious rituals, and prayers. Some parts of India became primarily Buddhist. In those places even Brahmans had to have jobs to support themselves, and they took jobs under the rule of duress that allowed people to work outside their caste if they had to do so.

Although the rules of ancient Indian social organization sound very strict, the Brahmanic rules were not followed as scrupulously as they are now followed by many Hindus. For instance, in the ancient world marriages between castes were common, and a stigma was attached to the marriage for two generations but no more. It was possible to find Brahmans doing jobs of any of the other castes, and they were sometimes important government officials. Clever Shudras could become rich and influential.

CHINA

Knowledge of the social organization of China before the Han Dynasty (202 B.C.E.–220 C.E.) is sketchy at present. Emperor Qin Shi Huangdi (r. 221–210 B.C.E.) tried to have the records of previous governments destroyed and even had Confucian scholars executed so that they could not transmit their knowledge to later generations. He did so because he wanted history to begin with him. He wanted to eradicate bad influences from the past, and he wanted the system of legalism to replace all previous systems of government. Legalism advocated laws to govern every action a person took, even trivial actions.

For a long time the Shang Dynasty (ca. 1500–1045 B.C.E.) was thought to be a myth, the primary records of existence being the transcription of histories from the memory of a 90-year-old scholar who survived Qin Shi Huangdi's purges. Archaeological discoveries have revealed the existence of the Shang, including their written language, but most of their known writings come from bamboo sticks that were used for magical records. Much about their society must be deduced from their physical remains.

Peasants made up the vast majority of Shang society. They lived primarily in the region of the Yellow River, and the food they produced kept the empire fed. When there were public works projects, such as building roads or city walls, peasants were conscripted to do the work. They formed the bulk of Shang armies and were often forced into war. Those who marched to a part of the empire far from home rarely returned. It seems that the Shang rulers learned that they were dependent on the peasants and may have made some efforts to care for the peasants, at least well enough to keep the peasants healthy and working. A peasant was expected to devote his or her life to work, laboring every moment possible.

Like the Shang, the Zhou were warlike. Much of society during their dynasty (1045– 256 B.C.E.) is still a mystery. As with the Shang, nearly everyone was a peasant. The Zhou placed nobles in charge of provinces, creating a feudal system in which the nobles had principal authority within their provinces. The lives of peasants were very hard. Nobles often took their land away from them, forcing them to pay rent for the land or to work the land as sharecroppers—people who have to give a share of their harvest to the landowner in order to be allowed to farm the land. Occasionally, a Zhou emperor would redistribute the land to the peasants, but the nobles would retake the land, often by making loans to peasants that the peasants could not repay, forcing them to forfeit their lands. During the second half of the Zhou Dynasty, the emperors had little military power and could not enforce their edicts, ending their ability to care for the peasants. The lives of peasants became so dire that some archaeologists and historians refer to their being slaves, but for all their miseries, peasants were not considered slaves. In fact, they were far higher on the social scale than were slaves.

During the Zhou Dynasty much of the pattern for Chinese social organization was set. At the top of society was the royal family, with the emperor ruling because he had been blessed by the gods. Below him were the nobles, who held their stations from the authority granted to them by the emperor. This situation meant that the nobles needed to keep the emperor even after the emperor had lost almost all his power because the nobles were accepted by the rest of the Chinese only as a result of the authority supposedly derived from a divinely appointed emperor. After the nobles came warriors, most of whom were minor nobility. After them came the peasants. During the Han Dynasty these would be the only true people of the nation. Everyone else, wealthy or not, was not socially recognized, including traders, craftspeople, servants, and slaves.

Perhaps the most socially significant change during the end of the Zhou Dynasty was the elevation of government officials in social standing. The period from 453 to 221 B.C.E. is known as the Warring States Period. During that time China's provinces had been combined into several large provinces, each competing with the others to rule all of China. The governors of these provinces took to calling themselves kings. One of these rulers was King Zheng of the Qin province in the western part of China. Qin had already adopted legalism as its philosophy of government. In its harsh organization of life, legalism had become the tool of scholars, men educated in the intricacies of running a government with complex rules. Some of these scholars traveled through China looking for sponsors; in Qin they had attained a standing below only that of King Zheng himself.

King Zheng became Qin Shi Huangdi, and his enforcement of legalism throughout China made him hated by nearly everyone. His government officials were loathed. Legalism sought to reorganize society so that no one except the emperor was exempt from the law. People would be persuaded to behave according to legalist principles by severe punishments for violating the rules and by rewards for obeying the rules. In theory, anyone could climb the social ladder by obeying the rules. In practice, legalism was corrupt, with people unable to avoid breaking at least a few laws every day, giving the emperor an excuse to send millions of unfortunate people into slave labor camps working on the Great Wall or other construction projects as punishment for their crimes. The legalist government officials became devoted to betrayal and political scheming.

When rebellion finally came, rebels slaughtered the entire royal family, even after the emperor surrendered. It is to Liu Bang's credit that when he finally emerged as emperor in 202 B.C.E., he did not continue the bloodbath, and he did not slaughter government scholars. He was a rough man with little respect for scholars, but he did see the good sense of having educated people run government. He chose Confucians. He often made fun of them, but he allowed them to reform the laws of the empire.

Liu Bang (r. 202–195 B.C.E.) founded the Han Dynasty, and the basic social organization of the Han remained the organization of Chinese society through civil wars and new dynasties throughout the rest of the ancient era. The basic social order was the emperor, then the nobles, then government officials, and then peasants. When disasters struck, these were the people who were to be saved because they were deemed essential to the survival of the nation. Although being a peasant was still usually miserable, the Han instituted new opportunities for social mobility. One of these was the institution of 20 ranks within society. Peasants had access to the first eight, while the others were reserved for members of higher social standing. Through contributions to community welfare, hard work, and acquisition of wealth, a peasant could ascend the first eight ranks, gaining prestige and rights with each rank. Whether the government officials who devised the 20 steps intended this result or not, the system was a powerful motivational tool because it gave hope to people in a culture where respect mattered greatly. A peasant at the eighth level was a significant member of his community. Further, the ranks allowed for downward mobility. A person in the highest ranks could lose so many ranks as punishment for a crime that he fell below the eighth level and could end up beneath the peasants he had once dominated.

Another opportunity for social advancement was through education. Schools open to boys from many walks of life began in 145 B.C.E. in the province of Shu, where modern Sichuan is, when Governor Wen Weng (ca. 1231–ca. 1135 B.C.E.) opened schools to boys from throughout the province because he needed a pool of educated people from which to hire government officials. The schools of China were Confucian, and students were expected to learn the principles of the philosopher Confucius (551–479 B.C.E.) and become skilled in the sciences and the law. If a student passed tests given by the government, he could gain a government job and rise through the ranks of government, acquiring higher social rank as he did.

Girls could become educated, too, but they had to be educated in private, usually by other women. This practice limited the opportunities for education to daughters of the wealthy, nobles, and government officials. Some women were marvelously gifted and even became influential advisers to emperors. Even so, they complained about restrictions placed on them because of their gender. The women of ancient China were notable for their industriousness and contributed greatly to the economy, but they were expected to submit to the authority of men. When they rose in rank, they did so usually because their husbands rose in rank. They may have found their greatest opportunities in trades and crafts because tradespeople and craftspeople were outside official recognition, but even a woman who made herself wealthy might find that her money was not her own if she married.

JAPAN

In Japan people did not begin building an agricultural economy until about 300 B.C.E. Even in the third century C.E. they had not yet learned to irrigate their farms; they did not plant rice as seedlings and, in fact, just scattered rice seed in wet areas, such as marshes. When they first formed governments is not known, but the earliest ruler for whom there are written records, mostly Chinese, is Queen Himiko (fl. third century C.E.), who ruled a nation called Yamatai, whose people the Chinese called Wa. This culture existed in the late second century and third century C.E. The Wa lived in more than 50 small chiefdoms. It is possible that Himiko ruled by the consent of the chiefs. That she was a sorceress suggests that women held high rank in religion. Although her being the monarch implies a matriarchal society, the effort to replace her with a man after her death suggests that male chiefs wanted a male leader.

Ceramic sculptures left by the Wa indicate that they had a society with many crafts because the sculptures portray many people in everyday work. It is easy to suppose that ceramics makers were highly respected because the people of Japan had produced magnificent pottery for thousands of years.

Jōmon Period pottery, Japan (about 13,000–300 B.C.E.); the development of production techniques and decoration of this style of pottery over such a long period suggests that the country was stable and enjoyed a continuity of social organization. (© The Trustees of the British Museum)

CENTRAL AND NORTHERN ASIA

Most of what has been recorded about the peoples of central and northern Asia was written by people who hated them. Historical records are of raids by central and northern Asians on farms and towns, of rampant slaughter of civilians and theft of a year's harvest as well as of valuable goods. However, the people of those parts of Asia were among the world's greatest explorers. Several times they crossed from Asia to North America, and their descendants populated two unfamiliar continents. Many in the far north of Asia followed nomadic animal herds, as some still follow reindeer. There is little record of these far northern Asians being warlike or raiding others. They seem to have had their societies organized around the herds they followed, which were regarded as owned by everyone in the society.

Those who raided the settled peoples of Asia had ethics so different from those of the settled areas that their points of view seemed almost incomprehensible to the settled peoples. In general, such groups as the Xiongnu, who lived north and northwest of China, regarded other peoples as prey. Their societies were organized around taking what they needed to survive, either from herds of sheep or cattle or from people who grew crops and manufactured goods they wanted. Efforts to reason with them by the Chinese and Indians failed for lack of a common ground of understanding.

The Xiongnu had kings, men selected from among many tribal chiefs. Their authority was limited because chiefs would sometimes choose to disobey them. Both men and women were trained from birth to be expert horsemen, and both genders held responsibility for carrying and raising tents, providing food, and defending their camps. Within a traveling group, there seems to have been social ranking, with some people owning more cattle or horses than other people. One way for someone to raise his or her social standing was to steal horses or cattle from another tribe.

Some nomads of central Asia moved into settled territories in order to find pasture for their herds. Central Asia had been drying out for centuries when Aryans moved into India and Iran to find new grazing areas. A growth in population may have provided additional pressure to move south into new lands. The best records of their societies known to exist are the Hindu religious works the Vedas, based on the ancient oral history of the Aryan invasion of India.

OCEANIA

Very little is known of the social organization of ancient Oceania. Thus, archaeologists and historians study the customs of people of Oceania of recorded history, from the 18th century C.E. to the present, and make inferences about social behavior. Sometimes they make assumptions about social organization that lack scientific foundation, based on what they know of similar societies in other parts of the world. Thus, much that is thought to be true of ancient Oceania is subject to sometimes radical change when new evidence is discovered. In general, the peoples of the ancient Pacific probably organized themselves by family relationships, with immediate relatives being the smallest social unit, followed by membership in a clan. The peoples of Tonga may have been organizing themselves into a larger social unit, a nation, during the last couple of centuries of the ancient era, when they were likely moving toward creating a monarchy and a kingdom. In Australia people probably moved across the landscape in family groups, forming larger groups only for religious observances. Elsewhere the social dynamics are murky. For instance, Indonesia almost certainly had cultures in which loyalty to one's clan was being replaced by loyalty to a monarch, but what form this change took is unknown. During the medieval era powerful kingdoms emerged on Java, suggesting that society was already organized and developing as distinct groups or nations earlier, during the ancient era.

EUROPE

BY AMY HACKNEY BLACKWELL

Although social organization is very difficult to determine from nonwritten sources, archaeologists use information from settlements and burials to infer how the ancient people of Europe structured their social relationships. The ice age hunter-gatherers before 10,000 B.C.E. were organized into bands that had only a loose connection to kinship and were based more on friendship and trust. Such groups may have coalesced at some times of the year and split apart at other times to take advantage of seasonal conditions for hunting and collecting. It is difficult to tell whether the family was a central element of social life at this time. The establishment of farming communities across Europe between 7000 B.C.E. and 3000 B.C.E. brought the emergence of distinct households, residential groups related by kinship and probably organized in a family structure. Such households were the basic building blocks of Neolithic society. Differences in status, power, and wealth were transient, and no lasting hierarchies appear to have formed.

Social structure changed in the late Neolithic and the Bronze Age, when we see for the first time clear differences in status, power, and wealth that persisted across generations. Farming households were still the fundamental basis for social structure, but starting in about 3000 B.C.E. in southeastern Europe and 2000 B.C.E. in northwestern Europe, there began to be rich burials and the accumulation of goods that marked social differences. Many archaeologists believe that the societies at this time took the form of what anthropologists call "chiefdoms," in which a small group of elite individuals and families were in control of a larger population of commoners. On the other hand, it is also possible that the lines of authority and status were not so hierarchical at first, and while some individuals may have been leaders in some spheres of activity (such as trade), others may have had leading roles in other activities (such as warfare and ritual). It is clear, however, that the complex social organization of Celtic and Germanic Europe that is known to us from written records emerged from these formative periods centuries and millennia earlier.

Most of what is known in written sources about ancient European social organization comes from the Celtic and Germanic peoples. The Celts, or more precisely the Celtic languages, spread through Europe during the first millennium B.C.E., radiating out from the Alps of Central Europe. By 400 B.C.E. most of the people in northwestern Europe and the British Isles spoke Celtic languages. The Germanic-speaking peoples appeared in northern Germany and southern Scandinavia around 500 B.C.E. and migrated throughout Central Europe over the next 1,000 years. Although there were other language groups and accompanying cultures, Celtic and Germanic peoples predominated in non-Mediterranean Europe.

Almost every ancient European culture was organized around a tribal structure. Both Celts and Germans organized their societies around two principles: family and war. Kinship determined tribal membership and battle companions. Family relationships and skill in battle also determined an individual's position in the social hierarchy. Social institutions were designed to help people behave within the hierarchy and to maintain the peace within a warlike society.

Ancient European social organization was also largely determined by the fact that Celtic and Germanic peoples moved around frequently. The Romans observed that the Celts and Germans sometimes wandered for generations at a time, loading their wagons with their worldly goods and traveling from place to place in the forests of Central Europe. They occasionally settled in small villages and farmed the surrounding land, but they often abandoned these settlements and wandered around. Social mores facilitated this frequent movement. For example, both Celtic and Germanic people would kill old people or newborn infants if keeping them around would slow down the group too much. By the time of the Roman Empire, Celtic and Germanic societies had become fairly civilized. People lived in cities and traded with people from several nations. In this period social organization was influenced by Roman and Greek practices.

CELTS

The Celtic peoples who occupied most of Europe by the fifth century B.C.E. had a loose social structure that revolved around family and warfare. Tribes, clans, and families were the primary social groupings. The largest grouping was the tribe, or *tuath* in Irish. This group provided people with their ethnic identity. Within the tribe, people belonged to a clan, an extended family that was the real source of social organization. Nuclear families formed the smallest social group but were less significant than clans.

Celts seem to have thought of themselves first as soldiers. The chiefs of Celtic tribes were expected to be extremely brave in battle to show an example to their soldiers. Soldiers grew very close to their comrades in arms and were expected to sacrifice their lives for one another or to avenge their fallen companions. It went without saying that clan members would

rally to the aid of their fellow clansmen. If a Celtic man was insulted or murdered by someone from another clan, his kinsmen would all assume the responsibility of avenging him. This practice resulted in extended feuds between families throughout the Celtic world.

Because feuds were so common, Celtic societies created a class of men who arbitrated disputes. These men were experts in the complex body of laws (called Brehon laws in Ireland) used throughout Europe in Celtic communities. Historians believe that these laws originated among European Celtic peoples during the Bronze Age, between 2300 and 900 B.C.E. For centuries Celtic legal experts memorized the body of laws so that they could interpret them and resolve disputes. One of the main purposes of Celtic laws was to prevent the frequent blood feuds from resulting in a never-ending string of murders by forcing murderers to compensate the families of their victims. This compensation would effectively end a feud, allowing the rival clans to resume peaceful relations.

Celtic society was organized into a number of different classes. Kings and noblemen sat at the top. These men were wealthy and counted in their clans large groups of powerful kinsmen who could support them in battle. Nobles often functioned as chiefs of their tribes. The people in the clan of a nobleman's tribe owed him allegiance. The nobleman himself might owe allegiance to a higher nobleman or a king. In Ireland a number of lesser kings would owe allegiance to a single high king. Anyone who owed allegiance to someone else was required to pay that nobleman tribute every year, in the form of grain, livestock, and military assistance.

Below the noble classes there were two classes of free people (as opposed to slaves). Members of the higher class owned some movable property, such as cattle, but they did not own land. Below them were free people who owned nothing. These freemen rented land from nobles, paying rent in the form of crops and fighting for their landlords during wartime. Below the free classes were slaves captured from other tribes and free clansmen who had somehow lost their tribal rights.

Celts also ranked themselves within classes, according to age, birth, and skill and courage in battle. This social ranking helped Celtic people know how to relate to one another. They knew who owed what to whom, who could own land and who could not, and who could testify in court. Social rank determined which crimes were prosecuted and how they were punished. It even determined the sort of funeral a person would receive; chiefs were often buried with chariots and weapons as well as gold jewelry.

Two categories of Celts operated somewhat outside the usual system of rankings. Priests, called Druids, maintained the calendar and determined the dates of festivals. Druids also memorized the body of mythology and taught it to people. They served as advisers to the kings and officiated at rituals. Professional poets, or bards, composed and memorized long poems describing mythical or historical events. Nobles and kings kept bards at their courts to serve as official historians and entertainers. Bards were allowed to travel more freely than other people and were often welcomed as visitors because they offered entertainment. Although Celtic society was patriarchal and kinship was traced through male lines, women had a fairly high position in society. They could own property, and they fought alongside men in battles.

During the first millennium B.C.E., settlement patterns varied from place to place. Many early Celts lived in small settlements that might house several extended families who farmed and hunted in the surrounding area. In the British Isles people lived in and around hilltop forts. Others lived in larger groups in towns. The people of the Hallstatt culture (1200–500 B.C.E.) lived in towns and in hill forts. Some Gallic tribes were large, amorphous groups of migrating warriors and families. They seem not to have believed that they had a homeland of their own and were willing to move long distances.

Several kings appear to have taken advantage of Celtic military skill and lack of national ties by buying their services as mercenary soldiers. In the days of the early Roman Republic (509–27 B.C.E.) the Gauls encroached on the Mediterranean world several times. Gauls of the Senones tribe, led by the chief Brennus (fourth century B.C.E.), attacked Rome in 387 B.C.E. and then immediately left; some historians believe that Brennus was hired by Dionysius of Syracuse (r. 405–367 B.C.E.) to attack Rome. In the late third century B.C.E. several thousand Gauls wandered through Thrace and were invited into Asia Minor by King Nicomedes I (r. 278–250 B.C.E.) of Bithynia, who wanted them to help him fight his brother. These Gauls settled in central Anatolia, where they became known as the Galatians.

Celtic people seem to have been trading with one another and with other Europeans long before the Romans arrived. Archaeologists have found prehistoric roads in Ireland and Germany that might have been used to transport goods from place to place. Celtic smiths used a variety of metals that had to come from other places. Celtic goods made their way throughout the Mediterranean region. Most trade among Celtic peoples was done by barter and exchange, and its primary purpose was the cementing of kinship ties and military alliances. Cattle were a particularly important form of wealth, and attempting to steal the cattle of enemies was apparently a fairly common enterprise among Celtic nobles.

The Celts did make some coins during the Roman Period, but these were of limited use, and most people preferred to hold their wealth in more tangible forms, such as gold jewelry, weapons, chariots, cloth, slaves, and livestock. As time went on and the Roman Empire grew, however, Celts became increasingly Romanized in their behavior and trading practices.

GAULS

By the time of the Roman Republic, the Celts in France and Belgium, known as the Gauls, had developed a complex society with defined territories and military alliances. Julius Caesar (r. 49–44 B.C.E.) wrote a lengthy description of Gallic life in his account of the Gallic Wars. Caesar describes three main groups of Gauls: the Aquitani, the Galli or Celtae, and the Belgae. The Belgae appear to have been at least part Germanic, though historians do not know much about them. They were particularly warlike because they lived far from the Mediterranean world.

According to Caesar, the Gauls of his time organized themselves into tribes, which were subdivided into *pagi*. Each *pagus* was a subdivision of the tribe's overall territory; the Romans also used the term to refer to the individuals who lived in a given *pagus*. Every tribe was led by a council of elders and a single leader, either a hereditary king or an elected official. The Aeduii tribe called their king Vergobret. These kings ruled together with the councils, preventing the kings from taking complete control of their tribes.

Tribes were also organized into larger groups that contained several tribes. Although these organizations, called "*civitates*" by the Romans, encompassed large amounts of territory and had large populations, they were not equivalent to nations. The Gallic tribes occasionally united to fight a common enemy, but generally they did not get along well enough to stay together for long. The chief Vercingetorix (d. 46 B.C.E.) of the Averni led a union of Gallic tribes in battle against the Romans in 52 B.C.E. Vercingetorix had enough authority to make alliances with other Gallic tribes and to hold supreme command of all the Gallic armies. He engineered an overarching defense strategy that would have been impossible with a looser arrangement. However, he was captured by Caesar, and the union of the tribes dissolved.

The Romans knew of numerous tribes. Gallic tribes included the Allobroges of the region near Geneva; the Aquitani of southwestern France; the Carnutes from modern Chartres, France; the Helvetii of Switzerland and southwestern Germany; the Nervii, a Belgic tribe from northern France; the Parisii, who lived on the site of modern Paris; and many others. Many of these tribes were "half-civilized," according to Roman estimations. They lived in well-organized towns and traded with their neighbors, but they did not value education as Romans did, and their governments were disorganized by Roman standards.

The Gauls who lived near the Mediterranean lived in cities, many of them elaborately fortified to serve as safe havens in battle. Gallic towns were often built on top of hills, the better to defend themselves. These cities were home to large numbers of people. Caesar calls these towns *oppida*. Each tribe might have several cities, but one would be more important than the others and serve as a capital of the tribe's territory. The Averni were centered in a city called Gergovia. The tribe known as the Mandubii called their capital Alesia. Alesia, in particular, left behind good archaeological remains, where historians have found evidence of a thriving town that traded with outsiders, including Romans. There were many large buildings, including a number of public buildings constructed during the Roman period. Contemporary writers mention the fine metalwork produced by smiths from Alesia, and archaeologists have found artifacts confirming this account.

GERMANS

The best source on Germanic social organization is the Roman historian Tacitus (ca. 56–120 C.E.), who describes the people in his work *Germania*. Tacitus observes that family and kinship formed the strongest ties among German people. Clans and families organized themselves into tribes. Male relatives fought together. Military squadrons were composed of clans and families instead of random groups of strangers, a bond that Tacitus claims gave the Germans great courage in battle. To add to the power of family, German women and children came to watch their men fight in battle, cheering on the brave and tending the wounds of the injured. Germans were said to have dreaded being taken captive and especially to have feared having to give noble women to enemies who beat them in battle.

German government was very loose, and the Germans had nothing that could be called a state. The only time they organized into large groups was during wartime, when large numbers of Germans might fight together under a single leader. This arrangement was very flexible, allowing them to adapt to threats as necessary; some historians believe it was this flexibility that helped the Germans avoid being conquered by the Romans.

According to Tacitus, the Germans had three types of leaders: chiefs or kings, generals, and priests. Kings were hereditary; the sons of a king could hope to become kings themselves. Kings were expected to provide a good example for their people, especially in battle, but their power was quite limited. They could make certain minor decisions on their own, but for major matters the entire tribe had to participate and make a group decision. Chiefs were required to be excellent soldiers and to lead the charge in battle. Their followers, who were also their male kinsmen, were expected to defend the chiefs with their lives. It was considered a disgrace for a chief to show cowardice or for a follower to walk away alive from a battle in which his chief had fallen.

Generals were chosen based on their ability. Soldiers who proved themselves in battle and who combined courage with intelligence and energy could win the admiration of their peers and thus become military leaders. Generals, like kings, lacked arbitrary power over their soldiers and civilians.

Tacitus wrote that German priests had the most real power. Priests alone were allowed to punish people by reprimand or flogging, typically for cowardice or other error in battle. Religion was the foundation of much of German social activity. Priests organized numerous festivals. Divination was a primary method of making decisions. Priests would perform various rituals to see what the future was likely to bring, and the Germans would base their decisions on the results.

German society was hierarchical, organized roughly according to birth, age, and military might. The various chiefs were ranked by birth and military prowess, so there was a chief of the chiefs. The highest-ranking chief was the man with the most followers. The followers themselves knew their respective ranks, determined by the nobility of their lord, their age, and their skill in battle. Young men vied to fight at the side of a chief because doing so was one of the best ways for them to advance. These young men would also walk around with a chief during peacetime because it was considered an honor for a chief to be surrounded by a large group of faithful soldiers. Chiefs solidified their power by giving large feasts for their followers. They also gave presents to their soldiers and to fellow chiefs.

Chiefs made minor decisions by themselves. For major matters, the entire tribe would consider the matter and make final decisions that the chiefs would respect. Tacitus notes that German tribal meetings were somewhat disorganized. The Germans did not have an accurate means of accounting for days and nights, so it was difficult for them all to assemble at once. Instead, they would take two or three days to assemble in one place. Then they would sit down, still wearing their weapons, and the priests would order everyone to be silent. The tribe members were then allowed to speak in order of rank, starting with the king or chief. The other participants ranked themselves by age, family, prowess in battle, or speaking ability, all of which were considered important and worthy of distinction.

According to Tacitus, German men had little to occupy themselves when they were not fighting. He wrote that they spent most of their free time either hunting or lying around sleeping. The women and old men were responsible for the daily care of the home and the production of food. Each German family had a nominal male head, usually the father, who could make decisions about family members, deciding who should marry whom and who would live where. German families lived in close quarters. Children had the run of the local clan area, whether they lived in a village or were in the midst of travels. Uncles, aunts, and other relatives were expected to help care for children. The relationship between men and the sons of their sisters was especially close; these men considered their nephews as important as their own sons. Germans also solidified family ties through the practice of fosterage, in which children went to live with relatives for a time.

The Germans had no cities. They did not even really have towns. Their villages sprung up with no plan, arising simply because groups of people all chose to build houses around the same site. Their homes were roughly built of timber, though the Germans were known to live in caves if they were convenient.

The Germans did not use actual currency, but they did have forms of wealth that allowed them to distinguish rich from poor. Germans loved gold and silver, which they wore as jewelry. Chiefs wore the best jewelry. Chiefs also used jewelry as a form of reward for faithful followers. Fine weapons were also appreciated. When couples married, they exchanged gifts of oxen, weapons, and horses.

Like the Celts, the Germans kept slaves. Slaves were typically prisoners taken in war. German slaves were allowed to live in their own homes and have families. They functioned more as tenants of their masters than as household servants.

By the end of the ancient period, the Germanic peoples had divided into numerous groups, including the Franks, the

Goths (who split into the Visigoths and the Ostrogoths), the Alamanni, the Vandals, the Suebi, and the Burgundians. The Visigoths and the Ostrogoths organized themselves into actual kingdoms in the third century C.E. Their social organization was heavily influenced by Roman culture over the next century. The two groups of Goths had kings and genuine governments and adopted Christianity, which added a church hierarchy to their society.

THRACIANS

The region north of Greece was home to various peoples who spoke Thracian languages. This area encompassed modern Bulgaria, Serbia, Romania, Ukraine, Hungary, and Slovakia. Homer wrote about the Tracians in the *Iliad*, describing Thrace as including the region bordered by the Black Sea and Hellespont to the east and the Vardar River to the west. According to the ancient Greeks, the people who lived in Thrace organized themselves into tribes led by kings or chiefs. These tribes were defined by kinship, military power, and geography.

Most people in Thrace lived in small villages and did not venture far from home. Thrace had no cities or large social groups. The region is mountainous, and travel was very difficult during ancient times. Therefore, groups of people were isolated from one another. The Greeks thought that the mountain tribes were the most warlike and uncivilized of the Thracian peoples. Tracians who lived in lower, flatter areas close to Greece were more peaceful and better informed about the larger world than those who lived in the mountains.

The only organized Thracian nation was the Odrysian Kingdom, which existed in Bulgaria, Romania, northern Greece, and the European portion of Turkey between the fifth century B.C.E. and the third century B.C.E. Its first capital was located in Edirne, Turkey. This kingdom was formed by King Teres (r. 480–440 B.C.E.), who gathered several tribes together in a rough union. Not all Thracian tribes joined the union, and though contemporary Greeks occasionally mentioned kings of Thrace, these kings did not control all tribes living in the region. Kings tried to unify the tribes, to increase both their own power within the kingdom and the power of the Thracians against kingdoms to the south, such as the Macedonians, but they had little success. In the fourth century B.C.E. the Thracian Kingdom divided into three smaller kingdoms. These smaller kingdoms proved easier for rulers to run. One of them moved its capital to Seuthopolis, Bulgaria, where its rulers kept it together for the century. The Greeks and Romans gradually colonized the area, influencing social structures. By 400 C.E. Thracian languages had disappeared, and the tribal structure had been replaced by Greek and Roman customs and styles of administration.

GREECE

BY JEFFREY S. CARNES

Greek societies were hierarchical, with clearly marked social classes and kinship groups. The place of an individual within society was defined by birth and family connections, property or other wealth, and status, particularly with respect to citizenship. Social structures varied from one polis (city-state) to the next but tended to fall into certain basic categories; they were, moreover, subject to manipulation and change over time; as always, ideology (of class, equality, or freedom) could cover over the actual social conditions under which people lived.

FREEDOM AND SLAVERY

The most basic social distinction at all times in ancient Greece was between the free person and the slave. Greeks prided themselves on freedom, and this freedom was defined by contrast with those who lacked it: slaves in Greek cities and the inhabitants of other, non-Greek nations. Slaves made up a large percentage of the population during the Classical Period (fifth and fourth centuries B.C.E.), perhaps as high as one-third in Athens and somewhat lower elsewhere. Inscriptions show the categories of liberty that the slave was denied: freedom to live where one chooses (including the possibility of migrating to another polis), freedom to act on one's own behalf in legal matters, freedom from arbitrary capture or seizure, and freedom of action. Greeks believed that other peoples, in particular, the Persians, also lacked such freedoms. It was common to portray the inhabitants of the vast Persian Empire as slaves to the Great King while the Greeks were their own masters.

As is always the case with ideological constructs, the simple free-slave, Greek-barbarian dichotomies masked a more nuanced reality. *Eleutheria* (freedom) became the rallying cry of Sparta in its imperialist struggles with Athens, despite the fact that citizens of Athens enjoyed far greater personal liberty than did Spartans. Nor was the distinction between slave and free always hard and fast. In addition to chattel slavery, a variety of types of limited servitude existed (such as debt bondage and serfdom). As Aristotle points out, the Greek ideal of freedom also included not having to work for the benefit of another person; however, a relatively small percentage of the population could make this claim, and many free laborers must have led lives more difficult and more constrained than those of some slaves (and in some instances may even have enjoyed lesser social status). In addition, the freedoms denied slaves were also denied women, and women of higher status were more subject to male scrutiny and control and thus enjoyed less freedom than did lower-class women.

SOCIETY IN THE HOMERIC AGE

The poems of Homer (ca. ninth to eighth centuries B.C.E.) present a vivid, if idealized picture of early Greek society as it existed in the years prior to the eighth century B.C.E., told from the viewpoint of the upper classes (though with a great deal of sympathy for others). The *Odyssey* shows a world in which the self-sufficient household (*oikos*) is the basic social and economic unit. Landholders with relatively large estates dominate the political and social landscape; Odysseus, as the largest of these landholders, is the king (*basileus*) of Ithaca. Other noble landholders compete for honor and power within Ithaca, but there exists as well the ethos of *xenia* (guest friendship), which governs relations between members of different households and different communities. *Xenia* demands that strangers be treated with respect and provides them protection, since it is viewed as a sacred bond protected by Zeus Xenios, the god of strangers. Moreover, *xenia* forges reciprocal bonds of friendship and obligation that last from one generation to the next. When a man of high status travels to a distant land, he will call upon other noblemen to provide him with shelter; the exchange of guest presents, often quite lavish ones, is customary. His descendants will be governed by the same obligations of *xenia*. The most striking example of this practice is in the *Iliad*, in which Glaukos and Diomedes meet on the battlefield. Upon learning that their grandfathers had entertained each other as *xenoi*, the two warriors refuse to fight each other and exchange armor in a gesture of mutual friendship. (Homer remarks that Diomedes gets the better of the exchange, receiving gold armor in return for bronze; this observation is perhaps a commentary on the rivalry and craftiness that might lurk behind the practice of gift giving).

The actual practice of *xenia* was perhaps less important than its ideological significance. For the upper classes it marked a way of life that set them apart from those below them. Contempt for merchants and those who make their living by trade is evident in the *Odyssey* and shows up in pro-aristocratic sources centuries later. Nevertheless, the Homeric worldview also exhibits sympathy for those of lower status. Those who overstep the limits of their class (the common soldier Thersites in the *Iliad* and the beggar Iros in the *Odyssey*) are treated harshly, but in general slaves and beggars are accorded sympathy. Being a wanderer or an exile is considered one of the worst possible fates (thus the poignancy of Odysseus's plight), especially for those who lack the safety supplied to the upper classes by the practice of *xenia*. Slavery was a condition to which anyone might be subject (piracy and warfare being common), and Homer expresses compassion for those who were subject to it. (The poems' dominant ruling-class ideology is reflected, however, in the expectation that slaves be loyal to their masters' interests.)

THE ARCHAIC PERIOD

In the eighth century through the sixth century B.C.E. the poems of Homer became the central texts for the Greeks' conception of themselves as a people (or group of peoples). During this time interest in genealogy grew, with oral or written genealogies becoming a way for noble families to trace their descent from the great heroes of the past as well as a foundation for the kinship systems that formed the basic social structures of archaic Greece. The poems of Hesiod (fl. ca. 800 B.C.E.) reflect the importance of heroic genealogies: Descent from a heroic or divine ancestor guaranteed the prestige of a particular group, whether a city or a family, and intercity alliances were made and unmade on the basis of such gene-

alogies. It was during this time that the distinction between Dorians and Ionians solidified. Greeks had always spoken a variety of dialects (Doric and Ionic among them), but it was during the early Archaic Period that these dialects took on an ethnic and political dimension. Thenceforward states could claim solidarity based on ethnicity and distant kinship, so that the fifth century B.C.E. conflict between the Spartan and Athenian Empires could be portrayed as a Dorian versus Ionian struggle.

The structure of Greek society was permanently altered by the events of the Archaic Period. A combination of factors led to material prosperity and expansion, in both colonization and trade. The influx of new wealth challenged the older aristocratic order, and colonization allowed more Greeks to possess more land, which remained the main source of wealth throughout antiquity. In many cities tyrants arose to champion the newly prosperous classes against the aristocracy; in others reforms kept the cities free from one-man rule. Material culture reveals a tendency toward equality. The rich tended to avoid ostentatious displays of wealth, and taste in art and handicrafts became relatively uniform throughout society. Literary sources reveal a flourishing debate on the nature of citizenship, wealth, and power. Some poets, such as Archilochus (seventh century B.C.E.), claim to represent the voice of the common soldier or citizen, while others, such as Theognis (sixth to fifth century B.C.E.), take a reactionary viewpoint, expressing disdain for poorer citizens' claims to social and political equality. This point of view was represented even into the fifth century B.C.E., with the odes of Pindar (ca. 522–ca. 438 B.C.E.) expressing a preference for inherited excellence over acquired skill and using the language of older aristocratic institutions such as *xenia* in an era in which they had long since lost their original significance.

The reforms of the statesman Solon (ca. 630–ca. 560 B.C.E.) in Athens illustrate the social developments of the Archaic Period. A rapidly changing economy led to a situation in which many small farmers had become heavily indebted to their landlords or even enslaved for debt. Solon abolished debt slavery, gave the tenant farmers ownership of their land, and divided the citizen body into four property classifications, with varying degrees of citizen rights. The top two classes, for example, could hold the major elected offices. The third could hold minor offices and the fourth none. All four classes could participate in the Assembly. Solon thus reestablished land ownership as the basis for citizenship, a tendency that continued throughout antiquity in many Greek states and was removed in Athens only with the advent of the democracy in 508 B.C.E. Land, however, remained the main source of wealth for citizens even in Athens, and various measures were enacted to prevent the concentration of land in too few hands.

PHRATRIES

The most significant kinship groups were the phyle (tribe) and the phratry. Membership in a phratry was determined by heredity and was normally linked to a particular place. Its members were *phrateres*, a word derived from the Indo-European root meaning "brother." The names of phratries normally used the patronymic (name derived from the father's name) ending *-idai* (thus Demotionidai, "sons of Demotion"), and while membership was inherited, the phratry was thought of as a larger unit than the family; "clan" is sometimes used to translate the term. Phratries were probably in existence in Mycenaean times (ca. 1600–1100 B.C.E.) but are first mentioned in the *Iliad* and existed in many Greek cities, both Dorian and Ionian. For citizens of the Ionian cities (including Athens), phratry membership was an essential component of their Ionian identity. The creation of the phratries was traced to Ion, the hero for whom the Ionians are named, and virtually all Ionian cities celebrated a festival known as the Apatouria, which was devoted mainly to enrolling new phratry members. In some instances, phratries seem to have been subdivisions of phylae, though in most cities it seems that the two institutions were separate and overlapped.

Membership in a phratry was a necessary condition of citizenship in Athens, even after the reforms of Cleisthenes (ca. 570–after 508 B.C.E.); this practice seems to be true for other Ionian cities as well. Their functions generally reflect the notion of phratry as brotherhood or extended family. They were responsible for enrolling citizens (usually young men coming of age and occasionally naturalized citizens) and oversaw questions of legitimate descent and inheritance. The Draconian law on homicide, which dated from the 620s B.C.E. and was the only one of Draco's (seventh century B.C.E.) laws reenacted in the fifth century B.C.E., provided that in a case of homicide, the victim's fellow *phrateres* were responsible for supporting his family and were to take on the responsibilities of his family (including prosecuting the alleged killer) if he had no family.

Phratry membership evolved with the changing needs of the polis. In the early days phratries may have been strongholds of aristocratic privilege (though the link of phratry membership to citizenship makes this theory somewhat less likely). Phratries could split up into smaller phratries or merge (whereas the number of demes, or local communities, and phylae were fixed). In democratic Athens phratries were themselves democratic: All members voted by secret ballot, and an official called a phratriarch was elected to a one-year term. There were perhaps 30 phratries in Athens, subdivided into *genē*, whose function is less clear. Not all citizens belonged to *genē*. They seem to be self-identified groups, claiming descent from a common ancestor. In some cases priesthoods were reserved for members of a particular *genos*.

PHYLAE

Later to develop than the phratry but ultimately more important was the phyle, or tribe. Unknown in the Homeric poems, phylae were in place by the eighth century B.C.E. in most but not all Greek cities. There were two main sets of phylae in the Archaic Period: the Dorian, consisting of the Hylleis, the Dymanes, and the Pamphyloi, and the Ionian, consisting of

the Geleontes, the Hopletes, the Argadeis, and the Aigikoreis in Athens and including the Oinopes and the Boreis in other Ionian cities. The names common to various cities most likely owe to the development of Dorian and Ionian ethnic identity, thus establishing the relatively late origin of the phylae.

Phylae often served as military units or as voting constituencies. Each tribe would be responsible for providing a certain number of soldiers or entitled to elect a certain number of magistrates. Like the phratries, phylae often had subdivisions—in some cases phratries themselves, or *genē*, but more often numerical subdivisions, such as thirds, hundreds, or thousands. Phylae were less stable than phratries, perhaps because they were viewed as more strictly political divisions, lacking some of the phratries' religious aura. Almost all cities for which we have evidence had altered their basic tribe structure by the start of the fifth century B.C.E. In some cases new tribes were added to accommodate an increase in population or an influx of immigrants; in others a political upheaval or a consolidation of several smaller communities (a process known as synoecism) provided the impetus for realignment. The Greek historian Herodotus (ca. 484–between 430 and 420 B.C.E.) tells the story of Cleisthenes (r. ca. 600–ca. 570 B.C.E.), who became tyrant of Sicyon and gave the local Dorian tribes insulting names (such as Hyatai, "pig-men") while naming his own tribe Archelaoi ("rulers of the people").

The best-known tribal reform is that of the Athenian Cleisthenes (grandson of the Sicyonian tyrant), which was effected in the years immediately following the establishment of the democracy in 508 B.C.E. The system was both complex and central to civic life. Attica (Athens and its surrounding territory) is one of the larger areas controlled by a polis, some 930 square miles. There existed within Attica a number of formerly independent cities (such as Marathon) that had been brought together via synoecism during the early Archaic Period. As a result, there were many local communities known as *demoi* (demes), representing villages or neighborhoods within the city. The demes were grouped into three main divisions: city demes, coastal demes, and hill demes (the inland parts of Attica), which had developed rivalries based on their perceived differences in economic interests. Cleisthenes made 30 groups (known as *trittyes*) out of contiguous demes (10 in each division), then formed 10 phylae by taking one *trittys* from each of the three divisions. The phylae were named after local heroes—Erechtheis for Erechtheus, Kekropis for Kekrops, and so on—thus distinguishing them from the older Ionian tribes (whose use was kept only for certain limited religious contexts) and marking them as a uniquely Athenian institution. The distribution of demes irrespective of geographic location had the effect of breaking down rivalries within the city so that any Athenian citizen would find himself sharing civic duties with citizens from far-flung parts of Attica.

A citizen in Athens, then, would find himself a member not only of a phratry but also of a deme, a *trittys*, and a phyle. The deme as a small-scale political unit had a substantial degree of autonomy; more important for social organization was its status as the basic unit of citizenship. Young men were enrolled at age 18 in their deme registers, thus becoming citizens; thereafter they would be known in formal contexts by name, father's, name, and deme affiliation. Thus, the statesman Pericles (ca. 495–429 B.C.E.) was known as *Perikles Xanthippou Cholargeus*, "Pericles, son of Xanthippus, of the deme Cholargos." Although it was geographic in origin, deme affiliation was inherited and did not change if a citizen moved from one locality to another. In practice, few did move unless compelled by circumstance. The Greek historian Thucydides (d. ca. 401 B.C.E.) speaks of the forced evacuation of the countryside during the Peloponnesian War (431–404 B.C.E.) as a time when citizens felt they were leaving their own native cities to move into Athens.

The *trittys* was by far the least important of the social units. It does not seem to have had an elected governing body or officials, although *trittyes* seem to have played some part in the organization of the navy and perhaps the army. The phylae, however, were central to civic life, and most state institutions were organized along tribal lines. The Boule, or Council, was composed of 500 citizens, selected by lot, 50 from each tribe; the 6,000 jurors for the law courts were selected in a similar way. The tribes became the basis for military organization, and the *strategoi* (generals) who led the army and became the de facto leaders of the city, were elected annually, one from each tribe. Civic competitions (in athletics, dancing, or singing) were contested according to tribal divisions; even the great tragic festivals chose their judges with equal representation from each tribe.

STATUS AND IDEOLOGY

There existed throughout the democratic era in Athens a strong ideology of equality, which emphasized that all citizens had an equal share in the government, enjoyed equal protection of its laws, and possessed an equal right to speak freely. The typical Athenian citizen believed himself to be *metrios*, "in the middle," neither extremely rich and powerful nor extremely poor or cut off from the governance of the city. The word does not exactly describe an economic middle class. Even well-off Athenians could be *metrioi* if they lived without extravagance or obvious arrogance. Rather, the term suggests a habit of equality and civic competence. The vast majority of Athenians were deemed capable of running the state (and, in fact, did so in turns, thanks to the large numbers of offices that were filled by lot). The free and equal status of the citizen was taken very seriously indeed. *Hubris* was the term used for the deliberate and gratuitous personal insult to a citizen's dignity, and such an insult was punishable by law. Those who committed certain crimes could be punished with *atimia* (loss of citizen rights), while those who were found guilty of making a false claim of citizen status could be taken and sold into slavery.

Officially, wealth brought obligation (higher taxes, usually in the form of expensive public services known as liturgies) rather than privilege; officially, noble birth likewise counted for little. Nevertheless, the rich and well-connected were, even in Athens, overrepresented in public life and enjoyed more comfortable lives. It is an open question as to what extent the rich were really in control of the state; certainly the ideology of equality guaranteed high status for middling Athenians, and most scholars believe that the common people really did have a large share in the running of the polis.

The ideology of equality among citizens was found in most other cities as well, though its practice varied greatly from one location to the next. In particular, cities with oligarchic constitutions (government in which a small number of people were in control) might restrict full citizenship to those who met certain property qualifications (often tied to their ability to undertake and pay for their own military service); in other instances, descent from some particular ancestral group was a requirement. In Sparta there was a radical social and economic equality among citizens, who were known as *homoioi* (equals). Together they owned the best land in Sparta, which could not be transferred to outsiders and which was worked by a subservient group known as helots ("the captured ones"). Spartan men devoted their lives to military training and service. After a rigorous and austere upbringing, they became members of *syssitia* (eating groups), to which each contributed produce from his ancestral land. Power was by no means equally shared. Two hereditary kingships, a body of elders, and a small group of annually elected officials essentially ruled the city, with the Assembly of Citizens having little more than veto power. Nevertheless, the Spartans viewed themselves as having an equal share in the state and remained a relatively harmonious political unit for several hundred years.

Sparta shows with particular clarity the ways in which citizenship and social status were defined in opposition to those on the outside. For Sparta to have its military society, a nonfree class of helots was necessary; in addition, there was a group called *perioikoi* ("surrounding inhabitants"), who, while free, lacked a voice in the governance of the polis. Indeed, every Greek city had in its midst a large number of noncitizens—slaves, women, local but disenfranchised freemen, and Greek and non-Greek foreigners. In the modern world, citizenship is a matter of birth or naturalization, and virtually every inhabitant of the planet is a citizen of one country or another (and sometimes more than one). For the Greeks, to be a citizen was a special and privileged status, one that entitled its possessor to a share in his government (a frequent turn of phrase in the ancient texts) and that guaranteed four basic abilities: to vote, to hold office, to fight for the polis, and to own land.

Greek cities marked out resident noncitizens in a variety of ways, often using the term *metic* (Greek *metoikos*, "dweller among"); the status of metics varied from place to place, and, as usual, Athens provides the best evidence. Any foreign residents in Athens who stayed longer than a month were required to register as metics—as such they had to pay a special tax of one drachma per month and needed to be sponsored by an Athenian citizen. The metic enjoyed the privileges of residence at Athens—admission to theaters and festivals as well as economic opportunity—but was also liable for military service or (if wealthy enough) for expensive liturgies, without the opportunity to have a voice in making the policies that might send him to war. Most metics were of modest means—traders and craftspeople, both male and female, Greek and non-Greek—who had come to Athens to make a better living. A few were wealthy and prominent, including the orator Lysias (ca. 445–after 380 B.C.E.), whose father had come to the city to set up a large shield factory. The literary sources show wealthy metics moving easily among the upper crust of Athenian society.

The status of women in Greek society presents several paradoxes. Women were excluded from citizenship and were thus automatically of lower political status than men, yet upper-class women enjoyed not only a comfortable standard of living but also privileges appropriate to their class. The chorus of women in Aristophanes' (ca. 450–ca. 388 B.C.E.) *Lysistrata* provides an example of the privileges enjoyed by wellborn women, mainly holding certain religious offices and fulfilling specific roles in the city's religious festivals. They go on to make a further point: Women contribute sons to the city and therefore have a share in the city's well-being. The language used is similar to that for citizenship and is designed to counter the argument (found in a variety of sources dating from the time of Hesiod) that women are an economic burden to the men who are responsible for them.

Indeed, women in Athens were treated as perpetual minors, unable to own property or exercise basic legal rights and in need of a legal guardian if not under the control of a husband or a father. However, while women could not be citizens, it makes sense to speak of women of citizen class, particularly in light of Pericles' citizenship law of 451 B.C.E. Under this law citizenship was restricted to those born of two freeborn Athenian parents; thus, women were capable of passing on citizenship to their sons but could not possess it themselves. Needless to say, one effect of this law was to give all metic women—who ranged in wealth and status from the poorest vegetable seller to the most celebrated entertainer or courtesan—the same permanent outsider status as male metics. And, as noted, both women and slaves were characterized by a lack of the basic freedoms that even the lowest freeborn male took for granted.

ROME

BY MICHAEL J. O'NEAL

Rome began its existence as a small settlement on the banks of the Tiber River. The possibility that it would rule a territory that stretched across the Mediterranean Sea and northward into Europe was remote. Still, over a period of a millennium, Rome would come to shape the culture, politics, and social organization of a vast empire.

THE LEGENDARY PERIOD OF KINGS (753–509 B.C.E.)

Historians often refer to the time from 753 B.C.E., the fabled year of the founding of Rome, to 509 B.C.E., the beginning of the Roman Republic, as Rome's "legendary period." This period of Roman history is not very well documented. Most of what is known about the kings who ruled during this period comes from the later writings of the Greek historian Herodotus (ca. 484–ca. 430 B.C.E.). While much of the history of this period is based on legend, including the story of the founding of Rome by the twin brothers Romulus and Remus, archaeological evidence suggests that at least some of what Herodotus and others wrote was true.

The social organization of the earliest Romans was strongly influenced by the Etruscans, who occupied a large portion of the western coast of the Italian peninsula and swatches of territory extending northward. Not much is known about the origins of the Etruscans, but they interacted with the earliest Romans and exerted considerable social influence on them. The Etruscans were ruled by kings, and cities were controlled by nobles. Etruscan women occupied a place of equality relative to men. In the fifth century B.C.E., as Rome was extending its reach throughout the peninsula, it defeated the Etruscans in a major sea battle, and the distinct Etruscan culture began a slow decline as it was assimilated into Rome.

During this early period Rome was principally an agrarian society. The pillars of its society were family and religion. Just as an absolute monarch ruled the state, so too the early Roman family was ruled by the senior male, the *paterfamilias*, who wielded absolute power (*patria potestas*) for life. Children and the fruits of their labor on a farm were regarded as belonging to the father. A father had the legal right to kill a son or sell him into slavery if he was guilty of disloyal behavior, and fathers frequently practiced infanticide when children were born with deformities or illnesses. The father was, in effect, the chief priest of his clan, and one of his major roles was to foster worship of the gods. Romans during this period tended to be conservative, frugal people who lived simple lives.

Despite the absolute power of the *paterfamilias*, evidence suggests that families in early Rome were bound by strong ties of loyalty and warm feelings. The family and clan were the basic units of social organization. Divorce was uncommon, and women enjoyed privileges that were denied to women in Greece, Rome's rival but also its role model at the time. Daughters inherited property equally with sons, and after they married, they managed the household with a level of authority that rivaled that of their husbands. Households of the affluent were likely to include slaves, usually people who were captured in war or who were in severe debt. Slaves were relatively well treated. They could save their own money and in many cases buy their freedom. Slaves who were freed were granted citizenship, and many stayed with the family that had owned them to work for pay in the fields or in the household.

THE ROMAN REPUBLIC (509–27 B.C.E.)

Historians refer to the period after 509 B.C.E. as the Roman Republic because in that year the monarchy came to an end and families of leading citizens ruled Rome. According to the Roman historian Titus Livius (ca. 59 B.C.E.–17 C.E.), better known to modern readers as Livy, the last of the Roman kings was Lucius Tarquinius Superbus ("Tarquin the Proud"). His son, Sextus Tarquinius, raped a Roman noblewoman named Lucretia (an event memorialized in William Shakespeare's long poem *The Rape of Lucrece*). She told her kinsmen what had happened and demanded justice before she committed suicide. Her husband and brother led a popular uprising that expelled the ruling house and established a republican form of government with elected magistrates.

The end of the Roman Republic and the beginning of the Roman Empire is a modern distinction that the Romans themselves did not make. Modern historians variously date the beginning of the empire at 44 B.C.E., when Julius Caesar was granted complete authority as emperor; 31 B.C.E., when Octavian defeated Marcus Antonius in the Battle of Actium; or 27 B.C.E., when Octavian was granted the title *Augustus*. The precise date is not important. What is important is that over a 500-year period, Rome grew in size and influence, primarily through military conquest.

The growth in the power and military prowess of Rome is relevant to its social organization. Repeated military victories lent a great deal of prestige to Rome's most important families and to its senators. Booty seized during military campaigns gave many Roman ambassadors and generals, who all served in the Senate, a great deal of wealth. With this wealth came a major shift in values and growing divisions and antagonisms in the social structure of the republic.

During the legendary period Romans valued frugality, modesty, public service, family, and worship of the gods. Among women, the ideal was the Roman "matron" who ruled her household and labored at crafts such as weaving. As the Roman Republic grew wealthier from conquest, a large class of nobility and statesmen became more arrogant and ostentatious. Many had traveled in the East, where they came into contact with the Greeks. They tried to imitate the Greeks by building large, elaborately decorated homes and massive public buildings. They seemed to compete with one another over who could hold the most lavish banquets or otherwise display their wealth. Women, too, began to imitate the Greeks by creating lavish lifestyles, often using inheritances from husbands or fathers who had died in warfare. This kind of ostentation got so out of hand that laws were passed allowing the state to confiscate excessive jewelry and gold.

During the Roman Republic considerable friction grew between the wealthy elites in the cities and the nation's rural population. Many men from the countryside were recruited into the military, meaning that they were not able to tend their fields. Then the republic embarked on a series of wars, called the Punic Wars, with the Carthaginians. During the Second Punic War, the Carthaginians' leading general, Hannibal (247–182 B.C.E.), led an army over the Alps from Spain into the Italian peninsula, laying waste to the countryside as he went. Meanwhile, Rome was cutting down the peninsula's forests to build ships for its navy. The result was that rural Rome was devastated. Its farms became far less productive, forcing the Romans to rely more heavily on imported grain from such places as Sicily. Many people tried to convert their farms into vineyards and olive orchards, but these types of operations required a large financial investment and years of work before they paid off.

With farm prices plummeting, many members of the Roman elite purchased land in the countryside. They used this land in part for recreational pursuits such as hunting and fishing. The also took over tracts of land that had been seized when Rome subdued other areas of the peninsula. In many cases they farmed this land, adding to their wealth, using thousands of slaves they had captured in war. Because of the greed of these landlords, the slaves were treated cruelly. The result was a series of slave revolts beginning in 135 B.C.E. The most famous of these revolts was the one led by Spartacus in 73 B.C.E.

Many rural Romans were unable to complete with the absentee Roman landlords whose land was worked by slaves. Many were forced off their land into the cities, where they could get jobs. Because of the immense amount of building taking place, jobs were plentiful, at least for a while. Most jobs were in the construction trades, as wealthy Romans built large homes and the government funded the construction of public buildings, aqueducts, and the like.

This new class of workers enjoyed the attractions that city life offered, but their relocation caused another problem for the republic: increasing difficulty finding military recruits. During the time of the Roman Republic a man had to own property to serve in the military, in part because he had to provide his own weapons and horses. As men left the countryside for the cities, they were no longer property owners, so the pool of potential military recruits was shrinking, and, given the farm crisis, those who remained on the land were reluctant to leave it for military service. The quandary for Rome was that this difficulty in manning the army came when Rome was essentially living off tribute (money paid by foreign rulers for protection and as a sign of submission) and booty seized in war. Making matters worse, Rome had to maintain armies of occupation in conquered territories. The result was a strain on the economy—Rome essentially spent its entire yearly revenue—and growing friction between social classes.

This friction between social classes not only affected the relationship between city elites and people in the countryside. It also affected social classes within the cities, especially the city of Rome itself. Two major social classes existed, the patricians and the plebeians. The patrician class included those who could trace their ancestry back to the first Roman Senate at the beginning of the republic. They were the aristocrats, the people who enjoyed wealth, status, and political influence. The plebeians consisted of everyone else (excluding slaves). During the early centuries of the republic, only patricians could hold public office. Intermarriage between patricians and plebeians was against the law. In general, patricians thought of plebeians as a mob, as the dregs of society who in many respects were barely human. In fact, however, many plebeians were themselves landowners, and some were fairly wealthy in their own right.

Over a period of some 200 years, conflict often erupted between the patricians and the plebeians (often called plebs). According to some historical accounts, this conflict led to a number of developments, including repeal of the laws barring plebs from holding public office and intermarrying with patricians. Further, the plebs frequently threatened, in effect, to go on strike and secede from Rome. Their interests were represented by the Plebeian Council (or Plebeian Assembly), which claimed the power to pass laws, giving rise to the modern word *plebiscite*, referring to a measure voted on by the population as a whole rather than its legislature. Collectively, these developments and threats are referred to as the Conflict of the Orders; the primary source of information about this conflict is Livy and his history of Rome, *Ab urbe condita* (From the Founding of the City).

Over time, the patrician class met many of the plebs' demands so that by the early third century B.C.E., the distinction between the two classes was eroding. In fact, many members of the patrician class were falling on hard times and petitioned the government to be reclassified as plebeians so they could reduce their tax bill. (Patricians, because of their alleged wealth, paid far higher taxes.) They also tried to reclaim their fortunes by marrying into plebeian families that had become affluent through trade and commerce. The political distinctions between the two classes diminished in the later years of the republic, though the social distinction between the two survived as a matter of prestige rather than law.

It should be noted that some historians dispute Livy's account of the Conflict of the Orders. While they agree that changes took place in the republic's social order, they maintain that nothing like an organized "conflict" took place and that the plebs never threatened to secede from the republic. Historians continue to dispute the exact nature of the events that took place.

THE ROMAN EMPIRE (27 B.C.E.–476 C.E.)

During the period referred to as the Roman Empire, Roman society remained exceptionally hierarchical, though historians know more about the lives of upper-class Romans than they do about the lower classes. It is known that "Rome" was a diverse entity difficult to define. It included not only descendants of Rome's founders and earliest citizens but also large numbers of people from conquered territories who were granted citizenship, slaves and former slaves who had

been able to buy their freedom and gain citizenship, rural immigrants who came to the cities for economic opportunity, people in conquered territories who were granted some citizenship rights, and large numbers of "easterners" from Greece and elsewhere who made Rome a cosmopolitan city. While aristocratic Romans looked down their noses at foreigners, former slaves, and rural immigrants, many Romans welcomed the mix of people, seeing it as a source of strength and vitality. Many of the legal distinctions between patricians and plebeians had been eliminated, but this did not mean that social distinctions ceased to exist.

The imperial court was the center of power and influence during the empire. Senators and knights were among the most important people at court. Historians estimate that at any given time there were about 600 senators and perhaps 30,000 knights, often referred to as equestrians, or *equites*. Numerous other people, including actors and astrologers, hung around the court seeking patronage and influence. The result was a kind of feudal system, where senators and knights rewarded the loyalty of their followers and retainers with offices and money, while the followers themselves often had a train of dependents who relied on them for their living.

So rigid was this sense of hierarchy that the Roman census actually divided people into six classes based on the amount of property they owned. The senatorial class (which did not necessarily mean that a person was a member of the Senate) required ownership of at least a million sestertii, referring to a silver or bronze coin. (A sesterti was equal in value to one-fourth of a denarius. It is difficult to attach a modern value to a sesterti, but using the price of bread as a standard of value, it was equal roughly to $5.00.) Membership in this class was based on estate ownership, and a person in this class was not allowed to engage in trade or commercial activity. The next class included the *equites*, who could engage in business and had to be worth at least 400,000 sestertii. These two were the most influential classes. Below them were three additional classes of property owners, followed by the *proletarii*, who owned no property. These census classes were important because they determined voting rights, with more voting power, of course, going to the higher classes than to the lower ones. Further, voting took place from the top down, and as soon as a majority was attained, the result was announced. Therefore, the *proletarii* rarely got to vote.

Social relationships were often based on the concept of patron and client. A patron (*patronus*) was typically a person of higher wealth, rank, status, or talent. In return for special attention and services from people of lower status, he provided them with benefits, which could include jobs or loans at low rates of interest. These patron-client relationships did not involve a single patron and a single client. These relationships formed a network, so the same patron would have numerous clients—a large retinue of clients was a sign of social status—and an individual client could have more than one patron. This social system emerged rooted in the belief that a network of mutual obligations based on status created a stable social order, one in which everyone knew their place.

The elite in Rome did not have to work. Because many owned large estates in the countryside, their source of income was secure, so they turned to public service. When they could, they lived in large villas on these estates. The elite received preferential treatment in many ways. They were able to eat fresh game meat and fish from the Mediterranean or specially stocked fishponds at lavish banquets and at everyday meals, while the diet of commoners consisted largely of beer, bread, lentils, processed fish sauce, and occasionally vegetables and bits of fruit. The elite often got away with criminal offenses and, unlike commoners, could not be tortured by the authorities if they were arrested. Even those convicted of a capital crime such as murder received preferential treatment. Commoners were thrown to beasts, crucified, or burned alive, but aristocrats were put to death relatively humanely with swords—assuming they were convicted. Among the top of the elite, the emperor heard cases and would probably have been reluctant to pronounce a death sentence on a member of his imperial court.

It has been estimated that the population of the city of Rome was about 500,000, but many scholars believe that the number was closer to a million, including a large population of slaves. An elite family lived in a single-story dwelling called a *domus*. Such a house typically had several rooms and a central courtyard. But as much as a quarter of the city of Rome was taken up with public buildings, so masses of commoners had to live in apartment buildings called *insula*. These buildings were a constant danger. The upper stories were supported by wooden beams that sometimes collapsed, and the threat of fire was ever present. Additionally, the streets were dark at night, making them dangerous and not just because of criminals. Commoners frequently discarded objects or emptied chamber pots through windows onto the street, often to the dismay of people walking below. Conditions were similar in other Roman cities, where aristocratic elites held power and commoners lived in less comfortable conditions.

Privilege among the upper classes extended to the education of children, especially boys. Early in the Roman Republic there was no system of education. Children learned what they needed to learn, usually farming, at home. But during the Macedonian Wars with Greece (215–148 B.C.E.), many Romans gained exposure to Greece and the system of education it had for its sons. Because many Romans wanted to imitate the lifestyle of the Greeks, they began to believe that Rome needed a similar education system as a means to a successful public career as an administrator or even a senator.

Wealthy Romans hired tutors for their children. For the less wealthy, private schools provided instruction in reading, writing, and arithmetic; the teachers in these schools were often Greek or Greek-speaking slaves. At the age of 12 or 13, talented students went on to attended a *grammaticus*, where they continued their studies in rhetoric, philosophy, history, literature, music, astronomy, geometry, and the Greek language. The very best students completed their studies in Athens, studying Greek oratory. In the wealthiest homes, books were highly valued and slaves were often employed as copyists to produce a copy of a book for the home.

The lower classes of the Roman Empire consisted of a diverse set of people. They included, of course, poor citizens, but also noncitizens, slaves, and freedmen, or people who had formerly been slaves. Manual laborers were regarded as lower class, but so too were large classes of people who in modern life would be regarded as professionals. These people included craftspeople, actors, musicians, and philosophers. Many people even scorned doctors as members of the lower classes. Doctors were often hated because they did not pay taxes.

To represent their interests, members of the lower classes joined *collegia*. These were similar to modern-day fraternal lodges. They gave poor people a place where they could find social relationships. They also functioned as burial societies to ensure that poor people received proper burials. They were often under the patronage of a wealthy citizen, who provided money for banquets and other activities. Patrons also gave members of a *collegium* some measure of legal protection. In return, the *collegium* honored the patron with prayers and respect. *Collegia* were open to slaves and freedmen as well as poor citizens.

Slaves were the lowest class of Romans. Estimating the number of slaves is difficult, but historians put the number between two million and 10 million, with as many as a half million living in and around the city of Rome. Slavery was an odd institution in ancient Rome. Slavery was never based on race or ethnicity. Slaves were prisoners of war, people in debt, or people who voluntarily sold themselves into slavery as a way of escaping debt or crushing poverty to a way of life that at least provided them with shelter and food. Many people treated their slaves with great kindness; others, especially in the countryside, were cruel. A slave had no legal status and was regarded as property. A male slave was responsible for his master's welfare to the extent that if the master was murdered, the slave was put to death for failing to protect him. Yet slaves could testify in court. Many were able to save their own money and eventually buy their freedom. Perhaps the oddest thing of all was that some Roman slaves themselves owned slaves.

Slaves served their masters in many capacities. The largest class included agricultural laborers. Many slaves worked on construction projects in and around cities. Still others worked in Roman households. Many slaves were relatively well educated and had talents that led to work as barbers, schoolteachers and tutors, accountants, secretaries, hairdressers, carpenters, messengers, goldsmiths, and even doctors. The most talented and educated slaves served as architects, business managers, and civil servants in the empire's bureaucracy. Owning slaves was a mark of status. While many Romans owned just one or two slaves, with 10 or fewer being a common number for middle-class people, others owned huge numbers; the historian Pliny claimed that one slave owner he knew owned 4,000 slaves.

Freedmen were slaves who had gained their freedom. In some cases, slave owners freed slaves for meritorious service. Some earned their freedom through service in the military. Still others were able to buy their freedom. Many freedmen continued to work for their former masters. The political rights of freedmen were limited in the early years of the empire, but their children were often able to enjoy all the rights of Roman citizenship, and the political rights of freedmen expanded later during the empire period. In some cases, the transformation from slave to prominent citizen took only one generation. Publius Helvius Pertinax, who became Rome's emperor in 193 C.E., was the son of a former slave. Many freedmen became quite wealthy through commerce, often wealthier than many members of the patrician class. Still others became wealthy through bribery and fraud in civil service jobs.

The experiences of women in ancient Rome were mixed. They did not have direct political power. While other nations in the region were at one time or another ruled by women, Rome never had a woman emperor. In some cases, such as that of Augustus and his wife, Livia, women served as advisers and could exert a great deal of indirect influence over public matters. Additionally, women could own property, including estates and commercial enterprises, giving them some measure of economic power. Otherwise, women were expected to serve primarily as managers of the home and family, which often included not only their own children but also the children's spouses and children. Women were highly visible in public; in contrast to Greece, they were never sequestered from life in public. Overall, upper-class women were expected to live up to the ideal of the virtuous, dignified Roman matron. In upper-class families, girls were given some measure of education, but they did not take part in advanced studies alongside men. Little is known about the lives of lower-class women, though archaeological evidence strongly suggests that many worked as midwives, food sellers, and nurses and in crafts production, including jewelry, leatherwork, and textiles.

THE AMERICAS
BY MICHAEL J. O'NEAL

Archaeologists and historians generally agree that the first human inhabitants of the Americas arrived about 30,000 years ago, possibly earlier. At that time the earth was much colder than it is today. Large glaciers, often a mile thick, had pushed southward as far as present-day Ohio and Indiana. Because so much of the world's water had turned to ice, sea levels were much lower than they are now. As the seas fell, a large bridge of dry land opened between the eastern tip of Asia and the western tip of Alaska in North America. That bridge is now submerged under the Bering Sea.

Historians speculate that the first Americans were Siberian hunters who were simply following game across the land bridge—entirely unaware that they were the first humans to set foot on a new continent. (Because the land bridge was roughly 1,000 miles wide from north to south, they would

not have thought of it as a "bridge" at all, but as a vast stretch of open country.) In time other hunters followed, and by about 8000 B.C.E. humans had migrated as far as the southern tip of South America. Clearly, when Christopher Columbus "discovered" America, he was only establishing contact between Europe and the Americas, which had been inhabited for thousands of years.

When the first migrants arrived, the Americas were entirely uninhabited. Groups of people were able to spread out and live in nearly total isolation from one another, although occasionally trade and barter took place between nearby groups. The result was the existence of a large number of distinct cultures and language groups, including the many tribes of Native Americans in what are now Canada and the United States and similar bands in present-day Mexico and Central America and South America. (In contemporary usage *Native American* refers to the tribes that inhabited, and still inhabit, the United States, such as the Apache, Sioux, and other familiar groups. In a larger historical context, though, the term refers to any of the many groups of people who occupied North, Central, or South America before the European contact—including, for example, the Maya and the Toltec.) Historians estimate that northern Mexico alone was home to between 300 and 350 distinct language groups. Because of the immense diversity of social groups any general statement about their social organization has to be supplemented with more specific statements about the organization of any particular group.

THE AMERICAS IN PREHISTORY

Unfortunately for historians, the archaeological record for the vast majority of early Native American groups is either sparse or nonexistent. Before about 12,000 B.C.E. most of the social groups of the Americas were hunter-gatherers. They moved from place to place following sources of food and left behind only the sparest evidence of their presence—for example, burial sites, bones, and a few stone tools. Almost everything they made with nondurable materials has long since decayed and disappeared. They had no writing systems.

From 12,000 to about 5000 B.C.E. the record holds a little more detail, giving historians a somewhat better picture of how people lived and enabling them to offer a few generalizations about social organization among ancient Americans. They believe that Americans in these years lived in hunter-gatherer bands of perhaps up to 100 members. The bands were based on kinship, and their members assumed that they all had a common ancestor. Occasionally, when they felt threatened by natural conditions or by aggression from other groups, several bands would forge alliances with one another, forming a loose community of perhaps 1,000 people. Neighboring bands sometimes traded with each other, and they also cemented alliances through intermarriage, primarily because each band wanted to maintain a rough equivalence in the number of men and women. Only in this way could they ensure the bearing of children to sustain the population and continuity of the band. For the most part, however, individual bands were self-sufficient.

The social organization of these bands was essentially egalitarian, meaning that no person or group of persons held a higher status or social position than others because of birth, though, of course, a person could achieve status through greater skill as a hunter. Because the groups were constantly on the move, following food supplies and seasonal changes, opportunities to accumulate possessions were few. People lived in caves or built temporary shelters out of perishable materials, and for the most part they owned only what they could carry.

Accordingly there was little sense of caste or social class within these bands. Men typically hunted, often leaving the settlement for days at a time (but carefully avoiding encroachment on the territory of other bands). Women stayed near the settlement to rear children and to gather plant foods. In coastal communities or those near major bodies of fresh water fishing and the collection of shellfish were important sources of food. (Parts of ancient Mexico and the southwestern United States were much cooler and wetter than they are in modern times, so the region contained larger and deeper inland bodies of water.)

To say that a culture is egalitarian does not mean that status differences do not exist. In what is today the southwestern United States along the Rio Grande there lived numerous Pueblo peoples. One of these groups made up the ancestors of a culture that came to be called the Tewa. The ancestral Tewa were an egalitarian society, and yet status differences were part of their culture. The Tewa identified levels of earthly beings, as well as levels of inhabitants of the spirit world. The top rung of earthly people, for example, included the *patowa*,

HOW DO ARCHAEOLOGISTS KNOW?

How can archaeologists detect something as abstract as an "egalitarian ethic" in a society with no written historical records and only a sparse and incomplete archaeological record? How can they look at bones or tools or pieces of pottery and make statements about the social relationships and organization of people who lived thousands of years ago?

In the case of a hunter tribe one specific technique that archaeologists use is to examine such objects as arrowheads and spear points. These points, made of stone, have survived through the millennia, while the wooden spear shafts, arrows, and the like have long since decayed and disappeared. These stone objects may not be writing, but they can tell a story about the people who made them in much the same way that a written account can.

In examining points used on hunting weapons, archaeologists are interested in at least three different things. First they examine the style of each point they find, looking for points that were probably made by the same person. An arrowhead or spear point is like a small sculpture, with a style unique to the person who made it. Such matters as size, shape, and the way the sharp edge was formed come into play. Archaeologists can sort the points found in an area according to the individual styles in which they were made.

Second, archaeologists try to determine how many people in a community made points for hunting weapons. Sometimes they find a number of points, but all seem to have been made by the same person or perhaps by just two people. In other cases they find a variety of styles, suggesting that numerous people made points and perhaps even that each hunter was responsible for making his own.

Finally, archaeologists are interested in where the points are located. If they find points made by a particular hunter in a narrow geographical zone, they can infer that use of those points was restricted to the hunter who made them, along with perhaps a limited number of others in his band. If the points are found over a wider geographic zone, they can infer that the points were used by a wider range of people in the band and perhaps even in other bands.

In Mexico's Oaxaca Valley, for example, archaeologists have discovered that the same small band of hunters made use of six or seven distinguishable styles of points. This tells them that each hunter in the band was responsible for making his own points; a smaller number, perhaps one or two, would suggest that one or two people had responsibility for making points for all the members of the hunting group.

In other societies the existence of unique points, each made by an individual hunter, suggests that a point could be used to identify the hunter who made the kill; this in turn could determine who got the meat. Among the people of the Oaxaca Valley, however, the existence of six or seven unique points found over a relatively wide geographic area strongly suggests that points were exchanged with friends and relatives. Points, then, could not have been used to identify the successful hunter, since several hunters may have been using the same point. For the same reason, the points could not have been used to determine who could lay claim to the meat. The effect was to diffuse meat distribution. Put simply, it did not matter who made the kill; the meat was equally distributed to everyone. Archaeologists can infer that the social organization of the band was egalitarian, with no one person seen as deserving more game meat than any other because of higher social status.

or "Made People." These were ritual leaders who earned their position through their skills and service to the community. They served as intermediaries between the earthly and spiritual realms. These people achieved their position by climbing through ranks or orders, starting with the "scalp" society and continuing through the "hunt," "warm clown," and "bear medicine" societies. These "societies" were in the nature of fraternal orders. At the bottom of the social order were the Dry Food People. These were ordinary citizens who had no official position. The Made People could choose to select ritual assistants from among the Dry Food People. While serving as assistants these people acted as mediators between the Dry Food People and the Made People. The key point is that rank and prestige were earned by service and skill, not birthright.

MESOAMERICAN SOCIETY

The most extensive archaeological record in the Americas exists for the people of Mesoamerica (Mexico and parts of Central America) beginning about 2500 B.C.E., although the roots of these civilizations extended even farther back in time. Some Mesoamerican civilizations were highly advanced. They built immense cities—cities larger than were, for example, Paris or London at the time the first Europeans arrived in the Americas—and had many of the characteristics usually thought of as belonging to modern societies, including government bureaucracies, systems of writing, calendars, sophisticated art and architecture. Because of the depth and detail of the historical and archaeological record, historians know more about the social organization of the Mesoamerican cultures than they do about those of other ancient American civilizations.

Between roughly 5000 and 2500 B.C.E. life in Mesoamerica began to change dramatically. The major change was a shift from hunter-gatherer societies to societies whose major source of food was cultivated plants. Plant cultivation required an entirely new way of life, for agriculture demands that people remain in one place for all or much of the year, rather than roaming from one place to another in search of game.

When people settle to grow food and tend plots of land, they form communities, and some of these communities eventually grow into cities. The cities, however, cannot provide their own food, so they come to rely on the surplus grown by surrounding rural areas. This surplus supports a larger and growing class of priests, artists, engineers, civil servants, and others who are not directly involved in the production of food. Further, it supports the existence of an elite that holds power, making decisions for the community as a whole. The result in the ancient Americas was the development among these cultures of a social order that differed from that of their hunter-gatherer ancestors, a social order that included a high-level class or ruling elites, a middle class of artisans and craftsmen, and a lower class of farmers and peasants.

Historians are not certain why this change took place. One theory emphasizes population growth: A larger number of people rendered hunting and gathering no longer practical, for

Double-spout-and-bridge vessel with pelican and fish, Nasca culture of Peru (ca. 200 B.C.E.-ca. 600 C.E.); birds played an important role for Nasca people, and bird feathers were used as ornaments for people of high social rank. (© The Trustees of the British Museum)

hunter-gatherer bands would be stumbling across one another, leading to competition and to the depletion of game. Others attribute the shift to ecological change. Much of the Mesoamerican region became more arid at this time, requiring people to find ways to produce and store their own food supply and to domesticate plants that could survive in the more desertlike climate. The best example is corn, which was developed from a wild plant (though botanists are not sure which plant). Over time people experimented with seeds from corn plants, developed varieties that could grow in the area's unique conditions, and turned corn into a major subsistence crop.

In discussing ancient Mesoamerica, historians conventionally identify three major periods. The first, the Preclassic, extended from about 1800 B.C.E. to about 150 C.E. (The Classic and Postclassic Periods came later and gave rise to the great civilizations of the Aztec and the Maya.) The Preclassic Period itself is typically divided into three subperiods: the Early Preclassic, from 1800 to about 1200 B.C.E.; the Middle Preclassic, from 1200 to 400 B.C.E.; and the Late Preclassic, from 400 B.C.E. to 150 C.E. These dates are approximate, and each Mesoamerican culture underwent changes at its own pace. The divisions, though, enable historians to make meaningful generalizations about the social organization and other characteristics of Mesoamerican culture.

During the Early Preclassic Period social organization remained much as it was during the region's prehistory. Cultures tended to be egalitarian, without any rigid social order or inherited social power. People lived in tribal communities consisting of hamlets of perhaps 20 or so huts built near the fields the inhabitants tended. No one's hut was much better or worse than anyone else's. Much of the society's activity centered on agriculture and seasonal changes in the weather. Most communities were entirely independent, but some contact and trade occurred as one community, because of ecological factors, was able to produce a commodity useful to a neighboring community that was unable to produce it for itself.

It was during the Middle Preclassic Period that a social order began to develop. Throughout Mesoamerica important changes took place, particularly in agriculture. People began to control the environment by building bridges, dams, and canals to store and channel water. They began not only to grow and harvest larger crops but also to grow a greater variety of crops. Further, they began to specialize. Each microregion increasingly focused on the crops that were best suited to the local conditions and then traded with other communities for crops that were better suited to those communities' environments. Ultimately, a greater abundance of food enabled some people to specialize in nonagricultural activities, such as pottery making.

Along with this increased prosperity and technical innovation came social stratification, meaning that a social hierarchy began to develop. (The word *stratification* comes from the Latin *strata,* meaning "layers.") For example, archaeologists studying the Olmec civilization of the Gulf Coast of Mexico have discovered that this society was the first in Mesoamerica to bury some people in more elaborate tombs, filled with richer funerary offerings, than they buried most of the population. Surviving art depicts people wearing sumptuous clothing, and it appears that the elite came to place high value on clothes made from exotic materials, often imported from far-flung locations. Further, archaeologists have discovered a considerable number of artifacts that could have been owned only by higher-class, wealthier people. These artifacts include ceramics made with rich and various colors, mirrors made with exotic minerals, figurines made of greenstone, cinnabar powder (used as a pigment), and jewelry made of semiprecious stones, shells, and bones.

Historians have offered many theories about why social stratification took place. Most of the theories have to do with the control of precious resources. Some people may have achieved a higher status because they had better access to valued resources. Others may have acquired special skills that had value as populations became larger and denser. Others may have possessed particular knowledge about agriculture or waterworks or some such useful subject. Still others may have acquired control over networks for trade and exchange with other communities, becoming the Americas' first entrepreneurs and business moguls. Finally, some belonging to a priestly class may have been thought to have special divine or supernatural powers.

No matter what the cause, it is likely that kinship groups played a role, as families acquired resources or means of so-cial control that were passed down through the generations. Thus power and social status were now inherited rather than earned, as they had been in earlier societies. Another important factor was the development of writing systems. The ability to write—and therefore to record history, myth, and political information—placed power and prestige in the hands of an educated few.

THE ZAPOTEC

The shift toward stratified societies is illustrated by the Zapotec people of the Oaxaca Valley of Mexico, whose civilization began to flourish in about 600 C.E. and who built a number of large cities. The Zapotec believed that there was a genealogical connection between people and the spirit world. In other words, they believed that certain people had divine origins. This belief was rooted in the Zapotec cosmology—the branch of thought that deals with the history and origins of the universe.

The Zapotec believed that there were two realms, that of the earth and that of the sky. The earth was generally kind, but it occasionally expressed anger, primarily through earthquakes. The celestial realm, too, was generally kind, but it expressed anger through bolts of lightning and thunder—a thunder roll was called "lightning's earthquake." Highly stylized images depicting earthquakes and lightning began to appear on the earliest Zapotec pottery. These images appear on burial pottery, but only for males—suggesting to archaeologists that the Zapotec believed that the earth and sky were the ancestors of some male descent groups.

Other evidence supports the notion that Zapotec civilization was marked by status differences. One is called the "mat" motif. It is believed that the civilization's rulers showed their status by not allowing their feet to touch the ground. Unlike ordinary people, the elite wore sandals rather than going barefoot; they sat on benches, thrones, or stools, and they placed reed mats on the floors when they held an audience with others. Pottery illustrates all of these behaviors.

Burial position also can provide clues about social status. Archaeologists have excavated a number of Zapotec cemeteries, and their findings shed light on the status of the people buried there. In one cemetery most of the people were buried in a prone position with a jade bead in the mouth and a modest collection of pottery in the tomb. Their arms were at their sides. However, six people, all men, were buried in a kneeling position. Archaeologists believe that these men, as well as people in other cemeteries who were buried in a sitting position or with their knees drawn up (perhaps seated on stools that have since decayed), were of higher status and probably rulers. Those buried prone were in a subordinate position. Similar differences in burial practices have been found in other parts of Mesoamerica. In Panama, for instance, the bodies of chiefs were first dried out in a smokehouse and then buried in common graves.

Cranial deformation, or reshaping of the head, is another mark of social status. In human infants the cranium (skull) is pliable and flexible. Among the Zapotec, cranial deformation was regarded as a sign of nobility. Typically, a few days after being born a noble infant was placed on a bed and its head was tightly compressed with boards. This gave the head an elongated appearance. The key point about this practice is that it shows hereditary rank. Clearly, an infant is not able to achieve high status through skills or service, so cranial deformation was practiced only on highborn children. Cranial deformation is easily spotted in skeletons found in tombs.

Differences in housing also suggest differences in status. Excavations of Zapotec hamlets have uncovered different types of houses. Some of the houses were modest; they were not very well made, the poles supporting them were slender, and walls were not covered with whitewash. Artifacts found in these structures suggest a simple life and include sewing needles, a few modest ornaments, and little in the way of minerals, pottery, and so on that would indicate affluence. Some other houses were larger, more elaborate, and more solidly constructed and had whitewashed walls. Some had lean-to roofs similar to the roof covering a deck or porch on a modern house. More important, artifacts found in these houses suggest a more affluent life. These artifacts include articles for use in crafts, such as minerals, basket-weaving tools, imported pottery, mother-of-pearl, jewelry, ceramic masks, shells, jade beads, and so on. Through their skill in crafts, the people who lived here occupied a higher status and thus had more comfortable and elaborate houses.

THE MAYA

One of the best-known ancient American civilizations is that of the Maya, whose roots extended back into the first millennium B.C.E. but who flourished from the fourth through about the tenth centuries C.E. For a long time archaeologists and historians believed that the Maya lived in an egalitarian society. They thought that Mayan rulers assumed positions of leadership on a rotating basis and that heredity was not a source of power. That view, however, changed after excavation of a major Maya site at Tikal, in modern-day Guatemala. The archaeological evidence strongly suggests that Mayan society was rigidly organized, with an elite class of rulers, a servant class, middle classes of artisans and civil servants, and a lower class of laborers and peasants.

Archaeologists discovered, for example, marked differences in housing, with elites commanding more space and privacy provided by stairways, screens, and gates. They also discovered elaborate royal residences. Burial practices, too, were stratified, with the elites buried in larger tombs, often engineered to keep earth from seeping in, and the tombs containing a larger number of decorative artifacts.

The skeletons of people buried in these tombs also reveal indications of class differences. Working much like the scientists who examine evidence at crime scenes, archaeologists have found differences in wear and tear on joints, differences in bone length, and cranial deformation, all suggesting an elite royal class that enjoyed a better diet, less physical labor, and longer life. Evidence of certain inherited diseases and other physical conditions suggests that certain families intermarried, indicating, in turn, that these were elite families who used intermarriage as a way of preserving power and status.

See also AGRICULTURE; ART; CHILDREN; CITIES; CLIMATE AND GEOGRAPHY; CLOTHING AND FOOTWEAR; CRAFTS; CRIME AND PUNISHMENT; DEATH AND BURIAL PRACTICES; ECONOMY; EDUCATION; EMPIRES AND DYNASTIES; EMPLOYMENT AND LABOR; FAMILY; FOREIGNERS AND BARBARIANS; GENDER STRUCTURES AND ROLES; GOVERNMENT ORGANIZATION; HUNTING, FISHING, AND GATHERING; LANGUAGE; LAWS AND LEGAL CODES; MIGRATION AND POPULATION MOVEMENTS; MILITARY; MONEY AND COINAGE; NOMADIC AND PASTORAL SOCIETIES; OCCUPATIONS; RELIGION AND COSMOLOGY; SETTLEMENT PATTERNS; SLAVES AND SLAVERY; SOCIAL COLLAPSE AND ABANDONMENT; TOWNS AND VILLAGES; TRADE AND EXCHANGE; WAR AND CONQUEST; WRITING.

Africa

∼ *Herodotus, excerpt from* **The Histories** (*ca. 430* B.C.E.) ∼

BOOK IV

The Libyans dwell in the order which I will now describe. Beginning on the side of Egypt, the first Libyans are the Adyrmachidae. These people have, in most points, the same customs as the Egyptians, but use the costume of the Libyans. Their women wear on each leg a ring made of bronze; they let their hair grow long, and when they catch any vermin on their persons, bite it and throw it away. In this they differ from all the other Libyans. They are also the only tribe with whom the custom obtains of bringing all women about to become brides before the king, that he may choose such as are agreeable to him. The Adyrmachidae extend from the borders of Egypt to the harbor called Port Plynus. Next to the Adyrmachidae are the Gilligammae, who inhabit the country westward as far as the island of Aphrodisias. . . . The customs

(continued)

(continues)

of the Gilligammae are like those of the rest of their countrymen.

The Asbystae adjoin the Gilligammae upon the west. They inhabit the regions above Cyrene, but do not reach to the coast, which belongs to the Cyrenaeans. Four-horse chariots are in more common use among them than among any other Libyans. In most of their customs they ape the manners of the Cyrenaeans. Westward of the Asbystae dwell the Auschisae, who possess the country above Barca, reaching, however, to the sea at the place called Euesperides. In the middle of their territory is the little tribe of the Cabalians, which touches the coast near Tauchira, a city of the Barcaeans. Their customs are like those of the Libyans above Cyrene.

The Nasamonians, a numerous people, are the western neighbors of the Auschisae. In summer they leave their flocks and herds upon the sea-shore, and go up the country to a place called Augila, where they gather the dates from the palms, which in those parts grow thickly, and are of great size, all of them being of the fruit-bearing kind. They also chase the locusts, and, when caught, dry them in the sun, after which they grind them to powder, and, sprinkling this upon their milk, so drink it. Each man among them has several wives, in their intercourse with whom they resemble the Massagetae. The following are their customs in the swearing of oaths and the practice of augury. The man, as he swears, lays his hand upon the tomb of some one considered to have been preeminently just and good, and so doing swears by his name. For divination they betake themselves to the sepulchers of their own ancestors, and, after praying, lie down to sleep upon their graves; by the dreams which then come to them they guide their conduct. When they pledge their faith to one another, each gives the other to drink out of his hand; if there be no liquid to be had, they take up dust from the ground, and put their tongues to it. . . .

Above the Nasamonians, towards the south, in the district where the wild beasts abound, dwell the Garamantians, who avoid all society or intercourse with their fellow-men, have no weapon of war, and do not know how to defend themselves. These border the Nasamonians on the south: westward along the sea-shore their neighbors are the Macea, who, by letting the locks about the crown of their head grow long, while

they clip them close everywhere else, make their hair resemble a crest. In war these people use the skins of ostriches for shields. . . . Adjoining the Macae are the Gindanes, whose women wear on their legs anklets of leather. Each lover that a woman has gives her one; and she who can show the most is the best esteemed, as she appears to have been loved by the greatest number of men.

A promontory jutting out into the sea from the country of the Gindanes is inhabited by the Lotophagi, who live entirely on the fruit of the lotus-tree. The lotus fruit is about the size of the lentisk berry, and in sweetness resembles the date. The Lotophagi even succeed in obtaining from it a sort of wine. The sea-coast beyond the Lotophagi is occupied by the Machlyans, who use the lotus to some extent, though not so much as the people of whom we last spoke. . . .

The next tribe beyond the Machlyans is the tribe of the Auseans. Both these nations inhabit the borders of Lake Tritonis, being separated from one another by the river Triton. Both also wear their hair long, but the Machlyans let it grow at the back of the head, while the Auseans have it long in front. The Ausean maidens keep year by year a feast in honor of Minerva, whereat their custom is to draw up in two bodies, and fight with stones and clubs. They say that these are rites which have come down to them from their fathers, and that they honor with them their native goddess, who is the same as the Minerva (Athena) of the Grecians. If any of the maidens die of the wounds they receive, the Auseans declare that such are false maidens. Before the fight is suffered to begin, they have another ceremony. One of the virgins, the loveliest of the number, is selected from the rest; a Corinthian helmet and a complete suit of Greek armor are publicly put upon her; and, thus adorned, she is made to mount into a chariot, and led around the whole lake in a procession. . . . These people do not marry or live in families, but dwell together like the gregarious beasts. When their children are full-grown, they are brought before the assembly of the men, which is held every third month, and assigned to those whom they most resemble.

Such are the tribes of wandering Libyans dwelling upon the sea-coast.

From: Herodotus, *The History,* trans. George Rawlinson (New York: Dutton and Co., 1862).

Asia and the Pacific

∼ *Arrian, excerpt from* Anabasis Alexandri *(Campaigns of Alexander, second century C.E.)* ∼

BOOK VIII (INDICA)

XI. The Indians generally are divided into seven castes. Those called the wise men are less in number than the rest, but chiefest in honour and regard. For they are under no necessity to do any bodily labour; nor to contribute from the results of their work to the common store; in fact, no sort of constraint whatever rests upon these wise men, save to offer the sacrifices to the gods on behalf of the people of India. Then whenever anyone sacrifices privately, one of these wise men acts as instructor of the sacrifice, since otherwise the sacrifice would not have proved acceptable to the gods. These Indians also are alone expert in prophecy, and none, save one of the wise men, is allowed to prophesy. And they prophesy about the seasons of the year, or of any impending public calamity: but they do not trouble to prophesy on private matters to individuals, either because their prophecy does not condescend to smaller things, or because it is undignified for them to trouble about such things. And when one has thrice made an error in his prophecy, he does not suffer any harm, except that he must for ever hold his peace; and no one will ever persuade such a one to prophesy on whom this silence has been enjoined. These wise men spend their time naked, during the winter in the open air and sunshine, but in summer, when the sun is strong, in the meadows and the marsh lands under great trees; their shade Nearchus computes to reach five plethra all round, and ten thousand men could take shade under one tree; so great are these trees. They eat fruits in their season, and the bark of the trees; this is sweet and nutritious as much as are the dates of the palm. Then next to these come the farmers, these being the most numerous class of Indians; they have no use for warlike arms or warlike deeds, but they till the land; and they pay the taxes to the kings and to the cities, such as are self-governing; and if there is internal war among the Indians, they may not touch these workers, and not even devastate the land itself; but some are making war and slaying all comers, and others close by are peacefully ploughing or gathering the fruits or shaking down apples or harvesting. The third class of Indians are the herdsmen, pasturers of sheep and cattle, and these dwell neither by cities nor in the villages. They are nomads and get their living on the hillsides, and they pay taxes from their animals; they hunt also birds and wild game in the country.

XII The fourth class is of artisans and shopkeepers; these are workers, and pay tribute from their works, save such as make weapons of war; these are paid by the community. In this class are the shipwrights and sailors, who navigate the rivers. The fifth class of Indians is the soldiers' class, next after the farmers in number; these have the greatest freedom and the most spirit. They practise military pursuits only. Their weapons others forge for them, and again others provide horses; others too serve in the camps, those who groom their horses and polish their weapons, guide the elephants, and keep in order and drive the chariots. They themselves, when there is need of war, go to war, but in time of peace they make merry; and they receive so much pay from the community that they can easily from their pay support others. The sixth class of Indians are those called overlookers. They oversee everything that goes on in the country or in the cities; and this they report to the King, where the Indians are governed by kings, or to the authorities, where they are independent. To these it is illegal to make any false report; nor was any Indian ever accused of such falsification. The seventh class is those who deliberate about the community together with the King, or, in such cities as are self-governing, with the authorities. In number this class is small, but in wisdom and uprightness it bears the palm from all others; from this class are selected their governors, district governors, and deputies, custodians of the treasures, officers of army and navy, financial officers, and overseers of agricultural works. To marry out of any class is unlawful—as, for instance, into the farmer class from the artisans, or the other way; nor must the same man practise two pursuits; nor change from one class into another, as to turn farmer from shepherd, or shepherd from artisan. It is only permitted to join the wise men out of any class; for their business is not an easy one, but of all most laborious.

From: E. Iliff Robson, trans., *Arrian, with an English Translation* (London: W. Heinemann, 1929–1933).

Europe

~ Julius Caesar, "The Germans," excerpt from De bello Gallico (The Gallic Wars, ca. 51 B.C.E.) ~

21. The customs of the Germans differ widely from those of the Gauls; for neither have they Druids to preside over religious services, nor do they give much attention to sacrifices. They count in the number of their gods those only whom they can see, and by whose favors they are clearly aided; that is to say, the Sun, Vulcan, and the Moon. Of other deities they have never even heard. Their whole life is spent in hunting and in war. From childhood they are trained in labor and hardship.

22. They are not devoted to agriculture, and the greater portion of their food consists of milk, cheese, and flesh. No one owns a particular piece of land, with fixed limits, but each year the magistrates and the chiefs assign to the clans and the bands of kinsmen who have assembled together as much land as they think proper, and in whatever place they desire, and the next year compel them to move to some other place. They give many reasons for this custom—that the people may not lose their zeal for war through habits established by prolonged attention to the cultivation of the soil; that they may not be eager to acquire large possessions, and that the stronger may not drive the weaker from their property; that they may not build too carefully, in order to avoid cold and heat; that the love of money may not spring up, from which arise quarrels and dissensions; and, finally, that the common people may live in contentment, since each person sees that his wealth is kept equal to that of the most powerful.

23. It is a matter of the greatest glory to the tribes to lay waste, as widely as possible, the lands bordering their territory, thus making them uninhabitable. They regard it as the best proof of their valor that their neighbors are forced to withdraw from those lands and hardly any one dares set foot there; at the same time they think that they will thus be more secure, since the fear of a sudden invasion is removed. When a tribe is either repelling an invasion or attacking an outside people, magistrates are chosen to lead in the war, and these are given the power of life and death. In times of peace there is no general magistrate, but the chiefs of the districts and cantons render justice among their own people and settle disputes. Robbery, if committed beyond the borders of the tribe, is not regarded as disgraceful, and they say that it is practiced for the sake of training the youth and preventing idleness. When any one of the chiefs has declared in an assembly that he is going to be the leader of an expedition, and that those who wish to follow him should give in their names, they who approve of the undertaking, and of the man, stand up and promise their assistance, and are applauded by the people. Such of these as do not then follow him are looked upon as deserters and traitors, and from that day no one has any faith in them.

To mistreat a guest they consider to be a crime. They protect from injury those who have come among them for any purpose whatever, and regard them as sacred. To them the houses of all are open and food is freely supplied.

From: Frederic Austin Ogg, ed., *A Source Book of Mediaeval History: Documents Illustrative of European Life and Institutions from the German Invasions to the Renaissance* (New York, American Book Company, 1908).

FURTHER READING

Géza Alföldy, *The Social History of Rome*, trans. David Braund and Frank Polluck (Baltimore, Md.: Johns Hopkins University Press, 1988).

Alfredo López Austin and Leonardo López Luján, *Mexico's Indigenous Past,* trans. Bernard R. Ortiz de Montellano (Norman: University of Oklahoma Press, 2001).

K. R. Bradley, *Slaves and Masters in the Roman Empire: A Study in Social Control* (New York: Oxford University Press, 1987).

Lionel Casson, *The Horizon Book of Daily Life in Ancient Egypt* (New York: American Heritage, 1975).

Barry Cunliffe, *The Ancient Celts* (New York: Penguin Books, 2000).

Geoffrey E. M. de Ste. Croix, *The Class Struggle in the Ancient Greek World: From the Archaic Age to the Arab Conquests* (Ithaca, N.Y.: Cornell University Press, 1989).

Ian Hodder, *The Leopard's Tale: Revevealing the Mysteries at Catalhoyuk* (London: Thames and Hudson, 2006).

Simon James, *The World of the Celts* (London: Thames and Hudson, 2005).

T. G. H. James, *Pharaoh's People: Scenes from Life in Imperial Egypt* (London: Bodley Head, 1984).

Nicholas F. Jones, *Public Organization in Ancient Greece* (Philadelphia: American Philosophical Society, 1987).

A. G. McDowell, *Village Life in Ancient Egypt: Laundry Lists and Love Songs* (New York: Oxford University Press, 1999).

Sarah B. Pomeroy, *Goddesses, Whores, Wives, and Slaves: Women in Classical Antiquity* (New York: Schocken Books, 1995).

Michael E. Smith and Marilyn A. Masson, eds., *The Ancient Civilizations of Mesoamerica: A Reader* (Malden, Mass.: Blackwell, 2000).

Miriam Stead, *Egyptian Life* (London: British Museum, 1986).

► sports and recreation

INTRODUCTION

The word *recreation* suggests the idea of "re-creating," or "creating again." In turn, this suggests that recreation serves to reinvigorate and strengthen people so that they can face life's trials. Sports and recreation in the ancient world were in many senses forms of "re-creation." Sports, for example, often served ceremonial purposes. Sporting events were frequently held in conjunction with religious festivals. Sometimes these events were staged to symbolize the creative powers of the gods. In other cases they reaffirmed the power and authority of a ruler and reinvigorated him to continue his rule. In some cultures, sporting events were held in connection with funerals as a way of honoring the dead. In the ancient Americas a ball game that bore characteristics of soccer and basketball held a ceremonial purpose. The participating teams were engaged in a literal life-and-death struggle, for the losing team might be ritually sacrificed to the gods.

While cultures throughout the world used balls for games, the ancient Americans, having discovered rubber, were the only ones to use rubber balls. In other parts of the world, balls were typically either stone or made by wrapping an animal skin around straw or a similar material. The ancient Chinese developed a game in which balls were hit with sticks into holes in the ground, a precursor of golf.

Sports and recreation were also regarded as a way of training a person for such activities as hunting and military service. The ancients knew what modern people know: that running, rowing, and other strenuous activities build muscle and increase endurance. Running, for example, was a necessary part of the training of couriers, who carried news of the progress of battles to commanders. Indeed, the modern 26.2-mile marathon recreates the legend (which is probably untrue) that an Athenian ran 26 miles to carry the news from Marathon to Athens that the Greeks had defeated the Persians in the Battle of Marathon in 490 B.C.E. In many cultures young men being initiated into the adult community had to prove their mettle by taking part in long races and similar challenging activities.

Some ancient cultures developed the concept of the spectator sport—that is, a sporting event people watched but in which they did not participate. In this regard the Romans led the way. In the Roman Empire people gathered in arenas that closely resemble modern football stadiums to watch mock hunts, contests between gladiators, chariot racing, animal exhibitions, and even brutal executions of criminals (suggested by the common phrase "throwing him to the lions"). For private recreation ancient Roman and Egyptian men went to gyms, often with the chief purpose of associating with other men.

Common sports in the ancient world included horse racing, boat racing, wrestling, track-and-field events (such as foot races and discus and javelin throwing), boxing, and archery. People who lived near bodies of water swam for sport and recreation. Other forms of entertainment included board games, dice, gambling, dancing, and bathing at public baths, where people could relax in the company of others.

AFRICA

BY KIRK H. BEETZ

In ancient Africa sports and games seem to have been important. What is known about African sports in earlier centuries, however, can be gleaned only from tenuous hints, some of which linger in the customs of modern Africans. For example, wrestling seems to have been a favorite pastime for some ancient Africans, because old wrestling traditions survive into modern times among some Bantu-speaking peoples. How prevalent wrestling was in ancient Africa and how important it was to society probably cannot be known. Still, it is apparent that young men in some places tried to prove their strength and social worthiness by grappling with others. Like ancient African warfare, wrestling matches could be very stylized events, with opponents moving as if choreographed by a set of rules designed to display their skills. Blood probably was rarely shed, and pinning an opponent's shoulders to the ground was enough for victory. It is possible that some groups—particularly those in which women chose their mates—used ritualized wrestling to show off marriageable men to marriageable women.

Racing was possibly a sport in ancient Africa; in North Africa especially, racing horses, camels, and elephants might have been popular. Among the ruins of ancient Kush, a kingdom along the Nile River south of Egypt, there is a large complex of buildings that may have housed elephants. The elephants would have been a type more easily trained than the African elephants from farther south. Near the ruined buildings is an area where these elephants may have been raced.

Most ancient African games involved numbers. Traders and nomads of North Africa, in the Sahara and along the steppes south of the desert, seem to have had games involving guesses at how long it would take to reach a certain place and word games involving the counting of words, perhaps to form a particular phrase. Number systems and number patterns were sometimes used in rituals for foretelling the future, and number and word games may have been played for the amusement of seeing what sort of predictions could be made with them.

Most ancient African games that modern people know anything about involved mathematics. There seems to have been a general cross-cultural fascination with mathematics that attracted people from all sorts of walks of life in almost all parts of Africa. Other sorts of games probably existed, but of those only game boards without rules remain, and it is possible that even boards that do not imply mathematical contests nonetheless involved mathematics. Boards from Kush and Axum are sometimes beautifully inlaid with ivory and variously colored woods. An interesting aspect of these boards is that even though their rules are long forgotten, the tradition of gaming with boards is so deep within modern cultures that a person seeing a relic from ancient Africa could easily recognize it as something people played games with.

Some African mathematical games were very simple, so lacking in complexity that whoever started first was the probable winner. Such games may have been used to teach children how to count and how to do simple addition and subtraction. Other games may have been intended to teach multiplication and division. Others involved such complex reasoning that they may have kept adult minds sharp for the complicated business of trading with outsiders, which could require people to keep in mind several different quantities of different goods along with how much they were asking or offering for the goods. Successful bargaining often depended on all the involved traders understanding and agreeing on numbers derived from hours of negotiations.

One of the oldest games is now called morabaraba. Its origins are obscure, but it spread through herding communities in northern, eastern, and southern Africa. It may be the ancestor of the European game called nine-man Morris. According to tradition, it was a way for African elders to teach young people how to steal livestock, especially cattle. The basic idea is to capture an opponent's cattle while moving one's own cattle toward the opponent's edge of the board. A cow is captured by lining up in a straight line three of one's own cattle in front of a cow of the opponent.

An interesting aspect of morabaraba and other ancient African games is that a game board could be drawn on the ground. All the players needed was a fairly flat, open area of sufficient size for both them and the board. Even when boards were fashioned from stone, clay, or wood, these materials were readily available, so play could begin at almost any time—an indication of how much some ancient Africans loved their games. Some boards were made to fold up to hold game pieces and be easily carried.

One of the most popular types of games in Africa is the sowing game, so named because its premise is planting seeds for crops. The general name for all such games is mancala. Although sometimes a game is sold in the Western world as mancala, the word actually was meant to refer to all sowing games. The name derives from *naqala*, which is Arabic for "to move." Sowing games probably originated in eastern Africa, perhaps in the ancient kingdom of Axum. They spread through most of Africa, along southern Asia to Indochina, and along the Mediterranean coast to southern Europe. In ancient Africa both men and women played these games avidly.

The games were probably originally played on the ground, with holes dug in rows and stones, seashells, or seeds used for playing pieces. Ancient boards made of stone and clay indicate that there were several variations of play, because holes would be arranged in different patterns on different boards. In general, the objective of the game was to force an opponent into a position in which no move was possible or to have more game pieces than one's opponent at the end of play.

Numerous variations evolved over many centuries, but a sowing game was usually played by two people, each controlling one side or end of a game board. Game pieces, called seeds, were usually gathered in a starting hole. A player could move seeds from his hole into neighboring holes, which usually meant that he controlled those holes and could, during a later turn, move seeds from them into other holes. Often a player was allowed to move to capture a hole controlled by her opponent, with the rules for how to capture a hole varying greatly depending on the variation of the game. A player's turn often ended when he ran out of moves, which could happen when he reached a hole he could not take. Moving seeds, choosing how many to move and where to move them, often involved complex thinking, requiring a player to have the ability to foresee an opponent's reactions to her moves, as well as the ability to thwart her opponent's strategy.

EGYPT

BY EMILY JANE O'DELL

Ancient Egypt was not all work and no play. In fact, there are many examples of sports and games from ancient Egypt. We know of the recreational habits of ancient Egyptians from surviving game pieces, written texts, and temple and tomb carvings. Although the ancient Egyptians had nothing like the Olympics of the ancient Greeks, they did participate in athletic and recreational activities that included throwing, running, wrestling, archery, boating, and board games.

We do not know very much about organized sports activity in ancient Egypt, but we do know that the pharaoh had a recurring athletic event that symbolically and magically rejuvenated him for the kingship. During the sed festival, a jubilee that traditionally occurred after 30 years of rule and thereafter every three years, the king was required to run around a special courtyard in front of his courtiers and the public. Such a court can still be seen at the step pyramid of the pharaoh Djoser (r. ca. 2630–ca. 2611 B.C.E.) at Saqqara. Relief carvings show royal guards running alongside kings' chariots, and some soldiers held the title "swift runner." However, we do not have evidence of competitive running until the time of King Taharqa (r. ca. 690–664 B.C.E.), when a stela (a carved standing stone) at Dashur records a government-sponsored footrace by units of the army, with prizes awarded to the best runners.

Many people associate horses and chariotry with ancient Egypt, but neither existed there until the Hyksos, a western Asian people who ruled much of Egypt during the Fifteenth and Sixteenth Dynasties (ca. 1674–ca. 1567 B.C.E.), introduced them, along with powerful new composite bows. These new elements of sport and war were quickly assimilated into ancient Egyptian culture. While target archery had been around since the Fourth Dynasty (ca. 2575–ca. 2465 B.C.E.), the addition of the composite bow and moving chariots made the sport that much more difficult and exciting. King Thutmose III (r. ca. 1479–ca. 1425 B.C.E.) claims on his stela in Armant to have pierced copper with his arrows, but the most famous example of such archery boasts comes from his son Amenhotep II (r. ca. 1427–ca. 1401 B.C.E.): Known as the most athletic of the kings, having been trained since childhood in many athletic pursuits, Amenhotep II claimed not only to have pierced four copper targets "as thick as a man's palm" while riding full-speed in a chariot but to have cleaved each target in two.

Wrestling appears in Egyptian art from the First Dynasty (ca. 2920–ca. 2770 B.C.E.) onward. During the Old Kingdom (ca. 2575–ca. 2134 B.C.E.) servant statues—statues buried with the dead to serve and entertain them in the afterlife—often depicted wrestlers. Naked boys who are wrestling are carved in relief in the tomb of Ptahhotep (a philosopher and high government official in the 24th century B.C.E.) at Saqqara. The most famous scenes of ancient Egyptian wrestling come from the Twelfth Dynasty (ca. 1991–ca. 1783 B.C.E.) tombs at Beni Hasan, which house more than 100 depictions of wrestlers. There is debate as to whether these figures are of recreational wrestlers or simply Egyptians fighting each other in one of the many civil conflicts of that time. However, at nearby Bersheh similar art clearly depicts sports wrestlers, as they are shown with a referee. During the New Kingdom (1550–1070 B.C.E.) wrestling became incorporated into royal ceremonies in which Egyptians wrestled foreign opponents. Art at Medinet Habu portrays stick fighting as another part of these competitions, with the fighters wearing shields on their forearms and padding on their faces.

Ancient Egyptians also played ball sports, and original balls from some of these games have survived. They were generally made by sewing a leather cover around a filling of clay or tightly packed straw, hair, papyrus, palm leaves, or yarn. In Twelfth Dynasty tombs women are shown juggling balls and throwing them back and forth, sometimes while sitting on the shoulders of other people. Some Egyptologists have read mythological meaning into the juggling games, but this explanation is speculative and not universally accepted. There are a few examples, however, of balls being used ceremonially and magically to stave off chaos. For example, during the Late Period (ca. 712–332 B.C.E.) the king would hit a ball with a stick as if he were striking the eye of Apophis (the god of evil and darkness), and in the edifice of Taharqa at Karnak the king is shown throwing four balls, each toward one of the four cardinal points of the compass. Apart from royal sports activity tomb art at Beni Hasan shows ancient Egyptians using a ball and long sticks in a manner that resembles field hockey.

In addition to juggling, ancient Egyptian art portrays women dancing and contorting in many different poses in gymnastic activity. For example, a painting from 2000 B.C.E. shows one woman doing a full backbend and another doing a front handspring or front walkover. Further, at Beni Hassan there are examples of ancient Egyptians holding certain yogic positions, including one in a headstand. Ancient Egyptians also had a unique form of weightlifting: They used bags full of sand that could be raised with one hand, much like dumbbells, to work their arm muscles.

Because most ancient Egyptians lived near water—along the Nile and its tributaries, as well as the Red Sea and Mediterranean—it seems probable that many people knew how to swim. The *Biography of Khety,* from the Eleventh Dynasty (ca. 2040–1991 B.C.E.), mentions swimming lessons given to the royal children. Both the Old Kingdom and the Middle Kingdom (ca. 2040–1640 B.C.E.) provide many carved depictions of men, women, and children fishing and hunting birds with throw sticks along rivers, and in some of these scenes men on papyrus rafts on the water are trying to push each other overboard with poles. Although there is no direct evidence of boat races, they must have occurred, as boating was part of daily life for people living on the Nile. Further, in the Late Egyptian text *The Contendings of Horus and Seth* the gods Horus and Seth compete against each other in a boat race, indicating that there must have been real-life precedents for such events.

Game pieces from ancient Egypt survive to this day. Egyptologists have identified four board games, but it is likely that more existed. The most popular was *senet,* played from the very earliest times all the way down to the Roman conquest. Besides recreational value, it had magical and religious significance: A person had to play a game of *senet* in the afterlife in order to proceed toward eternal happiness and peace. Thus, in effect, one played *senet* for one's life. The game appears in the Egyptian Book of the Dead, and a scene of the queen playing it for her life is beautifully painted in vibrant colors in the Tomb of Nefertari in the Valley of the Queens at Luxor. *Senet* was played by two players on a rectangular board of 30 squares (10 by 3). Each player had seven pieces, and flat two-sided dice sticks determined the moves that could be made. Much as in checkers, a player could jump the opponent's pieces to remove them and reach the opposite end of the board.

Another game, *men* (from the word for "endurance"), was contested by two players on a long narrow board divided into 13 or more sections. Not much is known about this game, but it seems that each player controlled five pieces and moved them according to throws of stick dice as in *senet.* After *men* disappeared at the start of the Old Kingdom, a somewhat similar game played with pegs became popular and lasted for 2,000 years. Players moved carved pegs on boards that had two tracks of 30 holes each. It is not known whether the peg game developed from *men* or was something new, perhaps imported from the Near East.

In the Old Kingdom tomb of the physician and scribe Hesy-Ra there is a depiction of a game called *mehen,* "serpent," named for the serpent god Mehen, who protects the sun as it sails across the sky. The board for the game is in the shape of a coiled snake and divided into six compartments, each holding six marbles of one color and a lion-shaped piece. In the tomb of King Reshepses at Saqqara four people are shown playing. The game, however, disappeared sometime around 2000 B.C.E., possibly because worship of the serpent god Mehen died out. A game called "20 squares" (for the number of squares on the board) became popular in the Seventeenth Dynasty (ca. 1640–1550 B.C.E.) and may have been introduced by the Hyksos. It was played by two people, each using five pieces.

In addition to board games children in ancient Egypt played with assortment of tiny figurines carved from wood and clay. Many such figurines and toys are found in the Cairo Museum. Children also played with hoops and sticks, engaged in jumping and whirling contests, and competed in tug-of-war.

THE MIDDLE EAST

BY MARK ANTHONY PHELPS

Defining what constitutes sports in the context of leisure activities in the ancient Near East is difficult before the advent of Greek colonization in Asia Minor and the later Hellenization of the region. What passes for sport by modern definition generally constituted three classes in the ancient Near East: children's games, military training, and professional acrobatics. All this changed after the conquest of the Greek king Alexander the Great (r. 336–323 B.C.E.), as sports and theater became a major component of social life.

Wrestling is the most widely depicted sport in Mesopotamian texts and artwork. The wrestlers are shown naked except for a type of belt. It seems that the belt was a necessity, owing to its ubiquitous artistic representation and its appearance in texts. It is not clear whether this equipment functioned as a grip for wrestling moves or served something in the capacity of a modern athletic supporter. The most famous literary image of the wrestler in Mesopotamia actually occurs as a simile in one of the earliest-known epic poems, wherein Gilgamesh, the legendary king of Uruk, and his foe Enkidu fight "like wrestlers." A copper vase from the third and fourth millennia B.C.E. shows the sculpted image of two wrestlers grasping each other's belts while balancing large vases on their heads.

Boxing is the next most commonly presented sport in iconography and textual evidence. A votive tablet from around 3000 B.C.E., found at Khafaje (in modern-day Iraq), shows a pair of boxers along with two pairs of wrestlers. Boxers almost universally wear the same belt as wrestlers, leading one to wonder if there was indeed always a strong division between the activities. Other representations show boxers wearing typical skirts with some sort of binding on their wrists, probably functioning in the same fashion as modern taping for strengthening the joint.

Life-and-death duels served as a spectator sport, if the Egyptian story of Sinuhe is to be believed. Sinuhe, stranded in Palestine, becomes adopted into a kin group and manages to become chief. He then is forced to encounter a "strong man from Retenu" (referring to Syria-Palestine), doubtless for the political control of a kin group. Challenged to single combat, he fights with his challenger before spectators, including women. The crowd initially roots for the man they thought was the underdog, the Egyptian, who soon proves his worth by killing the challenger.

This practice is in line with a scene depicted in the Hebrew Bible (2 Samuel 2:12–17). In this event, 12 representa-

tives each of the armies of David and Ishbaal, Saul's son and successor, meet near the pool at Gibeon to determine which army is favored by Yahweh, the Israelite deity, to rule Israel. These two dozen pair off, grab each other by the hair, and kill each other with the flint knives all were carrying. Divine favor unrevealed, open warfare begins. The story of David and Goliath, told in 1 Samuel 17, is also one of representational combat to the death through the use of weapons.

Sinuhe and the biblical examples are certainly not sport by modern definition, but the need for witnesses to validate the outcome of these life-and-death struggles for political supremacy finds some parallel in the "death for entertainment" context of gladiatorial shows. The fact that all ancient Near Eastern competition was a reflection of military training might suggest that these episodes may well be understood as sports writ large.

A Phoenician vase depicting runners, a Hittite tablet making reference to races at a New Year's festival, and references to the New Year's festival in Babylon call attention to another sport in the ancient Near East. The Bible (Ecclesiastes 9:11) states that "the race goes not to the swift," a reference in all probability to distance running. It is hard to fathom that there were no horse or chariot competitions, especially given the Hurrian manu-

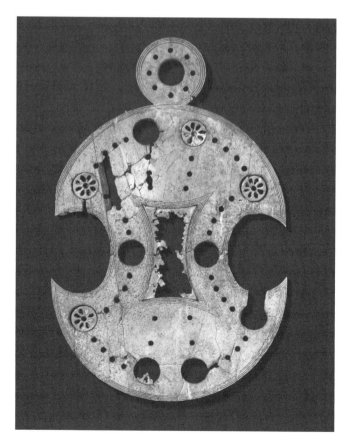

Game of 58 Holes, made of ivory inlaid with gold and blue paste, from Megiddo, Palestine, Late Bronze Age, 13th century B.C.E. (Courtesy of the Oriental Institute of the University of Chicago)

als translated into Hittite for horse training from the 13th and 14th centuries B.C.E. Likewise, there probably existed competition that involved lifting or throwing objects.

The king engaged in leisure pursuits that were calculated to increase his majesty. Domination over wild predators spoke well of his ability to deal with human adversaries. For example, Assyrian palaces were covered with scenes of the king killing lions for the benefit of the vassal delivering tribute. The ritualization of actual hunts by the king would involve animals that were typically captured or raised and then placed, perhaps bound, in a context that would present no actual danger to the ruler. A relief depicting a hunt by the Assyrian king Ashurnasirpal II (r. 883–859 B.C.E.) shows a lion being released from a cage. The depictions of hunting scenes on vessels used by individuals points to the hunt as being the activity of the elite as well. It is impossible to determine whether there was any influence of Egypt upon such activities as boxing, wrestling, or hunting. Although these activities doubtless developed independently of each other, the rules, social contexts, and individual moves could have been influenced from either cultural realm to the other.

Astragali, animal knucklebones, were an integral part of gaming. They functioned as four-sided dice, as each edge was distinct. These bones were also used in divination. Imitation astragali were made of stone, metal, or glass. Game boards, some with holes or depressions, have been discovered as well. One Babylonian game board included the signs of the zodiac. Among the best-known influences of Egypt upon leisure time is the presence of the board game *senet*, found throughout Syria and Palestine beginning in the Neolithic Period (ending ca. 3800 B.C.E.). The game board has been found from Cyprus to Iran and most points in between.

Musicians, dancers, jugglers, and acrobats are depicted in literature and artwork. Music was ubiquitous at work (as work songs), at festivals (as religious or wedding songs), and in daily life (as perhaps lullabies or taunts). Dancing accompanied many festivals. Watching acrobats and jugglers perform is probably as close to viewing spectator sports as the bulk of the population could come.

With the coming of the Hellenistic world, the face of ancient Near Eastern sports and leisure changed dramatically. Athletic competitions and theatrical performances became an integral part of the social life of at least some strata of the cities of the region. Hippodromes, gymnasiums, palaestrae (facilities for sports practice), and amphitheaters appear throughout the ancient Near East. Athletic competitions were spectator sports in this era, a big business that in turn spawned other affiliated businesses, such as concessions and prostitution. Fans of chariot racing arose in the provinces as well as the Roman heartland, evidenced by graffiti extolling both green and blue factions at Alexandria.

In addition to spectator sports and theater, the coming of the Greeks and Romans also provided for new types of games, new music, and other novel entertainment staples. Along with sports, the presence of public baths presented a cultural challenge throughout the ancient Near East as public nudity was nearly a universal mark of shame in the region.

ASIA AND THE PACIFIC

BY KIRK H. BEETZ

In ancient Asia and the Pacific sports and games served not only as entertainment but also to train players in physical and intellectual skills they needed to survive. Two sports, wrestling and archery, were common in most cultures. In China wrestling matches could attract large audiences in cities and were often part of celebrations staged by the rich and powerful. By the time of the Han Dynasty (ca. 202 B.C.E.–ca. 220 C.E.) the sport had become ritualized, taking a form similar to modern Japanese sumo wrestling. In India victors in even one tournament sponsored by a king not only became famous but indeed made their fortunes for the rest of their lives. These contests took place outside the gate to the king's palace, and individual wrestlers often were sponsored by nobles. The opponents began the contest by grasping each other around the waist, with their chins resting on each other's shoulder. Each then tried to force the other down or to break his hold, either of which brought victory.

Archery was a popular sport. In China nobles took excursions into the countryside to hunt game, usually birds, with their bows. These hunting parties could be extremely elaborate, with the nobles or kings accompanied by professional hunters and large retinues of servants. It was long the rule in Chinese society that no hunter take more than one of every two animals he killed, but during the Han Dynasty many of the rich or the nobility slaughtered every game animal they could find, ruining once-healthy forests. Hunting as a sport was open to people of every walk of life in China, with even poor peasants being able to show off their prowess occasionally with a bow. Archery contests, by contrast, were usually formal affairs, sponsored by a king or a provincial ruler, in which aristocratic participants shot at targets.

In India archery as a sport was reserved for the nobility. Only kings and nobles actually hunted for sport. By the Gupta Empire (ca. 320–ca. 600 C.E.) kings had hunting parks stocked with animals captured by professional hunters in the wild. A king's hunt was an elaborate undertaking, with the king riding a chariot, a horse, or an elephant, surrounded by dancing girls and assisted by servants and game wardens. Archery contests were open to nobles. A target was placed atop a tall pole. The winning archer received a prize, sometimes even marriage to a daughter of the king.

Spectator sports in China included horse racing, dog racing, and cockfighting. All involved gambling, with people wagering on the outcomes. The Chinese officially regarded gambling as a vice because it meant that people were gaining money without contributing anything worthwhile to society. High-stakes betting was particularly scandalous and sometimes resulted in even nobles being punished by the king or

Ceramic Liubo players, from China, Eastern Han Dynasty, first to second century C.E.; the board is marked with divination symbols, and the game pieces show the animals of the four directions. (© The Trustees of the British Museum)

emperor. Nevertheless, gambling was prevalent. One very popular betting game was *liupo*, which may have meant "six dice." It was a board game played by two or four people who shook six marked bamboo sticks in a cup and then spilled them out. Players moved pieces on the board according to what the sticks displayed. The pieces consisted of five pawns and one general, the objective of the game being to capture the opposing general. The board's design was meant to represent the universe. The game was played with much shouting and gesturing.

India had numerous games of chance, all condemned by the predominant religion, Brahmanism, because money changed hands without producing anything of social value. Governments regulated gambling, and players were forbidden to use their own dice. Gambling dens paid 5 percent of the value of their property in taxes, and both dice and stakes were taxed. Dice were sometimes made from seashells or the five-sided nut of the *vibhitaka* fruit or were sometimes cubes of ivory or wood. The game of *vibhitaka*, named for the dice that were used, called for a player to grab a handful of dice from a heap of them and declare how many he had grabbed while throwing them onto the ground. The number declared had to be a multiple of four. The player won when the number he or she shouted matched the total number of dice thrown. If more than one player guessed correctly during a round, play continued until only one correct guesser was left. Another popular game was *pasaka*, which used four-sided oblong dice. Gamblers agreed beforehand on a number, as well as on their bets, and winners were those whose throws resulted in the dice matching the agreed-upon number.

Board games in India dated from Harappan times (ca. 2600–ca. 1500 B.C.E.). Harappan boards were made of stone with grids etched on them. Playing pieces looked like mushrooms and towers. The most famous game of ancient India was *caturanga*, the ancestor of chess. Intended to teach people to think like military strategists, it was played by four people who sat around a board or a tabletop marked with a grid. Each player had four pawns and four other pieces representing a king, a horse, an elephant, and either a ship or a chariot. These last four pieces represented the traditional divisions of four corps in an army. Two dice were rolled to determine which moves could be made. *Caturanga* called for strategy and deception, with each player contending against three others, which required alertness and an ability to keep track of movements from multiple directions. Other ancient Indian board games include ones similar to modern backgammon and Parcheesi.

China had an ancient military strategy game of its own, called *yi* during the Han Dynasty but later called *weiqi*, ancestor of Chinese checkers and Go. Its first mention in surviving documents is from 559–548 B.C.E., but its origins probably extend back to the Shang Dynasty (ca. 1500–ca. 1045 B.C.E.), and it was played avidly throughout ancient times. Ancient Chinese tradition held that the game was invented in the 2300s B.C.E., during the legendary Xia Dynasty by the emperor Yao, as a way to teach his son how to think. The game was typically played on a wooden board etched or painted with a grid of black lines. Playing pieces were usually circular bits of stone or wood. The object of the game was to surround an opponent's playing pieces with one's own. It was easy to learn but could involve very complex strategy. A game between masters of *yi* could last several hours. In China emperors or nobles sometimes commissioned tournaments in which almost anyone, whether peasant or emperor, could participate. By the end of the ancient era the popularity of the game was spreading to Japan and Southeast Asia.

Little can be said with certainty about sports and recreation in the rest of Asia and Oceania during the ancient era. During the medieval era, counting games like those found in Africa became popular in Southeast Asia, but it is unlikely these games had as yet made their way along the southern coast of Asia to Southeast Asia before the ancient period ended. It is possible that Indian games made their way into Funan and that Chinese games made their way into Vietnam, but evidence for this is scant. The game of Go and sumo wrestling both had their origins in China, but documentary evidence for their existence in Japan before the medieval era is lacking. That the ancient Japanese played games is probable. Given the nearly universal popularity of wrestling, it probably existed in various forms throughout Asia and the Pacific. Surfing, the best known Polynesian sport, probably was not invented until after the ancient era, because the Polynesians had yet to colonize those islands where it seems to have emerged.

EUROPE

BY JUSTIN CORFIELD

The archaeological record of prehistoric Europe tells us very little about recreation and sport, and indeed these concepts as they are familiar to us in the modern Western world may not have existed. People probably found small amusements frequently in the course of their everyday life, but they may have involved telling stories, making music, or joking. Sports as competition in games and recreation as involving sport seem to have been relatively late developments in the human story; until modern times they seem to have been unknown in many parts of the world. At the Neolithic settlement at Skara Brae in the Orkney Islands of Scotland, a number of small well-carved stone balls have been found. Were they used in a game possibly similar to marbles, or did they play some ceremonial function? We can only guess.

Throughout Europe during the Bronze Age and the Iron Age many sports may have been connected with training boys and men for battle. Although there is little direct evidence for them, competitions in archery, javelin throwing, horse riding, and swordplay would have been natural accompaniments to training in these activities. It also seems probable that the Celts in Gaul and Britain engaged in chariot racing. Certainly their agility in battle, which Julius Caesar commented upon, meant that they had much practice, and it is reasonable to surmise that the development of these skills might have had a recreational aspect to it prior to their employment in combat.

A number of games and sports were limited to specific peoples or areas. Many Celts, for example, took part in games such as shinty, which seems to have been popular from the start of the Iron Age. Players on two opposing teams used

Bronze group of a bull and acrobat, Minoan, about 1700–1450 B.C.E., from Crete; bull jumping is frequently shown in Minoan art and was thought to be a sport associated with ritual activity. (© The Trustees of the British Museum)

sticks to hit a hard ball into a goal, much as in field hockey. A modern version of *shinty* is still played in Scotland, and hurling, a related sport resembling lacrosse, is still popular in Ireland. The ancient Celts seem to have believed that such sports provided good training for men and boys who were going to serve in battle.

In Scotland many men engaged in weight sports such as tossing the caber, which was popular among the Picts and remains a feature of present-day Highland games, as a test of strength. The sport, highlighting accuracy and skill rather than distance, consisted in throwing a long, tapered length of wood such that it turned over in the air and landed pointing at the thrower. In the Balearic Islands boys were trained intensively from a young age to use the sling.

As to indoor games and recreations, it seems likely that dice were used—certainly many dice have survived in Roman settlements, and it seems likely that enterprising traders would have sold dice to the Celts. Celts also played games with knucklebones as well as a form of chess.

In the area of music Europeans had been playing instruments such as flutes, drums, lyres, and cymbals for many centuries, and by around 1000 B.C.E. they were making bronze trumpets, as indicated by numerous finds in northern Germany, Denmark, Scandinavia, and especially Ireland. In addition to music there was spoken entertainment. Celtic bards, in particular, had a reputation for being able to recite stories of ancient times, former kings, and valorous deeds. During Roman times poetry reading and oratory became more important in cities throughout the Roman Empire.

Eating and drinking at large communal feasts was a popular recreation both in the Celtic world and after the Romans took control of Gaul and Britain, with some references in Roman works to similar events taking place in Germany, and archaeological evidence in Denmark also pointing to the use of large halls for eating. Feasts of this kind often provided a venue for dancing, music, and the telling of old stories. Women and girls danced for their own pleasure and also for the entertainment of others.

Large-scale spectator sports seem not to have existed in most of Europe before the Romans brought their gladiatorial shows, which became popular in larger cities throughout the conquered lands. Ancient Europeans attended these events as onlookers, and many who had been captured in war and enslaved fought in them as gladiators, with particular dress codes for those who were Germans, Celts, Thracians, and so on. A glass cup found at Colchester, England, clearly shows two gladiators fighting.

Other blood sports of the period included badger-baiting, bull-baiting, cockfights, and hunting. While much of the hunting was to provide food, there was also an element of sporting prowess, with trophies such as horns or the heads of the animals being displayed after the hunt. There are also descriptions of bullfighting taking place in Spain, with men in Baetica, Andalusia, in about 220 B.C.E. attacking bulls with a lance or an ax in an arena, after using a cloak or skins to confuse the bull.

GREECE

BY JOHN THORBURN

The Greeks were one of the few ancient cultures to engage in athletic activity for purposes other than religious ritual or training for either war or hunting. With few exceptions athletic competitions were limited to men, but some women (especially those from Sparta) did exercise for recreation or physical fitness. Although Greek athletics may originally have been connected with war, hunting, or worship, eventually people began to engage in sports for the joy of competition and the desire to display their *aretê* ("goodness" or "excellence").

The earliest evidence for athletic activity in the region near Greece comes from wall paintings found on the islands of Thíra (modern-day Santorini) and Crete. The fresco from Thíra (ca. 1650–1500 B.C.E.) shows two children boxing; the Cretan fresco (ca. 1500 B.C.E.) shows a person leaping over a bull, an activity that may have had some religious significance.

The next significant evidence for athletic activity among the Greeks comes from two epic poems attributed to Homer, the *Iliad* and *Odyssey*. First written down during the eighth century B.C.E., these poems contain several descriptions of athletic events. The competitions described in the *Odyssey* occur in Phaeacia, which cannot be identified with certainty as a Greek land, but the events—running, wrestling, jumping, discus throwing, and boxing—are comparable to those described in the *Iliad* where the hero Achilles honors a dead companion with athletic competitions: chariot racing, boxing, wrestling, running, sparring in battle gear, throwing the quoit (similar to a discus), and archery.

Although the historical accuracy of the *Iliad* and *Odyssey* is uncertain, about the same time they were written down the first athletic games took place at Olympia, in southwestern Greece (in 776 B.C.E.). By 500 B.C.E. several other athletic festivals were being held regularly: the Pythian Games at Delphi, the Isthmian Games near Corinth, the Nemean Games at Nemea, and the Greater Panathenaea at Athens. In each case these games honored a divinity, and except at the Panathenaea the victors received crowns of vegetation (for example, the olive crown at Olympia).

For the first five decades of the games at Olympia a footrace, the *stadion*, was the only event. The name (the source of the modern word *stadium*) referred both to the setting in which the race occurred and to the distance it covered (a stade). The length of the *stadion* varied somewhat from site to site, but at Olympia it was about 210 yards. As with most Greek athletic events, the athletes competed in the nude.

At Olympia and at the newer festivals other events were gradually added. A second running event, the *diaulos*, was named after a Greek musical instrument with a double pipe because the race covered two lengths of the *stadion*. The course was straight, not oval or circular, and it is uncertain how the runners turned at the race's midpoint. Apparently they started out in individual lanes and then turned around a single post at the opposite end of the *stadion*.

The *dolichos* and the *hoplitodromos* were grueling events. As the name *dolichos* ("long") indicates, this was a distance race. Its length differed at the various festivals; at Olympia it was 24 stades, or just under 3 miles. In the *hoplitodromos* ("running in armor") the athletes competed in military gear.

Hockey game, found in the Themistoclean wall, Athens (Alison Frantz Photographic Collection, American School of Classical Studies at Athens)

Ancient vase paintings show runners carrying shields and wearing helmets and other armor. The *hoplitodromos* appears to have been from 2 to 4 stades in length.

The Greeks also engaged in boxing, wrestling, and the *pankration* ("all fighting"), which combined boxing and wrestling. The opponents neither fought in a ring nor had rounds lasting for any specific time. Unlike their modern counterparts, Greek boxers, wrestlers, and pankratiasts, though divided into different age classifications, could be matched against opponents much heavier than themselves. Greek boxers and pankratiasts did not wear gloves but wrapped their hands in leather thongs. They won by either knocking out the opponent or having him give up. Wrestlers won when the opponent gave up or when a certain number of falls, probably three, occurred. What determined a fall is not completely clear, but causing an opponent's back or shoulders to touch the ground seems to have counted as one.

The Greeks also competed in a pentathlon (javelin, discus, jumping, *stadion*, and wrestling). An athlete who won three of the five events obviously would claim the prize, but otherwise the pentathlon's scoring system is debated. The javelins used in athletic competition seem to have been about 6 feet long. Unlike in the modern event, Greek athletes wrapped the shafts of their javelins with a strap that they looped around one of their fingers. The strap apparently caused a rifling effect that made the throws more accurate and possibly longer than they would have been without it.

Other events in the pentathlon also differed somewhat from their modern counterparts. Whereas the men's discus in the modern Olympics weighs 4.4 pounds, the Greeks threw disks whose weight probably varied from location to location. Modern competitors in the event whirl around two and three-quarters times before releasing the discus, but the Greek discus throwers apparently made only a single three-quarters turn. Meanwhile, Greek jumpers seem to have engaged in a standing broad jump rather than taking a running start. The most unusual feature of this event was that the jumpers held weights in their hands. Apparently swinging the weights forward and then dropping them after takeoff increased the distance of the jump.

Besides track-and-field events various equestrian competitions occurred. Greek riders, who had neither saddles nor stirrups, made six laps around an oval track about three-quarters of a mile long. The competition was divided into races involving horses either less or more than a year old. Chariot racing made the same age division but also had races for chariots drawn by two or four horses. Chariot races were twice as long as the horse races.

ROME

by Anne Mahoney

In ancient Rome spectator sports and individual exercises were distinct: The games people played on their own were not the same ones they watched other people playing. Spec-

tator sports included gladiator combat, wild-animal shows, and chariot races. Few Roman citizens participated in these events except as onlookers.

Gladiator combats began at least as early as the third century B.C.E. The Latin word for such a combat was *munus,* "duty," because at first they were held only at funerals, as an offering for the dead person. In about 50 B.C.E. Julius Caesar held a memorial service for his daughter Julia that featured gladiators, even though this was not her actual funeral. From then on gladiator shows were no longer necessarily connected with funerals. Most gladiator fights were between two combatants. A showy, expensive *munus* would involve several pairs fighting one after another. There were several styles of fighting, each with its special weapons and equipment. For example, a *hoplomachus* used the heavy armor and weapons of a Greek infantry soldier or "hoplite." A *retiarius* used a net (from Latin *rete*).

Gladiators were almost always slaves. The person putting on a *munus* hired the troop of gladiators from its owner. Fights might or might not end with the death of the loser. Sometimes the audience was asked whether the winner should kill the loser, and the spectators would shout and gesture their opinions. We know that they could give thumbs-up or thumbs-down, but the ancient evidence does not tell us clearly what these gestures meant.

Wild-animal shows included exhibitions, combats, and public executions. There were no permanent zoos in Rome, but travelers sometimes brought back exotic animals and showed them off. For example, Pompey the Great (Gaius Pompeius Magnus, 106–48 B.C.E.) showed elephants in his games of 55 B.C.E. celebrating the dedication of a theater he had paid for. More exciting were animal fights and staged hunts. In the hunts armed slaves called *venatores* ("hunters") chased down and fought various dangerous animals. *Venatores* were not as skilled as gladiators, and theirs was a less prestigious kind of combat.

Gladiator shows and animal shows took place in an amphitheater or arena much like a modern football stadium. The Colosseum in Rome is one such amphitheater, and others still exist in several former cities of the Roman Empire. A day at the arena might start with a staged hunt in the morning and finish with gladiators in the afternoon. In between there might be public executions. Criminals were often executed by wild animals in a spectacle much like the staged hunts except that the humans were not armed. Another form of execution was to perform a story from mythology with the condemned criminal in the role of a character who dies brutally. For example, the Roman historian Suetonius (ca. 69–ca. 130 C.E.) tells us that someone was made to act out the story of Icarus, the boy who in myth flew too close to the sun, which melted his artificial wings. Suetonius adds that the condemned man playing Icarus splashed the emperor with his blood when he fell.

Chariot races were the other major spectator sport. In these events chariots, usually pulled by two or four horses, raced around a track. The stadium was called a *circus*, "circle," although the track was an oval; the Circus Maximus ("biggest

DYRRHACHIUM

The Roman amphitheater in the port city of Dyrrha-chium (Durrës), in Albania, is the largest in the Balkans, the city being a Roman stronghold in their wars with the kings of Macedon. During the Roman civil war between Julius Caesar and the Roman Republic, Caesar's rival general Pompey used Dyrrhachium as his base, with a series of engagements fought there in 49–48 B.C.E. The famed orator and statesman Cicero had lived in the city 10 years earlier when he was exiled from Rome. However, it was not until the reign of the emperor Hadrian (r. 117–38 C.E.) that construction of the amphitheater began on the side of the rocky hill that overlooks the city. Although the city was formerly Greek, there is little trace of Greek design in the architecture of the building, which was primarily for gladiators, and the showing and killing of wild animals—a popular Roman pastime.

The amphitheater could hold some 15,000 to 20,000 spectators and was no doubt popular with the many landless, discharged Roman soldiers settled in the region. The whole of the structure has not yet been excavated, with some later buildings occupying the east and west sides of the arena, where many of the people would have sat during the gladiatorial performances. The amphitheater was used until 1081, when the town was attacked by the Normans, and then the stones became a source for building elsewhere in the city. Work did not begin on the excavation of the amphitheater until 1966, when Albania made great play of the Roman use of slaves and prisoners as gladiators. They opened up the underground tunnels where gladiators and wild animals had been held. The animal chambers were found to have neatly rounded corners to prevent the animals from injuring themselves when they charged out into the arena to be killed.

in games given in celebration of military victories or other special occasions.

At Roman sporting events, unlike most Greek ones, the audience included both men and women. Elaborate rules dictated who could sit where, with the best seats reserved for senators and the wealthiest equestrians (also known as *equites*, just below patricians in the Roman social order). Most cities in the provinces had amphitheaters and chariot racetracks: Gladiator combats and chariot races were popular throughout the Roman world. Although some intellectuals found the games boring or unsophisticated, most Romans seem to have enjoyed them. The emperor Augustus (r. 27 B.C.E.–14 C.E.) included the games he sponsored in his list of major achievements, and Suetonius in his biographies of the first 12 Caesars always tells us what kinds of spectacles they staged.

The sports and games that Romans played on their own were far less dramatic. Upper-class men might go to a Greek-style gymnasium or a palaestra (wrestling school) to exercise and socialize. The public baths were another place for recreation, open to Romans of all classes and both sexes. In all these places people would talk, have snacks, and play games. Mosaics from Ostia, Sicily, and Pompeii show people playing with balls ranging in size from softballs to large exercise balls. Although we do not know the rules of the games, the pictures and literary references indicate that there were throwing games and kicking games. Adults and children, men and women all played ball games.

The Romans also played games much like modern board games. There were gambling games with dice and games

Roman terra-cotta sculpture of two gladiators fighting, first to second century C.E. (© The Trustees of the British Museum)

circle") in Rome was the most famous example. The charioteers belonged to four different teams or "factions"—Blue, Green, White, and Red—which were part of an organization that covered the entire Roman world. (The emperor Domitian created Gold and Purple "expansion teams" in the late first century C.E., but they did not last.) A race might involve one chariot of each color, or there might be two or four of each color, which allowed for team tactics in the race. Charioteers were generally free or freedmen, not slaves; they got a share of the purse for races they won, and the best became fairly wealthy. Chariot races took place at the civic or religious festivals called *ludi* ("games") along with theatrical performances and other entertainments. They were a standard part of the major annual *ludi* and were also typically included similar to backgammon and checkers. The dice were typically made from the small bones of animals' knuckles but also could be blocks of wood or ivory like present-day dice. Game pieces varied from simple pebbles to elaborately carved figures. Romans played these games almost anywhere, in the baths, in taverns, and at home.

THE AMERICAS

BY RENEE McGARRY

People in the ancient Americas played a variety of sports and games. Many of these larger-scale sports, such as the ball game and the popular foot races, served ritual purposes. Other, smaller games often served the purpose of diversion and were leisure activities. Many games were played universally across the Americas, although the rules and practices of each varied greatly from civilization to civilization and group to group.

The ancient ball game is the oldest game known in the Americas. It originated about 1200 B.C.E. with the Olmec civilization and spread throughout Mesoamerica and even into the Caribbean islands. By about the year 1290 B.C.E. it was common for artists to dress figurines of Olmec rulers in ball-court costume, demonstrating the importance of the sport in society. Many ancient ball courts are still in existence, and scholars have used these courts and ancient figurines to determine the purposes, rules, and play of the ball game. While these remaining ball courts are principally located in areas where people played the game most frequently and extravagantly, archaeological evidence indicates that civilizations as far north as Arizona played less elaborate versions of the ancient ball game.

The Maya story of creation, the Popol Vuh, dates to the sixth century B.C.E. and illustrates the divine beginnings of the ancient ball game. In the story the gods known as the Hero Twins prove themselves to be extraordinary ball players, defeating even the Lords of the Underworld in a ball game. This early story establishes the game as more than simply a sport but indeed a contest of life and death, with the losing team ultimately suffering sacrifice to the gods.

The purpose of the ball game has been difficult to decipher. Many scholars believe that it was a fertility ritual that began as a simple game and evolved into a ceremony. This correlates with the blood sacrifice of the game, as many Mesoamericans believed that to perpetuate human life societies must take lives as offerings to their gods. These sacrifices could serve as a representation of a keeping of cosmic order, the victory of the sun over darkness, or an agricultural ritual.

The rules of the game varied by location, but many elements remained consistent across distance. Remarkably, each game was played with a rubber ball, a material entirely unique to the Americas in this period of history. Mesoamericans began harvesting and using rubber in approximately 1600 B.C.E., thousands of years before Europeans were familiar with the material. This rubber ball weighed 5 to 8 pounds and was bounced rapidly up and down the ball court during the game.

Stone hacha, Classic Veracruz, possibly as early as 300 C.E.; hachas were ax heads related to the Mesoamerican ball game and thought by some to be used as ball court markers. (© The Trustees of the British Museum)

In each culture the ball game was played with formalized teams and protective gear. From both depictions of the game and Spanish accounts, it is clear that neither the hands nor the feet were allowed contact with the ball. The body parts used to transport the ball varied across civilizations, though the manner of scoring points was rather consistent. A team scored a point with the use of two central hoops, or goals, midfield. Ball courts were generally large structures, complete with seating and a central field. Walls were decorated with depictions of the civilization's gods and often contained depictions of the ritual sacrifice at the end of the game.

The ball game was not the only sport played in the ancient Americas, but it is the one with the most remaining evidence. Foot races were perhaps the most popular and exciting sports for Native Americans. These races evolved out of a long tradition of running for transportation, but because little archaeological evidence exists there is no way to date the origin of the races. Much like the ball game, foot races have mythological origins. Several groups believed that races between their gods and the animals shaped the world, providing an explanation for constellations and the differentiation between species.

In advance of foot races participants took care to train and prepare themselves accordingly, which included such extreme measures as tying weights to their ankles for the weeks before the race. Runners also painted their bodies to identify themselves in the race and for ritual purposes. In many races wagering also became an important element, piquing interest in the sport.

Indigenous inhabitants of the southwestern United States and northern Mexico often participated in kick-ball races, long-distance races that involved kicking a ball for more than 25 miles at a stretch. Both men and women participated in these races, although women used a stick to toss a hoop ahead of them as they ran. Children began training for the kick-ball race when they were young, as it was seen as a religious ritual as well as a sporting event. Ceremonies were held the night before and the morning of the race, and there was a strong belief in supernatural intervention in these races. Many groups even believed that they were able to run faster while kicking the ball than without, as if a supernatural force were pulling each member of the team forward.

In Peru foot races were often included in the initiation of a boy reaching puberty. With other rituals, these foot races established each boy as a member of the adult community by showing his mental and physical fortitude. Foot races in North America were also run as part of growing up. Nations living in the Great Plains and along the Mississippi often viewed these races as preparation for future warfare.

For North American Indians in snowy climates, such as the ancestors of the Iroquois and Seneca nations (who can be traced to these regions to 4000 b.c.e.), the snow-snake game used the weather to its advantage. The object of the game was to toss an object called a snake (most commonly a pole) the farthest on ice or in snow. The lanes intended for the snow-snake were long and free from obstruction, but there were no specific rules about the paths or the snake itself. Snow-snake was generally an individual sport, although it could be played in teams, with each member tossing a snake and each team accumulating points for the longest throws. The game did not attract the attention of either the ball game or the races, nor did it have a supernatural or spiritual component. This game, then, seems to have been played simply for diversion and leisure activity.

Sports and games, then, did serve a purpose outside of a ritual one, particularly games of chance that originated in prehistoric times. In fact, the ancient dice playing of North American Indians can be traced back nearly 2,000 years using archaeological remnants of dice found in the southwestern United States. This prehistoric game did not use skill or calculation. Rather, each player relied on chance to win the game. As was the tradition with such games of chance, Indians often placed wagers on who would win. Some players were certainly luckier than others, and it was believed that those players had a special relationship with the gods or themselves had supernatural powers.

The dice that have been uncovered in Arizona, Utah, and Colorado are referred to as two-sided dice and are very unlike the six-sided dice of modern times. These dice resembled sticks and were decorated on each side, using light colors on one and dark colors on the other. As with most games of chance, the goal was to guess a number or a series of numbers involving the dice. The dice game has been found in more than 100 distinct groups in North America and is generally considered universal to nations in North America. As with the kick-ball race and the ball game, the rules and means of playing the game varied from nation to nation. Both men and women played the game in all nations, but they generally did so separately. Score was kept either with another set of sticks or using an abacus.

Ancient games were also played among children, and one of the best known is the skin or blanket tossing game of the Eskimo. In this game a large animal hide was spread, and a child climbed on it. When the hide was pulled taut, the child was thrown into the air. The object of this game was for each boy to land on his feet. Oftentimes the children were doing so after having been thrown more than 20 feet in the air.

Children all over the Americas also played with dolls, which were most frequently made using the most convenient materials. Those living in the region now occupied by the Chippewa used cattails in making their dolls, and clay figures were used in other parts of the Americas. Children often made their own dolls out of cornhusks where corn was most prevalent. Children played with dolls in much the same way as they do today, and these dolls were used by boys and girls alike.

See also ADORNMENT; AGRICULTURE; ARCHITECTURE; ART; CHILDREN; CRAFTS; CRIME AND PUNISHMENT; DRAMA AND THEATER; FESTIVALS; GENDER STRUCTURES AND ROLES; INVENTIONS; LITERATURE; MILITARY; MUSIC AND MUSICAL INSTRUMENTS; NUMBERS AND COUNTING; RELIGION AND COSMOLOGY; SOCIAL ORGANIZATION; TRADE AND EXCHANGE; WEAPONRY AND ARMOR.

Greece

~ *Pindar, Olympian Odes (ca. 470 b.c.e.)* ~

No. 9

Fit speech may I find for my journey in the Muses' car; and let me therewith have daring and powers of ample scope. To back the prowess of a friend I came, when Lampromachos won his Isthmian crown, when on the same day both he and his brother overcame. And afterwards at the gates of Corinth two triumphs again befell Epharmostos and more in the valleys of Nemea. At Argos he triumphed over men, as over boys at Athens. And I might tell how at Marathon he stole from among the beardless and confronted the full-grown for the prize of silver vessels, how without a fall he threw his men with swift and coming shock, and how loud the shouting pealed when round the ring he ran, in the beauty of his youth and fair form and fresh from fairest deeds.

No. 10

Ample is the glory stored for Olympian winners; thereof my shepherd tongue is fain to keep some part in fold. But only by the help of Zeus is wisdom kept ever blooming in the soul. Son of Archestratos, Agesidamos, know certainly that for your boxing I will lay a glory of sweet strains upon your crown of golden olive and will have in remembrance the race of the Locrians in the west.

No. 11

Who then won to their lot the new-appointed crown by hands or feet or chariot, setting before them the prize of glory in the games, and winning it by their act? In the foot-race down the straight course of the stadion was Likymnios' son Oionos first, from Nodea had he led his host: in the wrestling was Tegea glorified by Echemos: Doryklos won the prize of boxing, a dweller in the city of Tiryns, and with the four-horse chariot, Samos of Mantinea, Halirrhotios' son: with the javelin

Phrastor hit the mark: in distance Enikeus beyond all others hurled the stone with a circling sweep, and all the warrior company thundered a great applause. Then on the evening the lovely shining of the fair-faced moon beamed forth, and all the precinct sounded with songs of festal glee, after the manner which is to this day for triumph.

No. 13

Also two parsley-wreaths shadowed his head before the people at the games of *Isthmus*, nor does *Nemea* tell a different tale. And of his father Thessalos' lightning feet is recorded by the streams of Alpheos, and at *Pytho* he has renown for the single and for the double *stadion* gained both in a single day, and in the same month at rocky *Pan-Athenaios* a day of swiftness crowned his hair for three illustrious deeds, and the *Hellotia* seven times, and at the games of *Poseidon* between seas longer hymns followed his father Ptoiodoros with Terpsias and Eritimos. And how often you were first at *Delphi* or in the *Pastures of the Lion*, though with full many do I match your crowd of honors, yet can I no more surely tell than the tale of pebbles on the sea-shore.

From: Fred Morrow Fling, ed., *A Source Book of Greek History* (Boston: D. C. Heath, 1907).

Rome

∼ Suetonius, excerpt from The Divine Augustus (ca. 120 C.E.) ∼

43. In the number, variety, and magnificence of his public spectacles, he surpassed all former examples. Four-and-twenty times, he says, he treated the people with games upon his own account, and three-and-twenty times for such magistrates as were either absent or not able to afford the expense. The performances took place sometimes in the different streets of the city, and upon several stages, by players in all languages. The same he did not only in the forum and amphitheatre, but in the circus likewise, and in the Saepta and sometimes he exhibited only the hunting of wild beasts. He entertained the people with wrestlers in the Campus Martius, where wooden seats were erected for the purpose; and also with a naval fight, for

which he excavated the ground near the Tiber, where there is now the grove of the Caesars. During these two entertainments he stationed guards in the city lest, by robbers taking advantage of the small number of people left at home, it might be exposed to depredations. In the circus he exhibited chariot and foot races, and combats with wild beasts, in which the performers were often youths of the highest rank. His favorite spectacle was the Trojan game, acted by a select number of boys, in parties differing in age and station; thinking that it was a practice both excellent in itself, and sanctioned by ancient usage, that the spirit of the young nobles should be displayed in such exercises. Gaius Nonius Asprenas, who was lamed by a fall in this diversion, he presented

(continued)

(continues)

with a gold collar, and allowed him and his posterity to bear the surname of Torquati. But soon afterwards he gave up the exhibition of this game, in consequence of a severe and bitter speech made in the senate by Asinius Pollio, the orator, in which he complained bitterly of the misfortune of Aeserninus, his grandson, who likewise broke his leg in the same diversion.

Sometimes he engaged Roman knights to act upon the stage, or to fight as gladiators; but only before the practice was prohibited by a decree of the senate. Thenceforth, the only exhibition he made of that kind, was that of a young man named Lucius, of a good family, who was not quite two feet in height, and weighed only seventeen pounds, but had a stentorian voice. In one of his public spectacles, he brought the hostages of the Parthians, the first ever sent to Rome from that nation, through the middle of the amphitheatre, and placed them in the second tier of seats above him. He used likewise, at times when there were no public entertainments, if any thing was brought to Rome which was uncommon, and might gratify curiosity, to expose it to public view, in any place whatever; as he did a rhinoceros in the Saepta, a tiger upon a stage, and a snake fifty cubits long in the Comitium. It happened in the Circensian games, which he performed in consequence of a vow, that he was taken ill, and obliged to attend the Thensae [procession] reclining on a litter. Another time, in the games celebrated for the opening of the theatre of Marcellus, the joints of his curule chair happening to give way, he fell on his back. And in the games exhibited by his grandsons, when the people were in such consternation, by an alarm raised that the theatre was falling, that all his efforts to reassure them and keep them quiet, failed, he moved from his place, and seated himself in that part of the theatre which was thought to be exposed to most danger.

From: Suetonius, *The Lives of the Twelve Caesars*, trans. Alexander Thomson (New York: G. Bell and Sons, 1893).

The Americas

∼ *Excerpt from the Popol Vuh*
(oral tradition, unknown date) ∼

II. CHAPTER 2

THE messengers of Hun-Camé and Vucub-Camé arrived immediately.

"Go, Ahpop Achih!" they were told. "Go and call Hun-Hunahpú and Vucub-Hunahpú. Say to them, 'Come with us. The lords say that you must come.' They must come here to play ball with us so that they shall make us happy, for really they amaze us. So, then, they must come," said the lords. "And have them bring their playing gear, their rings, their gloves, and have them bring their rubber balls, too," said the lords. "Tell them to come quickly," they told the messengers.

And these messengers were owls: Chabi-Tucur, Huracán-Tucur, Caquix-Tucur and Holom-Tucur. These were the names of the messengers of Xibalba.

Chabi-Tucur was swift as an arrow; Huracán-Tucur had only one leg; Caquix-Tucur had a red back, and Holom-Tucur had only a head, no legs, but he had wings.

The four messengers had the rank of Ahpop-Achih. Leaving Xibalba, they arrived quickly, bringing their message to the court where Hun-Hunahpú and Vucub-Hunahpú were playing ball, at the ball-court which was called Nim-Xob-Carchah. The owl messengers went directly to the ball-court and delivered their message exactly as it was given to them by Hun-Camé, Vucub-Camé, Ahalpuh, Ahalganá, Chamiabac, Chamiaholom, Xiquiripat, Cuchumaquic, Ahalmez, Ahaltocob, Xic, and Patán, as the lords were called who sent the message by the owls.

"Did the Lords Hun-Camé and Vucub-Camé really say that we must go with you?"

"They certainly said so, and 'Let them bring all their playing gear,' the lords said."

"Very well," said the youths. "Wait for us, we are only going to say good-bye to our mother."

And having gone straight home, they said to their mother, for their father was dead: "We are going, our mother, but our going is only for a while. The messengers of the lord have come to take us. 'They must come,' they said, according to the messengers."

"We shall leave our ball here in pledge," they added. They went immediately to hang it in the space under the rooftree. "We will return to play," they said.

And going to Hunbatz and Hunchouén they said to them: "Keep on playing the flute and singing, painting, and carving; warm our house and warm the heart of your grandmother."

From: Delia Goetz and Sylvanus Griswold Morley, trans., *Popol Vuh* (Los Angeles: Plantin Press, 1954).

FURTHER READING

Carlin A. Barton, *The Sorrows of the Ancient Romans: The Gladiator and the Monster* (Princeton, N.J.: Princeton University Press, 1992).

Alan Cameron, *Circus Factions: Blues and Greens at Rome and Byzantium* (Oxford, U.K.: Oxford University Press, 1976).

Stewart Culin, *Games of the North American Indian* (New York: Dover Publications, 1975).

Wolfgang Decker, *Sports and Games of Ancient Egypt,* trans. Allen Guttmann (New Haven. Conn.: Yale University Press, 1992).

Irving Finkel, ed., *Ancient Board Games in Perspective* (London: British Museum Press, 2007).

Alison Futrell, *A Sourcebook on the Roman Games* (Oxford, U.K.: Blackwell, 2006).

H. A. Harris, *Greek Athletes and Athletics* (Westport, Conn.: Greenwood Press, 1964).

"History of Weiqi." Available online. URL: http://www.yutopian.com/go/misc/gohistory.html. Downloaded January 30, 2007.

Ulrich Hubner, "Games." In *The Oxford Encyclopedia of Archaeology in the Near East,* vol. 2, ed. Eric M. Meyers (New York: Oxford University Press, 1997).

George Jennison, *Animals for Show and Pleasure in Ancient Rome,* 2nd ed. (Philadelphia: University of Pennsylvania Press, 2005).

Anne Mahoney, *Roman Sports and Spectacles: A Sourcebook* (Newburyport, Mass.: Focus, 2001).

"Mancala." Available online. URL: http://www.search.com/reference/Mancala. Downloaded on November 29, 2006.

Stephen G. Miller, *Ancient Greek Athletics* (New Haven: Yale University Press, 2004).

Peter Nabokov, *Indian Running: Native American History and Tradition* (Santa Fe, N.M.: Ancient City Press, 1987).

Věra Olivová, *Sports and Games in the Ancient World,* trans. D. Orpington (London: Orbis, 1984).

Joseph B. Oxendine, *American Indian Sports Heritage,* 2nd ed. (Lincoln: University of Nebraska Press, 1995).

Michael B. Poliakoff, *Combat Sports in the Ancient World: Competition, Violence, and Culture* (New Haven, Conn.: Yale University Press, 1987).

D. S. Potter and D. J. Mattingly, eds., *Life, Death, and Entertainment in the Roman Empire* (Ann Arbor: University of Michigan Press, 1999).

Larry Russ, *The Complete Mancala Games Book: How to Play the World's Oldest Board Games* (New York: Marlowe, 2000).

David Sansone, *Greek Athletics and the Genesis of Sport* (Berkeley: University of California Press, 1988).

Judith Swaddling, *The Ancient Olympic Games,* 2nd ed. (Austin: University of Texas Press, 1999).

Malcolm Todd, *Everyday Life of the Barbarians, Goths, Franks, and Vandals* (London: Batsford, 1972).

E. Michael Whittington, ed., *The Sport of Life and Death: The Mesoamerican Ballgame* (New York: Thames and Hudson, 2001).

► storage and preservation

INTRODUCTION

Hunter-gatherers in prehistoric times paid minimal attention to long-term food storage and preservation. Their way of life dictated that they move about in search of food supplies and then consume what they found as they found it. Food typically would not have been preserved for more than a few days or perhaps weeks, depending on how long it would keep. Meat and fish, of course, had to be consumed within days, while plant foods could be kept on hand for a period of weeks.

It was with the advent of agriculture that ancient peoples turned more attention to longer-term food storage and preservation. Agriculture offered the possibility of making a community's food supply more consistent and predictable over time. By storing and preserving food, people could measure out their food consumption over the year and eliminate the need to pick up and move when food supplies ran out. Accordingly, they developed a number of techniques for storing and preserving food.

At the household level, food was stored primarily in such containers as woven baskets and clay pots; pots were also used for storing beverages. Grains (often ground into meal and flour), beans, and rice could be stored in this way for long periods of time. Foods more susceptible to spoilage were preserved principally by drying. The food was spread out on the ground or on racks and placed in the sun or over a fire. When its moisture content was low enough, it would be suitable for storage because microorganisms would not grow in it. In this way ancient peoples preserved fruits, berries, corn, vegetables, and especially meat and fish.

Smoking was another common method for preserving meats and fish. The smoke coated the food's cells with substances that inhibit the growth of microorganisms. Similarly, freezing was a good way to preserve food in cold-weather climates. North Americans, for example, killed game late in the fall and then allowed the meat to freeze, often grinding it up and mixing it with other foods such as berries. Another major way of preserving meat and fish was by salting them. Salt, inexpensive and taken for granted in the modern world, was a highly valued commodity in the ancient world, necessary not only for nutrition but for food preservation. In addition to salt, certain herbs and other plants were found to have preservative properties, particularly in discouraging insects and rodents. Enzymes from cow stomachs and some plants enabled people to preserve dairy products in the form of cheese. Pickling, too, used acids to preserve vegetable crops.

Larger, more advanced communities needed to find ways to preserve and store large quantities of food. The ancient Egyptians, for example, developed highly sophisticated techniques for growing grain in the silt left behind by the floodwaters of the Nile River. After the waters receded, millions of acres of grain crops were planted and then irrigated with water stored in a complex system of fields, dikes, dams, and sluices. Annual crop yields amounted to millions of tons, most of which was stored in community granaries for later distribution. On a smaller scale, some ancient peoples developed underground storage silos for grain, sealing the silos off from the air to prevent rotting, molds, and pest infestations.

AFRICA

by Kirk H. Beetz

Archaeological evidence for ancient African storage and preservation is patchy, known only from a smattering of sites scattered across the continent. Archaeologists have used physical evidence, records from ancient historians such as Herodotus (ca. 484–ca. 425 B.C.E.), and the practices in historical times of ancient ethnic groups to reconstruct a little of how ancient Africans stored food and valuables. There are hazards in using the practices of people in the present day to reconstruct what their ancestors may have done, because even a very traditional culture may change some of its practices over a period of thousands of years.

Even so, what little is known about storage and preservation in ancient Africa offers clues to the matters of ancient relationships among cultures and the diffusion of knowledge in ancient times. Grass-lined pits have been discovered in West Africa and in the central Sahara in which food, probably millet, would have been stored, and the peoples around ancient Lake Chad had silos made of mud bricks, possibly for storing grain. The pits of West Africa may date from about the early 4000s B.C.E., around the same time as similar ones found in Egypt, whereas the pits and silos of Chad date from about 1800 to 400 B.C.E. Some archaeologists take these finds as evidence of a shared culture that predated the ancient Egyptian culture and probably developed in the Sahara, then spread into the region of the Nile. Others suggest it is evidence that storage practices spread either from the newly agricultural peoples of the lower Nile region to the west or from central or western Africa to the region that became central Egypt.

Archaeological work in Chad is especially interesting because it is one of the few places in Africa where archaeologists have been able to begin constructing a record of continuous cultural development. Very early, people built villages near the shores of Lake Chad, which was much bigger before the Sahara dried. As the shores of the lake receded, people moved their homes to remain near the vital source of water. This has allowed archaeologists to go from one site to another, progressing ever more recently in history as they move ever closer to the modern lake. Thus there is evidence for the development of storage practices from about 1800 to 400 B.C.E.

The most significant finds have been pits. Some pits were dug to remove clay for building homes. Others were dug to provide clay for building defensive walls around villages. Still others are of a more mysterious purpose. Some probably stored valuables such as pottery and metal objects. Some of the pits may have stored food, especially cowpeas. Not yet securely dated are the silos, which were probably built after 1800 B.C.E. They were for grain, probably pearl millet, a type of grain that was durable when stored. The silos are taken as an indication that the ancient villagers were able to have surpluses of crops from their harvests and had the social organization to store the surpluses for periods of poor harvests. Given that pearl millet was a summer crop and that winters could be very dry, the silos and pits at least may have provided storage of food for use during the winter. People in the region still use storage pits, and archaeologists draw some of their conclusions about pits being used for storing food from the similarity of the ancient pits to the modern ones.

As the Sahara and much of northeastern Africa dried in ancient times, storing and preserving water became more and more important. Evidence for how this was done in the Sahara comes mostly from ancient rock paintings dating to about 8000 B.C.E. onward. Many of the paintings depict ordinary life, which has allowed archaeologists to trace some of the developments in Saharan culture as the climate changed. During the period from 2780 to 600 B.C.E. residents of the Sahara drew water from wells. One painting shows what appears to be a leather bucket being hoisted from a well. The belief that it is leather is based on the artist's depiction, which makes it look like animal hide, and the fact that the Saharans were longtime herders of cattle. From this it may be inferred that leather bottles were used to store and transport water much as the peoples of the Sahara have done in historical times.

In the kingdom of Kush (ca. 900 B.C.E.–ca. 300 C.E.), south of ancient Egypt, water management seems to have been more sophisticated. Cisterns made of stone have been found in Kush's towns and cities. Archaeologists debate about the use of the cisterns, suggesting that they were swimming pools, baths, or storage for drinking and cooking water. They tend to be located in or near homes, and the ancient Kushites boiled food extensively, both of which suggest that the cisterns were intended to store water for consumption.

South of Kush, along the coast of East Africa, lived people who seemed to put water to another use. According to the Greek geographer Strabo (64 or 63 B.C.E.–after 23 C.E.), fishermen of the region stored shellfish and fish in pools of water near the shore to keep for eating later, perhaps when catches were poor. This is a logical practice, and Strabo took greater pains than most ancient geographers to make his accounts accurate. A later development was the use of baskets to catch fish and keep them in water. This use of baskets was also found among Bantu-speaking peoples of West Africa.

The Bantu speakers were farmers, and by 200 C.E. they were advancing east and south out of West Africa, using their iron tools to carve out farms from forests. How they stored their harvests is not entirely clear, but inferences can be made from the recorded practices of their descendants. One is that their granaries were elevated above the ground on posts made of tree branches. This helped protect the grain not only from pests such as rats but also from flooding, a common problem in central Africa and parts of eastern Africa south of Kush. Another practice was that of making granaries out of walls of woven mats and conical roofs of long rushes that ran lengthwise from the peaks down to the edges, thus making rainwater flow out and away from the granary. Much of this inference is speculative because archaeologists have not made much progress in researching in Africa's forests; the central regions are remote and therefore hard to reach, and the region has been very dangerous for scientists because of bandits and warfare.

EGYPT

BY KATHARINA ZINN

Most food in ancient Egypt was not produced or consumed daily, and to be kept longer it had to be preserved. Methods of storage and preservation were designed to solve this problem and to accommodate the growing population of the region. Stored or preserved food could include grain, fruits, vegetables, meat, fish, poultry, and wine. The storage facilities in ancient Egypt showed a wide range of types and extended from single storage jars or basketwork containers for domestic use to large storeroom complexes. Meat, fish, and poultry were stored in pottery vessels. Plates or bowls were used to hold offerings (it was necessary to offer food to the deceased daily), and tightly closed jars were used for long-term storage. Oil, fat, and suet were stored in stoneware jars. Grain was stored in small domestic pits or jars as well as large-scale granaries controlled by the state or a temple, such as the Ramesseum (a mortuary temple in Thebes dedicated to the Egyptian king Ramses II [r. 1290–1224 B.C.E.]) and Medinet Habu (dedicated to Ramses III [r. 1194–1163 B.C.E.]). Storerooms for grain and other agricultural products were named *shenut* ("barns") and had a specific administrative structure devoted to their maintenance. Precious goods, such as herbs, spices, and salt, were kept in small leather or linen bags. Of further importance was the form of rations for food supply.

In a society without money, rations had a special significance; food had to be stored within the food circle from harvest or slaughtering to ration distribution.

Grain was stored in large quantities at the local, provincial, and state level in granary silos whose maximum capacity was calculated by scribes. Some silos are partly excavated, while others have been depicted in artwork or as model granaries in tombs. Depictions of stored grain or models placed in tombs were meant to guarantee a supply of food for the dead. Scenes portray people sacking up and carrying the grain from fields to the granaries, sometimes using donkeys. Grain was put directly into storage facilities after winnowing, sieving, recording, and measuring by scribes. At the granary porters carried the baskets up the stairs to the charging hole, where the grain was poured in. The process was supervised by a scribe or administrator who recorded intakes, storage, and removal. All harvested goods belonged not to the farmer but to the king or to the temples or nobles who had received the land as a gift from the king.

The first small-scale granaries were pits with basketry linens and a total yield of about 7.5 pounds. In El Faiyûm, a large oasis, Egyptologists have found well-preserved wheat and barley from the Neolithic Period (dating to about 5200 B.C.E.). This shows the long tradition of storage that preceded dynastic times. Other early examples are in El Badâri in northern Upper Egypt about 4500 B.C.E., where postholes, pits, and storage jars were found. The oldest large granaries were cones with round bases and domed tops that were made of mud brick or seasoned wood and sometimes plastered. The larger ones had steps or a ladder leading to a hole at the top

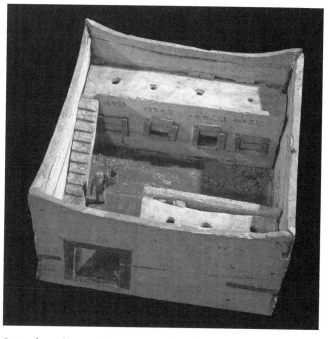

Painted wooden model of a granary, from Aswān, Egypt, Sixth Dynasty, around 2200 B.C.E. (© The Trustees of the British Museum)

where the grain was poured in. Another opening at the bottom was used to remove the grain. This structural form existed until the beginning of the Greco-Roman Period in 332 B.C.E. and was supplemented by trapezoidal structures used for storing cereals to be used for sowing in the next season. Quadrangular chambers, filled through small holes on the ceiling, also are evidenced by models and drawings. Sometimes terms for the contents were written on the models.

The Egyptian temples were given estates and royal endowments as offerings to the gods. The priesthood, in turn, received food and other offerings through an elaborate allocation formula called the Reversion of Offerings. Holding and redistributing the offerings required the use of large storage facilities, which belonged to the temples. The best-preserved set of large storage facilities is attached to the Ramesseum, which could support about 3,400 families (about 17,000 to 20,000 people) for a year with grain. The temple storehouses consisted of long mud-brick, barrel-vaulted halls of varying size with filling holes at the top, erected in groups with a shared vestibule. The temples built up substantial reserves for grain and other goods. From these or state granaries each farmer got his grain for sowing, again recorded by scribes. The granaries housed the food that was used as payment for the army, workers on building projects, and other citizens.

Egyptian houses, including palaces, also contained storerooms and granaries. Some of the houses of the planned towns in El-Lahun, Tell El-'Amârna, and Medina had a row of storerooms. El-Lahun shows evidence of several locations within the town rather than a central granary. Large estates had large private storerooms, while those who lived in the country had smaller, mostly conical ones that stored nearly everything in the Egyptians' diet.

As a form of preservation, most food was dried in air and sunlight. There is little evidence for smoking, probably for lack of wood. Pickling with brine, oil, or salt was common as salt draws out liquid. The use of vinegar is assumed but not evidenced. Meat and poultry were preserved through the use of fat, honey, or beer.

If meat was not consumed immediately after hanging, it was cut, wet- or dry-salted, dried in sun and air, possibly smoked, and cured in jars. As the food cooled inside the jars, a sort of vacuum was created that kept the food from spoiling. Some of these jars were made of marl clay, which kept their contents cool. The food was later cooked before it was eaten, which killed most bacteria in the process.

Another perishable food was fish. Much of the catch was cleaned, gutted, and dried in the sun on wooden frames. It sometimes was salted or pickled in oil. Roe was dried or pickled in salt and then pressed and dried. Drying, salting, and pickling were methods of preservation for small birds, too. Dairy products such as cheese were salted and sometimes preserved in oil, dried, and hardened. Dates, figs, olives, or grapes could be dried, ground, pickled, or pressed. Storing grain in spikelet form, rather than threshed, helped to protect it from attacks by insects or other pests. Herbs such as coriander, black cumin, and fenugreek were added as insecticides, as evidenced in a model granary of the Egyptian king Tutankhamen (r. 1333–1323 B.C.E.) containing emmer with other seeds.

THE MIDDLE EAST
BY LYN GREEN

The first permanent settlements appeared in the ancient Near East during the Neolithic Period. They were small and usually clustered around sources of water, as all later towns would be. These most ancient farmers tended to settle particularly along rivers, where alluvial soil carried by the water spread out and made fertile, easily cultivated agricultural land. Their houses and probably storage buildings were made of the same unbaked river mud. The crops grown by these earliest farmers did not have a high yield, since they were still essentially wild forms of the plants. The farmers, therefore, would not have been able to put aside large quantities of food between growing seasons. To supplement the grains and pulses such as barley, einkorn, emmer, lentils, peas, chick peas, and bitter vetch, they also ate wild fruits and nuts, fish, birds, and game. Because storage facilities did not need to be large or to keep food for extended periods of time, the earliest-known storage facilities (from the Pre-Pottery Neolithic A Period, perhaps as early as 8500 B.C.E.) were small bins and silos and probably baskets or sacks. The latter have not survived because they would have been made of rushes, reeds, or hide.

Later civilizations of the area, such as the Halaf culture (dating to as long ago as the sixth millennium B.C.E.), practiced agriculture and stored grain in beehive-shaped communal granaries. Many centuries later, granaries of the same shape were built at the sites of Arad and Beth Yerah. The Halaf storage facilities were small and shared only among a few dwellings. By contrast, the Bronze Age (ca. 3500–ca. 1200 B.C.E.) granaries of Arad and Beth Yerah were much larger and served whole communities. They rested on stone foundations and were usually from 13 to 30 feet in diameter. All of these storage buildings were built above the ground, but farmers of the fifth millennium B.C.E. in the Negev desert stored their food in below-ground chambers linked to each other and to the living quarters by a serious of subterranean tunnels. Within the underground storerooms were pits where grain, lentils, and other foodstuffs were stored. Underground storage in the desert was both cool and dry and proved so effective that these farmers continued to store grain underground even after they began to build their houses on the surface.

The earliest storage containers of the ancient Near East, dating to the early Neolithic Period, differ markedly from all later forms of storage because they appear before pottery was made. All later civilizations depended heavily on pottery storage jars in all sizes and shapes. These pottery pieces were almost always of undecorated fired clay, though they could be covered with a thin clay coating called a slip. Slip makes the surface of the pot less permeable to air and moisture and helps prevent the contents from spoiling. By the Chalcolithic Period (also known as the Copper Age, ca. 4500–ca. 3300 B.C.E.) pottery was becoming a specialized craft, and pots could be made in a variety of sizes and shapes. These new shapes became necessary because Near Eastern farmers from the Chalcolithic Period onward were experimenting with new ways of preserving foodstuffs. Around this time they began to crush grapes and olives for wine and oil, which obviously required quite different storage containers from whole olives or dried grapes (raisins). Scholars believe that around this time the farmers also began to dry figs and dates, though it is possible that in a hot, dry climate this sort of preservation would have been happening all along.

After the Chalcolithic Period centralized government arose in the Fertile Crescent, first in the form of city-states and later as kingdoms and even empires. It is often said that developments in food technology, including storage, are inseparable from this change. The evidence of texts and of archaeology makes it clear that the structures of the ruling elite were economic centers as well as residences or temples. In early Sumer, for example, where the priesthood often ruled the cities, storehouses were often located close to the temples. These government storehouses served multiple purposes: They provided long-term storage for grain and other foodstuffs for seed and as a guard against famine, and they were used as shorter-term storage for goods to be traded or redistributed as rations or wages.

Many different types of food were now being kept for a longer term, and this necessitated new preservation techniques. For example, while yogurt may have been made in the Chalcolithic Period, by Sumerian times the milk of sheep, goats, and cattle was preserved by being made into cheese and ghee (clarified butter). Grapes and dates were dried or pressed for their juice, which could be left to ferment into either wine or vinegar. The grape and date juice itself could also be boiled down until it became a synthetic form of honey. (Real honey was expensive and probably mostly imported.) The concentration of sugars caused by boiling down the juice inhibited the growth of bacteria, so the syrup would keep without spoiling. Pomegranates, another widely grown fruit, would keep without processing if stored carefully.

Pulses, legumes, and similar vegetables were dried for storage. Some other vegetables, such as mushrooms, could also have been dried. Drying, salting, and possibly smoking were used in various parts of the ancient Near East to keep meat and especially fish. The bones of saltwater fish found at inland sites in Sumer show that some sort of preservation of fish for shipment was taking place by the third millennium B.C.E. Sumerian texts show that they were making a kind of fermented fish sauce as well. Although most meat was eaten right away, the types that would have been available for processing included goat, beef, mutton, venison, and pork. Poultry such as ducks and geese were also raised and their meat dried or smoked.

As urban centers and the centralized control of commodities grew, larger storage facilities were needed. Grain, which was made into bread and (since the fourth millennium B.C.E.) beer, was stored in great quantities. The Middle Bronze Age (ca. 2000–ca. 1500 B.C.E.) silos at Beth Yerah are estimated to have held as much as 40 tons of grain. Other contemporary cities in this area, however, had a different solution to the problem of grain storage. They excavated downward rather than building upward to make their granaries. By the Iron Age (ca. 1200–ca. 586 B.C.E.) cities like Jericho and Megiddo were building rectangular storehouses and storerooms with thick walls to keep the grain and foodstuffs cool and dry. Archaeologists in Israel have uncovered storehouses in which the stored items were kept in pottery bins or jars. Occasionally, commodities such as grain were stored loose in these rooms. The remains of barley and wheat show that these were the main cereals grown and stored in the granaries.

ASIA AND THE PACIFIC
BY KIRK H. BEETZ

The need to provide food during lean times was met in many different ways in Asia and the Pacific, depending on the food that was available, the climate, and people's cultures. The first people in Australia found a fairly wet climate and big forests, but the continent gradually dried out, leaving only small forests in areas that remained wet. The Australians coped by spreading out in a thin population over the continent. By living in small, family-oriented groups with a great deal of space for hunting and gathering food, the ancient Australians were able to thrive when food was plentiful and still find enough food to survive when times were lean. Rather than store large caches of food, they made sure there were not too many people to use what food was available to them throughout the year.

In tropical climates storing food was difficult because the regions tended to be wet, and moisture helped to decay food. One way to preserve fish was to smoke it. This involved suspending fish over a low-burning, smoky fire that would rapidly dry the fish. Fish devoid of moisture could remain edible for weeks or even months. Cultures throughout the South Pacific and the Indian Ocean used this technique. In areas where tapirs or other sources of meat were available, meat was smoked. Techniques for storing smoked meat varied but usually involved hanging the dried meat either inside the home or underground in a chamber dug for the purpose of storing smoked meats, keeping the food away from scavenging animals.

Nomads in central and northern Asia hung meat from poles or skewers to allow the wind to dry it. It was important to allow the meat to dangle and to cut it thinly enough for the wind to dry it thoroughly. The climate of central Asia was drying out during the ancient era, creating excellent conditions for drying meat rapidly. It was difficult for the nomads to store bulky foods such as the grains most often grown in their regions: millet, wheat, and barley. Thus they sometimes took to raiding farming communities to steal the harvests when they wanted the food rather than producing and storing the food themselves.

Keeping grains dry was very important. The Harappan civilization of about 2600 to 1500 B.C.E. made the preservation of grain a science in which they engineered sometimes spectacular granaries for storing grain against hard times. The cities of Harappa and Mohenjo Daro had granaries that may have represented the apex of grain-storage technology. The granary in Mohenjo Daro was about 150 feet in length and about 75 feet wide, and it rested on a base of bricks about 20 feet high. Atop the base was a wooden, roofed structure perhaps 12 feet high. Although the city had mostly narrow streets, a large open space around the granary allowed easy access for carts bringing in grain or unloading grain for distribution. There was a loading platform along one side of the building where grain could be hoisted up or lowered down. Inside were wooden silos that held the grain. Under the floor were air ducts, channels that circulated air to keep the grain dry to prevent rotting. The granary looked like a fortress, which has inspired some archaeologists to speculate that the granary was like a bank that held the nation's wealth. The huge structure probably ensured that Harappans would have food to eat during poor harvests.

Insects and rodents were threats to stored grain. In ancient China their feasting in granaries sometimes resulted in a shortage of food. Keeping grain sealed helped keep out insects, and large ceramic jars with tight lids were used in China, India, and Japan to protect grain. Although the ancient Japanese typically built their structures with pits in the ground, they raised their granaries on posts to help keep the stored grain out of reach of mice and other pests. The shape of a granary was rectangular. Four holes in the ground were pounded until their bottoms were rock hard, then circular wooden posts were set in them. A wooden floor a few feet above the ground was installed, followed by walls attached to the posts and a roof that was probably peaked and covered with dried grass, although archaeologists disagree greatly among themselves about this detail. It seems that by 100 C.E. nearly every village in the Japanese islands had such a granary.

Another way to preserve food was to pack it in salt. The salt would keep meat from going rancid for a time, usually long enough to carry it through a season when food was scarce. Meat preserved with salt had something in common with dry grain: It needed water to make it edible. Rice is almost not chewable unless moistened. Salted meat needed to be soaked in water to wash out enough salt to make it digestible. In much of central and northern Asia water became increasingly harder to find throughout ancient times. For nomads, this left them their wind-dried meats. For farmers, this meant digging pits in which to store their foods, though this practice seems to have come late to northern China. The soldiers of the Great Wall had storage depots for food and other supplies, but the farmers of the region still needed to be taught about granaries and storage pits as late as the 100s C.E.

In India the need for water to make dry grain and salted meat edible created a dangerous problem. People from cities went to nearby rivers or to moats to fetch their water for cooking, and the rivers and moats were dreadfully polluted by 300 B.C.E. Diseases transmitted by human waste, garbage, and rodents lurked in the water, and underheated cooking water could result in outbreaks of disease that could kill thousands in crowded residential districts. The usually wet climate of most of India also made it difficult to keep foods dry. Indians got around some of their food preservation problems by tending gardens for fresh food. Even a small household usually had a garden from which fruits and herbs could be picked daily. Except for the cold and sometimes dry far north of India, it was possible to have something ripe and edible in a garden year-round. Both men and women were often master gardeners, and men who were professional gardeners took care to teach their daughters what they knew, because the girls would ultimately be responsible for caring for the food in their household gardens. It also was a good trade for a woman to know, to make money for herself and her family in the marketplace.

EUROPE

BY MICHAEL J. O'NEAL

The ancient Europeans faced the same storage and preservation problems that ancient peoples the world over faced. The enemies of food stored over a period of time include moisture, temperature, microbes (including molds), and pests. Without effective systems of food storage and preservation, the ancient Europeans would have found it difficult to fend off famine and starvation during the long, cold winters of the North. Moreover, without methods of storage and preservation, it is not possible to accumulate perishable goods, transport them, and trade them, activities that were a necessary means to the accumulation of wealth and status.

Many of the technologies that the ancient Europeans used to store and preserve food are still in use today. The only fundamental difference is that ancient Europeans did not have electricity to power the tools they used for the task. Accordingly, they relied on the tools that nature provided. One method of preserving such food as meat, fish, vegetables, and fruits was to dry them. With a low moisture content, food was not as susceptible to spoilage. To dry food, the ancient Europeans placed it in the sun and allowed warm air to circulate around it. A variant of drying is cheese making. The ancient Europeans were able to preserve milk in cheese form by coagulating it and draining out the watery whey, leaving behind the milk solids that had a much lower water content than the original milk. In cool temperatures, cheese would keep for many months. In Neolithic Britain residues of milk fats have been found on fragments of pottery that date from 4500 B.C.E.

The problem the ancient Europeans faced, though, was that for food to dry effectively, three to five days of high temperatures, bright sunshine, and low humidity were needed, so drying was not always possible. Accordingly, the ancient Europeans turned to a related technique, smoking, particularly for meat and fish. Smoke contains a number of substances that bind to the surface of the cells of meat products, allowing them to resist the action of bacteria. While meat and fish would normally spoil after perhaps a week, smoked meat and fish could be consumed safely for three months or more.

Similarly, storing meat, fish, and vegetables in brine—that is, a concentrated solution of water and salt—provided similar protection against microbes. Salt was a highly valued commodity in ancient Europe, and the salt-producing region of Austria near the modern-day city of Salzburg (*salz* means "salt" in German) enjoyed a great deal of wealth by mining it. The ancient Gauls sold salted pork to the Romans. Salt was especially valuable to the Scandinavian cultures of northern Europe, whose diet included a great deal of fish that had to be stored during winter months, when bodies of water were frozen over or too stormy to allow fishing. A related technique was the use of spices to preserve food; modern scientists have shown that some spices effectively fight the formation of harmful bacteria. In ancient Europe, however, spices were extremely valuable commodities, available only from Arab traders. The average person probably would not have had access to spices, although the elite would have.

The ancient Europeans, again in common with the rest of the world, needed reliable sources of wholesome beverages that would not become stale and brackish in storage. Fermented beverages, such as beer and wine, provided them with drinkable liquids throughout the year. Of course, the Europeans by no means invented fermented beverages, but they did introduce the wooden barrel as a way of storing and transporting wine and beer.

The ancient Europeans devoted considerable resources to the storing of food. In common with other cultures of the world, they used caves where they could. Caves have the advantage of being at a constant cool temperature, with reliable humidity levels. Caves were the earliest form of root cellars and were particularly useful for the storing of root vegetables as well as fruits.

Where caves were not available, the Europeans constructed granaries and other facilities for the storage of food, particularly for grain. Throughout the Celtic lands of western Europe and the British Isles, for example, archaeologists have uncovered a large number of hill forts and, in Scotland, brochs (circular stone fortifications) that date from the Iron Age. These hill forts were settlements that housed up to several hundred people, though sometimes they were occupied seasonally or provided a place of refuge for people and their livestock in times of war. These hill forts were administrative centers for the surrounding region, and one of the major functions they served was that of food storage and preservation.

In England, for example, hill forts such as Danebury have been found with massive grain-storage capacity. Many of these hill forts were built on chalk subsoil, and in their interiors were pits used for food storage, as underground grain silos. Normally, the moisture of an underground pit would cause any grain stored in them to rot. However, the Europeans may have found a solution to the problem. The grain was poured into the pit, and then the pit was covered with an airtight clay seal. The seal was then covered with dirt to keep the seal from drying and cracking. The grain in contact with the moist earth of the pit germinated, consuming all the oxygen in the pit and releasing carbon dioxide. Because the seal was airtight, no further oxygen could enter. The remainder of the grain, then, was preserved in a state of "suspended animation." In this way it could have been preserved for months, as long as the seal remained intact.

GREECE

by Lyn Green

From the Minoans and Mycenaeans (2600–1100 B.C.E.) of the Bronze Age to the Hellenistic Greek world more than a thousand years later there were many similarities in food storage and preservation. No matter what the time period, the storage needs of the people did not change. For the short term, food had to be stored before eating or before it was redistributed through rations. An example of medium-term storage was putting aside an amount of food to last through the gaps between growing seasons or before it was exported or otherwise used in trade. Farmers also had to put aside enough seed each year to plant the next season's crop, and prudent householders and city rulers put aside food in case of famine or war. These were examples of long-term storage in large volumes. Although both seed for planting and food put aside against famine were both problems in long-term and large-volume storage, there was one significant difference. When it was time for crop planting, the storage areas for seeds would be emptied until the end of season. There was no need to worry about contamination or spoilage of food that was now open to air. This may have affected the choice of container or structure for storage.

Tablets from the palaces of Crete and Greece in the Bronze Age show that palatial structures served as warehouses for goods and food items from the surrounding countryside. Olives, olive oil, grain, honey, fruit, and meat all were stored there. Grains such as wheat and barley were sometimes kept in palace courtyards in huge pottery vessels called *pithoi*. There were also other means of storing grain. The earliest forms of storage were probably pits lined with clay or stone. They would have been kept tightly sealed to keep out air and vermin, such as rats and mice. There is much disagreement among scholars about the purpose of some of the large pits excavated at places like Knossos and whether they would have been an efficient way to store grain, because it might have been difficult to keep out pests and mold-causing moisture. It is generally agreed, however, that these large pits would have been most suitable for long-term storage. Clay bins were also used for keeping grain. Sometimes, however,

Amphora, a ceramic vessel used for storing and carrying oil and wine and other commodities, from Athens (Alison Frantz Photographic Collection, American School of Classical Studies at Athens)

the grain was stored loose in a granary or in one room of a larger storage building.

Some of the earliest buildings solely dedicated to storage of grain were round, with dome-shaped roofs. These would have looked very similar to the images of granaries from Egyptian tombs from the same time period. Granaries from the later Geometric Period in Greece have an almost identical shape. Grain was poured into the granary through a window near the top of the dome and removed at the base through another gap. Thus, the older grain at the bottom of the pile would always be used first.

During the fourth and fifth centuries B.C.E. people actually made less use of large-scale and long-term storage fa-

cilities. During the Bronze Age goods had been taken to the palaces for redistribution, but in the Classical Period (480–323 B.C.E.) the system of storage and distribution was based on individuals and their farmsteads. However, even though the local farmers could not grow enough grain to feed the nearby cities, archaeologists have not been able to identify the storage places of the imported grain in urban centers or their ports. This has led some scholars to suggest that the grain was stored in the countryside.

At Knossos a building called the Unexplored Mansion contained a number of storage jars of untouched food, including legumes, figs, and several kinds of grain. Some of the grain in these jars was hulled, but a similar find of stored Bronze Age grain in Macedonia had spikelets of wheat. Centuries later, ancient authors would recommend storing grain without threshing it (removing the chaff or straw) so that if weevils did get in, they would be confined to the outer layers of the grain. In the eighth century B.C.E. the Greek writer Hesiod (fl. ca. 800 B.C.E.) stated that threshed grain should be kept in storage jars within the house.

The available methods of storing food meant that food had to be preserved by other means before being put into storage. Unfortunately, most of the ancient descriptions of food processing come from the Roman Period, and the archaeological evidence is often not of much help. The evidence seems to point to the fact that meat, which was expensive and therefore rarely eaten, was consumed right away. Fish, on the other hand, was eaten in larger quantities, both fresh and preserved. Based on the information available, it seems likely that the Greeks usually salted or smoked both meat and fish. There are, in fact, many terms for preserved fish, but all seem to describe the species of fish and the shape of the preserved pieces rather than the process. Milk from goats, sheep, or cows was preserved for short-term use by being made into butter and for longer periods by being made into cheese. Milk solids could be formed into small bricks, dried in the sun, and later rehydrated for use in cooking.

Lentils, peas, and beans of all kinds were dried for storage and were easily reconstituted with water in stews or ground up into flour. Other vegetables could have been dried or pickled in brine or vinegar. Olives and cucumbers were certainly pickled in these ways. Greens such as lettuce and cresses were difficult to keep for long periods and probably were eaten only fresh. However, it is known that the leaves of fig trees were pickled and were used by almost every cook. Fruits that had an outer rind (such as pomegranates) or were hard (like quinces) could be kept fresh by careful storage. If the fruits were placed in containers in such a way that they did not touch the sides of the container or especially each other, they would stay fresh for a longer time. Juicier, softer fruits such as figs, plums, cherries, and grapes could be dried or preserved in honey. Grapes, of course, were also preserved by being made into wine. Most fruits, in fact, could be pressed for their juice and the juice allowed to ferment and become cider or wine or to sour and become vinegar. Not only did this process preserve the fruit itself, but the alcohol in the fermented drinks (or the acid in the vinegar) could be used to preserve other foods.

ROME
by Lyn Green

Throughout the history of Rome, as capital of both a republic and an empire, the city faced the daunting task of keeping its growing population fed and supplied. However, unlike some other urban centers of the ancient world, the local countryside around Rome was inadequate to feed its massive population. To complicate matters further, as Rome grew in size and wealth, so did the demand for luxuries of all kinds. The growth of the Roman Empire and the spread of the Roman bureaucracy also increased demand for the same sorts of products throughout the vast territories as officials tried to maintain the lifestyle they had enjoyed in Italy. This demand necessitated a complex web of shipping routes and the facilities and techniques necessary to store goods of all kinds.

Although Roman writers liked to recall the good old days when their ancestors lived on *pulmentarium* (stew or porridge made of grains or beans), bread was the most important item in the Roman diet. Although spelt, barley, or rye could be used to make bread, wheat made the best loaves. Unfortunately, wheat was not a crop that grew well in Italy. North Africa and especially Egypt were the major exporters of wheat throughout the ancient Mediterranean, and trade routes from the ports of the African coast to Ostia were vital to the survival of Rome. However, as the wheat would first be stored, then shipped to Rome by boat, and then stored at Rome, some method of processing grain for storage was essential.

In order to avoid spoilage, grain must be kept in a cool, dry, and dark place. These places must also be designed to keep out such vermin as mice or rats, which would eat or contaminate the food. In the drier areas of the Mediterranean, such as Spain, the grain could be stored in underground pits that were lined with straw and tightly sealed. The Roman author Varro (116–27 B.C.E.) also mentions that the farmers of Thrace stored their grain in caves. In northern Spain and southern Gaul, the grain was stored in huge terra-cotta jars called *pithoi* or in silos. Varro also suggests using above-ground granaries that were ventilated by windows and raised up on wooden supports to allow air circulation. Another ancient description of these granaries mentions that they had brick walls 3 feet thick and were accessed from above. The author of that description also states that *amurca*, the dregs of pressed olives, should be incorporated into all the tiles and plaster used to seal the granaries in order to discourage vermin.

Wherever Roman legions went, they built large granaries, sometimes intended to hold enough food to last through a yearlong siege. These were originally built of timber, but after Trajan's (r. 98–117 C.E.) time stone granaries became more common. In either case, the grain was probably stored in sacks or baskets rather than piled loosely in chambers.

The containers would have made the job of measuring out rations much easier and would have served as barrier to vermin. The biggest civil granaries were undoubtedly those at Ostia, where the grain from Africa was delivered. Two types of granaries have been excavated at Ostia: a building consisting of long, narrow rooms facing a courtyard and two rows of rooms opening off a central corridor. Some granaries show evidence of stairs leading to an upper floor. Archaeologists are confident that grain was stored on the lower floors, but grain was of course only one of the items that could be stored in these buildings.

A number of methods of preserving food were known to the ancient Romans, and the choice of which one to use depended on the local climate and the type of food being stored. Drying, salting, smoking, and pickling were the most common ways of preserving food. Some fruits, like grapes, figs and dates, naturally lent themselves to drying without loss of flavor. They could also be packed in honey or in a mixture or honey and boiled wine. Beans, peas, lentils, and pulses were also dried, while cucumbers and olives were pickled in brine. Fish and meat were often salted by being immersed in brine, although in the hot, dry areas of the empire they could also have been wind-dehydrated. Pickling food could be done using beer vinegar, fig vinegar, wine vinegar, wine, and sour milk. The increased acidity of the food discourages the growth of bacteria, as does alcohol. As the Romans did not use distilled alcohol, wine or even beer could be used to preserve foods.

Pork was the most popular meat for upper-class Romans, but it did not keep well and care had to be taken to preserve it soon after slaughtering. To salt the meat, ancient authors recommend rubbing it with coarse salt each day for 12 days. For the first three days, between rubbings, it was kept pressed under weights to squeeze out excess moisture. Sometimes this step could be followed by further drying or smoking. Pork could also be salted in jars. The deboned pieces of meat were jammed into the jars and layered with salt until the container was crammed full. Then it was sealed tightly. The same methods were used to prepare salt fish. In the 1990s some archaeologists experimented with using spices to preserve food. They discovered that cinnamon, cumin, onion, and especially garlic slowed or even stopped the growth of microorganisms that would cause food to spoil. Black pepper, on the other hand, was not very effective in stopping bacterial growth.

Although there were ice houses in the ancient world, they were not always available. Therefore, the Romans developed other methods of keeping the color, scent, and shape of preserved foods: They prevented any air from reaching the food and starting the process of decay. There are a number of different techniques described by the ancient writer Columella (first century C.E.). For example, he states that if grapes are picked with their stems on, the ends of the stems should be sealed with pitch to keep out the air. This method is also recommended by other ancient authors for apples, quinces, cherries, plums, and pears. Quinces and pomegranates could be completely coated in a thick layer of potter's clay and left to dry. A quick wash would remove the clay from the fruits later. The Romans also understood the importance of keeping the fruits from touching one another, and fruits might also be stored in containers divided with wood into little compartments and filled with sawdust. However, all of these methods were very labor intensive and were probably most often used on the great estates that had hundreds of slave workers.

THE AMERICAS

BY AMY HACKNEY BLACKWELL

Ancient American peoples needed to store several things: wild food items that they had gathered, seeds for the next planting season, and water for daily use and in case of drought. They also needed to preserve food, both plant foods and meats, so that they would have a steady food supply throughout the year.

Drying was the most common method of food preservation throughout the Americas. People dried such grains as corn and other vegetables either by spreading them out in the sun or by placing them in a fire. How long grains would remain edible depended on local humidity; corn would last three years in the dry climate of the North American Southwest, but it lasted only one year in the humidity of the Yucatán peninsula. People preserved meat and fish by drying them as well. Women would cut meat into strips and lay it across open racks to dry in the sun. Meat and fish could be smoked by placing them in the smoke of a slow fire for several days. Dried and smoked meats would keep for many months, depending on humidity and temperature. Native Americans sometimes embellished their basic dried meats with different ingredients. For example, sometimes they would dip the meat in ground corn before drying it and then roll up the dried strips for ease of transport during travel. Pemmican was made by cutting fresh meat into chunks, mixing it with dried berries and rendered fat, and spreading it out to dry into bars.

Native Americans who lived in cold climates took advantage of natural freezing temperatures to preserve meat. They would kill animals early in the winter, cut them into pieces of meat, and allow the meat to freeze. They could then defrost it in a fire when they were ready to eat it. The people who lived in the Arctic commonly employed this technique with seal meat. People who lived in the Andes used freeze-drying to preserve some of their food, particularly potatoes. They would lay out their potatoes on the mountainside, where the potatoes would freeze; the water would then gradually sublimate out of them, resulting in very lightweight potatoes that lasted a long time. Although people ate dried foods as they were, they might also reconstitute them by soaking or cooking them in water.

Throughout the Americas people stored food in woven baskets. People throughout the two continents began making baskets about 6000 B.C.E. Both sexes wove baskets. People would sometimes weave baskets very quickly on the spot if they suddenly found a trove of food and wanted to carry it home. Basket styles and materials varied by region. People in the north made baskets of birch bark, ash, or sweetgrass. Native Americans in California used yucca, willow, or sumac. On the northwest coast weavers used spruce root, cedar bark, and swamp grass. People in the southeastern regions used pine needles. Basketry became more highly developed when people adopted the sedentary agricultural lifestyle, around 1 C.E. in North America and perhaps around 4000 B.C.E. in Central America.

Native Americans used baskets for a variety of purposes. They attached shoulder straps to conical baskets to make carrying baskets. Some baskets had an open weave; these baskets were lighter, good for carrying loads of firewood or large food items. Open-weave baskets were useful for catching and carrying fish or clams because they allowed the water to drain out of the basket. More tightly woven baskets could carry small items, such as seeds. When people harvested crops, they sometimes carried small baskets on their hips to hold the grain they picked, periodically emptying these small baskets into larger baskets on their backs. Different shapes of baskets were used for different food items. Baskets intended to hold fresh berries, for example, were shaped like cones to prevent the weight of the topmost berries from crushing the ones on the bottom. Baskets could be waterproofed with such substances as pine resin to make them suitable for carrying or storing water.

Native Americans throughout North America stored food in clay pots. Archaeologists have found pots throughout the continent, dating to the time when humans first lived in the area; numerous ancient pots date to between 25,000 and 8000 B.C.E. Plain mud can be formed into vessels that will dry hard, but unless they are fired, they will dissolve in water and crumble easily when dry. Baking clay in a hot fire makes it hard and more water resistant, though without some sort of glaze to seal the surface even fired clay will leak water. Archaeologists have found many unfired pots used by ancient Americans; these could have been used to store dry items, such as nuts and seeds.

Historians believe that the practice of firing clay pots was an outgrowth of basketry and food drying. One technique Native Americans developed to dry such food as corn was to place the grain in a basket lined with clay and then put it in or over a fire. The basket would burn, leaving behind a baked clay shell. As evidence for this practice, historians cite the many ancient pots with exterior textures that look as if they were formed in baskets.

Although Native Americans had used pots to store food for millennia before the advent of farming, it was when they settled down in agricultural settlements that potters gained real expertise with their art and different nations developed different designs for their vessels based on their storage needs. Women (who made most pottery) made water jars with bases designed to rest comfortably on the top of a human head in order to carry water from streams to homes. They built large pots with tight-fitting lids that could hold grain and protect it from insects, rodents, and moisture. They constructed large water pots with glazed interiors that would not leak. They also invented pots to store seeds for planting, using different designs to identify different types of seeds.

The Maya of the southern Yucatán peninsula in Mexico stored water in reservoirs in the ground. They dug holes in the ground and then plastered the bottoms to prevent water from running out the porous limestone bottoms. These reservoirs could hold enough water to last about 18 months with no rain.

See also AGRICULTURE; ARCHITECTURE; BORDERS AND FRONTIERS; BUILDING TECHNIQUES AND MATERIALS; CERAMICS AND POTTERY; CLIMATE AND GEOGRAPHY; CRAFTS; DEATH AND BURIAL PRACTICES; ECONOMY; FAMILY; FOOD AND DIET; GENDER STRUCTURES AND ROLES; HEALTH AND DISEASE; HUNTING, FISHING, AND GATHERING; INVENTIONS; MINING, QUARRYING, AND SALT MAKING; NOMADIC AND PASTORAL SOCIETIES; RELIGION AND COSMOLOGY; SETTLEMENT PATTERNS; TOWNS AND VILLAGES; TRADE AND EXCHANGE.

FURTHER READING

Daphne L. Derven, "Preserving." In *Encyclopedia of Food and Culture*, ed. Solomon H. Katz (New York: Scribner, 2003).

Salima Ikram, *Choice Cuts: Meat Production in Ancient Egypt* (Louvain, Belgium: Departement Oosterse Studies, 1995).

Hilary Wilson, *Egyptian Food and Drink* (Princes Risborough, U.K.: Shire Publications, 1995).

▶ textiles and needlework

INTRODUCTION

Archaeologists assume that the earliest clothing worn by humans were animal skins. With textiles, people were able to make clothing from hair such as wool and plants such as flax, the source of linen. Silk, which is made from cocoons of the silk worm, was an almost miraculous discovery made by people near the Yellow River in China in about 1900 B.C.E. One disadvantage all textiles had was that they each needed to be produced in the appropriate climate. Sheep, the source of most wool, needed open grasslands for their herds. Cotton required long hot seasons. Thus, the most common textiles of early times were those that traveled well—that is, ones that prospered in a wider variety of climates than most. This meant that hemp, in particular, was the common source of fabric used by the poor, because it was durable and would grow even in nutrient-poor soils.

Textiles did not pop up everywhere at once. Indeed, a newly appointed Chinese governor to far northern China in the 100s C.E. was dismayed to find that the people of the region wore few textiles and tried to keep warm by wearing grasses. Flax, which produced one of the most durable and comfortable of textiles, spread only slowly across the Old World, probably still not having reached Japan by the 300s C.E.

For ancient people in cold climates or places with cold winters, textiles were valued for their ability to hold in warmth. Thus, among the nomadic peoples of Asia, wool was especially valued. It might be itchier than cotton or linen, but where warmth mattered most, wool was preferred.

In warm climates, and even some with harsh winters but warm summers, people often did without textiles, because staying warm was not their highest priority for survival. In Sumer people often wore only wool skirts; in southeastern Asia and Japan, many people wore only loincloths, typically made of animal skin. In India the notion of wearing clothing for modesty did not arrive until the Muslim invasion. Still, in these places where textiles were not a necessity, they were valued for their decorative possibilities. Someone in India who might wear little in everyday life would nonetheless wish to wear colorful fabrics when attending a wedding or other important social event.

The earliest colors for textiles were paint and dyes. Painted textiles appeared in dry areas, such as the lands northwest of China. More common than painted textiles were dyed textiles, probably because dyes were preferred over paint. Whether dyeing textiles was an idea that originated in one place and then spread or was an idea that began in many different places is not clear, although the use of dyes by ancient Americans suggests that dyeing was an idea with different origins in different places.

The use of dyes says much about human beings and their needs. Although ancient textiles are hard to find, those that are extant are rarely plain brown or white. Usually the textiles are colored. Whether worn by the rich or the poor, they almost always have decoration, indicating that people wanted beauty in their lives even with simple textiles. Even embroidery, often associated with richly decorated robes for special occasions, would be used to brighten hems or add attractive images to textiles for everyday use.

AFRICA

BY SUSAN COOKSEY

Textiles produced on the continent of Africa in the period between 10,000 B.C.E. and 400 C.E. were made from both plant and animal fibers, including bark, reed, grass, cotton, and wool. Among textiles' many purposes were as clothing, sheets, blankets, bags, carpets, tents, and burial shrouds. Moreover, textiles were important items for trade, adornment, and markers of social, political, and economic status. Textile production in Africa and elsewhere indicates a sedentary society with skills in agriculture and husbandry; technologies used for dyeing, spinning, and various types of construction, such as weaving; and artistic ability to produce cloth that is both functional and aesthetically pleasing. Simply woven cloth probably served for everyday use, while more elaborately woven and patterned cloth was reserved for leaders and elite members of society.

In North Africa textile production was greatly affected by the influx of technologies and materials developed and distributed throughout the Mediterranean. The Phoenicians were some of the greatest purveyors of textiles, materials for textile productions, and textile technologies. After settling along the Tunisian coast, the Phoenicians introduced the eastern vertical loom to the urban Berbers, the indigenous people, around the 12th century B.C.E. In Carthage and other Phoenician towns local craftsmen wove linen and woolen rugs. In the rural areas of Tunisia textiles made of rush, reed, and alfa were produced and used for constructing tentlike dwellings for local inhabitants. Important people in rural societies may have owned woven wool textiles.

The Phoenicians are known to have traded in dyed wool by 1700 B.C.E. A purple dye derived from extracts from the murex, a shellfish, became increasingly popular in the Mediterranean world during the first millennium B.C.E. As the Phoenicians expanded trade in murex dye and murex-dyed textiles, they sought the shellfish from as far away as Africa's Atlantic coast. Evidence of textiles with murex-dyed fabric has been found in excavations of ancient Meroitic sites in Sudan, dating from 332 to 30 B.C.E. The Romans razed Carthage in 146 B.C.E. and, in the course of their occupation, taught the urban Berbers how to use a Latin loom to produce various textiles.

Cotton threads found in Dhuweila, in present-day Jordan, dated to 4450–3000 B.C.E. may have been imported across the Red Sea from India or from the area that is now the states of Sudan and Ethiopia, where a different variety of cotton was known at the time. Evidence of cotton cultivation and cotton fabrics dates back to the early fifth century B.C.E. in Meroë, located in the Nile Valley in the present-day state of Sudan.

Many Nile Valley textiles have been found in tombs. One collection from the areas of Ballana and Qustul includes burial cloths from three Nubian eras, beginning in 332 B.C.E. Textiles found in the tombs were made of various fibers, in-

cluding wool from sheep, camels, and perhaps goats as well as silk, linen, and cotton. The silk samples were imported and from a later era. A few burial cloths were made of horsehair or coarse grass or reed. However, most of the textiles were made of animal fibers. Both animal fibers and cotton were available in the area much earlier than the fourth century B.C.E. It is estimated that sheep were in the Nile Valley for thousands of years before that and were among the first domesticated animals in the region. The sheep brought to Nubia were probably a breed domesticated in Egypt. Goats and camels were imported to Egypt later and eventually brought to Nubia.

Cotton was introduced into Nubia later than animal fibers, though a type of cotton may have grown locally as early as 3100 B.C.E. The earliest samples of cotton cloth date from the fourth century B.C.E., but it is possible that cotton cloth was produced at an earlier time in Nubia. Early accounts of cotton—such as that of the Roman historian Pliny the Elder (ca. 23–79 C.E.), who referred to the "wool-bearing

Ugandan woman wearing a bark cloth dress; bark cloth began to be produced in Africa before 4000 B.C.E. (© Board of Regents of the University of Wisconsin System)

trees" of Upper Egypt and Ethiopia, and that of the ruler Ezana of Axum, who spoke of destroying crops of corn and cotton in the Nile Valley in 350 C.E.—prove the existence of cotton plants at this time. Linen textiles found in the tombs may have come from Egypt, where the flax plant was cultivated; linen weaving had been known much earlier; and, by the fourth century C.E., the trade in linen cloth was thriving. Egyptian texts of the New Kingdom (1550–1070 B.C.E.) refer to flax fields in Nubia, suggesting that at least flax may have been produced in Nubia, and perhaps linen was made there as well.

Many of the cloths used as burial shrouds were adapted for this use but were originally made for other purposes, such as clothing or sheets. Textile bags and carpets were also found in the tombs. Among them the plain-weave fabrics were locally made, whereas others were imported. It is also clear that in the earlier periods, plant fibers were used before animal fibers became prevalent. Later, in the Common Era, the use of plant fibers returned. Many of the textiles were decorated or dyed. Dyeing was done before the fibers were woven. Locally made textiles were dyed with local dyestuffs, yielding colors of brown, yellow, blue, and red. Yellow and blue were combined to produce green. The imported textiles, including carpets, were more elaborately colored with purple, yellow, and orange dyes.

Fibers were spun into yarn using various spindles and techniques. Three types of spindle were used for cotton and one for wool. Most yarn was spun so that the fibers twisted together in an S configuration. The art of weaving was well developed by the Meroitic period. Looms had been in use in Egypt since at least the Middle Kingdom (2040–1640 B.C.E). The earliest representations of looms in Egyptian art show women using horizontal types. The more complex vertical looms used by men were introduced later. Textiles found in Nubia show evidence of both simple and complex looms. Several types of techniques of weaving were used, including plain weave, twill, and pile weave. In some cases, textiles were woven into specific shapes of garments on the loom. Finely woven mats of reed and grass may have been made on a loom as well. The Nubian textiles were decorated with geometric motifs, foliate motifs (patterns representing trees or grain, for example), and stripes rendered in various colors. One surviving cloth has purple murex-dyed stripes and was obviously imported. Some textiles had tasseled edges. Decorative elements were created using various weaving techniques or needlework. Stitching was used to decorate the cloth and to bind cloth strips on the selvedges.

Bark cloth production began before 4000 B.C.E. and is still produced in Africa in the Ituri rain forest. Bark cloth is typically made of the inner bark of mulberry or ficus, which has been stripped and retted. The glutinous sludge resulting from the retting is beaten into large, thin sheets that could be colored by pigments such as ocherous earths and tannins. The finished sheets could then be fashioned into garments, coverings, or other items.

EGYPT

BY ERIN FAIRBURN

Egypt is unique among ancient cultures in that the desert location of funerary sites has preserved many objects of perishable nature that are infrequently, if ever, to be found at other ancient sites. Textiles are especially important among these rare artifacts. They shed light on how ancient peoples adapted to and utilized their environs, and their analysis can provide interesting insights into ancient technology. Egyptian textiles were used for garments, bedding, animal equipment, and lamp wicks, among other things, and were often recycled as mummy wrappings.

Almost all ancient Egyptian textiles were made of flax (*Linum usitatissimum*). Depending on when the flax was cut, the resulting threads and cloth would be a light or a golden brown color; however, the linen could be whitened by using a substance, such as natron, or by sun bleaching, as was often done to "royal" linen. The flax fibers were obtained through a process of beating and soaking the stalks until the soft interior was separated out. The fibers were then combed and dried.

Once the fibers had been thus prepared, they were ready to be spun. The spinning process began by roving, or rolling, the fibers on the thigh until they were loosely twisted. This rove would be rolled around a reel and placed in ceramic vessel or basket with a hole on the top. The fibers would be drawn from these vessels during the spinning process. They were spun onto a spindle of wood with a whorl (pulley) on top made of wood, stone, or ceramic.

Three types of spinning were used in ancient Egypt. The first technique produced thread by feeding the fibers onto the spindle with the fingers and rolling the spindle on the thigh to twist them. The second required a forked stick or ring through which to draw the thread while twisting the spindle between both hands. The third technique, the suspended spindle method, involved grasping the fibers with one hand while letting the rotating spindle swing free, thereby twisting the fibers. Counterclockwise spinning was the most common type in ancient Egypt; that is, the fibers were S-spun.

At this point, the spun fibers could be dyed. Dying does not appear to have been prevalent in ancient Egypt, but textile producers clearly knew how to produce a range of colors. Egyptian textiles contained threads dyed red, blue, yellow, brown, green, and purple. These colors were all created with vegetal (plant-based) colorants; brown, green, and purple were produced by overdying. While weavers did on occasion dye an entire piece of completed weaving, it was more common for them to embellish an undyed linen garment with colored threads.

Once the threads were prepared, they could be woven. Egyptians used two kinds of looms for textile weaving: a horizontal loom that was used throughout the Dynastic Period and a vertical loom that was used beginning in the New Kingdom (ca. 1550–ca. 1070 B.C.E.). Horizontal looms lay parallel to the ground with the beams pegged into place. Vertical looms

Tapestry made of multicolored wool on linen, from Egypt, fourth century C.E., *showing Artemis and Actaeon* (© The Trustees of the British Museum)

were perpendicular to the ground, with the warp strung onto beams attached to a frame.

Longitudinal threads, or warp threads, were attached directly to the loom. Every other thread was separated, forming two separate groups. Another thread, the weft, was strung between the two groups, or shed. Lifting a rod called the heddle switched the group to the fore, creating a counter-shed. Running the weft thread successively between the shed and counter-shed created an interlocking weave around the warp.

Several different weaving techniques were used to create textiles in ancient Egypt. The most common weave, and the simplest, was the tabby weave, where a single weft thread passes over and under individual warp threads. A variation on this is the basket weave, where the warp and weft threads are paired. Both of these methods were fairly easy to achieve on a horizontal loom. Warp- and weft-faced weaves, which

produced a two-to-one pattern that nearly hid the single threads, were also used in Egypt. Two tapestry weaves are also known, one that used the weft for the pattern and another that used the warp.

Weavers accommodated for broken or short threads by interweaving threads with either a long or a short splice. Short splices twisted together the ends of two threads and then twisted this back onto the main thread. Long splices were simply several inches of the two threads twisted together. Many preserved textiles have splices in them; finer linens seem to have mainly short splices, and coarser textiles often exhibit long splices.

A number of decorative and functional features were woven into Egyptian textiles. The most common was a fringe on the left selvedge (edge) of a textile. This was accomplished by extending the weft thread several inches beyond the last warp and seems to have been performed only on horizontal loom–made textiles. It may have served to prevent the weft from gathering in the warp, reducing the overall width of the textile. Decorative fringes were often added to the edges of a textile as well. These were usually created by letting the ends of the warp threads hang beyond the edge of the weft. These ends were loose or tied off. Occasionally, additional thread was woven into the edges and selvedges to increase the amount of fringe on the piece. Weft looping was also occasionally practiced. This process of letting the weft extend above the fabric surface at intervals created a sort of pile that probably increased the warmth of the resulting garment.

Weaving colors into textiles was a decorative technique commonly practiced. This usually extended only to weaving stripes into the edges of the textile. These stripes were usually in some combination of red, blue, and buff. Occasionally, what seem to be maker's marks were also woven into the textile at some point. Evidence for embroidery is slight in Dynastic Egypt, and most of what has been called embroidery by researchers was actually woven into the cloth. Tapestry weaving appears in the Eighteenth Dynasty (ca. 1550–ca. 1307 B.C.E.), beginning with pieces found in the tomb of Thutmose IV (r. 1401–1391 B.C.E.). In this technique the weaver used different color wefts in just the part of the design that demanded the particular color. These textiles were packed down to reduce the visibility of the warp.

Sewing was used to a minimal extent in Egypt, mostly for crafting garments. Seams and hems were usually rolled and stitched into place. However, textiles of all types were frequently mended, indicating their worth. Mending is found on common textiles as well as on the finer pieces found in royal contexts. The mending was accomplished by working new warp threads into the damaged area and then stitching across them. Patches were uncommon. As mentioned, embroidery was rarely used, and it was most commonly used to outline woven-in decoration.

THE MIDDLE EAST

BY AMY HACKNEY BLACKWELL

Few examples of ancient Near Eastern textiles exist. Because cloth decays quickly, most do not remain in the archaeological record. Likewise, few positively identified weaving and spinning implements survive, but archaeologists have found numerous drawings and paintings depicting spindles and looms and women working with them. Some ancient Mesopotamian sculptures convey the texture of the cloth worn by the subjects, but it is impossible to reconstruct colors or patterns. To guess what ancient cloth must have looked like, historians can only read contemporary descriptions of textiles and view examples of textiles from slightly later periods. Weaving and spinning techniques have not changed greatly over the centuries, so anthropologists can gain insight into ancient textile manufacturer by studying the weaving techniques of less developed societies.

Near Eastern people began making textiles as early as 25,000 B.C.E., braiding, twisting, spinning, and weaving strips of bark and plant fibers to make primitive cloth. When people domesticated sheep and goats around 8000 B.C.E., they began making cloth out of wool and goat hair. Wool was the most common fiber in the region. People started growing flax for linen about 8,000 years ago; linen was a luxury cloth used for expensive garments. In Mesopotamia textile manufacturing became a major business. Most cloth production was done in individual homes as a cottage industry rather than in large factories, but many households participated in the trade. Weaving factories at Ur and Lagash around 2100 B.C.E. employed thousands of women and children, producing cloth in five grades of quality. Most of the cloth was given out as rations to dependents of the great temple households, and only a small amount was ever traded abroad. In ancient Anatolia groups of women ran cloth-making businesses. After 1500 B.C.E. commercial weaving operations throughout the region employed men, but women continued to do most of the spinning and weaving for their homes and families.

The Assyrians brought cotton plants to the Near East from Egypt around 700 B.C.E., although Near Eastern people apparently were importing cotton cloth from other lands as early as 1000 B.C.E., as cotton fragments from Bahrain, in the Persian Gulf (ancient Dilmun), attest. Silk appeared in Mesopotamia and the Near East during Roman times, brought from China through Persia via the Silk Road.

Making fibers into cloth was a labor-intensive process. After the fiber was collected from the field or the animals, it had to be cleaned and untangled by combs. The fibers were then spun into thread on spindles—wooden spikes weighted on the bottom and used to twist and wind the fibers. Women throughout the Middle East used a kind of spindle called a drop spindle.

Archaeologists can tell where some textiles were made based on spinning patterns. Cotton fibers naturally wind to the right, and flax fibers naturally wind to the left. Spinners usually wound their threads according to the fiber's natural pattern. Wool, on the other hand, does not naturally twist in either direction, so it can be spun either to the left or to the right. In an area in which linen was common, spinners often spun wool thread to the left, using the same techniques on wool as they used on linen. In an area where cotton was common, wool thread was often spun to the right. Archaeologists who find wool thread spun in a direction opposite that most common in the area can assume the thread was made elsewhere. Archaeologists can also use microscopes to examine wool fibers to determine the type of sheep the wool came from and the textile's likely place of origin.

After spinning, thread was sometimes dyed. Archaeologists have found evidence that Middle Eastern people were dyeing cloth by 3000 B.C.E. and perhaps earlier. Dyers used roots, tree bark, leaves, nuts, lichens, and berries to achieve various colors. The indigo plant was used to dye cloth blue. The most expensive dye in the region was a purple color made from the

Wool textile fragment from Persepolis, Persia (modern-day Iran) (Courtesy of the Oriental Institute of the University of Chicago)

murex shell, found off the coasts of Lebanon and Syria. This region became known as Phoenicia, or "purple land," and its towns grew rich selling murex dye to Greeks, Romans, and other wealthy individuals; the town of Tyre was especially known for this color, which was often called Tyrian purple. To create the dye, fishermen collected thousands of the snails, cracked their shells, and dug out the veins that contained a purple mucus. It took nearly 9,000 snails to create one ounce of Tyrian purple dye, which cost more than its weight in gold.

After dyeing, the next step was to weave the thread into cloth on a loom. Early Middle Eastern looms were vertical frames on which weavers would stretch parallel threads to form the warp of the cloth. The weavers would then weave other threads through the warp, creating the horizontal fibers called the weft. The first looms had no mechanism for separating individual warp threads to create a space for the weaver to place the weft, but very quickly people discovered that it was easier to weave cloth if they used a rod to lift half the fibers at a time. Weavers wrapped the weft threads around a wooden block called the shuttle, which they could pass from hand to hand through the warp, and they used another rod to push the weft firmly together after each pass. By varying thread colors, weavers could create elaborate patterns in their cloth.

Ancient people throughout the Middle East decorated their cloth with embroidery. Persia, Babylonia, Phoenicia, Syria, and Israel were especially known for their embroidery. Embroiderers adorned cloth with traditional motifs; Persian decorations were known for being particularly ornate.

Groups developed their own unique embroidery patterns, many of which had ritual significance such as warding off evil or bringing good luck to a bride.

Carpet weaving is believed to have originated as early as 7000 B.C.E. in central Asia, where nomads wove carpets to create warm, soft, easily portable floors for their tents. Carpet making spread from central Asia into Anatolia and Persia. Anatolians were among the first Near Eastern people to weave carpets. They invented a double-knotted style of carpet weaving between the fourth and first centuries B.C.E. Village women carded and dyed their own wool and invented patterns that told stories as well as being decorative. Each group had distinctive designs. Mothers taught daughters how to weave carpets so that the young women could include them in their dowries and then produce more as married women. Carpet weaving was also important in Persia. People living on the Iranian plateau were knotting wool carpets by 500 B.C.E., though the art may have begun much earlier. Persian carpets depicted mythical events, objects from nature, or geometric patterns.

ASIA AND THE PACIFIC

BY JUSTIN CORFIELD AND MICHAEL J. O'NEAL

A wide range of textiles was used throughout ancient Asia and the Pacific, from elaborate silk and brocade (fabric with raised patterns) to coarse hemp. Very little material from this period survives, but much of it that does survive is silk and other more expensive cloths found in tombs dating from the Han Dynasty (202 B.C.E.–220 C.E.) and also outside China. However, much can be surmised from drawings, carvings, and statues of the period as well as from the small fragments of other materials that have been found by archaeologists.

The material used in China and nearby places for clothes was associated with three traditional styles of dress: the *pien-fu*, the *ch'ang-p'ao*, and the *shen-i*. The *pien-fu* was a two-piece ceremonial costume with a tunic, and underneath a skirt or trousers. The *ch'ang-p'ao* was a garment made up from one piece that covered the body from head to toe, and the *shen-i* essentially was a blend of the other two styles, usually with a *pien-fu* sewed together.

In China the most prized material was silk, which seems to have been used from about 3000 B.C.E. It was produced not only for use within China but also for export to other places, giving rise to the "Silk Road," as the major land trade route from China to Europe became known in ancient times. Silk served as a medium of exchange for the Chinese, and it appears that a large silk industry emerged in Persia and Syria, where dyeing and weaving took place. Some silk fabrics from the Han Dynasty have been found in tombs in Palmyra, Syria, dating from 83 to 273 C.E., where they were known as "damasks in Han weave." Similar material has been found in parts of central Asia, the Crimea, and other places along the Silk Road, indicating a flourishing trade. Besides being traded, silk was also given as presents to tribal chiefs loyal to China and was often taken by traders to cover their expenses. Indeed, in the later Han Dynasty it is known that some people paid their fines in silk.

The production of silk was heavily protected in China, and the export of silkworms was an offense punishable by death. Therefore, it was not until the sixth century C.E. that some silkworms were smuggled to Byzantium. This restriction on silk production kept the price of silk high, and as a result, many garments, even for wealthy people in China, were made with silk and also linings in other material, such as nettle cloth.

Poorer people in China and the areas around China used not only nettle cloth but also hemp and wool; many Chinese did not like wearing woolen garments although they were favored by many of the local tribal peoples. For patterns, traditionally cloth was dyed a particular color, such as blue, red, green or yellow, but by the Zhou Dynasty (ca. 1045–256 B.C.E.), some checked patterns began to be favored. All the "terra-cotta figures" from the tomb of Qin Shi Huang (r. 221–210 B.C.E.) were originally painted, with many fragments of different colored paints being found. By the Han Dynasty wealthier Chinese preferred geometric shapes, such as checks or diamonds, with the pattern repeated continuously; poorer people tended to have their garments made from cloth of a single color. Cotton does not appear to have been used in China until the 10th and 11th centuries C.E.

In addition to their use for clothes, many textiles were also used for drapes and awnings as well as for tents. Elaborate embroideries existed in the houses of the wealthy, with many other buildings having areas "curtained off," or separated using "silk screens," although these screens were not always made of silk.

Outside China and the surrounding areas very little cloth has survived. In Southeast Asia in the Funan Empire, located in southern Cambodia and the Mekong Delta, there are a few descriptions related to clothing. A Chinese embassy from 245 C.E. recorded that the people wore nothing but eventually were persuaded to wear clothing for reasons of modesty, beginning with small loincloths. However, by the 480s and 490s C.E. many people were wearing sarongs (long pieces of cloth wrapped around the body) made from brocade, showing an important Chinese influence. It is probable that this pattern was followed in other parts of Southeast Asia.

In central Asia many of the clothes included wool from sheep and goats, with more expensive materials imported from China. The major indigenous textile industries in the region were involved in the manufacture of tents and of carpets. The former involved the use of heavy material, such as wool. The latter varied between the hard-wearing carpets used by everybody, especially the nomadic peoples, and those for decorating houses, especially for the export trade. Prior to the arrival of Islam in central Asia, many carpets showed scenes of people, hunting, and festivities, although others had geometric patterns, which became very common after the sixth century C.E. Throughout the region needles were made

from bone or horn, and few have survived, though several have been found in China, dating back to 2000 B.C.E., with some estimated to be much older.

Like China, ancient India also had a rich tradition of weaving and textile production. Archaeological excavations from the Indus Valley civilizations (ca. 3000–ca. 1600 B.C.E.) have found spindles and needles that suggest that cotton fabric was woven in homes. Mention is made in numerous ancient Indian texts, such as the Rig-Veda and the epics Ramayana and Mahabharata, of weaving, textiles, and fabrics, and ancient sculpture and murals also attest to the wide variety of textiles produced in ancient India. The ancient Indians also traded their fabrics; cotton from India has been found in ancient Egyptian tombs, and in the first centuries of the Common Era, India exported silk fabric to Rome.

The ancient Indians were particularly adept at brocade work. *Brocade* refers to any kind of fabric made with silk or silk-cotton blends with raised needlework in gold or silver (or both). The designs made with this gold or silver needlework were called *nakshas*. These fabrics were dyed with vegetable dyes, and historically color has played an important role in Indian fabrics. Thus, for example, red was regarded as the color of love, yellow the color of spring, indigo (a shade of blue) the color of Lord Krishna, and saffron (a shade of orange to orange-yellow) the color of the earth.

Because textiles and fabrics do not survive through the centuries in the same way that artifacts made of stone or metal do, less is known about textiles in ancient Japan, where traditions developed later than they did in China and were strongly influenced by those of the Chinese. It is known that by the late ancient period and into the early medieval period, the Japanese had developed a number of textile traditions. One was the use of bast fiber, which was common before the introduction of cotton. Bast was a fiber that came primarily from the gampi tree and was used principally in papermaking. It was, however, also used to produce textiles.

Another type of textile work was called *rozome*, commonly referred to as "batik" in the West. *Rozome* was a process of dyeing fabric. Wax was used to create the designs by covering those portions of the fabric that were not to be dyed. A similar technique, called *kasuri*, created designs from dyed threads. *Sashiko* was a form of decorative embroidery used primarily for functional purposes to reinforce points of stress in a piece of fabric. Also common in Japan were various methods of tie-dyeing, called *shibori*, which created designs in fabrics by folding, stitching, twisting, or binding them. While the earliest examples that have been found date to the eighth century, the traditions and techniques developed over a period of hundreds of years prior to that.

EUROPE

by Judith A. Rasson

In ancient Europe cordage (thread, string, or yarn) was made by twisting fibers collected from plants or animals, most simply by rolling the fibers between one's palm and upper leg. Twisting fibers around a short rod or stick was the simplest way of spinning. The stick used to control the twisted thread was called a spindle. Cordage was used to tie things together. It was also interwoven in various ways to create cloth. Cloth was embellished by adding patterns while weaving or with embroidery. Floor and wall coverings were also made of mats, a basketry technique.

The first cordage was made in Europe during the Paleolithic Period, which coincided with the Pleistocene (up to 10,000 years ago). A piece of cordage was found in the Lascaux caves in France, famous for their Paleolithic wall paintings. The fibers were identified as bast—from a plant. No woven textiles have been found in Europe from this early period. As the climate changed at the end of the Pleistocene, people continued their nomadic lifestyles. Archaeologists call this cultural period the Mesolithic (up to 4000 B.C.E.). There is continued evidence for the use of cordage in this period. Fragments of nets made from tree bark bast have been found in waterlogged sites in Finland, Estonia, and Lithuania; the nets might have been used for fishing, but they might equally have been bags or hair coverings. No other Mesolithic textiles have been found.

As time passed, people began to rely on domesticated animals and plants, and they settled in villages. This period is called the Neolithic (up to 2000 B.C.E.). People increased their use of cordage, and this period seems to have been the time when cloth weaving was invented. People continued to use bast fibers; one example is a fishnet made of bast found in the waterlogged lake dwelling site of Zürich-Kleiner Hafner, dated from 1000 B.C.E. to 1000 C.E.

Weaving became more common during the Neolithic, and there is more evidence for both the weaving itself and the tools used. Most of the evidence for what was woven comes from impressions left in clay on pottery and elsewhere rather than the cloth itself (though a few cloth fragments have been recovered). The main fiber used was bast from flax or nettles. Plant stems, where the fibers are, had to be soaked in water and then pounded to release the fibers and combed to align them. Wool was probably not used during the Neolithic because sheep did not have fluffy coats but had many long hairs and short bristles mixed in the wool that made it difficult to spin.

Both flax and (later) wool were spun by hand on spindles. The person held the fibers in one hand or on a distaff (rod) and twisted them onto the spindle with the other hand. Spindles could be held by the thread and made to spin around to twist the fibers better. A small weight (often made of ceramic) on the spindle, called a spindle whorl, made it easier for the spindle to rotate. This method of spinning persisted into the 20th century C.E. in many parts of eastern Europe.

Weaving may have begun in Europe with belt weaving—weaving narrow bands—by fastening the end of a group of long threads (the warp) to a stable object, like a post or a tree, and maintaining the tension by fastening the other ends of the threads to the weaver's waist. Weaving would have been done by working another thread (the weft) crosswise over and under the long threads. This method is a small version of a loom.

Neolithic looms were upright, rectangular frameworks, with two legs and a horizontal bar across the top. Warp threads were attached at the top of the bar and hung down lengthwise. A stick called a shed rod separated the warp threads. Another rod, a heddle, moved alternate warp threads forward and back so that the weaver could slide the weft thread through. This process was faster than weaving each individual thread over and under. To help hold the warp threads taut, ceramic weights were attached to groups of warp threads. This process gives its name to the warp-weighted loom. It was used throughout Europe in prehistoric times and persisted in use until the 20th century C.E. in Norway, adding to our understanding of how the loom worked. Clay loom weights are found regularly at most Neolithic sites in eastern Europe.

Cloth could be woven in different patterns, depending on the over-and-under pattern of the weft and warp. A simple interlacing of the weft over and under the warp threads is called the plain weave. A patterned weave could be created by varying the number and order of warp threads skipped in each over and under. A pattern of over-and-under alternating pairs of wefts produces a twill pattern; these patterns have names like herringbone or bird's eye. Striped and plaid cloth and also embroidery began to be used in the Neolithic. Sometimes these variations were done while the cloth was on the loom by introducing extra threads in different patterns and colors. Excellent examples come from waterlogged sites like Pfäffikon-Irgenhausen in Switzerland.

Weaving plain and complex weaves continued in the Bronze Age (ca. 2800–ca. 700 B.C.E.), after the Neolithic, when there were some innovations. Wool came into use, collected by shearing or perhaps just by pulling it out when it became long and shaggy.

The technique of sprang first appears in the Bronze Age. Sprang is a type of weaving with the warp on a square frame, without weft thread. The warp threads are attached to the crossbars at the ends of the frame and twisted around each other, starting at both ends and working toward the middle. To keep the weave from springing apart, another thread is woven across the pattern when the weaving reaches the middle. Sprang fabric is stretchy, and the technique was used where stretch was important, as in socks and sleeves. It looks like knitting, which was not invented until later. Examples of sprang caps or hairnets have been found at the Danish Bronze Age sites of Skyrdstrup and Borum Eshøj. Sprang continued to be used in the Iron Age (ca. 1000 B.C.E.–ca. 500 C.E.), and knowledge of it has survived in Scandinavia until the present.

In the Iron Age, weavers added hemp to flax and wool for their textile needs. Loom weights abound on Iron Age sites in eastern and central Europe; they are also found in Scandinavia and in England. Weavers definitely used card weaving (or tablet weaving) to form narrow edges of large pieces of cloth

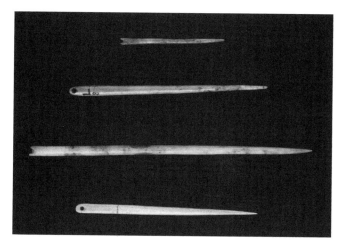

Bone needles from the cave of Courbet, Penne-Tarn, France, dating to about 10,500 B.C.E. (© The Trustees of the British Museum)

to be finished on a larger loom. In card weaving a number of cards (of wood, bone, or ivory), a bit larger than standard playing cards, had a hole drilled in each corner. The warp threads each passed through one hole. The warps were moved by flipping the cards from side to side and running the weft between them. This technique might have been used earlier, but the first unequivocal use was in the Iron Age. Iron Age skills were continued into the Classical Period, when writing and the increased use of figural depictions on ceramics provide evidence beyond archaeological deposits.

GREECE

BY SPYROS SIROPOULOS

Evidence confirms that textiles were used as far back as the Neolithic Period, although no findings of actual textiles have been preserved. Bone pins (as well as copper pins from the late Neolithic period) testify to the extended use of textiles in the area of Greece. The processing of wool and linen and the manufacture of tapestries and rugs appear to have been a major part of the Minoan economy. During the acme of the Minoan society (2200–1800 B.C.E.)—also known as the palace society because the palace was the central economic and political unit—many women offered their weaving services to the palace. Preserved on clay tablets from Pylos is information about 15 specialties of weavers. This specialization is equivalent to industry by modern standards. One tablet records 10,572 animals (goats and sheep), while others describe palace weavers also working with vegetable fibers, such as linen. Linen reached the palace by annual contributions twice a year: at the end of winter and at the beginning of spring. A series of clay tablets from Cnossus relates that 10 tons of wool were distributed to 30 workshops, where 600 to 900 female weavers labored. Other tablets from Cnossus mention the processing of 45 tons of wool, which would have required an estimated 2,700 to 4,000 workers.

Raw materials were not difficult to obtain. Out of the 3,000 tablets found at Cnossus, almost 1,000 are about goats and sheep, the number of which is estimated at 100,000. The average annual production of wool from these herds, which probably belonged to the palace, is an estimated 50 tons. A bolt of textile weighed roughly 22 pounds, so 50 tons should produce about 5,000 bolts. The L-series tablets, referring to the previous year's wool process, number about 5,000 bolts, the weight of which varies between 11 and 132 kilos, whereas their total weight reaches up to 45 tons. We are also certain that the textiles were dyed both at Pylos and Cnossus, though no traces of dying essences have been recognized by archaeologists today.

Herodotus (fifth century B.C.E.) reported in his *Histories* that in India a wild plant produced "fleece," obviously referring to cotton. It was Alexander the Great who introduced the cotton plant to Greece and made it part of the Greek economy. The two kinds of fibers—animal and vegetable—required different processing techniques. In the case of cotton and linen, the process went through the stages of opening the fruit, extracting the fibers, carding, combing, dyeing, and twisting them for the spinning frame. Women did most of the weaving at home, although specialized factories existed for processing wool. First the wool was washed with hot water. Then the yarns were combed and stretched. Workers stretched the wool over either their bare calves or a specialized tool called an *onos* or *epinetron*. The cylindrical clay tool covered the worker's knee and lower thigh.

Before the invention of the spinning wheel (around 500 B.C.E. in India), spinning was done by hand. Wool was bound loosely around a stick called a distaff. Many Grecian vase paintings depict women holding a distaff in one hand and using the other hand to draw the material onto a spindle—another stick with a weight at the bottom. Made to spin quickly,

Utensil used for unwinding balls of wool, called Ariadne's Clew Box (Alison Frantz Photographic Collection, American School of Classical Studies at Athens)

the spindle increased the pull on the fibers, turning them into workable threads.

The use of the loom is a topic of Homeric epics. The wise Penelope used a loom to trick her potential suitors by weaving a death robe for Odysseus's father, Laertes. She had promised to choose one of the suitors when the shroud was ready, but she undid each day's work during the night. The loom is a frame on which threads are passed over and under stable threads. With the help of a stem, a simple handheld device, women pulled the filling threads over and under the stable threads. Then, from the top of the loom, a kind of closely spaced comb was drawn, thus pressing the fibers together to form solid textiles. Of course, some techniques, such as knitting, were simpler.

In his *Republic*, Plato describes the work of the dyer. The first task was the lengthy and delicate process of preparing the dyeing materials, which were primarily barks, fruits, vegetables, animal products, or minerals. Before dipping threads into the dye, the dyer cleaned them by soaking them in potash and clay. Perhaps one of the best pictorial descriptions of the wool-working process is a painted vase dating from around 560 B.C.E. In five groups, women are shown combing wool, spinning thread, filling a basket with yarn, weighing balls of yarn, working on a vertical loom, and folding finished cloth.

Silk was also used in Greece. Through trade and colonization the Greeks had contact with people in the East who knew of the silkworm. The legislator Solon (ca. 638–559 B.C.E.) established sericulture—the farming of silkworms—to boost the economy of Athens. More than 5,000 cocoons of a silkworm are needed to produce about 2 pounds of raw silk. First the cocoons are boiled, and then their filaments are removed and twisted together into very long threads that are wound on reels.

ROME
BY LYN GREEN

Many of the surviving textiles of the Roman period are from the time of the empire and from the provinces, where, compared with Italy, the climate was often more conducive to the preservation of textiles. All the major fabrics used—cotton, linen, wool, and silk—have been found at sites in Egypt and the Near East. Of these, probably cotton was the rarest and silk the most valuable. Wool was the preeminent fabric of Roman culture. It was used for tunics, blankets, and of course, togas. It could be woven into various forms, including plain (tabby), twill, damask, and tapestry. Twill weave produced a hard-wearing fabric popular in the northern provinces. Damask weave is believed to have been developed in Egypt before the first century C.E. Tapestry weave was also used in Egypt, but often for fabrics of mixed fibers. The tapestry technique allowed wool decorations to be woven into the surrounding linen. These decorations were often colored.

One reason for the popularity of wool was that it was widely available, easily dyed, and relatively easy to prepare for weaving, even though much of the fleece was 50 percent dirt and grease. That problem was solved to some extent by washing the sheep before shearing. The next steps, probably performed by professional wool combers, were combing and teasing the wool to prepare it for spinning. Ancient Roman wool combs have survived, but teasing the wool to separate the fibers was done with the fingers.

To spin wool into thread, the Romans used a distaff and spindle; they appear not to have had spinning wheels. One technique for making thread easier to spin was wetting it and then spinning it in the direction that the fibers have a natural tendency to twist. Thus, cotton fibers were usually spun to the right (producing a *Z* twist), and linen fibers were usually spun to the left (producing an *S* twist). Wool, however, does not have a natural twisting direction and could be spun either clockwise or counterclockwise, though spinners in some areas seem to have preferred one direction to another. For example, the threads in many samples of wool excavated in Egypt were spun to the left, reflecting the Egyptians' preference for working with linen, which has a natural *S* twist.

The resulting wool thread was used for sewing, weaving, or knitting, depending on the thickness of the yarn. The number of knitted socks that have survived from various parts of the Roman Empire attest to the popularity of that method of producing clothing. However, Roman knitting was different from the modern technique of looping yarn around needles. An alternate method of working wool that did not involve spinning or weaving was felting. Felt was used primarily in army gear, however.

According to the Roman historian Pliny the Elder, flax was prepared for weaving into linen by being soaked in water to remove the bark of plants. Then the inner fibers of the plant were dried and beaten successively with a wooden mallet and a flat wooden blade. The beaten fibers were drawn through a wooden combing board with teeth. Egypt was one of the major linen producers of the empire. In Greco-Roman times cotton (*gossypium*) was introduced into Egypt to counteract the expense of importing it from India, but most of the cotton used in the empire was probably still brought from southern Asia. Silk was also brought overland from China at great expense. Once silk thread arrived in the Mediterranean, it might be rewoven with another thread, such as linen. That kind of silk was called *subserica*.

Several types of looms were in use in the vast Roman Empire: the warp-weighted loom, the two-beam vertical loom, and the horizontal loom. The warp-weighted loom was most common in Italy and the northern and western provinces of the empire. The two-beam vertical loom was used widely in the empire by the end of the first century C.E. The horizontal loom may have originated in Syria about the middle of the third century C.E.

The woven cloth was finished by fullers. In a large vat or tub filled with water, fuller's earth, urine (bought or collected from public urinals), and soapwort or other cleanser, the cloth was treaded or otherwise agitated to remove dirt.

LOOMS

A warp-weighted loom consists of two upright beams connected at the top by a bar, called the cloth bar, from which the warp threads are hung. Another beam one-third of the height of the uprights from the ground and parallel to the cloth beam is called the shed rod and helps to keep the threads separate. The warp threads are gathered and tied at the bottom to a cord strung through a warp weight. The two-beam vertical loom is very similar to the warp-weighted loom, except the warp threads are not weighted but anchored to a beam at the bottom of the loom. The horizontal loom is known to have existed only because of the types of weaving, such as damask, that were being done. No archaeological remains, pictures, or textual references to them seem to have survived. This is a complex loom suitable for professionals.

Wool was then brushed with a spiked brush to raise the nap, which was then sheared to produce a smooth cloth.

Different parts of the empire produced or imported cloth suitable to local tastes and climates. In northern provinces like Britain cloth was woven in checked patterns. Other areas, such as Egypt and Syria, favored plain garments decorated with bands or medallions of tapestry or embroidery dyed in various colors. In Italy braid was used to decorate clothing. Pliny the Elder credited the Phrygians with inventing embroidery, although it seems all they did was master the use of metallic thread.

The two most expensive dyes of the ancient world were saffron and Tyrian purple. Saffron was made from the stigmas of the saffron crocus. Tyrian purple was made from the secretions of the murex, a shellfish. Thousands of murex went into producing just a few drops of the dye; fortunately, only a drop was needed to dye a whole tunic. Also known as imperial purple, Tyrian purple has a dark reddish quality. Although the Phoenicians also produced a bluish purple from shellfish secretions, it was the redder shade that was more popular, especially in Roman times. Orchil was a kind of lichen that produced a bluish purple. Madder, woad, indigo, and safflower produced red, blue, and yellow dyes. In later Roman times the Egyptians used a technique for created multicolored scenes by repeatedly dyeing a fabric. Each time a different color was applied, the rest of the cloth was covered in clay or wax to prevent it from absorbing color.

Tapestry hangings were a specialty of the Alexandrian weavers and often depicted landscapes or mythological scenes. Embroidery, which the Romans called "painting with the needle," was also used to create the multicolored and often elaborate scenes. One of the masterpieces of ancient

embroidery dates to the fourth century C.E. and is part of a series depicting the seasons of the year. Its resemblance to the scenes on mosaics in other parts of the empire proves that artists of all types used pattern books, whether working in paint, stone, or thread.

THE AMERICAS
by Julia Marta Clapp

It is difficult to paint a broad picture about textile and needlework production in the ancient Americas. The inherently delicate and vulnerable construction of such materials has caused ancient textiles to disintegrate over time, leaving archaeologists with little to study. The conclusions at which they arrive can often be based upon a combination of two factors. First, archaeologists can make hypotheses based on any remaining textile artifacts that have been preserved from the ancient era. Such items are rare, much more so in certain areas than others. (For example, civilizations that existed in particularly damp climates are less likely to have preserved textiles than are civilizations in dry regions.) Second, archaeologists may examine evidence from more recent centuries and look at enduring traditions that may provide clues about the past. Any conclusions based on such observations must, however, be considered nothing more than speculation.

Among the Americas, South America arguably has the richest history of textile production. No other part of the hemisphere has left such ample or rich artifacts in this field. In general, the area that has yielded the most abundant artifacts is the northwest coast, or modern-day Peru.

The oldest textiles have been found in Huaca Prieta and are over 4,000 years old. As in North America, the majority of textiles have been excavated from gravesites that contain bodies and artifacts that are at times astonishingly well preserved. Also, similarly to the native North Americans, ancient South Americans wrapped their dead in layers of fabric, of which the inner layers have survived the best.

It is important to remember that as with some other ancient cultures, the ancient Peruvians did not have a system of writing. However, the absence of a writing system does not mean that they were unable to record thoughts or ideas. Although today we think of literacy in terms of reading and writing, some ancient cultures used other means to express themselves. In fact, weaving is an extraordinarily complex process that requires the ability to carry out intricate, advanced planning and to work with a mathematical sensibility.

We often think of textiles as being created by weaving pieces of dyed yarn together. The weaver devises in advance a color scheme, which eventually becomes a pattern. In the ancient Americas yarn was spun from either plant (for example, cotton) or animal (for example, wool) fibers. The warp consists of the strands over and under which the weft is woven. In the Chavín culture (ca. 900–ca. 200 B.C.E.), however, there is also evidence of textiles that did not have a pattern woven

Mantle border fragment made of cotton and camelid hair, first to second century C.E., *Peru* (Copyright the Metropolitan Museum of Art)

into them; instead, the pattern was painted on the surface. During this period ornamentation was an important part of textile production. Pieces of cloth with colorful, decorative borders and with embroidery have been found at burial sites from this era.

Stylistic developments can first be discerned in the Chavín culture. The weaving from this era represents not only abstract, geometric patterns but images of animals as well: jaguars, snakes, alligators, and birds. Many of the Chavín pieces depict the feline god, who appeared in textiles as early as 1200–700 B.C.E. The feline god was prominent in this civilization, and its presence remained throughout subsequent cultures in Peruvian history. The presence of this god indicates the strong religious significance of these pieces.

During this period the god was often represented in profile, but with its body depicted frontally. Later pieces, such as a burial cloth from around 300–100 B.C.E., represent animals in what we would consider a much more realistic or recognizable manner. This technique should not be mistaken for a development related only to the passage of time. In other words, stylistic representation did not become more realistic as time passed; later periods also occasionally used very schematic or abstract modes of representation.

In the Paracas Period (ca. 900 B.C.E.–ca. 300 C.E.) extraordinary and colorful textiles were still buried in gravesites. Both the quantity and the quality of the textiles of this period are a testament to the apparent value of this kind of production in the Paracas Period. In addition, new mythical and religious beings were introduced. As in other pantheistic societies, gods were designated to control various aspects of human life, such as agriculture or fertility. Such gods were represented on textiles, perhaps as offerings of appeasement. Such representations help us to understand the culture of this period as well; for example, the presence of an agriculture god in textiles indicates that agriculture was being practiced by ancient South Americans in Peru, and it was probably a significant part of their diet (relative to hunting and fishing, for example).

Certain prehistoric Native North American groups, particularly in the East and the Southeast, made for their elites elaborate burials, which are where most ancient textile re-

mains have been excavated. Many of these sites have been excavated and might offer clues regarding ancient textile production. Conclusions about tapestries and other forms of textiles must be made based on evidence available from garments. While such hypotheses may be less precise, such a study can at least provide information about what methods of textile production these civilizations used.

Artifacts from Late Archaic (ca. 3000 B.C.E.–ca. 1000 B.C.E.) excavations in what we now consider the southeastern United States have yielded small pieces of fabric. Through examination of these pieces, we have learned that early North Americans made both interlaced and woven cloth. Unfortunately, it is not possible to know what purposes these samples may have served outside of the burial context.

From the Adena culture (ca. 1000 B.C.E.–ca. 200 B.C.E.) archaeologists have found more woven textiles. These fabrics in particular have revealed that during that era the Adena people employed several different methods of weaving. Although many of these samples are items of adornment, such as headdresses, sandals, and skirts, woven cloth was also used to wrap other buried objects. These examples disprove any speculations that such early endeavors would have resulted in crude or unskilled production. On the contrary, archaeologists working in Adena sites have discovered cloth of very fine and delicate construction.

There is a disappointing lack of information from Mesoamerica during the ancient era. The earliest civilization that has been studied by archaeologists, historians, and art historians is the Olmec (ca. 1500 B.C.E.–ca. 400 B.C.E.). They inhabited the Gulf Coast region in Mexico, a particularly damp and swampy environment. Even generally durable stone artworks and architecture are rare, compared with that of other, later cultures. The Olmec civilization remains relatively unknown and has left us with more questions than answers.

However, before the Olmec, other traces of human life have been found, though information is sketchy at best. In the arid Tehuacán valley in central Mexico, archaeologists have found burial sites containing cloth samples made from cotton as well as human remains wrapped in woven blankets. Aside from burials, no one can be sure what use these items had in everyday life.

See also ADORNMENT; AGRICULTURE; ART; CLOTHING AND FOOTWEAR; CRAFTS; DEATH AND BURIAL PRACTICES; ECONOMY; EMPLOYMENT AND LABOR; GENDER STRUCTURES AND ROLES; HOUSEHOLD GOODS; OCCUPATIONS; RELIGION AND COSMOLOGY; TRADE AND EXCHANGE.

FURTHER READING

Ferdinand Anton, *Ancient Peruvian Textiles*, trans. Michael Heron (London: Thames and Hudson, 1987).

Alison Austin, "Spinning in Ancient Rome." Available online. URL: http://www.unc.edu/courses/rometech/public/content/survival/Alison_Austin/spinning.html. Downloaded on April 20, 2007.

Elizabeth Barber, *Prehistoric Textiles: The Development of Cloth in the Neolithic and Bronze Ages with Special Reference to the Aegean* (Princeton, N.J.: Princeton University Press, 1991).

Elizabeth Wayland Barber, *Women's Work: The First 20,000 Years: Women, Cloth, and Society in Early Times* (New York: W. W. Norton, 1994).

Margaret DeRamus, "Fibers and Fiber Preparation." Available online. URL: http://www.unc.edu/courses/rometech/public/content/survival/DeRamus_Durham_Laxton/margaret.html. Downloaded on April 20, 2007.

Margaret DeRamus, "Preparation of Finished Cloth." Available online. URL: http://www.unc.edu/courses/rometech/public/content/survival/DeRamus_Durham_Laxton/margaretfin.html. Downloaded on April 20, 2007.

Brian Durham, "Ancient Textiles as Evidence for Textile Production." Available online. URL: http://www.unc.edu/courses/rometech/public/content/survival/DeRamus_Durham_Laxton/brian.html. Downloaded on April 20, 2007.

Lallanji Gopal, "Textiles in Ancient India," *Journal of the Economic and Social History of the Orient* 4, no. 1 (1961): 53–69.

Jennifer Harris, ed. *5000 Years of Textiles* (Washington, D.C.: Smithsonian Books, 2004).

Kathy Laxton, "Looms and Weaving Tools." Available online. URL: http://www.unc.edu/courses/rometech/public/content/survival/DeRamus_Durham_Laxton/kathy.html. Downloaded on April 20, 2007.

John Mack and John Picton, *African Textiles: Looms Weaving and Design* (London: British Museum Publications, 1979).

Christa C. Mayer-Thurman and Bruce Williams, *Ancient Textiles from Nubia: Meroitic, X-Group, and Christian Fabrics from Ballana and Qustul; An Exhibition Organized by the Art Institute of Chicago* (Chicago: University of Chicago, 1979).

William Jay Rathbun, ed., *Beyond the Tanabata Bridge: Traditional Japanese Textiles* (London: Thames and Hudson, 1993).

Irmtraud Reswick, *Traditional Textiles of Tunisia and Related North African Weavings* (Los Angeles: Craft and Folk Art Museum, 1985).

Mary Schoeser, *World Textiles: A Concise History* (London: Thames and Hudson, 2003).

Gillian Vogelsang-Eastwood, *The Production of Linen in Pharaonic Egypt* (Leiden, Netherlands: Textile Research Centre, 1992).

Chen Weiji, comp., *History of Textile Technology of Ancient China* (New York: Science Press, 1992).

▶ towns and villages

INTRODUCTION

In general, archaeologists have specific qualities in mind for defining *villages, towns,* and *cities.* They tend to disagree with one another about what makes a city. Some insist that a city must have a certain minimum population to make it a city; otherwise it is a town. For these archaeologists, the Sumerian city of Uruk was the world's first true city because by 2700 B.C.E. it had a population of 50,000 people. Others believe the size of a settlement compared with others of its time matters most. Thus Çatalhüyük in Turkey, with several thousand people, would be the first true city in 7200 B.C.E., because at that time nearly everyone lived in settlements of 250 people or fewer. This means that defining towns is difficult, because it is unclear when a town is large enough to be a city.

Archaeologists usually see distinct differences between towns and villages. A town, like a city, needs to have a municipal government that organizes public works projects. It is expected to have leadership positions that form a hierarchy such as the *en* and *nin,* council of elders, assembly of citizens, and public employees of Sumerian towns. The *en* and *nin* were the male and female coleaders elected by the assembly. Archaeologists and historians devote much study to the organization of leadership in towns, because they believe the organization will tell them about how ancient peoples experimented with organizing their lives.

Where towns might have paved streets, areas for carrying on the business of civic government, and neighborhoods of homes, villages did not have those traits. They had human-made structures, even if those structures were just huts of mud or grass, and the structures would be intended to be used over a period of years rather than just a few days or a season. From this view, people who lived in caves did not live in villages, and therefore the development of the village itself was an important step for human societies.

A village almost certainly had a form of leadership, but it would not be as formal as that of a town. Very often villages were composed of members of one family or clan, with leadership belonging to family elders and with many decisions about village life being made with the involvement of all adults in the community. Villages did not have to be inhabited all year. Some ancient peoples had two places to live—one for the summer and the other for winter. In these cases, their villages were defined by the permanence of the homes, which would be sturdy enough to survive until the villagers returned.

After developing national governments, some cultures tried to regulate the organization of towns and villages. For instance, Romans insisted on ritually sanctifying the land before building. In ancient India villages and towns were intended to imitate the structure of the capital city, only smaller. In addition to villages organized around clans, they had villages and towns that were organized around crafts. For example, a village population could be all blacksmiths, who would be governed by their guild. Such villages were suburbs, because they usually existed to service a nearby city with their goods. Such details show villages and towns responding to developments of their cultures.

AFRICA

by Michael J. O'Neal

The emergence of towns and villages in ancient Africa writes in miniature the history of human development and civilization. The earliest hominids emerged in Africa some three million years ago and evolved into humans during the period historians call the Stone Age. During the earliest phase of the Stone Age, about one to three million years before the Common Era, the human population was small and scattered across the savannas of tropical Africa. People in small bands lived entirely by hunting and gathering, crafting primitive tools out of stone. The only thing approaching a town or village was a temporary encampment.

Later, up to 200,000 B.C.E., tools became more sophisticated, and populations increased. Greater intelligence enabled people to begin living in communities where they could share knowledge and pass that knowledge down to their offspring. As tools for digging, cutting, and carving became more specialized, and as these stone tools were attached to hafts to form spears and axes, ancient Africans were able to move off the savannas and into other regions, including forests, highlands, and more arid desertlike areas. After about 20,000 B.C.E. yet more specialized tools emerged, including fishhooks, awls, and bows and arrows, along with boats and pottery. These developments enabled people to live longer and contributed to population increases; therefore, they were crucial for the emergence of towns and villages.

Historians and archaeologists use the term *sedentary* to refer to this new, settled way of life, because people no longer lived in nomadic hunter-gatherer bands and formed relatively permanent communities. This change required the emergence of agriculture, which occurred in northern Africa beginning in roughly 16,000 B.C.E. The center of these new, more sedentary communities was the Upper Nile River. (The Nile flows from south to north, so the Upper Nile is to the south.) Throughout the following millennia the region was far wetter than it was after about 3000 B.C.E., so numerous lakes formed. Historians believe that it was in the region around these lakes, along the southern borderland of the modern-day Sahara Desert, that the first African settlements were formed. The region is called the Sahel, an Arabic word that means "shore," suggesting that the region formed the shore of the Sahara Desert, likened to a sea. The development of agriculture, including both herding and the planting of crops, paralleled the development of towns and villages because people gathered to pool their efforts in feeding themselves. Further, agriculture provided surplus food that enabled communities to support people who were not involved directly in food production, including artists, crafts workers, and the like.

In 2002 archaeologists discovered what may be the oldest agricultural settlement in the Horn of Africa, and perhaps Africa as a whole, near Asmara, the capital of Eritrea. The village is believed to be about 3,000 years old. Excavations of the site reveal that the people lived in stone houses. To conserve heat on the cool highland plateau, walls were shared, and the typical house did not have doors but was entered through a hole on the roof. Other evidence shows that the people herded and ate cattle and goats and brewed their own beer. For clothing they wore animal skins. Throughout Africa archaeologists have discovered similar villages, though buildings were more commonly constructed of mud and mud brick.

Numerous historical developments contributed to town and village life in ancient Africa. Agriculture was one. A second, which went hand in hand with agriculture, was climate change. Again the Sahel provides examples. In the 1970s archaeologists began to excavate the ancient town of Jenne-jeno, located in Sudan in the upper Niger River delta. Until about 300 B.C.E. the area was uninhabitable because of the high seasonal floodwaters of the Niger. Eventually the area began to dry out, and the floodwaters were lower and shorter lived. The result was the emergence of a fertile alluvial plain, where floodwaters left behind silt well suited to agriculture. The settlement of Jenne-jeno began in about 200 B.C.E. The original village was on a patch of high ground. People lived in circular huts made of straw covered with mud. By about 450 C.E. the village had grown to about 60 acres. The village continued to be a vital settlement until about 1200.

Jenne-jeno is a good example of two further developments that influenced the emergence of towns and villages in ancient Africa. One was an increasing amount of trade. Based on archaeological finds, Jenne-jeno appears to have actively engaged in trade. Artifacts found in the area demonstrate that Jenne-jeno imported goods from Greece and Rome. In fact, the entire Sahel, which stretches in an east–west band across the middle of the African continent, constituted a trade route. Goods from the east and from the Mediterranean area passed through the Sahel on the way to points south, where they were traded for African goods such as ivory, precious metals, and the like. The ancient Carthaginians established numerous trading posts along the northern and western African coasts. These posts were points of contact between the Carthaginians and their neighbors to the south. Along any trading route, towns and villages supported caravans of traders, providing them with food and water, forage for horses (and later, camels), markets, and resting places. Goods probably changed hands at numerous points along these trade routes, giving rise to villages.

A second development that contributed to the emergence of towns and villages was metalworking. Once again, Jenne-jeno was a site where a considerable amount of metalworking took place. Most of this work consisted of goldsmithing and jewelry. Archaeological evidence shows the presence of ironworking as well, yet the area itself holds no iron ore, suggesting that trade also took place for metals. One of the

Site of ancient walled town, Cameroon, Central Africa (© Board of Regents of the University of Wisconsin System)

peculiarities of the historical development of Africa was that the continent seems to have skipped the Bronze Age, passing from stone technologies directly to the production of iron. Good examples are provided by the Nok people of West Africa and the Soninke people of ancient Ghana. Both of these cultures developed sophisticated ironworking technologies, including blast furnaces. They also learned that the addition of carbon to iron produces the much harder steel. Just as in modern life, where towns and communities grow up around an industry, in ancient Africa towns and villages grew up as people gathered to take part in the mining, smelting, forging, and molding operations surrounding metalworking.

EGYPT

BY WOLFRAM GRAJETZKI

Over the centuries, forms and types of settlement in ancient Egypt changed considerably. An Old Kingdom town around 2500 B.C.E. must have looked radically different from one in the New Kingdom (ca. 1550–ca. 1070 B.C.E.) or from one in Roman times. At the beginning of the Naqada Period (ca. 4000–ca. 3000 B.C.E.) towns and villages were quite loosely arranged around certain areas, though always close to the Nile. Houses were built of light materials, such as straw, and featured spaces designated for economic purposes such as keeping animals, storing food, and producing handicrafts like

pottery. In the north of Egypt houses were often built deep into the ground. Little evidence suggests that fortifications or town walls were constructed. These ancient settlements had a variety of functions. Bigger towns, such as Naqada or Hieraconpolis, were local centers where, in the Naqada Period, local rulers had their residences and where at least one important temple could be found. Smaller villages, meanwhile, served as residential centers for farmers. Whether these ancient villages also had temples or small shrines for local gods is not known, but in later villages, at least, such features are present.

At the end of the Naqada Period towns began to feature walls and became smaller, probably not because of a reduction in population but because the population density was higher within the town walls. Houses were now built of mud bricks, with certain parts made in wood, and were situated quite closely together, with little indication of broader planning and very narrow streets. Houses are assumed to have quite often been two stories high. Regarding the expansion of such settlements, at Elephantine and Abydos, for example, next to the original walled town a new area was attached to the existing walls and enclosed by a new wall, and land lots were given to certain individuals and families.

With the advent of the Old Kingdom (ca. 2575–ca. 2134 B.C.E.), some towns remained centers of local administration. Such a center would have at least one temple, ancestor shrines for the local governors, and workshops supplying the populace with nonagricultural products. Local centers also featured marketplaces, which are as yet known to archaeologists only from depictions in tomb chapels. These markets were most likely located close to the Nile and to the town harbors, where incoming goods arrived. Despite such ready means of trade, scholars assume that even provincial capitals and larger towns had high proportions of the population directly involved in farming and producing food. Very close to the settlements, most often just beyond the town walls, were the town cemeteries.

Almost nothing is known about farming villages in ancient Egypt. The architecture and structure of houses and their arrangements within the villages might have been similar to those in the towns; villages may or may not have been enclosed by walls or other fortifications.

In the Middle Kingdom (ca. 2040–ca. 1640 B.C.E.) planned towns and settlements were built throughout Egypt. These towns follow rigid layouts, with the poorer populations living in small standardized houses in one section and the wealthier classes in larger houses in another section. The houses were arranged in rectangular blocks. In the larger houses the ruling elite used granaries to store grain and food, allowing them to supply the working population when needed. Many of these planned towns were erected around or next to temples; almost no other public buildings were constructed. However, in Elephantine, at least, an administrative building complex with many seal impressions could be found. Here, seemingly, food was collected and given to the populace, perhaps exclusively to those involved in locally organized state projects. In general, the settlements of the Middle Kingdom provide the impression of a highly organized and regulated society. Among the known pyramid towns from the Middle Kingdom, Lahun, located next to the pyramid of Sesostris II (r. ca. 1897–ca. 1878 B.C.E.), was quite expansive, with several thousand people living there. Lahun flourished under that king and then became a regional center.

From the New Kingdom not many towns have been excavated, and these few examples seem to be exceptional cases rather than regular settlements. Akhet-Aton, better known as Tell el-'Amârna, was built by Akhenaten (r. ca. 1353–ca. 1335 B.C.E.) to be the capital city. Deir el-Medineh was a workmen's village, built near the desert on the way to the royal tombs at Thebes, where the people of this village worked. These settlements do not show the tight planning of the Middle Kingdom towns. In Deir el-Medina, houses were arranged side by side along two narrow streets, with the village surrounded by a wall. Directly outside were the tombs of the workmen and several chapels and small temples. On Elephantine, a New Kingdom town featured tightly packed houses and several temples within the settlement, with no real planning in evidence. At Tell el-'Amârna, on the other hand, another workmen's village featuring rectangular blocks of houses was found, similar to the Middle Kingdom towns.

The New Kingdom town of Sesebi, in the Nubian province, is another example of a planned Egyptian town, with rows of house arranged in a checkerboard pattern, a town wall, and large temples. Next to the temple were large storage installations, indicating that the temples had strong economic functions. At the sites of several New Kingdom towns, no town walls are in evidence; in this period, perhaps, people simply felt safe. The situation changed in the Third Intermediate (ca. 1070–ca. 712 B.C.E.), during which time town walls are well known to have existed from both the archaeological record and from descriptions in texts. With the population rising, towns became densely populated places. During the Roman period, Hermopolis, in Middle Egypt, had houses seven stories high.

Especially in the Ptolemaic and Roman periods, the general picture of provincial towns changed drastically, with the appearances of new types of public buildings such as bathhouses, theaters, and other Greco-Roman-style public institutions. These buildings were in fair evidence in several provincial capitals but were less common in villages such as Karanis and other well-known villages in El Faiyûm. Many Egyptian villages from the Roman period were on the scale of medium-sized towns from other parts of the Roman Empire, by virtue of the high population density of the region.

THE MIDDLE EAST

BY AMY HACKNEY BLACKWELL

Towns and villages arose in the ancient Near East when people built homes near permanent sources of water and food. People kept living in towns and villages because agriculture required large amounts of communal labor and water supplies were limited, forcing people to share the same sources. The earliest towns appeared in the ancient Near East around 12,000 to 10,000 B.C.E., as people settled near reliable sources of wild foods such as natural stands of wild wheat and barley. These first settlements were small communities of about 100 to 200 people living in simple huts.

One of the first towns was Abu Hureyra in modern-day Syria. Abu Hureyra was established around 11,500 B.C.E. by hunter-gatherers who settled there to take advantage of edible plants growing near the banks of the Euphrates River. At the time the area had forests of oak, pistachio, and plum trees and was close to grasslands that provided edible seeds. Gazelles migrated through the area regularly, providing a reliable source of meat. The people who settled in the area built houses by digging shallow depressions into the ground and then sheltering them with branches and reeds placed atop wooden posts. They built additional shelters to store extra plant foods, keeping the surplus in reserve in case of drought or a poor year for nut cultivation. The women of the community used stone mills to grind grain into meal, a labor-intensive task that forced the entire group to stay in one place year after year.

By 9000 B.C.E. the town of Abu Hureyra contained several hundred inhabitants living in houses made of mud bricks. The people grew their own grain in fields surrounding the town, and the women continued to grind wheat in their houses day after day. The villagers also herded sheep and goats for milk, meat, and wool used to make cloth. The entire community existed to grow crops and raise children, generation after generation.

Over the next several millennia people continued to build towns and live according to the same pattern. By 6000 B.C.E. most residents of the Fertile Crescent lived in small villages near ready supplies of water. They were all located on or near sources of water that could be used to irrigate crops; most settlements rose along the Jordan, Tigris, Karkheh, and Euphrates rivers.

Mud was the main building material because both stone and wood were scarce. The agricultural seasons and daily necessities determined the activities of the residents. People experimented with and mastered irrigation techniques, such as canals, that allowed them to plant fields farther and farther from the rivers. When a town became too crowded to support itself, people simply moved into a free space and built new settlements.

Towns were occupied by family groups that helped one another with the labor of farming and other communal tasks, such as building. It would have been impossible for anyone to live alone; towns and villages made it possible to raise food and channel water in the harsh landscape. Living communally also made it easier to arrange marriages and raise children. Because they lived among relatives, village dwellers could always turn to someone for help. Living in towns fostered the beginnings of spiritual thought. Most towns remained in the same place for centuries, and many generations of dead were buried there. The inhabitants came to believe that dead ancestors continued to watch over the living.

Beginning around 3800 B.C.E. the towns at the mouth of the Tigris and Euphrates began to grow into cities such as Eridu, Ur, and Uruk. The climate was drier than it had been, and populations were too large for people to support themselves on family or village farms because there was not enough water or cultivable land for everyone in the area to farm for themselves. The people living in the cities developed governments to organize agriculture and distribute grain as well as to worship their gods. For the next 800 years or so, however, many people continued to live in towns and villages. Mesopotamian cities were surrounded by towns connected to the rivers by long canals extending in every direction from the cities. These towns specialized in various products, including metalwork, pottery, and fishing. They traded with merchants in the cities to get grain, and they relied on the cities for defense and religious ritual. By 3000 B.C.E., however, most of these villages had been swallowed up by the larger cities, and the residents were co-opted to work for the city's irrigation canals and farms.

By the first millennium B.C.E. towns and villages had been established throughout the Levant, Persia, and Anatolia as well as in Mesopotamia. Towns continued to be located near water sources and cultivable land. Most towns had a central area for people to meet and trade, and most contained a communal place of worship. Towns often sprang up along trade routes, such as the Persian Royal Road that ran across the Persian Empire. Some towns were quite small and simply organized, but as time went on they acquired more local government.

During the fifth and fourth centuries B.C.E. the Greek model of town organization spread into Asia Minor. Towns of this period were carefully planned, and the land was divided in a regular pattern. Each town contained an agora—an open space where people could gather to exchange goods or conduct business. The agora might contain a stoa—a building used for various purposes, including conducting courts of law and other civic activities. Later towns often had several stoas surrounding the agora, marking the space as an official public area. This type of town design spread throughout the Near East and Persia during the Hellenistic period, as Alexander the Great traveled through the region and founded numerous cities.

The Romans imposed their own form of order on Near Eastern towns during the empire. Towns were built on a rectangular grid pattern and included a forum—an open square used for business and politics. The local government organized the building of streets, sewers, and public water supplies. Many towns had fortifications to protect the residents from enemy attacks. The government also handled matters of taxation, grain distribution, and legal administration. During the late empire Rome's central administration deteriorated, and local people throughout the Near East took on more responsibility for their local government. In Asia Minor and the Levant local religious rulers gained power over towns and took on the financial responsibility of maintaining them.

ASIA AND THE PACIFIC
BY KIRK H. BEETZ

The region of Asia and the Pacific encompasses vastly varying climates, and the towns and villages built in ancient times varied according to people's needs for shelter from the weather, for protection, and for cooperative living. As early as 9000 B.C.E., and probably much earlier, people in Siberia and central Asia were using bones and skins from animals such as mammoths to build shelters. These people were cooperative hunters who probably gathered in small villages in order to easily form hunting packs for pursuing large game. The villages also would have allowed for greater numbers of people to deal with injuries and to gather together to keep warm in the often frigid environment.

Far to the south, in Southeast Asia, people were dealing with a very different environment: one that was warm and wet and becoming wetter. The coast offered opportunities for fishing, and people clustered together in villages to work together to harvest food from the sea. Not much is known of these ancient villages, partly because the rising ocean covered many of them with water and partly because the humid air quickly rotted the wood and leaves that were probably used for building homes.

Farther inland, in the rain forests, villages likely consisted of little more than lean-tos, shelters of branches raised on poles on one side and leaned against trees or large rocks. These villages would be found in forest clearings, perhaps beside rivers or streams. Living quarters such as lean-tos were favored in the construction of villages on the islands of the South Pacific, where warm weather made more sheltering structures unnecessary for most of the year.

Estimates for when agriculture began in the region of Asia and the Pacific vary widely among archaeologists, with some citing about 7000 B.C.E. in what is today far northern China, while others cite the more recent figure of about 4000 B.C.E. in both the Indus River valley and in far northern China. Early agricultural villages seem to have evolved out of villages constructed by hunter-gatherers who had assembled together as family groups. Along the Yellow River people who cultivated millet while still relying heavily on hunting and gathering formed villages of fewer than 40 people, probably constituting an extended family or clan. The land on both sides of the Yellow River was well suited to incipient agriculture, being easy to dig and rich in nutrients.

Who the villagers were in 4000 B.C.E. in the Indus River valley is not known, but their culture may have given rise to the Harappan civilization of 2600–1500 B.C.E. These early villagers almost certainly had contact with Sumerian cultures in the Near East, and the designs of their villages may have been influenced by those cultures. By 2600 B.C.E. these people were building numerous towns and villages, almost all along the several rivers that flowed through the Indus River valley at that time, as well as cities for up to 50,000 inhabitants. Towns and villages were usually well planned, with grids of streets and buildings made of fired brick. Granaries, for storing grain, seem to have been found in most towns and villages.

Although the Harappan civilization faded by 1500 B.C.E., the established methods of planning towns and villages did not. As Aryan invaders from central Asia spread southward into the heart of India, they imposed many of their customs on local peoples, but they were nomads without much skill in building settlements, and they seem to have adopted some of what they found among the Harappans and cultures farther south.

By about 500 B.C.E. the forms of Indian villages were generally set, with changes occurring only slowly during the rest of the ancient era. Both towns and villages were expected to be organized in the same manner as the capital cities in India's various nations. Towns and villages were often raided by bandits or other groups still living in forests, making defensive considerations important. Thus, settlements tended to have earthen walls and main gates through which people had to pass to enter. In the case of a town, the gates would

usually have buildings attached where local officials worked; these officials would collect taxes from people bringing goods into town. In the case of a village, such work was more likely performed by the village chief or his relatives. Towns would feature bigger houses than would villages, with houses in towns reaching two stories in height, whereas houses in villages consisted of one story only.

Indian villages were usually self-sufficient, as help from cities was generally slow to arrive because of the distances between locales and because the weather often made roads difficult to travel. Thus, villages were usually located near reliable sources of water and would typically have agriculture as their most important industry. Sometimes, a village consisted almost entirely of members of one profession, such as with metalworking or ceramics manufacture; children tended to enter the professions practiced by their parents, which meant that some small villages that had formed around extended families or clans became focused on a single industry. Such villages were dependent on the economies of cities for selling their products. Occasionally, a village was placed under royal protection, meaning that the villagers were not to be bothered by outside government officials.

In China living conditions in villages were poor during most of the ancient era. Villagers in the Yellow River region lived in circular homes, often wood and dried mud surrounding a pit. The roofs were probably made of thatch, with a peak in the center. The houses formed irregular patterns in villages. The villages themselves tended to be built wherever high ground could be found near a river. Although the villagers were farmers, so much of what they produced was taken from them in the forms of fees, taxes, and loan payments that they needed to hunt and fish to supplement their diet.

By the beginning of the Han Dynasty (202 B.C.E.–220 C.E.), towns featured houses that were significantly different from those in villages, which were usually one-room hovels; advanced Chinese construction methods were applied to town buildings, which were usually wooden with heavy posts on which walls were hung. Crucial to a town was its marketplace, where peasants brought their harvests and merchants sold their goods. A marketplace was usually located on a town's main road, where visitors were sure to pass after entering the town.

In Japan archaeologists have discovered numerous remains of circular houses, with the walls encircling pits. While the largest settlement yet discovered had about 1,500 homes, most settlements were much smaller. The larger towns were probably founded on agriculture, which allowed more people to live in one place than did hunting and gathering, but even at the end of the ancient era many Japanese were still hunter-gatherers living in villages in the vast forests that covered most of the islands of Honshu and Kyushu. Villages sometimes had protective ditches around them, and some may have had wooden walls, as warfare was common by 200 C.E.

EUROPE
BY KIRK H. BEETZ

The earliest Stone Age populations of Europe were mobile hunter-gatherers who lived in camps for short periods and then moved in search of game. Not until agriculture began in southeastern Europe around 7000 B.C.E. were settlements established with the permanence and character of farming villages. Archaeologists refer to people who live in permanent settlements throughout the year as sedentary. The practice of agriculture demands that people stay in one place to tend their crops and have a place to store the foodstuffs after the harvest. Eventually some hunter-gatherers who lived in rich environments displayed a few sedentary characteristics. An example from Europe is the communities of the Ertebølle culture that occupied the coasts of Denmark and Sweden between 6000 and 4000 B.C.E.

By 5000 B.C.E. farming had spread across central and southern Europe, and by 4000 B.C.E. it had reached the British Isles and Scandinavia. The earliest European farmers lived in various types of settlements. In the Balkans the houses made from mud were generally clustered into settlements that suggest true villages, whereas in central Europe the earliest farmers lived in farmsteads with timber houses that formed loose groupings along small streams. It is unclear whether these settlements had the organization of villages or whether each farming household functioned relatively independently. Whatever the structure of the settlement, its inhabitants were linked to other similar settlements through a network of trails and streams. Fields and pastures surrounded the houses.

By 3000 B.C.E. ancient Europeans managed to build villages even in the extreme climates of the far north. Perhaps the most famous of these villages is Skara Brae in the Orkney Islands, northeast of Scotland, where it is very cold and very windy. Skara Brae was one of many small villages made of stone near the northern seas. It was not the oldest stone village, because an older, well-developed village was found underneath it. However, Skara Brae was well preserved, allowing its remains to tell much about ancient village life. It was deliberately built in a midden, an ancient trash heap. Its walls were made of stone slabs, and there were passageways with stone walls between the village's houses, allowing people to walk from house to house without being exposed to the wind. The roofs of the houses were dirt with grass cultivated on them to hold them firmly together. Building the houses in the midden and covering both roofs and midden with soil in which grass was grown helped keep the village warm. Each house had a room set aside for a toilet, and beneath that room ran a channel that carried away the waste.

Skara Brae comprised only six houses. The climate was not good for most crops, but judging by the numerous bones found among the remnants of the village, grass grew well enough for the inhabitants to raise sheep and cattle. Villagers were likely related to one another. Some archaeologists believe that each house was closely associated with a particu-

lar family. Bodies of elderly women were found within the walls of houses, possibly an indication of villagers' belief that by revering their ancestors they could protect their houses. The village was occupied from about 3100 to 2480 B.C.E. and may have been abandoned slowly and voluntarily. Each house seems to have been ritually filled in with varying layers of debris. A common item found in the abandoned houses was antlers, which may have marked a house so closely associated with the family that no one else would have been allowed to live in it.

Other famous settlements of the early European farmers are the lake villages in central Europe, built in the foothills of the Alps between 4000 and 1200 B.C.E. At one time archaeologists thought these villages were constructed over lake waters, but it is now known that they were actually built over marshes near lakes. The levels of the lakes had risen to and sometimes over the dwellings after the villages were built, misleading early archaeologists. Piles were driven deep into the lakeside marshes until they hit a solid subsurface. Set on these piles were wooden houses with sharply peaked roofs to shed rain and snow.

Settlements that unequivocally have the character of towns began to appear during the final millennium B.C.E. One of the best known of these settlements is Biskupin in Poland, located about 143 miles to the west of Warsaw on a marshy peninsula along a lake. The town was a planned community from the start. Instead of the irregular arrangement of houses commonly seen in earlier villages, Biskupin had houses in several neat rows. They were built end to end as one long house divided by walls into many one-room dwellings. Because of the marshy character of the peninsula, the streets had to be paved with wood. In Biskupin the wooden streets stretched under the houses from one side of the town to the other, leaving no open spaces.

Around Biskupin was a wall of wood and dirt 20 feet high and 6 feet wide. Its sides and top were wooden, and the inside was filled with dirt. Within the wall were about 100 dwellings, housing roughly 700 people by about 720 B.C.E. Within the village all the crafts work took place, including metalworking. Fires either from blacksmiths or hearths burned part of Biskupin seven times. Whom the lake villagers feared is not known, though archaeologists in general speculate that raiders from the Baltic region or from the East pressed people into fortified villages like Biskupin.

By 600 B.C.E. the Celts were spreading through Europe. Along the Atlantic seaboard their villages tended to be made of stone, but inland they favored wood. Some Celtic towns were set on top of hills and were surrounded by wooden fences, but many villages were small and scattered through lowlands, usually near water but nearly always where farming was possible. Industrial centers with population densities and probably structures similar to towns were established in central Europe, where it was possible to carry out activities like ironworking and salt mining. Two of the most important centers of industry were Hallstatt in Austria, where salt was mined, and Stična in Slovenia, where iron was smelted and forged. To the west, wealthy and powerful chiefs and their retainers lived in hilltop settlements known as hill forts, such as those at Maiden Castle in England, Mont Lassois in France, and the Heuneburg in Germany.

By the time of the Roman invasion in the first century B.C.E. the inhabitants of western Europe were beginning to expand some settlements into fortified cities called *oppida*. Described by Julius Caesar in his account of his campaigns, *oppida* combined residential, industrial, commercial, and administrative functions. Some of the most famous *oppida* are found in France at sites like Alesia and Gergovia, while others in Britain eventually became the Roman towns of Camulodunum (modern Colchester) and Verulamium (modern St. Albans). The Roman towns were laid out in a grid pattern, with wooden shops and houses lining the streets. The Roman style of towns and villages dominated until the Germanic invasions of the 300s C.E. For protection nearly every village had a small fortress, and during the Common Era churches became standard in villages and towns.

GREECE

BY SPYROS SIROPOULOS

Greece is a mountainous country. Its irregular topography makes communication and trade difficult and led to the formation of many small, independent political units. Driven by social and economic necessity, some of these small communities united, which led to the formation of larger villages and towns. In *Politics* Aristotle argued that the city was the natural culmination of a series of associations and is the only environment in which the human being can reach completion. The first union, he argued, was between man and woman and then between master and slave; the result of these unions was the household or family (*oikia*). Households came to realize that to fulfill all their needs, they needed to consolidate into a village (*kome*). Eventually various villages joined together to form a city (*polis*), which ideally were self-sustaining, independent, and dedicated to meeting people's need to live the best possible life.

Thucydides was also aware that long ago the Greeks lived in wretched villages and the union of several of them led to the formation of cities. This process, known as synoicism, also occurred in Attica, when the people from the area confined by the Parnetha, Penteli, and Hymettus mountains were united in roughly 700 B.C.E. under the leadership of Theseus. The result was Athens, whose origins may explain its plural name.

A deme was the smallest political division of a city-state. Athenian demoi are the best documented, but demoi are also found in other city-states, like Eretria, Cos, and Rhodes. The Athenian politician Cleisthenes turned about 150 demoi into the basis for the arrangement of citizenry into 10 *phylai* (tribes). Archaeological excavations have shown that smaller-sized townships and secluded cottages and farms existed all over Attica, but residence there was seasonal. Possibly small unions of villages or farms were formed, but it is unlikely that the modern equivalent of a big village, secluded in the countryside, could be found in antiquity. The deme was the ancient equivalent of the modern village or small town.

The economic character of Greece remained essentially agricultural throughout the ancient period, which means that the civic centers, irrespective of their size, depended on the farming produce of the countryside. Many Athenians had their summerhouses outside the walls of Athens, in the country or the popular suburbs of Agryle. The countryside of the Attic Peninsula abounded with disparate cottages. For a long time the noblemen of Athens had large cottages and farms in the country, which gave them the right to excel in politics because the amount of crop a man had determined his political status. The statesman Pericles, of the fifth century B.C.E., had lands and houses in Attica, too, and he had promised to bequeath them to the state unless the invading Laconians burned them. In his *Oeconomicus* Xenophon describes vividly the life of country noblemen and praises agriculture as the source of all virtue, but he also hints at the sprawl of these cottages, with people building them anywhere they fancied.

Most farmers in classical times would have lived in the urban centers for protection and easy participation in politics. Fish was never the main course of the Athenian diet; therefore, small fishing villages around Attica never grew to considerable size, unless they turned into important trade and military centers. One example is Piraeus, which grew from a modest village to the largest port city in Greece.

Many people preferred to live outside the urban centers. For instance, in his comedy *The Clouds* Aristophanes describes the play's hero, Strepsiades, as a farmer from the deme of Acharnae who curses the fact that political obligations force him to leave his village at the break of dawn. Aristophanes makes clear the distinction between the *asty* (urban center), which Strepsiades hates, and the deme, which he longs for. In Boeotia it seems that people preferred to live permanently in the countryside. According to Thucydides, before Brasidas was received at Amphipolis he "had conquered the fortunes of Amphipolis' citizens who lived scattered all over the vicinity"—a clear description of people who resided in disparate farms and cottages rather than in organized towns and villages.

Like Strepsiades, most villagers and townsfolk had to commute to Athens if they wished to actively participate in the affairs of the state. Nevertheless, each deme maintained some form of independent local administration. A *demarchos* was elected as the head official and presided over a local council. The deme possessed land and had local cults. Most important, the deme maintained a list of its members, who were officially registered after being on the list 18 years. Like cities of the classical period, smaller communities pursued the ideal of self-sufficiency. However, to sell or buy products, the villagers had to go to Athens. In Argolis (in the area of the Peloponnese) scholars have observed that two of the area's small townships evolved into great cities from the beginning of the fourth to the beginning of the third century B.C.E. The distinctive sign of this evolution is the establishment of an agora, or marketplace. The agora was such a distinctive trademark of a city that Athens allowed only two other marketplaces to operate in all its vast territory.

ROME

BY KATIE PARLA

The first towns and villages in central Italy were Iron Age settlements later expanded by various groups such as the Villanovans, Etruscans, Latins, and, ultimately, the Romans. As Rome's territory began to grow, existing buildings in acquired towns were replaced with Roman models. Accordingly, certain common features emerged in towns and cities throughout the Roman world. These similarities were the product of town planning that combined Greek, Etruscan, and Roman elements.

During the Republican and Imperial ages, Rome expanded to include territories as far as Great Britain and the Near East. By imposing town planning on old and new settlements, the Romans were able to provide a common, unifying urban experience for all. By constructing public buildings that served as communal social and commercial spaces and by providing amenities to the people living in these territories, Rome was able to offer an unparalleled quality of life even in the smallest towns and villages.

Roman towns were typically laid out in grids; the organization of a town's streets into a grid system is called orthogonal planning. This model was borrowed from Greek town planning, but the Romans used square rather than rectangular city blocks. The streets running from east to west in such a design are called *decumani*, while those running from north to south are *cardines*. Where the principal *decumanus* axis (*decumanus maximus*) intersected the principal *cardo* axis (*cardo maximus*) is where the town forum would be located.

Romans built forums in towns and villages throughout their territory to provide a communal area to be used for political, economic, religious, and legal activities. Buildings and speaker's platforms would be constructed for meetings of the town or provincial government. Warehouses, banks, and shops would provide space for commercial exchanges. Temples dedicated to gods and emperors would reinforce the town's connection to Rome and its other settlements. Law courts, called basilicae, would be where Roman law was enforced and punishments doled out. Forums in Roman towns were public places where visitors would absorb the messages of unity and Roman primacy that were communicated through architecture.

Another important aspect of Roman towns and villages was their constant water supply. Aqueducts were built to bring water from lakes, springs, and rivers to settlements. These aqueducts were aboveground or belowground channels that delivered water over a distance at a low-grade angle using gravity. Some water sources were more than 50 miles away from the towns they supplied. This constant flow of water allowed for amenities like public fountains, public bath complexes, public latrines, and even running water in some residential complexes.

Waste management was another feature of Roman towns and villages. Sewers were built below street level to channel waste away from residential, commercial, and industrial sites. Also, groups of slaves would collect trash in the streets and rinse the streets regularly to keep public areas sanitary. This would help prevent the spread of disease.

Places for pubic spectacles were a major social component of Roman town planning. Theaters for cultural performances, as well as stadia and arenas for gladiator fights, chariot races, wild beast hunts, and public executions, could be constructed from wood or stone. Typically, these buildings were erected on the outskirts of towns, where more space was available. During the Roman Republic (509–27 B.C.E.) private individuals commissioned the buildings and the events held there. In the empire, the state financed such projects and produced structures of great scale and permanence. The sites for public spectacle found in ancient Roman towns were places where the masses, citizens and noncitizens alike, could reap the benefits of the government's generosity, since the events were free to the public.

Another Roman structure found in all towns and villages was the bathing complex. Public baths provided a common space where all members of society could relax, wash, exercise, and interact; the baths were social areas that guests would visit most afternoons for a minimal price. Like arenas and theaters, bathing structures were usually built by politicians during the republic and commissioned by emperors and the government during the empire.

One of the fundamental functions of Roman towns and villages was to provide secure areas for residential life. Since Roman towns were surrounded by defensive walls guarded by soldiers, residents would be protected from invaders. Police also patrolled the streets to protect private property within the town limits. The two main types of residential buildings were the *insula* and the *domus*. An *insula* was an apartment block with commercial spaces for lease on the ground floor and apartments on upper stories. A *domus* was a single-family home or villa that had reception and dining areas in addition to the private bedrooms and slaves' quarters. Sometimes the rooms of a *domus* facing onto a street would be used as commercial spaces. Many examples of this practice can be found in both Ostia and Pompeii.

Towns and village were located in all areas of Roman territory. Sometimes the Romans would reorganize existing settlements, adapting standing structures into the Roman layout that they would impose on conquered towns. This could result in established towns not adhering precisely to the orthogonal plan. Pompeii offers an example in which the original Oscan street plan, with its only occasional right angles, was incorporated into first the Greek, then the Roman grid system.

In other instances towns and villages were built in the absence of preexisting settlements. In such cases, religious authorities would be consulted in order to ascertain if the gods found a site acceptable. If so, the boundaries of the town would be officially established, including the *pomerium*, a ritual boundary within which magistrates could exercise power and outside of which burials, cremations, and military exercises could take place.

Aside from social and commercial functions, Roman towns and villages served certain military functions. The towns would protect Roman territory against invaders and offer bases from which military campaigns would be launched; these were the primary functions of Rome's first colonial settlements. Another military function of towns and villages was to provide a Roman presence in a distant part of Roman territory. Since many towns were conquered during military campaigns, the Romans would seek to maintain territory by populating areas with Romans. Members of the military might receive land as part of their war booty after conquest in or near newly conquered towns and villages.

As Rome grew during the late republic and the empire, a greater need for natural resources developed. By establishing settlements in a given area, local resources could be exploited, managed, and exported from the towns. This was an especially common practice in North Africa, where the majority of Rome's grain supply was grown. Commercial and agricultural development was managed and expanded from the towns and villages established throughout Roman territory.

THE AMERICAS

BY J. J. GEORGE

The establishment of village and town settlements, allowing people to live sedentary lives, is often but not always brought about by agricultural development. More than 100 species of edible plants were originally cultivated by Native Americans, the most familiar and widespread of which were maize, which came from Mexico, and potatoes, which were originally grown in the highlands of Peru. Other cultigens that were staples for many early communities included sweet potatoes, manioc, several kinds of beans, squash, tomatoes, and chili peppers. As farmers settled beside their crops, permanent villages were established. Surplus crops could be stored and traded with other communities; surpluses could also allow for certain community members to move beyond subsistence tasks and develop as craftsmen, merchants, priests, or ruling elite. Thus, many scholars argue that agriculture paved the way for social and economic stratification and for urban advances that laid the foundation for later complex cities and empires.

However, not all permanent villages developed as agriculture-based entities. For example, early large villages in regions as diverse as California, the Northwest Coast, and coastal Peru illustrate that sedentary civilization can develop in the absence of agriculture. In localities where resource-rich environments offered dependable food supplies, such as the salmon available seasonally along the Northwest Coast and the sardines and anchovies found in coastal Peru, villages developed and thrived according to nonagrarian initiatives. Generally, then, no single pattern defined or predicted the likelihood that a settlement would develop or succeed; each case was unique and subject to a variety of local factors. Changes in climate, for instance, could have dramatic effects on local populations, forcing massive resettlements or even causing the collapse of complex urban or semi-urban environments, as is thought to have happened when an extended drought struck the Moche towns in the Moche valley of northern Peru around the sixth century C.E. Similarly, climate change and associated decreasing yields of wild resources have been suggested as the causes of the collapse of the Hopewell in North America in the first centuries of the Common Era.

In the context of ancient civilizations, a *village* can be categorized as a settlement of as many as 30 or 40 dwellings occupying an area of several acres. A village would typically feature sturdy structures that remained in place and were occupied for extended periods of time; deep deposits of refuse, called middens; and some level of community planning. Early villages often had basic social hierarchies ruled by chiefs, as with similarly defined chiefdoms. *Towns*, by comparison, include many of the largest prehistoric communities, which covered hundreds of acres and featured housing structures numbering into the hundreds. Characteristic of towns were deep middens; heavy structures that were rebuilt or strengthened over time; dwelling units arranged in definite patterns, often in relation to ceremonial units or structures; and fortifications. All of these characteristics indicate long-term occupation of single sites.

In North America the ancestors of many peoples who would later settle into villages and towns were present as early as 7,000 years ago. While the archaeology suggests that town-level organization did not happen until after 500 C.E., examples of early North American village settlements are extensive. Such settlements include Hopewell Indian sites formed in the American Midwest by roughly 300 B.C.E.; coastal villages formed in British Columbia and southeastern Alaska, with evidence of plank houses, by 200 B.C.E.; and the villages of the Adena people, as affiliated with burial mounds and earthwork, which were formed in Ohio, Kentucky, and West Virginia between 1000 B.C.E. and 200 C.E.

Village life based on agriculture featuring intensive irrigation appeared quite suddenly in the southwestern United States around 300 B.C.E., as immigrants from Mexico established a Hohokam culture settlement in the Gila River valley at Snaketown, in southern Arizona. These people grew maize, beans, and squash and watered their crops by means of extensive canals. Early Hohokam houses were almost square, measuring 10 to 15 feet per side, and were loosely grouped together. The population of Snaketown is thought to have been about 100.

Neighboring Anasazi and Mogollon cultures also seem to have shifted from hunting and gathering to more sedentary modes of living. The establishment of pit-house villages and the production of pottery marked the transition of the Cochise in southeastern Arizona to the initial phase of the Mogollon tradition around 250 C.E. Early Mogollon villages were usually established at the ends of mesa tops, sometimes as high as 600 feet above the valley floor, at least in part for defensive reasons. One early Mogollon village referred to as the SU site had 28 houses; maize and squash were being cultivated, and some of the dwellings were of a significant size. The Anasazi of the region where New Mexico, Colorado, Arizona, and Utah meet represent a long-lived cultural tradition still extant today.

Many different settlement patterns occurred throughout Mesoamerica. Numerous villages featuring thatched-roof houses, as founded on improved maize productivity, rose during the Preclassic (ca. 1800 B.C.E.–ca. 150 C.E.) in the humid Pacific littoral of Guatemala and western El Salvador. Along the coast of the Gulf of Mexico the Olmec civilization (ca. 1500–ca. 400 B.C.E.) consisted of a series of towns and affiliated villages scattered across Mesoamerica as far as Honduras. Debate continues over the demographic identification of the primary Olmec sites of Tres Zapotes, San Lorenzo, and La Venta, all of which bear evidence of both ceremonial priorities and more advanced urban characteristics; some scholars claim these settlements as early cities. The Maya territory at this point in time comprised numerous towns and villages. The region around contemporary Guatemala City was characterized by a distribution of villages in relation to a large central town called Kaminaljuyú, which was believed to feature a core of several hundred temple mounds at its apex.

In South America evidence of maize cultivation and sedentism in Colombia and Ecuador occurs as early as 3200 B.C.E., and in Peru there is evidence of permanent village occupation at least as far back as 5000 B.C.E. at a site near the valley of the Chilca River. Analyses there have confirmed the existence of a permanent village of oval pit-houses apparently not founded on agriculture but on the efficient harvesting of the wild resources of the coast. By about 3000 B.C.E. Huaca Prieta, a modest fishing village on the north coast of Peru, had taken hold, with evidence there showing extraordinarily complex development of fiber arts. By about 2000 B.C.E. at least 100 villages like Huaca Prieta had been established along the Peruvian coast. Peruvian settlements with monumental architecture and more substantial population centers, indicating town-level development, include Caral, Asia, Salinas de Chao, El Paraíso, La Galgada, and Kotosh.

See also AGRICULTURE; ARCHITECTURE; BORDERS AND FRONTIERS; BUILDING TECHNIQUES AND MATERIALS; CITIES; CLIMATE AND GEOGRAPHY; CRAFTS; DEATH AND BURIAL PRACTICES; ECONOMY; FAMILY; GOVERNMENT ORGANIZATION; HEALTH AND DISEASE; HUNTING, FISHING, AND GATHERING; INVENTIONS; METALLURGY; MIGRATION AND POPULATION MOVEMENTS; MINING, QUARRYING, AND SALT MAKING; NOMADIC AND PASTORAL SOCIETIES; SACRED SITES; SETTLEMENT PATTERNS; SOCIAL ORGANIZATION; STORAGE AND PRESERVATION; TRADE AND EXCHANGE; TRANSPORTATION.

FURTHER READING
James C. Anderson, *Roman Architecture and Society* (Baltimore, Md.: Johns Hopkins University Press, 2002).
Norman Bancroft-Hunt, *Historical Atlas of Ancient America* (New York: Checkmark Books, 2001).
Gwendolyn Leick, *Mesopotamia: The Invention of the City* (London: Penguin, 2003).
Susan Keech McIntosh and Roderick J. McIntosh, "Jenne-jeno, an Ancient African City." Available online. URL: http://www.ruf.rice.edu/~anth/arch/brochure/. Downloaded on August 7, 2007.
Oswyn Murray and Simon Price, eds., *The Greek City from Homer to Alexander* (Oxford, U.K.: Oxford University Press, 1990).
Marc Van de Mieroop, *The Ancient Mesopotamian City* (Oxford: Clarendon Press, 1997).
J. B. Ward-Perkins, *Cities of Ancient Greek and Italy: Planning in Classical Antiquity* (New York: George Braziller, 1974).

▶ trade and exchange

INTRODUCTION

Systems of trade and exchange in the ancient world required first that civilizations had desirable goods to trade, goods that were otherwise unavailable to the trading partner. With the advent of agriculture and the rapid shift from nomadic hunting and gathering to more settled, permanent communities, most trade involved agricultural goods. Thus, as towns and cities emerged, those communities traded with outlying agricultural areas for food and other agricultural products like wool. In exchange, they provided desirable goods produced by craftspeople, including tools, leatherwork, pottery, rope, and numerous other items that would be useful in a rural agricultural community.

Later, other types of goods were commonly traded, particularly after the discovery of metals. First copper, then bronze (a copper-tin alloy), and finally iron became the basis of trade and exchange in many parts of the world. Economic activity was by no means limited to farm products and metalwork. In time, a wide range of commodities were traded, including glass and glasswork, jewelry, gold and silver objects, minerals, perfumes, dyes, silks, amber, oils such as olive oil, salt, herbs and spices, lumber, furniture, decorative objects, and many other types of goods.

Usually, the basis for trade was little different from its basis in modern life. One civilization discovered that it had resources that other civilizations wanted or that its craftsmen had developed a particular genius for producing certain types of goods. Thus, for example, Lebanon discovered that its cedar trees were in great demand because the lumber is easily worked and cedar's natural oils made the wood resistant to insects and decay. This natural resource became the foundation of Lebanese trade with other nations around the Mediterranean Sea. Ancient India had the resources and skills necessary for textile production, so its textiles were highly prized.

In addition to desirable goods, trade and exchange required trade routes and modes of transportation. The two choices, of course, were land routes and sea routes. Trade and exchange by land became more extensive after the domestication of pack animals. Caravans carried goods long distances, particularly in regions with broad grasslands, where transport was relatively easy and there was plenty of grass for pack animals to eat. In time, the ancient Romans constructed a vast network of roads connecting the imperial capital with its colonies, and the Chinese created a road network, often referred to as the Silk Road, connecting China with India, the Near East, and eventually Rome. As shipbuilding technologies became more advanced, nations that bordered the sea were able to maintain vigorous trade relationships both with their colonies and with other nations. In this respect, the ancient Greeks led the way, followed by the Romans and Chinese.

Trade and exchange involved more than just the exchange of goods. Trade and exchange played a major role in the diffusion of knowledge and ideas, as cultures made contact with one another through their business relationships and road networks enabled people to travel. Moreover, the wealth provided by trade and exchange led directly to some of the world's great civilizations, as bustling cities developed to support economic activity from all over the known world.

AFRICA

BY MICHAEL J. O'NEAL

Many ancient African societies engaged in trade, and some thrived on it. This was particularly the case in the northern sectors of the continent, where large settled communities developed earlier than they did in the southern half of the continent, where many groups still lived as wandering hunter-gatherers or herders. As settled communities grew, the people in them produced goods—food, metalwork, leather, glasswork, and numerous other things—they could trade with other communities far and near, and a number of kingdoms became crossroads for trade and exchange. These trading networks were a source not only of goods that were unavailable locally but also of tax revenues for kingdoms and their rulers.

One of the most vigorous trading communities was the region known as Nubia, just south of the Egyptian Empire. Nubia acted as a major crossroad for people from Egypt, the Near East, southern Africa, and later Rome, India, and the Byzantine Empire. The first civilization that developed in Nubia was the kingdom of Kush, which became a major center for trade. Goods from the southern part of Africa, including gold, ebony, ivory, exotic animals, and slaves, passed through Kush on the way to points north.

Throughout its history, though, Kush was unstable; the Kushites had to move their capital city on two occasions. Eventually an invasion by the Assyrians severely weakened Kush, and in about 350 B.C.E. the kingdom of Kush came to an end, giving way to the kingdom of Axum to the east. The Axumites occupied the highlands of Ethiopia near the Red Sea, along with parts of modern-day northern Ethiopia, Eritrea, Yemen, southern Saudi Arabia, northern Somalia, Djibouti, and northern Sudan. Axum was a mixture of indigenous Kushite people and immigrants from the southern Arabian Peninsula who had migrated to the region in about 500 B.C.E.

Like Kush, Axum derived its power from trade, primarily in such commodities as silk, spices, ivory, tortoiseshell, rhinoceros horn, hippopotamus hides, monkeys, gold, silver, cloaks and other garments, obsidian, spices, agricultural products, sugarcane, emeralds, salt, and slaves. The kingdom became immensely wealthy, and with a powerful navy on the Nile River and the Red Sea was able to extend its imperial power by establishing trading colonies throughout the region in the early decades of the Common Era. To foster trade, the Axumites developed a system of roads maintained and protected by the state. Also used for transportation and trade were riverbeds during the dry seasons and reed boats for carrying goods on lakes. Axum remained a major trading power until the rise of Islam in the seventh and eighth centuries C.E.

Among imported goods, both those from other nations and those that circulated within Axum itself, were iron, bronze, glasswork, ceramics, wood, leather, and livestock. While the bulk of Axumite trade was internal, with city centers trading manufactured goods for agricultural products from the countryside, much also was international. Most imported goods appear to have been luxury items for the elite. These goods had to pass through customs posts, where taxes were paid. Sometimes these taxes were in the form of coinage, but usually they were paid in kind—that is, a portion of the goods themselves were paid as taxes. These taxes were an important source of Axumite wealth.

One of the most important trade routes of ancient Africa ran in an east–west direction just south of the Sahara. This band, called the Sahel, was home to numerous cities and settlements that made their living primarily through trade. Goods from the east and from the Mediterranean area passed through the Sahel on the way to points south, where they were traded for African goods such as ivory and precious metals. One of these settlements was Jenne-jeno in Sudan in the upper Niger River delta. Beginning in about 200 B.C.E. Jenne-jeno actively engaged in trade. Artifacts found in the area show that the city imported goods from Greece and Rome. Along any trading route, including that of the Sahel, towns and villages supported caravans of traders, providing them with food and water, forage for horses (and later camels), markets, and resting places. Goods probably changed hands at numerous points along these trade routes.

Carthage, founded on the northern coast of Africa (in modern-day Libya) in 814 B.C.E. by Phoenician traders from the city of Tyre in Lebanon, became one of the great trading civilizations of its time. The basis of Carthaginian power was its navy, which included as many as 350 warships that continuously patrolled the Mediterranean, primarily to keep trade routes open and to drive off competitors. Carthage also maintained a large fleet of merchant ships, each capable of carrying 100 tons of goods. Much of the empire's trade was based on the Iberian Peninsula (present-day Spain and Portugal), which had rich deposits of lead, silver, and tin ore. Tin was especially important because it was mixed with copper to make bronze, the key material for weapons, armor, and other vital implements. The Carthaginians also traded for tin with Britain and possibly the Canary Islands, giving Carthage a monopoly on the tin trade and therefore on bronze.

Besides Iberian silver, Carthage had access to silver mines in North Africa, providing a solid foundation for Carthaginian wealth. But perhaps the single most-valued commodity carried in Carthaginian ships was a dye called Tyrian purple. Painstakingly made in tiny amounts from the secretions of certain marine snails, this dye was so esteemed in the ancient world that a pound of it sometimes brought a price equal in value to 20 pounds of gold. Other important commodities included textiles (silk, wool, cotton), spices, perfumes, pottery, incense, glasswork, wood, bronze, alabaster, precious stones, plows, mirrors, cabinetry, household items (pillows and bedding, for example), slaves, horses, and weapons. Food commodities included fish and a range of agricultural products, such as wine, olives and olive oil, grapes, dates, nuts, and fruits. Much of Carthage's wealth came from brokering trade in these goods. Carthage's influence also spread southward with caravans sent deep into the continent to trade for ebony, ivory, salt, timber, gold, hides, and such animals as apes and peacocks. To the north they obtained amber from the Scandinavian countries. The Carthaginians' skills in storage, transportation, and buying and selling (they invented the auction) brought their empire wealth and power.

EGYPT

BY PANAGIOTIS I. M. KOUSOULIS

The broader Mediterranean region, which includes 25 nations today, witnessed the development of some of the most important and magnificent cultures of the past: ancient Egypt, Greece, and Rome. The Mediterranean Sea facilitated this development through cross-cultural exchanges, which took the form of diplomatic affairs, wars and treaties, social, religious, and artistic imports and exports, and, of course, trade.

Even in very early times Egypt had an extensive network of direct and indirect commercial and cultural contacts with foreign populations. Egyptian ships sailed across the Mediterranean probably as early as the Second Dynasty (ca. 2770–ca. 2649 B.C.E.), mainly to obtain raw materials. We can only estimate the size of such ships, although a cedar ship built

in the Fourth Dynasty (ca. 2575–ca. 2465 B.C.E.) was said to have been 100 cubits, or 172 feet, long. Excellent representations of ships from the royal expedition of Queen Hatshepsut (r. 1473–1458 B.C.E.) to the mysterious land of Punt (perhaps in modern-day Somalia) are recorded in wall carvings at Deir el-Bahri in southern Egypt.

The main Mediterranean shipping routes follow sea currents and winds that go northward and westward along the Levantine and Anatolian coasts to the Aegean and those that go southward and eastward from Crete to Libya and Egypt. Ancient navigators considered May to September the best time for sailing the Mediterranean and might put out to sea as early as March or as late as November, but in winter the risk of storms made seafaring too dangerous, and captains kept their ships in port. Trade goods included amphorae (large clay jars used in ancient times for storage and transport) and other containers, jugs, bowls, and vases in ceramic, stone, and glass, and figurines of various materials, especially including scarabs, the carved stone beetles that Egyptians regarded as talismans. Besides ordinary trade there was considerable exchange of precious materials and other valuable items as gifts between royal authorities and foreign parties for diplomatic purposes. Many clay tablets excavated at Amarna in southern Egypt preserve lists of goods sent by Near Eastern rulers to the pharaoh as gifts.

Numerous other official writings, inscriptions, and carvings testify to an extensive trade network both within Egypt and externally. Some record expeditions to desert mines and quarries; others describe journeys to barter for goods with foreigners. The Egyptian sources report all royally authorized expeditions in standardized accounts that are all more or less alike. They record the date, the mission that the king set for the leader, and the destination. The accounts usually end with a happy and successful homecoming.

For modern readers perhaps the most striking thing in these accounts is the lack of interest in trade for the sake of profit. The aim of the expedition leaders seems to have been solely to carry out the orders of their superiors or to follow the divine will of whichever deity protected their missions. Thus the description of Hatshepsut's expedition to Punt emphasizes the god Amon's desire for the products of that land. Similarly, the Twentieth Dynasty (ca. 1196–ca. 1070 B.C.E.) *Report of Wenamun* tells the story of an official who went abroad to obtain wood for building a boat to carry the sacred image of Amon. He had no interest in buying wood for any other purpose, and he had no means of making a profit through the expedition, since he had sent from Egypt only enough commodities to obtain what he needed for the boat.

Royal control over the trade economy, especially during periods of powerful pharaohs and strong central government, left no place for private merchants. Private traders appeared only in times of weak or nonexistent central government, such as during the First Intermediate Period (ca. 2134–ca. 2040 B.C.E.) and the Second Intermediate Period (ca. 1640–ca. 1532 B.C.E.) or after the New Kingdom (ca. 1550–ca. 1070 B.C.E.).

But evidence from tombs indicates that even in times of strong central control, semiorganized barter did exist, particularly along the banks of the Nile. The most commonly exchanged items in the tomb depictions are vegetables, fish, figs, drinks, and metal containers. It appears that people engaged in this kind of trade for the purpose of enriching their diet or their home furnishings, not for profit.

Another characteristic aspect of the trade economy in ancient Egypt was gift exchange. It existed in two forms: gifts from the king to the people or vice versa and diplomatic gifts or tributes from allies and other foreign parties to the pharaoh and the Egyptian state, especially during the Middle Kingdom (ca. 2040–ca. 1640 B.C.E.) and New Kingdom. Gifts from the Egyptian populace to the pharaoh were conceived as a tribute to both the divine and the political attributes of the king. The Egyptians offered the king precious objects and commodities in order to receive from him internal peace and stability. Thus, in the step pyramid of King Djoser (r. ca. 2630–ca. 2611 B.C.E.) at Saqqara—the first monumental structure constructed exclusively from stone—a large number of inscribed jars were found, attesting to the continued practice of giving gifts to the king. Similar cases of gift giving are recorded in account papyri from the mortuary temple of the king Sesostris II (r. ca. 1897–ca. 1878 B.C.E.) at el-Lahun and in historical texts from the New Kingdom.

Tomb paintings, especially from Thebes (in southern Egypt), show porters bearing tribute to the pharaoh from almost all points of the compass. Elephant tusks, logs of ebony, and leopard skins arrived from tropical Africa. Copper ingots, amphorae filled with incense and other goods, flasks, and elephant tusks were among the items of tribute brought by Syrians and sometimes by Cretans. The gift exchange was reciprocal. The king honored the offerings and repaid the donors with equally valuable items.

A diplomatic gift carried social and cultural connotations more than it did mere economic value. Foreign rulers offered diplomatic gifts to the pharaoh as proof of the continuation of existing alliances or to offer the prospect of new ones. The custom of the diplomatic gift reached its peak during the New Kingdom, when the foreign expeditions of the pharaohs led to a greater intensity of contact with foreign lands, from Libya in the west to Nubia (modern-day Ethiopia) in the south to the countries of the Near East. Foreign tribute often included precious items and commodities that could not be found in Egyptian territory, but, again, these were not economic transactions. They were diplomatic expressions that acclaimed the pharaoh as the major delineator of action on behalf of the Egyptian society and in a superior position to the foreign emissaries.

THE MIDDLE EAST

BY FRANS VAN KOPPEN

One view of the exchange of goods and services is as a primary function of a social group, but from another perspective trade is the voluntary exchange of commodities between two parties for no reason beyond the acquisition of those goods. The two basic forms of trade are regional or domestic trade and foreign or long-distance trade. Regional trade is the exchange of raw materials and finished products inside a community or within the same region, whereas foreign trade is the movement of goods between different ecological regions that is motivated by the uneven distribution of raw materials in the natural world. The mechanisms by which commodities were distributed in ancient societies depended on particular social customs, and not all modes of exchange can be described as trade. Foreign trade focuses on the material aspect of long-distance exchange and is often considered the extraction of necessities from the periphery for the benefit of the center. In the ancient world, however, foreign trade was a function of intense interregional contacts and an essential factor in the diffusion of cultural and technological innovations, without which civilization would not have been attained.

Written sources and archaeological finds shed light on the conduct of trade. Archaeology indicates that trade predates the invention of writing by many millennia, revealing, for example, that in the Neolithic Period (ca. 8000 B.C.E.) obsidian, a volcanic glass suitable for sharp tools, was used many hundreds of miles away from its Anatolian source. Not all commodities of trade, however, are accessible in the archaeological record, and the interpretation of what has survived is often ambiguous because factors other than long-distance trade (for example, booty or tribute) also can explain the presence of artifacts of foreign material or manufacture. Ancient texts offer more conclusive evidence—in particular, cuneiform records from Mesopotamia, an area that depended on foreign imports for many essential resources, such as metals, stone, or wood, and where innumerable archival records pertaining to trade and commerce have been preserved. The existence of these records places Mesopotamia at the center of the study of ancient trade.

Ancient Mesopotamia, Persia, and other ancient Near Eastern regions were characterized by high levels of functional diversification among the population and clearly defined urban and rural sectors. These complex societies required efficient exchange mechanisms to link producers with consumers. Movements of food, craft products, and raw materials in early societies can be classified as reciprocal, redistributive, and commercial forms of exchange. Reciprocal exchange typically occurred between producers and consumers within a community and was based on long-term relationships and patterns of reciprocal obligations. Redistribution describes the collection of goods by a central authority and their disbursal to others on the basis of social status or kinship. Redistributive patterns occurred within the household and lay behind the functioning of Mesopotamian institutions that amassed agricultural produce to allocate them in the form of rations to dependents. The collection of vital resources as tribute in the Assyrian and Persian empires of the

Gold bracelet or diadem, Phoenician, seventh to sixth century B.C.E., from the Phoenician trading center of Tharros, Sardinia; such jewelery, with its mixture of influences, demonstrates Phoenician connections across the Mediterranean. (© The Trustees of the British Museum)

first millennium B.C.E. also has redistributive features and had a negative effect on commercial long-distance trade.

Finally, domestic trade conformed to a commercial type of exchange, with strangers trading goods or services on a market in accordance with freely varying prices. Economic value was expressed in quantities of certain goods, particularly silver, a commodity that fulfilled in antiquity many of the functions of our money. Pairs of scales and stone weights to weigh silver accurately, as well as the skill of converting into foreign weight systems, belonged to the toolkit of every ancient trader. Buying and selling, however, were often done by barter, with several items agreed on as the countervalue in a transaction, an ensemble that may include amounts of silver. Prices and commodity values fluctuated and were subject to supply and demand, but they usually adhered to customary rates attributable to social norms rather than government interference or market price fixing. Commercial, redistributive, and reciprocal modes of exchange existed alongside one another, depending on social context or transaction type, but their relative importance varied from place to place and through time.

Sellers on the domestic market were the producers themselves. Potters, for example, produced for clients but also sold their stock in marketplaces or from their workshops. Another example is people who made their living from retail. This group includes shopkeepers and vendors, occasionally specializing in products like salt or victuals. On a different scale, a class of wealthy merchants organized bulk transports of goods and relied on commercial networks for acquisition and distribution of merchandise. Those enterprises usually were undertaken on behalf of the state, with merchants collecting and selling agricultural taxes due to the state and repaying the state in silver or other commodities. Merchants held various positions; often they were entrepreneurs who entered into contractual agreements to undertake these tasks, but at other times and places they were more like government employees.

Some of these merchants also participated in long-distance commerce, but others dedicated themselves exclusively to trade expeditions to faraway destinations, exporting products of Mesopotamian manufacture, like textiles, vegetable oils, and foodstuffs, and importing resources, such as metals, stone, wood, aromatics, and slaves. City-states like Old Assyrian Assur (ca. 1900 B.C.E.) prospered as a result of long-distance trade, and merchants typically yielded much more political influence than did merchants in territorial states. Foreign commerce was based on family firms, with the younger male members traveling abroad or residing in foreign trade colonies like Kanesh, the central Anatolian settlement of Old Assyrian traders who sold Iranian tin and Babylonian textiles against Anatolian silver. Foreign trade depended on favorable political relations, and arrangements for merchants often were included in diplomatic treaties. Substantial volumes of wares also traveled abroad as diplomatic gifts between allied rulers—for instance during the Amarna Age (14th century B.C.E.)—but this exchange cannot be defined as trade as such, given that upholding social relations was its main purpose. Nevertheless, commerce and diplomacy often worked well together because diplomatic envoys took care of their trade interests during missions abroad.

The natural landscape dictates how long-distance communications and trade are conducted. Rivers are easy arteries of transport, and the Euphrates has throughout the millennia been the main pathway between the Persian Gulf and the Mediterranean coast, carrying large volumes of commerce that enrich ports of trade centers along its banks. Maritime trade over the Persian Gulf was particularly important in the late third millennium B.C.E., when traders from Mesopotamia met their colleagues from the Indus Valley on the island of Bahrain (ancient Dilmun). The Syrian and Phoenician cities of the Mediterranean coast were renowned trading centers from which the famous ship found at Uluburun (off the Turkish coast) sailed in the 14th century B.C.E. and where colonies were founded, such as Carthage in the ninth century B.C.E. An important overland trade connected Mesopotamia through the Zagros Mountains with the Iranian highlands; the same route became known as the Silk Road once trade contacts with China had been established during the Roman period.

ASIA AND THE PACIFIC
BY KIRK H. BEETZ

Trade helped build nations in ancient Asia and the Pacific, carrying with it ideas and inventions and encouraging people to learn about distant lands. Among the Pacific islands, trade was carried out using wooden boats. Near the Asian mainland, manufactured goods from China, Japan, and Korea went to islands like Sumatra, Java, and Tonga in exchange for spices, exotic woods, and rare seashells.

On the Asian mainland the economic giants were China and India. For most of ancient times China tended to look inward for trade. During the Shang Dynasty (ca. 1500 to 1045 B.C.E.) the Chinese believed that the world did not extend much beyond their borders in any direction. They focused on agriculture around the Yellow River. Important factors in the expansion of the Shang view of the world were attacks from outside and the discovery and then importation of goods from areas beyond China's borders. The most significant imported goods were wood and rice from the south. Instead of striving just to build good relations with their trading partners, the Shang adopted a policy that would remain typical of China's foreign trading for thousands of years: They tried to conquer the people who had the goods the Shang desired, making those goods part of the Shang Dynasty and thus goods at the command of the Shang king.

The Shang Dynasty and the Zhou Dynasty that followed (1045 to 256 B.C.E.) absorbed through warfare the Yangtze

Steatite seals from the Indus Valley, dating to 2600 to 1900 B.C.E. and thought to have been used in trading with other nations and cultures (© The Trustees of the British Museum)

River region and its rich rice fields. During the Zhou Dynasty, transporting the South's agricultural products to the north, where the national capitals were to be found, became a severe problem. The great rivers of China were not entirely satisfactory for shipping food; their winding and occasional shifting courses made transportation slow and unreliable. The government started building canals by the 400s B.C.E. to aid the movement of goods across the nation, but the almost ceaseless warfare among the provinces of China disrupted those public works.

The western province of Qin gained an advantage when it built a canal connecting its major rivers. This had begun as a scam: An eloquent civil engineer had been dispatched by Qin's rivals to persuade the ruler of Qin to build the expensive canal, drawing resources from Qin's military. Even after he learned of the scam, the ruler was so convinced of the value of the canal that he continued its construction. As a result, Qin was able to transport goods faster than it could earlier, thus strengthening its economy so much that it became China's foremost economic and military power.

The Han Dynasty (202 B.C.E. to 220 C.E.) was aggressive in building up trade within its borders, and it continued the practice of invading nations that had goods it wanted, such as horses from the west. More than had previous dynasties, the Han Dynasty looked outward for trading opportunities. Most of its efforts focused on overland trade. At the cost of the lives of hundreds of thousands of Chinese soldiers, the Han pushed nomadic raiders out of the northwest and extended the Great Wall westward to protect the Silk Road—a network of routes that led to Persia and through Persia to the Mediterranean world. China exported silks, ceramics, and metals to Rome, which paid in gold. Further, the Chinese pioneered trade routes into India. Some of the Chinese explorers left written records of their travels through India. Silk made its way from China to India in exchange for gems such as diamonds as well as fragrant woods.

Not until roughly the 300s C.E. did China began trading in earnest by sea. Before then it had traded mostly with Japan, which exported its own high grade of silk and probably animal skins and ceramics to China in exchange for Chinese metals—especially copper coins, which became Japan's medium of exchange. Otherwise, Malaysian seafarers had conducted most of the sea trade between China and other southeastern lands. The Malaysians were heavily influenced by the Indians.

The first great Indian civilization, the Harappan (2600–1500 B.C.E.), was a trading empire. Although it was focused on the rivers of the Indus River valley, it established trading posts hundreds of miles away in central Asia and Iran to import lapis lazuli, tin, and bronze, sending out copper, gems, and grain. The Sumerians dealt extensively with the Harappans, and archaeologists have found numerous Harappan artifacts at Mesopotamian sites. How much the trade influenced Harappans is a matter of much disagreement among archaeologists, but it is possible that the political organization of Harappan cities imitated that of the Sumerians.

Much of later Indian history focuses on the spread of Aryan nomads and their Vedic culture southward through India. These nomads were a warrior people who put great store in military honor and the conquest of rival nations, yet much of southern India developed nations because of trade, not war. The peoples of southern India conducted a lively trade with each other before, during, and after the rise and fall of the Maurya Empire of about 321–185 B.C.E. and the Gupta Empire of 320–499 C.E.

The Indians of the interior formed caravans of wagons carrying goods not only produced in their own regions but also imported from other lands, thus bearing Chinese silks westward and Roman pottery eastward. The wagons transported muslin, saffron, ivory, agate, diamonds, pearls, ebony, and teak across roads to seaports. Governments arose to regulate the trade and maintain the roads. Leaders called Shatavahanas, whom historians consider somewhat mysterious figures, arose to foster trade and lead disparate peoples who organized themselves into trading nations.

India became a great generator of wealth for the Old World, trading with Africa, Rome, Persia, China, southeastern Asia, and the Indonesian islands. They established trading centers on the Malaysian peninsula, bringing their culture with them. In Indochina, the kingdom of Funan emerged as a trading nation that may have been similar to those of India. According to Chinese records, Funan was cofounded by an Indian trader.

Along India's western and eastern coasts arose trading cities. The ancient Romans sailed through the Indian Ocean to establish trading centers on the western coast, and these centers thrived for hundreds of years. In about 170 C.E. the Roman Empire suffered a recession so severe that Indians suffered economically and the Shatavahanas withdrew their trade from the west coast. To the east trade continued to thrive, with Indians opening trade with the regions of present-day Thailand and Burma, overland and by sea.

Sri Lanka, a large island in Mare Erythraeum (the present-day Indian Ocean) off the southeastern tip of India, was a way station for explorers, travels, and traders from Europe, Africa, the Near East, India, Malaysia, Indochina, Sumatra, Java, and China. From the 200s B.C.E. to the 1200s C.E. Sri Lanka was ruled by the Sinhalese kingdom.

The Sinhalese kingdom became rich from charging fees to the traders whose ships stopped in its ports. Government officials managed port facilities and docks efficiently. Ports teemed with trading fleets from Rome, Axum, Arabia, Persia, India, and Malaysia. The docks and city streets were a colorful mix of the national garb of dozens of different lands. The visitors mixed with pious monks and local people selling their wares. Especially popular were the bountiful agricultural products of Sri Lanka, such as coconuts, bananas, mangos, passion fruit, papayas, oranges, and tamarinds. The exotic flavors of those fruits would have been welcomed by travelers after weeks at sea. In addition to fruits, the Sinhalese sold rice, sugarcane, and cotton. Thanks to an irrigation sys-

tem of 200 miles of canals, they had three harvests of rice per year. The Sinhalese were skilled water engineers who could build irrigation canals with only 6-inch rises per mile, and they knew the world was spherical and offered expert navigation skills to trading vessels.

EUROPE
BY FRANCESCO MENOTTI

Trade and exchange systems of the past have always been an important focus of research in archaeology. Studying trade and exchange can be difficult, however, especially within preliterate societies. In fact, scholars have available only what those societies left behind and time has preserved, such as archaeological artifacts. But useful information can be extrapolated from those seemingly useless remains. For instance, the materials from which artifacts are made can play a crucial role in identifying the movement of goods and reconstructing ancient exchange networks. Numerous methods of analysis have been developed to recognize and determine the origins of specific materials (stones, shells, metals, and so on) and to reconstruct production and distribution as well as the exchange system organization. Such analysis focuses on the various mechanisms of distribution that characterized ancient trade networks, from direct access to goods to down-the-line trade and eventually to a fully developed port of trade.

Beyond the simple economic value of traded goods, the meaning of exchange systems is also important. For example, in some instances symbolic elements might be predominant over other, more logical aspects. Circulation of ideas and communication of information imbedded in people's social behavior are therefore vital in understanding social contacts. To understand trade and exchange systems in prehistoric Europe, first it is necessary to divide the geographical area into conventional archaeological periods: Mesolithic (ca. 8000–4000 B.C.E.), Neolithic (ca. 7000–ca. 2000 B.C.E.), Bronze Age (ca. 2800–ca. 700 B.C.E.), Iron Age (ca. 1000–ca. 500 B.C.E.), and Roman times (ca. 400 B.C.E.–476 C.E.). Note that the dates provided apply to only the European continent as a whole and vary according to latitude and longitude.

Although it is flimsy and localized, evidence of trade and exchange in Europe does exist from the Mesolithic. The Mesolithic is an important transitional period in Europe, during which hunter-gatherer communities underwent significant changes in technology, economy, and social organization. The constantly changing environment triggered a steady development in tool technology, passing from bone and antler tools and the microlith (blade) industry common in the early Mesolithic to the various kinds of axes (first unpolished and then polished) in the later part of the period. In fact, the scarce availability of primary sources of raw materials in some areas was the primary factor initiating mobility, social interaction, and exchange systems. Despite evidence of material circulation on vast territories (obsidian in southeastern Europe and

Luxury imports from Italy, Rome, and the Near East, found at Hertfordshire, England, and dating to the Iron Age (20 B.C.E.–50 C.E.) (© The Trustees of the British Museum)

flint in northern areas), the exchange system was probably based on simple down-the-line trade involving balanced reciprocity. An event that changed Europe forever was the beginning of agriculture toward the end of the Mesolithic.

The first phase of agriculture diffusion occurred in a southwest–northwest direction, following the core–periphery model. Agriculture certainly brought changes in subsistence and the economy, but most significant was the social transformation. Another important event that took place in the late Neolithic was the discovery of copper. All this undoubtedly influenced social interaction and exchange systems. The quantity of traded goods increased, and some of them were seen as a way to gain social status. Significant movements of goods took place in the Mediterranean (obsidian); as far north as the Balkans (*Spondylus* shell); and in central, northern, and western Europe (axes, such as the Langdale ax in Britain and the Plussulien ax in France). Although organized long-distance trade was yet to develop, goods (especially nonperishable items) were circulated over vast distances through a system referred to as down-the-line trade. Food and other perishable materials were exchanged within much smaller areas.

Toward the end of the Neolithic, prehistoric Europe once again underwent a revolution brought about by a technological advance: metal alloying. At the beginning of the Bronze Age most artifacts, tools, and weaponry were made of bronze,

a copper and tin alloy. Consequently, exchange systems became linked to the desirability and accessibility of that metal (one of the main centers of bronze production and distribution was the Carpathian Basin). Further developments in transportation, on both water and land facilitated the consolidation of established long-distance trade networks. Although trade links over long distances were already present in the Neolithic Period, it is only in the Bronze Age that archaeological records show the presence of long-distance trade routes linking north to south and east to west. All sorts of goods—including axes, swords, and pottery—were traded over these networks, but some of the longest and oldest long-distance trade routes were the amber routes in the Baltic and Mediterranean regions.

Trade routes rarely stayed the same but changed directions through space and time. Thorough analyses of archaeological records show the kinds of events (socioeconomic and political instability, migrations, wars, and so on) that caused them. Exchange mechanisms improved considerably in the Neolithic. The down-the-line system still prevailed, but the first ports of trade started to appear, especially in the Mediterranean (for example, Gadir in Spain). Coinage was not yet in use, but certain categories of artifacts definitely operated as barter tokens. The later part of the Bronze Age was characterized by a new change in social context. The appearance of hill forts, flat cemeteries, and field systems suggest a more unstable and less ordered society, a social framework that would typify the next archaeological period: the Iron Age.

The parallel expansions of the Phoenicians and Greeks in the Mediterranean and that of the Romans in continental Europe later, undoubtedly played a crucial role in the formation of important trade networks in Iron Age Europe. Barbarian societies at the edge of the advancing powers reacted in different ways to the Mediterranean expansion, but all were fascinated by the new and exotic traded goods (wine, olive oil, and luxury items). At the same time, however, Mediterranean societies were interested in continental goods, such as metals (of which iron was becoming more and more widespread), amber, and salt. The unstable equilibrium that characterized the European Iron Age, with hill forts and competition for social status in the north and fighting for supremacy in the Mediterranean, did not hinder the trade systems. In fact, more and more ports of trade were established throughout the continent as far as Scandinavia (among them, the various amber ports of trade located in northeastern Poland and Lithuania). It is well known that the Romans conquered Europe economically well before it did so politically. Paradoxically, it was the existing pre-empire trade that facilitated the Roman conquest of Iberia (present-day Spain) and Gaul (present-day France) in the first century B.C.E.

Trade and exchange between Rome and the barbarian world continued throughout the empire. A trade buffer zone had even developed just beyond the empire's borders. That area was of great economic and political importance to both the Romans and the barbarians, with ports of trade between the two worlds located there. The barbarians would obtain prestigious and valuable items from the Romans and in return would acquire everything the empire needed, including cheap labor in the form of slaves (especially from eastern and northeastern Europe). Sadly, slaves became the "items" the barbarians most often exported to the Roman world during the empire's heyday.

The fall of Rome and the subsequent Nordic southward migrations created a period of serious instability within Europe's trading networks, but trade experienced no regression. In fact, some trade centers experienced further development and would become important emporia in early medieval times; examples are Lundeborg and Gudme in Denmark. Despite sociopolitical insecurity and massive migrations of peoples, goods continued to be moved all over Europe and beyond, linking even the most remote regions of the northeast in increasingly solid and sophisticated trade networks.

GREECE

by Edward M. W. A. Rowlands

From prehistoric times the Greeks were able to gain access to markets beyond their shores. By the sixth century B.C.E. Greek city-states had established colonies throughout the Mediterranean and into the Black Sea; this protected access to important goods such as grain, wood, and silver. Concurrently, coins developed into a popular means of exchange. In sharp contrast was the city of Sparta, which disapproved of trade and lived on the produce of its occupied territories. By 323 B.C.E. Alexander the Great from Macedon had conquered the Persian Empire, and on his death Greece became part of one of several Hellenistic kingdoms. The Hellenistic Period, and the later Roman dominance of the Mediterranean, opened up larger markets to the Greeks, but the economic power and influence of the Greek city-states were lost forever.

At Grave Circle A—a circle of six graves in Mycenae dating to the beginning of the Late Bronze Age—finds show that by 1600 B.C.E. people in the Peloponnese could import not only golden jewelry from Crete and the Aegean but also amber from as far as the Baltic Sea. At that time Greece and the surrounding islands were tied into European and Mediterranean trade networks. As a result, the powerful militaristic peoples known as the Mycenaeans were able to establish kingdoms throughout Greece, Crete, and the Aegean Islands. By controlling access to the items traded and through patronage of traded goods, the Mycenaean leadership could keep control over the elite of the kingdom.

Over the coming centuries the Greeks were to sail far and wide across the Mediterranean and into the Black Sea. Colonies were founded from the island of Sicily in the west to Crimea, in modern-day Ukraine, to the east. Through their colonies, trade centers like Athens, Thebes, Corinth, and Argos gained access to markets previously out of their reach. The Greeks imported goods such as wood, slaves, gold, silver, copper, and tin in exchange for products like wine, pottery, and olive oil. This trade increased the power of the trading centers, enabling them to monopolize production from their colonies and establishing them as powerful metropolises within their regions.

Most of the written evidence about trade and exchange that is available to modern classicists is from Athens. The city of Athens rose to serious power during the fifth century B.C.E. Western civilization has benefited from the art, drama, philosophy, and democracy developed at the height of the Athenian empire. Those developments were possible only because Athens, as a great sea power, could protect trade routes and colonies from attack. By the fifth century B.C.E. Athens had grown into a large city, and its surrounding territory of Attica could not supply enough grain to keep all Athenians alive. It was therefore imperative to maintain a route through the Bosporus and into the Black Sea, where large amounts of grain could be accessed. According to the Athenian statesman Demosthenes, in the fourth century from the Crimea alone Athens was importing 400,000 medimnoi a year, which in modern terms is equivalent to millions of gallons of grain. Athenian legislation was also written to make sure that grain produced in Attica could not be exported and that all grain coming into the port of Piraeus had to be sold in Attica.

Coinage came to Greece in the sixth century B.C.E. from cities situated on the coast of modern-day Turkey. It

Early Mediterranean Trade Routes

Ancient Greek trading routes extended throughout the Mediterranean.

© Infobase Publishing

Legend:
— Main Phoenician routes
- - - Main Greek routes
-·-·- Main connecting routes

0   400 miles
0   400 km

N

ATLANTIC OCEAN

Bay of Biscay

SCYTHIA

Tanais

Sea of Azov

Black Sea

Trapezus

Sinope

Heraklea

Istrus

Byzantium

Chalcedon

Bosporus

Propontis

Hellespont

Troy

LYDIA

Phocaea

Smyrna

Ephesos

Aegean Sea

Thera

Knossos

Crete

Al Mina

Posidium

Byblos

Tyre

Sidon

Gaza

Jerusalem

SINAI

Red Sea

Soli

CILICIA

Side

Salamis

Cyprus

Kition

Rhodes

Naukratis

Memphis

Nile R.

Halys R.

Tyras

Odessa

Apollonia

THRACE

Bug R.

(Dniester)

Olbia

Tyras R.

(Danube)

Ister R.

Drarus R.

Savus R.

ILLYRIA

Epidamnos

Epidaurum

MACEDON

GREECE

Corcyra

Corinth

Athens

Sparta

Ionian Sea

Rhegium

Syracuse

Sicily

Zancle

Segesta

Croton

Taras

MAGNA GRAECIA

Neapolis

Cumae

Rome

Hadria

Adriatic Sea

TYRRHENIA

Padus R.

Corsica

Sardinia

Cagliari

Mediterranean Sea

Malta

Leptis Magna

Sabratha

SAHARA DESERT

Leptis Minor

AFRICA

NUMIDIA

Carthage

Utica

Hippo Regius

Cyrene

LIGURIA

Nicaea

Massalia

Rhodanus R.

Liger R.

Emporiae

Balearic Is.

Tarraco

Iberus R.

Saguntum

Carthago Nova

IBERIA

Anas R.

Baetis R.

Malaca

Gades

Pillars of Hercules

Lixus

ATLAS MTS.

became common for coins to be made of silver and for Greek city-states to monopolize their formation. The Athenian historian Xenophon wrote in the fourth century B.C.E. that his city was assured of trade because of its good supply of silver coins, the result of the Athenian-controlled silver mines at Laurium in Attica. Coins gave city-states a valuable way to exchange goods within Greece and for great distances beyond its shores.

Port markets (*emporia*) and marketplaces (*agora*) served as locations for trade with people from other cities. The prosperity of some of these markets, especially in Athens and Corinth, increased significantly as trade between Greek cities and overseas nations increased. In the marketplace foreigners often had to pay a tax just for purchasing goods. City-states could also collect a duty on the cargo of ships with access to their ports. Written evidence at Athens shows that it taxed the value of vessels going through the Piraeus. Although trade between short distances was possible over land, the mountainous topography of Greece usually necessitated long-distance travel by ship. Toward the end of the Peloponnesian War in 413 B.C.E., Athens further exploited trade being carried out in the Aegean by imposing a 5 percent duty on all the ports within the empire.

A noticeable contrast to Athens is apparent in the city of Sparta. In the seventh century B.C.E. Sparta conquered the territory of Messenia and enslaved the entire population, turning them into what were called helots. Messenia was a fertile territory that provided Sparta with food supplies and a workforce of helots. A deeply militaristic society, Sparta was against the accumulation of personal wealth. Its military domination of Messenia meant that it was not forced into trading with cities for grain and was able to pass laws forbidding its citizens to trade.

The activities of Alexander the Great (336–323 B.C.E.) were to have a major effect on Greek economic activity. After his death the empire he created, which stretched from Macedon to India, was split into several Hellenistic kingdoms. The Macedonian generals of Alexander then ruled territories from Egypt, Syria, Anatolia (modern-day Turkey), and Macedonia. Greece benefited because Greek became the international language of business. The use of common currencies and the production of roads fostered economic expansion not just in Greece but throughout what became known as the Greek world. Yet Greece would not become the most important part of the greater Greek-speaking world because cities like Alexandria in Egypt were to be the main centers of manufacturing and imports.

The Roman Empire came to control Greece after the battle of Pydna in 168 B.C.E. Rome became the unquestionable trading and economic power, placing Greece in a politically united Mediterranean. In the second century C.E. the Roman author Lucian describes how he saw, in the Greek port of Piraeus, a Roman grain ship that was 180 feet long and 45 feet across, and "the crew was like an army." Greek culture and technology influenced the beginnings of Ro-

man society, but its ports remained important for trading throughout Roman times.

ROME

BY CHRISTOPHER SMITH

Rome was superbly positioned from its beginnings to take advantage of regional trade and exchange. The city of Rome is situated on the banks of the Tiber River; as one sailed up from the Mediterranean, from the first crossing point and alongside the river ran one of the oldest roads in Italy, the Via Salaria, or "salt road," which linked the salt pans of the coast with the interior. Salt was a vital commodity in antiquity, owing to its preservative function.

Some of the earliest archaeological evidence for the urban development of the city comes from an area adjacent to Rome's earliest port, called the Forum Boarium, which was primarily a cattle market. As of the eighth century B.C.E. imported pottery is in evidence at this site, signifying cults that originated in the east. The most apparent is the cult of Hercules, from the Greek Herakles, which also shows Phoenician features. These artifacts demonstrate the early growth of trade links, with key connections being formed with the East. Indeed, Greek and Phoenician traders moved westward from the eighth century B.C.E. onward, bringing such unfamiliar and exotic materials as gold, silver, and ivory, which became indicators of high social status. The Romans also learned from the Greeks the formal customs of banqueting. The Etruscans, who occupied areas both north and south of Rome, were a crucial intermediary in this process of social development.

Alongside the development of such long-distance trade, vigorous and important regional trade was conducted. The hinterland of Rome, the region called Latium, was populated

The Crawford Cup, Roman, dating to the first to second century C.E. and found on the border between Syria and Turkey; this goblet was made of fluorspar, a relatively rare mineral that in the Roman period could be found only in the kingdom of Parthia (modern-day Iran). (© The Trustees of the British Museum)

by a number of settlements scattered across a moderately fertile plain. Exchange among these settlements and Rome was frequent and enshrined in the legal concept of *commercium*: the right of any Latin or inhabitant of Latium to own Roman land and to enter into a contract with a Roman. Every ninth day in Rome was designated as a market day (*nundina*), and these days were inscribed on the formal calendars listing the annual festivals and events, which were found distributed throughout central Italy. Other calendars simply indicate the market days and their locations. The existence of these calendars demonstrates the importance of regular local markets in the economy of central Italy.

Agriculture was at the core of most of the commercial activity in the ancient world, in terms of the short-range movement of produce; long-range transhumance—or the movement of animals, typically sheep, from summer upland pastures to winter lowland pastures—and the exploitation of animals as resources, especially in terms of meat and wool; and the long-range movement of some staples, notably grain, wine, and olive oil, across the Mediterranean. As the Roman Empire grew, Rome became involved in existing trade patterns and began to influence their development. To the east, the long-established Greek cities and the Hellenistic empires already boasted sophisticated networks of trade and exchange. To the west and north, key centers such as Marseilles, in modern-day France, and Carthage, in modern-day Tunis, were already present, but the Romans may have had a similar impact on Spain, Gaul, and Britain in the first century B.C.E. as the Greeks and Phoenicians had on Rome in the eighth century B.C.E., stimulating social and economic development. One characteristic feature of this development was urbanization, which altered economic relationships by creating centers of consumption that drew from hinterlands.

With regard to modes of transport, the sea was a crucial conduit, and Rome expended significant effort, most notably through the campaigns of Pompey in 67 B.C.E., to clear the sea of pirates. The physical evidence for maritime trade consists most notably of shipwrecks, which give important information about cargoes. Also, Rome constructed roads to facilitate the movement of armies and of goods across the empire, sometimes utilizing preexisting structures and at other times applying their engineering skills to construct new roads, such as in Britain.

In time, Rome became the greatest center of consumption of all. Rome's population rose to a million by the end of the first century B.C.E., and a substantial number expected a stable supply of food, some of which was provided by the state and subsequently by the emperor. The demand for food was increasingly satisfied by the Roman provinces; huge grain ships plied the route from Egypt to Rome, and at Ostia and Portus (first created by Claudius in 46 C.E., with substantial redevelopment by Trajan in 103 C.E.) new facilities were constructed to cope with disembarkation, storage, and distribution. Another physical sign of the relatively enormous level of consumption in Rome is Monte Testaccio, a hill close to the Tiber some 160 feet high, entirely composed of broken oil amphorae, or containers. (Unlike wine amphorae, oil amphorae could not be reused.) Most of these amphorae came from the province of Baetica, in southwestern Spain, in the second and third centuries C.E., and the hill comprises more than 50 million amphorae, in which over 1.5 billion gallons of oil were imported into the city.

Other items in demand included building materials and metals. Quarrying was a major enterprise, and like many such enterprises was increasingly an imperial monopoly. At Mons Claudianus, in Egypt, marble was quarried for use in imperial palaces from Rome to Split, in modern-day Croatia. In addition to the masses of workers, the quarrying required an entire support network, such as to provide security over the transport route. Once imperial authority broke down at the end of the empire, quarrying ceased. The level of extraction of metal resources achieved during the empire was not matched again until the Industrial Age; the opencast Roman gold mine at Las Médulas, in Spain, was about 1.8 miles in diameter, and lead and copper pollution from the Imperial Period is detectable in the Greenland ice cap.

Metal was in demand, largely for coinage. After the introduction of coinage in Rome around 300 B.C.E. money became the dominant means of exchange with respect to taxation, wages, rent, and credit, although agricultural products also remained significant. Coinage was important at every level of the economy and grew increasingly centralized, with local mints disappearing and local currencies being phased out in favor of a central Roman currency. That currency was therefore vulnerable to debasement and consequent inflation, which became a problem in the third century C.E.

One commodity without which much of the rest of trading activity would have been impossible was human beings. Slaves were bought and sold across the empire—the Greek island of Delos had a notable slave market—and they contributed enormously through their labor to the productivity of the empire. A ratio of one slave to every three free persons has been suggested for Italy during this era. Owing to the Roman custom of freeing slaves, some could achieve substantial commercial standing themselves; this phenomenon is vividly portrayed in Petronius's fictional account, from the first century C.E., of the freedman Trimalchio, who was a substantial landowner, had diverse trading interests, and lent money to others, on the basis of which he sustained a comically excessive lifestyle. Roughly contemporary documents from Puteoli depict a family descended from a slave who for three generations engaged in loans and banking in a wide variety of enterprises, including ones run by other freedmen.

Regarding the overall nature of the Roman economy, scholars have long debated the extent of the impact of trade on the society and economy of the Roman Empire. In general, wealth derived from land carried more positive overtones than wealth derived from commerce. Some senators were engaged in trade, and a substantial wealthy elite across the empire had a diversity of commercial interests. In relation to growth, Rome's demand for taxes from the provinces may have meant that provincial economies were obligated to grow or suffer. Regardless, growth remained gentle and regionally distinctive in the first two centuries C.E.

Toward the end of the empire, both change and continuity were represented. Inflation led to attempts at price control by the Roman emperor Diocletian, and changes were made to the taxation system, but the volume of trade remained strong. After the fall of the Western Roman Empire, goods were exchanged and peoples were transported at much lower rates, with lesser degrees of sophistication, and without the levels of central control that had characterized the Imperial Period. In the sixth century C.E. some 5,000 cargo ships sailed in the eastern Mediterranean, indicating both the continued significance of trade and exchange and the considerably greater activity during the Roman Empire across the Mediterranean.

THE AMERICAS
BY J. J. GEORGE

Trade is typically defined as a two-way exchange—the business of buying, selling, or bartering commodities—motivated by profit or need. In a true market system, trade would be at least partially divorced from social or political entanglements, and the value of the commodities would follow laws of supply and demand, unencumbered by legislation. Trading activities in the Americas, however, were varied and complex, sometimes encumbered with political and social obligations and sometimes more freewheeling.

Generally, archaeologists consider the presence of nonlocal objects at a site to be evidence of trade, although other systems of exchange existed, including reciprocity and tribute. Reciprocity implies a mutual exchange of privileges or goods, often with socially acceptable gifts exchanged on a roughly equal basis with the aim of establishing or solidifying social or political relationships. Tribute, on the other hand, was often a one-way exchange between a dominant overlord and a subject polity. The later Aztec Empire (15th and 16th centuries) provides the primary Mesoamerican model of tribute exchange: Conquered territories were forced to contribute substantial amounts of prized goods in return for assurance that they would not be decimated. Exchange in its broadest sense also included the flow of art styles, religion, ritual, ideas, and technology as part of cultural diffusion. Although this form of exchange was often unidirectional and flowed from the impulses of empire, expansion, and diffusion, it also could be a shared enterprise and a means by which disparate political and social entities were united.

Mesoamerican cultures relied almost entirely on human carriers to transport goods, limiting the range for perishable commodities and resulting in high transportation costs. The wheel was a known concept, but there is no evidence yet of its use in transportation. Transport of items such as foodstuffs was limited geographically and reinforced localized trade in those items. Longer-distance trade emphasized high-value,

low-weight luxury goods often classified as elite items. In turn, the people who controlled trade and trade routes often solidified elite status or rulership roles for themselves.

Common Mesoamerican trade items included ceramics, lithic material such as obsidian and chert, textiles, perishable tropical goods, precious stones, metals, and foodstuffs. During Mesoamerica's Formative or Preclassic Period (ca. 1800 B.C.E.–ca. 150 C.E.) chiefdoms at several sites—such as Olmec sites on the Gulf Coast, sites in the Valley of Oaxaca and Chalcatzingo in Morelos, and several sites in Chiapas—exchanged items like jadeite, obsidian tools, ceramic vessels, shell ornaments, and animal products. Obsidian is a particularly useful material to document trade systems because the absence of metal tools meant it was used extensively in toolmaking and thus was highly valued. Additionally, obsidian has few sources, and its trace element composition is distinct, making chemical sourcing possible and allowing researchers to track its distribution. Major obsidian sources include Pachuca in central Mexico and El Chayal and Ixtepeque in highland Guatemala. Obsidian from these sources was found throughout Mesoamerica.

Other examples of trade items include high-quality chert from Belize, used to make tools throughout the Mayan lowlands of northern Guatemala and Mexico's Yucatán Peninsula. Basalt, andesite, and granite were used to make grinding tools such as mortars and pestles; such volcanic material was unavailable locally to people in the Mayan lowlands and was transported in from the highlands. Textiles, a highly valued but perishable item, were also traded. Although few survive, especially from the dense, tropical lowlands, the tools from which they were made, such as spindle whorls, first show up along the Gulf Coast and later throughout Mesoamerica, suggesting some system of diffusion through trade. Perishable goods like precious feathers from the quetzal bird of Guatemala and jaguar pelts—both symbols of royalty—were distributed throughout Mesoamerica. Precious stones, whose value in part derives from limited natural distribution, rarity, and symbolic importance, were used to make fine jewelry. Jadeite from Costa Rica and Guatemala and turquoise from the southwestern North America found wide distribution throughout Mesoamerica, as evidenced in various grave caches. Foodstuffs were limited locally in most periods, although empires such as Teotihuacán (ca. 100–700 C.E.), had infrastructures substantial enough to obtain grains, maize, beans, and amaranth as tribute from greater distances.

Many North American societies up to and beyond 500 C.E. were of the hunter-gatherer type, which makes data difficult to obtain. Various forms of trade were known. One example is from the first millennium C.E., which was a kind of golden age for the Arctic Eskimo, an era that saw brilliant creativity in both arts and manufacturing, and the perfection of skills and equipment required to hunt diverse northern animals. These developments originated along the shores of the Bering Sea and the Bering Strait and spread eastward, suggesting both population diffusion and exchange systems. Because distances were often great and contact infrequent between societal territories, trade probably happened spontaneously. In other northern locations, however, trade occurred regularly between coastal and inland groups to obtain staples that their own environments did not offer. For example, during the Mesoamerican Classic Period (150–650 C.E.) sea mammal oil and blubber were traded by coastal peoples to interior peoples in exchange for furs of the caribou, fox, and wolverine. A basic form of this exchange tradition probably dates back several thousand years. A similar geographic exchange principle between interior and coast also was thought to exist in the southeastern region of North America.

In the Adena-Hopewell interaction sphere, centered in present-day Ohio with satellites spread throughout the greater Midwest, mound builders gathered periodically for funeral ceremonies and construction. Evidence suggests that some form of exchange occurred, even if it was only labor. Craft specialization, including pipes and polished stone artifacts, all highly transportable, offered prime opportunities for trade. Researchers have found a surprising concentration of Adena-style artifacts, such as stone tubes, Adena points, birdstones, gorgets, and shell and copper beads as far east as the Chesapeake Bay. Materials for Hopewell grave goods were brought in from great distances. Other traded items include obsidian from what is today Yellowstone Park in Wyoming, conch and turtle shell, shark and alligator teeth from Florida, mica and chlorite from North Carolina and Tennessee, bluish flint from Indiana, and chalcedony from North Dakota. While down-the-line, or intervillage, exchange systems may

have accounted for some of the imports, long-range trading or mining expeditions also seem to have been involved.

Evidence throughout the Andes region supports a tradition of long-distance trade. In the period of 2000–1500 B.C.E. trade between coastal Ecuador and Amazonia is supported by ceramic developments, figurine traditions, and the presence in coastal Ecuador of a type of coca indigenous to the Amazon regions. In Peru evidence of long-distance trade is found in a medicine man's outfit discovered near Lake Titicaca and dated to the fourth century B.C.E. The outfit is attributed to a type of traveling herbalist called a *callahuayas*, whose business was the long-distance transfer of goods and ideas. Remains of food, arts, and crafts at Chavín de Huántar, the center of the northern Peruvian Chavín culture (ca. 900–ca. 200 B.C.E.), indicate extensive outside relations, including a far-flung trade network presumably facilitated by llama trains. In one example, obsidian from Huancavelica, some 290 miles south, was found at Chavín de Huántar.

See also AGRICULTURE; BORDERS AND FRONTIERS; BUILDING TECHNIQUES AND MATERIALS; CALENDARS AND CLOCKS; CERAMICS AND POTTERY; CITIES; CRAFTS; ECONOMY; EMPIRES AND DYNASTIES; EMPLOYMENT AND LABOR; EXPLORATION; FOOD AND DIET; FOREIGNERS AND BARBARIANS; INVENTIONS; LANGUAGE; METALLURGY; MILITARY; MINING, QUARRYING, AND SALT MAKING; MONEY AND COINAGE; ROADS AND BRIDGES; SEAFARING AND NAVIGATION; SHIPS AND SHIPBUILDING; SLAVES AND SLAVERY; SOCIAL ORGANIZATION; STORAGE AND PRESERVATION; TEXTILES AND NEEDLEWORK; TRANSPORTATION; WEIGHTS AND MEASURES; WAR AND CONQUEST; WRITING.

Greece

∾ The Periplus of the Erythraean Sea: Travel and Trade in the Indian Ocean by a Merchant of the First Century, *excerpt (ca. first to third centuries C.E.)* ∾

1. Of the designated ports on the Erythraean Sea, and the market-towns around it, the first is the Egyptian port of Mussel Harbor. To those sailing down from that place, on the right hand, after eighteen hundred stadia, there is Berenice. The harbors of both are at the boundary of Egypt, and are bays opening from the Erythraean Sea.

2. On the right-hand coast next below Berenice is the country of the Berbers. Along the shore are the Fish-Eaters, living in scattered caves in the narrow valleys. Further inland are the Berbers, and beyond them the Wild-flesh-Eaters and Calf-Eaters, each tribe governed by its chief; and behind them, further inland, in the

country towards the west, there lies a city called Meroe.

3. Below the Calf-Eaters there is a little market-town on the shore after sailing about four thousand stadia from Berenice, called Ptolemais of the Hunts, from which the hunters started for the interior under the dynasty of the Ptolemies. This market-town has the true land-tortoise in small quantity; it is white and smaller in the shells. And here also is found a little ivory like that of Adulis. But the place has no harbor and is reached only by small boats.

4. Below Ptolemais of the Hunts, at a distance of about three thousand stadia, there is Adulis, a port

established by law, lying at the inner end of a bay that runs in toward the south. Before the harbor lies the so-called Mountain Island, about two hundred stadia seaward from the very head of the bay, with the shores of the mainland close to it on both sides. Ships bound for this port now anchor here because of attacks from the land. They used formerly to anchor at the very head of the bay, by an island called Diodorus, close to the shore, which could be reached on foot from the land; by which means the barbarous natives attacked the island. Opposite Mountain Island, on the mainland twenty stadia from shore, lies Adulis, a fair-sized village, from which there is a three-days' journey to Coloe, an inland town and the first market for ivory. From that place to the city of the people called Auxumites there is a five days' journey more; to that place all the ivory is brought from the country beyond the Nile through the district called Cyeneum, and thence to Adulis. Practically the whole number of elephants and rhinoceros that are killed live in the places inland, although at rare intervals they are hunted on the seacoast even near Adulis. Before the harbor of that market-town, out at sea on the right hand, there lie a great many little sandy islands called Alalaei, yielding tortoise-shell, which is brought to market there by the Fish-Eaters.

5. And about eight hundred stadia beyond there is another very deep bay, with a great mound of sand piled up at the right of the entrance; at the bottom of which the opsian stone is found, and this is the only place where it is produced. These places, from the Calf-Eaters to the other Berber country, are governed by Zoscales; who is miserly in his ways and always striving for more, but otherwise upright, and acquainted with Greek literature.

6. There are imported into these places, undressed cloth made in Egypt for the Berbers; robes from Arsinoe; cloaks of poor quality dyed in colors; double-fringed linen mantles; many articles of flint glass, and others of murrhine, made in Diospolis; and brass, which is used for ornament and in cut pieces instead of coin; sheets of soft copper, used for cooking-utensils and cut up for bracelets and anklets for the women; iron, which is made into spears used against the elephants and other wild beasts, and in their wars. Besides these, small axes are imported, and adzes and swords; copper drinking-cups, round and large; a little coin for those coming to the market; wine of Laodicea and Italy, not much; olive oil, not much; for the king, gold and silver plate made after the fashion of the country, and for clothing, military cloaks, and thin coats of skin, of no great value. Likewise from the district of Ariaca across this sea, there are imported Indian iron, and steel, and Indian cotton cloth; the broad cloth called monache and that called sagmatogene, and girdles, and coats of skin and mallow-colored cloth, and a few muslins, and colored lac. There are exported from these places ivory, and tortoiseshell and rhinoceros-horn. The most from Egypt is brought to this market from the month of January to September, that is, from Tybi to Thoth; but seasonably they put to sea about the month of September.

From: Wilfred H. Schoff, ed. and trans.,
The Periplus of the Erythraean Sea: Travel and Trade in the Indian Ocean by a Merchant of the First Century (London: Longmans, Green, and Co., 1912).

Rome

～ *Petronius Arbiter (ca. 27–66 C.E.), "The Banquet of Trimalchio," excerpt from the* Satyricon ～

"When I came here first [as a slave] from Asia, I was only as high as yonder candlestick, and I'd be measuring my height on it every day, and greasing my lips with lamp oil to bring out a bit of hair on my snout. Well, at last, to make a long story short, as it pleased the gods, I became master in the house, and as you see, I'm a chip off the same block. He [my master] made me coheir with Caesar, and I came into a royal fortune, but no one ever thinks he has enough. I was mad for trading, and to put it all in a nutshell, bought five ships, freighted them with wine—and wine was as good as coined money at that time—and sent them to Rome. You wouldn't believe it, every one of those ships was wrecked. In one day Neptune swallowed up 30,000,000 sesterces on me. D'ye think I lost heart? Not much! I took no notice of it, by Hercules! I got more ships

(continued)

(continues)

made, larger, better, and luckier; that no one might say I wasn't a plucky fellow. A big ship has big strength—that's plain! Well I freighted them with wine, bacon, beans, perfumes, and slaves. Here Fortuna (my consort) showed her devotion. She sold her jewelry and all her dresses, and gave me a hundred gold pieces—that's what my fortune grew from. What the gods ordain happens quickly. For on just one voyage I scooped in 10,000,000 sesterces and immediately started to redeem all the lands that used to be my master's. I built a house, bought some cattle to sell again—whatever I laid my hand to grew like a honeycomb. When I found myself richer than all the country round about was worth, in less than no time I gave up trading, and commenced lending money at interest to the freedmen. Upon my word, I was very near giving up business altogether, only an astrologer, who happened to come into our colony, dissuaded me.

And now I may as well tell you it all—I have thirty years, four months and two days to live, moreover I'm to fall in for an estate—that's prophecy anyway. If I'm so lucky as to be able to join my domains to Apulia, I'll say I've got on pretty well. Meanwhile under Mercury's fostering, I've built this house. Just a hut once, you know—now a regular temple! It has four dining rooms, twenty bedrooms, two marble porticoes, a set of cells upstairs, my own bedroom, a sitting room for this viper (my wife!) here, a very fine porter's room, and it holds guests to any amount. There are a lot of other things too that I'll show you by and by. Take my word for it, if you have a penny you're worth a penny, you are valued for just what you have. Yesterday your friend was a frog, he's a king today—that's the way it goes."

From: William Stearns Davis, ed.,
*Readings in Ancient History: Illustrative
Extracts from the Sources.* Vol. 2: *Rome
and the West* (Boston: Allyn and Bacon,
1912–1913).

FURTHER READING

Edward Bleiberg, "The Economy of Ancient Egypt," in *Civilizations of the Ancient Near East,* ed. Jack M. Sasson et al., vol. 3 (New York: Scribner, 1995): 1373–1385.

Erik H. Cline, *Sailing the Wine-Dark Sea: International Trade and the Late Bronze Age Aegean,* British Archaeological Reports 591 (Oxford, U.K.: Tempus Reparatum, 1994).

Barry W. Cunliffe, *Facing the Ocean: The Atlantic and Its Peoples* (Oxford, U.K.: Oxford University Press, 2001).

W. Vivian Davies and Louise Schofield, eds., *Egypt, the Aegean, and the Levant: Interconnections in the Second Millennium B.C.* (London: British Museum Press, 1995).

J. G. Dercksen, ed., *Trade and Finance in Ancient Mesopotamia: Proceedings of the First MOS Symposium, Leiden, the Netherlands, 1997* (Leiden, Netherlands: Nederland Instituut voor het Nabije Oosten, 1999).

Francis Healy and Chris Scarre, eds., *Trade and Exchange in Prehistoric Europe* (Oxford, U.K.: Oxbow Books, 1993).

Panagiotis Kousoulis and Magliveras Konstantinos, eds., *Moving across Borders: Foreign Relations, Religion, and Cultural Interactions in the Ancient Mediterranean,* Orientalia Lovaniensia Analecta 159 (Leuven, Belgium: Peeters, 2007).

W. F. Leemans, *Foreign Trade in the Old Babylonian Period as Revealed by Texts from Southern Mesopotamia* (Leiden, Netherlands: E. J. Brill, 1960).

David Mattingly and John Salmon, eds., *Economies beyond Agriculture in the Classical World* (London: Routledge, 2001).

Michael McCormick, *Origins of the European Economy: Communications and Commerce, A.D. 300–900* (Cambridge, U.K.: Cambridge University Press, 2001).

Helen Parkins and Christopher Smith, eds., *Trade, Traders, and the Ancient City* (London: Routledge, 1998).

J. N. Postgate, *Early Mesopotamia: Society and Economy at the Dawn of History* (London: Routledge, 1992).

Nicholas K. Rauh, *Merchants, Sailors, and Pirates in the Roman World* (Stroud, U.K.: Tempus Publishing, 2003).

Andrew Sherratt, *Economy and Society in Prehistoric Europe: Changing Perspectives* (Princeton, N.J.: University Press, 1997).

▶ transportation

INTRODUCTION

Means of transportation limited empires in what they could do or expanded their horizons. The first significant empire, the Akkadian Empire (ca. 2350–ca. 2100 B.C.E.) fell apart partly because it was too large for efficient communications among its far-flung parts using the roads and transportation of its time. Good, safe transportation became a matter of importance for many civilizations.

The invention of the wheel was a crucial innovation for transportation. The earliest record for a wheeled vehicle comes from Uruk in the Near East, from about 3500 B.C.E. The wheel probably was derived from the potter's wheel and, like a potter's wheel, was originally solid. The wheel was improved and modified over centuries, with each change making the wheel capable of surviving ever-longer distances and moving faster. Speed and durability enhanced long-distance trade, enriching many cultures, and allowed ideas and technology to travel farther faster.

The first known indication of the domestication of the horse comes from Ukraine and dates to about 3000 B.C.E. The domestication of the horse presented problems that ancient peoples did not fully overcome. Although oxen have big, prominent shoulders to press against heavy yokes, horses do not. The best solution to harnessing a horse probably came from China, where a breast strap was invented. This strip of leather stretched around the horse's chest. It restricted the horse's breathing and could compress arteries that brought blood to the horse's brain, which meant the horse was limited in the loads it could haul. This meant that while horses were great for speed, oxen remained in use, as they are still, for hauling heavy loads.

The movement of people and goods were important to ancient governments, and they often tried to regulate transportation. Some tried to do it all at once, as did the Qin Dynasty of China of (221–207 B.C.E.), regulating even the lengths of axles so that the ruts in roads would be evenly spaced and could be used by all carts. Others built up their regulations through many years of traditions, as in ancient India. Still others, like the Romans, imitated the regulations of other peoples. Each culture reflected its customs in its transportation. For instance, the Romans regarded pedestrian traffic to be essential to their way of life, and they therefore forbad produce carts in their cities during the day and built sidewalks of raised stone that forced wheeled vehicles to slow down, protecting pedestrians.

When thinking of pedestrians, it would be well to remember that although the developments in ancient transportation were exciting and sometimes led to dramatic change in the fortunes of civilizations, most people continued to walk. The ancient world was one in which people mostly carried their needs themselves. Even in the advanced culture of China's Han Dynasty (202–220 B.C.E.) road workers were expected to carry all their tools and food themselves, even to remote parts of the empire. Many people were too poor to afford to ride or even to have an animal pull their goods. In some parts of the world, the use of the wheel and beasts of burden came very late or not at all, as in much of the Americas and Pacific islands.

AFRICA

BY JUSTIN CORFIELD

Inland travel in Africa was regarded as particularly hazardous, and most early traders seem to have preferred traveling by boat. Many of the large settlements in North Africa (excluding those in Egypt) were consequently close to the coast. In sub-Saharan Africa there were also large settlements along rivers and around lakes, so it seems probable that vessels were constructed primarily for navigating rivers. Goods were clearly traded along the river Niger from an early date.

Horses were domesticated in the European steppes around 4000 B.C.E. and in Egypt by 3000 B.C.E., so it seems likely that the use of horses for transportation would have come to the rest of Africa through Egypt. The horses people initially used were much smaller than the modern domesticated horse and were better for pulling carts or chariots than carrying riders. The use of the larger cavalry horses came later, and their use quickly spread throughout North Africa

where the Carthaginians, Numidians, and others made extensive use of them for relaying messages. Horses or donkeys could be used as pack animals to carry people and important messages or to pull carriages or carts, which were made with solid wheels in Egypt and neighboring areas from at least 3000 B.C.E. Bullocks and oxen were also used for this purpose. The carts they pulled were large wooden ones; some had solid wooden wheels, while others had spoked wheels.

For long-distance travel across deserts and inhospitable terrain (as opposed to forest travel) caravan routes were fairly clearly defined. Camels were the principal beasts of burden in these conditions, and because their feet are sensitive, their escorts cleared paths through the stones that normally litter a desert. In this way routes were established. On shorter journeys where feed was available, horses and donkeys would be used. Oases, wells, and trading posts lay along these defined routes; for reasons of safety and security, these would be no more than one day's journey apart.

Crossing rivers was a task often solved by rafts guided by ropes. The Greek historian Polybius (ca. 200–ca. 118 B.C.E.) refers to the Carthaginians making rafts for their elephants to cross the river Rhône in Europe, and it seems likely that similar rafts would have been used to carry elephants, horses, wagons, people, and goods across rivers in North Africa.

Because the empires of Carthage and Rome were supported largely by slave labor, the used of manual labor for loading and unloading goods from ships would have been commonplace. For some vessels at small ports, it might also have been necessary to load things onto barges for transportation between the ship and its final destination or from the quay to the ship. Many items were transported in barrels, making it comparatively easy to roll them to their destination. Large numbers of slaves would have worked at the docks and in the mines and quarries around Carthage, and they would have carried tools, stones, and other materials by hand. The Carthaginians were well known for their use of elephants,

Petroglyph of camel and horse, from the Sahara Desert at Tassili, Algeria, North Africa (© Board of Regents of the University of Wisconsin System. Photographer: Jeanne Tabachnick)

and some could have been used for moving large amounts of stones or other items. Elephants also could have been used to help pull rafts across rivers.

An early method of transportation in the Sahara region was the chariot. Many pictures of chariots appear on wall paintings and on pots. They tend to indicate the prevalence of chariots along several established trade routes. One runs from Essaouira in Morocco through the deserts of modern-day Mauritania to Timbuktu. Another from the region around Edjele in southeastern Algeria also goes through to Mauritania and, halfway through, connects with another route that comes from the Al-Kufrah group of oases in southeastern Libya. Although these chariots are similar in all places—with horses pulling a chariot, often with semicircular sides, on which a person is standing—there have been doubts cast by historians about whether a chariot was a common method of transportation or merely a military vehicle or something for public entertainment, as in chariot racing.

Many people traveling together had to travel by foot. From the description of many North African towns of the period, it appears that people heading from one town to another would gather in the morning at a particular gate or market so they could cross the farmland or desert in a large company to inhibit assault or robbery. Bandits, violent peoples, and other problems often made traveling by foot hazardous, and it appears that there was little land contact between many of the sub-Saharan civilizations in the ancient world. This can be clearly seen through the transmission of technology such as the use of iron. The use of iron outside Egypt started in Nubia and progressed over many centuries down the east coast of Africa, missing many of the powerful inland kingdoms such as that of the Buganda in modern-day Uganda. As a result, knowledge of the technology traveled from Nubia to the coast of southern Africa far more quickly than the comparatively shorter distance to the kingdom of Buganda.

EGYPT

BY AMR KAMEL

Written and pictorial sources from as early as the Predynastic Period (ca. 5500–3100 B.C.E.) of Egypt record land and water transportation. Besides its obvious importance in everyday activities, transportation was deeply rooted in Egyptian religious ritual and beliefs, notably the solar cycle: The sun god, Ra, who was born in the east, sailed during the day across the "celestial wasters" (the sky) in his "day boat" before descending at sunset in the west into the hereafter and the womb of his mother, Nut. Then he sailed from west to east in his "night boat," to be reborn again at dawn.

Approaching the hereafter was a favorite theme of the Egyptians, who in their tomb art often represented this final journey as a boat ride that took the mummy from the Nile's east bank (the living world) to the west bank (the realm of the dead—the "Beautiful West," as Egyptian texts called it), where the gate to the hereafter waited to be entered.

Three factors especially affected the development of transportation throughout the history of ancient Egypt: trade, warfare, and mining and quarrying activities. The creation of an extensive network of routes and highways spanning the whole country facilitated not only the transportation of goods but also the movement of military forces, specifically along Egypt's southern frontier with Nubia and its northeastern one with the Near East. These routes included fortifications and way stations, which also formed part of a communications system. As for mining and quarrying, a government office established as early as the Third Dynasty (ca. 2649–ca. 2575 B.C.E.) and known as Masters of the Roads was responsible for coordinating and maintaining the land routes through the desert to quarries and mines. These roads required water stations and wells at regular intervals.

Besides these overland routes Egypt maintained a sea road into the eastern Mediterranean. From the inland port of Memphis large cargo ships descended a branch of the Nile to the sea, carrying trade goods or, in wartime, military supplies to Syria and Palestine. Because of the dominant influence of the Nile, water transportation played a much greater role in Egypt than in some other ancient civilizations. The Nile was the principal communication artery and provided the easiest and cheapest means of transportation. When population centers or other important areas lay distant from the Nile, the Egyptians linked them to the river by digging canals. Weni, a Sixth Dynasty (ca. 2323–ca. 2150 B.C.E.) administrator of the southern province (modern-day Aswān), mentioned a canal he built at the first cataract of the Nile to ease the movement of boats past these rapids. Presumably this was the same canal later cleaned by Sesostris III (r. ca. 1878–ca. 1841? B.C.E.) to facilitate his military campaign into Nubia. Necho II (r. 610–595 B.C.E.) dug a canal to connect the Nile with the Red Sea. This waterway was later maintained and deepened by the Persians and by the Ptolemaic pharaohs of the Greco-Roman Period (323 B.C.E.–395 C.E.). The Greek historian Herodotus remarked that two large ships could navigate the canal side by side.

The ancient Egyptians used boats and barges to carry people all along the Nile (or simply to ferry them across it) and to transport grain, cattle, and many other kinds of cargo. Water transportation linked the royal capital with all other cities and villages along length of the river. It aided in collecting grain or taxes from these places and transporting them to the central storehouses. River transport also figured prominently in religious festivals. During the famous Valley Feast, for example, statues of the god Amon; his consort, Mut; and their son, Knonsu, were carried in an elaborate boat procession from the Karnak temple down the river to Deir el-Bahri on the west bank to visit their ancestors. Art from private tombs at Thebes as well as textual evidence show that this festival was also an occasion for the public to cross the Nile and visit their relatives' tombs on the west bank. An echo of this custom still exists in present-day Egypt, where people celebrate certain feast days in cemeteries in which their relatives are buried.

Although many boats on the Nile were conducting official government business, apparently there were other craft operating for private profit. Texts from the New Kingdom (ca. 1550–1070 c.e.) mention lump-sum payments given to captains of these vessels as freight fees, part of which were portioned out among the crew at the captain's discretion. Literary sources regularly portray ferrymen as greedy and their fees as exorbitant. Even the goddess Isis had to give the ferryman Nemty a golden ring to see her son Horus in his competitions with his uncle Seth. In the Book of the Dead ferrymen make all sorts of excuses to the deceased about the unreadiness of their boats to cross the celestial river, presumably to extort higher pay. The New Kingdom writer Amenemope described the character of the evil person in a telling comparison: "He acts like the ferryman in knitting words: He goes forth and comes back arguing." Most of the mummies found in Egypt from the Greco-Roman Period gripped golden coins in their hands to pay the ferrymen in the hereafter.

The primary mode of land travel throughout ancient Egypt was by foot; even high government officials and armies normally traveled that way, as a set of model figures from the tomb of Mesheti at Assiut from the Eleventh Dynasty (ca. 2040–ca. 1991 b.c.e.) reveals. Art from temples and tombs shows ancient Egyptians walking in funerals, in holy processions during festivals, and the like, in which the distance involved was relatively short, but for many centuries there was no alternative to walking for long land journeys as well.

Donkeys have been the principal beasts of burden in Egypt from prehistory to the present. Art at Deir el-Medina shows donkeys carrying water, wood, grain, straw, hay, dung, and in one case an offering to a goddess up steep paths from the riverbank. No depictions survive from ancient Egypt of people riding donkeys as their descendants do in modern-day Egypt, although one scene preserved on an Old Kingdom (ca. 2575–2134 b.c.e.) tomb at Saqqara shows the tomb's owner supervising his farm activities while riding in a litter borne by donkeys.

Several texts describe caravans of donkeys used for long-distance overland transport. The biography of Harkhuf, a Sixth Dynasty caravan leader, reports that he returned from one of his many trips to Nubia with 300 donkeys laden with all sorts of trade goods. Sabni, Harkhuf's contemporary, mentions using 100 donkeys in his mission to the south to recover the body of his father, who had been murdered there.

Wheeled vehicles apparently originated in Sumer during the early fourth millennium b.c.e. and were later adopted by the Egyptians. The earliest example, from the New Kingdom, is a gold model of a four-wheeled wagon carrying a boat. Although it is unclear whether the model is realistic or merely symbolic, heavy wagons must obviously have existed in order for it to be made at all. Scenes of Ramses II (r. ca. 1290–ca. 1224 b.c.e.) at the battle of Kadesh show an ox-drawn wagon, presumably being used to transport supplies needed on the battlefield.

Horses and the light horse-drawn chariots were introduced to Egypt from the ancient Near East around 1700 b.c.e.

as a means of transportation and quickly became invaluable military resources. New Kingdom texts and pictures indicate that kings and nobles used horses for riding and to draw chariots for travel and in hunting expeditions in the desert. However, horseback riding apparently was not greatly favored by the Egyptians.

The animal that many people automatically associate with desert transportation, the camel, was a relative latecomer to Egypt. Domesticated centuries earlier in the Near East, the single-humped camel or dromedary came into widespread use in Egypt during the Greco-Roman Period. Able to carry about five times as much as a donkey and to travel for extended periods without water, camels became invaluable for the long-distance transport of both riders and trade goods across the Egyptian deserts.

THE MIDDLE EAST

BY KIRK H. BEETZ

In the ancient Near East early roads consisted of trails pounded flat by the feet of travelers over the course of centuries. Here, as elsewhere in the prehistoric world, for many thousands of years transportation simply meant people walking, carrying on their backs such loads as they could bear. The first pack animal (meaning an animal used to carry loads on its back) in the region was the donkey, which was domesticated in Africa or the Near East sometime before 3500 b.c.e. Oxen, domesticated in the same general timeframe as donkeys, were used mainly as draft animals, pulling plows and towing carts in farm fields. Although they were very strong, oxen were too slow to be of much use for long-distance hauling. The first Near Eastern vehicles for carrying cargo were probably sledges. A sledge is essentially a framework of wood on which loads are dragged across the ground. Early sledges were soon improved by adding runners, which significantly reduced the resistance met in pulling them. It is likely that the first wheeled vehicle was a modified sledge.

The peoples of Mesopotamia were not the only inventors of wheels: Wheeled toys have been found at ancient sites in the Americas. The Mesopotamian insight was to use wheels for transportation. The old notion that the idea for the wheel came from using logs as rollers for moving heavy objects, with the logs eventually wearing thin in the middle where the weight rolled over them, leaving wider "wheels" at the sides, is probably mistaken, because wheels cut horizontally out of tree trunks quickly fall apart. Solid wheels needed to be made from planks cut vertically from tree trunks. The actual inspiration for the wheel as transportation may have been the potter's wheel.

The first known depiction of a wheeled vehicle comes from the Sumerian city of Uruk (in what is now southern Iraq) and dates to around 3500 b.c.e. It shows a sledgelike body fitted with solid wheels. The wheels were made of three boards laid side by side and held together by two boards that crossed them on the inside of the wheel. They were fixed to axles, and the axle and wheels rotated as one unit. This made maneuvering difficult, but it still allowed two or more animals to pull together as a team and thus to haul much heavier loads than ever before. Wheeled vehicles quickly became vital to the growth of cities, to which supplies had to be carried from the countryside. By 3000 B.C.E. wheeled carts had become common.

Also around 3000 B.C.E. wheelwrights added rims to their wheels to reduce wear. At first they simply studded the outer edges of the wooden wheels with nails. This made the solid wheels more durable, but even heavier. In about 2000 B.C.E. rims made of bands of copper were introduced. At about the same time, people discovered that heated wood could be bent. This discovery led to the spoked wheel. The rim became a circle of bent wood protected by a band of copper and connected to the hub by spokes. The first spoked wheels had two wide spokes. Wheelwrights experimented with different numbers of narrow spokes, with four- and six-spoked wheels becoming common. Spoked wheels were much lighter than solid ones and thus allowed greater speed.

Transportation technology advanced still further with the making of wheels that turned independently of each other and of the axle. This innovation greatly increased maneuverability (although many simple wagons and farm carts continued to use the cruder construction of fixed wheels and axles). Among other things, the combination of light spoked wheels and independent rotation led to the development, sometime around 2500 B.C.E., of the chariot. This most famous of ancient vehicles had two wheels and eventually took a wide variety of forms. At one extreme were light, swift models used for racing or for delivering messages. At the other were heavy, armored war chariots that carried, in addition to the driver, archers and lancers.

Neither the improvements to the wheel nor the invention of the chariot would have meant much without a fast, strong animal to pull the new vehicles. That animal was the horse. Horses may have been domesticated in Ukraine in the fourth millennium B.C.E. Although the nomadic peoples of central Asia rode horses, the animals may not have appeared in the Near East until about 2500 B.C.E., when Sumerians hitched them four abreast to pull four-wheeled battlewagons. The value of horses must have been obvious throughout the region after about the 1700s B.C.E., when the Hyksos, a southwest Asian people who migrated as far as Egypt, used them to great effect in both war and peace. At about the same time, the Hittites swept down from what is now north-central Turkey aboard horse-drawn battle chariots and conquered much of northern Mesopotamia and modern-day Syria. Their enemies soon adopted this same lethal combination. When the Egyptian pharaoh Ramses II finally dealt the Hittite Empire a crushing defeat, at Kadesh, in Syria, about 1275 B.C.E., it was in one of the greatest horse-and-chariot battles of all time.

Of all the people of the ancient Near East the Persians may have made best peacetime use of the horse's potential. Persian rulers created a large network of roads to connect their empire, including the Royal Road, which spanned the Near East from the city of Susa near the Persian Gulf to the

Achaemenid Persian gold model chariot dating to the fifth to fourth century B.C.E. from the region of Takht-i Kuwad, Tadjikistan (© The Trustees of the British Museum)

city of Sardis near the Aegean, covering 1,600 miles. The Persians developed a system of way stations where horses could be cared for and exchanged, allowing messengers to cover about 180 miles a day, riding from Susa to Sardis in nine days—a rate of travel unheard of at the time. Although it was not as fast as the horse, the mule—a cross between a female horse and a male donkey—contributed greatly to transportation as both a pack animal and a draft animal. Mules tolerated heat and cold well, had tough hides, and could carry heavier loads than donkeys could. The Sumerians were using mules by the third millennium B.C.E.

For long-distance travel in the desert, however, neither horses nor mules could compete with a later arrival in the Near East, the camel, which was far better adapted to hot, dry conditions. The one-humped dromedary was probably domesticated in Arabia around 1200–1100 B.C.E., quickly revolutionizing long-distance trade. Camel caravans made it possible to transport aromatics like frankincense and myrrh from the southern Arabian kingdoms northward to Mesopotamia, Syria, and the Levant. In Iran two-humped Bactrian camels were used for similar purposes. These animals originated in the Mongolian area, but by the third millennium B.C.E. they had reached the Iranian plateau. In addition, dromedary-Bactrian hybrids were being bred by the early second millennium B.C.E. These animals became the heavy-duty trucks of antiquity, capable of carrying loads of half a ton and with far greater tolerance of extremes of heat and cold than either purebred dromedaries or Bactrians.

Inland water travel was rare in the Near East except on the Tigris and Euphrates rivers. Both rivers posed problems for people who traveled on them, because they tended to fill with silt as well as to jump their banks periodically to forge new courses to the sea. By the Early Dynastic Period (ca. 2900–ca. 2340 B.C.E.) barges moved up and down these rivers, carrying goods and people. Sometimes oceangoing ships sailed up the rivers, transporting goods from the east. Smaller boats made of animal skins stretched over wooden frames were commonly used on the rivers to transport only a few people or for fishing.

ASIA AND THE PACIFIC
BY KIRK H. BEETZ

Most ancient peoples of Asia traveled on foot. Even after the domestication of draft animals and the introduction of the wheel, transportation usually meant people walking, carrying loads on their shoulders and backs. One of the remarkable things about ancient peoples was the large amounts of goods they transported in this manner, trekking through dangerous, frequently very dry or very cold environments. The paths they wore in the earth on these journeys often became the roads of empires.

On the many large Asian islands between the Indian and Pacific oceans dense tropical forests often impeded land transportation. On such islands as Sumatra and Java water transportation was the better choice for moving goods over any but the shortest distances. People poled or paddled boats such as dugout canoes and bamboo rafts over the sinuous waters of rivers, streams, and swamps. Even on the mainland, in Indochina and much of southern Asia, dense forests inhibited travel. People walked the trails of tapirs and elephants to make their way to streams where they could use boats. On many Pacific islands, forests were thick enough to inhibit travel. The islanders often found it easier to travel by boat in the ocean around their islands than to try to travel great distances inland. For large islands, such as New Guinea, islanders made their ways to streams and used dugout canoes to carry themselves and goods. In open areas such as those in Australia, people of the Pacific continued to rely on transportation on foot through the ancient era.

The amount of goods a walker could carry was obviously limited by his or her strength. In many parts of Asia poles were set across the shoulders of two people, enabling them to carry weights greater than one person could bear. From very early times people also used sledges for heavy loads. The early sledges, little more than rough wooden frames on which goods were dragged across the ground, were soon improved by the addition of sledlike runners. This innovation may have occurred in the far north of Asia. Even after the introduction of the wheel, sledges remained the preferred mode of transportation over mud, marshes, snow, and ice. For the nomadic peoples of Siberia sledges became essential to their way of life because they frequently had to pack up and move their heavy animal-skin-and-wood tents and other goods to new places.

When the domestication of draft animals reached Asia is not known, but by 3500 B.C.E. farmers near the mouth of the Yangtze River were using oxen to pull plows. The wheel as a means of transportation was first used in Sumer, in the Near East, before 3500 B.C.E. and spread from there. The original wheels consisted of three boards held together by two boards fitted crosswise on the inside of the wheel. These solid wheels were very heavy. The Harappans of the Indus River valley (2600–1500 B.C.E.) probably used four-wheeled wagons pulled by two oxen apiece. These heavy vehicles enabled them to transport enough grain to fill the huge granaries in their cities, providing a food reserve against hard times.

For many centuries in ancient India oxen remained the favored animals for hauling carts and wagons. They were so valuable that in some places in India it was punishable by death to kill one. Even long after the domesticated horse was introduced to India, oxen were preferred for pulling wagons. By 300 B.C.E. Indian traders formed long caravans of hundreds of wagons pulled by oxen. Ox-drawn carts of supplies followed Indian armies to war. Oxen were slower than horses but tolerated India's climate better. Thus horses served mainly to carry riders or to pull light chariots.

Two-wheeled chariots had the advantage of being faster than four-wheeled wagons. They transported elite warriors to battle and the rich through cities. Sometime after 2000 B.C.E. spoked wheels—lighter and therefore faster than solid wheels—were introduced to India. Another innovation improved maneuverability: Originally, axles and wheels formed one unit, rotating together, which made chariots, carts, and wagons difficult to turn. Eventually, wheelwrights found ways to allow wheels to turn independently of each other. The wheels could thus rotate at different speeds, allowing fast, tight turns without skidding.

By 2600 B.C.E. wheeled vehicles had appeared in China, probably introduced by nomads from central Asia who had learned this technology from Mesopotamians. Solid wheels and wheels fixed to axles presented the same problems to the Chinese as they did to the Indians, but the use of solid-wheeled carts persisted in southern China and southern Asia as they did in India, probably because of their durability and ease of construction. Although China had two great river systems, the Yangtze and Yellow River, the rivers wound through the landscape so much that the Chinese found it took longer to move on the rivers than to travel by land, which led to many road building projects to improve land transportation.

It was probably also nomads of central Asia who introduced war chariots to China. By 2000 B.C.E. people in what is now northern China were using wheels with 18 spokes. Chariots with spoked wheels, pulled by horses, were of great value to the Shang Dynasty (ca. 1500–ca. 1045 B.C.E.). The chariot, even a heavy, lumbering one, gave Shang armies a big advantage in battle and in the transportation of military supplies against enemies who often were limited to being on foot. The advantage became even greater when Chinese wheelwrights, like those in India, discovered how to let wheels turn independently. Meanwhile, Shang four-wheeled wagons appear to have remained clumsy vehicles because the forward axle was fixed in place and could not easily shift to follow a winding road, but they were nevertheless important for transporting heavy cargoes.

The Scythians of central Asia introduced the stirrup to the Chinese. A Scythian stirrup was just a leather loop, but it gave a rider greater stability and greater control of his mount. In about 380 B.C.E. the Chinese made a stirrup of metal rather than leather. It allowed a rider to stand up in his or her stirrups and provided enough stability that an archer could shoot accurately while riding. Until this innovation chariots had been the best mobile platform for archers. The Scythians also introduced the use of a blanket for padding under a saddle; the Chinese modified this idea by padding the saddle itself.

The Chinese were probably the inventors of the double shaft for vehicles, introducing two-wheeled carts with double shafts and one horse. The shaft of a cart or wagon is a pole extending forward, to which animals are hitched so that they can pull the vehicle. Before the introduction of the double shaft, carts had one shaft. A single shaft, however, required two draft animals, one on each side of the shaft, because a single animal would naturally pull the shaft toward the side to which it was attached. The double shaft had poles to each side of one draft animal, allowing it to pull a cart and keep it in a straight line. After 100 B.C.E. double-shafted carts became common in China.

Despite the great advances in technology, much transportation of goods was still a matter of humans carrying loads. China had many regions where the only roads were merely footpaths. Sometime around the first century C.E. an unknown Chinese inventor introduced the wheelbarrow. Essentially a small human-powered cart, this humble vehicle soon became an invaluable tool for transportation, carrying goods not only along country lanes but through the narrow streets of big cities as well, hauling tools and produce between fields and homes and moving countless tons of supplies and raw materials for the building of roads, dams, and other public projects.

EUROPE

BY MICHAEL J. O'NEAL

During the Palaeolithic, Mesolithic, and most of the Neolithic periods people in Europe traveled mainly by foot. In most cases they did not travel great distances, but sometimes they went on long treks. The frozen so-called Iceman found in the Alps in 1991 was traveling north from Italy, perhaps to escape pursuers, and was crossing the Alps when he died around 3300 B.C.E. Rivers and large lakes posed obstacles, and dugout canoes were the best means of crossing these bodies of standing water. Wetlands were crossed with wooden trackways.

In northern Europe skis were used by travelers at a very early date. They were probably invented in many different places once people began to adapt to modern climatic conditions after the ice age. Skis were found preserved in a bog in Hoting, Sweden, dating back some 4,500 years, and hundreds of others have been found throughout Scandinavia. Further, a 4,500-year-old rock carving depicting a man skiing with a hunting weapon in his hands has been found on the island of Rodoy in northern Norway, and numerous other rock carv-

ings illustrate groups of people on skis. Russian researchers found skis in the Altay region of central Asia that are at least 6,000 years old. The word for *ski* is similar in language communities as distant as Finland and Siberia, suggesting that skis were developed across most of Eurasia very long ago.

During the fourth millennium B.C.E. two developments had a profound effect on transportation in prehistoric Europe: the domestication of the horse and the invention of the wheel. Around 3500 B.C.E. the inhabitants of the steppes (vast, open grasslands) of eastern Europe and western Asia began to keep horses as livestock, initially just for food. They subsequently discovered that horses could be ridden. Archaeological evidence includes bit marks on teeth found in horse skeletons from the third millennium B.C.E., though saddles were not used until after the fall of the Roman Empire and the stirrup was a still later innovation. The domestication of the horse and the invention of horse riding had an enormous impact on the mobility of the peoples of Eurasia. It enabled them to migrate over immense distances. It transformed warfare. In particular, it contributed to the spread of the Indo-European language, the ancient common tongue from which numerous languages in Europe and parts of the Middle East and Asia descended.

Skis and the horse can transport one person, but they are of little use in transporting goods or agricultural produce. To that end, Europeans discovered that they could use animals to pull wagons, carriages, and carts. The earliest European wagons, which date to the end of the fourth millennium B.C.E., were clumsy, lumbering vehicles. They were probably first pulled

Horse harness fittings from Iron Age Britian (1–100 C.E.) (© The Trustees of the British Museum)

by oxen and only later by horses. The wheels were solid and heavy, typically constructed out of three joined pieces of wood. The axle was fixed so that only the wheels turned. In time the Europeans discovered ways to make wagons and carts more maneuverable. One chief innovation, dating from the second millennium B.C.E., was the use of spoked wheels rather than solid wheels. The earliest wheels were made entirely of wood, but Celtic metalworkers in central Europe learned to attach a metal band around wheels, making them far more durable on rough roads. Another innovation was the development of axles that turned, making wagons and carriages much more nimble.

Wagons pulled by oxen were used primarily by farmers in their fields and around their settlements during the Bronze Age. The archaeological record provides enough evidence for archaeologists to make good guesses as to what such carriages looked like. Among the most important finds are portions of wagons discovered in Holland. These wagons were constructed with solid wheels (that is, wheels without spokes), a forked undercarriage, a forked shaft, axles, and a large wickerwork "basket" on top for passengers or materials. Wagon technology improved during the Iron Age. The tomb at Hochdorf in Germany that dates to approximately 530 B.C.E. contained a four-wheeled wagon about 6.5 feet long, with a pole for attaching it to a team of oxen or horses extending over 6.5 more feet. Each wheel had 10 spokes. A similar wagon was found in a tomb at Vix in France.

Horses and particularly lightweight carriages were used primarily by the social elites. Among the most important carriage finds are six carriages called the Dejbjerg carriages, named for the bog in western Denmark where they were found. These carriages might have been built by the Celts in central Europe, who developed a tradition of expert carriage making. These wagons were probably used by headmen, and probably on ceremonial occasions primarily. They were much lighter than agricultural wagons and featured spoked and iron-banded wheels and bronze ornamentation. They were constructed of ash and beech, both of which are especially durable woods.

In addition to carriages and wagons the Europeans developed a type of chariot. The ancient Celts in Ireland drove a vehicle called a *carpat*, a word similar to the Latin word *carpentum* used by the ancient Romans, to refer to these vehicles. Historians long believed that these words and the vehicles they named were unrelated, but more recent research suggests that they are in fact related. The chariot was a light, two-wheeled, horse-drawn vehicle mounted on a flexible suspension. Above the suspension was a platform on which the rider stood and a seat—all protected by a fabric covering called a tent. Examples of these chariots, dating from as far back as 500 B.C.E., have also been found both in Yorkshire in England and on the Continent.

The chariot was used for purposes of warfare, but that was not its primary purpose. As a military vehicle, it served to transport soldiers and their gear, but actual fighting was done on foot. The chariot, rather like a modern-day sports car, was a mark of status. Members of the elite class used chariots to travel about or visit their neighbors in stately fashion. They were also used by young men who wanted to display their style and daring, for the chariot was used in races and, in particular, for such feats as riding pell-mell over creeks or ditches; the flexible suspension enabled the rider, at least most of the time, to make a relatively soft landing.

The use of wheeled vehicles for long-distance transportation required the improvement of the road system of ancient Europe, which had existed for millennia as beaten tracks through the forest. Roads connected the Celtic *oppida*, or towns, which greatly facilitated trade and movement of military groups. The invading Romans made use of this road structure as well as improving it further. The Roman Empire relied on efficient transportation for administration and trade, so in addition to building roads, the Romans built some canals in Europe. In the first century of the Common Era, the Roman general Drusus built a canal that connected the Rhine River with the IJssel River in Holland. In England the Romans built the 11-mile-long Fossdyke canal near Lincoln, connecting the river Witham with the river Trent, and the 40-mile-long Caerdyke canal in the same area. Otherwise, the Romans found canal building to be impracticable in their northern colonies.

GREECE

BY CHRISTOPHER BLACKWELL

Transportation in the ancient Greek world was dominated by the sea. Overland travel was arduous and often unnecessary. The Greek mainland is mountainous and rugged, and the Greek population was concentrated in the coastal areas to the east and west of the northern Balkan Peninsula, around the edges of the southern peninsula of the Peloponnese, and scattered across the islands of the Aegean Sea and along the coast of Asia Minor.

The many separate population centers of Greece were not politically unified in any sense of the word until the late fourth century B.C.E., and even then only into a relatively loose structure of military dominance by Macedonia. Greek communities, isolated by geography and largely self-sufficient, had no need for swift overland commerce—in contrast, for example, to the Persian Empire, whose bureaucracy required and provided a network of "Royal Roads" with well-maintained stations set at intervals and supplying food, rest, and fresh animals for official travelers.

Land transportation among the ancient Greeks was largely a matter of walking. Horses were not common outside the plains of Thessaly in the northeast of Greece and were not prized as draft animals. Along the few main roads mules or oxen were the preferred beasts of burden. Oxen (cattle trained to the harness) were stronger than mules or horses but very slow. Mules (the offspring of a female horse and a male donkey) afforded the best combination of strength and speed.

Overland travel was made perilous by bandits, especially in places where roads passed far from centers of population. The myth of the Athenian king Theseus emphasizes the heroism

TURNING SEA INTO LAND AND LAND INTO SEA

When Xerxes, the great king of Persia, was planning to invade Greece in the early decades of the fifth century B.C.E., he faced a number of challenges of transport. His army numbered at least 100,000—the numbers are not known precisely, and ancient sources are notoriously unreliable in these matters—and it was supported by a vast naval fleet. Xerxes had to get his army across the Hellespont, the channel of water connecting the Black Sea with the Aegean. He also had to get his fleet safely along the coast of Thrace, the territory to the north of the Aegean, and particularly past the Chersonese, an area of peninsulas extending into the sea, regularly wracked by storms.

Xerxes' famous solution was to "turn sea into land and land into sea," as the Greek historian Herodotus reports. He built a bridge over the Hellespont, a line of barges secured by cables woven from papyrus. His first attempt succumbed to the currents of the Hellespont, whereupon he had his servants flog the body of water with whips. His second attempt succeeded. To avoid the storms around the capes of the Chersonese, he had his engineers dig a canal across the promontory of Mount Athos (today the site of a famous monastery), allowing his fleet to make the Thracian crossing without entering the Aegean proper. To Herodotus and evidently many of the Greeks, these feats of engineering represented excessive pride, an affront to the gods, and Xerxes' eventual defeat, on sea and on land, seemed only fitting.

of his choice to travel overland between Troezen in the Peloponnese and Athens (a relatively short journey). In historical times, when cargoes of any value were transported overland they tended to go in well-armed caravans, following river valleys. But there were few cargoes that needed carrying long distances by land, and so mule- or ox-drawn wagons were mainly limited to local transport, bearing produce from the countryside to urban markets or cargoes from harbors into cities. The chariot appears in poetry as a vehicle of war but was not used, in war or peace, to any significant extent by the Greeks during the historical period. Most warfare among the ancient Greeks was between neighbors and was dominated by soldiers on foot, who marched to their battles and back home again.

Trade was by sea, with bulky cargoes (most often grain) or valuable cargoes (luxury goods such as particular vintages of wine or fine pottery or textiles) moving from one end of the Mediterranean to the other and beyond. Ancient Greek trade goods have been found in England and Sweden, perhaps brought that far north by merchants looking for tin, a

metal alloyed with copper to make bronze. (Copper was common in the Greek world, but tin was not.)

Ironically, given the relative unimportance of land transport, there were occasions when ancient travelers preferred to carry their ships overland rather than sail them on the sea. Ships traveling between east and west in the Mediterranean could choose to round the southern end of the Peloponnese, risking bad weather from the open sea to the south, or to cross the Isthmus of Corinth by land. The Corinthians had constructed a dragway across the isthmus and would (for a fee) carry merchant ships across that narrow strip of land on rollers (today there is a canal).

ROME

BY KIRK H. BEETZ

The earliest remains archaeologists have found at the city of Rome are graves dating from the 800s B.C.E., but Roman tradition held that the city was founded in 753 B.C.E. By this time many of the ancient world's most important innovations in transportation had already been made, primarily in the Near East, and much of this Near Eastern technology had found its way into Italy. At the same time, Celts in Europe were making marvelous carts and chariots, experimenting and innovating in their design and uses. Still, even though the Romans acquired all the advanced transportation technology, the favored Roman method for hauling even heavy goods was humans trudging along under their burdens. Slaves were abundant, and it was easier to load them up with whatever needed to be transported, whether it was bricks or wheat, than to invest money in beasts of burden and their maintenance. Even the Roman army was apt to carry what it needed on foot. Most of its soldiers were farmers used to long hours on their feet, and the army tended to favor infantry over cavalry. Walking remained the most common mode of transport for the poor throughout the history of ancient Rome

Transporting goods by water was usually much less expensive than hauling them over land. In the time of Diocletian (r. 284–305 C.E.), it was less expensive to transport goods across the Mediterranean from Spain to Syria than to transport them over 75 miles of land. But when it came to personal travel, Romans preferred to go overland rather than travel by ship. Many did travel by ship, especially if they were in a hurry, but dry land seemed more secure to most Romans. They were also avid tourists who liked to see the sights wherever they went.

Oxen were the primary beasts of burden for pulling carts. For small farmers, oxen and a cart were essential for bringing produce to markets in towns or cities. The carts were heavy affairs, made of thick planks of wood with either two or four solid wheels. On most big Roman carts the axles were fixed to the carriage body, making turns very difficult. It required the strength of oxen to maneuver them. When taking produce to a city, the farmer walked beside the oxen rather than riding on the cart. He traveled at night, because carts carrying farm products were forbidden to be in cities during the day.

Cities were designed to favor pedestrians. There were sidewalks, and cities often had laws requiring people who owned property next to a sidewalk to provide awnings that protected pedestrians from the sun and rain. Crosswalks consisted of large flat stones laid a step apart across streets. Cart and carriage drivers had to guide the wheels of their vehicles slowly between the stones. Streets were often full of people, further slowing wheeled traffic. Wealthy people rode in palanquins, using them like battering rams to force their way through streets. The palanquin was adopted from the Near East and consisted of an enclosed carriage body on two poles. The poles were carried on the shoulders of four or more slaves or servants. In large cities it was common to see these palanquins and their bearers marching through crowds, their passengers hidden behind drawn curtains. Palanquins were often marked with the symbols of their owners and would be followed by clients of the owners, hoping for a handout whenever the palanquins stopped.

The Romans were probably the greatest road builders of the ancient world. Not only were their city streets paved and well maintained but so were the roads and highways that connected the regions of the empire. Such roads had advantages for commerce, and entrepreneurs established carriage

Chariot with horse and rider, from a sarcophagus at Heraklion (Alison Frantz Photographic Collection, American School of Classical Studies at Athens)

services for transporting passengers in cities and around the countryside. A common sight was the *raeda*, a four-wheeled cart that was large enough to hold several passengers. It was heavy, slow, and difficult to maneuver, but Roman engineers tried to lay out roads as straight as possible, which minimized the number of turns a vehicle would need to make if it stayed on a main road without making detours. There were lighter carts that also carried passengers. Lighter carriage bodies and light, spoked wheels meant that every bump in the road was felt, but with spoked wheels and teams of four horses drawing them, light carriages could cover as much as a hundred miles a day on Roman-built roads. Sometimes Romans chose to ride in a light, two-wheeled carriage called a *cisium*, which could function like a taxicab. Many Romans chose to ride horseback when traveling. Inns and even whole villages arose along major thoroughfares to provide services for all kinds of freight and passengers, with cartwrights and stables available.

The lightest cart, the *birota*, could carry about 150 pounds, and the heaviest, the *angaria*, could carry about 1,100 pounds. Neither was well suited for carrying the monumental stones that the Romans used for building. Such stones were often fitted with posts in their sides on which wheels were placed, and the whole was towed as if it were a huge cart. Liquids were transported in wooden barrels seated in wheeled frames. For pulling their carts, Romans used oxen, mules, and horses. They lacked an efficient towing harness for horses, which limited horses to light carts and chariots. Oxen were common throughout the empire, although mules seem to have been favored in dry areas because they could better tolerate hot, dry conditions. Pack mules were extensively used for carrying goods in bad weather and on narrow paths.

For moving heavy goods, Romans preferred watercraft whenever they could avail themselves of them. Although they occasionally built canals in Europe, by and large they relied on existing waterways. For instance, the city of Rome itself depended on the Tiber River. Ships laden with grain and other goods from North Africa would dock at the nearby port city of Ostia at the mouth of the Tiber, where cargo would be transferred either to barges or to land transportation. The barges were hauled upstream by slaves pulling thick, heavy ropes along the riverbank.

Horses were favored by Romans for pulling chariots and other light vehicles. Horses often worked in teams of four not only in chariot races but also in pulling transport vehicles outside cities. Individual riders rode horses for hunting as well as for travel. Romans began using spurs and riding boots in the 300s B.C.E. They also invented horseshoes. The first was the *hipposandal*, which consisted of an iron plate tied to the hoof with leather strips. They eventually developed a horseshoe made of iron that was nailed to the underside of the hoof, much like that used today. The padded saddle was introduced only late in the empire, in the 300s C.E., and was marketed to riders by Roman merchants as a way to reduce the possibility of getting hemorrhoids.

THE AMERICAS

BY MICHAEL J. O'NEAL

Horses, donkeys, and oxen were not introduced to the Americas until the time of European contact. Meanwhile, the large native animals, such as buffalo, were poorly suited to domestication either for riding or for pulling loads. Some smaller animals, such as the llamas of South America, could be trained to carry modest burdens on their backs but were too small to ride or to use as draft animals. Wheeled vehicles existed only in the form of a few toys, since there were no animals to pull the real thing. Thus, for thousands of years, when ancient Americans traveled by land, they went on foot, carrying whatever they needed with them.

Prehistoric Americans traveled along routes that were determined primarily by two factors. One was the movement of wild game, which they followed in search of food. Migratory animals such as mastodons, deer, elk, and bison created trails through forests and over plains, and ancient Americans followed these trails in search of food. They became adept at reading the signs that nature provided, including hoofprints and the droppings the animals left behind. From these signs they could tell when animals had passed and what they were eating, which provided hunters with clues about where to look for them.

The other factor that determined the footways of ancient Americans was the terrain. Throughout the Americas people were confronted with different types of terrain, from the Rocky Mountains of the American West and the Andes Mountains of South America to the tropical forests of Central America and the woodlands of the eastern half of what is today the United States. When the first Americans crossed the land bridge between Siberia and Alaska and then moved southward, their movements were channeled by a path between two glaciers. They faced changes in elevation, marshes and swamps, ravines, rivers and streams, mountains, and other natural obstacles. Naturally they sought to avoid these obstacles in their travels or, if that was not possible, at least to find the easiest way over them. Many modern roadways, as well as hiking trails in national parks, follow the same tracks left behind by ancient Americans.

During prehistoric times, when people survived by hunting and gathering, they moved about in search of food, often following similar routes each year as the seasons passed. The advent of agriculture required those who adopted this way of life to settle in more or less permanent communities, remaining in one place year-round or at least for much of the year. But circumstances often caused even settled farmers to pack up their belongings and travel, sometimes for great distances. In some cases they were motivated by the basic human need to explore. In other cases changes in climate conditions forced them to seek new farmland, or perhaps a natural disaster such as a flood, earthquake, fire, or volcanic eruption forced them to move.

In time the roadways that people had worn into the ground over generations became used for trade and cultural contact. Roads led to the diffusion of languages and ideas and to the construction of cities that served as administrative centers and hubs for the movement of goods and people. Roads enabled rural people to transport their goods to the cities. Empires such as those of Central America needed roads for communication and in some cases military conquest. In many cases roads were needed to transport raw materials used for building cities. They also led to ceremonial centers, where people gathered for religious purposes.

As time passed, some early Americans traveled by water. Those who settled along waterways or in coastal areas used canoes and small boats, usually for hunting purposes but sometimes to transport goods for trade as well. Most of these early boats were dugout canoes; that is, they were carved out of a single log. Numerous examples of dugout canoes dating to ancient times have been found in the southeast of what is now the United States, with its long coastline and numerous rivers and lakes. Archaeologists have discovered 400 such canoes, and although some date from the later medieval period, others are thousands of years old. In Mesoamerica water became important for the transportation of goods late in the ancient period, and the peoples of the Caribbean islands relied on seacraft to travel from island to island trading goods. By about 300 C.E. the Moche of Peru in South America were using canoes to hunt mammals at sea. This growing reliance on waterways for transportation, however, was a late development in the ancient period. Transportation by foot remained the norm for many millennia.

See also AGRICULTURE; ART; ECONOMY; FESTIVALS; INVENTIONS; METALLURGY; MIGRATION AND POPULATION MOVEMENTS; MILITARY; RELIGION AND COSMOLOGY; ROADS AND BRIDGES; SEAFARING AND NAVIGATION; SHIPS AND SHIPBUILDING; SLAVES AND SLAVERY; TRADE AND EXCHANGE.

FURTHER READING

Lionel Casson, *Travel in the Ancient World* (Baltimore, Md.: Johns Hopkins University Press, 1994).

Jac J. Janssen, *Donkeys at Deir el-Medina* (Leiden, Netherlands: Nederlands Instituut voor het Nabije Oosten, 2005).

M. A. Littauer and J. H. Crouwel, *Wheeled Vehicles and Ridden Animals in the Ancient Near East* (Leiden, Netherlands: E. J. Brill, 1979).

Robert Partridge, *Transport in Ancient Egypt* (London: Rubicon Press, 1996)

Stuart Piggott, *The Earliest Wheeled Transport* (Ithaca, N.Y.: Cornell University Press, 1983).

Stuart Piggott, *Wagon, Chariot and Carriage* (London: Thames and Hudson, 1992).

D. T. Potts, "Camel Hybridization and the Role of *Camelus bactrianus* in the Ancient Near East," *Journal of the Economic and Social History of the Orient* 47, no. 2 (2004): 143–165.

Steve Vinson, "Transportation." In *The Oxford Encyclopedia of Ancient Egypt*, ed. Donald B. Redford, vol. 2 (Cairo: American University Press, 2001): 450–453.

► war and conquest

INTRODUCTION

In general, historians writing about the ancient world tend to define war as a military enterprise that required long-term preparation and planning and was carried out by one state or national government against another state or government. For the purposes of the definition, nomadic peoples united under a single leader or governing council count as a nation, which is why some historians will refer to nomadic peoples as "nations" even though they did not live in one place with defined borders.

Most anthropologists believe that people have been killing people from the beginning of modern humans. Those very ancient disputes may have begun over offended honor, a mistreated daughter, or the claiming of rights to a fertile territory. Rock paintings dating to tens of thousands of years ago, from Europe, Africa, and Asia, show people killing one another with bows and spears. Some of the combat looks organized, with figures wearing special clothes or body decorations specifically meant for battle.

Exactly when small conflicts became large ones is unknown. For a time the rise of cities in Sumer was thought to have brought about the beginning of war. As the cities grew, they needed more lands to feed their people, and they became envious of each other; for this reason they started killing each other to acquire land and to steal one another's wealth. This would not have begun before 3500 B.C.E. Yet Çatalhüyük in modern-day Turkey dates from about 7200 B.C.E. and was built for defense against large-scale attacks. Between 10,000 and 8000 B.C.E. the residents of Jericho built massive walls and an extraordinarily well-designed tower. Those battlements would seem to have been pointless wastes of valuable time and labor unless they were meant as defense against a large and dangerous threat, such as an army with leadership that would devote time to planning how to defeat such a stronghold. It is possible that someday the exact place and time the first war was fought will be discovered, but at present archaeologists and historians can study only the wars they know about.

War was expensive. It required a large investment of time, people, and goods to wage war. For a society to invest its energy in war, it needed to see value come from war. People had to believe that they were either gaining something valuable through aggression or keeping something valuable through defense. War had objectives that were perceived as valuable, and those objectives could be met only by sacrificing other valuables, such as human lives, money, and labor for public works. In societies in which people had to spend almost every waking moment working just to feed themselves, taking time for war was a great sacrifice. Some societies solved the problem by giving up making their own food and goods and devoting themselves to taking food and goods from other people. In northern China and northern Mesopotamia, for instance, there were nomadic peoples whose lives focused on war and whose societies' efforts centered on annual raids for looting farming communities to the south. In China hundreds or thousands of lives, much labor, and a great deal of wealth was spent on such defenses as tall, wide walls around every city.

The constant warfare that marred much of the ancient world generated an arms race in almost every culture. The classic example comes from ancient Sumer, where warriors used stone clubs to bash in heads, so people made metal helmets to absorb the blows, so weapons makers created metal axes to cut through metal helmets, so armorers styled larger, thicker, and more resilient metal helmets, so weapons makers developed new casting techniques that allowed them to make stronger, larger axes with curved blades that could smash through metal helmets, and so on. Many of the technological advances of ancient peoples were put to use in war, and many advances came from people trying to find better ways to fight wars.

This race in technology was paralleled by changes in military organization and strategy. Whereas the technology of the composite bow made Sargon I ruler of most of the Near East, the strategy of the phalanx helped make the Hittites the military masters of their era. The Neo-Assyrian Empire (1050–609 B.C.E.) combined its weapons and armor technologies with sophisticated deployment of highly trained units devoted to one kind of warfare, such as sappers for bringing down enemy walls, archers for long-range attacks, light infantry for responding quickly to events on the battlefield, heavy infantry to push massed enemy troops out of the way, and chariots for shock attacks to break up enemy formations.

Some historians argue that every great empire of ancient times was built through war. This may be too much of a generalization. For instance, there are the trade empires of ancient southern India to consider, but even those required some military power to keep trade routes free of bandits. What may be noteworthy is that war had its limits. Ancient Rome prospered while its armies looted newly conquered territories, but it declined when it did not continue to do so. During the Han Dynasty (202 B.C.E.–220 C.E.) of China, there was a period in the 100s B.C.E. when its army crushed opponents to the south, the west, and the north but at such a high cost of lives and wealth that its economy nearly collapsed. Even the Neo-Assyrians ended up fighting wars mostly using mercenaries and vassals because it was running out of its own men to fill its armed forces.

Perhaps it is most important in studying the wars of ancient peoples to note how people struggled to meet each day, to feed themselves and their families, and to endure the pain and sorrow that war inflicted on them. For most people most of the time war was something to be survived. Some cultures developed strict rules of warfare that minimized bloodshed, allowing for glory for the leaders and for victories while also allowing most warriors or soldiers to return home unharmed. Still, such cultures eventually either adopted the waging of war as massive bloodshed or were overwhelmed by the armies of cultures that made war a matter of slaughtering enemy troops. Those who failed to learn the lessons of advancing technology and improving military strategy tended to perish. Survival seems to have depended on vigilance, sacrifice, discipline, and sound military doctrine.

AFRICA

BY KIRK H. BEETZ

Rock paintings in southern Africa and in the Sahara show people fighting with bows and spears. The identification of these early people is not clear, but the depictions of conflict continue for thousands of years. By 9000 B.C.E. the people in southern Africa were probably the San, often known as Bushmen. It is not clear what the Bushmen fought over. As hunter-gatherers, they probably did not have much property to defend or covet, but they may have had territories they considered their own. In the often dry plains that many Bushmen inhabited, even a small family group of hunter-gatherers would have needed a wide territory in which to find food. Raids for marriageable women might have been another purpose for conflict. The combat probably involved no more than a dozen fighters at a time. At no time did the Bushmen number as many as 300,000 people, which meant they were so thinly spread over their lands that it would have been very unlikely that they could have gathered together enough people to form anything resembling an army. The same would be true for the small-statured peoples often referred to as Pygmies, who inhabited most of central Africa and much of the east and south.

For the ancient peoples of the Sahara the issue of war and conquest is more complex than for southern Africa. Their rock paintings hint at an evolution of warfare not found elsewhere in Africa. Most depictions of conflict prior to the Herdsmen Period (ca. 5095–ca. 2780 B.C.E.) show naked men in small skirmishes. During the Herdsmen Period some men in battle seem to wear robes, and there may even have been a hierarchy, indicated by a single figure wearing robes that were colored or tailored differently from those of others in his command. It seems that for the cultures depicted, the wearing of clothes may have been reserved for war or other official functions.

During the Herdsmen Period the rock paintings show a diverse ethnic population, with pale figures mixing with dark ones. The primary occupation of people seems to have been herding cattle. It is probable that conflicts focused on stealing cattle. Prestige could be won in a village or group by successfully stealing cattle from another village or group. Wars in which cattle were considered important booty continued into the medieval era. In any case, as time passed, the paintings of battles became increasingly common.

What happened to the ancient warriors of the Sahara grasslands is not entirely known. Some of the pale people and the dark people seem to have mixed, perhaps becoming the Berbers. Others retreated to Egypt. Some retreated to oases as the Sahara slowly dried and created farming communities. Around them developed nomadic groups who created their own culture of war in which they mastered horses and the use of weapons. These groups preyed on the farmers at the oases, forcing them to pay tribute or die. Sometime late during the Horse Period (ca. 2780–ca. 600 B.C.E.) the attacks on the farmers became too much. Apparently, raiders using chariots swept out of the northern Sahara and drove the farmers out. The Greek historian Herodotus (ca. 484–between 430 and 420 B.C.E.) suggested the attackers were the Garamantes, a Berber group from the northern coastal area of North Africa. The fighting was probably very one-sided, with the attackers using not only chariots but also javelins and shields against farmers who had only bows. The farmers were probably part of an ethnic group that already occupied much of West Africa. Their descendants may have been the Bantu-speaking people who eventually spread over most of the continent.

Warfare as modern people think of it, with large numbers of warriors or soldiers united in a single cause, may have taken place in Africa in many places, but this is not known because of the lack of archaeological or written evidence. The earliest records of war tend to come from the earliest literate peoples of Africa, the Egyptians, Kushites, and Axumites of northeastern Africa.

NUBIA

Egyptian culture may have begun around 5000 B.C.E. in farming communities in Upper Egypt—the southern half of what became ancient Egypt. By 3500 B.C.E. the culture was spreading north. At the same time, a strong local culture was developing in Nubia, which was south of Egypt. The Nubians of this time were several different groups, some farmers and others pastoralists. By about 2250 B.C.E. a Nubian confederation had formed under one chief just south of Egypt in an area called Wawat. This confederation and Egypt traded with each other. Nubian warriors were noted for their ferocity, and for most of their history after 2250 B.C.E. they were in demand as mercenaries in armies as far away as Mesopotamia. Nonetheless, Wawat and much of the region around it were rich in gold, and for this prized commodity Egypt sent an army to occupy Nubia.

This was not easily done, even though the Nubians' military technology was inferior to that of the Egyptians. The Egyptians had composite bows, an import from the Near East. A composite bow had an inner lining of bone, a middle lining of wood, and an outer lining of animal skin. It sometimes was made of more than one kind of wood, each kind intended to provide strength or springiness. The composite bow was powerful, and the arrows it launched could penetrate the animal-skin shields of the Nubians. Some of the nomads among the Nubians continued to fight for decades by raiding the Egyptians, but the Egyptians built several forts in the region that eventually enabled them to defeat efforts to drive them away.

KUSH

There seems to have been much activity south of the Egyptian conquests in Nubia. A kingdom called Karmah, after one of its most important cities, became an important trading center for eastern Africa. Whatever Karmah's military problems, they were significant enough for the kingdom to fortify its cities with walls. By 1650 B.C.E. Karmah had extended its territory almost as far north as the first cataract on the Nile. Karmah had taken advantage of a period of political chaos in Egypt, the Second Intermediate Period (ca. 1640–ca. 1532 B.C.E.). The Egyptian king Thutmose I (r. ca. 1504–ca. 1492 B.C.E.) invaded Karmah. His army sacked the city and extended Egyptian influence south of the fifth cataract of the Nile. Over the next 400 years Egypt tried to make the land it called Kush into a cultural disciple of Egypt. The children of the political elite of Kush were raised in Egypt, where they were taught to worship Egyptian gods, to follow Egyptian customs, and to speak, read, and write Egyptian. By 950 B.C.E. the Kushites had developed a strong kingdom, and its leaders regarded themselves as the true inheritors of ancient Egyptian culture.

Egypt had fallen again into chaos, having become divided among many petty kings who contended for power. The Nile Delta had several independent city-states. A strong dynasty had been founded in Kush by King Alura (r. ca. 780–ca. 760 B.C.E.). The wars in Egypt had cut the Kushites off from worship at important sites of their religion. Thus, Alura's successor, Kashta (r. ca. 760–ca. 747 B.C.E.), sent his son Piankhi (r. 751–716 B.C.E.) in 748 B.C.E. to secure Thebes.

The exact details about the army Piankhi took with him are not known, but it probably numbered more than 10,000 troops. Its principal soldiers were spearmen, still mostly equipped with spears with stone tips. They had chariots but not in great numbers. The Kush had war elephants of a species now probably extinct that was easier to train than the notoriously irritable African elephants from farther south. Piankhi himself probably rode an elephant; at least, Kushite kings are depicted in Kushite art as riding elephants. Their bows were probably still not composite. The organization of the army probably was into infantry, chariots, and elephants. Women could be military leaders in Kush, and it is likely that some of Piankhi's officers, including generals, were women. This suggests that women played other roles in the army, but evidence is scant for their participation in infantry or other units.

Regional Egyptian governors and chieftains usually submitted to Piankhi on his way to Thebes. His object was not to destroy but to preserve, so he did not loot and sack. Instead, he secured access to Thebes, where he worshipped. When he assumed the throne of Kush, he made his capital in Napata, far to the south of Egypt, along the Nile. Napata was a major site for the worship of the Egyptian god Amun, who at the time was the principal deity in Kush.

In the early 720s B.C.E. the Egyptian chief of the city of Saïs in the Nile Delta, Tefnakhte (r. ca. 724–717 B.C.E.), raised an army and navy and marched and sailed south along the Nile. King Nimlot of the city of Hermopolis surrendered to Tefnakhte. Tefnakhte then sent his fleet toward Thebes. How Piankhi actually regarded these events is unclear, but he may have viewed Tefnakhte's aggression toward Thebes as a threat to Kush's influence in Upper Egypt, of which Thebes was the capital. Piankhi sent an army into Egypt. He divided it into two parts, one to intercept Tefnakhte's fleet before it reached Thebes and the other to take Hermopolis from Tefnakhte.

While he had managed to take Hermopolis, Tefnakhte had problems to his rear, because the city of Heracleopolis, south of the river delta, was holding out against a siege by Tefnakhte's forces. Piankhi's army met Tefnakhte's fleet north of Thebes. A little of the battle that followed can be reconstructed. The Kushites were accomplished sailors on the Nile, and they could transport infantry quickly on their boats. The Egyptians' principal weapon was the bow and arrow. Their other weapons, which were bronze, were mostly superior to those of the Kushites. Overall, in a fight on a river, the Egyptians should have had the upper hand. The Kushites were daring fighters, however, noted for their ferocity in combat. If their spearmen could press the Egyptians into close-quarters fighting, they could overwhelm their enemy. Even at this late date, neither side's troops wore much armor. That the Egyptian fleet was decisively defeated suggests that the Kushites managed to board the Egyptian boats and force both sailors and archers into a confrontation best suited to Kush's infantry.

Piankhi then journeyed to Thebes, where he celebrated the Festival of Opet. It may have been at this time that he proclaimed himself pharaoh, thereby establishing the Twenty-fifth Dynasty of Egypt. He then joined his army at Hermopolis, where he directed the siege that resulted in the city's surrender. The wife of Nimlot asked one of Piankhi's wives to persuade him to spare Nimlot's life, which he did. Thereafter Piankhi's army sped to Heracleopolis, which was near surrender. The advantages of Tefnakhte's forces were their superior knowledge of the terrain and their bronze technology. Piankhi's forces had elephants, some warriors equipped with bronze or copper weapons, and a clear chain of command. Tefnakhte had allies and petty princes to supervise, whereas Piankhi was the undisputed commander of his troops, with a clear hierarchy of officers.

Tefnakhte's forces were driven from the field, and Heracleopolis was saved. Its people were starving. Piankhi was said to have been furious at what he saw. The starving of the city's horses especially galled him, perhaps because the horse was his emblem. Tefnakhte and his allies made a stand at the city of Memphis. For the battle Piankhi brought both his fleet and his army to the city. Instead of laying siege, which would have been the accepted military practice for Egyptians, Piankhi led an assault on the city's defenses. Apparently, attacks from both land and river overwhelmed the defenders. Again, Piankhi arrived as a savior of Egyptian culture, not as a conqueror, and it seems that civilians were not harmed.

Piankhi continued first to Heliopolis and then to Athribis, where he defeated allies of Tefnakhte. The chiefs of the cities of the Nile Delta, including Tefnakhte, then paid him homage. Piankhi was content to allow the chiefs to continue to rule their cities as long as they paid him tribute, and he returned to Napata. This made Piankhi the ruler of one of the largest empires of the ancient world, extending more

than 1,400 miles north to south, eastward to the Red Sea, and westward to oases in the desert.

What happened militarily over the next several years is unclear. It seems that Nimlot rebelled against Piankhi. Tefnakhte declared himself ruler of Lower Egypt; he died in 717 B.C.E., but his son Bekenrenef succeeded him. Piankhi died in 712 B.C.E. and was succeeded by his brother Shabaka (r. 712–698 B.C.E.), who was a less forgiving conqueror. His army of spearmen, chariots, and elephants ruthlessly crushed the enemy army, and Bekenrenef was burned alive. Shabaka brought a shift in attitude to his rule of Egypt; whereas Piankhi viewed himself as a savior of Egypt, Shabaka viewed himself as the one and only rightful ruler of Egypt. Thus, he took power away from Egypt's chiefs and established a central government bureaucracy led by Kushites to run the empire, and he moved his seat of government about 500 miles north of Napata, to Thebes.

The pharaohs of the Twenty-fifth Dynasty seem to have seen it as their duty to return Egypt to the power and glory it had held during the New Kingdom (ca. 1550–ca. 1070 B.C.E.), a period marked by great public works and Egyptian control of much of Palestine. They rebuilt decaying monuments and temples and built many new ones, and Egypt returned to some of the prosperity it had once known, but Palestine was to be their undoing.

Shabaka and his successor, Shabatka (r. 698–690 B.C.E.), had maintained an alliance with Assyria, but in about 701 B.C.E. the kingdom of Judah, led by Hezekiah (r. ca. 715–ca. 686 B.C.E.), rebelled against Assyrian rule and asked Shabaka for aid. Shabaka responded as a New Kingdom pharaoh might have; he sent assistance. The Kushite-Egyptian army met the Assyrian army at Eltekeh in Judah. The Assyrians lived for war; their society was geared toward waging war. Their army was better equipped with armor and weapons than the Kushite-Egyptian army, and it was better organized into combat units. It was more mobile and more experienced. Even so, the Kushite-Egyptian army inflicted heavy losses on the Assyrian army before having to withdraw. Some Assyrian vassals took this as a good sign, and they rebelled. The Assyrian army became afflicted with a disease that killed more than 15,000 troops, and it was unable to finish the war.

The Assyrian rulers regarded the Kushite pharaohs as irritating upstarts, but they had their hands full quelling rebellions in Palestine, delaying their eventual attack on Egypt. In 674 B.C.E. an Assyrian army met a Kushite-Egyptian army in northern Palestine and was decisively defeated. In 671 B.C.E. King Esarhaddon (r. 680–669 B.C.E.) of Assyria led an army to Egypt using camels as pack animals to transport goods through the hot, dry Sinai. His army inflicted a series of defeats on Kushite-Egyptian forces. The decisive factor may have been Assyrian armor, which was made of resilient iron and was mass-produced so that every soldier had armor and iron weapons. The Kushite-Egyptians could not supply all their troops with metal weaponry and armor, and they were still living in a Bronze Age military world, whereas the Assyrians had the superior military organization of troops on the battlefield that was necessary for victory in the Iron Age world, as well as much superior discipline among their troops.

Pharaoh Taharqa (r. 690–664 B.C.E.) retreated to Thebes and then to Napata. His family in Thebes was murdered by the Assyrians. The Assyrians made the cities of Egypt north of Thebes their vassals. Taharqa was succeeded by Tantamani (r. 664–657 B.C.E.), who believed himself to be the only true ruler of Egypt. In 664 B.C.E. he led a Kushite force against an alliance of Egyptian vassals and Assyrians. The key to his success seems to have been mastery of the waters of the Nile; boats may have moved his forces swiftly into position.

By this time the Kushites had probably noted the value of the iron technology of the Assyrians, and Kush had already begun to establish an iron industry. In 664 B.C.E., however, the Kushites had to rely on their ferocity to overcome their enemies, which they did in a battle at Memphis. Tantamani regained control all the way to the Mediterranean Sea, but too much had changed in the Near East. His allies in Palestine had been defeated by the Assyrians, and combat had depleted his military's resources. Despite waging a stubborn defense, his army was driven ever southward by a determined counterattack of Assyrian forces commanded by Ashurbanipal (r. 668–627 B.C.E.). Thebes was sacked, its women raped, its children slaughtered, and its men enslaved.

Although Tantamani's line would survive until about 300 C.E. and its monarchs would call themselves the rulers of both Upper and Lower Egypt, they would not again rule Egypt. There is some indication that they tried again in about 601 B.C.E., when Babylon attacked Egypt. The Kushite army fought an army composed of Greek and other mercenaries near Abu Simbel, about 250 miles south of Thebes. The battle was ferocious, but the Kushites were forced to withdraw. Although the rule of Kush over Egypt was short, it had a long-lasting effect on Egyptian society: It reinvigorated Egypt's religion, arts, and economy for hundreds of years.

This was not the end for the Kushite military. Most Kushite kings and queens proved to be capable rulers who incorporated what had been learned from the Assyrians into their army. The Kushite iron industry focused on the city of Meroë, south of Napata, just south of where the Atbara River flows into the Nile. After an Egyptian army sacked Napata, the capital of Kush was moved to Meroë. The principal duties of the army became protecting Kush's trade routes that ran deep into southern Africa, west along the Sahel steppes south of the Sahara, and east to the Red Sea. Kushite inscriptions depict numerous battles, mostly against nomadic peoples. Kush assumed the role of protector from raiders for small tribal lands to its south. Elephants seem to have faded out of use in the army, as did chariots. They were replaced by horseback-riding cavalry armed with lances and bows. Spearmen remained the core of the army.

Specific military actions for Kush reappear in the historical record in 24 B.C.E. By then Rome controlled Egypt, and the Romans had built a series of forts south of Egypt, possibly infringing on territory that Kush regarded as its own. At that time Kush was ruled by a queen, called a *candace*, which Greek writers mistook for a given name rather than a title. This was probably Queen Amanirenas, a big woman with an imposing personality. The Roman governor responsible for the forts left with most of his troops to aid in fighting in the Near East. Although Amanirenas was probably present for the attack on the fort at Aswān, her army was led by a general, perhaps a Prince Akinadad, who is linked with her in inscriptions found in Meroë. Using boats and infantry the Kushite army assaulted and seized forts at Aswān and Philae. In the marketplaces there the Romans had installed statues of the emperor Augustus (r. 27 B.C.E.–14 C.E.), which the Kushites took home. A head that may have been from one of these statues was found by archaeologists hidden in clean sand under the entrance to a building in Meroë.

When the Roman governor, Gaius Petronius, returned, he counterattacked. Although the Kushite army dominated regional African groups, it was no match for the Romans, and despite stubborn fighting the army was driven south by the Romans. Amanirenas tried to negotiate with the Romans, but the Romans persisted until they captured and sacked Meroë. Several Kushite towns were left in ruins.

How Kush fell is not known. A rival kingdom, Axum, left some hints, and archaeologists have found additional clues. In about 300 C.E. Kush lost its constant war against nomads. Among the nomads were the Red Noba, who were in control of Kush when Axum invaded in 350 C.E. The key to the nomads' victory may have been camels, which enabled them to travel farther more quickly in dry climates than could horses, and Kush was drying up as the desert of the Sahara continued its spread. Where the Kushites went is a subject historians and archaeologists like to debate, but at present what happened to the Kushites is unknown.

AXUM

Axum was located where Ethiopia is today. At its height it was one of the great powers of the Indian Ocean, where its navy transported its army to fight in distant lands. Although Axum had a distinct culture of its own by 1500 B.C.E. and developed a written language, less is known about it than about Kush.

Axum's focus was on trade, and throughout its history it was a mercantile nation. Thus its military's primary duty was to protect trade. By about 400 B.C.E. Axum's navy was large, and it sailed along the coast of eastern Africa and as far east as Sri Lanka. In the Red Sea and along Africa's east coast it protected merchant ships from pirates. By maintaining safe waters Axum attracted the sea trade to its ports. Visitors to the ports saw imposing stone forts on hilltops along Axum's coast. These forts apparently represented a military class that held much political power in Axum society.

The king of Axum was the commander in chief of the military, and he sometimes led his army into battle. The army was run by nobles who based their operations in the hill forts. Beneath them were trained officers who oversaw a well-disciplined infantry and cavalry. It is possible that Axum's army included elephants. Part of Axum's ability to protect its people from harm was its ability to project its power overseas. Its navy could transport divisions of the army throughout the Red Sea and along the southern coast of Arabia and the Near East, and Axum used this ability to effect wars and rebellions in areas it considered important to its well-being. Often when a rebellion or war of conquest disrupted Arabia, Axum would send its army to restore order and place its friends as rulers.

On the continent of Africa, Axum shared power with Egypt, Kush, and various small groups. Beginning around the 1470s B.C.E. it maintained trade relations with Egypt, which were sometimes interrupted by wars and civil wars in Egypt. Whether it meant to or not, Kush contributed to Axum's security by protecting African trade routes from bandits and nomadic marauders. Perhaps Axum's greatest king, 'Ezānā, was in power when the kingdom of Kush expired under the effects of farmland lost to desertification and attacks from nomads of the Sahara. 'Ezānā forged peace treaties with the nomads that were meant to protect Axum's borders and its trade, but the nomads who gave up their nomadic ways to settle in the remains of Kush persisted in attacking trade caravans. The breaking point seems to have come when the Red Noba mistreated ambassadors of Axum in 350 C.E. 'Ezānā led a punitive expedition into Kush, destroying villages along the way. At Meroë his army defeated the Nobu. Losses on his side seem to have been light, but his army may have killed as many as 15,000 enemy warriors. He took home with him several thousand head of cattle, many horses, and slaves.

THE BANTU SPEAKERS

Although Axum persisted as an important power for another thousand years, a people who would reshape Africa to the present day were on the move to the west by 200 C.E. These were the Zande-speaking and Bantu-speaking peoples of West Africa, probably the descendants of the farmers of the Sahara who had fled south 1,000 or more years earlier. They had iron technologies, and their blacksmiths had learned how to carbonize iron with charcoal to make steel. This was tricky, because too much or too little carbon could result in metal that was too soft or too brittle to be of good use. They were an agricultural people, and as they pushed the Pygmies and the Bushmen out of their ancient territories, the Bantu speakers, in particular, made the land permanently their own by settling and farming it. Even though it is unlikely that the Bantu speakers could summon huge armies, they could call upon more warriors on short notice than could either the Pygmies or the Bushmen.

Among themselves, the Bantu speakers at the end of the ancient era fought wars that had well-understood rules. Warriors, rarely more than 100 on each side, would gather on open land. They carried shields made of animal skins, and their weapons were usually spears. They painted their faces

and their bodies to make themselves look frightening. Actual combat seldom took more than a few lives before one side fled. In the event that neither side fled, the side that was winning would refrain from wholesale slaughter by leaving an opening for the losers to use for running away. It was against the rules for one side to surround the other because it was understood that trapped warriors would fight to the death, increasing casualties for the winners as well as the losers. It was from these warriors that the important military powers of medieval central and southern Africa would evolve.

EGYPT

BY MARIAM F. AYAD

Perhaps no other civilization survived as long as that of the ancient Egyptians. In its long history Egypt not only invaded and annexed foreign territories but also was occasionally the subject of military conquest by invading armies. In discussing the development and organization of Egypt's armed forces and Egypt's imperialistic role in history, it is important to clarify terminology. The Egyptian word *mesha*, traditionally translated as "army," is used in reference not only to a body of soldiers but also to any kind of expeditionary force, such as a mining expedition or similar peaceful endeavor. Thus the meaning of the word is not inherently militaristic but much broader, perhaps even referring to any organized group of individuals who undertake state-sponsored excursions to achieve a state-sponsored objective, militaristic or peaceful. Avoiding use of the word *army* when describing Egypt's military force might be prudent, because the term would imply the existence of a national body of soldiers from the beginning of Egyptian history until the demise of pharaonic civilization, which was not the case.

OLD KINGDOM (CA. 2575–CA. 2134 B.C.E.)

The earliest reference to a war in ancient Egyptian evidence appears on the Narmer Pallet. On one side of the pallet is a highly stylized pictorial representation of a king grasping the hair of an enemy in one hand and holding a mace in the other upraised hand. The king is shown in the process of hitting the fallen enemy, a pose that became associated with smiting enemies throughout Egyptian history. The other side of the pallet depicts the king marching in a victory procession. The representation preserved on the pallet has been interpreted as a record of a single militaristic action that led to the forceful unification of Egypt by a king of Upper Egypt. Although most scholars subscribe to a theory of a more gradual unification process, this scene, one of the earliest preserved, records some kind of a militaristic internal struggle.

As early as the Old Kingdom, Egypt wanted to acquire the natural resources of the region immediately south of its border, Nubia. To expand their kingdom's boarders southward, Egyptian forces occasionally mounted campaigns into the southern region. Egypt's southern expansion came as a

Frieze in the temple of Ramses II, listing captured cities in Nubia (Courtesy of the Oriental Institute of the University of Chicago)

natural consequence of its unique geography. Running the entire length of Egypt from its southern border to the Mediterranean shore, the Nile River was Egypt's highway. The strong river current carried the ships effortlessly north, while winds blowing from the Mediterranean enabled boats to sail south. Moreover, originating in the Ugandan mountains, the Nile facilitated easy access to the African heartland.

Evidence suggests, however, that Egypt did not have a standing army during this period. Instead, various local governors were called on not only to join military expeditions but also to recruit troops from among their local constituents. The autobiography of Weni, an official under the Sixth Dynasty king Pepi I (ca. 2289–2255 B.C.E.), details an expedition to Nubia, Egypt's southern neighbor. Preserved in his tomb at Abydos, the autobiography lists Weni's many titles, including several hereditary positions (Weni had the social rank of an *iry-paet*, a title often translated as "hereditary nobleman" or "count.") In addition, Weni held several high-ranking administrative positions: He was both a governor and a chamberlain of Upper Egypt, the warden of Nekhen (a cultic center in Upper Egypt), and the mayor of Nekheb (an equally important cultic center).

Much like Weni, the officers under his command were hereditary noblemen and members of the civil administration of Egypt; among those Weni listed in his autobiography are "counts, royal seal bearers, sole companions, chieftains and mayors of towns of Upper and Lower Egypt" as well as chief priests and chief district officials. Remarkably, neither

Weni nor his officers bore any specifically militaristic titles. The high-ranking administrators among them were required to recruit their own troops from the villages and districts they governed or administered. Farmers comprised the bulk of the Egyptian military force.

Indeed, Weni's autobiography recounts the marshaling of "tens of thousands" of troops against the "Asiatic Sand-dwellers," which was the Egyptian way of referring to Bedouins who subsisted along Egypt's eastern border. Troops were recruited from all the districts of Upper and Lower Egypt as well as from Nubia, the area immediately to the south of Egyptian border, and even included some Libyans. As the leader of this very diverse force, Weni was proud of the discipline of his forces, which he attributed to his own rectitude. In his autobiography he boasts that while he led the troops, "no one attached his fellow, . . . no one seized a loaf or sandals from a traveler, . . . no one stole a cloth from any town, . . . no one took a goat from anyone."

Weni roughly sketched the route of the campaign, but his autobiography focuses primarily on the victorious outcome of the campaign, ending in a poetic refrain that recounts the safe return of the troops, "having slain thousands. . . [and] having carried off many troops as captives." The successful outcome of the campaign ensured that Weni would head the military force sent to fight against the Bedouins five more times. At least once Weni traveled to the battleground aboard a ship, while half of his troops proceeded on land.

Middle Kingdom (ca. 2040–ca. 1640 b.c.e.)

Soon after the long reign of Pepi II, a period of political turmoil ensued in Egypt. Known as the First Intermediate Period (ca. 2134–ca. 2040 b.c.e.), the tumultuous period following the collapse of the Old Kingdom lasted from the Seventh Dynasty through the middle of the Eleventh Dynasty. Egyptian literature describing this period implies that it may have witnessed some form of civil war. In particular, the "Instructions to King Merikare," a text written in Middle Egyptian and surviving in three Eighteenth Dynasty copies, describes the following conditions: "Troops will fight troops. . . Egypt fought in the graveyard." Traces of hieroglyphs preserved in this document suggest that the text refers to King Khety, a possible conflation of Akhtoy, a name commonly held by rulers of the Ninth and Tenth dynasties.

This text belongs to a larger corpus known collectively as pessimistic literature and comprising literary works dating to the Middle Kingdom. Works belonging to this genre describe how Egypt went through a period of turmoil until order was finally restored by a savior king. The "Instructions of King Amenemhat," founder of the Twelfth Dynasty, belong to this genre. After a lengthy account of the chaos in which he found the land, Amenemhat describes how he was able not only to restore order in the land but also to vanquish Egypt's southern neighbors in Wawat and Medajj (two districts in Nubia). Amenemhat also claimed that he "made the Asiatics do the dog walk."

However, even in the Middle Kingdom and despite many campaigns into Nubia, the Egyptian military force lacked the many ranks and titles characteristic of a regular standing army. Similarly absent was a formal division of the military into units and subunits. Egypt's strategic location in northeastern Africa, lack of a formal standing army, weakened governmental authority, and lax control of the northeastern border eventually led to the occupation of the delta region by nomadic groups of western Asiatic descent, known as the Hyksos (the name is a Hellenized version of the Egyptian term *heqa khasut*, meaning "rulers of foreign countries"). The Hyksos are credited with the introduction of several technologies and inventions, not the least important of which were the wheel and its use in the military chariot.

New Kingdom (ca. 1550–ca. 1070 b.c.e.)

As founder of the Eighteenth Dynasty (ca. 1550–ca. 1307 b.c.e.), King Ahmose is famous for the successful campaign he launched against the Hyksos strongholds in the delta. Among the several texts recording the events leading to the expulsion of the Hyksos from Egypt is the autobiography of an officer in the Egyptian military, also named Ahmose, who started his military career as a crew commander under King Ahmose and later served in the Nubian and Syrian campaigns of Amenhotep I and Thutmose I. The autobiography, inscribed in the officer's tomb at El-Kab, records his early career and provides a vivid account of his involvement in the battle against the Hyksos. Ahmose portrays himself as a courageous "crew commander" who climbed the ranks of the military and was rewarded for his bravery and prowess with gold (seven times) as well with tracts of arable land. As part of his reward Ahmose the officer also received male and female slaves, some of whom he had captured himself in battle and some whom others captured.

It is clear from his autobiography that Ahmose was an infantryman who "followed the sovereign on foot when he rode in his chariot." In one episode the soldier records going to the battlefield aboard a ship called the *Wild Bull* while he was still an unmarried young man. As an infantryman Ahmose actively participated in the siege of the town of Avaris, the delta stronghold of the Hyksos. He was then appointed to serve aboard a ship named *Rising in Memphis* and took part in some "fighting on the water." This episode, however, should not be taken to indicate that a naval battle took place. Rather, the fighting occurred on a lake or perhaps a tributary of the Nile near Avaris. The ship merely served as a platform from which archers could aim their arrows. During the battle Ahmose captured a prisoner of war, and when the captive tried to escape, Ahmose waded into the waters and recaptured him.

It is clear from his autobiography that although Ahmose was aboard ship to reach western Asia, he was an infantryman who fought on land. Thus he could be considered a marine who mainly engaged in infantry warfare. The text also suggests that Ahmose fought using primarily short-range weapons, such as the club or mace for clubbing; the spear, straight sword, or dagger for stabbing; and the battle-ax or broadsword for slashing and cutting.

Ahmose's vivid descriptions of the fall of the cities of Avaris and Sharuhen indicate that he also engaged in siege warfare. Whenever forces could not infiltrate a fortified city or fortress by tunneling under, climbing over, or smashing into its walls, they would launch a siege that would continue until the inhabitants began to starve and surrendered to the attacking forces. Ahmose describes how Sharuhen was besieged for three years.

Two other types of warfare, not mentioned by Ahmose but attested to elsewhere are naval warfare, in which battles took place on water, and chariotry warfare, in which combat occurred from horse-drawn chariots. These two types of warfare, though not as well documented in the archaeological and pictorial records, are depicted on the walls of a few temples.

Although it is emblematic of ancient Egyptian warfare in popular culture and art, the chariot was rarely used in Egyptian battles. Appearing soon after the expulsion of the Hyksos, the chariot enabled a soldier to fight aboard a wheeled vehicle. A unit of mounted troops, or chariotry, was limited in size and thus considered elite. The main function of the two-wheeled, horse-drawn chariot was to provide military intelligence and reconnaissance. Protected by its mobility, a chariot would travel along the front lines of the enemy, learning the organization of its infantry forces and bombarding them with arrows. However, the chariot's use as a mobile platform from which archers could shoot their targets was only secondary. Chariots were expensive to maintain. Each vehicle required at least four horses, which needed fodder, tending, and specialized care. Eventually, the chariot became "a status symbol, and in the case of the king . . . a surrogate throne."

A mid-Eighteenth-Dynasty title, commander of horsemen, suggests the existence of a sort of cavalry or mounted troops. This is further corroborated by scenes from the tomb of Horemhet from Saqqara, which clearly depict the cavalry as an arm of the chariotry. Further evidence suggests that the cavalry unit was used extensively in Sheshonq I's Palestinian campaign of around 925 B.C.E.

Egypt's location on the Mediterranean subjected it to repeated attacks from the Sea Peoples, first during the reign of King Merneptah (ca. 1224–ca. 1214 B.C.E.) and later under Ramses III (ca. 1194–ca. 1163 B.C.E.). These invaders were groups of migrants who swept through the Mediterranean world in the 11th century B.C.E. Although the exact reason for this massive population movement remains elusive, possible reasons include severe climatic changes in the northern and western Mediterranean.

Pictorial evidence of Ramses III's naval battle against the invading Sea Peoples survives on the walls of his mortuary temple at Medinet Habu. The evidence preserved there constitutes the only known example of an active naval engagement. The scenes indicate that during the Twentieth Dynasty of the New Kingdom the Egyptians commanded large seafaring vessels. The evidence also suggests the existence of naval ranks and titles, and military ships had specific designations. Earlier in the struggle against the Hyksos and later during Piye's 25th march into Egypt, ships were used to transport troops north. But the reliefs of Medinet Habu clearly depict troops fighting from onboard ships, although the specifics of conducting naval battles cannot be reconstructed.

Along with distinct naval ranks and titles, the evidence suggests that during the New Kingdom the Egyptian forces were finally divided into distinct units, each exhibiting a clear hierarchy of ranked officials. The units were organized according to their modes of transportation. Foot soldiers, or infantry troops, made up by far the largest units. Indeed, the evidence suggests that this was the only type of unit up to the beginning of the New Kingdom.

The accounts of two major battles (Megiddo and Kadesh) shed light on New Kingdom warfare. The two accounts are propagandistic in nature, concerned primarily with the exultation of the king and expounding on his role as the great warrior-savior in great detail. Although their propagandistic tone makes the reliability of the numbers (of troops as well as booty) mentioned there quite unreliable, they remain our only primary source on warfare, strategy, and battle moves in ancient Egypt.

Prompted by rumors of a coalition of western Asiatic rulers, Thutmose III launched a preemptive campaign into Syria-Palestine in his first year of sole reign (ca. 1458 B.C.E.). The confrontation between the two armies took place on the plains of Jezreel across from the Canaanite city of Megiddo. Written in literary form, numerous accounts of the battle of Megiddo were engraved on Egyptian temple walls, the most extensive preserved on the walls of the Amun temple at Karnak. As in similar works of this literary genre, the author goes to great lengths to demonstrate the king's military prowess and strategic brilliance. The propagandistic tenor of the text is clear in its introductory lines, which give the complete titles of the king: "Mighty Bull, Shining in Thebes; King of Upper and Lower Egypt, Lord of the Two Lands; Menkheperre; Son of Re." The text then relates how all the victories he enjoyed in battle were granted him by "his father Re [the sun god]."

Under the pretext of quenching perceived rebellion, Thutmose III decided to march against the Asiatics at a time when they seemed to have "fallen into disagreement," when their infighting would have made them an easy target. The account engraved at the Amun temple details the events of the battle: the troops marched "out of Egypt to Gaza, then along the coast of Canaan to the entrance of the Aruna Pass" (probably the Wadi Ara near modern Hadera). Giving this account its particular historical appeal is the seemingly accurate date provided at the beginning of the narrative. The troops set out in Thutmose III's 22nd regnal year, on the 25th day of the fourth month of *Peret* (the winter season). The text also records the date that the king arrived at his destination at the city of Yehem in western Asia: year 23, first month of *Shemu* (the summer season), on the 16th day.

On his arrival, however, Thutmose III convened a council of war and received bad advice: to take "a safer route toward Megiddo." The king ignored the advice of his courtiers, deciding instead to take the dangerous crossing of "the Carmel ridge via the Aruna Pass" and enter the Jezreel Valley just outside of the city of Megiddo. He "commanded his entire army to march on that road, which threatened to be narrow. His majesty swore, saying, "None shall go forth in the way before my majesty. . . . He went forth at the head of his army himself, showing the way by his own footsteps; horse behind horse, his majesty being at the head of his army."

At seeing the king, considered a divine being, the enemy troops fled into disarray. According to the inscription preserved on a stela in Napata (a city in Nubia, in modern Sudan), the Egyptian forces then laid siege to the city of Megiddo until its leaders surrendered. The text gives a vivid description of the surrender and details the booty carried off by the Egyptian troops, giving exact numbers for prisoners of war captured (340), enemy troops killed (83), mares taken (2,041), and stallions seized (6). The text further details the finery of a gold chariots seized and records that 200 suits of armor were taken. Significantly, it does not mention the number of Egyptian troops deployed for battle, and there is no mention of how long the march (or the battle) lasted.

The battle of Qadesh, fought in the fourth year of the reign of the pharaoh Ramses II (ca. 1274 B.C.E.) at Tell Nebi

Mend on the Orontes River, was widely publicized, with many scenes of the battle engraved on the walls of several temples in Egypt and Nubia. The scenes, which proclaim the military prowess of Ramses II, propagate a version of events that claim Egyptian victory in the battle. Like Thutmose III at the battle of Megiddo, Ramses II was misled by false intelligence. The Egyptian forces were ambushed, and although both sides fought ferociously, the Hittites did not yield the land. In fact, extant Hittite records of the battle indicate that the Egyptian troops suffered a severe defeat and fled in chaos. The ensuing peace treaty between Ramses II and the Hittite king Mutewalis preserved the status quo, with both sides suffering considerable losses.

The Egyptian account of the battle of Qadesh is most significant because it indicates that the Egyptian military was subdivided into four battalions, each named after one of the major Egyptian deities. Indeed, the Egyptian versions focus on the bravery of Ramses II who, having been deserted by his infantry and chariotry, continued to fight gallantly. The poetic version of the battle surprisingly preserves a passage in which Ramses II complains that the god Amun-Re had deserted him in battle. Despite the lack of divine support, however, Ramses II is able to single-handedly defeat thousands of enemy troops. Indeed, this seems to be the sole purpose of the numerous inscribed versions of the battle: the glorification of the reigning king and the further establishment of his bravery and divinity.

Egyptian military forces were not always on the offensive. In its long history Egypt also experienced several invasions by the armies of other Near Eastern nations: the Nubians, Assyrians, and Persians, and later the Greeks and Romans, all invaded Egypt. At the end of the New Kingdom, Egypt witnessed a period of political fragmentation known as the Third Intermediate Period (ca. 1070–ca. 712 B.C.E.). During this period several rulers simultaneously claimed the kingship of Egypt. Occasionally these rivaling dynasts fought over territorial hegemony. Sometime in the early to mid-seventh century B.C.E. Egypt's southern neighbor in Sudan, the kingdom of Napata, rose to power. One of its earliest rulers, Kashta, marched north and may have controlled all the area to the south of Egypt up to Aswān. Located at the first cataract, Aswān was Egypt's traditional southern border. Kashta's sons, Piye and Shabaka, invaded Egypt several times: Piye twice in his fourth and 20th regnal year and Shabaka in his second year. The Nubians eventually succeeded in having a firm grip on Egypt; from 715 to 671 B.C.E. they fully controlled Egypt as its Twenty-fifth Dynasty. The penultimate ruler of that dynasty, Taharqa, was a military man who had spent the early part of his career leading his predecessor's armies. Taharqa tried to expand Egypt's northeastern frontiers.

Assyria was the main military force in the ancient Near East at the time, with a strong presence in Palestine. Taharqa's ambitious military intervention in western Asia may have prompted several subsequent Assyrian invasions into Egypt (in 674, 671, and 667–666 B.C.E.). The Assyrians' invasion of

Egypt was a natural consequence of its need to secure Palestine's southern boundary. They left Egypt only after installing their Egyptian ally, Psammetichus I (664–610 B.C.E.), as a vassal king. Psammetichus I succeeded in driving Tantamani, the last Nubian ruler of Egypt, from Egypt, having chased his armies all the way to Nubia in the Sudan. Psammetichus I and his successors of the Twenty-sixth Dynasty relied heavily on the use of mercenaries. Cretans, Greeks, and Jews were among the many nationalities employed in the Egyptian military at the time.

But perhaps the most devastating of all invasions was the Persian invasion of Egypt in the spring of 525 B.C.E. Having swept through the Near East, the Persians conquered Egypt and ruled it for more than a century. An Egyptian revolt in 401 to 399 B.C.E. led to the expulsion of the Persians from Egypt. Shortly thereafter, in 343 B.C.E., the Persians reconquered Egypt. This time their rule of Egypt was short lived. After a brief decade Alexander the Great invaded Egypt in 332 B.C.E.

After Alexander's sudden death his generals divided the territories he had conquered. Egypt fell into the hands of General Ptolemy, who declared himself king of Egypt. His decedents constitute the Ptolemaic Dynasty, and the period from 305 to 30 B.C.E. is known as the Ptolemaic Period. The last Ptolemaic ruler was none other than the famous Queen Cleopatra VII. Egypt was finally annexed to the Roman Empire after Cleopatra and Marc Anthony's defeat at the naval battle of Actium in 30 B.C.E.

THE MIDDLE EAST
BY KIRK H. BEETZ

In the ancient Near East the objective of warfare was the capture or defense of a capital city. The original cities of Mesopotamia were sacred, the homes of specific gods in the religions of the peoples of the area. When a city became the urban center of a state consisting of towns and villages, it retained its central place in the hearts of its populace. To capture a capital was to capture the hearts of its people and usually to bring the end of resistance.

Until about the era of the Neo-Assyrian Empire (1050–609 B.C.E.) another objective of war was to slaughter the enemy, and prisoners of war were typically executed. Even though the Neo-Assyrians were especially bloodthirsty, they changed the practice of routinely killing prisoners, because they valued their prisoners as potential slaves and tended to ship them off to parts of their empire where labor was wanted.

The archaeology of Near Eastern warfare before about 1200 B.C.E. is sketchy, but the scant physical evidence is often all that speaks of wars. Even after writing became common, war records usually contained the statistics of victory—such as how many of the enemy were killed, how many were captured, and what sort of loot was found—rather than descriptions of tactics, military organization, or even the reasons for the wars.

Before 3500 b.c.e.

Warfare seems to have been a constant preoccupation for Near Easterners, even as far back as the end of the last great ice age. One archaeological site that indicates this is Jericho. Sometime between 10,000 and 8000 b.c.e. a giant stone wall was erected around a settlement at Jericho. It seems to have been intended to protect a small population and a spring. Of special interest to military historians is a stone tower attached to the wall. The tower was about 35 feet high and built solidly, with a stone staircase up the middle. The great antiquity of the tower is significant because of the tower's sophisticated design, which suggests that its builders drew on a tradition of erecting similar towers. The reason Jericho was fortified at such an early time is unknown, as is the identity of the enemy. Speculation has tended to focus on the spring and the likelihood that Jericho was a farming community. Nomads may have coveted the harvests of Jericho, and traders traveling the ancient trade route that passed through Jericho may have coveted the water flowing from the spring.

The physical remains at Jericho offer some idea of what warfare may have been like. An important point to consider is the significant expense of fortifications. Instead of farming more land or producing more goods, valuable time and thought were devoted to building walls and at least one large tower. It is logical to suppose that if the massiveness of the walls and tower were unnecessary, the society of Jericho would have built a less imposing fortification. Thus the structures' heavy-stone construction, great height, and massiveness indicate that the enemy could bring down or penetrate walls built of wood or small stones. This suggests that at that early date, attackers already knew about using sappers to undermine walls and fire to burn walls and may have even used battering rams. The tower's height may have been for guards to watch for enemies, which would mean that attacks could come unexpectedly. On the other hand, the tower was situated so that people on it could fire arrows or hurl stones at anyone attempting to scale the walls. Altogether, the evidence indicates that people were already thinking carefully about how to wage war.

Farther north, in present-day Turkey, another city offers hints about war. Çatalhüyük, established before 7200 b.c.e., was built to resemble a beehive. The city had no roads or footpaths, and its interlocking buildings had few, if any windows and no conventional doors. People moved from place to place by climbing ladders through openings in their ceilings and walking across roofs, occasionally climbing or descending where buildings were of different heights. The dominant theory about why the city was built as it was focuses on military defense. An enemy, whether bandits or a full army, would have had no clear entrance to attack. Attacking and entering an outer building would have left the enemy with nowhere to go but up a ladder, and defenders could heap stones, arrows, and burning oil on them. Seizing the city would have required fighting to take each building. Archaeologists believe that the lack of evidence that Çatalhüyük was ever taken by force indicates that its defensive layout was successful.

Early Dynastic Period (ca. 3000–ca. 2350 b.c.e.)

By 3000 b.c.e. the numerous Sumerian cities established in southern Mesopotamia were already warring against each other. For several reasons the waging of war was not a simple matter of a king deciding to take his army to battle. First, there were no standing armies. Early Sumerian armies consisted of militias of free male citizens. Second, kings were not absolute rulers and had to gain consent from a council of elders or an assembly of citizens. For instance, during the rule of Gilgamesh (r. ca. 2700 b.c.e.) the city of Uruk received a demand to surrender itself to the dominance of another city-state. Gilgamesh wished to fight for his city's freedom, but Uruk's council of elders voted to surrender. Gilgamesh called for an assembly of Uruk's free citizens, and the assembly overruled the council of elders and voted to fight to remain free.

Another difficulty was that typically citizens were expected to provide their own weapons: spears, daggers, stone maces, bows and arrows, and slingshots. Although shields were available, a warrior usually carried his weapon in both hands and had a dagger strapped to his side. Protective armor was typically no more than a hat of cloth or leather. Battles in open land consisted of barrages of arrows when armies were less than 300 feet apart, because the bow of the time was accurate only up to that distance. The barrage could be followed by a charge. The enemy would meet the charging warriors with spears and rocks hurled from slingshots. A battle between big city-states could result in 10,000 dead.

Gilgamesh was famous as a city builder. Songs and poems lauded him for the great wall he directed to be built around Uruk. It was constructed from fired clay bricks, which were expensive but durable for the time; good stone for building was hard to find in southern Mesopotamia. The wall was wide enough for two chariots to pass side by side, and it had many towers. Such defenses were necessary because military leaders were learning how to organize their troops for coordinated attacks that could overwhelm lesser defenses with the sheer number of warriors scaling the walls.

By the end of the Early Dynastic Period, an arms race had developed. Bigger walls meant bigger weapons for knocking walls down. Skulls crushed by maces led to the development of metal helmets, which in turn resulted in the invention of a battle-ax that could crash through metal. This, in turn, created the need for sturdier helmets, leading to the development of new casting techniques and then sturdier ax blades that curved, making cutting through helmets easier.

Old Akkadian Empire (ca. 2350–ca. 2100 b.c.e.)

The king who founded the Old Akkadian Empire may have been history's first military genius. Sargon I (r. 2334–2279 b.c.e.) established what is thought to have been the first could return fire, he forced opponents into disastrous charges against well-organized formations of warriors with spears at the ready, or opponents fled because they could not come to grips with his warriors.

Sargon's successors continued to innovate. Perhaps their most significant contribution to military history was the development of specialized units within the army. Rather than having every warrior fight with every weapon, they developed units of archers, spearmen, slingshot specialists who backed up the spearmen, and charioteers.

NEO-ASSYRIAN EMPIRE (CA. 1000–CA. 626 B.C.E.)

The foremost practitioners of war of the ancient Near East were the Assyrians. They did not begin that way. Originally they settled in a mountainous region through which several trade routes passed, making their living as traders and farmers. Both trading and farming would remain vital to the economy that funded the Assyrian military. During the Old Assyrian Period (ca. 1813–ca.1365 B.C.E.) Assyria's wars tended to be reactions to aggression. Their mountains did not afford them much protection, and their harvests attracted the greed of nomads to the north and city-states to the south.

The archer was the most important weapon in the Assyrian army. The Assyrians developed a pairing of an archer with a shield bearer. The shield was composed of reeds with an outer covering of animal skin or metal. It rose higher than the heads of the shield bearer and archer, curving up over the bearer's head. It was intended to allow the archer to focus on his job of shooting the enemy while someone else worried about keeping him alive. Both bearer and archer were usually armed with daggers for hand-to-hand fighting, but it was the Assyrian commander's intention to keep his archers away from direct contact with the enemy.

During this period the Hittite Empire (ca. 1650–ca. 1200 B.C.E.) had developed to the west, in present-day Turkey. The Hittites introduced the phalanx to warfare in the Near East. The Hittite phalanx consisted of a block of soldiers who marched toward the enemy in lockstep with spears evenly spaced. The soldiers were heavy infantry, wearing weighty uniforms draped with iron plates. The Hittites' tactics involved trapping enemies into direct encounters with the heavy infantry, whose skills and armor surpassed those of others in the Near East. Further, the Hittites used chariots as true offensive weapons. Their units of chariots moved swiftly across battlefields, pulled by horses and using spoked wheels.

In about 1200 B.C.E. the Hittite Empire collapsed. Raiders whom modern historians call the Sea Peoples cut off some of the Hittites' trade routes to the south, and the Assyrians cut off their trade routes to the east. Their capital was sacked. This left openings for lesser kingdoms to expand, and it left much of the territory to the west of Assyria open for conquest.

In 1595 B.C.E. Assyria had become a vassal of the Mittani Kingdom, but that kingdom was absorbed by the Hit-

Clay prism of King Sennacherib, ca. 689 B.C.E., upon which are recorded eight successful military campaigns against various peoples who refused to submit to Assyrian domination (Courtesy of the Oriental Institute of the University of Chicago)

standing army, consisting of 5,400 men, with whom he ate daily. The Sumerian battlewagon was a clumsy vehicle, with four heavy wheels and pulled by onagers—wild asses from central Asia. In battle Sargon and his commanders would ride the wagons more for transportation around the battlefield than for use in combat, but from the battlewagons archers could fire on the enemy while staying out of the way of counterattacks.

The use of formations in battle and one great advance in weaponry may have been behind Sargon's ability to crush his enemies and build the world's first great empire. The advance was the composite bow. It consisted of an inner layer of bone, a middle layer of wood, and an outer layer of leather. Sometimes more than one kind of wood was used, all to give the bow more power. The result was that Sargon's archers had a range almost 200 feet greater than that of enemy archers. By having his army fire on the enemy long before the enemy tites during the 1300s B.C.E., giving Assyria a chance to assert its independence, which it did under King Ashu-uballit I (r. ca. 1365–ca. 1330 B.C.E.). Thereafter, the Assyrians embarked on centuries of military adventures, not all successful. King Shalmaneser I (r. ca. 1273–ca. 1244 B.C.E.) secured Assyria's northern frontier with wars in central Asia. King Tikulti-ninurta I (r. ca. 1244–ca. 1208 B.C.E.) attacked Babylonia in 1220 B.C.E., occupying the city of Babylon until 1213 B.C.E., and he spread his conquests into the Zagros Mountains to the east before he was assassinated by one of his sons.

The Assyrian Empire thereafter fell apart, pulled itself together, and fell apart again. As the Neo-Assyrian Empire it reached its zenith and gained the military reputation that it now has. The Neo-Assyrian society was geared toward making war. Its people came to rely on war as a source of luxury goods. Their boys were trained almost all their lives to be warriors, and military service was not only expected of all young men but also considered the best thing a man could do. At the same time women were repressed. They were required to wear robes that totally covered them when they were out in public, and their principal purpose was to bear boys for the military. Newborn girls were often killed because they were considered valueless.

The Neo-Assyrian military machine was a master of propaganda. It advertised its victories, spreading accounts of the horrors it had visited on its opponents. Before attacking a major stronghold such as Jerusalem, it would attack surrounding villages and towns, slaughtering the inhabitants as a display of power to discourage the defenders of the stronghold. Typically, an Assyrian envoy would stand outside the stronghold to ask in the Assyrian language that the defenders yield to the greater might of Assyria. This would involve detailing some of the horrors visited on those who resisted Assyria. Sometimes the authorities of the stronghold would agree to surrender, and usually the Assyrians would let the residents live, though they would require a very heavy tribute and force some of the men to join their army.

Often the authorities of the stronghold refused to surrender. Then the Assyrians would speak to the defenders in their native language, telling them of how they would suffer once the Assyrians won the battle. The hope was that the common people would rebel rather than endure the misery of an Assyrian victory. Thereafter tall stakes would be driven into the ground within view of the defenders, and captured soldiers and civilians would be impaled on the stakes. This was intended to demoralize the defenders. Then prisoners would be taken in view of the defenders and tortured in ways that Assyrian scribes recorded in agonizing detail. Sometimes the victims would be put in cages on carts that were pulled in circles around a besieged city to display to as many people as possible the torture being inflicted. Such events were recorded on stone walls and monuments throughout the empire to frighten anyone who might wish to rebel.

By about 722 B.C.E. the Assyrian government had adopted a policy of avoiding fighting as many of the enemy as possible. The extraordinary cruelties inflicted on people were intended to inspire others to surrender rather than fight. Typically, in a city that did not surrender, the Assyrians raped every woman or girl they found and killed the military-age men. Boys would be made slaves. Captive populations would be shipped to parts of the empire where the Assyrian government could watch them and where they were wanted as forced labor, because the Assyrian government was depleting its lands of workers through its relentless warfare.

The Assyrians established storehouses throughout their empire, where their army could find supplies when it moved. At the core of the army was the *qurbuti*, the royal guard. This consisted of elite troops from Assyrian nobility. Assyrian kings often led their troops in battle, and the *qurbuti* accompanied them. When the king was not present, the commanding officer was the *tartanu*, who was to be obeyed as if he were the king. The army also had cavalry, called *pethallu*. However, the principal fighting units were the infantry and the chariot regiments. The most important fighters in the infantry remained the archers, who carried 50 arrows in their quivers. Most of the rest of the infantry was supposed to protect the archers. Sometimes the Assyrians fielded an army whose infantry consisted only of archers and their shield bearers. Of greatest importance were the chariots.

The Assyrian chariot was a swift vehicle, with a metal undercarriage making it tough and durable. Its spoked wheels had metal-studded rims and blades projecting from their hubs. Assyrian chariots moved as units and were used to break up enemy infantry lines. With two horses pulling each, the chariots would charge not as a line parallel to the enemy line but as a column perpendicular to the enemy line. One after another the chariots would smash into the line and then disperse as they spread the enemy line apart, their bladed wheels chewing through enemy infantry. Assyrian tactics were intended to terrify an enemy, and the chariots were truly frightful.

The driver of an Assyrian war chariot had to press forward against the front screen of the chariot to hold himself steady. On a light chariot the only other passenger was an archer or a lancer. On a heavy chariot the car would be rectangular to hold one or two shield bearers or a warrior to defend the rear of the chariot. The lancer would be armed with spears or javelins, usually tipped with iron. Sometimes lancers were used as infantrymen.

Eventually Assyria faced a shortage of men of any age; for this reason, boys younger than military age and retired soldiers often were pressed into service. The vassal troops, rarely happy about serving far from home in wars not of their own making, were unreliable. Rebellions broke out on the fringes of the empire, the Medes to the east invaded Assyria, and the army was spread too thinly to cope with all the demands at the same time. The Babylonians and Medes raced each other to the capital of Assyria, with the Medes getting there first. Over a period of about 10 years, the surviving Assyrians were hunted down and exterminated.

PERSIAN EMPIRE (CA. 538–CA. 331 B.C.E.)

The Persian Empire is also known as the Achaemenid Empire, named for its founder Achaemenes (r. ca. 600s B.C.E.). The first great Persian military leader was Cyrus the Great (r. ca. 559–ca. 529 B.C.E.). Persian soldiers were especially skilled in the use of slings and bows and arrows, perhaps a result of their origin in mountains in Iran, where hunting with such weapons would have been important. Although the Persians borrowed much of their military organization from that of the Assyrians, horses were rarely used by them in Cyrus the Great's era, relegating chariots to minor roles, whereas the infantry was of primary importance.

As was the case with the Assyrians, archers were very important to the Persian Empire. The Persians imitated the combining of shield bearers with archers, but they massed their archers behind a line of shield bearers. The shields were made of rectangles of leather stretched over rodlike willow twigs called osiers, and then the leather was allowed to harden, creating a tough but easily lifted shield. The shield bearers would form a line, one next to the other, allowing their shields to create a long, tall wall, behind which archers, also arrayed in lines, fired their arrows in volleys. Unfortunately, the shield bearers lacked weapons other than daggers for close-quarters fighting, a problem the Persian army continually tried to solve by experimenting with different kinds of weapons such as spears and curved swords.

The core of the army was the king's spearmen, the *arstibara*. After them came the *amrtaka* ("immortals"), a division of troops that gained its name from its never being allowed to be short of troops; its strength was always at 10,000. The major unit of the army was the *hazarabam*, the regiment, which had 1,000 troops. Its commanding officer was the *hazarapatis*. The *hazarabam* was divided into 10 units of 100 troops. Each unit was a *satabam*, commanded by a *satapatis*. Each *satabam* was divided into 10 companies of 10 men each. A company was a *dathabam*. On the battlefield each *dathabam* would be lined up in a column perpendicular to the front line, with its leader, the *dathapatis*, in front. The *dathapatis* carried a 6-foot spear or a large protective shield. The other nine soldiers in his company carried either bows or falchions, which were curved swords. When all the men behind the company leaders had bows and arrows, the company leaders would form a protective line of shields.

All Persian men were expected to serve in the army. A boy lived with his mother, apart from his father, until age five and then with his father, apart from his mother, until age 20, during which time he learned skills important to combat. From 20 to 24 years of age a man served in the army. His period of enlistment could be extended, and he was subject to recall to military service until he was 50 years old.

As he conquered much of the Near East, Cyrus the Great relied on vassal troops to supplement his core of Persian infantry, especially vassal cavalry. Cyrus the Great decided that his army should have a cavalry composed of Persians. Thus he established a new unit of the army composed of horseback riders. When horses and their supplies were captured in his campaigns, he distributed them among his nobility. Then he declared that it would be considered a disgrace for any noble to be seen walking rather than riding. The cavalry would be considered an elite unit. The most prestigious unit of all would be the 1,000 horsemen drawn from the nobility and called the *huvaka* ("king's kinsmen").

Not much is known about the organization of the Persian navy. It was developed during the reign of Cambyses (r. ca. 529–ca. 522 B.C.E.) as a response to the Egyptian navy, which had helped thwart Persian efforts to invade Egypt. It apparently borrowed ideas from the Corinthian navy, dividing its ships into units of 30 as the Corinthians did. When it was sent into battle against the Greeks in the 400s B.C.E., the Persian navy was decisively defeated. Military historians debate why this happened, but it appears that the Greek navy was more ably led and its sailors more skilled at the techniques required to disable enemy ships.

The failure of the Persian army to defeat the Greeks, first at Marathon in 490 B.C.E. and later with a massive army of between 700,000 and 1,500,000 troops, seems to have been a shock to the Near East. The perplexing methods of combat of the Scythians had been only an annoyance. The Scythians used archers on horseback, who attacked and then rode away, attacked again and rode away, and so on until the Persians stopped chasing them. In the case of the Greeks the Persians fought an enemy willing to engage in large battles of massed infantry and horsemen.

The Persian soldiers were courageous and determined fighters, but their commanders had no answer for the Greek soldier called a hoplite. The hoplites were members of heavy infantry, armed with spears and protected by shields that strapped to their forearms, allowing for a wide range of motion. Holding their shields high for protection from the Persian archers and covered by the fire of Greek archers, the hoplites were swiftly able to take advantage of changing conditions on the battlefield to close in on Persian units of archers. When the Greek style of fighting combined with the genius of Alexander the Great, the Persians often found their units outmaneuvered. From 336 to 328 B.C.E. Alexander the Great fought Persia, conquering the country just five years before his death in 323 B.C.E.

IRANIAN EMPIRES

One of Alexander the Great's generals, Seleucus I (r. ca. 311–ca. 281 B.C.E.), founded the Seleucid Kingdom (ca. 311–ca. 140 B.C.E.). The Seleucid army was most notable for its cavalry, which was probably the best in the Near East in the 100s B.C.E., but they were overcome by the Parthians, who were also famous for their cavalry. The Parthians had migrated into Iran from central Asia. The Arsacid Dynasty of Parthia was founded by Arsaces I (r. ca. 250–ca. 248 B.C.E.) and lasted from about 250 B.C.E. to 226 C.E. It was King Mithridates I (r. ca. 174–ca. 136 B.C.E.) who toppled the Seleucid Kingdom.

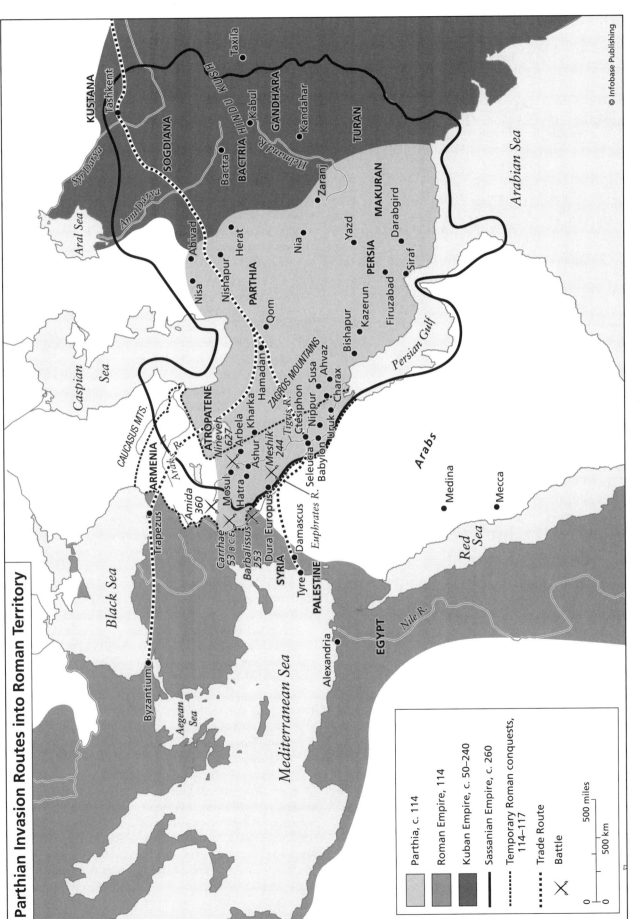

Parthian Invasion Routes into Roman Territory

KUSTANA

Tashkent

SOGDIANA

Syr Darya

Amu Darya

Aral Sea

Abivad

Nisa

Nishapur

Herat

PARTHIA

Qom

Hamadan

ZAGROS MOUNTAINS

ATROPATENE

Nineveh

627

Arbela

Ashur

Kharka

Mosul

Hatra

Araks R.

ARMENIA

Amida
360

CAUCASUS MTS.

Caspian
Sea

Black Sea

Trapezus

Byzantium

Aegean
Sea

Carrhae
53 B.C.E.

Barballissus
253

Dura Europus

SYRIA

Damascus

Tyre

PALESTINE

Meshik
244

Seleucia

Ctesiphon

Nippur

Susa

Ahvaz

Charax

Uruk

Babylon

Tigris R.

Euphrates R.

Mediterranean Sea

EGYPT

Alexandria

Nile R.

Red
Sea

Arabs

Medina

Mecca

Bishapur

Kazerun

Firuzabad

PERSIA

Yazd

Nia

Siraf

Darabgird

MAKURAN

Persian Gulf

Zaranj

Bactra

BACTRIA

Helmand R.

HINDU KUSH

Kabul

GANDHARA

Kandahar

TURAN

Taxila

Arabian Sea

© Infobase Publishing

Legend

	Parthia, c. 114
	Roman Empire, 114
	Kuban Empire, c. 50–240
	Sassanian Empire, c. 260
-----	Temporary Roman conquests, 114–117
•••••	Trade Route
✕	Battle

0   500 miles

0   500 km

The Parthian and Roman armies battled each other for nearly 300 years, from the first century B.C.E. to the third century C.E.

The Parthians organized their army into 1,000-man units called dragons. The most important part of the army was its cavalry. The Parthians were master horsemen who developed the Parthian shot. A Parthian shot occurred when a horseman pretended to be fleeing and then twisted in his saddle to shoot backward at his enemy. The army combined unarmored horse archers with cataphracts—cavalry with heavy armor and arms. The light cavalry harassed the enemy while the cataphracts hammered enemy lines. Cataphracts were recruited from the retainers of Parthian nobility. Sometimes mercenaries were employed for other units.

The effectiveness of Parthian tactics and troops was shown in the Battle of Carrhae in 53 b.c.e., in present-day Turkey. A Roman army invaded Parthia, led by Marcus Licinius Crassus (115–53 b.c.e.). When he learned where the Parthian army awaited him, he had a choice of two routes. He took the route that crossed open land. The Parthians had anticipated his taking the other route, and their main army was waiting there for him. Mostly light cavalry was all the Parthian army had to fight Crassus's army in the open route. The Parthians gamely attacked, harassing the Romans with arrows. Crassus pulled his army into a square, open in the middle. The Parthian cavalry circled the Romans and fired without taking care to aim; the Roman formation was dense, and its troops were easy targets. After losing 20,000 men without ever coming to grips with the enemy, the Roman army retreated.

The Parthian Empire eventually fell to an insider rather than from invasion from the outside. Ardashir I (r. 224–241 c.e.) overthrew the last Arsacid king, founding the Sassanian Empire (226–641 c.e.). The Sassanian army had infantry, horse cavalry, and war elephants. The infantry mostly comprised spearmen who were ordered to hold their positions against attack. The cavalry were well armored and responsible for breaking up enemy formations. The elephants carried towers containing archers. Before battle the army arrayed itself into three parts. In the center, typically the largest part, were archers and the elephants. Although horses were armored, the elephants were not; they were protected instead by an escort of infantry.

ASIA AND THE PACIFIC
by Michael J. O'Neal

Warfare in the modern world is typically waged between nation-states. For various reasons one of these states, with its own clearly defined borders, chooses to go to war with another. While civil wars continue to plague some countries, modern warfare has most often been between nations rather than within nations.

Warfare in the ancient world, including Asia, often had a different purpose. Modern nations such as China, India, Korea, and Japan did not always exist as clearly defined nation-states, with fixed borders and a central government accepted by the entire population. These regions tended to be more in the nature of collections of smaller kingdoms. Sometimes these kingdoms united to form larger states. Just as often, though, they fought with one another as one tried to extend the reach of its authority and influence. While external enemies remained a threat, internal enemies often were the target of warfare and conquest. The result was a long, bloody process of uniting regions into larger nations.

CHINA

The dominant military power of ancient Asia was China. In the absence of any records, little is known about war and conquest—or any other topic—in prehistoric China. China as a nation began to emerge during the era called the Three Sovereigns and Five Emperors, followed by the Xia Dynasty. Most of what is known about these eras is legendary, even mythical, although archaeological finds have confirmed that at least some of what was written about them by later Chinese writers is probably based in fact. The known history of China begins with the Shang Dynasty (sometimes referred to as the Yin Dynasty), which ruled from about 1500 to about 1045 b.c.e. Much of the history of the Shang and the dynasties that followed into the Common Era is a history of internal warfare and rebellion.

The Shang Dynasty itself began in war, for historians believe that the dynasty's founder was a rebel who overthrew the earlier Xia Dynasty. Over the next several hundred years the Shang emperors fought a series of wars to defend their realm, which encompassed primarily northern China, from invaders from the steppes (vast, open grasslands) of inner Asia. At this point China as a nation was by no means fully formed. The region consisted of numerous settlements and city-states that did not coalesce into a unified nation until much later. Thus, warfare was typically a matter of conflict between neighboring city-states as they jockeyed for power and tried to extend their authority over a broader region.

The Shang Dynasty was overthrown by the Zhou Dynasty in about 1045 b.c.e. The Zhou were a people who had settled to the west of the territories ruled by the Shang, and for a long period they submitted to Shang authority. But as the Zhou population grew, its region became more powerful than that controlled by the Shang, particularly since the Shang were continually waging war with northern invaders. Thus, the Zhou defeated the Shang and established a dynasty that ruled 200 to 250 city-states until 256 b.c.e.

Their reign was not without complications, however. Barbarians from the north, particularly the Xiongnu, a nomadic people who controlled a large central Asian empire, continued to invade Chinese lands. (The Xiongnu are frequently referred to in the literature as Huns, but they are not to be confused with the Teutonic Huns of Europe.) In 771 b.c.e. they successfully overran the western portion of the Zhou lands, including its capital city. The king was killed, and his son fled to the east. Thus, the Zhou Dynasty is divided into two periods, the Western Zhou (1045–771 b.c.e.) and the Eastern Zhou (770–256 b.c.e.) The Eastern Zhou is further divided into two periods. The first, called the Spring and Autumn Period, was a time of great instability. Among the large number of Chinese city-states, no single state had much power. Thus, they joined into a series of continuously shifting alliances as a way of defending themselves from the northern barbarians.

The name of the second phase of the Eastern Zhou, the Warring States Period, gives a clear indication of the nature of Chinese life during this time. Many of the military and political alliances that had been forged during the Spring and Autumn Period fell apart. China descended into considerable chaos as various states tried to fill the power vacuum and absorb other states, and the Zhou emperor ruled in name only. Warfare between states was nearly constant. By the end of the period, instead of hundreds of city-states, the number was eight or nine, with each vying to gain control of all of China. The nature of warfare changed dramatically during this period. Earlier, war had been conducted in feudal fashion, with aristocratic nobles each leading his own small army. During the Warring States Period armies became much larger and were made up of professional warriors.

It was during the brief, but ruthless Qin Dynasty that China's kingdoms merged for the first time into an imperial nation. The Qin emperors, who ruled from 221 to 207 B.C.E., confiscated all weapons, including those of the nobles who had fought during the Warring States Period. This step was taken to prevent uprisings. The Qin rulers also expanded China's borders by going to war against the northern barbarians. During the Warring States Period nobles had built walls and fortifications to defend their realms. The Qin emperors ordered that all these walls be linked to form China's first great wall to keep out foreign invaders. (The Great Wall of China familiar to tourists was built much later, under the Ming Dynasty.)

Despite the efforts of the Qin rulers to quell dissent and rebellion, they were unsuccessful. Near the end of the dynasty the nobles began to reassert their power. Peasants, prisoners, and soldiers rebelled. The result was the overthrow of the Qin Dynasty and the creation of the Han Dynasty, which ruled until 220 C.E. The Han Dynasty, however, began with an interregnum period from 206 to 202 B.C.E. called the period of Chu-Han Contention. During this period, in the vacuum created by the overthrow of the Qin Dynasty, two factions emerged that went to war to determine which would lead the kingdom. One faction was the Han people; the other was the Chu. These factions were led by the nobles who had been stripped of their power during the Qin Dynasty. The numerous battles these two sides fought—the battles of Julu, Pengcheng, Lingbi, and Xi River, for example—became part of the cultural identity of the Chinese and are still depicted in Chinese movies, television shows, and even board games. The power struggle was fierce; at times the warring armies were as large as half a million men. After the tide shifted back and forth several times, the Han, led by Liu Pang (r. 206–195 B.C.E.), emerged victorious and created the Han Dynasty.

The Han Dynasty tried to scale back the level of warfare. To the north the rulers paid tribute to the Xiongnu and tried to buy peace through intermarriage. The dynasty also tried to appease other neighboring nomads, which continued to be a threat. At the same time, the Han Dynasty used its superior military force to extend its borders into the regions of present-day Vietnam and Korea. The military also functioned to keep open the Silk Road, the trading route that eventually extended westward all the way to Rome. In 154 B.C.E. the military had to put down the Rebellion of the Seven States, led by several minor princes who objected to the Han Dynasty's efforts to centralize the government. The rebellion was marked by initial ferocious fighting, but in the end it lasted only three months.

Less than three decades later the Han Dynasty concluded that its treaties with the Xiongnu were ineffective and costly. In 129 B.C.E. a force of 40,000 Chinese cavalry attacked. Warfare persisted intermittently until 119 B.C.E., when a Chinese force of 100,000 cavalry and 200,000 foot soldiers drove the Xiongnu into the Gobi Desert. The campaign, while successful, was costly; the Chinese took 140,000 horses into the desert, but fewer than 30,000 returned. The Xiongnu, however, just would not go away. In the first century of the Common Era, China dispatched one of its most famous generals, Pan Ch'ao (31–101 C.E.), to subdue them and drive them out of the Tarim Basin to China's west. In 97 C.E. he commanded an army of 70,000 men to drive them even farther west; he went as far as the Caspian Sea, where he struck an alliance with the Parthian Empire. Despite all of China's successes against the Xiongnu, in 311 C.E., 100 years after the end of the Han Dynasty, the Xiongnu sacked Luoyang, the capital of the Han.

One of the last military actions of the Han Dynasty was the suppression of the Yellow Turban Rebellion, sometimes called the Yellow Scarves Rebellion. The rebellion took place in 184 and was led by Daoist peasants who objected to the regime's decision to make China a Confucian rather than a Daoist state. Despite fielding an army of 360,000, the rebels were unsuccessful and were put down in 185. Fighting erupted again in 186, 188, and 192, when the rebellion was finally ended.

For many historians, the Yellow Turban Rebellion, so called because of the yellow headscarves the rebels wore, was the unofficial start of the Three Kingdoms Period (220–263 B.C.E.) that followed the Han Dynasty. Again, China was wracked by instability. The "three kingdoms" were those of Wei, Shu, and Wu, though they were not really kingdoms but regions whose emperors each claimed to be the legitimate heir to the Han Dynasty. The period was marked by a great deal of infighting, which eventually led to the defeat of the Shu by the Wei. The Wei, in turn, were then defeated by an alliance of the Wu and the Jin Dynasty (265–420 C.E.). The period was extremely bloody, with a large percentage of the population killed during the wars that raged from about 190 to 280. On the heels of these civil wars came the War of the Eight Princes (also called the Rebellion of the Eight Kings or Rebellion of the Eight Princes), another period of civil war from 291 to 306 C.E. The rebellion was centered in northern China. Again, it led to huge population losses, which greatly reduced the power of the Jin Dynasty. The dynasty itself was rent by divisions, leading to the creation of the Western Jin Dynasty (265–316 C.E.) and the Eastern Jin Dynasty (317–420

C.E.). One of the most important battles in ancient Chinese history was the Battle of Fei in 383 C.E., when the numerically inferior eastern Jin army defeated the surviving western Jin to claim control over the throne.

One of the results of this long history of warfare was the production of texts about military strategy. One is referred to as the "Thirty-Six Strategies." The origin of the book is shrouded in mystery. Historians generally believe that it was compiled by a General Wang during the Warring States Period. It consists of a number of proverbs about warfare, many of which were probably traditional by that time. The number 36 is a figure of speech used to refer to "numerous" strategies, divided into six sections. To cite one example, the text advises military commanders to "deceive the sky to cross the ocean." The text explains this precept by saying that the clever commander hides his true intentions by going about daily activities in full view of the enemy; hiding or moving about in the darkness only attracts suspicion.

The other great military text from ancient China is *The Art of War*, written, it is thought, in the sixth century by Suntzu. The book has 13 chapters and is still regarded by military planners as the definitive treatise on military strategy—particularly on how to win a battle or war without actually fighting but rather by outsmarting the enemy. The book continues to be required reading for officers in Asian militaries. Many of the book's statements have become proverbial, such as the famous quote "All warfare is based on deception." The book was rediscovered in the West in the 1980s when corporations and political candidates began using its precepts to plot business or campaign strategies and outsmart their rivals. The book has also entered the popular culture in the West, with numerous references to it in movies, plays, sports, music, board games, and television shows.

Based on these and other texts, as well as on the archaeological record, historians and archaeologists have been able to reconstruct the nature of warfare in ancient China. They know, for example, that weapons during much of ancient China's history were made of bronze. Examples include the spear, whose point was made of bronze, and the dagger-ax, which was primary weapon of foot soldiers. A dagger-ax consisted of a dagger-shaped blade mounted perpendicularly on a wooden haft, or handle. Often the blade consisted of a dagger on one side and a scythe-shaped blade on the other. Other weapons included the sword, many quite elaborate and ornate, and the crossbow. Chinese soldiers also wore armor, which tended to be light and flexible rather than heavy and thick, trading the stopping power for speed and maneuverability. The Chinese invented gunpowder, probably in the third century C.E., but gunpowder was not used as a component of military weapons until much later.

The horse-drawn chariot was a primary instrument of war. Ancient China was a feudal society, and there emerged a warrior class that emphasized the skills of horsemanship and the handling of the chariot. Horseback riding tended to be difficult for Chinese men, who wore robes rather than trousers, but skills in military horsemanship were highly developed among members of the aristocratic warrior class, and many troops stormed into battle on horseback. In about the fifth century C.E. the stirrup was introduced, allowing mounted warriors to retain stability and balance and so fight on horseback with swords and lances.

Early warfare tended to be ceremonial and ritualized. As time went on it became more brutal and bloody. Much emphasis was placed on deception and tricking the enemy. Also common was siege warfare, where an attacking army surrounded a city, bombarded it with missiles launched by catapults, and wore down the residents over time. In more conventional battles the norm was not to arrange regiments of troops in a fixed order of battle but rather to rely on firepower using crossbows. Large numbers of archers loaded their weapons, took aim on the order of their commander, and then fired simultaneously, in this way overwhelming the enemy by the sheer number of arrows that had to be ducked.

Naval warfare played a major part in the history of ancient China. During the Qin Dynasty, for example, China had a fleet of ships capable of transporting close to one million pounds of grain to feed troops during war. The Qin also had a fleet of *lou chuan*, or "castle ships," with large, elevated decks. The Han continued to build warships, and its fleet reached 2,000 castle ships able to carry 200,000 seamen.

INDIA

The history of warfare and conquest in ancient India in many ways parallels that of China. Rather than being a unified nation-state, India was a collection of numerous smaller kingdoms. At times the number of kingdoms was as few as 16. Such was the case during the Iron Age in about 500 B.C.E., when the 16 kingdoms were collectively called the Mahajanadapas. At other times the number of kingdoms and principalities was much larger, as many as 100 or more. As in China, these kingdoms often competed with one another for territory and resources, so they often went to war. Warfare, though, was conducted on a smaller scale than it was in China and consisted primarily of border skirmishes.

India, however, faced more external threats than did the Chinese. Like China, India was subject to invasion by barbarians from the north. One of the greatest civilizations of the ancient world, the Indus Valley civilization, was destroyed by northern Aryan invaders in about 1600 B.C.E. Additionally, in the fifth century B.C.E. India was invaded by the Persians under the king Darius the Great (r. 522–486 B.C.E.) and was ruled by the Persian Empire for nearly 200 years until Macedonia, under the leadership of Alexander the Great (r. 336–323 B.C.E.), conquered the Persian Empire, including its holdings in India. One of the key events in this conquest was the Battle of the Hydaspes River (now called the Jhelum River) in 326 B.C.E. Alexander invaded to subdue the various Indian kings, but one, Porus (d. between 321 and 315 B.C.E.), who ruled the area around Punjab, resisted. Alexander sent a large army against him. Porus and his army put up fierce resistance, but eventually Alexander won and made the area the eastern border of his empire.

India as a unified empire did not flex its military might until the Maurya Dynasty, which maintained a standing army of three-quarters of a million troops, most belonging to a warrior caste. The empire, founded about 321 B.C.E. by Chandragupta, was based in eastern India but in time stretched across western, central, and portions of southern India. One of the greatest achievements of the Maurya was the liberation of those parts of the country that were occupied by the Macedonians. One of Chandragupta's ministers, Kautilya (fl. 300 B.C.E.), wrote a text called the *Arthashastra*, a book that examined the military arts along with politics, economics, and other subjects.

One of the most important rulers of the Maurya was Chandragupta's grandson, Asoka (r. ca. 265–238 B.C.E. or ca. 273–232 B.C.E.). Early in his reign Asoka was a talented military commander. His major achievement was to lead a large army against the Kalinga, one of the kingdoms of southern India. Although he triumphed, he lost an estimated 10,000 troops, and when he saw the devastation the war had caused both to the armies and to the civilian population, he renounced war and accepted the teachings of Buddhism. However, as many historians note, he had no further reason to go to war, for he had successfully united most of what is modern-day India.

Stone figure of the war god Skanda, from eastern India, eighth to ninth century C.E.; Skanda was a poular deity in ancient India. (© The Trustees of the British Museum)

In the centuries that followed the end of Maurya rule, India again fragmented. The invading Kushans established an empire that stretched across the center of India. The later Gupta Empire, which ruled from C.E. 240 to 550, again united India, primarily because of its strong military organization.

One of the most important military weapons of the Gupta Empire, as well as the empires of its predecessors, was the chariot. Indian chariots were more like troop-transport vehicles, in contrast to the light Roman and Egyptian chariots that normally come to mind. They carried at least two men—the driver and an archer—but many carried up to seven and were so heavy that four and even six horses were needed to pull them. Sometimes the chariots were simply driven at high speed into the middle of a fight, where their large wheels crushed enemy infantrymen. Meanwhile, the archers were as high as six feet off the ground, giving them a tactical advantage over enemy troops on the ground.

Another important tool used by Indian armies, which came into use in about 1500 B.C.E., was the elephant, which Indians continued to use in war until the 19th century. Elephants were a measure of wealth and prestige; Candragutpa's army had more than 21,000. Elephants were analogous to modern-day tanks. They were covered with armor and often had long daggers, sometimes poisoned, attached to their tusks. Each elephant provided protection for as many as six infantrymen, who fought with bows and arrows, lances, and javelins and then retreated behind the elephant when necessary. Elephants were also used to break down walls and enemy fortifications. One battle tactic, used by Porus at the Battle of Hydaspes, was to range the elephants in a line, providing a kind of moving fortress or wall. Like chariots, they were often driven directly into the battle, crushing enemy troops underfoot as archers mounted on the elephant's back shot at men below. Some elephants were even trained to swing weapons such as balls and chains back and forth.

Unlike China, which made extensive use of horse-mounted cavalry, Indians did not in general fight with cavalry. One exception was the Rajput Kingdom, which had an extremely skilled cavalry. Otherwise, the main force of an Indian army was its infantry, which fought primarily with bows and arrows and hundreds of different types of swords. The armies of India tended to be huge, much larger than the armies fielded by other empires at the time. Even though the kingdoms at war might have been small, it was not unusual for their armies to number in the hundreds of thousands. India maintained a navy for military purposes; during Maurya rule the navy became quite extensive. Although the navy was used to subdue islands and provinces along the coast, naval warfare was not a prominent feature of India's military history.

India was particularly noteworthy for its use of planned battle tactics and formations. Some of these battle formations were complex and included the *chakra* (wheel), *suchi* (needle), *chayana* (hawk), *mala* (garland), *garuda* (eagle), and *padma* (lotus). These terms reflected the shape of the formations. Thus, for example, in the *padma* formation archers (as well as the commanding general) were on the inside, surrounded by cavalry and infantry in the shape of a lotus flower, protecting the archers. If enemy troops managed to force their way into the area between the "petals" of the flower, the two petals would swing together, crushing the troops between them. The *garuda* formation featured elephants and the most skilled archers at the "beak," archers who were almost as good at the "head," "wings" of swift cavalry and infantry troops, and a "body" of reserves behind.

KOREA

Like China and India, Korea consisted of a number of city-states, except that the number was much smaller, reflecting the small size of the Korean peninsula. During the first millennium B.C.E., the three city-states that dominated were Koguryo Paekche, and Silla, though other minor city-states existed as well. Within each of these city-states were several groups. Historically, these city-states have been called the Three Kingdoms, and the Three Kingdoms Period extended from the first century B.C.E. to 668 C.E., when Silla defeated Koguryo.

Militarily, the most powerful and dominant of the kingdoms was the Koguryo (the name from which *Korea* evolved). Beginning in 37 B.C.E. and into the first centuries of the Common Era a succession of monarchs united the kingdom, extended the kingdom's boundaries and, in particular, resisted the Chinese. During the reign of Taejo (53–146 C.E.) the Koreans mounted a number of well-conceived attacks on the Chinese garrisons at Lolang, Xiantu, and Liaodong. Their efforts were successful, and Koguryo became entirely independent. The regime also launched attacks against smaller states to absorb them. Later, under King Gwanggaeto the Great, who reigned from 391 to 412 C.E., the kingdom further expanded its territories through military conquest; in fact, the king's name means "great expander of territory." His army conquered at least 64 walled cities and 1,400 villages against a group called the Buyeo. He subdued additional peoples, annexed portions of the peninsula, conquered Silla, and waged war against Japan. The result of his efforts and those of his son was to turn Korea into a unified country for some 50 years.

Less is known about the tactics and organization of ancient Korean armies. Although there was a measure of internal warfare, Korea did not engage in extensive armed conflict with neighbors, and weapons technology was not as highly advanced as it was among the Chinese. In general, Koreans fought using farm implements and other common objects. Among them were the *ji pang e*, a cane; the *jang bond*, or long staff; the *jung bong*, a staff of middle length; the *tahn bong*, or short stick; the *jang tan-do*, or long dagger; and the *nat*, or sickle. Koreans, though, did not carry these simple weapons into battle without training. Martial-arts training provided warriors with the skills the needed, including the *hyungs*, or patterns, to turn these objects into lethal weapons. Accompanying this was training in hand-to-hand combat. Many of these Korean martial arts continue to be taught in the modern world.

The ancient Koreans, especially those in the kingdom of Silla, maintained a strong warrior class. Boys and young men were sent to schools that emphasized training in military tactics and the use of weapons, and the most promising ones were given further training and became members of the warrior class.

JAPAN

Warfare was infrequent during the Jōmon Period, the earliest period of Japanese history, which began about 13,000 B.C.E. and extended to about 300 B.C.E. During the fourth and third centuries B.C.E. waves of immigrants from Korea and China changed the fundamental makeup of Japan. From about 300 B.C.E. to 300 C.E. the Yayoi Period of Japanese history (named after the modern Tokyo suburb in which archaeological remains of the culture were found in the 19th century) was marked by the introduction of metal weapons and the rise of an aristocratic warrior class. Most of the warfare in which Japan took part was internal. Japan at the time was not a unified nation-state but a collection of villages and small cities. Japan was an agricultural society, and imbalances in the productivity of its numerous communities led to conflict. The basic unit of society was the clan (*uji*), and each clan, led by a noble, fielded an army to defend its interests. This emphasis on an aristocratic warrior class continued into the Yamato Period that followed the Yayoi. The Yamato emperors continued the process of subduing groups and even attacked part of Korea in 391 C.E. The pattern, then, was similar to those of China, India, and Korea, as small kingdoms warred with each other over resources and in the attempt to forge a larger kingdom.

Little is known about ancient Japanese battle tactics or military organization. It is known that some warriors fought on horseback, but most were foot soldiers. The archaeological record shows arrow points, swords, knives, and axes made of iron. Bronze weapons included halberds, swords, and spears. Because ancient Japanese society was feudal and clan based, no nation-state mounted a centralized army; rather, military forces were small, and their members consisted of the men that the feudal overlord could press into service.

OCEANIA

Social organization throughout Oceania, including Micronesia, New Guinea, and Australia, was highly fragmented in ancient times. None of these peoples built an empire or even a nation. The basic unit of organization was the tribe. Tribes were typically run by a "big man," the tribal leader. Geographically, the unit of organization was the island or, on larger islands, the village. Sometimes primitive warfare broke out as populations grew and tribes competed for resources; at times they resorted to cannibalism. Also, population pressures often forced islanders to leave to find new lands.

EUROPE
BY KIRK H. BEETZ

Violence was a large part of life in ancient Europe. Evidence of interpersonal violence first appears in the Mesolithic Period (ca. 8000–ca. 4000 B.C.E.), and mass burials such as those found at the Neolithic (ca. 7000–ca. 2000 B.C.E.) sites of Asparn in Austria and Talheim in Germany contain skeletons that bear signs of blows from stone axes. Traumatic injuries on bones are common features of Neolithic skeletons throughout Europe. The nature of this violence is difficult to determine, but from about 5500 B.C.E. onward banks and ditches around Neolithic settlements are common. Sites like Darion in Belgium were very clearly fortified with palisades and ditches, and movement into the sites was channeled through gates that could be defended. Since Darion was located on the frontier of Neolithic settlement at the time, it could be speculated that the site was defended against the hunter-gatherers on whose territory the farmers were encroaching.

Warfare in prehistoric Europe did not involve the conquest and control of territory because this would entail organized political units that did not yet exist. Instead, warfare primarily took the form of raids to obtain livestock or other resources, or they were factional struggles between the adherents of one chief or leader and those of another that turned violent. They probably involved techniques such as ambushes in the forest and the terrorization of the inhabitants of isolated settlements and farmsteads rather than large, organized groups of warriors. Violence may also have been directed at individuals rather than groups, as the wounds on the frozen, 5,300-year-old "Iceman" found in the Alps in 1991 suggest.

During the Bronze Age (ca. 2800–ca. 700 B.C.E.) and Iron Age (ca. 1000 B.C.E.–ca. 500 C.E.) the increased effort expended in the fortification of settlements as well as the many types of weapons that could be manufactured from bronze and iron indicate that conflict and warfare may have increased. Sites without much evidence of permanent settlement but with elaborate fortifications may have served as refuges in times of threat. The emergence of chiefs who could command their retainers to take up arms against communities loyal to their enemies shifted warfare to a new level of organization, and the chiefs themselves may have owed much of their status to their accomplishments in battle. Such values may have resulted in further escalation of warfare throughout the Bronze Age and Iron Age as individuals sought prestige and wealth.

Soon after 2000 B.C.E. the bow and arrow almost disappeared from European warfare. This was an odd development because the bow and arrow remained very important instruments of war in and near Asia. Throughout much of Europe, however, small projectile points that could have served as arrowheads almost disappeared from the archaeological record. There may be two reasons for this, one cultural and the other technological. By 2000 B.C.E. Europeans were adopting what archaeologists and historians call a heroic culture. They usually point to the epic poem the *Iliad* by the Greek poet Homer (eighth or ninth century B.C.E.) as an example of what a heroic culture was like. In a heroic culture warriors dominate. The apex of society is the individual leader who has distinguished himself or herself in combat. For Europe this may have encouraged the use of hand-to-hand weapons that were suited to contests between two easily identifiable warriors rather than long-range weapons in which death and victory came anonymously.

The key technological development was the sword. In southern Europe and the Near East small swords and daggers were favored for combat, but in the rest of Europe swords grew increasingly longer. By 900 B.C.E. the Celtic peoples were conquering Europe, and their weapon of choice was a slashing sword. Celtic masters of metalworking found ways to make long swords tough and durable. In the Near East swords remained short partly because metalworkers could not keep a sword strong and durable after it reached the length of about 2 feet; their swords would snap when they became too long. Short swords were intended more for stabbing than slashing, and they were used only for fighting in very close quarters, as in the combat favored by the Romans.

THE CELTS

By the time the Romans and Celts came into direct conflict in the late 400s B.C.E. the Celts had developed a style of warfare that favored the long sword. When they met and slaughtered a Roman army near the city of Rome in 390 B.C.E., they were using long swords with blunted points that were intended entirely for slashing. They also used spears, which they made in three lengths. The longest spear was designed for thrusting, the medium-length spear was made for throwing, and the short one was used for close combat. There seems to have been no loss of prestige for using spears, but the sword was the weapon of preference for most Celtic warriors.

The Celts of that era had fully developed their warrior culture. The best way for someone to advance in Celtic society was through heroic victories in combat. Also prestigious was the taking of the heads of fallen heroes and bringing home loot. An interesting aspect of Celtic looting was that they often gave their best loot to gods or goddesses, frequently dumping what they brought home into lakes and rivers as gifts to the gods who had aided them in battle.

Headhunting by the Celts appalled many of the Greeks and Romans who explored Celtic Europe before Rome's invasions of central Europe in the middle of the first century B.C.E. The heads of cowards were not taken. There was no glory in killing someone who ran away or froze in fear. Instead, Celtic warriors cut off the heads of people they had killed face to face. Although these heads were usually those of men in the male-dominated Celtic society, some were probably of women who had earned reputations as fearsome sorceresses or masters of combat. Celtic oral tradition has many tales of warriors being taught the skills of combat by women who were masters of battle, and killing them in armed combat was considered just as glorious as killing a great male warrior. The greater the warrior, the more prestige would come from having his head. The heads were hung on the walls of Celtic homes, and the family in the home would recite the many glorious achievements of the former owners of the heads, just as they would of the ancestors or living family members who had slain them.

In battle Celtic horsemen hung the heads from the necks of their horses as part of the intimidation of opponents that was always a part of Celtic warfare.

Celtic homes offer some indication of what Celtic wars were usually like. Most Celts lived in homesteads, which were houses on farms. The ground around the houses was fortified with a wooden wall. Although the defenses of a homestead would not protect residents from large armies, they were adequate for keeping out raiders. Most Celtic warfare consisted of raids, mostly for stealing cattle. Cattle were a form of booty that successful raiders could show off to others. Young men in small groups often wandered Celtic Europe looking for adventure, gaining experience in combat skills while fighting warriors at homesteads. This activity was treated more as a sport than serious warfare.

More serious were disputes over land, insults, or large numbers of stolen cattle. Protecting one's land and defending one's honor or the honor of one's group were considered imperative. Stealing a few dozen cattle was seen as excessively greedy. To settle these disputes, sometimes hundreds of warriors met for combat. The two sides would agree to meet at a place with sufficient open ground for everyone to see and to fight. Honor came from being seen to overcome a foe.

Until about the time of the Roman general Julius Caesar (100–44 B.C.E.), chariots figured prominently in Celtic warfare in continental Europe, and they lingered in Britain and Ireland for about 100 years after Caesar's era. The chariot had a driver who was a follower of the warrior who owned the chariot. He would stand out on the shaft that thrust out between the two horses from the car, maneuvering the chariot quickly to take his warrior through battle. In doing so, he won merit for his skill and for the great courage that it took for him to be vulnerable to the enemy. In the 200s B.C.E. the Celts invented the four-pommel saddle, which had two pommels in front of the thighs to hold them in place and two at the rear of the saddle. This gave the Celtic cavalryman the stability that allowed him to become a fighting machine, protected by chain-mail armor and shield while wielding an assortment of weapons that would be given to him by two mounted followers. The team was called a *trimarcisia*, which meant "three horses" in Celtic.

Sometimes these battles ended without bloodshed. A warrior might take charge of his chariot and put on a display of acrobatic daring—handstands, leaps, and tumbles—while racing in front of the enemy. Often, the warrior rode out on horseback and performed a variety of impressive stunts. Sometimes the skill of such a warrior was so great that both sides agreed to settle the dispute in favor of the side of the outstanding performer. Roman soldiers were amazed at the skill of such warriors before combat, but they had no idea the demonstrations were intended to substitute for actually killing people. On the other hand, the Romans well understood the idea of duels between champions to settle battles without additional bloodshed.

Before battle the champions would step forward from the ranks of their sides. The champions would proclaim their heroic deeds and the deeds of the warriors they had killed. The objective was to overawe the other side. The Celts believed that the spoken word was as powerful as the might of a well-armed warrior, and they took boasting seriously. Sometimes no one would emerge to answer the boasting of the opposing champion, and the battle was settled without bloodshed. If the boasting was answered by a champion, then each would compete in oratory, trying to make the other back down. If neither backed down, then they would fight.

During the duel the other warriors of both sides would shout and blow their *carnyxes*, which were horns with the heads of animals on one end. They made a great din of harsh sounds. Many of the warriors would have drunk alcohol before battle to make themselves reckless. Once one champion or the other won, the battle could be settled, and everyone could go home. Sometimes a new challenger emerged. One oral account tells of a warrior who killed more than 100 challengers before everyone agreed to stop fighting. Sometimes after a duel was over, the warriors of both sides would charge at each other in a frenzy of bloodlust, each hoping to be seen to be heroically felling enemies. This charge was intended to settle the battle; the Celts had no backup strategy if the charge failed. Thus, the losers in a charge often ran away. The Romans learned to take advantage of this: If they could withstand the first charge of the Celts, they could win, because the Celts had no idea what to do next.

There was another kind of war for the Celts, and this was the war of conquest. When a tribe grew too big for its territory or was driven from its lands by an invader, the members sometimes abandoned their homes and carried their property on carts. If attacked while carting across country, the men would engage the enemy in combat. If they were overcome, the women would fight next. To actually seize the carts meant having to defeat the children, who would guard them. A Greek explorer, Posidonius (ca. 135–51 B.C.E.), was awed by the size and strength of Celtic women. He and others noted that if a Celtic man fell in combat, the fighting was not always over, because his wife was skilled in hand-to-hand combat and could deliver tremendously powerful blows with her feet and her fists as well as with weapons. Children were trained in fighting almost from birth.

When Caesar invaded central Europe in 58 B.C.E. he introduced a form of warfare that was unfamiliar to the Celts. The Roman troops fought as tightly structured units. Like the Celts, their objective was usually to fight hand to hand, using their superior skill, armor, and weapons to overcome their adversaries. Further, the Roman objective was to annihilate the enemy. Over hundreds of years the Celts had developed a structure for combat that usually allowed them to avoid much bloodshed. The objective was to make one's point, dazzling friends and foes, and then go home and feast, exaggerating one's heroism while telling about the battle. The Romans rarely quit, but just kept coming. Celts often panicked and ran after their initial charge if this failed to put the Romans to flight.

When the Celts had competent leadership and worked together, they were almost more than the Romans could handle.

During the Roman conquest of Europe the Romans lost an entire legion near Belgium when a group of Celtic tribes under unified leadership fought them. The charismatic Celtic leader Vercingetorix (d. 46 B.C.E.), who had recently become chief of the Averni tribe, persuaded tribes from all over Europe to join into one army under his command. He lost battles to the Romans but kept his alliance intact, and he switched to guerilla warfare, which the Romans were ill equipped to handle.

The Celts burned their farms so the Romans would not find food, and they killed Roman units that were sent away from their main army to forage. Vercingetorix's crucial mistake was to take his army to Alesia, a fortified city in central Europe. It is likely that he did not know enough about Roman tactics to grasp that Roman engineers would build a fortification to surround Alesia to starve him out. He probably hoped that the Romans would be caught between relief forces from the north and his army in Alesia. The fractiousness of the Celts contributed to their downfall. Some refused to help and were later overwhelmed by the Romans. Others refused to send all their warriors. Three times the Celts attacked the Roman fortifications simultaneously from inside and out, twice nearly penetrating Roman lines and overwhelming the Romans. More warriors might have been enough for success, but the Celts were forced to surrender. Vercingetorix was imprisoned and later executed in 46 B.C.E.

Another able leader undone by Celtic customs of war was Queen Boudicca (d. 60/61 C.E.). She was the widow of a king of the Iceni, a tribe in eastern Britain. The Romans governed the Britons harshly, but her tribe had managed to keep the peace. The spark that touched off a firestorm was the rape of two Iceni girls by Roman soldiers. How old Boudicca was is unclear. She was old enough to have had a 12-year-old daughter, but she could still have been in her late 20s. She is usually imagined as middle-aged. She was described as big, but Celtic women in general looked big to the Romans. Nonetheless, she was either imposingly tall or heavy or both. Her blazing red hair hung down to her waist. In battle she painted half her body green and wore a large robe. She was said to be a sorceress.

In western Britain 10,000 Roman troops were slaughtering Druid priests. Perhaps as many as 10,000 marched to suppress Boudicca's rebellion. She had drawn to her about 100,000 warriors from homesteads across Britain. Instead of their usual frontal charge, the Celts quietly surrounded the Romans in a forest and then attacked from all sides at once. They killed nearly every Roman soldier. Their attacks on Roman towns and fortifications were similarly disciplined. They seemed unconcerned with taking trophies but fought the Roman way, totally destroying the enemy. The Roman governor fled London with his troops, leaving it to Boudicca's army.

By the time Boudicca brought her army to bear on the 10,000 Roman soldiers marching from the west, having exterminated the Druids, she had more than 200,000 warriors, along with supply wagons and fierce Celtic women to defend them. The Romans were holed up in a small valley. Boudicca arrayed her forces in a line to face them. Charioteers put on traditional Celtic shows of skill and bravery. The Romans stepped forward in a jagged line of V formations designed to break up the Celts' solid line, allowing Roman soldiers to hack at their foes from the front and the sides. The Celtic mistake was to allow themselves to be provoked. They charged as a mass, making a din so frightening that the Romans nearly panicked. Then the Celts pressed in on each other, trying to get at the Romans. Chariots overturned. Warriors suffocated. The Roman line held, and the Celts panicked. Following a longstanding tradition for Celtic war leaders, Boudicca committed suicide when it was clear the battle was lost.

THE GERMANS

By Caesar's era the Celts were beleaguered not only by the Romans from the south but also by the Germans from the north and east. In fact, Caesar began his campaign to conquer Gaul by first driving away Germanic invaders. These Germans came primarily from the north but were conquering their way through northeastern Europe and would eventually threaten Roman Europe from both north and east. Their motivations for conquest varied. Sometimes a tribe's population grew so much that the tribe chose to expand its territory to accommodate its growth. Sometimes a natural disaster or an invasion of its territory drove a tribe from its homes and into territory claimed by someone else. Often the conquest was inspired by a desire for loot. At other times a leader wanted glory.

War chiefs tended to serve only while a war lasted. Customs varied among Germanic tribes, with some choosing one leader while others chose two. One reason for choosing two might have been to prevent either one from using his power to make himself the permanent king. In early campaigns against Germanic armies the Romans noted that the Germans seemed wild and ill equipped. A German warrior was expected to supply his own weapons and armor. This meant that German armies of the first century B.C.E. often featured warriors wearing only breechcloths (loincloths), without even protection for their heads. Often they had no shields. They just carried spears and rarely axes or swords. In the close hand-to-hand combat that both Romans and Germans favored, the Romans cut the Germans to pieces.

The Germanic fighters differed from the Celtic warriors in an important way: They knew how to fight as units and were accustomed to having a long-term strategy. Like the Celts, they liked to show off their courage, toughness, and prowess. In the dead of winter men would ride naked and bareback on horses to display their contempt for discomfort. They were used to being cold, tired, and uncomfortable, and in the long run they would prove to be formidable opponents for other Europeans.

The basic Germanic fighting unit was the family. Family members stayed together during marches and battles and were responsible for each other's well-being. If a war chief failed to satisfy his troops with his leadership, families could desert, choosing to return to protect their homes rather than serve someone they did not trust. An army could disintegrate this way. Family groups were organized into clans composed of their relatives. The clans were organized into tribes. The tribes often had their own chiefs, and a war chief needed to address their worries and their ambitions, keeping those factors in check while trying to keep everyone focused on the military campaign.

Summoning warriors family by family was a slow process, and it depended on the mutual obligations between family members and their chief. Germanic armies tended to bunch together, which made them difficult to maneuver on the battlefield and hard to organize into efficient marching. Poor scouting and a focus on internal discipline among the troops meant that German armies were often taken by surprise. When surprised, they might not flee, but they were slow to respond and poorly organized at such times; they might stubbornly fight where they stood until they were cut down. Even so, when they were assembled and units were properly sorted out by family, clan, and tribe, the Germans could form large, formidable armies.

Generals were usually men from well-known warrior families. During the first century c.e. the leaders of these families became nobles, and their status and political power continually increased as their tribes forged national identities over the next several centuries. These nobles were usually dedicated full time to preparing for and waging war. Around them grew the *comites*, full-time warriors who served a noble. During the ancient era Germanic warriors were primarily infantry. They did not have the exceptionally sophisticated cavalry gear that the Celts had, making it hard to use horses as mobile battle platforms the way the Celtic cavalry did, although those few who fought from horseback were extraordinarily skilled and not to be taken lightly.

The waging of war was the preoccupation of most Germanic peoples. Their sons were taught throughout childhood how to kill their enemies, and if the family could afford it, a son's coming-of-age ceremony included a gift of weapons, helmet, and shield. Even poor families could give a son a *framea*, a light spear. Leadership in a tribe was often determined by who was the most successful warrior. In some tribes the chiefs were elected by the warriors of the tribe, but in others a notion of kingship was developing that would evolve into the system of mutual obligations that became the feudal system of the medieval era.

After Caesar's time many German tribes became *foederati*, or tribes that were federated with Rome and helped protect Roman borders. By the year 9 c.e. the Romans were making good progress advancing their borders east and north into German lands. The Germans in Roman-held territory were beginning to speak Latin as their primary language, were wearing Roman-style clothing, and were adopting Roman customs. A Roman governor, however, abused and overtaxed the Germans in Roman territory, making it easy for German nationalists to recall days when their ancestors roamed the land, terrifying their enemies. In 9 c.e. the Germans rose in revolt.

The Romans had many Germans in their armies. One was Arminius, a member of the Cherusci tribe. He had proved so valiant in battle that he had been awarded Roman citizenship, but he was still German at heart. He hoped that through warfare he would win enough glory to become chief of the Cherusci. The Roman emperor Augustus (r. 27 b.c.e.–14 c.e.) appointed a successful diplomat, Publius Quintilius Varus (d. 9 c.e.), as commanding officer of the Roman army in Germany. In September 9 c.e. he led three Roman legions, composed of 15,000 troops, toward their winter quarters through lands that were unfamiliar to him. Although other Germans with him warned that Arminius was untrustworthy, Varus followed the guidance of Arminius.

In what followed can be seen the strengths of German tactical thinking. Arminius led the Romans through muddy grounds, weakening the soldiers' legs and making them weary. Ahead of them was a large German army. As the Romans marched between a large bog to their right and a 300-foot-tall hill to their left, about 10 miles north of the modern German town of Osnabrück, they confronted a wall of mostly sand, about 4 feet in height and several feet deep. Behind it were German warriors, coordinating their defenses through cooperation. The site was discovered in 1987. The area in front of the wall shows that the Romans tried to storm it several times. The wall was a zigzag shape that broke up the Roman line and allowed defenders to stand on the wall and use their spears to strike Romans from their sides as well as their front. The absence of debris on the German side of the wall suggests that the Romans never made it over the top.

Behind the Roman column Germans who had hidden in the woodlands to the left of the Romans tried to block a Roman retreat. Others waited to storm the column from the woods. What resulted was a well-timed, carefully coordinated ambush in which an experienced army of 15,000 troops was trapped. Varus fell on his sword to avoid being captured, as did several of his officers. This left junior officers and regular soldiers to fight without a center of authority to coordinate their actions as they faced an enemy that fought with discipline. Many Roman soldiers fought as Romans often did, determinedly holding their ground when the Germans finally charged into them. The German strategy had broken up the Roman column so the German warriors could penetrate it and take on individual soldiers. Romans were very good at one-on-one combat, and this strategy by the Germans probably resulted in unnecessary deaths for many of them. But Arminius was leading Germans, not Romans, and to keep German warriors satisfied with his leadership, he probably had to let them have their battlefield glory.

Some Romans made their way into the woods and slowly went back home. Others were captured, tortured, and taken to altars set up in the woods. When Romans visited the site six years later, they found Roman heads dangling from trees and blood-drenched altars as well as the bones of Romans piled across the battlefield. Almost all died, about 15,000. Romanization of much of Germany was halted, and the Romans eventually withdrew back into Gaul. Arminius became chief of his tribe and a war leader of several tribes. He was assassinated by relatives in 21 C.E.

GREECE

BY MICHAEL M. SAGE

Warfare in ancient Greece, though it changed over time, always spanned the full range of possibilities from small-scale raiding to full-scale pitched battles. As the most dangerous of activities, it was marked by formal declarations, special religious rites, and a number of symbolic acts whose character changed over time, such as the erection of battlefield trophies, thanksgiving and victory sacrifices, and the use of special burial rites for the fallen.

Early Greek warfare tended to pursue restricted goals. City-state governments remained relatively simple and lacked the means to control large blocks of territory. Hoplite warfare focused on gaining control of the enemy's agricultural land, and normally that was enough to bring victory. Greek arms and tactics were not well suited to siege warfare, which was the only way to achieve complete victory. For the most part, warfare centered on boundary disputes, raids, and in certain cases, hereditary feuds.

It is difficult to gauge the frequency of organized warfare. The absence of sources makes any estimate impossible from the Mycenaean Period (ca. 1600–ca. 1150 B.C.E.) until the fifth century B.C.E. For the period from 500 to 338 B.C.E. Athens was at war two out of every three years. However, no comparable figures exist for other Greek states, and Athens was a special case. In all periods warfare on any scale is the most costly of activities, and Athens during this period had resources not available to most Greek states. Sources give the impression that warfare was common until the imposition of Roman domination in the mid-second century B.C.E. For the period after 400 B.C.E. there is scattered evidence in the form of inscriptions for frequent warfare among smaller communities in Crete and elsewhere.

ATTITUDES ABOUT WAR

The attitude of the Greeks toward warfare was, as is the case for most societies, ambivalent. On one hand, war was recognized as an evil. The historian Herodotus (ca. 484–between 430 and 420 B.C.E.) blames war for overturning the natural order of things: "In peace, sons bury their fathers. In war, fathers bury their sons." In his *Laws*, Plato (ca. 428–348 or 347 B.C.E.) asserts that that we should pray to be spared from war and civil strife and that no man can be a true statesman unless he prepares for war only as a means to peace. Despite the misery it brought, war could also be viewed as desirable. The earliest Greek literature that we possess, the *Iliad* and the *Odyssey*, composed by Homer (ninth–eighth? century B.C.E.), suggests that excellence as a warrior is a man's most important quality. The growth of the city-state, which consisted of an urban core with its dependent towns and village,

Bust of a warrior known as Leonidas (Alison Frantz Photographic Collection, American School of Classical Studies at Athens)

and the associated stress on the importance of the community, altered this "heroic code." The emphasis shifted to a warrior's contribution to his city in battle, but the significance attached to an individual's prowess in battle remained the same. Warfare also had more tangible attractions. The normal Greek view was that the conquered and their possessions passed into the hands of the victor and were his to dispose of as he pleased. Slaves brought the highest profit, but other items, such as personal valuables or temple treasures, also brought wealth. It was the capture of cities and temples that gave the greatest returns.

In politics war always remained an option and was pursued when it offered some advantage, especially among the more powerful states. There was a change in the fourth century B.C.E., first visible in 371 B.C.E., when the notion of a common peace among Greek states developed; however, the idea had little practical effect and never excluded warfare against non-Greeks. Peace among the Greeks was achieved only by Roman control.

THE MYCENAEAN PERIOD

There is little available evidence for the earliest period of Greek warfare, the Mycenaean Period. It is generally assumed that the Greek mainland and islands were divided into a number of small kingdoms centered on heavily fortified citadels. Given the absence of any contemporary description of warfare, inferences have to be made on the basis of archaeological finds of weapons and contemporary pictorial representations of fighting in frescoes and reliefs. An additional source of information is provided by the Linear B tablets. These tablets are accounting documents produced by the palaces and written on clay. They highlight the importance of chariots in this period. Large numbers of tablets as well as replacement parts for them were maintained. In addition, a set of tablets from the kingdom of Pylos in the southwestern Peloponnese details the organization of a coastal watch in response to an unknown threat. It is clear that there was technological development in the period, especially in producing more effective swords, but we do not have the data to trace the interaction between changes in technology and the development of new forms of war making.

The importance of chariots in the tablets poses a problem. Mainland Greece, with its rugged topography, is not well suited to the use of the chariot, especially in the mass formations found in the contemporary Near East. It may be, given some later parallels, that chariots served as elite transport to the battlefield and that their primary function was to display the high status and importance of their owners. The weapons finds and portrayals of fighting indicate the importance of the heavy thrusting spear. Although the sword is found in all periods, the thrusting spear is found most frequently. The use of such a weapon implies some type of compact formation, though its organization eludes us.

THE DARK AGES

The end of the Mycenaean Period in about the middle of the 12th century B.C.E. witnessed profound changes on the Greek mainland and islands. The palaces were destroyed and with them the writing system used to keep their accounts. The archaeological finds paint a picture of a depopulated and fragmented society based primarily on small villages with a much reduced economy during the dark ages (ca. 1100–ca. 750 B.C.E.). Most political units centered on a local chief, who functioned with the support of local nobles. The amount of surplus wealth that such a society could devote to warfare was small, and it is probable that most of the fighting centered on raiding and small-scale conflict.

The same difficulties in reconstructing warfare in this period arise as for the previous one. We have to rely on weapons finds, and from about 850 B.C.E. there are vases that show fighting. Evidence points to the importance of missile warfare, with javelins and an open and fluid manner of fighting. Chariots are pictured, and there have been occasional finds of chariots in graves dated to after 1000 B.C.E. These must have belonged to the elite, but their function remains unknown. Based on evidence from the Homeric poems, these armies must have consisted of relatively small war bands operating under the leadership of a local chief or prince whose primary adversaries were small armies of a similar nature. These formations were too small and lacked the organization to achieve permanent conquest. Warfare for the most part must have consisted of raiding and border warfare.

THE ARCHAIC PERIOD

The warfare of the *Iliad* and the *Odyssey* has been a particular focus of discussion. There has been debate about realism and the period in which the works are set. It seems that they reflect the period towards the end of the dark ages and the beginning of the following period, the Archaic (ca. 600–ca. 480 B.C.E.). They portray a world of small-scale states controlled by kings and the nobility, where war is the primary means of enhancing one's prestige and status. The kings and nobles, such as Achilles and Hector, dominate the combat and display superhuman strength.

Despite the presence of gods and other fantastic elements, Homer's works do present a comprehensible picture of warfare. The poems reveal a style of warfare close to that of the dark ages. The elite lead individual war bands that often function independently. Combat is normally in loose formation and mostly involves the exchange of missiles. This formation responds to circumstances. Under pressure from the enemy or in pursuit, it can compact, and battles between closely formed groups of warriors occur. These masses are important in determining the course of combat despite the focus on the actions of the elite. The elite function primarily as front fighters and often fight before the masses of their men, challenging enemy leaders. The poems portray their successes as the key to victory.

The use of chariots in Homer has evoked further controversy. They are used singly and often serve as transport for warriors who drive into battle, fight dismounted, and then use the chariots as transport to the rear. The movement of these vehicles in and out of the battle has no parallel elsewhere. Chariots were normally used elsewhere in massed formations as missile platforms or as transport to the battle but were not used to fight along with the infantry. Although the use of intermingled chariots and infantry is not impossible, it seems likely that the poet's use of chariots for his heroes is the product of an attempt to emphasize his heroes' superhuman nature.

From the second half of the eighth century B.C.E. Greece underwent a profound change. Population increased dramatically, there was extensive colonization around the Mediterranean, external trade resumed, and writing was reintroduced. Accompanying these developments was the formation of a new political organization: the city-state. In essence, the city-state consisted of an urban core based on a defensible citadel surrounded by public and religious spaces. It served as the political, social, and economic center for the surrounding countryside and its dependent towns and villages. In conjunction with these changes, royal government disappeared and was replaced by aristocratic rule and a political structure consisting of magistrates, council, and assembly. The higher population of these communities as well as their greater wealth allowed them to mobilize far more resources for war than had been possible earlier.

These profound developments in Greek society provided the context for a momentous change in warfare. The decisive arm on Greek battlefields over the next four centuries was to become the heavily armored infantryman (hoplite) using the heavy thrusting spear as his main offensive weapon and fighting in a dense, rectangular phalanx formation. This transition was accompanied by changes in equipment. Metal helmets, corselets (armor covering the torso), and a new type of shield appear. Hoplites were drawn from the better-off farmers and landowners and served at their own expense. Mass, weight, depth, and cooperation among the members of the phalanx became the decisive elements in this simple type of warfare in which masses of heavily armed men engaged each other on flat, level plains. It was a form of warfare developed to protect a city's agricultural land on which it depended for its food supply. The short, sharp engagements and the ample defensive equipment were designed to limit warfare's destructive effects.

These developments were limited to central and southern Greece. Elsewhere older forms of warfare persisted. Whatever the connection between these developments and political change, it was only in areas where the city-state was common that hoplite warfare came to dominate. The evidence does not permit a firm date to be assigned to the development and spread of this type of warfare. Elements of the equipment that later became typical appear around 700 B.C.E. and the first portrayals on pottery of warriors in a phalanx-like formation occur in the middle of the seventh century B.C.E. A date around and after 600 B.C.E. is reasonable, though some hold that its full form emerged only around 500 B.C.E. How quickly it spread is unknown.

THE FIFTH CENTURY B.C.E.

The dominance of this form of fighting led to changes in other arms. Light-armed troops whose main offensive arm was missile weapons lost their importance, and their main functions were now to act as a screen for the deployment of the phalanx and to aid in pursuit. Contemporary with these developments in infantry fighting, the cavalry also experienced significant changes. From the seventh century B.C.E. there are portrayals of warriors on horseback, but they appear to be mounted hoplites rather than true cavalry. The transition to true cavalry, that is, troopers who fight from horseback, may be as late as the first half of the fifth century B.C.E. under the impact of the Persian invasion of Greece in 480 B.C.E. The first organized cavalry appear in Athens in the 450s B.C.E., while Sparta had none until the 420s B.C.E., and few major states remained without such formations. This cavalry was useful for flank and rear attacks on organized infantry and for protection from enemy cavalry forces. In addition, it was employed in pursuing broken infantry and in protecting foraging parties.

The Persian War of 480 B.C.E. marked a watershed. For the first time a substantial number of Greek states served under the unified command of a single state, Sparta. Athens, building on an earlier decision to expand its navy, became the most important maritime power. The Greek victory had momentous consequences. Sparta remained focused on its supremacy in the Peloponnese, but Athens was able to create an alliance against the Persians that within a generation would develop into a naval empire of subject states. Unlike the Spartans, who demanded only military service, the Athenians demanded tribute, and the empire became a substantial contributor to the maintenance of its fleet and its citizens.

At Athens all Athenians who were between the ages of 18 and 60 and who possessed a certain level of wealth were entered in a list of those eligible for military service, with the wealthiest serving as cavalry. Athens was unique in providing pay for military service from 456 B.C.E. on. Army organization was based on units of 1,000 and 300. The larger units had their own officers, but nothing is known of the organization of the smaller ones. The cavalry had its own commander and subordinate officers, and the same must have been true of the light-armed troops, though they are not mentioned. Overall command was vested in an annually elected board of 10 generals. Normally, two or three generals exercised command on a campaign. The historian Thucydides (d. ca. 401 B.C.E.) informs us that in 431 B.C.E. the hoplite army totaled 29,000 men out of a population of about 180,000, with 13,000 serving in the field army and the youngest and the oldest defending the city.

There was no parallel to the Spartan army elsewhere in Greece. All other armies were citizen militias; only Sparta possessed a professional army. As a result of a unique social and economic system, all full Spartan citizens were freed to devote themselves to full-time military training. This was an extraordinarily rigorous training that began in childhood and continued until the end of adolescence. The army was organized on the basis of age groups and geographical districts within Sparta. This army was far better articulated than any other Greek force. The largest units of 600 men were composed of four successively larger units, each with its officers. Normally, overall command was vested in one of the two Spartan kings, though occasionally detached forces could be commanded by other officers.

Sparta's unique military system fueled a policy of expansion that resulted in the acquisition of extensive lands on the western flank. Sparta's attempt to expand its control to the north was checked by the mid-sixth century B.C.E., and a new policy of alliance in the Peloponnese was adopted. Sparta was clearly the controlling member, and the allies were bound to follow where Sparta might lead. Despite Sparta's military superiority, several large and important states in the Peloponnese, such as Argos, remained out of the league and were at times openly hostile. After its initial expansion Sparta's main military preoccupation was to ensure its local dominance.

In Boeotia and a few other areas where federalism had emerged, there were federal armies with member states contributing troops according to population, and command was held by federally elected officers. Elite units are mentioned at Thebes in Boeotia and at Argos in the fifth and fourth centuries B.C.E., but we know almost nothing of their organization. Given that most Greek armies were militias, it is probable that they were commanded by each city's magistrates.

The Peloponnesian War (431–404 B.C.E.) between Athens and Sparta and its allies precipitated a number of changes. For the first time mercenary troops from the poorer regions of Greece were employed on a large scale as well as specialist troops drawn from non-Greek sources. The dominance of the hoplite outside of decisive battles was reduced. Combined forces of light-armed troops, cavalry, and hoplites were shown to be effective in small-scale actions. The length of the war and the employment of mercenaries led to a growing professionalism, visible both at the level of the individual soldier and in positions of command. The greater professionalism and frequent warfare in the fourth century B.C.E. led to the development of new tactics and changes in hoplite equipment.

In these years Greek politics had essentially become bipolar, with most Greek states aligned with either Sparta or Athens. In addition to the war's effect on the nature of warfare, this conflict also had profound political consequences. It destabilized a number of states, leading to internal factional fighting, which was often bloody. A number of cities were destroyed and the population enslaved. It led to the Spartans' realization that the older strategy of laying waste to an opponent's agricultural land as the key to victory no longer held in Athens's case, since as long as Athens dominated the sea, it could supply itself from overseas. This realization led the Spartans to solicit Persian money to subsidize their navy and so involved them in the affairs of the Greeks of Asia Minor.

By the end of the war Sparta stood supreme. Athens was subordinated but not destroyed so that it could serve as a counterweight to the ambitions of Thebes. However, Spartan blunders created a number of coalitions of major Greek states to oppose Sparta. Sparta's supremacy lasted until 371 B.C.E. and Sparta's defeat in battle by Thebes, which now assumed Sparta's role. By 362 B.C.E. Sparta's ascendancy had ended, and no state emerged as dominant; rather, there was a series of combinations in an attempt to limit the power of any one state.

THE FOURTH CENTURY B.C.E.

The rise of Macedonia radically changed the situation. The most crucial development of the fourth century B.C.E. was the rise of a powerful and expansive monarchy in Macedonia. Its creation was the work of Philip II (r. 359–336 B.C.E.). Philip consolidated a weak state rent by faction and in the process created an army superior to any the Greek world had yet seen. Macedonia had always had effective cavalry, but it was Philip's achievement to develop a superb infantry. Its organization must be inferred from Alexander's army, whose structure is far better known. The cavalry was organized into eight units, one being the royal cavalry of 300, which also served as a bodyguard. The other seven units were each 200 to 300 men strong. The infantry phalanx was levied by geographical areas and by the end of Philip's reign was 24,000 strong and divided into sections of 1,500. Two other infantry units are known, one of 250 and one of 16. There were also substantial numbers of light-armed troops of all types drawn from Macedonian and subject populations, who also provided specialized units. The king was normally in command and had a number of senior commanders drawn from the Macedonian nobility, who commanded units on the battlefield and in independent expeditions. The Macedonian army represented a departure from traditional Greek forces. For the first time a force was created that effectively used different modes of fighting in combination in large-scale battle.

The army that Philip's son, Alexander the Great (r. 336–323 B.C.E.), led against Persia in the spring of 334 B.C.E. was essentially the force his father had created except for a substantial presence of allied Greek contingents. It probably differed only in having a higher proportion of cavalry, since the main Persian strength was concentrated in that arm. One innovation Alexander may have made was the creation of an elite infantry guard, the hypaspists of 3,000 men who were armed in the same manner as other heavy infantry and under the direct command of the king. Attrition, distance, and Alexander's own vision led to an attempt to incorporate Oriental troops into his army. Oriental cavalry were added to the army as Alexander advanced eastward, but they were kept separate from Macedonian troops. Orientals were denied positions of command except in special circumstances.

Alexander's conquests of the Persian Empire and northwestern India created the initial conditions for a massive movement of population from Greece and Macedonia to the Near East. This movement, over by about 250 B.C.E., led to the spread of Greek culture and the extensive urbanization in the Near East. The kingdoms of Alexander's successors were controlled by Greeks and adopted Greek political practices. The military forces continued and completed a military revolution. The use of professional soldiers culminated in the professional standing armies of the Ptolemies and the Seleucids. Militia-based armies continued to exist on mainland Greece and in Macedonia, but even there professional soldiers were employed on a substantial scale. These were much more heterogeneous armies than those of the Classical Period (480–323 B.C.E.), consisting of Greeks, Macedonians, and mercenaries drawn from all over the Mediterranean as well as levies of subject peoples. War and conquest had created Greek states on a far vaster scale than earlier. Despite these advantages, none of the monarchies created in the wake of Alexander's death was capable of resisting the advance of a Roman army based on the militia system.

Alexander's death in 323 B.C.E. led to a half century of struggle, which ended in the establishment of three large successor kingdoms: the Ptolemaic based in Egypt, the Seleucid, whose territory stretched from the seacoast of Asia Minor to northwestern India at its greatest extent, and the

Antigonid, centered in the Macedonian heartland. Their armies were direct descendants of Philip's and Alexander's. There were changes in scale; armies were now much larger, and cavalry declined in importance. An innovation of the period was the institution of an elephant corps. Europeans had first met the elephant in battle in northwestern India and were quick to adopt it for their own use. Elephants were used to screen against cavalry, to attack infantry, and to break into fortifications. After 300 B.C.E. they were equipped with towers manned by troops armed with missile weapons. Little is known of how these elephants were organized. Difficulties in breeding as well as the general ineffectiveness of elephants in European warfare led to their disappearance from Western battlefields by the middle of the second century B.C.E.

The major Hellenistic armies, except for the Macedonian, which relied on its own population for its main military forces, used mercenaries. Greeks serving as mercenaries in the Near East are known as early as the seventh century B.C.E. However, in Greece the use of a militia as the main military force meant that mercenaries appear infrequently. The first large-scale use of such forces dates from the Peloponnesian War and continues into the fourth century C.E. Economic troubles caused by the war and by the growing need for specialist troops whose fighting techniques required extensive training spurred their use. Philip and Alexander employed them as well. The Hellenistic monarchies had an enormous need for manpower, and although the core of their armies consisted of Greek and Macedonian settlers, they hired large numbers of mercenaries from all over the Mediterranean. A parallel development can be seen in naval forces, where professional rowers had to be hired.

ROME

BY JAMES A. CORRICK

By tradition the doors to the temple of Janus in the Roman Forum were closed in times of peace and open during times of conflict. During the centuries of the Roman Kingdom and Roman Republic, these doors were shut only twice, and after the formation of the empire they were open far more often than they were closed. War was indeed a constant throughout Rome's history, for Rome was built on war and conquest. Its dominance of the Mediterranean world was through force of arms. Its treasury and many of its prominent citizens and leaders were periodically enriched through the loot of conquest and the governance of conquered provinces, whose inhabitants were forced to pay tribute under the threat of Roman military reprisal.

ROMAN ATTITUDES TOWARD WAR

The Romans were a militaristic people who saw war as a natural—indeed a proper—way of establishing their dominance over others. Thus for much of its history Rome spent half of its revenues on maintaining its military and on waging war. It gave its top officials—consuls, praetors, proconsuls, propraetors, and the occasional dictator—the imperium that gave

them the authority, among other things, to command troops in battle. It demanded that its elected officials not only serve in the military but also have combat experience. Further, it elevated Mars, who had been a minor agricultural god, to the second most powerful deity in the Roman pantheon, just after Jupiter, by making him the god of war.

The Roman character itself was shaped by war and the demands of war. The Romans were a people who valued discipline, endurance, and courage and who saw duty to the state as among the highest goals to be achieved. They praised those who rejected luxury for austere living and who took no notice of physical hardship. They admired the pragmatic. All of these characteristics made for good, reliable soldiers.

Yet despite their belief in the rightness of combat and battle, Romans did not take war lightly. They knew, as the Roman poet Virgil (70–19 B.C.E.) wrote in the *Aeneid*, that war was horrible. Accordingly, the centuriate assembly was to debate the justness and necessity of any proposed military action, which its delegates then had to approve through majority vote. Nor were Romans reluctant to use other means of gaining their ends. Roman officials, for instance, often negotiated with states to avoid war; sometimes they brought these states under Rome's influence through treaties, sometimes through large bribes to foreign rulers.

Still, Rome was mostly at war somewhere in the Mediterranean, the Middle East, or along its northern European border. The deliberations of the centuriate assembly were often short-circuited by aristocratic influence over delegates who voted as their patrons desired; patricians could enrich themselves only through agriculture or war and were thus often inclined to go to war. Occasionally, Roman leaders simply ignored the assembly altogether. Diplomatic efforts were often feeble or filled with demands the Romans knew would be rejected.

In the end, successful wars of conquest led Romans to see themselves and their culture as superior to others. They were convinced that Rome's destiny was to be ruler of the world. They had no hesitation in pursuing that destiny through warfare and military occupation of other lands, nor did the Romans question that they had a right to plunder and loot their fallen enemies for the enrichment of Rome.

EARLY ROME

Nothing is known about Roman warfare prior to the eighth century B.C.E. Beginning in the eighth century, according to Roman historians such as Livy (ca. 59 B.C.E.–17 C.E.), the Roman Kingdom fought a number of wars with neighboring peoples, among them the Albans, the Fidenae, and the Sabines. The latter were defeated in several battles after they attacked in response to Romans supposedly seizing Sabine women for wives. To what extent these accounts of early war are factual is difficult to know because no actual records survive from this early period. For the most part, Rome's early wars were probably minor affairs, in general being no more than skirmishes with neighbors that consisted of border disputes or raids to seize livestock, slaves, and plunder.

Little is known about the Roman army of the early kingdom. Probably small, the army was led by the king and consisted of the royal bodyguard and a few hundred citizens of the city. By the end of the seventh century B.C.E. the army, a militia of citizen soldiers, had grown, with its organization deriving from the supposed three tribes that inhabited the Roman kingdom: the Ramnes, the Tities, and the Luceres. Each tribe contributed 1,000 soldiers, who supplied their own weapons and armor and who were under the command of a tribune, or tribal officer. Further, each tribal subdivision provided 100 men to form a unit known as a century. The total 3,000-strong body was called the *legio*, or levy, better known as a legion. Attached to the legion was the cavalry, numbering some 300.

The infantry would remain the core of all Roman armies. Infantry units could move more quickly and readily than cavalry through the often mountainous Italian terrain and in later centuries were more easily transported by sea to distant conflicts. Chariots, popular in other parts of the ancient world, were impractical and rarely employed by the Romans in war because of their legacy of fighting in rugged Italy. Because of their reliance on infantry, the Romans would always favor close-quarter, or hand-to-hand, fighting. Roman cavalry would act primarily as scouts and as protection from enemy cavalry as well as for rear attacks against opposing troops.

War for early Rome was a seasonal business, with the summer being the traditional battle season for the city. Winter conditions were generally too poor for combat, and the Roman soldiers, being mostly farmers, had to plant in the spring and harvest in the fall. At the end of summer campaigning, the legion was disbanded to be reformed the following year.

A Change in Strategy

Beginning in the fifth century B.C.E., the first years of the republic, Rome used its army to conquer and dominate its Etruscan neighbors north of the Tiber. This initial series of conquests culminated with Rome's victory over its archrival Veii in 396 B.C.E.

This series of conquests marked a change in Roman strategy that would dictate the course of all Rome's wars until the time of the later empire. Prior to the fifth century B.C.E. Rome's strategy was primarily defensive, countering specific threats posed by neighboring peoples. However, in the fifth century B.C.E. Roman warfare became almost exclusively offensive with the Romans coming to view war as a means of subjugating others and thus expanding their territory. From the fifth century onward the Romans engaged in wars of conquest that in the end would give them control first of Italy and then of much of the Mediterranean. This expansion would offer Rome increased protection from attack by pushing its enemies farther from the city itself. Expansion in Italy also brought more farm land under Roman control. An important consequence of this larger food supply was the growth of the city of Rome.

Gaining dominance over other states required a battlefield strategy of not just defeating an enemy army on the field but also destroying the enemy force by killing as many opposing warriors as possible. Without the protection of its own army, many enemy states surrendered to the Romans. Any that continued to resist through use of their remaining soldiers or by arming noncombatants suffered bloody reprisals from the Romans, who often killed many of the surviving adults and sold the rest along with children into slavery.

Rome sometimes resorted to other means of winning a war that did not involve direct combat. Roman soldiers might burn enemy fields and thus force surrender through the threat of starvation. They might wait until an enemy army disbanded, either because the soldiers had to return to tend their fields or because they ran out of money to pay mercenary troops. On the whole, however, Romans preferred meeting and besting their enemies on the battlefield.

Phalanxes and Sieges

The Roman army of the early republic had grown to a legion of 6,000 infantry, to which 18 centuries of cavalry were attached. The legion was still divided into centuries, but the number of soldiers in each century varied. (Exact numbers are not now known.) Soldiers were recruited from five social classes of citizens, with those of the top class being able to afford to equip themselves with the best weapons and armor and with those of the lowest class lacking armor and armed only with slings and stones. Additionally, the Roman army was now modeled on the Greek hoplite forces, in which warriors carrying long thrusting spears and with shields overlapping marched in a succession of rows, varying in number from eight to 16, toward the enemy. These massed lines were called a phalanx, Greek for "roller," and allowed fallen soldiers in the front line quickly to be replaced from the lines behind.

Although they continued to prefer close-quarter infantry engagement during this early period of expansion, Romans learned siege craft when they attacked the Veian city of Fidenae. Unable to breach the city's defenses, the Romans laid siege. The purpose of a Roman siege, like any siege, was to cut the enemy off from supplies—food, weapons, and sometimes water—and then through repeated attacks to wear down resistance until Roman soldiers could gain entry to the besieged city. In later centuries the Romans would employ siege engines such as battering rams to bash in gates or to knock holes in defensive walls and ballista and onagers capable of hurling large rocks against enemy walls (the latter could also throw flaming pitch into an enemy city). The use of these engines helped bring a siege to a quicker end. At Fidenae the lack of such engines led to a siege lasting six or seven years.

Defeat and Reorganization

By the fourth century B.C.E. Rome was the strongest military power in central Italy. In terms of weapons and armor, Romans were generally no better equipped than their enemies. Rather, they owed their success in war to a stress on teamwork and esprit de corps over individual heroics. Additionally, the hard—sometimes brutal—training of Roman soldiers led to proficiency in the use of arms and to disciplined obedience. At all times on the battlefield, Roman soldiers were expected to maintain their formation and to stay sheltered behind their body-length shields, from behind which they delivered quick stabbing blows with their short swords.

Nonetheless, Romans were not invincible. Indeed, in 390 B.C.E., six years after its final victory over the Veii, Rome suffered one of its most humiliating defeats at the hands of Celts from Gaul. These Gauls first destroyed a Roman army and then went on to capture Rome and to demand an exorbitant tribute before retreating back north. The weakness that the Gauls exploited was the phalanx formation. Roman training and teamwork made the phalanx effective against other massed enemy infantry. Nevertheless, it did not allow Roman soldiers much flexibility of movement on the battlefield, while the Gauls who fought as individuals or in small groups were more mobile and thus were able to outflank the Romans.

The Romans quickly abandoned the phalanx and adopted a new battlefield formation that divided the legion into units called maniples. A maniple, from a Latin word meaning "handful," consisted of 160 soldiers, or two centuries of 80 each. Each maniple acted semi-independently and was arranged in three lines. The front line would engage the enemy and then, after about 15minutes, would fall back and be replaced by the second line, which in turn would be replaced by the third. This maneuver gave the soldiers a period of rest before rejoining the fight. The single legion of the army was also replaced by first two, then three, and finally four legions. Each legion had 60 centuries or 30 maniples.

PYRRHUS AND WAR ELEPHANTS

Although the defeat by the Gauls left Rome weakened, it soon grew militarily powerful again and, with its restructured army, brought the Italian peninsula under its control over the next century. In doing so, Rome had to fight three wars with the Samnites, beginning in 343 B.C.E. It was in 312 B.C.E., during the second of these wars (326–304 B.C.E.) that the Romans, realizing that they needed a method of moving troops and supplies rapidly, built the first of their roads, the Via Appia, or Appian Way, Roman roads would be one of the keys to Rome's success in waging successful war in the centuries to come, as they were able to rush troops relatively quickly to trouble spots in their holdings.

In 280 B.C.E. Roman expansion in Italy brought war with the Greek colony of Tarentum, to whose aid Pyrrhus, ruler of the Greek city-state Epirus, came. This war was the first time that Rome faced one of the Mediterranean superpowers and the first time that its soldiers encountered war elephants. It was these latter that gave Pyrrhus a victory in his first two battles with the Romans.

The Romans may have lost the first battles, but as would be their practice in the centuries to come they refused to concede defeat. Instead, they regrouped and continued the war. They allied themselves with the other major Mediterranean power, the Carthaginians, and they adapted their battlefield tactics to deal with enemy elephants. In 275 B.C.E. the Romans met Pyrrhus for the final time and defeated him by routing his elephant corps through the use of javelins and fire and perhaps at times by hitting the animals on the head.

THE FIRST PUNIC WAR

The defeat of Pyrrhus left the Greek colonies open to Roman conquest, and Rome quickly defeated each in battle. As the Romans were finalizing their control of Italy, they became embroiled in a war with Carthage over Sicily. Rome and Carthage would fight three wars, the first from 264 to 241 B.C.E. Known as the Punic Wars, these conflicts would leave Rome with the beginnings of its overseas empire and as the strongest state in the Mediterranean world. Carthage would be destroyed.

Bronze statuette of Mars, god of war, Roman Britain, second century C.E., from Earith, Cambridgeshire; Mars wears the armor of a general, including an elaborate helmet, sheet-metal leg guards decorated with thunderbolts, and an embossed chest plate moulded to the form of the body. (© The Trustees of the British Museum)

The outcome of this conflict was by no means assured, particularly since Carthage was the great naval power of the period and Rome had no navy at all because the city's wars had to date been conducted on the Italian mainland, generally inland. When water transport was necessary to carry troops along the Italian coast, Rome turned to its allies on the Bay of Naples for ships and crews. In order to win the First Punic War, Rome built its first fleet, modeling its ships on captured Carthaginian vessels. The Romans developed a new device to aid them in this new type of warfare. The corvus was a large gangplank that could be dropped onto an enemy ship. A large spike at its end drove deep into the enemy's deck. Army legionnaires then crossed over the corvus to take the other vessel. The device worked very well, allowing the Romans to use their greatest battle strength, close-quarter infantry fighting. With the aid of the corvus the Romans defeated two Carthaginian fleets and won the First Punic War.

Despite two more wars with Carthage and other sea engagements, the republic never maintained a permanent navy. When a fleet was needed, it was built, as for Pompey's expedition in 64 B.C.E. against the pirates of the Mediterranean. Even when they existed, republican fleets often came to grief. Led by commanders with no nautical experience, entire fleets were lost to storm and shipwreck. It would not be until the empire that Rome would maintain a permanent navy, and even then the seafaring service would remain secondary to the army.

The Second and Third Punic Wars

During the Second Punic War (218–202 B.C.E.) the Carthaginian general Hannibal (247–183 B.C.E.) crossed the Alps; after inflicting a series of devastating defeats on the Romans, most notably at Cannae, he and his army ravaged the Italian countryside. Hannibal made no attempt to attack the city of Rome, perhaps because its walls, built after the Gauls' capture of the city in 390 B.C.E., made Rome a difficult target. Instead of continuing in its attempt to defeat Hannibal's army, Rome tried a new tactic: It launched an attack on the city of Carthage. Hannibal was recalled to defend his home, where he was overcome by the Roman general Scipio Africanus Major (236–184 or 183 B.C.E.).

Carthage was destroyed in the Third Punic War (149–146 B.C.E.). Following their strategy of annihilating their enemies, the Romans captured the city of Carthage after a brief siege, sold into slavery those Carthaginians not killed, and razed the city to the ground. When the Romans finished, nothing remained of the Carthaginians or their culture, and Rome was the most powerful state in the Mediterranean.

The Punic Wars left Rome in control of Sicily, North Africa, and parts of the Iberian Peninsula. Over the next century they conquered and occupied the southern part of Gaul, Macedonia, Greece, and much of the Middle East. Although Rome was still technically a republic, it was by the first century B.C.E. an empire in all but name.

Social Change

Roman war and the conquest brought power and wealth to Rome, but they did even more. They changed what was a small farming community, more town than city, into one of the largest and most cosmopolitan cities of the ancient world. Rome became a place where people from all over the Mediterranean lived, worked, and traded. Roman society itself was, if not softened, altered by exposure to other peoples, most notably the Greeks, whose literature, art, and philosophy were embraced by many Romans.

War also brought to Rome millions of slaves, whose cheap labor led to economic dislocation for many Roman citizens. By the first century B.C.E. the small farms of early Rome had mostly given way to large farming estates owned by wealthy individuals and worked by slaves. The small Roman farmers were left landless and without a livelihood. Occasionally, one of these estates was broken up and its land distributed to soldiers, such as those who served Pompey and Julius Caesar. However, such redistributions were not given to Roman peasants, many of whom made their way to Rome, where they lived in tenements and depended on food from the state grain supply. There was little but poverty for these Roman citizens, for as in the countryside, most work in the city was done by slaves.

Political Change

War and conquest also led to political change. The political organization of the republic, designed to rule a single city, was not capable of handling the administration of such a large realm. The Roman Republic lacked any true central authority and had virtually no state employees with which to handle the day-to-day details of government. Its ruling officials, two consuls, served for only one year, a period that was often insufficient to study and then handle problems in Rome's far-flung provinces. Additionally, the consuls could overrule each other and be overruled by other elected officials, so important matters frequently were left unattended for years at a time. Although they had fewer checks on their power, Rome's provincial governors, the proconsuls and propraetors, also rarely had more than a yearlong appointment, sometimes a goodly amount of that time being eaten up preparing for the job and then traveling to the assigned region. The strain of governance was one of the contributing factors leading to the eventual disintegration of the Roman Republic and the emergence of the Roman Empire, with its single source of authority, the emperor, and its elaborate bureaucracy.

This political change was also aided by the rise at the end of the second century B.C.E. of generals whose troops were more loyal to them than to the state. These generals, among them Marius (ca. 157–86 B.C.E.), Sulla (138–78 B.C.E.), Pompey (106–48 B.C.E.), and Julius Caesar (100–44 B.C.E.), became rich from the plunder of successful campaigns and used this money to buy the favor of many Roman citizens. Caesar, for instance, for one year paid the rent of everyone living in

Rome. These generals also vied with one another for power. They fought pitched battles until in 31 B.C.E. Octavian, later Augustus Caesar (ca. 27 B.C.E.–14 C.E.), emerged victorious, soon becoming the first emperor.

MILITARY CHANGE

The army also underwent changes during the growth of Rome as an imperial power. The Punic Wars and those fought elsewhere required an increase in the number of legions to 20, along with the creation of several urban legions made up of the old and underaged, whose duty it was to protect the city of Rome. Over the final three centuries of the republic, the number of legions would fluctuate according to military demands; the number appears not to have dropped below six.

At the end of the second century B.C.E. further changes were made to the structure of the legion. These changes would remain in place until the late empire. According to tradition, under Gaius Marius each legion was divided into 10 cohorts rather than 30 maniples. A cohort was made up of 480 soldiers divided among six centuries, thus giving each legion a complement of 4,800. When combined with a new weapon, a long spear called a *pilus*, the cohort was felt to retain flexibility in combat while increasing the strength of the Roman force. At the beginning of battle each legionnaire threw his *pilus*, the point of which was designed to bend so that it could not be used against the Romans. A *pilus* was capable of piercing light armor, and if it stuck in an enemy soldier's shield, its weight would make the shield too cumbersome to carry.

Over time, each legion was also augmented by a body of troops that came from various Latium and other Italian communities. Generally, some 500 soldiers and cavalry were drafted from each town until each legion was accompanied by an auxiliary, known as an *ala sociorum* (wing of allies), which was of equivalent size to the legion itself. Attached to each legion was also an elite group of allied fighters, the *extraordinarii*. Mercenaries, particularly archers from Crete, also fought with each legion. When on campaign, then, each legion fielded a total of between 8,000 and 10,000 troops along with 750 to 1,250 cavalry.

THE NATURE OF ROMAN WAR

Over the centuries the nature of Roman warfare itself changed. The skirmishes and raids of the kingdom and the early republic—brief affairs at best—turned into long offensive campaigns of conquest that required extended marches or sea voyages just to reach the enemy. Once engaged, Roman soldiers might have to fight several battles in succession. Sometimes campaigns lasted years and involved not only battle but lengthy sieges of enemy cities and strongholds. Once a region was conquered, it had to be occupied by permanent garrisons. These extended campaigns and occupations also changed the character of the Roman army. By the end of the first century C.E., what had started as a seasonal, volunteer militia made up of part-time soldiers had transformed into a standing army with a core of career professionals.

When in the second century C.E. the empire reached its farthest extent, the nature of Roman war once more changed. Instead of large offensive campaigns, the army was engaged mostly in consolidating the frontier areas that were still in the process of becoming Roman—indeed, many never really did— and in patrolling and defending the imperial borders.

THE AMERICAS
BY MICHAEL J. O'NEAL

As communities of people migrated and spread throughout the Americas in ancient times, they inevitably came in conflict with one another. The usual source of the conflict would have been territory and resources. As one nation encroached on another's territorial hunting grounds, the earlier inhabitants very likely would have resisted, and conflict would have erupted. The problem for historians, as is often the case with the ancient world, is the lack of any kind of documentation for warfare. Accordingly, historians have to rely on other tools. One such tool consists of oral legends about warfare that were transmitted over many generations. Sometimes, archaeological findings can shed light on ancient conflict. In South America, for example, tombs have been found with inscriptions, weapons, and battle dress that shed some light on ancient warfare.

NORTH AMERICA

Among the many nations of North America, conflict was inevitable and probably frequent. Numerous examples could be cited, but one that dates back to at least 1000 B.C.E. is the conflict between the ancient ancestors of the Lenape and the Allegewi (the source of the name given to the Allegheny Mountains and the Allegheny River in the eastern United States)—though again, historians have to rely on oral tradition and archaeological finds. The Lenape, also known as the Lenni Lenape, migrated eastward until they came to the Mississippi River, which they called Namesi Sipu ("River of Fish"), the source of the word *Mississippi*. Here they met up with and formed a peaceful alliance with the Mengwe, who had migrated from the north in the region around the source of the river.

On the other side of the River of Fish were the Allegewi. The Lenape sent scouts across the river to reconnoiter, and the scouts came back with tales of giants who lived in walled cities and appeared to be warlike. The Lenape had no wish to do battle with the Allegewi, so they sent emissaries requesting permission to travel through Allegewi territory to points farther east. The Allegewi granted permission, so the Lenape began to cross the river in great numbers. The Allegewi, not knowing that so many people would be crossing their land, felt threatened, and they attacked, killing a large number of Lenape. The Lenape, in turn, fought back and, according to oral legend, routed the Allegewi and drove them southward. The Lenape then occupied the region around the Ohio River valley, while the Mengwe returned to the north. In time the

Lenape continued their eastward trek into the forested regions of the eastern United States, giving rise to at least 40 nations, including the Delaware, which found homes in New York and along the eastern seaboard. The Mengwe in time evolved into the Iroquois. Ironically, the two nations that had formed an alliance during war and lived in harmony for many centuries after defeating the Allegewi themselves became bitter enemies.

Native North Americans did not mount "armies" as the term is conventionally understood. Rather, the war party generally constituted the fighting forces of Native Americans. Generally, the leader of a war party was a chief or another member of the nation who had shown courage in battle on a former occasion. Usually, such a person was said to have "medicine," meaning a kind of spiritual power that would make him and his force victorious. Individual warriors also had medicine, and this medicine was typically symbolized by an object, such as an amulet, that the warrior carried into battle. Interestingly, it is believed that among some nations, women as warriors were as fierce as men. Warfare among ancient Native Americans was not always intended to vanquish the enemy and seize his territory and resources. Rather, warfare was often regarded as a kind of ritual activity with spiritual implications. The number of casualties in these types of conflicts was often quite low, and in some cases, the goal of a warrior was merely to touch an enemy soldier and perhaps seize his weapon.

The most common battle tactic of Native Americans was stealth. Because large bodies of soldiers did not take part in battles, smaller bands of warriors moved swiftly and silently over the landscape, finding ways to sneak up on or ambush the enemy. Retreat was not considered a form of dishonor; rather, retreat was often a strategic move designed to lure the enemy to a place where he could be confronted and defeated. Related to strategic retreat was the principle of force concentration. Rather than allowing the line of battle to be spread out, it was common to lure enemy forces into a ravine, a small valley, a narrow mountain pass, or some other similar place where the attacking force could focus its attack. In many respects ancient Native American warfare was similar to guerrilla warfare. The goal was usually not to overwhelm the enemy with a large, superior force but to harass the enemy and pick off enemy soldiers one at a time or in small groups.

Weapons differed depending on the types of tools and materials that were available to a given tribe. Thus, for example, the groups of the Arctic North used spears—the same spears they used for fishing and hunting for sea mammals—often tipped with points made of bone. Other groups used spears that were otherwise used for big-game hunting, though they were likely tipped with stone. Other weapons included the bow and arrow, the club, the sling, and the tomahawk—any hatchetlike implement with a stone head, used primarily by eastern North American nations, whose soldiers threw it at enemy soldiers. Sticks and knives were also common weapons.

Also important was hand-to-hand combat, and Native American warriors were skilled at forms of martial arts that enabled them to overcome enemy soldiers in close quarters. Some Native American nations adopted forms of armor and helmets. A form of psychological warfare that was implemented involved throwing weapons that were elaborately decorated with feathers and other objects; masks with fierce grimaces were often worn. Native American war paint on the face, arms, and upper body was also common. It should be noted that ancient Native Americans did not fight on horseback. Horses did exist in ancient North America prior to at least 6000 B.C.E., when they became extinct on the continent, but they were not domesticated, meaning that ancient peoples probably used them only as a food source. The horse became a weapon of war only after the arrival of the Europeans and their domesticated horses in the 16th century C.E.

MESOAMERICA

Archaeologists for many decades believed that the societies of ancient Mesoamerica were relatively peaceful. More recent findings, however, suggest otherwise—that warfare was a way of life for some Mesoamerican cultures, at least during portions of their history. Among the Maya, the most dominant culture of ancient Mesoamerica, warfare was conducted to capture victims for ritual sacrifices and to control trade routes and resources. Additionally, warfare was a source of slaves for building temples and other monuments.

The Maya defended their cities with earthworks and walls—often systems of double walls, where enemy invaders were trapped and slaughtered after breaching the outer wall. In common with other warriors in North and South America, they fought primarily with weapons they could hurl. The atlatl was a device that gave greater impetus and range to spears; it consisted of a shaft in which the spear rested, enabling the warrior to hurl the spear by propelling the atlatl, giving the spear much more energy. The *macahuitl* was a wooden weapon that was used like a club or a sword; sharp blades made of obsidian were inserted into the wood, making the weapon lethal. Blowguns were also used, and while bows and arrows were sometimes employed, they were not common weapons. Ordinary warriors wore no helmets, but they carried shields made of wood, animal skins, or woven mats. Leaders, on the other hand, dressed themselves for battle in padded armor and elaborate headdresses, all decorated with religious symbols designed to inspire fear in the enemy.

At the head of Maya military forces was the ruler of each city. Each city had a small group of soldiers who captured sacrificial victims; this group was supplemented by a militia during times of war. Commoners were often recruited to fight, but since they had no military-style weapons, they used hunting tools and rocks. On some occasions, women took part in battles. A chief strategy was to use the forests as cover, luring in enemies and then ambushing them. Sometimes canoes were used to approach enemy cities located on rivers and lakes.

Among the Mesoamericans, warfare was very much a religious ritual activity. Warfare was sanctioned by the gods, and leaders were men of religious authority. Warriors called on help from the gods by singing, blowing horns and whistles, and beating drums as battles began. Religious items were carried into battle. Death in battle was regarded as a far more desired fate than capture by the enemy, for it was common for captured soldiers, especially their leaders, to be degraded with cruel treatment and for their religious symbols to be desecrated.

Mesoamerican warfare was much more sophisticated than warfare among more northerly Native Americans. Very often Mesoamericans fielded large armies, perhaps as many as 20,000 troops and often more. The Mesoamericans conducted warfare in a way that seems more modern. Armies sacked cities, but very often, too, they conducted field operations in open areas; in other words, while northern Native Americans conducted more guerrilla-type warfare, Mesoamericans conducted war based on superiority of forces. Further, Mesoamericans trained for war. Many young boys went to schools that emphasized not only academic subjects but the arts of warfare as well, particularly the use of weapons, such as the spear, the shield, and the others discussed earlier. When they turned 17, they were assigned to military regiments. Armies were highly organized, with trained generals, units, couriers, porters, flag bearers, bodies of foot soldiers, bodies of archers, and the like. Like modern armies, Mesoamerican armies had ranks of soldiers; a person moved up through the ranks by showing courage and skill, and a soldier's rank was indicated by an elaborate flag on his back that identified his clan, family, or city.

SOUTH AMERICA

Historians and archaeologists long believed that warfare in ancient South America was not common. They pointed to the fact that South American societies tended to be small and decentralized. Thus, dominant societies did not mount armies of conquest. However, much of the archaeological record shows defensive remains, such as walls, moats, ditches, and parapets, though some archaeologists question whether these "defenses" could possibly have been effective and suggest that they served more ritualistic purposes. For example, they note that "forts" had no source of water, suggesting that they could not have been used as refuges for armies for more than brief periods of time. Further, the forts had numerous points of entry and even gaps, making them inadequate for defense.

However, more recent archaeological thinking suggests that warfare may have been more common than was previously thought. These scholars emphasize, though, that South American warfare tended to be prosecuted not by large armies

in open fields of battle. Rather, it was conducted more like the wars of Native North Americans, with emphasis on guerrilla tactics. Further, warfare tended to be ritualistic and even relatively bloodless—more a form of social negotiation rather than an effort to destroy an enemy. The word used to convey this idea is *tinku,* which means something like "ritual battle." Scholars draw these conclusions by looking at the archaeological remains, which include many pictures of ritualized war and in particular ritualized conflict between people who are not adult males. This record shows that the most common weapons in ritualized warfare were clubs, slingshots, and even whips.

The practice of capturing enemy soldiers for ritual sacrifice was common in South America. Among the Moche, for example, the purpose of warfare was not to conquer enemies so much as it was to obtain captives for ritual sacrifices conducted by warrior-priests. Surviving decorations on pottery, for example, show these sacrifices being conducted, with enemy soldiers having their throats slit and warrior-priests drinking goblets of the soldiers' blood. In conducting war South Americans used weapons that were in most respects similar to those used in North America and Mesoamerica: knives, lances, and particularly clubs. Bows and arrows do not seem to have been as widely used.

South America also provides a clear example of the relationship between warfare, resources, and climatic conditions among the Andean people of Peru. Recent archaeological findings show that the Andeans developed a complex, thriving civilization beginning in about 3000 B.C.E. They built cities, including the city of Caral, pyramids, monuments, and plazas that have only begun to be explored fully. For about 1,200 years the Andeans lived peaceably with their neighbors. Very early on ocean currents provided rich marine life along the coast as well as a climate for growing fruits and vegetables. But at some point the climate turned much drier, so the Andeans built canals to irrigate what was becoming desert. Their problem was that over time the soil became progressively less productive, leading to a decline in their civilization. By about 1800 B.C.E. the region had been conquered by neighboring states.

See also ADORNMENT; AGRICULTURE; ARCHITECTURE; BORDERS AND FRONTIERS; BUILDING TECHNIQUES AND MATERIALS; CHILDREN; CITIES; DEATH AND BURIAL PRACTICES; ECONOMY; EDUCATION; EMPIRES AND DYNASTIES; FAMILY; FESTIVALS; FOREIGNERS AND BARBARIANS; GENDER STRUCTURES AND ROLES; GOVERNMENT ORGANIZATION; HUNTING, FISHING, AND GATHERING; INVENTIONS; LITERATURE; METALLURGY; MIGRATION AND POPULATION MOVEMENTS; MILITARY; NOMADIC AND PASTORAL SOCIETIES; RELIGION AND COSMOLOGY; ROADS AND BRIDGES; SEAFARING AND NAVIGATION; SETTLEMENT PATTERNS; SHIPS AND SHIPBUILDING; SLAVES AND SLAVERY; SOCIAL ORGANIZATION; TOWNS AND VILLAGES; TRADE AND EXCHANGE; TRANSPORTATION; WEAPONRY AND ARMOR.

Africa

~ *Herodotus: "The Carthaginian Attack on Sicily,"*
excerpt (The Histories, fifth century B.C.E.) ~

VII.165: They, however, who dwell in Sicily, say that Gelo, though he knew that he must serve under the Lacedaemonians, would nevertheless have come to the aid of the Hellenes, had not it been for Terillos, the son of Crinippos, king of Himera; who, driven from his city by Thero, the son of Ainesidemos, king of Agrigentum, brought into Sicily at this very time an army of three hundred thousand men—Phoenicians, Libyans, Iberians, Ligurians, Helisykians, Sardinians, and Corsicans, under the command of Hamilcar the son of Hanno, king of the Carthaginians. Terillos prevailed upon Hamilcar, partly as his sworn friend, but more through the zealous aid of Anaxilaos the son of Cretines, king of Rhegium; who, by giving his own sons to Hamilcar as hostages, induced him to make the expedition. Anaxilaos herein served his own father-in-law; for he was married to a daughter of Terillos, by name Kydippe. So, as Gelo could not give the Hellenes any aid, he sent (they say) the sum of money to Delphi.

VII.166: They say too, that the victory of Gelo and Thero in Sicily over Hamilcar the Carthaginian fell out upon the very day that the Hellenes defeated the Persians at Salamis. Hamilcar, who was a Carthaginian on his father's side only, but on his mother's a Syracusan, and who had

been raised by his merit to the throne of Carthage, after the battle and the defeat, as I am informed, disappeared from sight: Gelo made the strictest search for him, but he could not be found anywhere, either dead or alive.

VII.167: The Carthaginians, who take probability for their guide, give the following account of this matter: Hamilcar, they say, during all the time that the battle raged between the Hellenes and the barbarians, which was from early dawn till evening, remained in the camp, sacrificing and seeking favorable omens, while he burned on a huge pyre the entire bodies of the victims which he offered. Here, as he poured libations upon the sacrifices, he saw the rout of his army; whereupon he cast himself headlong into the flames, and so was consumed and disappeared. But whether Hamilcar's disappearance happened, as the Phoenicians tell us, in this way, or, as the Syracusans maintain, in some other, certain it is that the Carthaginians offer him sacrifice, and in all their colonies have monuments erected to his honor, as well as one, which is the grandest of all, at Carthage. Thus much concerning the affairs of Sicily.

From: Herodotus, *The History*, George Rawlinson, trans. (New York: Dutton and Co., 1862).

Egypt

~ *Pen-ta-ur: "The Victory of Ramses II over the Khita,"*
inscription on the wall of five temples, one at Karnak (ca. 1326 B.C.E.) ~

THEN the king of Khita-land,
With his warriors made a stand,
But he durst not risk his hand
In battle with our Pharaoh;
So his chariots drew away,
Unnumbered as the sand,
And they stood, three men of war
On each car;
And gathered all in force
Was the flower of his army,
for the fight in full array,
But advance, he did not dare,
Foot or horse.

So in ambush there they lay,
Northwest of Kadesh town;
And while these were in their lair,
Others went forth south of Kadesh,
on our midst, their charge was thrown
With such weight, our men went down,
For they took us unaware,
And the legion of Pra-Hormakhu gave way.

But at the western side
Of Arunatha's tide,
Near the city's northern wall,
our Pharaoh had his place.
And they came unto the king,

And they told him our disgrace;
Then Rameses uprose,
like his father, Montu in might,
All his weapons took in hand,
And his armor did he don,
Just like Baal, fit for fight;
And the noble pair of horses that carried Pharaoh on,
Lo! "Victory of Thebes" was their name,
And from out the royal stables of great Miamun they
    came.

Then the king he lashed each horse,
And they quickened up their course,
And he dashed into the middle of the hostile, Hittite
    host,
All alone, none other with him, for he counted not the
    cost.
Then he looked behind, and found
That the foe were all around,
Two thousand and five hundred of their chariots of war;
And the flower of the Hittites, and their helpers, in a
    ring—
Men of Masu, Keshkesh, Pidasa, Malunna, Arathu,
Qazauadana, Kadesh, Akerith, Leka and Khilibu—
Cut off the way behind,
Retreat he could not find;
There were three men on each car,
And they gathered all together, and closed upon the king.
"Yea, and not one of my princes, of my chief men and my
    great,
Was with me, not a captain, not a knight;
For my warriors and chariots had left me to my fate,
Not one was there to take his part in fight."

Then spake Pharaoh, and he cried:
"Father Ammon, where are you?
Shall a sire forget his son?
Is there anything without your knowledge I have done?
From the judgments of your mouth when have I gone?
Have I e'er transgressed your word?
Disobeyed, or broke a vow?
Is it right, who rules in Egypt, Egypt's lord,
Should e'er before the foreign peoples bow,
Or own their rod? . . .
Let the wretch be put to shame
Who refuses your commands,
But honor to his name
Who to Ammon lifts his hands.
To the full of my endeavor,

With a willing heart forever,
I have acted unto you,
And to you, great God, I call;
For behold! now, Ammon, I,
In the midst of many peoples, all unknown,
Unnumbered as the sand,
Here I stand,
All alone;
There is no one at my side,
My warriors and chariots afeared,
Have deserted me, none heard
My voice, when to the cravens I, their king, for succor,
    cried.
But I find that Ammon's grace
Is better far to me
Than a million fighting men and ten thousand chariots
    be. . . .
To you my cry I send,
Unto earth's extremest end,
Saying, 'Help me, father Ammon, against the Hittite
    horde.'"

Then my voice it found an echo in Hermonthis' temple-
    hall,
Ammon heard it, and he came unto my call. . . .

Then all this came to pass, I was changed in my heart
Like Monthu, god of war, was I made,
With my left hand hurled the dart,
With my right I swung the blade,
Fierce as Baal in his time, before their sight.
Two thousand and five hundred pairs of horses were
    around,
And I flew into the middle of their ring,
By my horse-hoofs they were dashed all in pieces to the
    ground, . . .

Then the wretched king of Khita, he stood still,
With his warriors and his chariots all about him in a ring,
Just to gaze upon the valor of our king
In the fray.
And the king was all alone,
Of his men and chariots none
To help him; but the Hittite of his gazing soon had fill,
For he turned his face in flight, and sped away. . . .
Then his princes forth he sent,
To battle with our lord,
Well equipped with bow and sword
And all goodly armament, . . .

(continued)

(continues)

Then, like Monthu in his might,
I rushed on them apace,
And I let them taste my hand
In a twinkling moment's space.
Then cried one unto his mate,
"This is no man, this is he,
This is Sutek, god of hate,
With Baal in his blood;
Let us hasten, let us flee,
Let us save our souls from death,
Let us take to heel and try our lungs and breath."
And before the king's attack,
Lands fell, and limbs were slack,
They could neither aim the bow, nor thrust the spear,
But just looked at him who came
Charging on them, like a flame,
And the King was as a griffin in the rear.
Behold thus speaks the Pharaoh, let all know,
I struck them down, and there escaped me none
Then I lifted up my voice, and I spake,
Ho! my warriors, charioteers,
Away with craven fears,
Halt, stand, and courage take,
Behold I am alone,

Yet Ammon is my helper, and his hand is with me now."
. . .

When my Menna, charioteer, beheld in his dismay,
How the horses swarmed around us, lo! his courage fled
    away,
And terror and affright
Took possession of him quite;
And straightway he cried out to me, and said,

"Gracious lord and bravest king, savior-guard
Of Egypt in the battle, be our ward;
Behold we stand alone, in the hostile Hittite ring,
Save for us the breath of life,
Give deliverance from the strife,
Oh! protect us, Ramses Miamun!
Oh! save us, mighty King!" . . .

Then the king, he hurried forward, on the Hittite host
    he flew,
"For the sixth time that I charged them," says the
    king—and listen well,
"Like Baal in his strength, on their rearward, lo! I fell,
And I killed them, none escaped me, and I slew, and
    slew, and slew."

From: Eva March Tappan, ed., *The World's Story:
A History of the World in Story, Song and Art.* Vol.
3, *Egypt, Africa, and Arabia*, trans. W. K. Flinders
Petrie (Boston: Houghton Mifflin, 1914).

The Middle East

∾ Excerpts from Accounts of the Campaign of Sennacherib ∾

FROM THE SENNACHERIB PRISM (CA. 701 B.C.E.)

In my third campaign I marched against Hatti. Luli,
king of Sidon, whom the terror-inspiring glamour of
my lordship had overwhelmed, fled far overseas and
perished. . . . As to Hezekiah, the Jew, he did not submit
to my yoke, I laid siege to his strong cities, walled forts,
and countless small villages, and conquered them by
means of well-stamped earth-ramps and battering-rams
brought near the walls with an attack by foot soldiers,
using mines, breeches as well as trenches. I drove out
200,150 people, young and old, male and female, horses,
mules, donkeys, camels, big and small cattle beyond
counting, and considered them slaves. Himself I made a
prisoner in Jerusalem, his royal residence, like a bird in a
cage. I surrounded him with earthwork in order to molest
those who were his city's gate. Thus I reduced his country,
but I still increased the tribute and the presents to me as
overlord which I imposed upon him beyond the former
tribute, to be delivered annually. Hezekiah himself, did
send me, later, to Nineveh, my lordly city, together with
30 talents of gold, 800 talents of silver, precious stones,
antimony, large cuts of red stone, couches inlaid with
ivory, nimedu-chairs inlaid with ivory, elephant-hides,
ebony-wood, boxwood and all kinds of valuable treasures,
his own daughters and concubines.

From: Oliver J. Thatcher, ed., *The Library
of Original Sources*. Vol. 1, *The Ancient
World* (Milwaukee, Wis.: University
Research Extension Co., 1907).

FROM THE HEBREW BIBLE, 2 KINGS 18:13–15, 19:35–37

In the fourteenth year of King Hezekiah, Sennacherib, king of Assyria, went on an expedition against all the fortified cities of Judah and captured them. Hezekiah, king of Judah, sent this message to the king of Assyria at Lachish: "I have done wrong. Leave me, and I will pay whatever tribute you impose on me." The king of Assyria exacted three hundred talents of silver and thirty talents of gold from Hezekiah, king of Judah. Hezekiah paid him all the funds there were in the temple of the Lord and in the palace treasuries. . . . That night the angel of the Lord went forth and struck down 185,000 men in the Assyrian camp. Early the next morning, there they were, all the corpses of the dead. So Sennacherib, the king of Assyria, broke camp and went back home to Nineveh. When he was worshiping in the temple of his god Nisroch, his sons Adram-melech and Sharezer slew him with the sword and fled into the land of Ararat.

From: The Bible (Douai-Rheims Version)
(Baltimore: John Murphy Co., 1914).

Rome

∼ Polybius: "The Roman Maniple vs. The Macedonian Phalanx," excerpt (The Histories, ca. second century B.C.E.) ∼

In my sixth book I made a promise, still unfulfilled, of taking a fitting opportunity of drawing a comparison between the arms of the Romans and Macedonians, and their respective system of tactics, and pointing out how they differ for better or worse from each other. I will now endeavor by a reference to actual facts to fulfil that promise. For since in former times the Macedonian tactics proved themselves by experience capable of conquering those of Asia and Greece; while the Roman tactics sufficed to conquer the nations of Africa and all those of Western Europe; and since in our own day there have been numerous opportunities of comparing the men as well as their tactics, it will be, I think, a useful and worthy task to investigate their differences, and discover why it is that the Romans conquer and carry off the palm from their enemies in the operations of war. . . .

Many considerations may easily convince us that, if only the phalanx has its proper formation and strength, nothing can resist it face to face or withstand its charge. . . .

It is clear that in front of each man of the front rank there will be five sarissae projecting to distances varying by a descending scale of two cubits.

With this point in our minds, it will not be difficult to imagine what the appearance and strength of the whole phalanx is likely to be, when, with lowered sarissae, it advances to the charge sixteen deep. Of these sixteen ranks, all above the fifth are unable to reach with their sarissae far enough to take actual part in the fighting. They, therefore, do not lower them, but hold them with the points inclined upwards over the shoulders of the ranks in front of them, to shield the heads of the whole phalanx; for the sarissae are so closely serried, that they repel missiles which have carried over the front ranks and might fall upon the heads of those in the rear. These rear ranks, however, during an advance, press forward those in front by the weight of their bodies; and thus make the charge very forcible, and at the same time render it impossible for the front ranks to face about.

Such is the arrangement, general and detailed of the phalanx. It remains now to compare with it the peculiarities and distinctive features of the Roman arms and tactics. Now, a Roman soldier in full armor also requires a space of three square feet. But as their method of fighting admits of individual motion for each man—because he defends his body with a shield, which he moves about to any point from which a blow is coming, and because he uses his sword both for cutting and stabbing—it is evident that each man must have a clear space, and an interval of at least three feet both on flank and rear if he is to do his duty with any effect. The result of this will be that each Roman soldier will face two of the front rank of a phalanx, so that he has to encounter and fight against ten spears, which one man cannot find time even to cut away, when once the two lines are engaged, nor force his way through easily—

(continued)

(continues)

seeing that the Roman front ranks are not supported by the rear ranks, either by way of adding weight to their charge, or vigor to the use of their swords. Therefore, it may readily be understood that, as I said before, it is impossible to confront a charge of the phalanx, so long as it retains its proper formation and strength.

Why is it then that the Romans conquer? And what is it that brings disaster on those who employ the phalanx? Why, just because war is full of uncertainties both as to time and place; whereas there is but one time and one kind of ground in which a phalanx can fully work. If, then, there were anything to compel the enemy to accommodate himself to the time and place of the phalanx, when about to fight a general engagement, it would be but natural to expect that those who employed the phalanx would always carry off the victory. But if the enemy finds it possible, and even easy, to avoid its attack, what becomes of its formidable character? Again, no one denies that for its employment it is indispensable to have a country flat, bare, and without such impediments as ditches, cavities, depressions, steep banks, or beds of rivers: for all such obstacles are sufficient to hinder and dislocate this particular formation. . . . If the enemy decline to come down into it, but traverse the country sacking the towns and territories of the allies, what use will the phalanx be? For if it remains on the ground suited to itself, it will not only fail to benefit its friends, but will be incapable even of preserving itself. . . .

For no speculation is any longer required to test the accuracy of what I am now saying: that can be done by referring to accomplished facts. The Romans do not, then, attempt to extend their front to equal that of a phalanx, and then charge directly upon it with their whole force: but some of their divisions are kept in reserve, while others join battle with the enemy at close quarters. Now, whether the phalanx in its charge drives its opponents from their ground, or is itself driven back, in either case its peculiar order is dislocated; for whether in following the retiring, or flying from the advancing enemy, they quit the rest of their forces: and when this takes place, the enemy's reserves can occupy the space thus left, and the ground which the phalanx had just before been holding, and so no longer charge them face to face, but fall upon them on their flank and rear. If, then, it is easy to take precautions against the opportunities and peculiar advantages of the phalanx, but impossible to do so in the case of its disadvantages, must it not follow that in practice the difference between these two systems is enormous? Of course, those generals who employ the phalanx must march over ground of every description, must pitch camps, occupy points of advantage, besiege, and be besieged, and meet with unexpected appearances of the enemy: for all these are part and parcel of war, and have an important and sometimes decisive influence on the ultimate victory. And in all these cases the Macedonian phalanx is difficult, and sometimes impossible, to handle, because the men cannot act either in squads or separately.

The Roman order on the other hand is flexible: for every Roman, once armed and on the field, is equally well-equipped for every place, time, or appearance of the enemy. He is, moreover, quite ready and needs to make no change, whether he is required to fight in the main body, or in a detachment, or in a single maniple, or even by himself. Therefore, as the individual members of the Roman force are so much more serviceable, their plans are also much more often attended by success than those of others.

From: Polybius, *The Histories of Polybius*,
2 vols., trans. Evelyn S. Shuckburgh
(London: Macmillan, 1889).

FURTHER READING

Elizabeth Arkush and Charles Stanish, "Interpreting Conflict in the Ancient Andes," *Current Anthropology* 46, no. 1 (2005): 3–28. Available online. URL: http://www.ioa.ucla.edu/stanish/pubs/arkush_stanish.pdf. Downloaded on May 1, 2007.

Matthew Bennett, *Dictionary of Ancient and Medieval Warfare* (Mechanicsburg, Penn.: Stackpole Books, 2001).

Fergus M. Bordewich, "The Ambush That Changed History," *Smithsonian* 36 (September 2005): 74–81.

Alfred S. Bradford, *With Arrow, Sword, and Spear: A History of Warfare in the Ancient World* (Westport, Conn.: Praeger, 2000).

M. Kathryn Brown and Travis W. Stanton, eds., *Ancient Mesoamerican Warfare* (Walnut Creek, Calif.: AltaMira Press, 2003).

Prithwis Chandra Chakravarti, *The Art of War in Ancient India* (Delhi, India: Oriental Publishers, 1972).

Pierre Ducrey, *Warfare in Ancient Greece*, trans. Janet Lloyd (New York: Shocken Books, 1986).

John Hackett, ed., *Warfare in the Ancient World* (New York: Facts On File, 1989).

William V. Harris, *War and Imperialism in Republican Rome, 327–70 B.C.* (Oxford, U.K.: Clarendon, 1979).

Lawrence H. Keeley, *War before Civilization* (New York: Oxford University Press, 1996).

Steven A. LeBlanc and Katherine E. Register, *Constant Battles: The Myth of the Peaceful, Noble Savage* (New York: St. Martin's Press, 2003).

Stuart C. Munro-Hay, "Warfare." In *Aksum: An African Civilisation of Late Antiquity* (Edinburgh: Edinburgh University Press, 1991). Available online. URL: http://users.vnet.net/alight/aksum/mhak4.html#c11. Downloaded on May 13, 2007.

John Rich and Graham Shipley, *War and Society in the Roman World* (London: Routledge, 1993).

Michael M. Sage, *Warfare in Ancient Greece: A Sourcebook* (New York: Routledge, 1996).

Pat Southern, *The Roman Army: A Social and Institutional History* (Santa Barbara, Calif.: ABC-CLIO, 2006).

Hans Van Wees, *Greek Warfare: Myths and Realities* (London: Duckworth, 2004).

► weaponry and armor

INTRODUCTION

Warfare has been a constant element of life since ancient times, yet relatively few ancient weapons and armor have survived to be studied. Iron decays easily, as does the wood and other organic materials that early people used for weapons. Bronze has a better rate of survival, but this material was not used in southern Africa, the Americas, and Oceania. The study of ancient weaponry is further complicated by confusion over how weapons were used. While surviving art and literature from Europe, the Near East, and Asia contains descriptions of weaponry and armor, the same sources are not available for other regions of the world.

In Europe weapons were used almost exclusively to kill enemies and prey. A few daggers and swords, highly decorated and in the possession of high-status men, had ceremonial purposes. Daggers, swords, and spears were typically used for combat, with only daggers intended strictly for attacks upon humans. Slings were the first missile weapon, followed by the enormously popular bows and arrows. The Greeks invented chemical warfare in the form of Greek fire and sulfur gas. Metal, wood, skins, and leather were employed to construct head and body coverings as well as shields. The users of weaponry and armor in Europe were almost exclusively male.

In the Near East warriors used the same sorts of weaponry and armor that were found in Europe. The Assyrians are the earliest warriors of history of whom we have detailed knowledge. They were armed with spears, battle-axes, maces, swords, and shields as well as bows and arrows. Assyrians show liquid fire on bas-relief artwork. Along with other people of the region, they employed simple incendiary materials such as blazing arrows, pots of boiling oil, and naphtha. Babylonian spearmen protected themselves with square shields held edge to edge, as did the Greek phalanxes and Roman legions 3,000 years later. The Assyrians were the first to develop scale armor that consisted of many small metal plates sewn on a leather jacket so that the rows overlapped.

In the Americas some of the aboriginal people used copper and bronze, but they never developed wrought iron or steel for weapons. Stone arrowheads and spearheads continued to be used century after century, as they were in Oceania. In Asia the Hindus became renowned as the best temperers of steel in the ancient world. Few clues to the weaponry of ancient Africa remain. The Africans passed from the Stone Age directly into the Iron Age, missing the Bronze Age entirely. In the context of ancient Africa a weapon has to be viewed as part of a highly complex system of interdependent actions and beliefs. Some weapons were empowered by the application of magical substances. No matter how thick the hide of a shield or well tempered the blade of a sword, both were considered incomplete without the symbolic designs applied to them. Even accessories such as sword sheaths seem also to have had great importance.

AFRICA

BY CARYN E. NEUMANN

Western understandings of weaponry have limited application to Africa. In ancient Africa the separation between military and civilian life was not as distinct as in the West. While European weapons were made to kill, ancient African weaponry came in a wide variety of forms developed for use in political, religious, or other ritual or ceremonial contexts; not all were designed to kill.

Weaponry in Africa began with rock. The oldest surviving weapons in the world are pebbles chipped into blades that were found in Africa. These weapons also could double as tools or perhaps were an adaptation from tools; their use as tools no doubt preceded their use as weapons. These rough weapons advanced into knives made of sharpened rock, spears with stone tips, and hand axes shaped like almonds. One type of hand ax, the cleaver, has been found only in Africa. It had a hefty blade used for hacking, slashing, and cutting.

A wide variety of raw materials, including quartzite, hornfels, mudstone, and chert, was used in southern Africa for stone point production. Herodotus reported that Africans used spears with heads constructed from the sharpened horns of antelope. The points, with distinctive tangs, were bound to spears with plant twine, bark, leather thongs, and sinew. The binding materials would have been moistened before application. Moistened bindings expand and become more pliable before contracting to their original size upon drying. This shrinkage, and the fact that individual strands on drying tend to adhere to one another, leaves the point firmly secured on the haft.

The first long-range missile weapon was probably a sling, although no ancient African slings have survived. Slings were originally used by ancient shepherds to scare predatory animals that were attacking their herds. They gradually became weapons of warfare, used by light-armed troops against similarly defenseless warriors. The sling consisted of two leather or sinew straps. Each strap was attached at one end to the sides of a small piece of leather or cloth. The other end of one

Stone ball, Lower Palaeolithic, about 1.2 million years old, found in Olduvai Gorge, Tanzania; such stone balls might have been tied to a leather thong and used in hunting to bring down game. (© The Trustees of the British Museum)

strap, held by the slinger, was looped securely around a finger or wrist, while the other strap, usually knotted to provide a grip, was held freely between the thumb and forefinger of the throwing hand. The missile, a stone, was placed on a piece of leather, and the straps were pulled taut, creating a pocket for the stone. A rotary motion of the wrist, usually three or four rotations, gave the stone momentum when the unlooped, held strap was released. A skilled thrower could be very accurate, and the high-speed missile could kill.

Copper technology indicates that ancient Africans mastered a considerable degree of the pyrotechnology needed for copper smelting. Evidence of early copper metallurgy has been radiocarbon dated from 4140 B.C.E. to 2700 B.C.E. in western Africa. Copper products included thin arrowheads. There is evidence of iron production in East Africa from about 1400 B.C.E. The date suggests that iron production might not have been introduced from elsewhere but instead developed in the region. Iron ore is distributed widely across Africa. Stone artifacts were always present at early Iron Age sites in the form of arrow points and axes, with metal weapons used as status objects. Africans employed iron to make tools, weapons, and points for weapons. Many central African people believed that, except on a few designated occasions, women should not come into contact with iron. To do so could render a woman barren and destroy the power of the iron products with which she came into contact. However, other parts of Africa accepted women warriors, and the Teda of the Tibesti region developed weaponry specifically for women.

The Iron Age brought the use of throwing knives as missiles. Throwing knives, additionally used as long-distance currency, were more popular than javelins. The sharp spikes of these weapons could inflict severe wounds on practically nude enemies. The classic form of the northern variety of throwing knife consists of a narrow piece of iron, up to 2½ feet in length, with a projecting spur a little over halfway up. Below this spur are a straight shaft and a grip, which, if not made of bare iron, is usually made of hide or reptile skin. Above the spur is the blade, often broader than the shaft and curving forward in the same direction as the spur. Weapons of this type were distributed across a wide area of Sudanic Africa from northern Nigeria to the Blue Nile province of Sudan and deep into the Tibesti region of the Sahara.

The typical southern variety of throwing knife is generally smaller than the northern variety. It usually has a number of blades radiating from the central shaft and a grip of plaited vegetal material or, occasionally, of wire or hide. It is found in a small area of northern Gabon and in a broad belt from eastern Cameroon almost to the White Nile. The Zande kpinga, a southern type of throwing knife, is one of the few varieties whose aerodynamic qualities and consistent use as a missile have been well documented. The heavier northern throwing knife was used more often than the lighter southern variety for ceremonial purposes.

Not every weapon was intended for war. Weapons of various types were widely used in dance and masquerade throughout Africa. The musele, a Kota throwing knife conceived as a bird in profile with a long bill, was not designed to be thrown. The Kota, of the eastern Ogooué River region, saw the musele as a prestigious weapon of chiefs to be used in dances. Throwing knives of the Wadai region were also ornithologically inspired and designed for ceremonial purposes. Among the Kota and the Fang spears, knives, and swords were considered to be emblems of the owner's status and were left on tombs of chiefs after death.

To protect against weapons, Africans used light armor that befitted their hot climate. The protective armor of the Benin warrior was a large wooden shield with a curved top and straight bottom. It was designed to be set on the ground to cover a kneeling man. The shields in the Sudan were made of hippopotamus or elephant hide. The shields of the Dinka were oval in outline and reinforced by a staff threaded through loops cut into the hide. The staff served as a handgrip. The Shuli had shields of a more nearly rectangular form, while the Shilluk and Nuer both had shields that could serve as clubs. The club shields were reinforced with a log with a cutout for the grip. The skin cover of ox hide was applied tightly in order to keep the wood from splitting when delivering blows with this shield club. Chiefs and other distinguished warriors throughout Africa wore helmets of padded basketwork or crocodile skin. For body armor they had quilted ponchos covered with leopard skins.

EGYPT

BY AMR KAMEL

Ancient Egyptian weapons apparently were manufactured in the workshops attached to royal palaces, great temples, and military headquarters. There are a few scenes from the Old and Middle Kingdom (ca. 2575–ca. 1640 B.C.E.) that depict bows and spear shafts being smoothed and others that show arrows. From the New Kingdom (ca. 1550–ca. 1070 B.C.E.) there is much pictorial evidence showing various techniques used in weapons manufacture. Scenes include a craftsman straightening the shaft of a spear over a fire after wetting it from a cup of water beside him, a bow being tested for resilience, arrows being made, metal helmets being weighted, bow cases being sewn up with an awl (a pointed tool for punching holes), and an arrow being checked for straightness by one workman while a second uses an adze (a bladed tool) to plane out another arrow resting on his knees.

A letter sent by Dhutmose, a scribe who was on a military mission in Nubia, to his son, Butehamun, the scribe of the Necropolis at Deir el-Medina, requests "fresh supplies of copper spear-heads" made by the local coppersmiths as well as spare parts for war chariots, new material for clothing, and old material "for bandages," a rare sign of concern for the wounded. Several New Kingdom tombs include representations of carpenters, joiners, and leather workers, all working on a chariot together. In addition to wood, they required large amounts of leather for fastening parts together, covering the body, tiring the wheels, and making reins, blinkers, and bits.

During the New Kingdom the Egyptians imported highly developed weapons from the Near East and adopted Near Eastern military technology. There is perhaps some evidence that non-Egyptian craftsmen participated in weapons manufacture. Bows and arrows, the most important long-range weapons, can be dated to the Late Paleolithic Period (ca. 12,000–10,000 B.C.E.). During the Second Intermediate Period (1640–1532 B.C.E.) the composite bow was introduced from the Near East. It was made from laminated wood, horn, and sinew and had a much improved range and power. It had an effective range of 500 to 600 feet, and an exceptional shot could attain a distance of 1,500 feet. Because of the laminate construction of composite bows, they were sensitive to heat and moisture and thus were usually stored in cases. Two types of cases have been discovered from New Kingdom Egypt: One was carried, and the other was attached to the body of a war chariot. They could be made of leather or wood and were sometimes ornamented.

Handheld stabbing weapons can be traced to Paleolithic times. The earliest artistic representation of a spear is on the Hunters Palette. Spears were regularly used in military contexts in later times as well. For example, the Egyptian soldiers on Hatshepsut's (r. 1473–1458 B.C.E.) mission to Punt are shown carrying spears and shields on the Deir el-Bahri reliefs, as are troops following Tutankhamun (r. 1333–1323 B.C.E.) as he drives his chariot on the "painted box." Some of the Near Eastern men in the Beni Hasan tomb painting carry spears, and the Shasu Bedouin in the Seti I (r. 1306–1290 B.C.E.) reliefs at Karnak brandish spears and axes against Egyptian forces. Spears were ideal defensive weapons in siege warfare.

A spear with much longer shaft, known as a lance, is illustrated in siege scenes from the Middle Kingdom Beni Hasan tombs. In these scenes a portable defensive structure covers a group of soldiers who attack a fortified city with a large lance, in the manner of a battering ram. Maces with mace heads of varying form were the most powerful weapons of close combat in the Predynastic Period (before roughly 3000 B.C.E.). In the Late Period (712–332 B.C.E.) and into Greco-Roman times (332 B.C.E.–395 C.E.) kings are shown brandishing maces in the head-smiting motif on temple walls. Disc- and oval-shaped mace heads are found in the Naqada I and II periods of the Predynastic Period. These shapes continued to be used through pharaonic history and beyond. The mace (and club) probably had a more ceremonial function after the Old Kingdom, despite Thutmose III's (r. 1479–1425 B.C.E.) boast on the Gebel Barkal stela regarding his victories in the Near East: "It was my mace which overthrew the Asiatics, my club which smote the Nine Bows."

The earliest form of ax was the handheld implement from Paleolithic times. When the stone blade was first affixed to a handle is not known, but at that point of development the ax became a deadly weapon. During the Old Kingdom copper blades were introduced. The ax blades were long and rounded and continued to be used during the Middle Kingdom. The duck-bill blade is the ax shown in the tomb of Khnumhotep at Beni Hasan. In two Old Kingdom battle scenes the ax is used by Egyptian soldiers to repel their enemies and to hack up the city wall. In the New Kingdom the blade is much more narrowly shaped.

Swords and daggers were of great military importance throughout Egypt's history. These weapons are similar in construction but different in length and usage. A sword is generally defined as longer than 16 inches, and a dagger is shorter. The Third Dynasty relief of King Sekhemkhet (r. ca. 2611–ca. 2603 B.C.E.) at Wadi Maghara (Sinai) shows a dagger tucked in the monarch's belt. These early daggers were made of copper and had no midrib (thickening down the middle for added strength). The dagger's usefulness as a weapon would have been in hand-to-hand combat. As copper gave way to bronze in the third millennium B.C.E., daggers in Egypt evolved into swords. Preserved examples from the Middle Kingdom resemble the daggers of earlier periods. However, swords were not commonly used in Egypt until the New Kingdom, when longer, double-edged swords were introduced from Anatolia.

Shields were the oldest means of defense and were made of wood covered with leather. They were used first by infantry. In the New Kingdom they were held by drivers of war chariots, to protect the archers standing beside them. The tomb of Tutankhamun contained wooden shields, some of which had leather or animal skins over them. Combining wood and leather made the shield a more effective defensive tool, and a metal protective surface was especially useful against arrows fired from composite bows. Helmets appeared in the Eighteenth Dynasty (ca. 1550–ca. 1307 B.C.E.), when some troops acquired helmets of bronze or leather in imitation of the Asiatic model. Other troops wore shirts made of leather strips sewn together in rows. Armor made of iron lamellae (thin plates) appeared in the reign of Sheshonk I (r. ca. 945–ca. 924 B.C.E.).

The two-wheeled, horse-drawn chariot was introduced to Egypt from Asia in the Second Intermediate Period. From that time onward the chariot significantly contributed to the art of Egyptian warfare, useful for its mobility and the element of surprise. It was constructed of wood with some leather and metal elements, making it a light vehicle on the battlefield. It was manned by two soldiers: the charioteer, who held a shield, and the chariot-warrior, who was armed with a bow and a spear. The chariot was not armored in any way and therefore was not suitable for a direct attack. Once the enemy lines were broken, the chariot was ideally suited for pursuing and harassing the scattered infantry.

THE MIDDLE EAST

by James A. Corrick

Through the sixth millennium B.C.E. weapons in the ancient Near East were made from stone and wood. Spears with long wooden shafts and arrows made from reeds or wood were tipped with chipped-flint heads. Some crude spears and arrows lacked heads, with one end being nothing more than a fire-hardened point. Axes with stone blades were also used. During the fifth millennium B.C.E. the flint and stone heads of these weapons were often replaced by copper, and by 3500 B.C.E. bronze was in use for weapons. Around 1200 B.C.E. the Hittites were among the first to use iron for armaments. However, the quality of this iron was not good, and bronze weapons were still stronger and better made. Good-quality iron weapons did not become common until after 1000 B.C.E., with steel—iron hardened by the addition of carbon—appearing in arms manufacturing after 500 B.C.E.

Many of the weapons that became common throughout the ancient Near East were first used by the armies of Sumer. By 2500 B.C.E. infantry troops were armed with 5- to 6-foot-long thrusting spears and lightweight throwing spears, or javelins. Others carried bows with an effective range of between 150 and 300 feet. Many also carried daggers, ranging in length from 6 to 12 inches. Some weapons carried by Sumerian soldiers were everyday tools. Hunters brought slings for throwing stones that could down either game or enemy warriors in battle. Fishermen brought their nets, using them to entangle their opponents, whom they then either speared or stabbed. Nets did not long remain a part of the Near Eastern battle equipment, but slings would be used by most Near Eastern armies through the early centuries C.E., although the ammunition would sometimes be clay or lead pellets rather than small stones.

Another important Sumerian weapon was the socket ax. The bronze head of this battle-ax was narrow for better cutting and had a socket that slipped down over the end of the ax's wooden handle. A rivet driven through the socket into the handle held the head in place and allowed the wielder to deliver a strong blow without dislodging the head, as often happened to axes with heads tied to the haft. Able to cut through most forms of armor, the socket ax, its head made of iron during the last centuries B.C.E., would remain one of the most deadly ancient Near Eastern weapons.

The composite bow was the next important advance in personal weaponry, appearing sometime after 2300 B.C.E. during the Akkadian reign. Until this time bows had been carved from a single piece of wood. The composite, however, was built by gluing together different types of wood, along with bone and sinew. The resulting bow was stronger and capable of shooting an arrow twice as far as the older bows. The composite eventually became the bow of choice throughout the ancient Near East and was still being used by the Persians of the Sassanian Dynasty (224–651 C.E.).

Both Sumerians and Akkadians carried the sickle-sword, which had a curved blade much like the sickle used in harvesting crops. The straight-bladed sword eventually developed from the dagger, and Assyrians began carrying straight-bladed swords during the first millennium B.C.E., as later did Persian and other Near Eastern armies. The sickle-sword, however, continued to be used in the ancient Near East into the early centuries C.E. Its curved blade was designed for slashing at an enemy and was sharpened only on its outer edge. The straight-bladed sword might have either one edge sharpened for slashing or both edges for thrusting and stabbing as well as slashing. Long swords, measuring more than a yard, were found in the arsenals of many Near Eastern armies, but short swords, normally ranging in length from 2 to 2.5 feet, were more common. The Persian infantry of the Achaemenid Dynasty (550–330 B.C.E.) carried a very short, straight-bladed sword called an *akinakes*, which was made of iron and measured between 14 and 18 inches in length, making it not much longer than a dagger; indeed, the difference between a long dagger and a short sword was vague. Sword blades were often leaf-shaped, swelling in the middle and then tapering at the end. Bronze and iron blades were formed from a single piece of metal, while steel blades had a core of iron over which was layered a coat of steel.

The primary defenses against all weapons were armor, helmets, and shields. Sumerian armor was a linen or leather cloak to which copper or bronze disks were sewn. The most common form of armor in the ancient Near East was that worn by the Assyrians and later the Achaemenid Persians. Known as scale armor because it resembled the scales of a fish, this protective gear was made by sewing overlapping small oblongs of bronze or iron to a shirt of linen or felt. Originally, among the Assyrians, an armor shirt reached to the knees or lower, but later it was shortened so that it reached only to the waist. This short armor was also preferred by the Persians, probably because it allowed for more maneuverability. The sleeves, even on the longest armor shirts, ended well above the elbow. Sometimes Near Eastern armor was nothing more than quilted linen, as was the case with some Achaemenid Persian troops.

The first helmets were worn by the Sumerians and were either cloth or leather caps. The Sumerians eventually began using headgear made from copper that looked like metal caps. Bronze helmets appeared later. The Assyrians were among the first to wear iron helmets, although both copper and bronze helmets would remain in use in the ancient Near East throughout the last millennium B.C.E. The Assyrian helmets were noteworthy for their conical shape. They were designed so that a blow by a sword or ax, unless aimed directly, would slide down the side of the helmet. A curtain of scale mail also hung from these helmets. Modifications of this design would be adopted later by the Parthians (250 B.C.E.–226 C.E.) and the Sassanian Persians, among others.

Achaemenid Persian troops generally wore tight-fitting helmets, when they wore any headgear at all. Indeed, it was not unusual for ancient Near Eastern warriors to fight without helmets or armor. This was particularly true of archers, who might be hampered by the weight of protective gear. Instead of armor worn on the body, these troops were protected by shields, often carried for them by others known as shield-bearers. But armored and helmeted troops also generally carried shields. The earliest shield, and one that would be used as late as Sassanian times, was the wickerwork shield. It was made of woven reeds or twigs, supported by a wooden frame and sometimes lined with leather for extra protection and given additional strength by bands of metal. Even the Assyrians, with their iron scale armor and helmets, used these wickerwork shields because they were lightweight. Metal shields, made first of bronze and then of iron, also existed during this period. Shields were rectangular, circular, or oval and could be small (no more than 2 feet across) or large enough to tower above a warrior's head. The smallest shields were normally made of metal, but large metal shields were too heavy to carry into battle.

ASIA AND THE PACIFIC
BY AMY HACKNEY BLACKWELL

The basic weapons in ancient Asia were spears, swords of various designs, and bows and arrows. In prehistoric times weapons were made of wood, bone, horn, stone, and hide; bones and stones can be fashioned into very sharp points. As people learned how to work metals, they started making weapons out of them. Bronze weapons appeared during the early second millennium B.C.E. Iron weapons gradually replaced them in the next millennium, although people continued to make bronze weapons until the early years of the Common Era. Chinese weapons makers became experts at metallurgy; weapons produced during the Qin Dynasty (221–207 B.C.E.), for example, are made of carefully composed alloys of copper, nickel, chrome, iron, and several other metals. Some arrowheads contain lead, presumably for its poisonous effect. Chinese weapons makers of this period coated their blades with a thin layer of chromic salt oxide to prevent rust; this coating has preserved many weapons in good condition for more than 2,000 years.

Most ancient weapons were meant for hand-to-hand combat. Projectile weapons were harder to use and supply because they needed a stream of ammunition in battle. The sling was the most basic projectile weapon; throughout ancient Asia people used slings made of leather or some other flexible material to fling rocks or other projectiles. Bows and arrows were more effective and could propel weapons farther than slings, but the simplicity of the sling kept it in use throughout the ancient period, especially in the more remote islands of the Pacific.

The spear, or *qiang*, is one of the oldest Chinese weapons. Spears were simple to make; affixing a small, sharp tip to a long shaft did not require technological expertise. Chinese warriors began using spears in prehistoric times. Spears with bronze tips became popular starting in the 17th century B.C.E. Weapons makers started using steel instead of bronze for spear tips during the Eastern Zhou Dynasty (770–256 B.C.E.). The *qiang* spear was the most important long weapon of the Western Han Dynasty (202 B.C.E.–9 C.E.).

One of the classic Chinese weapons was the saber, or *dao*. These early *dao* were more like knives, with a straight or slightly curved blade. The oldest *dao* were made of bronze. Smiths began to make them of iron and steel between the sixth and third centuries B.C.E. As the *dao* evolved, its blade became curved, and it was often attached to a long handle, though many types of *dao* existed. The *dao* was especially popular during the late Qin Dynasty and early Han Dynasty. During the Han Dynasty cavalry became more important, and warriors took to carrying long *dao* that had single-sided blades attached to long shafts, which they could wield on horseback. Infantrymen of this time often carried short *dao* or broadswords.

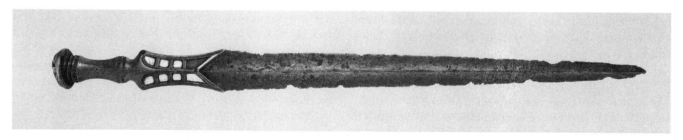

Short sword of steel, bronze, and gold from east-central Asia, ca. fourth to first century B.C.E. (Copyright the Metropolitan Museum of Art)

The *jian* was a straight sword. The earliest *jian* date to the sixth century B.C.E. This weapon was most popular during the Zhou Dynasty and the Western Han Dynasty, when famous sword makers developed their craft to an art form. After the first century C.E. the warrior's *jian* grew less popular than the *dao*, which became the preferred combat weapon, especially of the cavalry. Men still wore *jian* as part of their ensembles and as a status symbol, and some warriors continued to use *jian* in combat. Martial artists of this time adopted the *jian* as a weapon to use in symbolic martial arts.

The *ji*, or halberd, was a sort of combination spear and sword; it consisted of a long shaft with a bronze point at its tip and a curved blade parallel to the shaft close to the spear tip. Sometimes a *ji* had two blades affixed opposite each other. The *ji* could be used for slashing and stabbing, and it could be wielded by men on foot or in chariots. It was popular during the Shang Dynasty (ca. 1500–ca. 1045 B.C.E.) and Zhou Dynasty. During the Han Dynasty the *qiang* spear gradually replaced the *ji* as the long weapon of choice, relegating the *ji* to martial artists.

Crossbows with bronze mechanisms are common in the archaeological record in China beginning in about 600 B.C.E. Chinese historians started mentioning crossbows in the fifth century B.C.E. Soldiers used crossbows at the battle of Maling in 341 B.C.E. During the Han Dynasty the crossbow was commonly used in infantry battles and also was occasionally deployed during fighting on horseback. Early crossbows were made of cast bronze parts attached to a wooden frame.

In India the people who lived in the Indus Valley between 2500 and 1500 B.C.E. made numerous weapons that they used for war, war games, and hunting. The Vedic sacred texts of this period describe warfare and the weapons that soldiers were expected to master. These weapons included the bow and arrow, the discus (the god Krishna was said to be an expert with the discus), the javelin, the ax, the mace, and the dagger. Archery, in particular, was highly esteemed as a soldierly skill. Indian weapons makers were among the first to build bows out of steel. Indian peoples also used swords in battle. The chariot played an important role in Indian warfare. Indian chariots were large, heavy, four-wheeled devices made of iron and wood and pulled by several horses. They could carry several soldiers, including a driver, an archer, and up to five foot soldiers. The chariots themselves were heavy enough to crush enemy soldiers, and the soldiers who rode on them used the chariots' height and speed to overpower their enemies. Indian armies also used elephants in battle starting in about 1500 B.C.E. The elephants could carry several soldiers on their backs and were themselves armed with long blades attached to their tusks.

In Japan during the Jōmon Period (ca. 13,000–ca. 300 B.C.E.) people made simple weapons from chipped and polished stone, but it was not until the Yayoi Period (ca. 300 B.C.E.–300 C.E.) that people engaged in large-scale organized warfare. During this time Japanese people began using swords and spears made of bronze and iron. Japanese weapons of this period are similar to contemporary Chinese weapons, and historians believe that Japanese weapons makers might have borrowed bronze- and iron-smelting techniques from China. The basic weapons of spears, slings, clubs, bows and arrows, and blades were used throughout the Pacific region. Australian aborigines used boomerangs, curved wooden blades that could be thrown, both for hunting and in warfare. Pacific islanders made weapons out of locally available materials. In Hawaii, for example, soldiers used slings to fling volcanic rocks. They made daggers out of swordfish spears, hammers out of stone, and spears with points made of shark teeth.

EUROPE

BY CARYN E. NEUMANN

War shaped the ancient world, with weaponry and armor determining the success of the combatants. The sheer number and wide range of military artifacts that have been unearthed speak of large-scale production and large-scale deposition of arms and armor in Europe. During the Paleolithic, Mesolithic, and Neolithic periods weapons generally included whatever blunt object was close at hand as well as any sharp object that could be thrown. Skeletons in the Neolithic mass grave at Talheim in Germany bear the traces of blows from stone axes on their skulls, and many other skulls in Neolithic burials also have evidence of blows from hard objects. Sometimes the victim survived to fight another day, but often these blows were fatal. The bow and arrow was invented during the Mesolithic, but it was some time before bows were strong and accurate enough to deliver a lethal shot to a vital organ. More often, a lucky shot would wound the victim, who then would have to be finished off by spear or ax if he had not escaped. The so-called Iceman found frozen in the Alps in 1991 had an arrowhead lodged in his shoulder, either a fatal wound or a debilitating injury that contributed to his eventual demise. He was also carrying a bow (but it was unfinished, so of no use to him) and a quiver of arrows as well as a flint dagger.

During the Copper Age, between about 3500 and 2000 B.C.E., depictions on rock carvings and finds of arrowheads indicate that the bow and arrow had increased in accuracy and killing power to become apparently the most popular weapon throughout western and central Europe. Yew and elm were the favored woods for making bows, while arrow shafts were generally made from the straight twigs of hazel. Bowstrings could have been made from animal sinew, but the Iceman's bow had a flax string. Arrowheads were often made of flint, bone, or bronze and were attached to their shafts with resin and pitch. Thus, many different raw materials had to be procured and integrated to make an effective bow and arrow. Some of the metal arrowheads were barbed to inflict more substantial wounds. Curiously, arrowheads become less common after about 2000 B.C.E., suggesting that the bow and arrow declined in popularity.

Daggers were one of the most popular weapons of the Bronze Age (2800–700 B.C.E.) and were still in common use

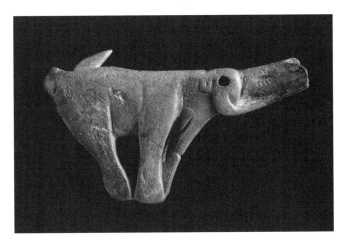

Spear thrower carved in the shape of a mammoth, Late Magdalenian (about 12,500 years old), from the rock shelter of Montastruc, Tarn-et-Garonne, France (© The Trustees of the British Museum)

in the Early Iron Age (beginning in 1000 B.C.E.). While some elaborately decorated daggers were apparently intended only for ceremonial use, most daggers were employed for fighting at close quarters. Unlike the bow and arrow, daggers probably were meant only for human fighting rather than hunting. It is possible, however, that they were used to deliver a coup de grace to wounded animals and people and, in the absence of other implements identifiable as knives, daggers also might have been used to butcher prey. Daggers typically had rounded pommels.

Two types of weapons emerged early in the Bronze Age that would have a substantial impact on warfare for many centuries. The sword and the spear were critical elements in combat. The spear developed out of a daggerlike blade with a long tang (attaching the blade to the handle) that might have been mounted on a long shaft rather than held close to the body. By 1800 B.C.E. the socketed version, fitting over the shaft, was in use in central Europe. With only small differences, this is the form that existed throughout the ancient era. Depictions of spears do not clearly indicate whether they were typically held or thrown. In Europe small and large spearheads were used, as were those of intermediate sizes. It is most likely that small spearheads were intended for light javelins that could be thrown over long distances. Large spearheads were probably used for heavy spears that were held firm by a warrior or group of warriors under close-quarters thrust at an opponent. Collective finds of spears in Scandinavia indicate that spear owners acted and fought in collaboration, with some throwing their spears and then taking cover behind others, who advanced holding their spears. At the moment of encounter the throwers could then have emerged to use cutting or thrusting weapons (daggers, rapiers, swords) in hand-to-hand combat.

While spears were obviously important, they were not usually decorated or given the appearance of prestige weapons, unlike swords. Early versions of the sword were in existence by 1800 B.C.E. The cut-and-thrust sword developed several centuries later. In combat, swords were usually accompanied by daggers or knives and sometimes by spears. Not everyone relied on a sword—a few relied on spears or daggers. Still, swords were the commonest weapon.

To fend off arrowheads and the blows of blades, ancient Europeans devised various types of armor. Most of the earliest examples of body armor in Europe date to the 13th century B.C.E. Leather and wood were the most popular materials for protection. Wooden shields were produced in Ireland around 1800 B.C.E. Leather, always in use, had more flexibility than bronze, and it was considerably cheaper and easier to produce. Few warriors were protected entirely by bronze, but hammered sheet bronze is so thin that it would have been relatively useless as protection against a spear or sword.

Pelts were also used as a sort of armor that offered not only the physical protection of the animal's fur and hide but also the psychological reinforcement brought about by taking on the animal's fighting skills. Warriors wore the pelts of wolves, bears, and other fierce animals when going into battle. The head of the animal sat on the warrior's head like a helmet. The animal's front legs ran down the warrior's arms, protecting them from sword blows, while its hind legs were attached to the warrior's legs. In this way the warrior inhabited the animal and took on its spirit, often in an intensely ecstatic state that made him relatively impervious to wounds and to fear and, consequently, very hard to stop.

There was another kind of ecstatic warrior that fought wearing no armor—indeed, no clothes at all. A representation of such a naked warrior has been found carved into a stone slab left by the Kemi-Oba culture at Kernosovka in Ukraine. It is the oldest-known image of a European warrior and dates from 4000 to 3000 B.C.E. The warrior is dressed in nothing but a belt, but he is heavily armed with a club, a knife or spear, and three axes. His hair is long, his arms are held tightly to his chest with his shoulders pulled up, and his penis is erect, all indicating a heightened state of passion and alertness. The same representations of tightly held arms, tense shoulders, and erect penis are also found on a Celtic statue of a "berserk" warrior. The Celts adorned their nakedness with golden neckbands, which served the double purpose of accenting their white skins and taunting their enemies to come and take the bands off their necks if they dared. They wore their naked paleness with similar bravado, as a kind of psychological armor that showed off the red blood of their wounds. Without the burden of armor, they were also faster than ordinary soldiers. At the battle of Cannae in 216 B.C.E. the Romans ran in terror from the troops of bare-chested Gauls that Hannibal had assembled. In these cases, the most effective armor was no armor. Berserks scared their opponents into fleeing the field of battle. When men did fight, wooden shields and leather coverings offered little protection against arrowheads and swords. In ancient Europe weaponry advanced more quickly than personal defenses against it.

GREECE

BY CHRISTOPHER BLACKWELL

The wall and vase paintings from the Minoan and Mycenaean Bronze Age, during the second millennium B.C.E., are the earliest evidence of the existence of weaponry and armor in the ancient Greek world. These paintings show warriors carrying shields in the shape of a figure eight, an oval with semicircles cut out on either side of the middle; these warriors wear helmets and carry long, narrow swords.

The Homeric epics, composed in their present form around the seventh century B.C.E., present a backward-looking view of warfare from an earlier age. They describe warriors armed with bronze helmets—although Odysseus, in book 10 of the *Iliad*, goes on a nighttime raid wearing a leather helmet studded with boars' tusks, bronze breastplates, and greaves (metal armor covering the shins) and carrying one or two spears and a sword. These Homeric warriors would throw their shields, either from chariots or while standing, and then engage the enemy, one on one, with their swords.

The Archaic Period (ca. 600–ca. 480 B.C.E.) saw the so-called hoplite revolution. The term comes from the Greek word *hoplon*, or "weapon; a *hoplitēs* was a soldier outfitted with heavy bronze armor and trained in the tactics of the phalanx. The phalanx was a line of infantry in close formation, each man's shield covering half of his own body and half of his neighbor's, trained to present a theoretically impregnable mass of spear points and shields. Victory depended on numbers and on the discipline of the individual soldiers.

The hoplite's armor consisted of a breastplate, or *thorax*, made of bronze; a bronze helmet, *kranos* or *korus*, closely fitted and covering the whole head and with a T-shaped slit exposing the eyes and mouth (and often a noseguard descending

from the brow); bronze greaves, *knēmides*, for covering the shins; and the bronze and leather shield, *aspis* or generically *hoplon*. The hoplite's weapons were the sword (or *xiphos*), a short-bladed stabbing weapon for close combat, and the spear (*doru*), a longer thrusting weapon. Hoplites typically did not fight with the thrown spear, *akontion*, although mounted cavalry and some more lightly armed units did.

Because each soldier was responsible for providing his own armor, at his own expense, there must have been a certain amount of diversity in the style and quality of arms. The historian Thucydides, in recounting how the Athenians prepared for their invasion of Sicily in 415 B.C.E., describes a certain competition among soldiers to show off by acquiring the best armor, saying that "the land forces had been picked from the best muster-rolls, and vied with each other in paying great attention to their arms and personal accoutrements."

The cost of this armor limited participation in land combat to those who could afford to arm themselves; these were generally men who owned land and who therefore had the most at stake in any conflict between neighboring states. But in contrast to the Bronze Age "heroic" warfare described by Homer, which was a series of acts of single combat between champions, hoplite warfare was communal, requiring cooperation and mutual trust. Historians see connections between the rise of this form of fighting and the increasing broadening of political participation in the Archaic Period, as power moved out of the hands of individual kings and into the hands of aristocracies or oligarchies, with governance being shared by those who were in a position to fight on behalf of the state.

The weight of metal that provided protection presented its own problems, and vase paintings of soldiers from the sixth, fifth, and fourth centuries show them, more often than not, with their heavy helmets perched back on the top of their heads, leaning on their shields, or standing by their unworn armor. Historical accounts, particularly those of Xenophon, a historian and mercenary commander of the fourth century B.C.E., contain many anecdotes of soldiers waiting to put on their armor until literally the last minute before engaging the enemy.

Cavalry did not have a large role in land warfare among Greek states until the period of Macedonian supremacy in the fourth century B.C.E. Likewise archery played a limited role, except when Greeks fought as mercenary units in the larger armies of Asia Minor. Archers, *toxitai*, do appear in accounts of siege warfare, as well as in the Homeric epics, where the Trojan Alexandros (Paris) is shown using a bow, as is the Greek Odysseus.

During the fourth century B.C.E. some Greek armies experimented with units of more lightly armed foot soldiers, called *peltasts*, some armed mainly with throwing javelins or slings. But the most significant improvements to arms came through innovations among the armies of Philip of Macedon, who arrayed his phalanxes several rows deep and armed each row with the Macedonian spear, the *sarisa*, using different

Vase from Mycenae depicting warriors in battle gear (Alison Frantz Photographic Collection, American School of Classical Studies at Athens)

ARMING SCENES

A common feature of ancient Greek heroic poetry was the "arming scene," a description of the hero putting on his armor and gathering his weapons before entering battle. The Homeric *Iliad* has many such scenes. Book 3 of the poem describes the Trojan Paris arming for single combat with the Greek Menelaus. According to this description, Paris first "covered his legs with greave of good make and fitted with ankle-clasps of silver; after this he donned the breastplate of his brother Lykaon, and fitted it to his own body." Then "he hung his silver-studded sword of bronze about his shoulders, and then his mighty shield. On his comely head he set his helmet, well-wrought, with a crest of horse-hair that nodded menacingly above it, and he grasped a redoubtable spear that suited his hands."

The poet's vivid descriptions of the opulence of the metal and often of the history of the various pieces indicate a hero of elevated status—these heroes are rich and from illustrious families. The descriptions serve to build tension in the narrative as well: The weapons hold potential for death and destruction, but only battle itself would reveal the outcome. In the *Iliad* the arms of a hero hold talismanic powers, and fierce battles rage over the bodies of fallen warriors, with each side trying to strip the dead hero of his weapons.

The narrative technique of including an arming scene before battle, used to such good effect by Homer, is not unique to Greek poetry but appears throughout literature and art, from antiquity to the present. They range from the somewhat comic scene of King Saul arming David before his battle with Goliath (I Samuel 17: 38–40 in the Bible) through medieval epics such as *Sir Gawain and the Green Knight* to modern depictions of historical battles in literature and film.

exander the Great's campaigns against the Persian Empire in the last years of the 330s B.C.E.

By the Hellenistic Period, the period after the death of Alexander in 323 B.C.E., Greek armor had become light and tactics more fluid. Soldiers abandoned greaves and increasingly adopted a helmet with a more open face, the so-called *pylos* helmet instead of the older, more closed Corinthian style. The new helmets increased the soldier's field of vision, made breathing easier, and weighed less, and these advantages seem to have outweighed the reduced protection afforded by the open face. The old Corinthian style continued to appear on vase paintings, however, and seems to have been an iconic symbol of the warrior tradition extending back through the Classical Period to Homeric times.

ROME
by Michael M. Sage

Little can be said about Roman arms, armor, and other military equipment before the middle of the sixth century B.C.E. Literary sources offer scant evidence, and the site of Rome has provided few archaeological finds of a military nature. There are a few fragmentary pieces of metal protective equipment and a number of spearheads, which point to the importance of the javelin.

The middle of the seventh century B.C.E. saw a profound change in military equipment in central Italy, especially to the north of Rome in Etruria. Again, there is little evidence at Rome, but given the close cultural ties of Rome and Etruria, there is every reason to suppose that the same developments took place at Rome. Greek heavy infantry equipment of the hoplite type appears in Etruria, probably under the influence of the Greek colonies of southern Italy. This hoplite equipment consisted of a metal helmet, a metal cuirass (body armor) made up of back and front plates, and the hoplite shield. The hoplite shield was usually a convex circular device, 3 feet in diameter, made of a wooden core with metal facing, usually of bronze. The arm was inserted through a curved metal band, and the hand gripped a strap on the rim of the shield. This holding mechanism distributed the weight of the heavy shield along the length of the arm, allowing the shield to be held for long periods. The usual offensive weapon of the hoplite was a heavy thrusting spear with a short slashing sword as a secondary weapon.

By 550 B.C.E. the literary sources show that the hoplite style of fighting had been adopted at Rome. Despite the artificial character of the descriptions that survive, it is clear that at Rome, as elsewhere in central Italy, there was a greater variety of equipment than in Greece. Especially important is the reference to a type of shield later known as the scutum. The construction of this shield is described in detail by the Greek historian Polybius (ca. 200–ca. 118 B.C.E.). It was 4 feet long and 2.5 feet wide, made of two wooden boards glued to each other. Its convex outer surface was covered in linen topped by leather. It was rimmed with iron and had a central iron spine

lengths for the different ranks. The longest of these spears measured 17 feet and had a leaf-shaped iron tip, a change from the straight-sided tips of earlier hoplite spears. To offset the weight of these long spears, and reflecting the added unlikelihood of enemies penetrating the bristling hedge of iron points that the phalanx presented, the shield was reduced from a large, full-body-size rectangle to a smaller, more maneuverable disk. The supremacy of Macedonian tactics, which combined this newly re-formed phalanx with *peltasts* and cavalry, appeared most dramatically at the battle of Chaeronea in 338 B.C.E., when Philip's army defeated the forces of Athens and Thebes, and even more dramatically during Al-to strengthen the shield and to aid in warding off blows. This type of shield first appeared in Italy in the mid-eighth century B.C.E. and eventually became the standard Roman heavy infantry shield with some modifications until the end of the ancient world.

The early Roman army fought in the manner of the Greek phalanx as a dense rectangular formation that relied on its weight and the points of its heavy thrusting spears to achieve victory on the battlefield. During the fourth or perhaps as late as the early third century B.C.E. the Roman army underwent a tactical revolution. In place of the phalanx it adopted a three-line formation, which depended not on the heavy thrusting spear but on a combination of javelin and sword for its offensive power. The front two lines carried two javelins, called *pila*, one heavy and one light. The heavy *pilum* weighed about 10 pounds, and the lighter one was about half that weight; both were about 6 feet long. The barbed spearhead and its metal tang were made as a single piece, and the head was attached to its wooden shaft by driving the tang into it. The sword that eventually became standard was a short sword with a blade, approximately 2 feet long, with two cutting edges and a long, sharp point. It was well adapted for both slashing and stabbing strokes. The third line retained the heavy thrusting spear.

The legionnaire was protected by a bowl-shaped metal helmet of bronze with a short neck guard at the rear and attached cheek pieces. His chest was protected by a small square metal pale held on by straps and worn over a leather tunic. Wealthier legionnaires provided themselves with a mail shirt. A greave (shin armor) was worn on the left leg, which was thrust forward in combat.

Each legion also contained light-armed troops. They were equipped with a light wicker shield 3 feet in diameter and a leather helmet; they carried the legionary sword and a number of light javelins. Little is known about Roman cavalry equipment during the republic. The cavalry probably carried a round shield, wore some form of chest protection, and carried a lance and a sword. Although there was some variation in equipment down to the end of the first century B.C.E., the only major change was the standardization of offensive weaponry for all legionnaires.

For the first two centuries of the empire until 200 C.E., changes in legionary equipment were evolutionary. From the middle of the first century C.E. the sword point was shortened to make it more effective in stabbing, and helmets evolved to provide increased protection for the nape of the neck and the forehead. Toward the end of the second century C.E. a longer sword with a blade of between 32 and 40 inches appeared and eventually replaced the traditional legionary sword. The most striking change was visible in chest protection. Several types appeared. The mail shirt was now standard for legionnaires, with scale armor also found. A new type of body armor was developed, consisting of metal strips attached to leather straps for both the chest and the back; this new armor was more flexible and provided greater

Sixteenth-century shield depicting Roman battle scene; the scene shows accurate armor and clothing of the time, as drawn from antique coins and sculpture. (Copyright the Metropolitan Museum of Art)

protection against blows. The scutum, though constructed in the same way, now became rectangular instead of oval to increase the protection it offered.

There appears to have been a tremendous variety in the body armor of the Roman cavalry of this period. Mail shirts frequently appear in pictorial representations, but other types of cuirasses are also found. Helmets display a similar diversity. Offensive weapons also varied greatly, as many units were highly specialized, such as archers from the eastern provinces. One striking development beginning in the mid-second century C.E. was the appearance of a new type of cavalry patterned on eastern models. These were the Clibanarii, who wore a tight-fitting conical iron cap and a coat of either mail or scale armor, which covered the upper body and the thighs; the lower body was protected by metal bands. This cavalryman's main offensive weapon was a heavy lance.

Artillery was used in siege and naval warfare and on the battlefield. Roman artillery evolved from Greek models. Its propulsive force was supplied by torsion, that is, the building up of energy in some elastic material, such as braided ropes of hair or animal sinew, by twisting them and then suddenly releasing them. These devices were generally constructed of wood, though in the Imperial Period there was a greater use of metal for increased strength and durability. These machines varied in size and were used to propel either arrow-shaped projectiles or large stone balls. The larger catapults were could hurl stones of up to 60 pounds with devastating results.

THE AMERICAS

BY J. J. GEORGE

The principal weapons used by ancient indigenous North Americans were the spear-thrower, or atlatl; the sling; the spear; and the club, all of which were used in both warfare and hunting. Instruments used only for hunting included the harpoon, the bola, the blowgun, the rodent skewer, and the reptile hook. Shields and rudimentary body armor were used defensively in warfare. Weapons were normally made of stone, bone, horn, and wood. Often they were composite, the point, head, or blade being made of stone or bone and the handle or shaft of wood. Metal was rarely used for weapons because metallurgy was limited to softer metals, such as gold and silver, and largely only for decorative rather than utilitarian purposes. In Mexico, where metallurgy was most highly developed, there was an abundance of obsidian and other igneous stone, which was superior to copper and copper alloys for weapon points and blades. Iron and steel tools and weapons arrived with the Europeans in the 15th and 16th centuries C.E.

The earliest projectile points discovered in North America date from about 11,000 B.C.E.; they are attributed to the Clovis culture and were probably spear points because they are too large for arrows. The blade's unique design, a narrow, tapering profile with sharpened side edges and a technically challenging "flute" at the base for hafting, was intended to maximize the lance's ability to pierce hide or skin. The lance would have been used in close proximity to the intended target. In several instances, recovered Clovis points were found hundreds of miles from where they had been quarried, sometimes in burial caches, leading to continued speculation about who made them, how the technology was transferred, and what it meant when they were ceremonially buried. It is not until about 500 C.E. that chipped stone points, comparable in size and workmanship to modern arrowheads, first became known.

The atlatl, a device that supplies leverage by adding length to the user's arm and increases the range, force, and accuracy of the spear, seems to have been distributed throughout the world by migration or diffusion. It was used by the polar Eskimo in the Arctic, the Tlingit of the Northwest Coast, groups in Baja California and northwestern New Mexico, and Native Americans at the mouth of the Mississippi; it was also used throughout Mesoamerica and by many people of the circum-Caribbean area. The spear-thrower has existed in Europe for at least 20,000 years, but the oldest-known examples from the Americas date to about 5000 B.C.E. The spear probably preceded the bow by many thousands of years; indisputable evidence of the bow is not known until about 500 C.E.

The decline of Hopewell sites in the Illinois Valley around 400 C.E. coincides with the disappearance of finely made atlatl weights from the archaeological record, which seems to reflect the replacement of the atlatl by the new weapon system of the bow and arrow; small points, probably from arrows, occur at Illinois sites at this time. The greater range and accuracy of the bow and arrow may have affected hunting practices and probably altered the way warriors engaged. Also, an increased incidence of warfare in the Ohio Valley has been inferred from the seemingly defensive location and layout of some hilltop enclosures, a change in site planning possibly necessitated in part by changes in weapons technology.

Handheld spears varied greatly in length, diameter, and type of point. They were employed more in hunting than in warfare and appear to have been in use by at least 8000 B.C.E. in the Pleistocene to kill bison in North America. In areas where atlatls and the bow and arrow were present, it appears that the spear was not used javelin style and tended to be reserved for heavy duty at close range. Recent excavations at New Haven Harbor in Connecticut have uncovered more than 5,000 stone artifacts dated to before 1000 B.C.E., including unfinished points and dart points made of fashioned quartzite that could have been used to form the lethal end of an atlatl dart. Used primarily in hunting, the projectiles would have proved lethal against enemies.

In Mesoamerica early examples of defensive armor include quilted or rolled cotton. At Teotihuacán (ca. 1–650 C.E.) spun cotton body armor, called *escupil*, and helmets were introduced to protect the head, body, and limbs. Some scholars have tied the sudden increase in the need for and use of cotton to acceleration in the downfall of Teotihuacán. One argument suggests that because the military was essentially a state enterprise, the state's decline was facilitated by its inability to provide armor to everyone due to its cost. The art historical record also provides insight into the nature of Teotihuacán weaponry. Warriors are depicted wielding atlatls and rectangular shields or thrusting spears and bucklers. The depictions suggest standardized weaponry, which typically indicates state control, formations, and complimentary arms use. One likely scenario inferred from the depictions of warriors and weaponry suggests that the atlatlists would first engage the enemy with projectile fire, and then the spearmen would close and engage the enemy in hand-to-hand combat.

For a long time scholars believed the Mayan civilization to be peaceful and idyllic. A brief inventory of their weaponry dispels that notion: Spears, atlatls, darts, and arrow points used as weapons were common in Mayan civilization of the Classic Period (ca. 150–ca. 650 C.E.). The art historical record shows that the Maya were clearly equipped to fight. Stela 31 from Tikal records Stormy Sky, the name of a ruler in the mid-fifth century C.E., flanked by two guardians dressed in Teotihuacán-style military garb, carrying shields, spear-throwers, and feathered darts. Spear and dart points found at the rapidly abandoned fortified city of Aguateca, Guatemala, suggests that both the royal family and elite scribes and artists used them for intergroup warfare as well as for artistic and craft production under enemy threat. An important implication is that the ruler and elite scribes and artists were also warriors. In another example, an unusually high concentration of identifiable weaponry at the hilltop center of

Cerro de las Mesas indicates that warfare was critical in the development and downfall of classic Mayan civilization.

Weaponry prevalent throughout South America, including the Chaco region, which comprises territories in northeastern Argentina, eastern Bolivia, and western Paraguay, shows that warfare was a main concern, and weapons like bows and arrows, spears, and clubs, mostly made of wood, were quite common. Bolas, stones connected by cords, thrown to entangle and fell prey or an enemy, were a typical weapon. In northern Peru's Moche culture painted pottery dated to the sixth century C.E. provides a stylized glimpse of the Moche warrior and his weaponry and armor. Two animated warriors, their faces covered with fox face masks, wearing decorated helmets and belted tunics, carry round shields and war clubs. Celebrating warriors on painted pottery shows clear veneration of the warrior culture.

See also ART; BORDERS AND FRONTIERS; CERAMICS AND POTTERY; DEATH AND BURIAL PRACTICES; EMPIRES AND DYNASTIES; FOREIGNERS AND BARBARIANS; HUNTING, FISHING, AND GATHERING; METALLURGY; MILITARY; WAR AND CONQUEST.

FURTHER READING

Simon Anglin, Rob S. Rice, Phyllis Jestice, et al., *Fighting Techniques of the Ancient World (3000 BCE to 500 AD): Equipment, Combat Skills, and Tactics* (New York: St. Martin's Press, 2002).

M. C. Bishop and J. C. N. Coulston, *Roman Military Equipment from the Punic Wars to the Fall of Rome*, 2nd ed. (Oxford. U.K.: Oxbow Press, 2006).

John Carman and Anthony Harding, eds., *Ancient Warfare: Archaeological Perspectives* (Stroud, U.K.: Sutton, 1999).

James T. Chambers and Spencer C. Tucker, *Ancient Weapons: An Illustrated History of Their Impact* (Santa Barbara, Calif.: ABC-CLIO, 2007).

Arthur Cotterell, *Chariot: From Chariot to Tank, the Astounding Rise and Fall of the World's First War Machine* (Woodstock, N.Y.: Overlook Press, 2004).

Will Fowler, *Ancient Weapons: The Story of Weaponry and Warfare through the Ages* (Darby, Penn.: Diane Publishing Company, 1999).

Sir John Winthrop Hackett, ed., *Warfare in the Ancient World* (London: Sidgwick and Jackson, 1989).

Victor Davis Hansen, *The Western Way of War* (Berkeley: University of California Press, 2000).

Lawrence H. Keeley, *War before Civilization* (New York: Oxford University Press, 1996).

Eric W. Marsden, *Greek and Roman Artillery: Historical Development* (Oxford, U.K.: Clarendon Press, 1969).

John R. Mixter, "Man's First Long-Range Missile Weapon, the Sling Was a Deadly Military Asset in Skilled Hands," *Military History* 18, no. 3 (August 2001): 12–13.

Helmut Nickel, *Arms and Armor in Africa* (New York: Atheneum, 1971).

Daithi O'Hogain, *Celtic Warriors: The Armies of One of the First Great Peoples in Europe* (New York: St. Martin's Press, 1999)

Robert B. Partridge, *Fighting Pharaohs: Weapons and Warfare in Ancient Egypt* (Manchester, U.K.: Peartree Publishing, 2002).

H. Russell Robinson, *The Armour of Imperial Rome* (New York: Scribner, 1975).

Ian Shaw, *Egyptian Warfare and Weapons* (Princess Risborough, U.K.: Shire Publications, 1991).

Anthony Snodgrass, *Arms and Armor of the Greeks* (Baltimore: Johns Hopkins University Press, 1997).

Christopher Spring, *African Arms and Armor* (Washington, D.C.: Smithsonian Institution Press, 1993).

Jwing-Ming Yang, *Ancient Chinese Weapons* (Jamaica Plains, Mass.: YMAA Publication Center, 1999).

▶ weights and measures

INTRODUCTION

For a prehistoric hunter-gatherer a system of weights and measurements would likely not have been very useful. It was enough to know that an object was so heavy that it required two people to move it or that it would take a day to move to an encampment on the other side of a distant hill. The development of systems of weights and measures coincided with the development of civilization itself. As people settled into permanent communities that evolved into towns and cities and as they developed trade relationships with other communities, they needed agreed-on systems for measuring and weighing food and other goods. While these systems differed from culture to culture, they all had common elements and served common needs.

The earliest units of measurement were often based on the human anatomy. Thus, hand spans, forearms, fingers, feet, and other parts of the body were used to specify length. By extension, distance could be measured by, for example, how far a person could walk in a day, while area could be measure by the amount of land a worker could plow in a day. Similarly, ancient cultures used natural objects as the basis for specifying weights and measures. A reed, for example, could have been used to measure length. The people of ancient India used such natural objects as louse eggs and dust particles to measure very small units of length. Other cultures used such objects as mustard seeds as units of measure.

The problem with these units of measurement, of course, is that they varied from person to person and place to place. Accordingly, ancient civilizations made efforts to standardize their weights and measures. Often, this was a task assigned to the king or other ruler. The king had a vital interest in accurate weights and measures. Taxes, for example, were collected on volumes of grain or, in the case of ancient India, bolts of cloth. Similarly, agriculture required some agreement on land boundaries. Ancient builders had to have a common basis for measuring building materials. If a building was to be made of bricks, then calculating the number of bricks needed to construct a building of a given size required agreement on the dimensions of a brick.

Usually, systems of weights and measures developed in connection with systems of counting and numbers. Indeed, counting emerged because people had to weigh and measure. Systems of mathematics provided people with common units of measurement, which could then be divided by common factors to produce smaller units or multiplied by common factors to produce larger units. In this way, for example, the modern yard consists of 3 feet, a foot consists of 12 inches, and so on.

Trade and exchange, too, required systems of weights and measurements. If one country was trading wine for lumber, the merchants making the trade needed some way of measuring and agreeing on the volume of wine and lumber to determine prices. The result was that systems of weights and measures were often imported and exported along with the goods they measured. When the value of commodities came to be measured by money as a medium of exchange, it was vitally important for merchants to be able to weigh accurately coins and the gold and silver with which they were made.

AFRICA

BY MICHAEL J. O'NEAL

Historians, archaeologists, and scientists use the term *metrology* to refer to the study of weights and measures, particularly as it applies to the premodern world, when weights and measures were not universally standardized. Metrology, though, does more than simply seek to discover which specific units of measurement and weight the ancients used. It also seeks to understand the underlying system that gave rise to weights and measurements.

Thus, the types of questions metrologists ask include: Were units of weight and measure arbitrary values, or were they based on some phenomenon from the natural world? How was one unit divisible into, or a multiple of, some other unit? How did ancient traders and others convert units of weight and measure into those of another people in the process of striking trading bargains? To what extent were units of measure and weight standardized in a kingdom or region? Did royalty have one unit of measurement or weight and common people another? What can ancient artifacts, such as buildings and their dimensions, reveal about systems of measurement? What was the relationship between systems of weights and measurements and mathematical, astronomical, calendrical, timekeeping, and other systems?

The grandest question of all, however, is this: Did ancient systems of measuring weight, volume, distance, and the like derive from some common system that was spread throughout much of the ancient world, including parts of Africa? Many metrologists have devoted careers to finding common units of measurement that underlay the construction of artifacts as widely dispersed as the pyramids of Egypt and Stonehenge in England. Some claim to have found commonalities, in various cases based on common astronomical observations from which the circumference of the earth at the equator may have been deduced. Many of these conclusions, though, are highly speculative.

Few of these questions can be answered with any certainty about ancient Africa (other than Egypt). The absence of written records inhibits the work of metrologists who focus on the continent. Further casting a veil over the subject is the fact that ancient African kingdoms, cities, and settlements rose and fell with great frequency. People migrated throughout the continent, often in response to climatic change, taking with them their culture and knowledge systems and mingling them with the culture and knowledge they found in their new homes. Warfare wiped out some African cultures—the kingdom of Kush, for example, fell to the kingdom of Axum, and the Carthaginian kingdom was totally destroyed by the Romans—contributing to the lack of records and artifacts.

At the same time, more powerful empires, including that of Egypt and later the Roman Empire, would have imposed their systems on tributary people in Africa; in particular, Egyptian units of measurement probably became the norm throughout much of northern Africa. Later, Roman units probably became accepted. These units were derived from Greek measurements, which the Greeks in turn had adopted from numerous cultures in the Near East, who in turn had adopted them from such places as Mesopotamia. Furthermore, because much of Africa, particularly the northern stretches of the continent (as opposed to the nomadic southern portions), engaged in trade and other activities with a large set of other civilizations who routinely passed through the region known as the Sahel, a strip of settlements that spanned the continent below the Sahara Desert, the notion of any kind of standardized, "African" system of weights and measures remains elusive.

Despite these problems, historians and archaeologists can make some inferences. It is highly likely that ancient Africans, in common with numerous other ancient peoples, measured distances using, at least as a starting point, the human body. Thus, for example, hand spans, knuckles, arm length, feet, and forearms were probably used as units of distance. Indeed, the cubit is a unit of measurement used throughout the entire region of Africa, Rome, the Near East, and eventually Europe. The cubit was a unit of length that originally measured the distance from a man's elbow to the tip of his longest finger, although eventually the cubit settled into a measurement of about 18 inches. Such a unit of measurement, of course, would necessarily be imprecise, since the unit would be longer for a taller man than for a shorter one. In the case of royalty, the "royal cubit"—a slightly larger unit of measure—would have been longer than that used by others, in an effort to suggest that royals were larger than common mortals. Similarly, it is little accident that in the modern world, the foot continues to be a common unit of measurement. The foot was used throughout the ancient world to measure a unit of distance that was, in fact, just about a foot, or 12 modern inches. The knuckle of the thumb could be used to measure relatively small distances, and thus corresponded to a modern inch.

Longer distances were probably measured by human activities. Thus, for example, distances corresponding to modern miles were probably measured in a way that gauged the amount of ground a person could walk in a certain period of time. Similarly, a unit of area probably was measured by the amount of ground, for instance, that a farmer could plow in a given period of time.

Ancient Africans undoubtedly used natural objects in the calculation of weights. Indeed, the modern word *grain*, still used in weighing precious metals, reflects this ancient heritage. Thus, any African culture probably would have developed a system that used small stones or quantities of seed, such as wheat seed, as a unit of weight. Other objects included items such as bird claws, feathers, and, for large weights, elephants. The ancient Egyptians used a system of weights called beqa weights to measure quantities of gold. Examples have been found of beqa stones, which standardized weights, and some of these bear royal insignia. Given Egypt's dominance over much of northern Africa, this system for weighing precious metals and perhaps other commodities probably was imposed on trading kingdoms to Egypt's south and west. Such a system would have governed coinage, which ancient Africans would necessarily have had to accept.

Another natural object that played a role in ancient weights and measurements was water. Thus, for example, a cubic foot of water represented a unit of weight called the talent, divisible into various units. The Romans divided the talent into 60 minas, and various Mediterranean cultures that accepted the talent and the mina subdivided the mina into varying numbers of shekels. These units were used by Syrians, Phoenicians (the ancestors of the African Carthaginians), and others, who carried them into Africa for purposes of trade and exchange.

EGYPT

BY AMR KAMEL

With the emergence of the centralized government in the Nile Valley as early as the Third Dynasty (ca. 2649–ca. 2575 B.C.E.), Egyptians formed accurate systems of weights and measures. They developed methods for weighing grain, counting cattle, drawing up building projects, and sizing huge slabs of stone as well as issuing rations and materials to workmen and, above all, measuring the level of the annual Nile flood, on which the levying of taxes depended. This system was valid throughout the whole country and remained active until the Greco-Roman Period (332 B.C.E.–395 C.E.), without real significant changes. In general, the system that the Egyptians set up included three main subsystems that measured capacity, length, and weight.

In their literary texts ancient Egyptians frequently express quantities of products counted either by the piece or by a usual grouping of pieces, such as bunches of flowers, jars of wine, baskets of grapes, pots of honey, bundles of vegetables or flax, handfuls of reeds, and even pairs of geese. Nonethe-

less, ancient Egyptians used many other measures that are still obscure, such as the gsr, which was used only for milk, the g3t, which was used for cream, and the thab, which was used for salt.

Several pieces of textual evidence suggest that the measures used for official purposes, such as tax payments, were checked on a regular basis. In conducting personal business Egyptians apparently preferred to use their own measures. For example, Hekanakhte, a farmer of the Eleventh Dynasty (ca. 2040–ca. 1991), sent a messenger to his family in the delta to bring to him his own corn measure to use in measuring his grain in Thebes (modern-day Luxor) rather than using other local measures, which might not be wholly accurate.

The Egyptian capacity system was apparently grounded on the hnw for measuring fluids, now reckoned conventionally at around 1 pint. The Egyptians used multiples of 10 hnw to describe greater units: 40 hnw, 50 hnw, 100 hnw, 160 hnw, and 200 hnw. The basic unit for cereals and other dry goods was the hekat, or bushel, of 4.3 quarts. In the Old and Middle Kingdoms (ca. 2575–ca. 1640 B.C.E.) 10 ghar made the larger unit khar, or sack, of 11 gallons. With the beginning of the New Kingdom (ca. 1550–ca. 1070 B.C.E.), the value of the khar was increased to equal 16 hekat, or 17.5 gallons. This increase reflected not an economic crisis but rather the change of a decimal system to a new binary system, which made accounting easier. These 16 hekat were later subdivided into units of 4 hekat, 4.36 gallons each.

Smaller quantities were expressed as fractions of oipe, more precisely as one of the fractions of the geometric progression ½, ¼ (the former hekat), ⅛, 1/16, 1/32, and 1/64. The last quantity equaled 0.2 quarts and was divisible into 5 ro, or parts, of 0.05 quarts each, reflecting the ancient division of the hekat into 80 and of the 4-hekat into 320 ro. In the Greco-Roman Period the artabe, a Persian unit, played a major role, varying in size from 29 to 40 of the Greek choinix, a capacity unit of about 0.9 quarts.

For general length measurement the standard unit was the royal cubit. The cubit represented the length of the forearm, from the elbow to the tip of the fingers, estimated conventionally at 18 inches. The measure was composed of 7 palms, (the hand's width without the thumb), each consisting of 4 fingers, ¾ inch each. Apart from the cubit of 7 palms, there were the small cubit of 6 palms (about 17.64 inches), the remen of 5 palms (14.7 inches), the djser of 4 palms (11.76 inches), the great span of 3.5 palms (10.29 inches), the small span of 3 palms (8.82 inches), the dopple or double palm (5.88 inches), and the fist of 1.5 palms or 6 fingers (4.4 inches). Furthermore, Egyptians of the New Kingdom sometimes used a larger unit, called a nebi ("pole"); its length has been estimated at 1.25 cubits.

Land surveying required a longer unit than the cubit; thus, the ancient Egyptians seem to have used the khet, or "rod," of 100 cubits (160 feet) as the base, since a land-measuring rope was 100 cubits long, stretched between two rods driven in the ground. A larger unit, itrw, or "river," measured

20,000 cubits (6.5 miles) and was used to measure land distances, originally representing the length of a day's towing of a boat along the Nile. Textual evidence from the Twelfth Dynasty (ca. 1991–ca. 1783 B.C.E.) refers to an official estimation of the Egyptian land, from Elephantine in the south to Tell el-Balamun in the delta, at 106 itrw (670 miles), divided into 86 itrw for Upper Egypt and 20 itrw for Lower Egypt.

The basic measure of area was the stat, which represented a square of land of 100 by 100 cubits, or 1 khet by 1 khet (3,271.38 square yards). Multiples and submultiples were not defined by squaring multiples or submultiples but rather by multiplying or dividing the width while retaining the length as 100 cubits.

Volume measures were based on the denit, which was a cubic cubit (0.187 cubic yards). In the Ptolemaic Period (304–30 B.C.E.) volume and capacity measures seem to have been linked, but the absolute norms on which this relationship was based are still uncertain. This measure was used exclusively for calculating the progress made by workers in the excavation of a tomb.

The saqed expressed the slope of a masonry massive, such as a pyramid, by giving the length in palms of the horizontal base of a right triangle of 1 cubit high, whose hypotenuse was a section of the expected or measured slope. In Old Kingdom construction, for instance, there is clear evidence for the use of a saqed of 5.5 palms or 5.25 palms, corresponding to slopes of 51°51′ and 53°7′, respectively, as notably illustrated in the Giza pyramids.

Ancient Egyptians' basic unit of weight was called a deben. From the Old Kingdom the deben seems to have been around 0.48 ounces; it increased during the Middle Kingdom to 3.2 ounces. In the New Kingdom it was divided into 10 qite of 0.32 ounces each, with lesser weights expressed as fractions of qite.

As early as 1300 B.C.E. the Egyptians had developed accurate balance-beam scales that could weigh small quantities or materials with an accuracy of plus or minus 1 percent. The scales were simple in concept and consisted of a horizontal beam centered on a vertical post. Suspended from the ends of the beam were the platforms. One platform held the object or material to be weighed. The other held an object of known weight.

THE MIDDLE EAST
BY AMY HACKNEY BLACKWELL

People living in the ancient Near East standardized weights and measures so that they could accurately measure quantities—by weight and volume—of commodities important in their lives. These included seed, precious metals like silver and gold, base metals like copper and lead, and liquids like oils, beer, and wine. In conducting transactions with other peoples, traders used their own systems of weights and measures and calculated conversions to other systems developed by their trading partners, such as Egypt and the Indus Valley,

referring to such alien systems in their economic texts with a phrase like "according to the standard of Land X."

Archaeologists and Assyriologists have been able to reconstruct the weights and measures of Mesopotamian civilizations because of the survival of both the weights themselves (and occasionally balance mechanisms as well) and written sources that give detailed calculations of commodities, everything from gold to grain. In some cases, annotations were inscribed on the rims or shoulders of storage jars, indicating a vessel's capacity in volumetric terms.

The shiklu, or shekel, was the basic unit of weight. One shekel weighed about 0.3 ounces. Small items were measured in she, which was 1/600 ounce and originally represented the weight of a single grain of barley. Larger items were measured in manu, usually called minas in English, which was a unit of 60 shekels, or in biltu, which was a unit of 60 minas. Although these terms were used widely throughout the ancient Near East, the absolute value of these weights varied so that the mina of Ur around 2000 B.C.E. is not necessarily the same as the mina of Ugarit 500 years later. Most weights were made of stone, many in the shape of a duck with its head and neck lying on its back, as though the bird were asleep. Fine, barrel-shaped weights of hematite were also common.

The Old Testament mentions seven different kinds of weights, which were equivalent to coins. In biblical times people used units of weight to barter goods for silver, long before silver was minted into actual coins. One Mesopotamian biltu was equivalent to 1 talent, the largest measure of weight in biblical and ancient times. One talent of gold was somewhere between 50 and 100 pounds of gold; it represented either a man's weight in gold or the amount of gold one man could carry, depending on who was defining it. The biblical

Bronze duck weight, found in the treasury at Persepolis, Persia (modern-day Iran) (Courtesy of the Oriental Institute of the University of Chicago)

talent was equal to 3,000 shekels instead of the 2,600 shekels of the Mesopotamian talent.

Ancient Mesopotamians measured volume in sila or qa; 1 sila was equivalent to about 1.5 pints. A sila was made up of 60 gin, each equal to about ⅔ ounce. Sixty sila made 1 massiktu or pi, which was about 11 gallons or 1.3 bushels. One hundred sila made 1 imeru, which was about 18.3 gallons or 2.25 bushels and was the amount one donkey was expected to be able to carry. A qurru or gur was 180 sila, about 33 gallons or 4 bushels.

The basic Mesopotamian measurement of length was the ammatu, or cubit, which was about 15 inches long. It originally was the length of a man's arm from elbow to fingertip, a convenient measuring device for merchants anywhere. An ubanu was about ⅔ inch, the length of a finger joint; 24 or 30 ubanu made up 1 ammatu, depending on the time and place. A kanu was 6 ammatu (around 8 feet), and a gar was 12 ammatu. One ashlu consisted of 10 gar. A beru was 1800 gar, about 5.25 miles.

Fields and land were measured in iku, which consisted of about ⅚ acre. One musaru was equal to 1 square gar, about 27.5 square yards; this was the standard measurement of a garden plot. One buru was equal to 18 iku, or 15 acres. One shar was equal to 1,080 iku, or 25.3 square miles.

During the Hellenistic Period (323–31 B.C.E.) Greek units of weights and measures spread throughout Mesopotamia and the Near East. During the Roman Republic and Empire (509 B.C.E.–476 C.E.) many people in the Near East and Mesopotamia used the Roman system of weights and measures. Throughout the ancient world there was much flexibility of weights and measures. For example, archaeologists have found objects in Greece and Rome that appear to have been made according to Persian weights and measures. Although these objects could have come from Persia, historians believe it is more likely that people in Greece and Rome occasionally used foreign measurement schemes to make certain objects. Even within the well-regulated Greek and Roman systems, there was a great deal of local variation, as individual towns customized weights and measurements to fit their needs.

ASIA AND THE PACIFIC

BY AMY HACKNEY BLACKWELL

The earliest documented systems of precise measurements were created in the fourth and third millennia B.C.E. in the Indus Valley, Mesopotamia, and Egypt. Chinese people are known to have developed precise weights and measures by the late second millennium B.C.E., though they may have done so several centuries earlier. Chinese systems of measurement spread throughout the rest of eastern Asia toward the end of the ancient period.

The peoples who lived in the Indus Valley between 3300 and 1500 B.C.E. developed precise systems of measurement. They divided weights and measures into units of 10. The basic unit of weight was about 10 ounces. Weights were multiples of this unit; the standard weights were 1, 2, 5, 10, 20, 50, 100, 200, and 500 units. Smaller weights were measured as fractions of the basic unit; the main fractional weights were 0.5, 0.2, 0.1, and 0.05 units. The Harappan people who lived in the Indus Valley at this time built cities and houses according to precise plans, which required them to measure bricks, boards, streets, and other units carefully. Bricks were made according to a ratio of 4 to 2 to 1; that is, a brick was twice as wide and four times as long as it was tall.

By the late first millennium B.C.E. in India, overseeing weights and measures was considered the government's responsibility. The *Manusmriti*, a book of Hindu laws written around the first or second century B.C.E., observes that one of a ruler's duties was to ensure that weights and measures remained constant. During the Maurya Dynasty (321–185 B.C.E.) the government established a system of measurements that was used throughout the realm. Despite standardization, all measurements were somewhat flexible; it is impossible to know exactly how long any of these measurements really were because they varied somewhat from place to place. Many of them were determined by body proportions and so would naturally vary from person to person.

The smallest unit of length under the Indian system was a parmanu, which was microscopically small and could not be subdivided; the parmanu was a strictly theoretical unit because no one had the technology to work with such small items. From there, units were generally defined by groups of four or eight. Eight parmanu equaled 1 rajahkan, the length of a dust particle. Eight rajahkan equaled 1 liksha, the length of a louse egg. Eight liksha equaled 1 yookamadhya. Eight yookamadhya equaled 1 yavamadhya.

Eight yavamadhya equaled 1 angul, the width of a finger, or about ¾ inch. Eight angul equaled 1 dhanurmushti, the length of a fist with the thumb sticking out, or about 6 inches. Four angul were the width of a bow grip, called dharnugrah. Twelve angul made 1 vitastaa, about 9 inches, or the distance between a stretched-out little finger and thumb. Four vitastaa equaled 1 aratni or hast, about 18 inches, or the distance from an elbow to an outstretched middle finger, a unit known as the cubit in European systems. Four aratni made 1 dand or dhanush, about 6 feet, or the length of a bow. Ten dand made 1 rajju, which was about 60 feet. Two rajju equaled one paridesh, about 120 feet. Two thousand dand equaled 1 krosh, which was about 2 or 2.25 miles. Four krosh made 1 yojan, which was about 9 miles.

The system of weight measurement in India was closely tied with ayurveda, the main type of medicine. Ayurvedic medicine used many herbs and oils as treatments, and ayurvedic practitioners developed a precise system of weights and measures to ensure accuracy in their preparations. Doctors typically needed to weigh very small amounts of substances, and they used natural seeds as standards. Mustard seeds, sesame seeds, and madatiya seeds were all common weights. Texts on ayurveda list tables describing numerous weights and measures to be used in making drug preparations.

China may have developed systems of weights and measures around the same time as the Indus Valley civilizations. According to Chinese tradition, the Yellow Emperor (ca. 2697–ca. 2598 B.C.E.) was the first ruler to issue guidelines for weights and measures, but little is known about this system. The first well-known official units of Chinese weights and measures were invented and standardized between the 13th and 10th centuries B.C.E.; these units became the basis for measurement in China for the next three millennia. The actual lengths and weights that went with the standardized measurements varied over the centuries. Governments would occasionally step in and define units; for example, during the Qin Dynasty (221–207 B.C.E.) the Chinese government standardized weights and measures.

The basic Chinese unit of length was the chi, which is about 9 or 10 inches long and served as an equivalent to the English foot. It was determined by the distance between the thumb and middle finger of an outstretched hand. One cun was equivalent to about an inch. Ten chi made up one zhang. One li was equivalent to about ⅓ mile. Long distances were generally expressed in li. One important measure was the length of one bolt of cloth, or one pi, which was about 40 feet long; most households had to pay some of their taxes in cloth, which was measured in pi. The most common unit of land area was the mu, equivalent to about 733 square yards. One qing was 100 mu.

The standard units of weight in China were the qian and the liang. The liang was a small amount, ½ ounce in the ancient period. The qian weighed between 7.7 and 9.2 ounces. These weights were based on the actual weight of coins used as cash; the minting of coins was not done according to a uniform weight standard, so weights fluctuated. The Chinese people did not use coins as currency very much, preferring to keep their gold as valuable property. Weights were more important in trade, for buying and selling specified amounts of goods. Chinese medicine, like ayurvedic medicine in India, required precise measurements of herbs and other medicinal items.

During the centuries between about 500 B.C.E. and the fifth century C.E., the Chinese system of measurement gradually spread through Southeast Asia, Korea, and Japan. The people of these nations adapted the Chinese measurements into their own languages. For example, in Japan the main unit of length was 1 shaku, equivalent to the Chinese chi. It was broken into 10 sun and 100 bu. Six shaku made up 1 ken, slightly less than 6 feet. Three hundred sixty shaku equaled 1 cho; 36 cho made up 1 ri, which was about 2.6 miles. The most common measurement of land area was the tan, which was about ¼ acre.

EUROPE

BY MICHAEL J. O'NEAL

Systems of weights and measures throughout the ancient world were highly complex, and historians have been able to decipher them only in part. In many cases they have to rely on archaeological evidence; for example, they can make inferences about systems of weights and measures from regularities they find in the measurements of surviving buildings or the volumes of containers. An essential requirement for any system of weights and measures is the ability for a community or a society to come to common agreement about their values. At the boundaries between systems of weights and measures, some understanding must be established about how these values will be converted from one system to another.

Understanding systems of weights and measures before the advent of writing is nearly impossible. The Scottish engineer Alexander Thom (1894–1985) claimed the existence of a "megalithic yard" of about 2.72 feet that served as a unit of measurement in laying out monuments such as Stonehenge, although this is impossible to document conclusively and also does not seem to be supported by evidence outside Britain. With the emergence of metallurgy, prehistoric European people appear to have developed some common understanding about units of weight. For example, copper and tin ingots of standard sizes are often found in Bronze Age shipwrecks in the Mediterranean Sea. In northern Europe bronze and gold artifacts such as axes and neck rings may have served as standard units of exchange, a sort of primitive currency. Although it is likely that there were rules for measuring and weighing commodities, we simply cannot do more than speculate about their nature.

Some ancient civilizations, including the Greeks, Romans, Egyptians, and Mesopotamians, were able to develop fairly regular, stable systems of measurement largely because they ruled over extensive empires. Because so many people from diverse areas were under their control, particularly in the extensive Roman Empire, they adhered to standards of weights and measures imposed on them from a central authority, usually by royal decree. Because of the importance of trade to these empires, both between countries within the empire and between the empire and other regions, merchants and public officials needed accurate ways of measuring volumes of goods and determining their price. They also needed accurate ways to measure the weight of gold and silver coins minted by other nations and used to pay for goods.

While the Romans were expanding their empire in western Europe, northern and eastern Europe were peopled by largely autonomous extended tribes: the Scandinavians, an assortment of Germanic tribes, the Celts, various Slavic peoples, and others. Without a central authority, each of these communities developed its own standards for weights and measures, and these standards often changed gradually over time. In time the Romans, who adopted many features of the Greek system, imposed their system of weights and measure on portions of Europe, particularly Italy, Gaul (France), and the British Isles. Many of these standards survived and were imported eventually to the New World, where such measurements as the inch and foot continue to be used. In other respects the standards shifted and have presented a challenge to historians.

Many of the measurement units known to us from historical accounts in medieval Europe probably had their roots deep in antiquity. In Europe, as elsewhere in the ancient world, early units of measurement typically had some relationship with the physical world. The ancient Europeans started with the human body, using such standards as hand spans, the width of a finger, the length from the elbow to the tips of the fingers, and the length of a foot to measure linear distance. In this regard, their units of length were little different from those of the ancient Egyptians and Babylonians. Thus, for example, the ancient Irish had a unit of measure called the troigid, which was the length of a man's foot, so a troigid was a "foot." A troigid was made up of 12 ordlochs, or inches, with 1 ordloch being the width of a man's thumb. Sometimes objects were used. The Germans measured length by the ell, which was the length of a bolt of cloth.

Also commonly used to measure distance was the stride. The Romans, for example, used the pace of a marching soldier, based on two consecutive positions where the right foot landed, to measure a Roman mile, which consisted of a thousand paces. This measurement was imposed throughout the empire, and it remains fairly close to the British mile that survives in modern life. Evidence also suggests that ancient peoples had a fairly accurate understanding of such large measurements as the circumference of the earth and the distance between the poles. These measures were then broken down to provide smaller units of measurement that were used, for example, in determining the length and width of monumental buildings. Again, the ancient Europeans inherited some of these systems by a process that historians do not fully understand.

To measure weight, the ancient Europeans used the materials that surrounded them. In the British Isles, for example, the stone, or 14 pounds, is still commonly used to measure a person's weight, though in the past the stone was probably more like 16 pounds. Further, agricultural commodities, often the basis of trade, were used to determine weights. Throughout the ancient world people were able to develop growing, stable civilizations because of a major staple crop. In Asia the crop was rice. In the Americas it was maize, or corn. In Europe and around the Mediterranean wheat was the staple crop, so grains of wheat were often used to form a common standard of weight. Thus, for example, the weight of a certain number of grains of wheat equaled a certain measure of silver; in turn, these measures were used to determine such measures as the ounce, from the Latin word *uncia*. This system is preserved in modern medicine, where pharmaceuticals are still often measured in grains, as well as in modern measurements of precious metals. The carob seed was often used to measure silver and gold, giving rise to the modern word *carat*.

Grains of wheat were also used to measure length. Again, in ancient Ireland measurements based on wheat ran as follows: The length of three grains of wheat equaled 1 ordloch,

Bronze steelyard with lead weights from Roman Britain, first to second century C.E.; such weights were used by shopkeepers and traders. (© The Trustees of the British Museum)

Some historians argue that the standards of weights and measures used in ancient Europe, as well as around the Mediterranean Sea and among the Slavic peoples of eastern Europe and Russia, all descended from a common root system, probably that of the ancient Babylonians. Thus, as people spread northward and westward throughout Europe, they based their system of weights and measures on an earlier one. Historians base their argument on sophisticated mathematical analysis that shows that these systems often had common arithmetical factors. Mathematicians refer to the science of weights and measures as metrology, and an important component of metrology is the notion that a particular unit of measurement is divisible into smaller units or can be multiplied into larger units. Ancient Europeans may have developed different standards of measurement, but those standards were convertible into the standards used by other cultures in much the same way that, for example, American dollars can be converted into Japanese yen according to an agreed-on exchange rate. Without common arithmetical factors, it would have been nearly impossible for far-flung communities to engage in trade or determine the value of gold and silver coins.

or an inch; 4 inches were regarded as 1 bas, or hand palm; 3 palms were a troigid, or foot; 12 troigids were a fertach, or rod; 12 fertachs were a forrach; and an area 12 forrachs in length and 6 in width was a tír-cumaile. The last of these measures was significant because it represented an area sufficient to graze a cumal, or three cows. Property was often measured according to the amount of work that could be performed on it. The acre, for example, developed as an amount of land that a worker could plow in a day.

GREECE

BY SPYROS SIROPOULOS

The ability to measure and compare physical objects and to express their attributes in symbols easily understood by everyone constitutes a standard of communication and provides a way to relate abstract thought to reality. To define a measurement, it is necessary to establish a *metron*, a unit with which to count objects and various subunits or multiples. Various metrical systems have developed to measure elemental dimensions such as length, area, capacity, and weight.

From an early stage of their communal life, people realized the need for specific measurements. Representations of simple forms of balances or scales have been discovered at Knossos in Crete. The Egyptians had used scales since 2500 B.C.E., and it is possible that the use of such mechanisms passed from Crete to Greece. In any case, the first units of measurement were inspired by the human anatomy. The finger, palm, and foot were the first natural measures. Needless to say, the degree of standardization varied from place to place. Furthermore, there were situations in which these measures were inadequate; for example, in the case of measuring longer distances, the cast of a stone or spear or the distance covered by a walker in one day were used as basic units. The Greek poet Homer (eighth or ninth century B.C.E.) uses phrases like these to describe long distances.

People also needed to measure the fields they plowed, the liquids they stored or exchanged in trade, and the amount of grain they produced. Various metrical systems developed, all of them based on local conditions, habits, and needs, yet all of them interdependent and volatile because of international trade and the contact of people with their neighbors. In classical Athens the prototype measures of capacity used for market inspection were kept in the dome of the Athenian Agora (market).

The principal unit for measuring length was inspired by the foot, or pous, but its length was not standard and varied greatly from place to place. The foot of Olympia was 1.050 modern feet, the foot of Pergamon was 1.083 modern feet, and the foot of Aegina (which was used more frequently) was 1.093 modern feet. The subdivision of the pous is called daktylos, or a finger breadth, which is equivalent to $\frac{1}{16}$ of the pous, or 0.063 modern feet (0.76 inch). Further subdivisions are taken by the fingers. Thus, 4 daktyloi = 1 palaesté (palm);

8 daktyloi = 1 dichas or hemipódion (half foot); 11 daktyloi = 1 orthódoron; 12 daktyloi = 1 spithamé (span of all fingers); 16 daktyloi = 1 pous (foot). Measures for higher dimensions are taken from the arm: 18 daktyloi = 1 pygmé (the length between the elbow and the beginning of the fingers); 20 daktyloi = 1 pygón (the length between the elbow and the knuckles of the fist, used by the Greek writers Homer and Herodotus); 24 daktyloi = 1 péches (the length between the elbow and the fingertips).

From farming life the Greeks developed the measure of a stádion, the distance covered by the plow in a single draft. Originally the stádion contained 600 feet, irrespective of the foot's size. The Attic stádion was therefore 606.889 modern feet; the Olympic stádion was 630.807 modern feet; and the odoiporikón (pacer's stadium) was 516.732 modern feet. The stádion produces further units, such as these: 2 stádia = 1 diaulos; 4 stádia = 1 hippikón; 12 stádia = 1 dólichos; 30 odoiporiká stádia = 1 persian paraságes; 40 odoiporiká stádia = 1 Egyptian schoinos.

The minimum measure for area was the amount that a pair of oxen could plow in the course of one day. This was called pléthron, a square of 101 by 101 modern feet. Divisions of the pléthron were the árura ($\frac{1}{4}$ of the pléthron) and the

Red porphyry 1-talent weight, from Knossos (Alison Frantz Photographic Collection, American School of Classical Studies at Athens)

héktos (⅙ of the pléthron). A different measure introduced to Athens from Sicily and Cyrenaica was called médimnos, and it represented the amount of land that could be sown by a certain quantity (a médimnos) of wheat.

Since corn and wine were two of the main agricultural products, two different measuring units were established for measuring dry or wet products. The measuring unit for dry products was called kýathos. According to different local systems, it varied from 0.048 to 0.075 gallons (or 0.191 to 0.300 quarts), although it most usually was 0.055 gallons (0.218 quarts). The following units are derived from the kýathos: 6 kyathoi = 1 kotýle; 3 kotýlai = 1 kséstes; 2 ksestai = 1 choinix; 4 choinikai = 1 hemiekton; 8 choinikai = 1 hekteus; 6 hekteis = 1 medimnos (88.19 pounds).

The Athenian statesman Solon (ca. 630–ca. 560 B.C.E.) used the medimnos to calculate the citizens' wealth and to classify citizens according to their economic position. The social classes of the Athenian citizens were ordered thus: The *pentakosiomedimnoi* were those with 500 medimnoi of annual produce; the *triakosiomedimnoi* or *hippeis* were those with 300 medimnoi of annual produce; the *diakosiomedimnoi* or *zeugitai* were those with 200 medimnoi of annual produce; and the *thetai* were the poorest citizens, without land of their own.

During the Archaic and the Classical periods (ca. 600–ca. 323 B.C.E.) Greeks used the kotýle for measuring both wet and dry products. The measuring units for liquids are formed thus: 1.5 kyathoi = 1 oxýbaphon; 2 oxýbapha = 1 hemikótylon; 2 hemikótyla = 1 kotýle; 2 kotýlai = 1 ksestes; 16 ksestai = 1 chous; 12 choai = 1 metretés (10.41 gallons).

Various measures were used for weight in Greece. Clay tablets from Knossos, Mycenae, and Pylos present a weighing system in which the largest unit was about 66 pounds. The typical weight of historic Greece was a lead plaque, sometimes with the name of the issuing city or badge. Solon introduced to the Attica region the weighing measure of the Greek island of Euboea, called obolós. Initially the obolós was in the shape of a spit, or the sharp end of a lance (*obelos* in Greek), and it was ⅙ of a drachma (0.159 to 0.212 ounces of silver coin in Attica). A drachma indicates the amount that can be held in the palm of the hand, equivalent to six such spits, or oboloi. The weight of the obolós either in silver or gold depended on the local value of the coin. Thus, in Athens and Euboea the obolós was 0.026 ounces, while in Aegina (the second most established measure) it weighed 0.037 ounces. Various values of the obolós are formed thus: 1 dióbolos = 2 oboloi = ⅓ drachma; 1 dekábolon = 10 oboloi; 1 hemiobólion = ½ obolos; 1 tritemórion = ⅔ obolos; 1 tetartemórion = ¼ obolos; 1 chalkens = ⅛ obolos (copper).

There was also the mina, equivalent to 100 drachmae, and the talent, equivalent to 100 minae. A talent represented a man's load, and it would be relevant to the local standard used. An Attic-Euboic talent would weigh approximately 57 pounds, while the Aeginitic talent would weigh approximately 83.33 pounds.

ROME
BY KATIE PARLA

The use of a sophisticated system of weights and measures was born in the Middle East. As far back as the third millennium B.C.E., the Mesopotamians used common units for calculating weight, area, volume, and distance. The development of such a system was due to a growing territory and economy as a result of increased conquest and commerce. A standardized system of weights and measures was needed to ensure smooth trade across vast distances. Persians, Egyptians, and Phoenicians also implemented standardized weights and measures that would later be adapted by Greeks and Romans.

As a city-state or empire grows, it is necessary that all people in that territory have a common vocabulary in order to facilitate commerce. This vocabulary applies not only to the quantity of commercial goods but also to the monetary system, provided it is based on the gold or silver standard. For this reason the Romans, like so many civilizations before them, instituted a system of weights and measures that was used throughout their territory. While Rome's many standards of measurement were influenced primarily by Egypt and Greece, the Romans also developed their own native units.

The Romans were the first to employ the mile to measure long distances. The word *mile* comes from the Latin mille passum, or 1,000 paces. Each mile was equivalent to 1,000 double paces (2,000 individual steps) for a total of 5,000 Roman feet. The Roman mile was standardized in the first century B.C.E. by the emperor Augustus (r. 27 B.C.E.–14 C.E.) as part of his legendary administrative reform. He erected a pillar in the Roman Forum known as the Milliarium Aureum. This "Golden Milestone" listed the distances in miles from that point in Rome to important cities in the empire.

The Romans borrowed the concept of short-length measurements from the Egyptians. In Egypt finger digits, palms, feet, and arms were all used to measure short distances. These body parts were convenient rulers that could be used in daily life and casual commerce. However, for building and trade, the units were rigidly standardized, so these units would be uniform all across the Egyptian sphere of influence. The Romans used digits, palms, feet, and cubits (the distance from the elbow to the tip of the middle finger) for measuring lengths, although their values were slightly different from the Egyptian standards and also varied across Roman territory, particularly during the republic (509–27 B.C.E.). There was also a slight difference between the length of feet and their units during the republic and the length of feet and their units during the empire.

A Roman foot, or pes was divided into 12 equal units called unciae. During the republic the Roman foot measured 11.65 inches, and during the empire it measured 11.5 inches. A cubit was equal to 1.5 Roman feet, and a passus, or a double step, measured 5 feet. A stadium was another unit of measurement for greater lengths derived from the distance

Roman cup or bowl depicting a man carving the number 7 on a nilometer, a device used to measure the water level of the Nile's annual flood (© The Trustees of the British Museum)

around a Greek racing stadium. It was equal to 625 Roman feet, ⅛ of a Roman mile.

Romans measured weight in a unit called a libra, which was divided into 12 base units of equal weight, also called unciae. A libra weighed 11.5 ounces, just short of a modern pound. Accordingly, each uncia weighed just a bit less than an ounce. Another term for libra was as. Asses or librae were not just units of measurement for weighing commercial goods; they were also used to establish the value of Roman currency, emphasizing just how critical a standard of weights and measures was to the Roman economic system.

Liquid volume was measured in a unit called an amphora. Borrowed from Greece, this unit was equivalent to 6.8 gallons of liquid. In the ancient Mediterranean terra-cotta vessels called amphorae were used to transport liquids like oil and wine. The volume of the amphora is equivalent to 1 cubic foot of liquid and is thought to be derived from the amount of liquid a human being can comfortably carry. The Romans also employed smaller volume units. For example, 1 amphora was equal to 8 congii, each of which had a volume of 0.85 gallons. One congius contained 12 heminae, each of which had a volume of 0.57 pints. A sextarius consisted of 2 heminae. For measuring either dry or liquid volume, the Romans used the modius (pl. modii). This volume was equivalent to 2.4 gallons of liquid. The modius was further subdivided into 16 units for liquid measure called sextarii; each had a volume of 1.1 pints.

Romans used four main units to measure land area. They were used in land division and distribution for colonial, agricultural, and military endeavors. The basis for these calcula-

tions was the actus, a unit of length equal to 120 feet. A square actus, actus quadratus, was equivalent to 14,400 square Roman feet, or about ⅓ acre. Next was the jugerum, possibly derived from the average area two oxen could plow in a single day. One jugerum equaled 2 actus quadrati. Two jugera made a heredium, which measured approximately 1.25 acres. The largest denomination of land area was the centuria, which was equivalent to 100 heredia, approximately 125 acres during the republic but up to 200 heredia in the empire. The origin of the centuria was the approximate area occupied by an encamped century of the Roman military.

The Roman system of weights and measures was partially standardized during the late republic. Although there were slight regional variations in units, the basic units of distance, length, weight, volume, and area were uniform throughout republican and imperial territory. Elected officials called aediles were responsible for regulating the system of weights of measures in towns and cities throughout Roman territory. In Rome the standards for weights and measures were kept at the Roman Forum in the Temple of Castor and Pollux. Employing a uniform system of weights and measures, Rome was able to divide its land, mint money, and exchange commercial goods over a vast territory while using a common vocabulary from Britain to the Persian Gulf.

THE AMERICAS
BY KIRK H. BEETZ

Exactly what the weights and measures were for ancient Americans is among the mysteries of ancient American life. For most ancient cultures archaeologists rely heavily on written records for identifying weights and measures, and most ancient Americans left no such records. Some ancient American cultures did have written languages, but it seems that they did not deem their weights and measures worthy of recording. For instance, merchant transactions among the ancient Maya were written on the ground, in dirt, with stones, seeds, or other small objects serving to mark numbers, presumably including those that stood for weight, volume, and length; the transactions were then memorized and the dirt and markers reused for other transactions. A lack of physical evidence adds to the mystery. For instance, in other parts of the world metal scales for weighing objects have been found and their uses identified, but Americans made little use of metal in the ancient era. They may have used wooden measuring devices or devices that combined wood, bone, and stone. If both the wood and the bone decayed, archaeologists would have only the stones, and the stones may look like nothing special.

Researchers expect weights and measures to appear in cultures that trade extensively among themselves and with outsiders and that have a central government which can impose standards for weights and measures on people. This assumption would seem to leave the cultures of the Innuits and the people of the plains of North America out of the picture.

They may have formed weights and measures of their own, but it seems unlikely that they did.

Cultures that might have had weights and measures existed in northeastern North America, along the Mississippi River, in Mesoamerica, and in northern South America. In each case, between 1000 b.c.e. and the end of the ancient era, cultures created urban areas, the most sophisticated of which were in Mesoamerica. Towns of as many as 30,000 people may have been built in North America in the northeast and along the Mississippi River, and they seem to have had extensive trade networks, implying a need for weights and measures, as well as the opportunity for the formation of central governments that could establish weights and measures; however, evidence for these is absent at present.

One way for archaeologists to gain hints about ancient customs is to study modern descendants of the ancient cultures in the hope of finding practices that can be dated back to ancient times. In northeastern North America the cultures of the ancient towns were long gone by the time people who could read and write arrived. Along the Mississippi disease wiped out the town dwellers, who may or may not have been descended from the ancient town builders, before they could be studied. In northern South America the ancient builders of impressive monuments and towns were gone before the coming of Spanish record keepers. Nevertheless, in Mesoamerica the Mayan culture still exists. However, by the time anyone wrote about Mayan weights and measures, the Maya had adopted Spanish weights and measures. Only something to measure distance overland has survived, called a "pace."

The Aztecs known to the Spanish seem to have adopted many practices from the Maya, probably including some weights and measures. Some of their records for payments of taxes and tribute have survived, indicating a few of their measures. Gold was made into disks about 2 inches in diameter and 1 finger thick. Cotton was traded in bales, although the size of a bale is as yet unknown. Maize and other grains may have been measured by baskets, although again the exact size is not known. In each of these instances, it is possible to visualize ancient Maya making similar measurements.

There are good reasons to believe that the ancient Maya had systems of weights and measures. Their cities levied taxes on their subjects, and they exacted tribute from conquered lands. In each case, being able to weigh and measure goods would be necessary for making sure the correct amounts of taxes and tribute were paid. Further, the ancient Maya had complex legal systems that included the ability of people to file lawsuits against merchants they believed had cheated them. Weights and measures would be useful for determining whether someone was overcharged or shortchanged. In addition, kings were expected to ensure that resources were properly distributed among their people; managing the distribution of food, cloth, and other goods would be made simpler if a system of weights and measures were employed. Complicating matters is the possibility that every city or perhaps every king may have had a unique set of weights and measures.

With all those possibilities in mind, archaeologists use generalized words to represent weights and measures they hope to identify someday. For example, the word *load* may be used to represent the weight or size of goods. This term does not represent a random weight or size; instead, it represents what archaeologists believe was always a fixed amount. The term *loads* would apply to large weights or sizes, such as harvests being brought to the city from farms. Smaller sizes would be packets, articles, and bundles, which would be traded in marketplaces to families. The word *length* applies to cloth. For the Aztecs, 20 lengths would be equal to 1 load, although such may not have been the case for the ancient Maya. Such terms allow archaeologists to discuss the use of weights and measures without knowing their exact amounts.

Cotton was traded extensively among the Maya and neighboring cultures. Cotton was almost certainly baled for ease of transport, and it may be assumed that the bale was a standardized unit of measure. Of all Mayan goods, the likeliest to have been weighed or measured was cacao. The cacao bean was treasured because it could be made into a variety of drinks that were valued for their taste, either bitter or sweetened with sugar or honey, as well as incorporated as flavoring into foods. The beans were probably traded by how many there were, but they may have been traded by weight. Ground cacao would have been either weighed or measured by volume. So highly valued was cacao that it was almost certainly measured down to tiny grains. It is with cacao that archaeologists have their best hope of discovering a Mayan weight or measure because the consumption of cacao was something the Maya deemed worthy of recording, even on their monuments.

See also AGRICULTURE; ARCHITECTURE; ASTRONOMY; BUILD-ING TECHNIQUES AND MATERIALS; CLIMATE AND GEOG-RAPHY; ECONOMY; EMPIRES AND DYNASTIES; HEALTH AND DISEASE; METALLURGY; MILITARY; MONEY AND COINAGE; NO-MADIC AND PASTORAL SOCIETIES; NUMBERS AND COUNTING; SCIENCE; SOCIAL ORGANIZATION; TRADE AND EXCHANGE; WAR AND CONQUEST.

FURTHER READING

"Ancient Weights and Measure." ArchaeologyExpert.co.uk. Available online. URL: http://www.archaeologyexpert.co.uk/AncientWeightsAndMeasures.html. Downloaded on May 12, 2007.

François Cardarelli, *Encyclopedia of Scientific Units, Weights, and Measures: Their SI Equivalences and Origins*, trans. M. J. Shields (New York: Springer, 2003).

Paul Cartledge, Edward E. Cohen, and Lin Foxhall, eds., *Money, Labour, and Land: Approaches to the Economies of Ancient Greece* (London: Routledge, 2002).

Anita Ganeri, *The Story of Weights and Measures* (New York: Oxford University Press, 1996).

Pierre Grandet, "Weights and Measures." In *The Oxford Encyclopedia of Ancient Egypt*, vol. 3, ed. Donald B. Redford (Oxford: Oxford University Press, 2001).

Mabel Lang and Margaret Crosby, *Weights, Measures, and Tokens* (Princeton, N.J.: American School of Classical Studies at Athens, 1964).

Andy Meadows and Kirsty Shipton, eds., *Money and Its Uses in the Ancient Greek World* (Oxford, U.K.: Oxford University Press, 2001).

Helen Parkins and Christopher Smith, eds., *Trade, Traders and the Ancient City* (London: Routledge, 1998).

Karl M. Petruso, "Early Weights and Weighing in Egypt and the Indus Valley," *Bulletin of the Museum of Fine Arts, Boston* 79 (1981): 44–51.

► writing

INTRODUCTION

The earliest writing systems, often referred to as proto-writing, emerged during the Neolithic Period, probably in about the seventh millennium B.C.E. Archaeologists have found this type of writing, which consisted of symbols that stood for objects or ideas, inscribed on tablets or such objects as tortoise shells. Not much information, however, could be recorded by this type of writing. Writing proper is believed to have originated in ancient Sumer in the Near East during the Bronze Age, in about the fourth millennium B.C.E. At roughly the same time, a form of writing called Proto-Elamite developed in Persia (modern-day Iran), and by 3200 B.C.E. the ancient Egyptians had a form of writing. By 1900 B.C.E. writing had developed in India. The Chinese, meanwhile, produced proto-writing as far back as 6000 B.C.E. and had formed a script by 1600 B.C.E. Other early writing systems that historians have discovered (and in some cases have been unable to decipher) include Anatolian hieroglyphs and writing from the island of Crete, both from around the second millennium B.C.E., and various Semetic languages that emerged in the Near East in roughly 1800 B.C.E. With only very few exceptions, such as the writing system of the ancient Maya in the Americas, all writing scripts throughout the world descended from the writing systems of the Near East or China.

Writing in the ancient world took various forms. The earliest is called *logographic,* from the Greek word *logos,* meaning "word." Logographic writing consisted either of pictographs (symbols that were essentially pictures of the thing represented) or ideographs (symbolic representations of concepts). Later, more flexible writing systems consisted of syllabaries, or lists of symbols that stood for syllables.

These types of writing systems, however, were cumbersome and difficult to learn, for they required the use of hundreds, if not thousands of symbols. A major step forward was the development of alphabetic writing during the Iron Age. Now a small number of symbols could be used to represent the sounds contained in a word. The earliest-known alphabetic systems of writing were those of the Semitic languages, and the written languages of ancient Greece and Rome were alphabetic. Some ancient writing systems were a mixture or two or even all three of these types of writing.

Two other terms are often used in connection with ancient writing systems: *cuneiform* and *hieroglyphs.* The writing of the Sumerians was cuneiform, a word that derives from a word meaning "wedge." Cuneiform writing consists of wedge-shaped symbols that took this shape because they were pressed with a stylus into wet clay. The word *hieroglyphs* is commonly used to refer to the writing of ancient Egypt as well as the Anatolian script mentioned earlier. While the word is widely used, specialists in Egyptian archaeology and history discourage it, primarily because the word is of Greek origin and does not have a precise meaning. Generally, though, hieroglyphs refers to the complex artistic writing of the ancient Egyptians, typically practiced by trained scribes and the priestly class. This system consisted of three classes of symbols: phonetic symbols that functioned like an alphabet, logographs, and a third set of symbols called determinatives that narrowed the meaning of a logograph.

AFRICA

BY DIANNE WHITE OYLER

Writing in the African society and culture of the ancient world dates back to 3000 B.C.E. in the Nile River valley after the political unification of Upper and Lower Egypt by King Menes. *Hieroglyphics*, a Greek word meaning "sacred text," is the first indigenous African writing system.

Along the upper Nile River, south of Egypt, Nubia had been influenced by Egypt in the use of the Egyptian language and writing system through trade and conquest. Although hieroglyphics were known by people living along the upper Nile, the region was not receptive to adopting a writing system. The more rural part of the river lacked the urban, centralized government that required detailed record keeping. Both Nubia and the kingdom of Kush adopted the hieroglyphic writing system from Egypt. However, although the kingdom of Kush and the kingdom of Kush at Meroë possessed literate societies, not everyone was able to read and to write. Members of the royal and upper classes, priests, and scribes enjoyed an education through which they controlled society by possessing written knowledge. Everyone else lived in a preliterate world that coexisted in a symbiotic relationship with the literate one.

The Egyptian hieroglyphic writing system was adapted between the eighth and fourth centuries B.C.E., during the Napatan Period, when a form of hieroglyphic writing was used in texts. The Kushite rulers of Egypt's Twenty-fifth Dynasty—Kashta, Piye, and Shabaka—used hieroglyphics to write about their conquests on steles placed throughout the combined kingdoms. In 170 B.C.E. Queen Shanakdakhete became the first female ruler of the Meroitic Period. During her 10-year reign she used Meroitic hieroglyphs to inscribe texts on stone and brick walls. These texts represent the oldest-known Meroitic hieroglyphs, which were adapted from Egyptian hieroglyphics and changed to meet Nubian needs. Although the two forms of hieroglyphs appear similar, they do not represent the same meanings. Based on their connection to Egyptian hieroglyphics, the written Meroitic marks can be deciphered; however, the Meroitic language has not been translated, so it is impossible to understand what has been written.

The kingdom of Axum created its own indigenous alphabet and imported other alphabets through trade and migration. Axum's indigenous Ge'ez language and alphabet were based on the language and script of migrants from southern Arabia; the Sabaen alphabet dates from about sixth century B.C.E. The Hebraic alphabet also may have been migratory. According to one origin myth, Menelik I, son of the Queen of Sheba and Solomon of Israel, brought the alphabet from Israel in the 10th century B.C.E. Another myth proposes that the Hebraic alphabet was brought in the ninth century B.C.E. by the Hebrew tribe of Dan living in the Ethiopian highlands. In the 12th century Jewish clerics dated to antiquity the Torah used by the descendants of the tribe of Dan. The Egyptian Coptic missionaries brought the their alphabet to Axum during the fourth century C.E., and the Greek language and alphabet and Latin language and Roman alphabet came through the Port of Adulis through the Red Sea trade.

Present-day Ethiopia's Ethiopic script reportedly originated in Axum in the second century C.E. and is based on the ancient writing system of Ge'ez. This writing system was used in religious and secular inscriptions on stone and metal objects. During the fourth century C.E. King Ezana adopted Christianity as the religion of the state, and biblical texts were translated from the Coptic language and script to the Ge'ez language and Ethiopic script.

In the North African region of Maghreb inscriptions in an indigenous Berber writing called Tafineq date from as early as 500 B.C.E. This writing system was used to communicate messages, for funerary inscriptions, and to mark property lines. Tafineq may have been influenced by the Punic writing system based on the Phoenician alphabet used in the colony of Carthage. In addition, the Greek language and alphabet and Latin language and Roman alphabet were imported first through trade and later through Roman conquest in the Punic Wars (264–146 B.C.E.). From 155 to 160 C.E. the Latin language and Roman alphabet were used by the Roman Catholic Church to spread Christianity in North Africa.

Ancient African writing is the second oldest in the world. Written hieroglyphics changed as the need arose to streamline complex writing system. Egypt's gift to the world was its writing system, which was adapted by other civilizations to meet their unique needs, and papyrus, on which texts covering various subjects and in various languages and scripts are preserved for posterity. Other writing systems were imported through cultural diffusion as various groups traded with, migrated to, or conquered civilizations on the continent.

EGYPT

BY LEO DEPUYDT

Egyptians wrote their language in the pictorial hieroglyphic script. *Hieroglyphic* is a Greek word meaning "pertaining to holy carving." The unit of the writing system is the hieroglyph. Hieroglyphs are stylized but realistic pictures of beings and objects. The earliest hieroglyphic writing dates to about 3000 B.C.E. Early attempts are imperfect and difficult to decipher. Full-fledged hieroglyphic writing emerged around 2500 B.C.E. The hieroglyphic tradition steeply declined in the second century C.E., and the latest surviving texts date to the fourth and fifth centuries C.E. The last scribe presumably died sometime in the sixth or seventh century C.E. In 1822 the French Egyptologist Jean François Champollion deciphered hieroglyphic writing.

Because writing represents language, any description of a writing system must be preceded by a description of the language system. Language is composed entirely of signs. Signs have two sides, the signified and the signifier. An example of the signified is a person's image of a dog. The signifier attached to this signified is the sound pattern consisting of the three sounds written *d + o + g*. In other words, the signifier is the code in the brain that prompts the speech organs to produce the sounds. Signified and signifier are independent. The proof is a comparison of languages. French speakers also know the signified of a dog but use different sounds as the signifier, namely *chien*. In English and French the image of a dog is about the same, but the sound pattern changes. Language is neither signifieds nor signifiers but rather the links between the two. English speakers tacitly agree to link the image of a dog always to the sound pattern written *dog*. The biochemical configurations of signifiers, signifieds, and the links between them in the brain are unknown, but their existence seems certain.

Hieroglyphs can refer to either signifieds or signifiers. The hieroglyphic script is one of the few scripts that does both. A hieroglyph denoting a signified is an ideogram—that is, an "idea character." A stroke included in a hieroglyph indicates that the hieroglyphs meet two conditions: They are ideograms, and they denote a whole word by themselves. A hieroglyph denoting a signifier (one or more sounds linked to a signified) is a phonogram—that is, a "sound character." Phonograms represent one, two, or three consonants. They are therefore uniliteral, biliteral, or triliteral. Vowels are not written. Phonograms also function as phonetic complements.

Pictures come to denote sounds through the rebus principle. *Rebus* is Latin for "representing sounds by depicting objects." In English the sound made by the letter *I* might be represented by a picture of an eye. It is in this way that phonograms are derived from pictures. In rebus derivation a hieroglyph that denotes a signified as an ideogram—and that secondarily denotes the signifier attached to that signified—is cut loose from the signified and left to express only the signifier as a phonogram. Like any language, Egyptian consists of a limited set of distinctive sounds, about 25. Each sound can

Abu Simbel—hymn in praise of King Ramses II (Courtesy of the Oriental Institute of the University of Chicago)

be represented by its own phonogram. The group of phonograms in the language is called the alphabet. But hieroglyphic writing is not purely alphabetic. It uses other signs besides the alphabet. Still, about half of the signs in any hieroglyphic text are those of the alphabet.

Ideograms always denote both sound and meaning. Phonograms always denote sound but only sometimes denote meaning. The result is asymmetry. An ideogram denotes the signifier of a word. The signifier is linked to the signified in the sign. That is why an ideogram indirectly denotes a sound. In referring to both sides of a word—that is, a whole word—an ideogram is always a logogram, or a "word character." Only a full sound pattern as signifier is linked to a signified. Therefore, only a phonogram denoting a full sound pattern is also a logogram.

A third type of hieroglyph is the determinative. It appears at the ends of words and determines the meaning class to which a word belongs. Hieroglyphs often function in more than one capacity. Ideogram, phonogram, and determinative are therefore functions rather than types of hieroglyphs. A word can be written in many combinations of one or more of the three types—ideogram, phonogram, and determinative—and contains from one to five or six hieroglyphs, sometimes more.

Hieroglyphs normally exhibit their full pictorial quality only when chiseled or painted. This is hieroglyphic writing proper. When writing with a pen on papyrus, scribes used cursive variants. Pen-written hieroglyphs are called hieratic, which is derived from the Greek word for "priestly." The distinction between hieroglyphic and hieratic appears first in the religious writings of Clement of Alexandria (ca. 250–210 C.E.). Hieratic was by that time used mainly in religious texts inscribed by priest-scribes on papyri. Earlier, hieratic had been used for all pen-written texts composed in the first three stages of the language: Old, Middle, and Late Egyptian.

From about 650 B.C.E. onward an extremely cursive variant of hieroglyphic writing called demotic was used for more than a millennium. It denotes the fourth stage of the language, also called demotic. Demotic means "of the people." The name first appears in the writing of Herodotus (fl. fifth century B.C.E.). Hieroglyphic proper and hieratic had by then become limited mainly to monumental and religious texts. In demotic the hieroglyphs of a word often merge into a single composite sign taking on a life of its own. Therefore a demotic word was often written with its own signs. Demotic therefore makes great demands on a reader's paleographic memory.

Hieroglyphic writing as a rule runs from right to left, with people and animals facing right. Texts were mostly written in lines. Columns of hieroglyphs were commonly used in monuments and were the norm in hieratic in the third millennium B.C.E. The sign list in A. H. Gardiner's *Egyptian Grammar* contains fewer than 800 signs. The number of signs used frequently is less than that.

THE MIDDLE EAST

BY BRADLEY SKEEN

The cuneiform script is the oldest form of writing in the world. Its earliest form was semipictographic, devised around 3400 B.C.E. to record the language used by the ancient inhabitants of Uruk in southern Mesopotamia. This so-called protocuneiform may have been developed to write the Sumerian language (which is related to no other known language), but early cuneiform writing was not used for Sumerian until the middle of the third millennium B.C.E. After 2500 B.C.E. it was quickly adapted to record the east Semitic Akkadian language of people living in the same area. Eventually many other linguistically unrelated languages used cuneiform, including Elamite, Hittite, Ugaritic, Canaanite, Hurrian, Urartian, and Old Persian.

Writing was invented at Uruk in the context of a complex society that produced a large agricultural surplus and needed to record the incomings and outgoings of that produce and other commodities. The invention of writing at Uruk by administrators managing the large agricultural estates and workshops of Eanna, the household of the goddess Inanna, was thus a very specific, pragmatic development driven by the need to record estate activities. Because of its difficulty, the cuneiform writing was used only by professional scribes, educated bureaucrats, and other elites whose positions in society were bolstered by their access to writing, especially in the form of legal and religious documents.

The precursors of cuneiform writing began to develop as early as 8000 B.C.E. The first step was the use of tokens—small clay objects marked with simple symbols—to record business transactions, such as the transfer of livestock from a shepherd to a temple estate. Eventually traders documented transactions by sealing tokens inside a large hollow clay ball known as a bulla. Seeing the specifics of what was recorded, however, required breaking the bulla, thus making it useless. The solution was to impress another symbol on the outside of the bulla for each token it contained. In time the documentation system was simplified by writing transactions on flat clay tablets of various sizes. Once this became common practice, the set of signs expanded, enabling people to write longer texts.

Cuneiform is a Greek word meaning "made of wedges" and is used by modern scholars to describe the Sumerian script and its offshoots. Although the writing system began as schematic drawings of things named, the images, called logograms, were quickly abstracted and reduced to a set of a few hundred signs, each composed of a unique group of wedge shapes impressed in the wet clay with the tip of a stylus made from a reed. Typically a sign had a syllabic value, and a series of signs strung together formed a word. Much cuneiform literature has survived because the clay tablets on which it was written were very durable. Even when ancient cities were burned by enemy armies, tablets survived because the fire of the burning libraries actually hardened and preserved the clay. Thus, large collections of tablets are preserved from Nineveh, Assur, Ur, Uruk, Mari, Ebla, Ugarit, and many other cities that were destroyed by fire.

Egyptians learned of cuneiform through trade contacts with Mesopotamia and, after 3000 B.C.E., created their own hieroglyphic script that shared many features with cuneiform. When Indo-European Hittites and Persians conquered Mesopotamia, they adopted cuneiform for writing their languages, which previously had been without any form of script. Because of the prestige of the Mesopotamian empires, even the Egyptian court had to maintain an office of scribes trained in the cuneiform languages to handle diplomatic correspondence. In the Iron Age (1000–550 B.C.E.) languages written in alphabetic scripts became predominant, but Akkadian and Sumerian survived as scholarly, religious, and literary languages until the first century C.E., in much the same way Latin did in western Europe after the fall of the Roman Empire.

As early as 1900 B.C.E. many people who spoke northwest Semitic languages developed the first alphabetic writing. This ancestor of the alphabetic scripts used in the modern world is known as the Proto-Sinaitic script because it was first discovered in graffiti and other inscriptions left by copper miners in the Sinai Peninsula. It has since been found in inscriptions from all over Egypt. Rather than a simple transliteration of words into hieroglyphs, the Proto-Sinaitic script comprises roughly 30 hieroglyphs that began with the sound of the consonants in Semitic languages; systems of adding vowels in Semitic languages were not developed until the Middle Ages (ca. 1000 C.E.).

The city of Ugarit on the Mediterranean coast of modern Syria was destroyed by invaders about 1200 B.C.E. Several surviving clay writing tablets show that many languages were spoken and written in that cosmopolitan trading city, but texts in the native language, a northwest Semitic dialectic called Ugaritic, were written in an alphabetic script that was adapted from cuneiform and inscribed on clay tablets. The influence of the cuneiform script among northwest Semitic speakers was so great that every city would have had scribes and scribal schools trained in cuneiform. The new form of writing, therefore, must have been developed in an appeal to the prestige of cuneiform writing while maintaining the relative ease of an alphabetic script. Ugaritic also reveals the first use of alphabetic letter order.

By 1000 B.C.E. the Phoenician cities developed their own form of alphabetic writing based on both the Proto-Sinaitic script and the Ugaritic script. This was important because all later alphabetic writing was derived from the Phoenician script. It was from the Phoenicians that Greeks learned the alphabet for trading purposes (before 900 B.C.E.), after which they devised their own version of the alphabet to write the Greek language (no examples of Greek texts survive from much before 700 B.C.E.). In fact, the term *alphabet* comes from the names of the first two letters of the Greek alphabet, *alpha* and *beta*. Needing fewer signs to write their consonants than did the Phoenicians, the Greeks used the spare signs to represent vowels, thus completing the development of the elements associated with the alphabet. The Greek alphabet was passed on to the Etruscans and then the Romans, who modified it into the Latin alphabet that is still used for many Western languages.

The Phoenician alphabet was adapted by people all over the Near East and turned into a different alphabet by the speakers of each Semitic language. The most important language in the Iron Age was Aramaic. People in Mesopotamia and many other areas spoke Aramaic, and its alphabetic script was written on sheets of papyrus or vellum in ink with reed pens. Because it was more convenient than writing cuneiform on clay tablets, most written pieces, such as personal letters, were probably composed in this way. Because papyrus and vellum are highly perishable materials, however, very

Clay tablet with Babylonian inscription, found in the treasury of Persepolis, Persia (modern-day Iran) (Courtesy of the Oriental Institute of the University of Chicago)

few manuscripts of any northwest Semitic language remain from before the Common Era (although inscriptions in stone survived). Hebrew developed its own version of the alphabetic script and used it to write the Hebrew Bible (the Old Testament). The Hebrew language, script, and biblical texts became important factors in forming and maintaining Jewish identity.

ASIA AND THE PACIFIC
BY KIRK H. BEETZ

Writing in Asia and the Pacific seems to have developed and evolved to answer specific needs of societies. For example, the ancient Australians did not develop a writing system but painted rocks with images of their history and religious beliefs. Similarly, the Chinese of the Shang Dynasty (ca. 1500–ca. 1045 B.C.E.) used pictures to represent words. Although the pictorial lexicon of the ancient Australians could be interpreted only by people specially acquainted with them, it seems to have been enough to satisfy the religious needs of the ancient Australians. It was not enough for the Shang, however, because their religious beliefs included the ability to contact dead ancestors and ask them questions. These questions had to be written down on animal bones or the shells of turtles, which seers would transmit to the dead for their answers. A seer would drill a hole in the bone or shell and then touch a red-hot bronze pin to the hole, making the bone or shell crack. These cracks were the replies of the ancestors, which the seer would read and then record in writing.

Religion was not the only motivation for developing a written language. In the Harappan civilization (ca. 2600–ca. 1500 B.C.E.) of the Indus River valley, the creation of writing seems to have followed a path similar to that of the first written words of the Near East. Harappan writing is almost universally associated with commerce, with most of it being found on seals used to mark goods. As was probably the case for the Near East, writing appears to have begun as symbols representing goods and ownership of goods for trade. As time passed, those symbols may have evolved into symbols for words, which may have separated into symbols for syllables and then symbols for spoken sounds. Harappan seals were carved in tiny stones, usually soapstone, and they were impressed into clay. Although about 2,000 seals have been found, almost all in or near marketplaces, the words written on them have yet to be translated.

About 5,000 characters for the Shang written language have been found, with about 2,500 having so far been translated. Each Shang character represents a single word. Linguists call the characters logographs. They were not only written on bones and turtle shells but also on bamboo and wood. The writing implement was probably made of metal, with a sharp edge used to incise the logographs.

During the Zhou Dynasty (ca. 1045–ca. 256 B.C.E.) the Chinese written language became more complicated and versatile. Characters represented things or ideas, and when new things or ideas were to be expressed, the Chinese writers combined two or more characters to form a new image. Characters that represent things or ideas are called ideograms. The Zhou favored writing on wood, bamboo, and silk. For writing on wood and bamboo they used sharp writing implements. Silk required new tools: brushes and ink. Silk was expensive, but it was possible to write something long on silk and be able to roll it up and store it. The oldest silk scroll found dates from about 500 B.C.E.

It was during the brief Qin Dynasty (221–207 B.C.E.) that Chinese writing took on its modern form. During the Zhou Dynasty many languages were spoken in the empire, and in various parts of the empire new ideograms were added to Chinese writing to express words from the local languages. Had this process been allowed to continue, written Chinese probably would have split into several distinct and mutually incompatible written languages. The Qin Dynasty pulled together all the diverse strands of writing that had developed during the Zhou Dynasty, eliminated about 25 percent of the ideograms, and created a standard script that the law required to be used for all official business. This script has undergone little modification since.

As a matter of political policy during the Han Dynasty (202 B.C.E.–220 C.E.), government officials had to be scholars. To assume a position in government, a person had to read and write Chinese fluently; it took about 10 years for a student to learn enough ideograms to be fluent. Every scholar carried a writing toolkit—a wooden box containing a brush, a knife, sticks of solid ink, and a mortar and pestle. Ink was usually carbon made from soot, with pine soot being the most common. Ink makers made sticks of ink that were often works of art designed to remind the writer to do his best because he was destroying a beautiful object to create a written work. At the start of the Han Dynasty most brushes were tipped with horsehair, but rabbit hair came to be favored during the middle of the era. When the writer wished to erase writing on wood or bamboo, he used a knife to peel away a layer from the wood. The wood or bamboo would be prepared for writing by being dried and then cut into slats, which were then stitched together by string or thongs so that the slats could be wrapped around each other into a tube for carrying. Calligraphy was considered an art as well as an important skill; the written work, even a simple one, was supposed to be beautiful.

Less is known about the development and evolution of writing in India than about the Chinese writing system. The Indians did not have a single written language that remained intact or changed slowly. They had many. Until the 1830s scholars thought that the history of India began at about 1200 C.E., because no readable government or historical records survived from before the Muslim invasion. In 1837 a British civil servant in India released a translation of writings found on pillars. The written script is called Asoka Brahmi, after the emperor who had the pillars erected. Since then archaeologists have searched for more such inscriptions.

Pillar edict of Emperor Asoka dating to 238 B.C.E., from Uttar Pradesh, India: an example of the earliest readable Indian script (© The Trustees of the British Museum)

Scribes were a standard part of ancient Indian governments. Every court of law was required to have one. Kings had them for recording government business. Professional scribes attended births to record the predictions for the infant made by the attending astrologer. That Asoka had his edicts placed all over his kingdom in prominent places suggests that Indians were mostly literate. Some writings on stone, copper, and gold have survived, while those committed to bamboo and leaves have disintegrated.

The Harappan script seems to have died sometime after the Aryan invasion of the 1000s B.C.E. In about 500 B.C.E. Brahmi script emerged, becoming a robust written language by the era of Asoka (r. ca. 268–ca. 233 B.C.E.). The letters are beautifully graceful. From the end of the Maurya Empire in 185 B.C.E. to the start of the Gupta Empire in 320 C.E., Brahmi split into two or three written scripts. By the end of the ancient era the scripts derived from Brahmi were being split into new scripts to suit the languages of southern India.

EUROPE

BY BRADLEY SKEEN

Writing was invented about 3000 B.C.E. in Mesopotamia and spread from there through contacts between cultures. Writing that uses the alphabet—a small number of signs representing the various distinct sounds of speech—was developed by Semitic-speaking peoples living in Egypt after 2000 B.C.E. This system spread through the Near East and then to Greece. From there it was adopted after 800 B.C.E. by the Etruscans and Romans. Writing came to northern Europe from the Roman Empire.

By the end of the Roman Empire (476 C.E.) most societies in northwestern Europe had some familiarity with the Latin alphabet and language. The Latin alphabet is the system of writing still used for English and other modern European languages. Literacy was not very widespread and was limited primarily to churchmen and government officials. Literacy in northern and eastern Europe came with the spread of Christianity into those areas.

Before writing, ancient European peoples expressed their ideas visually through a variety of media. Their modification of the landscape and the size and positions of monuments and tombs provided signals of group identity and territorial ownership. In Scandinavia and the Alps, beginning around 5000 B.C.E. but especially during the Bronze Age after 2000 B.C.E., people inscribed figures on boulders and rock outcrops to depict people, animals, and objects that had symbolic and ritual significance. Pottery designs were another important medium of communication about group identity. Other claims for writing in prehistoric Europe, such as the Tărtăria tablets from Romania, do not stand up to scholarly scrutiny.

Paper made from cotton fiber was a Chinese invention that did not become widely used in Europe before 1100 C.E. The main writing material used in classical antiquity, papyrus, was made from reeds grown in Egypt and was not widely available outside the Roman Empire. The most common writing material used in northern Europe, therefore, was parchment. This was made from animal skins. The skins were not tanned as for making leather but were stretched and scraped while held tightly in a frame. The parchment was typically cut into single sheets or bound into a book, or codex. More permanent documents, called inscriptions, were made by carving letters into stone or metal plaques. Inscriptions were sometimes made on wood, but because wood is highly perishable, they have not survived in large numbers.

Runes are the earliest system of writing the Germanic languages. They exist only as inscriptions. The runic characters appear for the first time on artifacts such as combs and jewelry dating to the middle of the second century C.E. The runic letters are clearly a variation of the Latin alphabet, but they bear a close similarity to older forms of the alphabet that were used in northern Italy as early as the fifth century B.C.E., suggesting that runes might have been invented and used

Painted pebbles from cave of Mas d'Azil, Ariége, France, dating to 8,000–10,000 B.C.E.; the decorations, which include dots and bands, are thought to represent a kind of writing. (© The Trustees of the British Museum)

for some time before the oldest surviving examples of runic script were written. Early runic inscriptions consist for the most part only of names, perhaps of the person who made the object bearing the inscription or the object's owner. In the Middle Ages some longer inscriptions were made to record, for example, the lives of important people. Once a particular German tribe was converted to Christianity, the people generally ceased to use runes and began to use the standard Latin alphabet of the new Christian writings.

A major effort was made in the ancient period to equip a language from northern Europe with its own alphabet. It was carried out by Christian missionaries in connection with translating the Bible into the target language. This was the Gothic alphabet, created to accommodate the language spoken by the Germanic tribe of the Visigoths. They originated in southern Sweden and migrated as far as the Crimean Peninsula in the southern Ukraine before turning to the Roman Empire and eventually conquering and settling in Spain. This language is not ancestral to modern German and died out not long after 700 C.E. This was because Gothic speakers gradually adopted the Latin language that was spoken by their Spanish subjects. However, in the mid-fourth century C.E. Bishop Ulfilas (ca. 311–ca. 382 C.E.) translated the Greek text of the Bible into the Gothic language for the benefit of Visigoths then living in Moesia (modern-day Bulgaria). Most of the Bibles transcribed in Gothic were eventually destroyed because Ulfilas was later denounced as an Arian heretic (that is, as holding disapproved ideas about the Christian Trinity), but a few hundred pages have survived from various handwritten manuscripts of the Gothic Bible. These texts are extremely important for the study of the history of languages (philology), since they are by many centuries the oldest substantial texts written in any Germanic language.

Ulfilas invented a new alphabet for writing the Gothic language, which before had never been written. (A very small number of runic inscriptions, however, are possibly Gothic.) In general he used contemporary Greek letters. In some case the pronunciation of a letter was changed to fit the needs of the Gothic languages. A small number of other letters were borrowed from Latin, such as the *F*, whose sound did not precisely exist in Greek. Some scholars suspect, however, that these letters may instead have been borrowed from the runic alphabet since the runes were themselves derived from Latin. The names of the Gothic letters, in any case, are derived from those of a runic alphabet. Furthermore, these Gothic letters are different from the style of handwriting in the Latin alphabet commonly called Gothic in the sense of belonging to the medieval period.

GREECE

BY MICHAEL J. O'NEAL

Among the nations of Europe the Greeks were the first to write using an alphabet rather than such writing systems as pictographs used in other ancient cultures. The Greek alphabet formed the basis of the Roman alphabet, which in turn spread throughout Europe and much of the world. Thus the ancient Greek alphabet was the foundation on which western writing systems were built.

The genealogy of the Greek alphabet begins with the Proto-Sinaitic script, sometimes called Proto-Canaanite, which emerged from Egypt and spread throughout the western regions of the Middle East that Egypt controlled. Beginning in about 1100 B.C.E. an important trunk of this family tree of languages was developed by the Phoenicians, who wrote using a 22-letter alphabet with no vowels. The Greeks adopted the Phoenician alphabet and later adapted some of its letters to form vowels. Interestingly, many of these letters had pictographic meanings of their own, meanings that, with a little imagination, can still be seen in the Greek and Roman alphabets. Thus the letter *M* (Greek *mu*) originated in the Phoenician script as the letter *mem*, which means "water" and was formed to suggest the peaks and troughs of a wave. Similarly, the Phoenician letter *heth*, which means "fence," evolved into the *H,* which bears some resemblance to two fence posts with a cross rail. The ancient Phoenician letter *O* also meant "eye." These similarities are not accidental.

In about 800–750 B.C.E. numerous dialects of Greek began emerging, each using a variant of the ancient script, though the dialect called Ionic and its script became the standard in the fifth century B.C.E. Another important dialect was the Eurobean, which the Greeks carried to their colonies on the Italian Peninsula, where it was adopted by the Etruscans and eventually evolved into the Roman alphabet. A third important dialect of Greek that predated these, called Mycenaean, was spoken on the island of Crete and parts of the southern Greek mainland. The only record of this dialect is a written script called Linear B, which was written from about 1500 to 1200 B.C.E. This script consists of many symbols that represent variously letters and syllables. Historians regard it as a kind of "proto" Greek, and deciphering it was a lengthy and laborious process. (Linear A is the name given to the written script that predated Linear B on Crete.)

Writing, along with art and architecture, was one of the highest achievements of ancient Greek civilization. Originally, Greek was written right to left. Sometimes written texts "snaked" their way down the page, with the text going from right to left, continuing on the next line from left to right, and so on. The ancient Greeks used writing materials common among ancient civilizations, including the Romans. One was a metal stylus, similar to a pen, for inscribing letters on tablets covered with wax. The letters could be rubbed out with the flat end of the stylus, making the wax tablet reusable.

The ancient Greeks also wrote on papyrus, a type of early paper that came from the papyrus plant. To make papyrus, first long slits were made along the length of the plant, and then the material was unrolled. Material from the pith, or center, of the plant worked particularly well. The unrolled strips were placed side by side vertically, and then additional strips were affixed horizontally to hold the materials together.

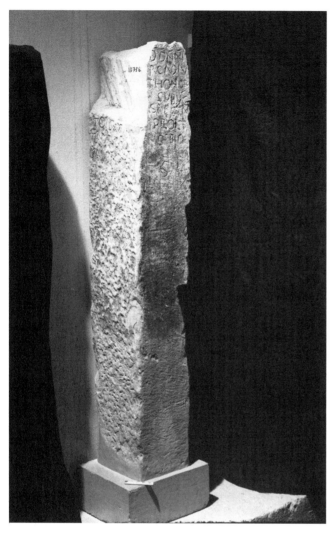

Bilingual milestone marker (Alison Frantz Photographic Collection, American School of Classical Studies at Athens)

Generally, the writing was done on the horizontal strips. Sheets made in this way were joined into scrolls about 5 or 6 yards in length, though longer scrolls were not uncommon. Sometimes single sheets were used for business documents, letters, and writing instruction. Papyrus was typically purchased from Egypt and sold by vendors.

Papyrus, though, was stiff; it could not be folded, and writing on it with pen and ink could be difficult because the writer had to fight the grain of the material. Thus parchment was often used because it was easy to write on and its light color formed a readable contrast with dark ink. The disadvantage of parchment was that it was even more difficult to make than papyrus, so it was more expensive. Parchment was made from the hides of domesticated animals, preferably very young or even unborn animals. The hide was washed to remove hair, soaked in lime, and then stretched on a frame. The stretched hide was scraped, wetted, coated with chalk, rubbed with pumice, and then allowed to dry. Another disad-

vantage of parchment was that the ink was easily erased. Historians believe that many important Greek documents have been lost simply because the parchment on which they were written was recycled.

Ink was often made of soot, charcoal, or resin. Examinations of many ancient Greek manuscripts reveal that their inks contained a high concentration of iron. Of course, Greek writing techniques were not limited to using a stylus on wax tablets and pen and ink on papyrus or parchment. Carving inscriptions in stone on buildings and tombs was also common.

Additionally, in roughly 440 B.C.E. the Greeks invented a form of writing called steganography, which means "covered or hidden writing." Steganography differs from modern cryptography in that the latter encodes messages that can still be seen but cannot be deciphered unless the reader has a key to the code. Steganography, in contrast, is the writing of messages that literally cannot be seen. The ancient Greeks used it for military communications, when the sender was concerned that the message could fall into the enemy's hands. The simplest form of steganography was scratching a written message on a board and then covering it with wax. The board looked like nothing other than an unused wax tablet. Some military commanders were more inventive. The Greek historian Herodotus records the story of a military commander who shaved the head of one of his slaves and tattooed his message on the slave's head. The message was hidden as the slave's hair grew out and then retrieved when the recipient reshaved the slave's head.

ROME

BY MICHAEL J. O'NEAL

The Roman alphabet has had an enormous influence on writing systems worldwide. In the modern world, languages from Afrikaans to Zulu, with scores of others in between, are written using the Roman alphabet. For ancient Romans the alphabet made the task of writing simpler compared with earlier pictographic writing systems used by other cultures. Because of this relative ease of writing, combined with fairly high literacy rates among upper-class Roman citizens, large numbers of written texts survive from Rome, though the ones that survive are only a fraction of the number produced. These texts survive not only as written documents but also in such forms as inscriptions on buildings, monuments, and even coins.

No examples of writing on the Italian Peninsula existed before the Greeks established colonies there in about the eighth century B.C.E. The native Etruscans then adopted and modified the Greek alphabet during the seventh century B.C.E. The Roman alphabet in turn developed out of the Etruscan alphabet. (Note that the word *alphabet* is composed of the first two letters of the Greek alphabet, *alpha* and *beta*.) In time the Roman alphabet spread through the earliest Roman settlements and from there throughout the Roman Empire.

Writing was important for official and military communication throughout the vast empire. One of the most important archaeological finds pertaining to ancient Rome's written communications with its colonies are the so-called Vindolanda tablets, found at the site of the Vindolanda fortress near Hadrian's Wall in ancient Britain and now housed at the London Museum. When Christianity, based in Rome, spread in the vacuum left by the collapse of the Roman Empire, it continued to use the Roman alphabet, making the alphabet a fixture of Western life.

The alphabet the ancient Romans used to write Latin consisted of 23 letters. The letters *J*, *U*, and *W* were added later, *J* as a variant of *I*; *U* as a variant of *V*; and *W*, or double *V*, added to distinguish the sounds of *W* and *V*. Also, the ancient Romans used the letters *K*, *Y*, and *Z* only in transcribing Greek words. The ancient Roman alphabet comprised only capital letters. Most look similar to modern-day letters, although because of the nature of ancient writing tools many, such as *B*, *D*, and *P*, had an angular rather than rounded look.

In ancient Rome children learned to write using boards covered with wax. They wrote in the wax using a stylus—a pointed metal tool similar to a pen—and could rub out what they had written with the flat end of the stylus. In this respect tools for teaching writing were similar to the modern blackboard or ink board. Otherwise, documents were written on wax tablets or very thin pieces of wood. The wax was poured into hollowed-out slabs of wood or sometimes into bronze frames. People who wrote letters often used wax tablets made of wood or ivory, which were then tied together and sent in a box called a seal box. More important documents, such as legal contracts, government proclamations, and such, were written with pen and ink on papyrus, a kind of paper extracted from the pith of the papyrus plant and then pressed into a flat material to write on. Because this stiff material could not be folded, documents were stored and transmitted in the form of rolled-up scrolls. Parchment—made from the skins of domesticated animals like sheep and goats—was also used as an early form of paper. Ink was made from various substances, including charcoal, soot, and gum. It is unclear what was used to bind these materials together, though vinegar may have been used. Other ink ingredients included copper, burnt resin, various minerals, and glues made from remains of animals such as oxen.

Ancient Roman books were nearly always preserved in the form of scrolls, formed by attaching single pieces of papyrus into long, continuous texts. A reader moved on to a new page by rolling it out and then rolling up the part that had already been read. The chief disadvantage of scrolls was that it was difficult for the reader to browse or go back to an earlier page; the entire scroll had to be unrolled and rolled up. In about the first century of the Common Era the Romans invented the book, using flat sheets that were sewn together. This type of book, called a codex, made storage much easier. Scrolls had to be stored in boxes or baskets, whereas flat books could be arranged on shelves.

Ancient Rome produced a large number of writers, many of whose works continue to be read for their insights into art, philosophy, history, politics, religion, and other areas of thought. These works were some of the highest cultural achievements of the Roman Empire. But much writing, too, survives in the form of tomb inscriptions, inscriptions on the walls or capitals of monumental buildings, and even in the form of *graffiti*, a word that comes from the Italian for "scratch," as in scratching an inscription on a wall or other surface. The ancient Romans were lovers of graffiti, even on the walls of their homes. Many poets enjoyed writing epigrams, or short, pithy sayings, on walls.

The ancient Romans carried the writing of personal letters to great heights. Roman letters were highly stylized, with a system of abbreviations used in the salutation and closing, initials similar to the kind of abbreviations used in modern e-mail communications. Thus, for example, *S.P.D.* stood for *salutem pluriman dicit*, or "sends very fond greeting." Because Rome had no postal system, wealthy letter writers hired messengers to deliver letters, often at great distances. One concern was that a letter intended as a personal communication might go astray and be revealed to a larger public. For this reason, Roman letter writers devoted considerable attention to the literary style of their letters in an attempt to avoid embarrassment if someone other than the addressee read them. Sometimes recipients of letters replied by writing notes in the margins of letters they received. Also, because of the danger that letters and other documents might be lost or missent, copies were generally made and kept. In the case of official documents a class of scribes and copyists did the work. It

Pottery inkwell from Roman Britain, inscribed with its owner's name, Iucundus (dating to first to third centuries C.E.) (© The Trustees of the British Museum)

could be said that ancient Romans lived in a culture of letter writing, often using daily letters and replies as a way of keeping in touch with friends, loved ones, and business colleagues throughout the empire.

THE AMERICAS

BY MIGUEL ARISA

The indigenous languages of the North and South American populations produced a diversity of writing systems, the most important of which were the hieroglyphic writings that evolved in the Mesoamerican zone. In the region of modern Canada and the United States, Native American writing systems did not develop fully until the advent of the Europeans, when syllabaries became the norm. These were symbols representing syllables, but they did not become widespread until the 19th century C.E.

Mesoamerican writing is believed to have developed with religious and political ends in sight. Writing was cunningly used for political advantage in identifying rulers and deities and driving the propaganda machine of the powerful. The calendar and a number system may have been the earliest examples. Bar-and-dot numerals made an early appearance and spread quickly. With time the ideographic signs became logographic, representing whole morphemes (collections of speech sounds) or words; finally, by the time of the Spanish conquest, logophonetic systems had developed, representing speech.

Some of these writing systems date to as early as 1500 B.C.E. At a very early stage in the Formative Period (as early as 1800 B.C.E.), elaborately carved icons in stone served the purpose of representing concepts, and they seem to have been sufficiently conventionalized to have been understood in a widespread area. This area includes a number of cultures, such as the Olmec, the Aztec, the Maya, the Zapotec, the Mixtec, and others whose writing systems evolved in tandem with reciprocal influences at different times over a millennium.

The major systems of the so-called Late Formative Period, from 400 B.C.E. to 150 C.E., were the Zapotec, the Epi-Olmec, and the Mayan. The earliest forms of writing were highly pictorial, and their most important function was to record dates and the names of government officials and rulers. The illustration of myths, liturgical instructions, and mnemonic devices cannot be ruled out in the more developed stages.

The Olmec, a culture that flourished in the Gulf not far from the Yucatán peninsula, are generally considered to have developed the first system of writing. Hieroglyphs carved in basalt columns at La Venta have led scholars to conjecture that they represent the name of a person, since the image of a bearded man is also present. Notwithstanding, glyphs in a cylinder seal and on carved greenstone discovered in San Andrés, an Olmec site in the vicinity of La Venta, have been dated to about 650 B.C.E. and are now regarded as the earliest artifacts reflecting a system that combines pictures and glyphs and that may represent oral speech patterns. The glyphs show lines coming from the mouth of a bird, in fact rendering the act of speaking. One of the symbols is *ajaw*, which means "king" or "lord," and the other is *three ajaw*, a day in the calendar.

A stone discovered in Veracruz has revealed a new system heretofore unknown, predating the Olmec but with obvious references to that neighboring culture. The 62 signs inscribed on a stone slab, called the Cascajal stone, have been dated to around 900 B.C.E., the earliest yet for such a complex set of symbols. An insect, an ear of corn (representing perhaps both deity and ruler), inverted fish, and various other pictographs displayed in repeated patterns show a distinct language system whose arrangement seems analogous to sentences. These signs show patterns that can be deduced to be syntactical (that is, making up an orderly and connected arrangement or structure) and whose repetition can even be construed as representing poetical forms, as in a couplet.

The Zapotec seem to have followed the example of the Olmec and developed a system of writing around Monte Albán, their capital, from 600 to 200 B.C.E. Carved images of dancing men now thought to be captives ready for sacrifice appear next to what some scholars deem is their names; others interpret the images as calendrical signs. Other pictographs found in tablets in a Late Formative building at Monte Albán have been considered a record of conquest and the submission of nearby towns. Not conducive to phonetic writing like the Mayan system, Zapotec inscriptions are more logographic, like Chinese, in which a symbol represents a word.

Another early form of writing is called the Isthmian script, a precursor of the Mayan. A stela found at La Mojarra, near Veracruz, contains 465 glyphs in 21 columns with the image of a ruler. It is structurally similar to the Mayan because it is logophonic and uses morphemes for meaning. Mayan writing is thought by some to predate even the Olmec system. New research from Guatemala on fragments inside a pyramid at the Mayan site of San Bartolo reveal that one hieroglyph sign may be an early version of *ajaw*. Carbon dating demonstrates that the paintings and the glyph were made around 300 B.C.E. The script next to an image of the maize god evidences the relationship between writing, kingship, and religion.

Even though Mesoamerican writing systems had undergone a long process of evolution by the time the Spaniards arrived in the New World, the conqueror's zeal in eradicating the cultures they considered heathen resulted in widespread burning and destruction of their records. Anthropologists, linguists, and art historians continue to decipher the inscriptions in temples and tombs and the few extant manuscripts from before and after the Conquest.

See also ADORNMENT; ARCHITECTURE; CALENDARS AND CLOCKS; CERAMICS AND POTTERY; EDUCATION; GOVERNMENT ORGANIZATION; INVENTIONS; LANGUAGE; LITERATURE; MIGRATION AND POPULATION MOVEMENTS; MILITARY; MONEY AND COINAGE; NUMBERS AND COUNTING; OCCUPATIONS; RELIGION AND COSMOLOGY; SLAVES AND SLAVERY; SOCIAL ORGANIZATION; TRADE AND EXCHANGE; WAR AND CONQUEST.

FURTHER READING

David N. Carvalho, "Forty Centuries of Ink." World Wide School. Available online. URL: http://www.worldwideschool.org/library/books/tech/printing/FortyCenturiesofInk/toc.html. Downloaded on May 14, 2007.

Michael Coe and Mark Van Stone, *Reading the Maya Glyphs*, 2nd ed. (London: Thames and Hudson, 2005).

Florian Coulmas, *The Blackwell Encyclopedia of Writing Systems* (Oxford, U.K.: Blackwell, 1999).

"The Development of Old Germanic Alphabets." Available online. URL: http://titus.uni-frankfurt.de/didact/idg/germ/runealph.htm. Downloaded on May 11, 2007.

A. H. Gardiner, *Egyptian Grammar: Being an Introduction to the Study of Hieroglyphs*, 3rd rev. ed. (Oxford, U.K.: Griffith Institute, Ashmolean Museum, 1988).

Jean-Jacques Glassner, *The Invention of Cuneiform: Writing in Sumer*, trans. and eds. Zainab Bahrani and Marc Van de Mieroop (Baltimore, Md.: Johns Hopkins University, 2003).

Jack Kilmon, "The Scriptorium." Available online. URL: http://www.historian.net/target.html. Downloaded on November 22, 2006.

Lawrence Lo, "Greek." Ancientscripts.com. Available online. URL: http://www.ancientscripts.com/greek.html. Downloaded on May 14, 2007.

John Man, *Alpha Beta: How 26 Letters Shaped the Western World* (New York: Wiley, 2000).

Joyce Marcus, *Mesoamerican Writing Systems: Propaganda, Myth, and History in Four Ancient Civilizations* (Princeton, N.J.: Princeton University Press, 1992).

Anna Giacalone Ramat and Paolo Ramat, eds., *The Indo-European Languages* (New York: Routledge, 1998).

Michael Trapp, ed., *Greek and Latin Letters* (Cambridge, U.K.: Cambridge University Press, 2003). Available online. URL: http://assets.cambridge.org/052149/5970/sample/0521495970ws.pdf. Downloaded on May 14, 2007.

Vindolanda Tablets Online. Available online. URL: http://vindolanda.csad.ox.ac.uk/. Downloaded on May 14, 2007.

Glossary

abacus A device used for making calculations by sliding beads or counters along rods attached to a board.

abax A flat board with vertical columns, used for calculation; the Greek version of the abacus.

ablution vessel A vessel filled with alcoholic, herb-infused, or other liquids for physical purification before encounters with spirits.

acephalous society Human group in which there is no designated political leader.

acrophonic notation A Greek system of numbering using letters to represent the initial sounds of numbers.

acropolis Literally, "high city," which was in many Greek cities the central, elevated, and fortified part of the town.

acupuncture A Chinese medical practice in which needles are inserted into various points in the body to free blocked energy, bringing the yin (the female principle) and the yang (the male principle) back into balance in the attempt to cure injury or illness.

adobe Bricks made of sun-dried mud and used for constructing buildings.

adze A bladed tool that is used to smooth wood.

aedes To ancient Romans, any site where a deity dwelled.

aedile In ancient Rome, a plebeian official in charge of various of Rome's public works and functions, among them, streets, traffic, water supply, and markets and the organization of religious festivals and cult observances.

aerarium The Roman treasury.

ager publicus Public land confiscated from Rome's enemies that could be leased by Roman citizens for farming, grazing herds, or performing other activities.

agger Rampart or embankment; the sloping of a Roman road from a high point in the center to a lower point at the roadsides to facilitate drainage.

agni Indian word for "fire," one of the three basic elements described in the early Upanishads, or religious texts of Hinduism.

agora An open space in a Greek town or city, serving as a marketplace and a political forum; typically the main business district.

agrarian Characterized by farming.

agropastoral subsistence A livelihood based on a combination of farming and herding, often involving migration of herds among pasturelands.

aguada Small water reservoir lined with clay in the ancient Americas.

ahauob Mayan term for nobility.

ahaw Mayan word meaning "lord" or "king."

aivan A type of veranda, or open-air entrance hall that leads into a reception hall.

akhet The inundation, or flooding of the Nile River, which ran roughly from July to December.

ala (**pl.** *alae*) Open rooms off the atrium of a Roman house, used for storage or work.

alchemy The quest to create sought-after substances, such as artificial gold or an elixir of eternal life, by experimentally combining chemicals or minerals or both.

alfa A wild grass (*Stipa tenacissima*) used for weaving.

alliteration The repetition of the initial sound of one or more words in a line of verse.

alloy A combination of two or more pure metals.

altiplano A high plateau or plain.

ambergris A waxy material originating from the innards of sperm whales.

amelu A class of patricians in Babylonia that also included skilled artisans.

amphitheater A large, oval-shaped, freestanding Roman structure designed for the staging of gladiatorial contests and other spectacles.

amphora A ceramic vase with two handles used in the ancient world to transport and store wine, oil, olives, and other goods.

amulet A charm, typically carved or engraved with a magical incantation to ward off evil.

amurca   The dregs of pressed olives.

ancestor worship   The spiritual veneration of one's deceased parents, grandparents, and so on, practiced widely in many ancient cultures.

andrôn   Living quarters for men in ancient Greek homes.

animal husbandry   Breeding, feeding, and management of animals, or livestock, for the production of food, fiber, work, and pleasure.

animism   A religious belief that many (or even all) places, objects, and living things have their own spirits.

ankh symbol   The Egyptian hieroglyphic sign for *life*, consisting of a loop-topped cross.

annealing   A process in which metal is heated to reduce the hardness and brittleness that result from hammering, making the metal easier to shape.

antediluvian   Dating to the period before the Flood, described in the Bible.

anthropomorphic   Having human attributes or a human-like form.

Antikýthēra device   An ancient instrument that used numerous interconnected gears to calculate the motions of the planets and stars.

antiphonal   Containing musical verses to be sung in alternation.

apiculture   The cultivation of honeybee hives in order to collect honey and beeswax.

apoikia (**pl.** *apoikiai*)   The standard term for an official Greek colonial settlement, laid out according to specific procedures, which became an independent polis.

apotropaic wands   Wands having the power to ward off evil or bad luck.

appliqué   A decorative ornament made in a material such as needlework applied to another fabric surface.

apron moldings   Joint stones that slightly hang over the bottom stonework of a wall.

aqueduct   A man-made channel or pipeline designed to transport water across long distances; often raised above the ground, moving water by gravity.

aquifer   An underground rock bed yielding groundwater.

archaeoastronomy   The field of archaeology that focuses on sites with astronomical importance.

archaeological culture   An assemblage of artifacts (and their stylistic attributes) that tend to be found together in a particular region at a certain time.

archaic lyric   The earliest Greek poetry that expresses subjective thoughts and feelings, often in a songlike style or form.

Archimedian screw   An irrigation device that uses a screw in a pipe to raise water from a river or pool to a field or container.

archipelago   A group of islands.

architrave   In architectural design, a beam that extends across a row of columns.

archon   A chief magistrate of the Greek city-states.

ard   A simple form of plow used to cut a furrow though the soil without turning it over.

aristocracy   A political system under which a few prominent extended families share power and pass power from generation to generation.

armillary sphere   An astronomical device that mirrors the positions and movements of the heavenly bodies.

armlet   Band worn around the arm but not around the wrist, which would be a bracelet.

Arretine ware   Ceramic wares from the region of Arezzo, Italy, made of fine red clay.

artifact   An object created by human beings, especially one of interest to archaeologists.

artisan   A skilled worker who performs a specific trade or craft.

asafetida   The resin of a plant related to fennel, used to flavor Roman dishes.

asbestos   A nonflammable substance, made from fiber extracted from certain rocks, that was used in the ancient world for lighting as well as fireproof clothing.

ascetic   A person who forsakes comforts to live a life of severe self-discipline.

asclepeion   A Greek sanctuary built to honor the god Asclepios and as a health retreat where the sick and injured were treated.

ashlar   A style of building walls in which shaped stones are laid out in regular rows, one on top of another (as opposed to the more complex, but often stronger, techniques using irregular stones).

aspect   Feature of a verb that describes the duration or completeness of an action.

assimilate   To absorb into a culture.

asterism   A small grouping of stars.

astrolabe   An early astronomical instrument used in navigation.

ataraxia   In ancient Greece, considered to be a life without disturbance, fear, and worry

atimia   Loss of citizen rights, used as a punishment in ancient Athens and other city-states.

atlatl   A hand-held stick used as an arm extension for throwing a spear or dart.

atrium   The open interior area of a Roman house that was the center of domestic life.

augur   A member of ancient Rome's College of Pontiffs; a priest whose role was to interpret the will of the gods through signs and omens.

aulos   A reed instrument with two pipes, capable of a great range of dynamic effects; used in many contexts in ancient Greece but particularly to accompany choral poetry.

auroch   A type of prehistoric giant cattle that is now extinct.

autochthony   Belief in origin from the earth or in having inhabited the same place since time immemorial.

automata   Devices that use hidden mechanical forces (steam, water, pulleys) to move objects in such a way that they appear to be moving of their own accord.

auxilia   Mercenaries hired by Rome to serve in its legions and protect its frontiers.

avatar   A physical form, human or otherwise, taken on by a deity.

axis mundi   Center of the world.

axone   A wooden table or roller used to record ancient Greek writings

ayurveda   A system of medicine used in India that emphasizes diet as a means of correcting imbalances within the body.

azimuth   The angle measured from north, eastward along the horizon to the point where a vertical circle through a celestial object intersects the horizon.

ba   For Egyptians, the soul.

band   The simplest form of political and social group, consisting of members (from eight to 100, though typically less than 30).

bandolier   A flat band worn over the shoulder and across the chest, often as official or ceremonial dress.

barbaros (**pl.** *barbaroi*)   A word used by the ancient Greeks to describe a foreigner—specifically one who did not understand the Greek language; often used with reference to someone rude or rough.

bard   A tribal poet-singer who gave recitation performances of ancient tales and epics.

barrel vault   Solid, semicircular ceiling supported and framed by horizontal arches that rise from piers along the walls.

barter economy   Trading goods for each other without the use of money.

basalt   Gray-black volcanic rock.

basileus (**pl.** *basileis*)   A king in ancient Greece, though one who typically enjoyed limited powers.

basilica   A large Roman meeting hall for commerce.

bas-relief   A technique of decorative sculpture in which the artist carves away unwanted material and allows the elements of a scene to emerge from a flat background.

bast fibers   The outer stems of certain types of plants, including jute and flax, that can be extracted and used in textile production.

beasts of burden   Animals that transport burdens such as goods or people.

benben   In Egyptian cosmology, the first place the sun fell on earth when it emerged from the primordial waters and possibly the name of the mound itself.

benu bird   A heronlike bird associated with the sun in Egyptian mythology.

berm   A mound of earth.

berserk   A warrior who fought, often naked, in an ecstatic state.

beveled   Cut at a slant such that two surfaces do not form a right angle.

bident   A two-pronged spear.

bipod mast   A mast that is forked into two projections at the base.

bireme   A ship with two banks of oars.

birrus   A woolen hood.

bitumen   A substance derived from oil deposits that was used in the waterproofing of porous material.

black-figure pottery   Pottery painting in which black figures are placed on a red background.

blank   A coin-shaped piece of metal without a stamp indicating its value and place of origin.

bodhisattva   A person who can ascend to oneness with God but who chooses to put off salvation in order to help other human beings reach nirvana.

bolas   Stones connected by cords, thrown to entangle and fell prey or an enemy.

boule   A Greek city council elected by the citizens to serve as a lawmaking or advisory body.

breechcloth   Sometimes called a "breechclout," a strip of cloth that hangs between the legs from a waistband.

bride-price   Money or property given to a bride's family by the prospective groom.

brine   Seawater that was commonly heated and evaporated, leaving behind salt for seasoning and preserving food.

broad-cella   A central hall or room designed to be accessed through a maze of halls.

brocade   Fabric with raised patterns.

brochs   Circular stone fortifications in ancient Scotland.

bronze   An alloy of copper and tin, with tin added to strengthen copper.

brooch   A large, decorative pin or clasp.

buckler   A small, round shield held by a handle at arm's length.

bucolic   Relating to the countryside.

bulla (**pl.** **bullae**)   In the ancient Near East, a spherical clay container into which were placed tokens to record quantity of goods held in storage.

burial goods   Objects that are placed in or around a grave to either protect or serve the dead person.

burnishing   The rubbing of the walls of a vessel with a smooth stone or similar implement, creating a smooth finish and making the vessel less permeable to liquids.

burnoose   A one-piece hooded cloak.

butt joint   The ends of two pieces of wood placed at a 90-degree angle and held together with pegs or tied together with leather threaded through drilled holes.

buttress   A projection from a wall that prevents a wall's collapse, either under its own weight or under the weight of a roof.

byre   A stable for cattle.

caber   A pole or a young tree trunk used for tossing as a test of strength.

cacao   Beans used to make chocolate, cocoa, and cocoa butter; in the Americas in ancient times, they were used as currency.

cadastral   Relating to a register recording property ownership boundaries, typically used to apportion taxes.

caementum   A mixture of sand, lime, and crushed volcanic stone known as pozzolana that provided the basic construction material for public and private buildings in ancient Rome.

caesura   A break or pause in the middle of a line of verse.

caiman   A small crocodile native to Central and South America.

cairn   A mound of stones, often piled on top of a burial chamber.

calcei   Formal laced shoes worn with the Roman toga outside the house.

caldera   A crater formed by the collapse or explosion of the central part of a volcano.

camelid   Any mammal from the camel and llama family Camelidae.

cameo   A material, such as gem, shell, or glass, carved in relief, where the design and the background are of layers of contrasting colors.

canon of human proportions   A technique used by Egyptian artists to guide them in maintaining the proportions of human figures, using a square grid and allocating a specified number of grid squares to the parts of the figure.

canopic jar   In ancient Egypt, one of four jars holding the liver, stomach, lungs, and intestines of an embalmed person for entombment with that person.

capital   The top of a column.

caravan   A group of people, vehicles, or supervised animals that are traveling together for safety.

carbon steel   An alloy of iron and carbon that is harder than pure iron.

cardo   A north-to-south road that formed part of the central axis of a Roman city, crossing the *decumanus* (east-to-west road) at the city's center.

carnyx   A European war or ceremonial trumpet with a stylized animal head at the bell end, usually made of beaten sheet bronze; played while being held vertically over the musician's head.

cartouche   In ancient Egypt, an oval figure that enclosed the pharaoh's name.

cash economy   An economy in which money rather than barter is used for buying and selling goods.

cassava   A starchy root used in baking breads or cakes.

caste   In ancient India, a social class based on birth that restricted the professions, civil rights, and marriage possibilities of people born into it

casting   A process in which molten metal is poured into a mold and allowed to cool, taking the shape of the interior of the mold.

castros   Ancient fortified towns inhabited by the Celtiberians.

cataract   A rocky outcrop that produces rapids when water runs over it; there are six major cataracts along the Nile south of modern Aswān.

catasterism   The transformation of a mortal into a star, constellation, or other celestial object.

cauterization   Burning tissue with a very hot metal instrument in order to stop infection.

cavetto cornice   A concave molding shaped like a quarter circle.

cella   The inner chamber, or sanctuary, of a temple.

celt   A prehistoric ax of stone or metal.

cenotaph   A symbolic place of burial not containing the remains of the owner; these false tombs were erected to perpetuate the mortuary cult of the deceased or simply to have an additional tomb in a sacred place.

cenote   Freshwater-filled limestone sinkhole.

censor   The most senior magistrates in ancient Rome, with less power than consuls because they lacked imperium, the authority to lead an army and the power of life and death over citizens.

centaur   A mythical creature that is part human and part horse.

centuriation   The process ancient Roman surveyors used for marking out plots of land for Roman settlers.

centurion   In the Roman army, the officer in charge of a century, a group of foot soldiers.

century   In the Roman army, a group of foot soldiers, originally set at 100.

chadar   A heavy strip of cloth worn by ancient Indians to protect the upper body.

chaff   The husks of grain removed during threshing.

chaitya   In Indian architecture, a building consisting of a set of halls that people could use when an outdoor stupa, or shrine, could not be used because of inclement weather.

chamber pot   Small tublike pot specially made to be kept in the bedroom for use at night as a toilet.

champlevé   An enameling technique where colored enamels fill channels cut directly into metal.

chantress   A female singer engaged in religious rites.

chappal   A type of sandal worn in ancient India.

characters   The symbols representing concepts or words used to write ancient and modern Chinese (and some other languages) and borrowed to write Korean, Vietnamese, and Japanese.

charnel   A building in which human remains are deposited.

chasing   A way of working silver by hammering in a design from the outer surface.

chassis   Framework attached to the axles of a cart.

chattel   In law, personal portable property; in the context of slavery, a condition of ownership of slaves that included the owner's right to sell, donate, or devolve them to his heirs but also to liberate them at will.

cheng   Chinese word for "city" or "wall."

chi   Usually translated as "energy," the Chinese concept of the most basic physical element in the world.

Chi-Rho   A symbol formed by the first two letters of Christ's Greek name (*Christos*), consisting of the letter *Rho* superimposed onto the letter *Chi*.

chiton   A belted, knee-length tunic of seamless cloth worn by the ancient Greeks.

chlamys   A short cloak worn by the ancient Greeks.

chóra   The countryside surrounding a city.

chorobates   A device resembling a long wooden bench, which allowed ancient builders to ensure that floors and other horizontal elements were correctly aligned and level.

chorus   A group of performers who sang and danced in Greek dramas.

chronometer   An accurate clock, particularly one used in seafaring and navigation.

chultune   An underground chamber that ancient Americans used to collect water.

chun   A Chinese skirt with pleats.

cinerary urn   Containers used to hold the ashes of the dead.

cinnabar   Red pigment derive from mercury.

cist   A burial chamber formed from stone slabs set on edge.

cistern   Rain collection device, usually cut out of rock and sealed with lime plaster.

citadel   A city's fortress or stronghold.

civic calendar   A calendar based on the sun and recognized for use in ordinary affairs.

clan   A group of related lineages or kin groups tied together to a distant ancestor; often several lineage groups are contained within one clan.

clepsydra   "Water thief," a term for water clocks of ancient Greece.

cleruchy   A type of Greek colony in which settlers received shares of land (*kleroi*) but maintained citizenship in their native polis.

clibanus   In ancient Rome, a portable oven for baking bread.

clientage   A social system in ancient Europe whereby a member of the nobility provided a person or community protection in exchange for services.

clogs   Blocks of wood used in hunting, intended to trip a running animal.

cloisonné   An enameling process that uses thin wires to create settings for precious stones.

cob   A mixture of wet clay and straw used as a building material.

codex   A book in the modern sense of several groups (called quires) of pages stitched together between a stiff cover.

cohort   The basic tactical unit that replaced the maniple around 100 B.C.E. and consisted of 400 to 600 heavy infantry.

coil-build   To lay rolled lengths of clay, shaped into rings, on top of each other to form pottery.

cold cutting   Carving a piece of glass with hammer and chisel in the same fashion as one would carve stone.

collegium (pl. collegia)   A Roman society whose members paid into a common fund to cover the expenses of their funerals.

colonnade   An outdoor walkway or gathering place, lined with columns and generally roofed, at least partially, to provide shade.

colonus (pl. coloni)   A Roman peasant who was tied to the land despite being legally free.

colophon   An inscription at the end of a text, citing the facts of its production.

columbarium   An underground chamber housing the remains of the Roman dead within small niches, which held funerary urns marked by plaques and inscriptions.

combined arms   The use of differently equipped soldiers in a single fighting force.

commercium   The right of any Latin or inhabitant of Latium to own Roman land and to enter into a contract with a Roman.

compluvium   A rectangular opening in the roof of the atrium that admitted light and rainwater into a Roman home.

composite bow   A bow made by gluing together bone, sinew, and different bones for added strength, with a consequently longer range than a bow carved from a single piece of wood.

concentric   Having a common axis or center point.

conciliar calendar   A political calendar, in which the number of *prytaneis*, or months, varies with the number of phylai, or groups of citizens.

concubine   A woman who is acknowledged as the sexual partner of a particular man; the man typically supports her and acknowledges her children as his own.

confarreatio   The ancient form of marriage practiced by the Roman nobility.

confinement pavilion   An ancient Egyptian structure made of plant materials and used to seclude a mother after the birth of a child and possibly for the birth itself.

conscript   In Egypt, free people forced into government service for a week to a few months; their labor would substitute for paying taxes, or they would be paid.

conscripted   Forced into public service.

consul   The highest-ranking Roman official; this magistrate held imperium, the power to command Rome's armies anywhere and the power of life and death over citizens.

contagious magic   Magic that looks to achieve its ends by using an object that has come into contact with the person or thing that a person is trying to influence.

contour rivalry   Technique in which one set of lines creates two different images, as perceived by the viewer.

controversia   In Roman rhetoric, an argument for or against a particular legal case.

copal   A resin obtained from certain tropical trees.

corbel vaulting   A method for building rough arches or domes; for a dome stones are laid in circles of successively smaller diameter until the stones meet at the apex and can lean against one another for support.

cordage Twisted fibers that form thread, string, or yarn.

cordillera Parallel chains of mountains.

core forming Forming of glass by placing vegetal matter or animal dung mixed with clay and sand at the end of a wooden handle and either dipping it into molten glass or drizzling molten glass onto it, after which the core is rolled on flat stone or metal to even and smooth the surface.

core tools Tools that are shaped by striking off flakes from the central portion of a large pebble or cobble.

core–periphery model Economic and political relationship between well-developed centers and less-advanced ones that are in contact with them.

Corinthian One of the three orders, or styles, of Greek architecture, distinguished by long, slim columns and elaborate and detailed carvings on the capital.

cornice A molding at the corner between the ceiling and the top of a wall.

corroboree Australian Aboriginal festivity with singing and dancing, usually at night, to celebrate important occasions.

corvée Unpaid labor exacted in place of taxes by a governmental authority, usually for public works.

cosmogony The study of the origin of the cosmos or universe.

cosmology A system of beliefs used to describe the origin of the universe.

cosmopolitan At home with many different cultures of the world; having a worldwide scope or composed of influences or peoples from many parts of the world.

coulter A blade placed in front of the plowshare in order to cut a vertical slice through the soil.

course A horizontal layer of brick or stone; courses are laid on top of one another in building walls.

courtesan A prostitute who associates with socially elite people.

cowrie shells The shells of a sea mollusk from the family Cypraeidae, having shiny, colorful shells that are still used as money in parts of the South Pacific.

cranial deformation The practice of using boards, mats, or vices to shape the cranium or skull of an infant before the bone has fused together and hardened.

crannog Found in prehistoric Ireland and Scotland, a fortified island in inland waters or marshes built to protect a settlement.

crucible A heat-resistant container in which ores or metals are melted or heated.

cruciform Shaped like a cross.

cubicula Bedrooms opening from the atrium of a Roman house.

cubit A unit of length that is equal to the distance between a person's elbow and his outstretched middle finger.

cuirass Body armor that covers the neck and chest.

cult statue A statue of a god, believed to contain the god's essence and housed in a temple or sacred site to be used as the focus of worship and ritual actions.

cultic calendar The schedule of interaction between a community and its deity.

cultigen A cultivated or domestic organism which has diverged enough from its closest wild relatives to be classified as a species, subspecies, or major variety.

cuneiform A form of writing invented in Mesopotamia around 3400 B.C.E. that used a reed pen called a stylus to make triangular marks on clay tablets.

cupellation A process used to purify silver by heating it to remove lead and other impurities.

curia A building where the Roman Senate met.

cursive A form of writing Chinese characters in which brushstrokes for one character flow into the brushstrokes for the next character.

curule aedile In ancient Rome, patrician officials in charge of various of Rome's public works and functions, among them, streets, traffic, water supply, and markets and the organization of religious festivals and cult observances and also for public games.

cyfarwyddiaid Professional bards of ancient Wales.

cylinder seal A small object made of stone or other hard material in which a scene or symbol is carved away from the surrounding material; the seal is rolled across wet clay or papyrus to leave a permanent impression.

dactyl A poetic foot that has one long syllable followed by two short ones.

dais A raised platform that may be used for a table.

damask Thick, heavy cloth with a pattern woven into it; the weave is named after the city of Damascus, where silks were woven in this pattern after the first century C.E.

daub Mud or clay mixed with water as a kind of plaster.

daughter language Descendent languages from a protolanguage, or "original language."

dead reckoning A method for estimating a ship's position through its speed, the distance that it has covered, and the direction of its travel.

deben Egyptian unit of weight for measuring metals, mostly copper, the equivalent to about 3.5 ounces.

debt bondage A condition in which one who owes another money or goods is forced to work until the obligation is paid off.

decimal A system of representing numbers by assigning values to different places, such as 10s, 100s, 1,000s, and so on in the base-10 system.

declamatio In Roman rhetoric, practice speeches given to fellow students.

declension An inflection of a noun or an adjective—a change in its form to indicate a change in its grammatical function.

decumanus An east-to-west road that formed part of the central axis of a Roman city, crossing the *cardo* (a road running north to south) at the city's center.

deferent A hypothetical circle along which moves the epicycle, a theoretical orbit of the earth, sun, moon, and planets.

Delphi The most sacred and famous oracle of ancient Greece, dedicated to Apollo, god of prophecy.

deluge A flood; often used to refer to the Flood mentioned in the Bible in the story of Noah and his ark.

demagogue A leader who rises to power through playing on people's prejudices or one who champions the cause of the people.

deme Basic geographic unit of Athens, equivalent to a neighborhood or ward.

democracy A political system in which governing power rests broadly on the population generally.

demography The study of a population's characteristics, such as birth and death rates, density, growth, distribution, and breeding patterns.

demos The citizen body of Athens.

demotic A simplified form of Egyptian hieroglyphic writing.

denarius (pl. denarii) A Roman silver coin.

denomination A specific class of coin with a specific value.

derrick A tall platform over an underground well that is used to raise and lower drills and containers.

desertification Process that causes fertile land to become desert.

deshret "Red land" in the Egyptian language, referring to desert, in contrast to *kemet* (cultivatable land), or "black land."

desiccation The process of drying something out thoroughly.

determinative A hieroglyph placed after the phonetic spelling of an ancient Egyptian word relating to the meaning of that word, like an ear placed after the verb meaning "to hear."

deterministic A theory or belief that any event or set of events is the inevitable consequence of what precedes and causes it and cannot be avoided.

devaraja The Hindu concept of the divinity of secular rulers.

devolution of property The transfer of land from one generation to the next.

dharma In Hindu and Buddhist philosophy, divine law as associated with the moral duty of individuals.

dhoti A wrapped Indian garment resembling loose, short trousers.

dhow A sailing vessel with triangular sails that was heavily used beginning in ancient times in the Indian Ocean, especially for trade between Africans and Arabs.

di indigetes Ancient Rome's native gods.

di novensides In ancient Rome, "newcomer gods" imported from foreign cultures.

diadem A headband, like a crown, worn as an adornment by the royalty.

dialect A subgroup of a language usually (but not always) comprehensible to speakers of the parent language.

diaspora Dispersal of a people from its homeland.

diaulos A running event in ancient Greece covering roughly a quarter mile.

dictator In ancient Rome, a special kind of magistrate appointed by the Senate to act in times of emergency and who had almost unlimited power but whose term was limited, usually to about six months.

didactic poetry Poetry that teaches a lesson.

die An engraved metal device for stamping a design into a softer metal such as a coin.

dikai demosiai In Athens, public lawsuits in which prosecution could be initiated either by magistrates or by private individuals not directly connected to the case.

dioptra In ancient Greece, a sighting rod used in mapping and surveying.

diorite A hard, grayish stone that was commonly used in ancient Mesopotamia for freestanding obelisks and commemorative slabs. Diorite could be polished to a glossy sheen.

diphros A simple stool or low chair in ancient Greece, without arms or a back.

diploidion A piece of material left long in front and folded at the shoulders worn by the ancient Greeks.

distaff Any tool used to hold fibers for spinning; in the Roman period it was a stick of wood, bone, metal, or even ivory.

distributive economy An economy in which a central authority collects food and other goods, stores the collections, and then redistributes them according to the people's social positions or needs.

dithyramb An impassioned choric hymn and dance of ancient Greece, performed in honor of Dionysus.

divination A ritual observation of nature for signs that the will of the gods is favorable or unfavorable to a specific action, as a way to determine whether a contemplated action should be taken.

dolichos In ancient Greece, a race of about 2.5 to 3 miles.

dolmen A type of stone monument in which a horizontal stone slab lies atop a set of upright stones.

domestication A process by which plants and animals are altered by human selection, resulting in loss of the ability to survive in the wild.

domus An ancient Roman home, especially in the cities.

Doric One of the three orders, or styles, of Greek architecture, distinguished by thick, sturdy columns and plain capitals.

dowel A pin fitted with holes to hold two pieces in place together.

downcutting Stream erosion that deepens a valley.

down-the-line trade A pattern of exchange whereby goods are passed from one person (or group) to another.

dowry Payment of property accompanying a bride to her new house, available for the husband's use but repaid to the wife's family should the marriage dissolve.

drachm   Ancient Greek silver coin equal to the weight of a drachma, or approximately one-eighth ounce.

drachma   A weight of metal in ancient Greece; a drachma of silver represented a reasonable day's wage in fifth-century Athens.

draconian   Unusually harsh or severe

draft animal   An animal used to pull plows, wagons, or other heavy loads.

draft   The depth of a vessel's keel below the surface of the water.

dressing stone   Carving stone into a desired shape and smoothness.

Druid   An ancient Celtic priest or religious leader.

drystone   Stones fitted together, as in a wall, without mortar.

Duat   The netherworld in ancient Egyptian religion.

dux bellorum   A military governor of the Roman Empire.

dynasty   A succession of rulers from the same family.

earspool   Circular ear ornaments that are hollow at their centers and worn by being placed within a hole in the earlobe.

eaves   Roof edges that project beyond the walls of a building.

eccentric   Rotation around a point that is not the center of the cosmos.

ecliptic   The circle representing the apparent annual path of the sun.

edge species   A species of plant or animal that lives at the edge of an environment, where it can take advantage of two different environments.

effigy   An image or representation especially of a person.

efflorescence   The process of developing and unfolding.

egalitarian   Offering equal social and political rights, with no special privileges or status conferred by birth.

einkorn   A kind of wheat (*Triticum monococcum*).

ekklesia   The Assembly in Athens, responsible for all major state decisions and made up of all citizens who wished to attend.

ekphora   The funeral procession from the deceased's house to the gravesite.

El Niño   A recurrent warming of waters in the Pacific Ocean.

electrum   an alloy made by combining gold and silver.

elegiac couplet   A line of dactylic hexameter followed by one of dactylic pentameter and forming a complete thought.

elegy   A short poem generally concerned with the passion of a lover and employing the elegiac couplet.

elite   A group with higher status in a society that is differentiated by status, power, or wealth.

embedded economy   An economic system in ancient Celtic Europe in which the aristocracy laid claim to a portion of a farmer's produce or a craftsman's goods in exchange for providing the worker with protection.

embroidery   Threads added to cloth after it is woven, often in decorative patterns or colors.

emmer   A kind of wheat (*Triticum dicoccum*).

empire   Sometimes limited to government by a ruler known as an emperor but more generally rule over a wide area by a single political entity, such as a single nation ruling over many other nations.

empiricists   Doctors in ancient Greece who relied upon observation and experience only, not on theory.

emporion   The Greek word for a "market," also used to describe overseas settlements devoted to trade but lacking the status of formally established *apoikiai*.

en   An official who oversaw the administration of a Mesopotamian city-state and who sometimes became a king.

enceinte   The inner ring of fortifications enclosing a town.

endemic   Belonging to a particular region or people.

endogamous   Pertaining to the custom of marrying only within a tribe or clan.

ensi   A governor who took over from an *en* the secular duties of running a Mesopotamian city-state; the office may have evolved into a kingship.

entablature   The horizontal row of stone blocks under the roof of a building between the tops of the columns that support the building, often carved with friezes.

ephebeia   A compulsory program of public education during the years of adolescence, designed to train young male citizens of the Greek democracy, especially in military arts.

ephors   Board of overseers, five in number, who exercised control over the kings and Assembly in Sparta.

epic   A long narrative poem that tells the story of the deeds of a single hero or a band of heroes and that can involve intervention by and conflict with the gods.

epicyclic   Rotation around a point that is itself rotating around a different center.

epigram   A short poem expressing a single thought or observation.

epistemology   Theory about knowledge.

epode   The third part of a three-part lyric ode.

equinox   One of the two days in the year when the sun crosses the celestial equator. On these days, there are approximately equal amounts of sunlight and darkness.

equites   The equestrian, or knightly class, of ancient Rome.

eschatology   The usual modern scholarly designation for such religious themes as the fate of the human being after death, the end of the world, warfare between the powers of good and evil, the resurrection and judgment of the dead, the end of the world and related ideas.

escupil   Spun cotton body armor used in ancient Mesoamerica.

eskers   Long, narrow ridges of sand and coarse gravel deposited by glacial meltwaters.

estuarine   Relating to an estuary, the section of a river that meets the sea and where freshwater mixes with saltwater.

Etesian winds   The dry, relatively cool winds that regularly blow from north to south in the Mediterranean during the summer months.

ethnocentrism   The concept that one's group, however defined, is superior to all other groups.

ethnography   The study and systematic recording of human cultures.

ethnologist   Someone who studies cultural and biological relationships among large groups of people.

etymology   The structural and semantic history of words.

eunomia   "Good laws," the Spartans' favorite phrase to describe their system of government.

eunuch   A castrated man typically employed in a palace, often taking charge of a harem.

eustasy   The phenomenon of rising and falling sea levels.

excarnation   The practice of allowing a body to decay before burial.

execration text   List of foreign kings and peoples written on Egyptian pottery and statuettes of prisoners of war.

exomis   A short, sleeveless tunic with the right side open worn by the ancient Greeks.

exorcist   A "magician" skilled in warding off disease and the other effects of evil demons.

faience   Earthenware decorated with glazes.

fauces   The hall leading into a Roman house.

felt   Cloth made from wool treated with water, heat, and an alkaline.

fenestration   Cutting out sections of a vessel wall in decorative patterns.

feng shui   An ancient Chinese worldview that sought harmony and balance between the opposing forces of nature and between the physical environment and humans; its principles were applied to the siting, design, and construction of buildings.

feria (pl. *feriae*)   The Latin word for "festival."

fetch   The distance wind travels over water unimpeded.

fetiale   In ancient Rome, a member of a priestly order whose job was to ensure that war was declared properly.

feudal system   A social and economic system in which land is held on condition of loyalty to a higher authority, as in nobles holding land on the condition of their loyalty to their king.

fibula   A clasp or brooch used to fasten clothing in the ancient world.

fief   An estate ruled by a lesser lord within a greater feudal kingdom.

filial piety   In Confucian philosophy, the unquestioning devotion to and respect for one's parents.

filid   Ancient Irish bards.

fillet   A ribbon used for binding the hair or as a headband.

finial   An ornamental projection from the top of a wall or column or at the peak or corner of a roof.

fired brick   Clay bricks that have been hardened in fires or ovens, making them much more water resistant than clay bricks dried in sunshine.

firing   The practice of cooking clay vessels in a fire in order to make them harder.

fishtail point   A ancient projectile point that takes the form of a fish.

fjord   An inlet to the sea with high cliff walls, created by the retreat of a glacier.

flagon   A type of drinking vessel with a handle and spout and typically a lid.

flake tools   Tools that are made from the flattish pieces that are knocked off in the formation of core tools.

flamen   In ancient Rome, a member of a class of priests who ensured that proper observances and sacrifices were made to the gods.

flax   A plant material that is the basis for linen.

fletching   The feathers on an arrow.

fluting   Concave, semicircular grooves carved into an architectural column.

fodder crops   Plants grown specifically for animal consumption.

foot   A division of a line of verse that contains a specific number of long and short syllables.

forging   Shaping metal by hammering, often when heated to white hot or red hot.

forum   An open plaza at the center of a Roman town, used for commercial, legal, political, and religious activity.

frame   A timber oriented perpendicular to a ship's keel, to which a ship's hull planking was fastened.

fresco   Decorative wall painting on plaster with water-based paint applied when the plaster is wet, allowing the color to permeate the plaster and become permanent.

frieze   A horizontal band of carved stone, typically depicting a progression of events and procession of figures.

frontality   The convention of always having a statue of a human facing to the front.

fundamental note   The lowest or most dominant note that an instrument is designed to play.

funerary cult   Provisions a person makes before death to provide everything the deceased would need in the afterlife, such as food offerings.

funerary priests   Religious officials who oversaw burial rituals and other offerings and sacrifices in honor of the deceased.

futhark   Runic script of the ancient Germans.

gables   Triangular sections fastened to the top of end walls in houses with double-pitched roofs.

game drives   Hunting practices that involved preparing and setting nets for migratory fish and birds.

gangue   The surrounding rock in a metal ore.

garum   A condiment popular in the Roman world and produced mostly in Spain, made by allowing salted fish intestines to ferment in the sun for days or weeks.

genos   A Greek family or clan that shared a common ancestor and family name.

geocentric   Having the earth at the center of the universe, orbited by the sun, moon, planets, and stars.

geoglyph   Large-scale earth drawing created using simple geometric principles and surveying techniques.

gerontocracy A form of social organization in which the oldest men and women in a society are expected to guide and lead the community because of their wisdom.

gerousia A council of elders in Sparta, made up of 28 prominent citizens over the age of 60.

ghee Clarified butter, created by boiling unsalted butter and drawing off excess water; used as lamp fuel in ancient India.

glacial maximum The time of maximum extent of ice sheets during an ice age.

glacier A river of ice flowing slowly downhill.

gladiator A slave who fought as a professional soldier in combats staged for entertainment.

glaze A glasslike coating that seals the surface of a ceramic object and decorates it.

glyph A symbol, such as a hieroglyph, carved into stone.

gnomon "Indicator," the vertical bar that casts the shadow of the sun on the face of a sundial.

gorget An ornamental collar or throat covering.

gourd Dried and hollowed out shell of a fruit from the squash or pumpkin family that is converted into a vessel.

grafting The practice of attaching the stalk of one plant to the root stock of another to provide strong roots to a plant that would naturally have weak roots.

grammaticus In ancient Rome, a public secondary-school teacher.

grammatistes A teacher of reading, writing, arithmetic, and poetry in ancient Greece.

granary A storehouse for harvested crops.

granulation A method of decorating metal with patterns made up of small balls of the same metal, usually gold.

gravitas A dignified bearing, one of the Roman virtues.

greave Armor that protects the legs below the knees.

griot In ancient Africa, an oral historian who recounted cultural tradition through song.

groin vault A ceiling formed by the intersection of two barrel vaults, which are in turn supported by piers that are either freestanding or set into a wall.

groma A device that allowed Roman builders to ensure that vertical elements, such as columns and piers, were set at right angles to the horizontal.

grotto A cave enclosing a body of water.

guano Bat dung; used as fertilizer.

gur In the ancient Near East, a measure of the value of an item that was approximately equal to 43 gallons of barley.

guru A teacher in the Hindu tradition, seen as a god in human form and as the sole source of knowledge for his students.

gurukula A school in the Hindu tradition.

gymnasium An area devoted to intellectual and athletic pursuits.

gymnastics In ancient Greece, any athletic training.

gynaikeion Living quarters for women in ancient Greek homes.

haft The handle of a knife, an ax, or another weapon or tool.

halberd A battle-ax mounted on a long handle.

handfasting Engagement to marry.

hangul The system instituted in 1446 to write Korean phonetically; originally used along with Chinese characters but now generally used exclusively.

haniwa Small ceramic figures, usually depicting people, made by the ancient Japanese to surround tombs, protecting the tombs from evil spirits.

harmika A finial, or ornamental projection from the top of a wall or column, found in the architecture of India.

harpy eagle A large bird of prey native to Central and South America.

haruspex (pl. haruspices) Literally, "men who look at guts": Roman diviners who read the will of the gods by examining the entrails of sacrificed animals.

heddle A rod on a loom used to guide threads.

heliacal rise The first appearance of a star near the eastern horizon just preceding sunrise, following a period of nighttime invisibility due to proximity to the sun.

heliocentric Having the sun at the center of the solar system, orbited by Earth and other planets.

Hellenization The process of "becoming Greek."

helot In ancient Greece, a slave of the Spartans.

hemp A tall herb with tough fibers used to make durable cloth and ropes.

hen In ancient Egypt, the measure of a volume equal to half a quart or less, with a value that could vary according to the substance or liquid to be measured; generally regarded as equal in value to one deben.

henotheism The worship of a single most important deity without denying the existence of others.

hep Egyptian term for law, abstract moral order, normative custom, and every kind of rule, either natural or juridical, general or specific, public or private, literary or oral.

herm A statuette of the god Hermes, usually placed at house gates or as a marker on roads.

hero In ancient Greece, a great mythical or legendary human being who was usually considered the offspring of a god and a mortal and whose spirit was worshipped much like a god.

hestia A Greek cooking stove.

hetairai (or hetaerae) In ancient Greece, courtesans, often valued for wit and education as well as beauty; these women occupied a social space between that of a prostitute and a mistress.

hexameter A poetic meter that has six feet per line.

hierarchical society A society characterized by multiple levels of authority and status.

hieratic Sacred; associated with priests; also a cursive form of Egyptian hieroglyphs used for all domestic texts and records.

hieroglyph The Greek word for "sacred carving," describing the Egyptian writing system, which consisted of pictorial signs, used phonetically and pictorially.

himation   A rectangular outer mantle draped in various ways and worn by the ancient Greeks.

Hippocratic bench   A bench with moveable posts and straps, used for reducing dislocations and for traction.

Hippocratic oath   A statement of basic principles followed by students and physicians at the ancient school of medicine on the island of Cos and which survives to this day as a foundation of modern medical ethics.

historical linguistics   The study of the derivation, changes, and relationships of languages over time.

ho boulomenos   A Greek term literally meaning, "the one who wishes," a definition of who could initiate a public lawsuit.

hogging trusses   On a ship, thick ropes that could be tightened to keep the bow and stern from sagging.

homoioi   Literally "equals," a term applied to the citizen body in ancient Sparta.

honestiores and *humiliores*   Two broad classes into which Roman citizens were divided during the empire. The *honestiores* were aristocrats, soldiers, and public office-holders; they suffered lighter punishments than *humiliores*, who made up the rest of the population.

hoplite   A heavily armed Greek foot soldier, protected by a metal helmet, breastplate, and large round shield.

hoplitodromos   A race in ancient Greece that the athletes ran while wearing armor.

hoplomachus   Gladiator armed with Greek heavy-infantry weapons.

horos (pl. *horoi*)   Stones used to mark boundaries for various types of spaces: temple precincts, public spaces, and the edges of poleis, or city-states.

hubris   In ancient Greece, an outrage or a deliberate affront to the dignity of another, particularly a citizen.

humor   One of the elemental fluids of the body in Hippocratic, Galenic, and medieval medicine; the four canonical humors after Galen were blood, black bile, yellow bile, and phlegm.

hunter-gatherers   People who survive by hunting wild animals and gathering wild plants, without agriculture.

hybris   Any act that went beyond the established moral codes or surpassed human capacities, usually followed by *nemesis*, or divine punishment.

hydraulics   The study of the mechanics of fluids, especially with respect to engineering.

hydraulis   A water-powered pipe organ developed in ancient Greece; the world's first keyboard instrument, it used bellows or a hydraulic pump to force air through pipes.

hydria   A vessel to hold water mixed with concentrated wine.

hydrostatics   The branch of mechanics dealing with the equilibrium of weights in water.

hypaspists   Members of an elite infantry guard in the army of Alexander the Great.

hypocaust   The space underneath the floor of a building from which heat rose to warm the floors above it.

hypostyle hall   A hall with a flat ceiling supported by columns.

iamb   A poetic foot that has one short syllable followed by a long.

ibw   Tent in which bodies underwent ritual purification before embalming in ancient Egypt.

ice core   a sample of the various layers in large ice sheets taken by drilling a long, hollow tube down into the ice sheet and used for research purposes, such as the study of past climate change or ecological conditions.

iconography   Symbolic representation, especially the conventional meanings attached to an image or images.

ideogram   A written character that represents an object, image, or idea.

ideographic   In a writing system, having symbols that denote ideas rather than words.

idiophone   An instrument producing a specific, unusual, often atonal sound.

idolatry   The worship of images or statues of gods instead of the gods themselves.

igneous rock   A type of rock that has been subjected to extremely hot temperatures, to the point of becoming molten, and then cooled to a hardened form.

imagines   Images of the Roman dead carried by the living in the form of masks during a funeral procession.

Imperial Cult   During the Roman Empire, the belief that the emperor was divine, usually declared after his death.

imperium   The power of military and civilian command belonging to certain magistrates and promagistrates such as consuls and proconsuls.

impiety   The crime of violating religious law in a way that was viewed as injurious to the nation.

impluvium   The shallow pool in the floor of an atrium that collected rainwater directed through an opening in the roof of a Roman house.

incertum   An early technique of Roman masonry in which blocks of tufa were inserted randomly into drying concrete blocks.

incised or raised relief   Symbols, images, or writing cut or hammered into metal surfaces to distinguish them from the plane surface.

infinitesimal   A number smaller in absolute value than any positive real number.

inflected language   A language in which words take different forms to reflect grammatical information such as gender, tense, and singular and plural.

inflection   Change in the form of a verb, noun, or adjective (for example, the adding of *s* in English to form a plural).

ingot   A metal casting that is shaped for easy working or for recasting, typically oblong in shape.

initiation   Any ritual, ceremony, or cultural practice that marks the transition from childhood to adulthood.

inscription   Writing carved into a solid substance such as stone or bronze.

insula   A Roman apartment building, usually multistoried.

interaction sphere   In prehistoric cultures, groups that had social interaction and exchanged material goods.

intercalation   The addition of an extra day in the month, or an extra month in the year, to ensure that the months remain synchronized with the seasons.

interstadial   A short period of relatively warmer climate within an ice age.

inundation   Predictable annual flooding events that renew the soil and sustain ecosystems; often used to refer to the flooding of the Nile.

Ionic   One of the three orders, or styles, of Greek architecture, distinguished by slender columns and capitals ornamented with spiral scrollwork called volutes.

isegoria   The principle in Athenian democracy under which all citizens had an equal right to speak in the Assembly and other public gatherings.

isolate   An ancient language that has no similarities with other languages and thus may have developed independently.

isonomia   "Equality under the law," the basic idea of Athenian democracy.

isostasy   The rebounding of the earth's mantle after it has been depressed.

ius privatum   Private law that was concerned with the legal dealings between individual Roman citizens or groups of citizens, as well as between citizens and noncitizens.

ius publicum   Public law that regulated the relationship between the Roman state and its citizens.

jamb   One of two uprights in a door frame that together supports a crosspiece, or lintel, and that transfers the weight of the wall above the door to the ground.

jaundice   A yellowish discoloration of the skin symptomatic of diseases affecting the processing of bile.

javelin   A lightweight spear designed to be thrown.

joinery   Techniques or processes used to join pieces of wood, usually referring to ways of cutting the wood so that nails or screws are not required.

ju   A Chinese shirt with a stiff, upright collar.

Julian calendar   A solar calendar purportedly created by the Greek astronomer Sosigenes of Alexandria and instituted by Julius Caesar in 45 BCE.

k'uhul ajaw   Mayan term for divine king.

kalasiris or *calasiris*   A thin linen tunic.

karma   In Indian spirituality, the positive or negative energy created by people during their lifetimes, determining the states they will take in future lives.

kataginu   A Japanese vest with broad, stiff shoulders.

keel   A large timber running longitudinally at the bottom of a ship from which the hull is built up and that provides stabilization.

keep   A fortress within a fortress.

kemet   "Black land" in the Egyptian language, referring to land that could be cultivated, in contrast to *deshret* (desert), or "red land."

khapusa   A heavy, knee-high boot that was worn in northern India.

kinship   Ties (either biological or cultural) that determine human groups.

kitchen middens   Accumulations of food and other debris of human occupation, such as discarded tools and ashes from hearths.

kithara   An ancient stringed instrument used by the Greeks and Romans, similar to the modern guitar.

kitharistēs   A music teacher in ancient Greece, who taught singing and playing the lyre, a stringed instrument like a harp.

klinē   A bed or couch in ancient Greece, consisting of a wooden frame across which a webbing of leather or rope would be woven to support the occupant.

klismos   A chair in ancient Greece, with curved legs, no armrests, and a curved, reclined back.

knight   A member of the second-highest Roman social class, rated by the value of property according to the census. Knights were required to serve in the cavalry since they could afford to buy their own horse and equipment.

knot   A measurement of speed at sea equal to 6,076 feet per hour.

kohl   An eye cosmetic often composed of ground galena (a black mineral), sulfur, frankincense, and powdered antimony, which contains lead.

koine   The "common" dialect based on Attic that developed starting in the third century B.C.E. and became the basis for Byzantine and Modern Greek.

kore (pl. *korai*)   Representations of standing female nudes from the Archaic Period of Greek art.

kouros (pl. *kouroi*)   A figure of a standing male nude from the archaic period of Greek art.

krypteia   An annual secret campaign of assassination conducted by the Spartans in ancient Greece against their slaves, the helots.

ku   Loose Chinese trousers.

kudurrus   A boundary stone, which carried emblems and symbols of the gods.

kurios   The legal lord of a Greek household, with power over and responsibility for all its members.

lacquer   A coating used to made an object glossy; in China, lacquer at first came from the resin of the lacquer tree, *Rhus verniciflua*.

lamassus   Large-scale architectural sculptures of human-headed winged bulls that abutted the entrance walls of Assyrian palaces.

lamellae   Thin iron plates that were used in the construction of armor.

lapis lazuli   Semiprecious blue stone used in creating jewelry and other objects.

latifundium   Originally, in ancient Rome, a large estate relying largely on slave labor.

latitudinal   Having to do with latitude, the geographic distance of any point on the earth north or south of the equator.

laudatio   The Roman ceremony of displaying and eulogizing a dead person before cremation or burial.

lay   Song of the Anglo-Saxon bard.

lead line   A rope to which was tied a lead or stone weight and that was used to measure water depth; often the weight had a depression filled with tallow so that a sample of the sea bottom could be brought to the surface.

lector priest   A ritual specialist who carried out ceremonies according to the secret books in ancient Egypt.

lee shore   A shore toward which the wind blows, constituting a danger to a ship in a storm.

legion   The largest independent formation in the Roman army, consisting of heavy infantry, light infantry, and cavalry and varying between 4,200 and 6,000 men.

legionary sword   A short sword, used in ancient Rome, with a blade about 30 inches long with two parallel cutting edges and a long, sharp point.

legionnaires   Members of a legion, or the basic unit of the Roman army.

legume   A plant related to the pea family, notable for its protein content.

léine   A long linen tunic worn in Ireland.

leishmaniasis   A protozoan skin disorder carried by female sand flies.

lekythos (pl. *lekythoi*)   A Greek vessel used to store olive oil for the anointing of the dead in preparation for burial or as a burial offering

leprosy   Chronic progressive bacterial infection affecting the skin and nerves, acquired by close personal contact over a long period, often among members of the same family.

levee   An embankment or barrier meant to prevent flooding.

lex frumentaria   In ancient Rome, a grain law, which provided grain to each citizen at a subsidized price.

lex talionis   A legal concept of punishment based on equal and direct retribution, often popularly expressed as "an eye for an eye."

lexicology   A branch of linguistics concerned with the study of words and their application.

libation   The act of pouring liquid as a sacrificial offering, typically to the gods but also to one's ancestors.

lignified   Hardened; used in reference to the hardening of the outer husk of corn.

limes   A border defensive system of the ancient Romans.

limestone   Stone formed from sediments laid down over eons; usually easier to carve than granite.

limitanei   Light troops of the late Roman Empire who guarded the borders and frontiers to hold off invaders until heavier troops could arrive.

lineage burials   Burials in grounds set aside for a single family lineage.

lineage   Family ancestry traced through a line of parenthood, either fathers or mothers but not both.

linen   A flexible, durable, and usually soft cloth made from flax.

lintel   A beam that rests on the uprights, or jambs, of a doorway and that transfers the weight of the wall above the door to the uprights and from them to the ground.

lithic   Of, relating to, or being a stone tool.

litter   A chair or similar vehicle suspended from poles carried by either humans or animals to transport one or more riders.

litterator   In ancient Rome, a teacher of basic literacy and numbers.

littoral   A region near a shore, especially of the sea.

liturgy   An institution whereby private citizens in ancient Athens were obliged to pay for public works from their own resources.

loan word   A word that one culture borrows from another, either as is or with modifications, suggesting contact between the two cultures.

lodestone   A piece of magnetite, having magnetic properties.

loess   Chalky clay or silt created by layers of wind-blown dust over a long period of time.

logic   A system or principles of reasoning.

logographic   In a writing system, having symbols that denote a whole word or a morpheme, a minimal language unit.

logophonetic   In a writing system, having symbols that denote the actual sounds of speech.

loincloth   A strip of cloth wound about the waist and between the legs.

long barrows   Elongated burial mounds.

lost-wax casting   A method of creating metal objects by use of a wax cast set within a clay mold; the wax is heated and runs out of the mold to be replaced by molten metal.

ludus (pl. *ludi*)   A show or performance; from the Latin for "play, game."

lugal   Literally, "great man"; in ancient Sumer, a leading citizen chosen to take charge in times of crisis.

lunar calendar   A calendar that is based on the cycles of the moon, defining one month as the time it takes the moon to complete one revolution around the earth.

lunation   The interval from new moon to new moon.

lungi   An Indian skirt that resembles a loincloth.

lunisolar calendar   A calendar that combines aspects of lunar and solar calendars, basing units of time on the earth's movements relative to both the sun and the moon.

lur   Cast bronze horns from northern Europe, made in distinctive pairs and thought to have been used for ceremonial purposes.

lustratio   A purification ceremony performed for a Roman male infant at the age of eight days.

lute   A stringed instrument with a long neck, rounded body, and flat front.

lyra   A small type of Greek lyre, often with a sound box made out of a tortoiseshell.

lyre   A stringed instrument like a U-shaped harp with strings fixed to a crossbar at the top of the U.

lyric poetry   Short, very personal poetry that deals with the poet's feelings or state of mind.

maat   In ancient Egyptian cosmology, cosmic harmony (personified as a goddess) as established by the creator god at the beginning of time, including truth, justice, moral ethics, and social and political order.

mace   A ceremonial staff.

madder   A plant used to make red dye.

magic lantern   A device used to illuminate and project images and silhouettes onto a screen.

maguey   A plant from the cactus family indigenous to Mexico, used for a variety of purposes, particularly for its fibers to create cloth.

mail shirt   A body covering composed of interlaced rings or chain work and normally extending below the waist.

major lunar standstill(s)   The moon's farthest rising and setting points north and south on the horizon over an 18.6-year cycle.

malakaras   Garland makers in ancient India.

malaria   Epidemic infection caused by a parasite transmitted through the bite of a mosquito and causing recurring chills and fever.

mammoth   Any large, elephantlike mammal of the extinct genus *Mammuthus*.

mangroves   Woody trees that live in coastal habitats.

maniple   The basic unit of the Roman army, consisting of either 120 or 60 men.

mantle   A large, rectangular cloth arranged around the neck and over the shoulders.

mantra   A sacred word or phrase that a person chants over and over to achieve spiritual effects.

manumit   To free a slave.

manus   The power that a husband held over his wife in ancient Rome.

manuscript   Writing on a sheet of papyrus or vellum.

mastaba   Underground tomb carved down into rock and topped aboveground with a square masonry platform.

material culture   The material remains (artifacts, dwellings, and other constructions) of past societies.

matriarchal society   A society in which women hold dominant positions or in which inheritance follows the maternal rather than the paternal line.

matrilineal   Descriptive of a culture in which lines of descent are traced through the mother and her ancestors rather than through the father.

matron   A woman in the most legitimate and respected form of Roman marriage.

mattocks   Digging tools or picks.

maul   A heavy stone hammer used to break up rock.

mead   An alcoholic beverage made by fermenting honey and water.

meander   An ornamental pattern resembling a labyrinth.

mechane   In ancient Greece, a cranelike device used to lift a performer above the ground.

mechanics   The expertise of making and designing machines.

medicine wheel   Large patterns of linear stone alignments, many of which have the appearance of a spoked wheel.

medium of exchange   Any class of objects used by people as if it were money.

megalith   Literally "great stone," referring to the use of large stones in the construction of Neolithic tombs and other features (for example, geometric figures, such as circles, as well as lines or avenues for which the massive stones served as markers), especially in central and western Europe.

menhir   A single tall megalith, often posited as part of a sightline for astronomical observation.

meridian   A great circle on the surface of a sphere that passes through both poles.

meter   The rhythmic pattern of a poem.

metics   Resident "aliens," or foreigners, with no rights of citizenship in a Greek city-state; this group was made up largely of immigrants and former slaves and was concentrated largely in Athens.

Metonic cycle   A lunar calendar devised by the Greek astronomer Meton, using 19-year cycles totaling 235 months.

metope   A pictorial panel, part of the frieze on the entablature of a building.

metrological   A system of counting that separates the unit of measurement from the thing being counted.

metropolis   A large and densely populated urban area.

miasmas   Impurities floating in the air and resulting from any kind of pollution.

microliths   Small retouched blades or blade segments usually made of flints and commonly used in composite tools or weapons such as knives, arrows and harpoons.

microtonal scale   A musical scale that contains more notes within an octave than the traditional 12 notes of the Western scale.

middens   Heaps of refuse, especially kitchen waste.

midrib   A thickening down the middle of a dagger for added strength.

midwife   A woman who helps other women give birth.

millet   A small-seeded grass that is used for food.

milpa   A form of agriculture in which a clearing is cropped for one or more seasons, then abandoned.

mime   In ancient Rome, a popular form of theater that featured skits, songs, dances, magic acts, and acrobatics while emphasizing sexual jokes and parodies.

mina   A weight of metal in ancient Greece, equivalent to 100 drachmas.

miter joint   The ends of two pieces of wood cut at complementary angles and fitted together to create a 90-degree angle.

mode   A set pattern of notes played over an octave using the white keys of a keyboard.

model A small-scale reproduction of an object that could magically be animated.

moiety One of two units into which a tribe or community is divided on the basis of unilineal descent.

mold making Producing glass objects by pouring molten glass into a hollow form, in order to make a certain shape or decoration.

molding A decorative recessed or relieved surface on an edge; a decorative strip used for ornamentation or finishing.

monarchy A political system under which a single king or queen holds supreme power, which is passed through the family line by hereditary descent.

monotheism The belief in the existence of only a single divinity.

monsoon A wind pattern that follows the same course every year, bringing predictable weather, such as rain, with it; also the intense rainfall or the season o rainfall associated with this wind.

monstra "Prodigies," or a natural but strange occurrences, such as the birth of a calf with two heads, regarded by Romans as a warning from the gods.

moraine An accumulation of stones and debris carried and deposited by glaciers.

morpheme A collection of speech sounds considered to be the smallest language unit.

mortar A substance used as an adhesive to fasten courses of bricks or stones together or as a plaster to protect the surface of a wall.

mortarium A heavy Roman bowl with sharp stone fragments embedded in its interior surface, used to grind food.

mortise and tenon A method for joining two planks of wood by means of a series of projecting tongues cut into the edge of one piece and slots cut into in the other.

mos maiorum A sense of tradition, one of the Roman virtues.

mosaic A design made with small pieces of colored glass or tile.

mud brick Bricks made from mud and straw and then dried in the sun.

mummification The Egyptian process of preserving the body by the removal of internal organs, drying out the corpse, and protecting it with linen wrappings.

mummy portrait Painting on a wooden panel made to cover the face of an Egyptian mummy, usually done in encaustic (wax) technique.

mundus A hole in the ground near the center of a Roman city that was usually covered but when uncovered allowed earth spirits to communicate with the city.

munus Gladiator show; from the Latin for "duty."

murex An aquatic snail that lived in the Mediterranean near Lebanon and was used as a source of purple dye.

murus gallicus "Gallic wall," a type of rampart found at many defended sites in ancient Gaul, consisting of timbers, filled with earth and stone, backed by stone walling, and often fronted by a ditch.

music In ancient Greece, any of the arts associated with the Muses: music, poetry, dancing, and drama.

musk A perfume originating from a sac inside the male musk deer.

nadir The point on the celestial sphere directly below the place on which the observer stands and opposite the zenith.

natron A mineral form of hydrated sodium salts found in dried lake beds.

necromancy Conjuring of the spirits of the dead in order to communicate with them.

necrophilia Sexual attraction or contact with a dead body.

necropolis A cemetery, especially one of large size and usually of an ancient city.

nexum Debt bondage.

niche A setback or indented enclosure; a small concavity.

Nilometer A series of steps that were used to mark the height of the Nile inundation as well as regular water levels

nirvana In Hinduism, the union of the human spirit with Brahma (the god of creation) and in Buddhism the state of blessedness in which the human spirit is released from the cycle of reincarnation.

nomad A member of a people who move seasonally from place to place to search for food and water or pasture for their livestock.

nomadic pastoralism A form of pastoralism in which all or most of the people move with their herds year-round to find pasture, living in temporary encampments and often traveling great distances.

nomarch The ruler of a nome, a political and geographical division of territory in ancient Egypt similar to a state in the United States.

nome A Greek term for an ancient Egyptian province, of which there were 42.

nomoi In Greek, "laws; the word could denote formally enacted laws as well as to established customs ("unwritten laws").

noncultic Nonreligious.

nopal A type of cactus eaten cooked or raw by ancient Mesoamericans.

numerology The study of the occult, or mystical, influence of numbers on everyday life.

numina A term early Romans used to refer to their gods, usually translated as "presence" or "power."

numismatics The study of coins and coinage.

nun The waters of primordial chaos in Egyptian cosmology.

nundina A market day in Rome.

obelisk A tall, tapered, four-sided monument with a pyramid at the top.

oblate A category of dependent person attached to the temples of the gods.

obol A weight of metal in ancient Greece, equivalent to one-sixth of a drachma.

obsidian A volcanic glass that was used in making tools.

obverse The "heads" side of a coin; this side of a coin often, but not always, contains a portrait bust.

ocarina A wind instrument, often oval in shape, with finger holes and a projecting mouthpiece.

ocher A powdery form of iron-rich earth or clay widely used as a pigment.

octant A navigational device used for measuring angles to a celestial body as a way to calculate position, with a calibration of 45 degrees.

odeion A Greek roofed hall used for musical performances

oenology The science of making wine.

offering formula A text inscribed on some funerary goods to magically provide sustenance for the deceased in the afterlife.

offering table A place where Egyptian priests or family members could place provisions for the deceased, often in the shape of a cone-shaped loaf of bread on a table.

oikistes **(pl.** *oikistai***)** The founder of a Greek *apoikia*, responsible for establishing the city walls and distributing land among its settlers.

oikonomia A Greek word translating roughly to "household regulation," from which the English word *economy* derives.

oikos **(pl.** *oikoi***)** In Greece and the ancient Near East, a great household, typically a temple, palace, or large estate, that controlled the labor, production, and consumption of its many members, most of whom were not related; a basic economic unit.

oligarchy A form of government in which rule resides jointly in the hands of a few people, usually the wealthiest and most powerful.

olla **(or** *aula***)** A deep, round-bottomed Roman vessel used for boiling stews or porridge.

omen Any event in nature that provides insight into the future.

onomastica Catalogues of things arranged under their kinds, not alphabetically.

opening of the mouth ceremony Funerary ritual that enabled the deceased to breathe, eat, and talk in the afterlife.

oppidum **(pl.** *oppida***)** A type of fortified town that was developed before the Roman Iron Age in western Europe and was a center of residential, administrative, commercial, and industrial activities

oracle bones Bones of animals, typically shoulder blades (usually of oxen), and also turtle shells that were heated to produce cracks, which were analyzed by those seeking to divine the future.

oracle A person, such as a priest, through whom a god is believed to speak.

oratory The art of public speaking.

orature Oral literature in ancient Africa.

orchestra A flat, circular area in which much of the action of a Greek drama occurred, situated between the spectators' seating area and the stage.

order The three ancient Greek styles of building design.

ore A naturally occurring mineral from which metals can be extracted.

orrery A mechanical model that reproduces the movements of heavenly bodies.

orthogonal planning City plan in which the perpendicular axes of streets create square city blocks.

orthostat An upright stone or slab used by architects in buildings.

osteomyelitis Bacterial infection of the bones and bone marrow.

ostracon (pl. ostraca) A fragment of pottery, typically carrying an inscription or drawing.

outcastes A person in ancient India who had no caste or had been ejected from a caste for violation of customs and rules.

outlier A language geographically detached and possibly remote from the range of the languages closely related to it.

outrigger A float attached by spars, or poles, to a watercraft.

overdying Successively dying a thread with individual colors until the desired color is reached.

overtone series In music, a number of higher notes produced simultaneously above a lower continuous drone.

oxidize To combine with oxygen.

pack animal An animal used to carry loads on its back.

paedagogus In ancient Rome, an educated slave who served as a tutor in ancient Rome.

paidotribēs In ancient Greece, a gymnastics teacher, working on physical fitness and the vigorous games that formed the basis of public competition and prepared young men for war.

palaestra Facility for training in wrestling and boxing in ancient Greece.

palanquin A litter or carriage body on poles, carried on the shoulders of men or women.

paleoclimatologist A scientist who studies long-term changes in climate on the earth throughout the planets four-billion-year existence

paleographic Having to do with ancient writings.

paleopathologists Scientists who study disease in prehistoric populations through examination of skeletal and tissue remains, coprolites, and works of art.

palette A flat stone tray, often decorated with carved designs, upon which colored minerals (such as malachite or hematite) were ground to make cosmetics.

palisade A fence made of upright stakes or posts set very closely together; a stockade.

pallium A rectangular woolen mantle worn by lower-class Romans.

panchayat In India, a council at the village level, responsible for dealing with local crime and punishment.

panegyric   Laudatory written or oral poem.

pankration   An event in ancient Greece that combined elements of boxing and wrestling.

pantheistic   Relating to the worship of all gods.

pantheon   The group of gods worshipped by a particular culture.

papyrus   A tall aquatic plant used mainly by the Egyptians to make a writing material resembling paper.

parapegma   A calendar that lists annual celestial events, such as the rising and setting of specific stars or constellations on given days of the year; a star calendar.

parrhesia   In ancient Greece, frank or open speech, a cherished Athenian principle.

passage tomb   A tomb where the burial chamber is reached through a low passage; secondary chambers may lead off from the main chamber.

pastoral nomadism   An economic lifestyle that revolves around entire families or kin groups following domesticated animals during yearly cycles.

pastoral poetry   Poetry that presents an idealized portrait of country life, often concerning the love between shepherds and shepherdesses.

pastoralism   The breeding, tending, and exploitation of domestic herd animals as a principal means of livelihood for a community or society.

paterfamilias   In ancient Rome, the male head of a household.

pathogen   Any agent capable of causing disease.

patria potestas   The legal authority (including the power of life and death) of a Roman head of household over his family (including slaves and other dependents).

patriarch   A male head of a family.

patrician   The upper social class of Rome, consisting of those who held social, political, and economic power.

patrilineal   Descent traced through the male ancestors.

patrilocal   A residence pattern in which married couples live with or near the husband's family.

patronus   A Roman of wealth and status who extended his patronage and protection to one or more lower-status clients.

pavimentum   Concrete foundation of a Roman road.

Pax Romana   Term used to describe the relative peace and stability that the Romans imposed on their empire.

payment in kind   The offering of crops, animals, and textiles, and other goods instead of money to pay taxes or a debt.

peat   Partially carbonized plant matter, usually found in bogs.

pectoral   A breastplate or breast covering.

pederasty   An erotic relationship common in Greek culture between a youth (usually between the onset of puberty and the full growth of the beard) and an adult man.

pediment   The triangular section just below a sloped roof, which may contain decorative or sculptural features.

peltast   A Greek lightly armed infantry soldier.

pemmican   A mixture of dried meat, dried berries, and rendered fat.

pentameter   A poetic meter that has five feet per line.

pentecontor   A 50-oared ship, rowed by arranging 25 oarsmen on each side of a vessel.

peplos   A loose gown worn over a tunic by the ancient Greeks.

peret   The "growing season," one of three seasons in the Egyptian calendar, based on the stages of the Nile's transformation.

perioikoi   In ancient Greece, people from neighboring towns, especially those subject to the people of Sparta.

periplous (or periplus; pl. periploi)   In ancient Greece, a narrative of discovery containing details of navigation, such as ports and coastal landmarks.

peristyle   An open area or courtyard surrounded by columns.

permafrost   Permanently frozen ground.

petasos   A hat with a broad, floppy brim worn by the ancient Greeks.

petroglyph   An image that is carved or pecked into a rock surface with a hard stone or some other tool.

phalanx   A rectangular formation of heavy infantry, densely arrayed so that each man's shield protected both himself and his neighbor to his left.

pharmaceutical   Having healing properties.

pharmacology   The study of drugs, especially their effects.

phonetic   Having to do with the sounds of languages.

phonogram   Written symbol used to express a sound.

phratry   A kinship group found in many Greek cities.

phyle (pl. phylae)   One of the main divisions of the citizen body in most ancient Greek cities; in ancient Athens the 10 phylae provided the organizational basis for many government functions.

physis   Greek word for "nature"; can refer to the overall state of the physical body and its health and well-being.

pictograph   Picture symbol representing by way of an illustration a person, idea, object, activity, event, or place.

pietas   A sense of duty, one of the Roman virtues.

pilaster   A rectangular column that projects from a wall to which it is attached.

pile weave   Weaving that produces raised loops rather than a flat surface.

piles   A beam of timber driven into the ground to be part of a foundation for a building.

pilum (pl. pila)   The standard missile weapon of the ancient Roman legionnaire, similar to a javelin.

pips   Small fruit seeds.

pit house   An ancient form of dwelling consisting of a pit excavated in the earth and roofed over.

pitch accent   In language, the form of accentuation in which the accented syllable does not receive additional emphasis (as in English) but instead is pronounced at a musical pitch different from the rest of the word.

pitched roof   A two-sided, sloped roof.

pithoi Large terra-cotta jars used for storage in ancient Greece and Rome.

placebo effect The effect seen when patients improve as a result of their positive expectations about the treatment rather than as a result of the treatment itself.

placer deposits Glacial deposits that contain valuable minerals, especially gold.

plain weave A technique of passing weft threads alternately over and under the warp threads.

plaiting Braiding a number of strips of leaf to create one long strip for use in a basket or mat.

plano-convex A shape comprising five flat sides, each one forming a plane, and one side curved upward, or convex.

plaza Large open-air area for public gatherings, created by the enclosure of buildings or mounds.

plebeian In Roman society, a commoner.

plinth An architectural support or base, such as small stands for statues and larger platforms for entire buildings.

plowshare The metal blade of a plow.

pneumatics The study of the mechanical properties of gases.

pneumoconiosis A disease of the lungs caused by inhalation of other irritating particles in the environment.

polestar Known as Polaris, the star that hangs above the North Pole and is a useful navigational guide at night.

poliomyelitis Severe viral infection that affects the spinal cord and brainstem and can lead to muscle wasting and partial or complete paralysis.

polis (pl. poleis) A ancient Greek city-state.

polity A politically organized unit.

pollen analysis A type of analysis that studies pollen that has survived for many thousands of years in waterlogged or acid conditions in the soil to gain a picture of plants growing in the vicinity the sample was taken from.

polychrome Multicolored.

polyculture The practice of planting several different crops in the same place, such as growing wheat among the trees of an orchard or lentils between the rows of vines in a vineyard.

polygamy The practice of marrying more than one spouse.

polyglot A person who speaks several languages and, hence, a place where several languages are widely spoken.

polygyny The practice of having two or more wives.

polyreme A large, multi-oared warship.

polytheism A religious system based on the belief in and worship of multiple gods.

pomerium A ritual boundary that separated the sacred space of the Roman city from the nonsacred world beyond.

pommel A knob on the part of a bladed weapon that is held in the hand.

pontifex maximus The chief religious figure in ancient Rome.

porcelain A white, hard, almost transparent ceramic coated with colored glazes.

pornai Prostitutes in ancient Greece.

port of trade Place where emissaries from central places trade and exchange goods.

portico A porch with regularly spaced columns, or colonnades, often surrounding the sanctuary of a temple.

portoria Customs duties.

post mast A simple mast made of one long timber.

post Vertical timber joined to a ship's keel at the bow (stem) and the stern (sternpost) to receive the hull planking.

post-and-beam construction An important early architectural design in which vertical posts, made of wood or stone, support horizontal beams anchoring the walls and roof; also called "post and lintel."

potsherd A fragment of a clay vessel or other object.

potter's wheel A circular platform that spins, on which wet clay is shaped by a potter's hands.

pozzolana Hard volcanic stone that went into Roman *caementum,* or cement, helping to make the walls of Roman buildings impervious to fire and moisture.

praetentura The quarters of elite troops within a Roman camp or fortification.

praetor In the government of ancient Rome, officials who held imperium, or the authority to lead an army and the power of life and death over citizens, and who were in charge of litigation and courts of law.

Praetorian Guard The Roman emperor's private military troops.

praetorium The headquarters of a Roman camp or fortification, built to house the legionary commander and the unit's symbolic banners.

precentor A person who leads worshippers in singing or chanting prayers.

precession The movement of an axis of a rotating body, causing it to "wobble" slightly in its orbit.

primogeniture The legal right of inheritance belonging to the first-born child, most often the eldest son.

proconsul A Roman consul whose imperium was continued after his year in office as a promagistrate.

proletari, **(pl. *proletarii*)** People in ancient Rome who owned no property.

pronominal A term use to describe the nature of a pronoun.

propylon A porchlike structure that typically served as an entrance to the grounds of temples in ancient Greece.

prothesis A ceremony in which the corpse was laid out for mourning at home.

protohistoric Historical era immediately preceding the emergence of writing.

protolanguage An ancestral or root language, the basis for a family of languages.

provenance Place of origin.

proyet The period when the waters of the Nile receded, literally meaning "the emergence."

prytaneion A Greek city hall.

prytanis (pl. *prytaneis*) Member of the executive committee presiding over the Athenian *boulē*, or citizens' council.

psephismata Decrees, that is, decisions of the Assembly in Athens that pertained to a specific situation and did not establish a permanent law.

pseudepigraphic Having a false title.

publicani Wealthy partners in Roman companies that invested large sums in bidding for state contracts to collect taxes or operate facilities like state-owned mines.

pueblos Native American communal dwellings built in cliff faces.

pulmentarium In ancient Rome, stew or porridge made of grains or beans.

pulque An alcoholic beverage made by ancient Mesoamericans from the fermented juice of various agave plants, such as the maguey.

purdah An Indian woman's garment that covers the entire body.

pututu Traditional Andean musical instrument made by drilling a large seashell at its point to make a mouthpiece.

pylons Large gates with two abbreviated pyramids on each side.

pyrotechnology The process of transforming a raw material such as clay into its final form using fire.

Pythagorean theorem A technique for finding the length of a side of a right triangle if the other two sides are known, based on the fact that the area of the squares made from any two sides have a known relationship to that made by the remaining side ($a^2 + b^2 = c^2$, where c is the hypotenuse).

qanat An irrigation system of underground tunnels developed by ancient Persians.

quadratum A building technique in which blocks of dressed stone were fastened to a concrete wall to form a regular facing.

quaestor In the government of ancient Rome, an official who handled financial matters: collecting customs or duties at ports and rent for Rome's public lands, running the city's treasury, and helping a provincial governor administrate his province.

quay A wharf built parallel to the shoreline.

quern A smooth stone used as a surface for grinding grain.

quetzal A bird indigenous to Guatemala with feathers greatly favored for making ancient ceremonial garments.

quinoa A pseudograin, consisting of the seeds of a herb from the goosefoot family and used by ancient Mesoamericans in making bread.

quinquireme A large multi-oared vessel; the oars are thought to have been arranged in sets of three, with two men pulling each of the top two oars.

quotidian Relating to common, everyday life.

radiocarbon dating (carbon-14 dating) A method that relies on the carbon-14 isotope (a specific form of carbon), which has a predictable rate of decay over time, to date historical artifacts based on the amount of carbon-14 remaining within a particular sample

raised relief A form of stone carving where the background is cut away, leaving the figures to stand out from the surface of the stone.

raja Indian title of nobility.

rampart A raised fortification resembling a wall and surrounding a township or other area to be protected.

rebate A continuous rectangular recess along the top or bottom edge of the face of stonework.

recession agriculture A way of scheduling agricultural production by planting crops after the recession, or receding, of annual floodwaters in a river valley.

reciprocity Type of exchange that takes place between two individuals when neither is dominant.

rede A Germanic word meaning "leadership" or "governance," especially if favored by the gods.

regent Someone who rules in a monarch's stead, especially when the monarch is a child.

regimen Lifestyle, largely diet and exercise, prescribed by ancient Greek physicians to treat ill health.

reincarnation The rebirth of a soul into a new human being (or other creature).

relics Objects venerated by Christians, often fragments of a saint's body or objects related to a saint's martyrdom or life.

relief Artwork that projects outward from a flat background; a coin, with its raised forms, is a common example of relief work.

rendered Melted; used in connection with animal fats melted for use as fuel.

repoussé A method for creating designs in relief on metal by hammering on the reverse side.

retentura The quarters of ordinary soldiers and cavalry, placed at the rear of a Roman fort or camp.

retiarius Gladiator armed with a net; from the Latin for "net."

reticulum A pattern of stones or bricks laid into a wall in regular, rectangular blocks.

retting A process in which fibers that make up the stems of certain plants, such as jute and flax, are detached from their woody core by soaking the fibers in water for several days.

reverse The "tails" side of a coin, with a wide range of design types and images.

revetment A decorative thin slab of stone, or facing, on a wall.

rhetor In ancient Rome, a teacher of public speaking.

rhetoric The study of principles and techniques that aid in the effective presentation and defense of a line of reasoning; also simply eloquence in speaking.

rhizome An elongated, underground (or underwater) horizontal stem from which roots and shoots emerge.

rhizotomoi Pharmacists or herbalists (literally "root cutters") in ancient Greece.

rites of passage Rituals used within a community to mark the transition of individuals from one status to another, including weddings, funerals, and rituals of initiation.

river ordeal A method used in the ancient Near East to reach a verdict when all else failed; the accused was thrown into a river, being judged innocent if he or she survived and guilty if drowned.

rock gong A large rock that produces a resonant tone when struck.

Romanitas A sense of belonging to a great empire felt by many of the conquered peoples of the Roman Empire.

Romanization The process of culturally changing foreigners into Romans.

rondo A piece of music that has a central theme repeated between contrasting sections.

rope stretchers Ancient Egyptian land surveyors who used essentially modern surveying tools to remeasure individual property lines on the farmland washed free of all distinguishing features by the annual Nile inundation.

rudder A large paddle at the rear of a vessel that is manipulated in order to steer the vessel.

rudus Mixture of components such as sand, soil, clay, or concrete, which is used as a foundation for a Roman road.

runes Form of writing in ancient Germany and medieval Scandinavia.

rushes Marsh plants with hollow stems.

rushlight A type of early candle, consisting of the pith of a stalky plant stem soaked in oil.

sacred barks Boats that carried the shrines of the gods in ancient Egypt.

sakkia An Egyptian animal-powered waterwheel.

salient A segment of the wall that projects outward from the wall.

salting A method of drying and preserving food.

san An ancient Chinese jacket.

sand-core technique Threads of molten glass are wound around a shaped core of sand; after the glass hardens, the sand is removed.

sapper Engineer used to undermine or dismantle walls.

saqiya A waterwheel powered by a domestic animal, used to collect water in buckets and raise it to an irrigation ditch or container, used in ancient Egypt and the Near East.

sarcophagus A coffin made of stone, often decorated with relief sculpture.

sari A long, wrapped Indian garment.

sarisa The long Macedonian spear, an innovation of Philip of Macedon.

sarongs Long pieces of cloth that are wrapped around the body.

saros cycle A period of about 18 years after which eclipses of the sun and moon reoccur.

sastras **and sutras** Books of rules for conduct that formed the foundation for ancient Indian law.

satire Verse, prose, or a combination of the two that with humor, and sometimes harshness, criticizes bad behavior, hypocrisy, and other failings of society.

satrap A political office in the Persian Empire and later in the eastern kingdoms ruled by the successors of Alexander the Great.

satrapy A Persian province, administered by a royally appointed governor, who was known as a satrap.

Saturnian A native Roman poetic meter that was composed of two feet separated by a caesura, or pause, and that fell out of fashion in the late third century B.C.E.

satyr play An ancient Greek farce on a mythological subject, with a chorus representing satyrs, deities that have characteristics of horses or goats.

satyr A mythological creature that is usually part man and part goat, known for excessive drinking and lechery.

savanna A flat tropical or subtropical grassland.

scale armor Armor named for its resemblance to fish scales and made by sewing small oblongs of bronze or iron to a linen or felt shirt.

scale In music, a series of notes differing in pitch, varying with the frequency of vibration.

scarab A beetle used as a charm to ward off evil.

scarification Deliberate scarring of skin to create decorative patterns.

schenti A fabric loincloth or skirt.

schistosomiasis Parasitic infection acquired by immersion in water containing a certain species of worm; infection can result in fever, fatigue, serious anemia, and even liver damage.

scop Anglo-Saxon bard.

scoria Light volcanic ash that was used to extend concrete and make it capable of supporting longer arches and vaults.

scribe A man of letters in the ancient world who was capable of writing and who often worked as a teacher, a copyist, or a public official in the capacity of a clerk.

script A handwritten language.

scrivener A professional copyist or scribe.

scutum A rectangular or cylindrical shield.

scytale An encryption device consisting of rods and leather straps.

seal A carved piece of stone pressed into moist clay to leave an image that would be preserved when the clay was fired.

secondary burial Burial (or reburial) of bones from which the flesh has already decomposed. This practice implies that the corpse was originally buried elsewhere or exposed aboveground deliberately to reduce it to bones.

sedentary pastoralism A herding economy practiced by people living in permanent settlements.

sedentism A culture's shifting from living in nonpermanent settlements to living in   permanent settlements.

sediment core A sample of layers of sediment, taken from lake bottoms or dry lands using a long cylinder, for the purpose of studying past environmental or human conditions

sedimentary rock Rock formed from sediment that has drifted down and settled in a seabed.

seine A fishing net that hangs vertically in the water via floats at the top and weights at the bottom.

seismic Relating to an earthquake.

selvedge Edge of a textile created by the looping of the weft around the warp.

senator The highest-ranking Roman class, consisting essentially of former magistrates. Their wealth lay in land, since they were banned from engaging in trade.

senyu In ancient Egypt, a weight in silver equal to one-half deben, or 1.75 ounces.

sepulchre A tomb.

serf A category of dependent person attached to the soil.

sericulture The breeding and raising of silkworms.

serpentine A soft, blue-green stone, sometimes used by the Olmec as an apparent substitute for more valuable jade.

sesterti (pl. sestertii) A Roman coin, made of silver or bronze, equal to one-fourth of a denarius.

sexagesimal In a mathematical system, relying on the base number 60.

sexireme A ship with six rows of oarsmen.

sextant A navigational device used measuring angles to a celestial body as a way to calculate, with a calibration of 60 degrees.

shabitib **(pl.** *shabitii***)** Small figure placed in an Egyptian tomb used as a substitute workman in case the spirit of the deceased is called on to do work in the afterlife.

shaduf A tool for irrigation made of a long branch or pole on a frame, with a bucket at one end and a counterweight at the other, allowing the operator to lower the bucket into the water and then easily raise it out with the help of the counterweight.

shaman A person who acts as intermediary between the natural and supernatural worlds, using magic or sorcery for purposes of healing, divination, and control over natural events.

shed rod A stick that separates warp threads into over-and-under groups.

sheet bronze Bronze that has been beaten or compressed into a thin sheet, which can then be fashioned into tubular and other shapes.

shemu The "drought season," one of three seasons in the Egyptian calendar, based on the stages of the Nile's transformation.

shinty A game resembling field hockey and dating to ancient times in the British Isles.

sibbe An ancient Germanic clan.

sickle sword A sword with a blade that curves so that it resembles the sickle used in harvesting crops.

sidelock of youth A long ponytail, worn to one side by youngsters.

sidereal Having a relation to or based on the stars.

silt Sand or earth, usually fine grained, carried by flowing water and then deposited.

singlet A loose shirt made of one layer of cloth.

sirocco A warm, moist Mediterranean wind.

sistrum (pl. sistra) An ancient Egyptian hand-held percussive musical instrument consisting of a handle and a U-shaped frame with crossbars holding loose rings that would jangle or tinkle when the instrument was shaken.

situla **(pl.** *situlae***)** A bronze vessel, similar to a bucket.

skene A rectangular building with one to three doors at the rear of the Greek stage, often representing a house, palace, military tent, cave, or other enclosure.

skyphos **(pl.** *skyphoi***)** A deep, two-handled cup.

slag What remains after ore is smelted and metal is removed.

slash-and-burn agriculture The practice of felling and burning trees to clear land for planting.

slip A thick clay-based liquid coating applied to the surface of a ceramic vessel, either for decorative purposes or to make the vessel surface less porous.

smallpox A highly contagious and deadly viral disease that produces fever and skin eruptions.

smelting A method of separating metal from surrounding rock or soil through heating or mixing with chemicals; also the process of heating and transforming mineral ores into more refined and usable finished metals and alloys.

social stratification The division of people into classes; from the word *strata,* meaning "layers."

socket ax A battle-ax with a bronze or iron head possessing a socket that slips over the end of the ax's handle to which the head is fastened with a rivet.

soil resistivity testing Detecting changes in the electrical resistance of the soil in order to find the remains of structures hidden beneath the ground.

solar calendar A calendar that bases a year on the time it takes the earth to complete one revolution around the sun.

solar year A year based on the time it takes the earth to complete one revolution around the sun; a calendar year of 365 days.

solar zenith passage The day of the year when the sun passes directly overhead and casts no shadow on vertical objects.

solstice The point at which days are longest or shortest, depending on the earth's tilt to its orbital plane. The winter solstice occurs in December in the Northern Hemisphere and in June the Southern Hemisphere, and the summer solstices are the reverse.

sophistēs A sophist, or professional teacher of rhetoric in ancient Greece; literally "professional wise person."

sorghum A cereal grain crop.

sound box On a stringed instrument, the hollow shell that amplifies the sound of the strings.

souterrain Underground chambers lined with stone.

spar   A pole used for support on a watercraft.

speakers of the laws   Legal specialists in the Persian Empire who explained the ins and outs of the law to those involved in court cases as well as helping to conduct those cases.

spear thrower   Also called by its Aztec name, *atlatl,* a weapon used as an extension of the thrower's arm to add force and speed to a hurled spear or dart.

spelt   A kind of wheat (*Triticum aestivum spelta*).

sphere of influence and **sphere of interest**   A means of reserving a portion of territory from the political interference of another state; *interest* is assumed to be a less significant claim than *influence.*

spillway   A channel carrying water around an obstruction.

spindle whorl   A circular object that weights a spindle for spinning to improve rotation.

spindle   A pointed stick about 12 inches long, used for spinning.

sprang   Stretchy fabric woven of intertwined warp threads only.

squinch   A small arch built across the interior angle of two walls.

stadion   A term denoting both the rectangular ground upon which the Greeks ran in competition and the name of a race covering one length of this track.

stalactites   Mineral deposit, often shaped like a spike, hanging down from the ceiling of a cavern.

stalagmites   Mineral deposit, often shaped like a spike, pointing up from the floor of a cavern.

standard   A wooden pole surmounted by an image used to represent a town or province in Egypt.

stasis   A political faction in Greece, or the strife caused by such a faction.

statics   The branch of mechanics dealing with weights in static equilibrium.

statumen   Mixture of stones used as a foundation for a Roman road.

steganography   A writing system used for hidden messages; the message is literally hidden from readers other than the intended recipient.

stela (pl. stelae)   A carved stone slab, usually installed vertically and used to commemorate an event or person.

steppe   A vast treeless grassland

stepped fret   A zigzag form resembling a mountain, especially the terraced mountainsides of the Andes—a prominent feature in later Andean art and a symbol of prestige.

stereometry   The measurement of solid figures or volumes.

stoa   A narrow hallway often found in the commercial districts of Greek towns, with an open colonnade, where merchants set up shops.

stola   The long garment worn by married Roman women over the tunic.

strategos   "General," one of the few elected officials in democratic Athens, with authority that often extended beyond military matters.

stratification   Division of people into social groups or classes

strut   Bar used to draw weight down to a central point.

stucco   A fine plaster used to cover walls.

stupa   A dome-shaped mound serving as a Buddhist shrine.

stylus   An instrument, often made of reed, used by the ancients for incising or inscribing on clay or wax tablets.

suasaria   In Roman rhetoric, an argument made to justify or condemn a course of action.

subligaculum   Also called a *campestre,* a garment worn under the tunic and toga as underwear and as a sports garment.

subsistence farming   The practice of agriculture that provides enough food to eat without an excess for sale.

suffets   Nonroyal magistrates who were granted control over a Punic city-state.

sumptuary laws   Laws designed to limit excessive consumption or use of luxury goods.

sunk relief   A form of stone carving where the background is left as it is and the figures are carved into the stone.

supernova   A star's explosion, producing an exponential increase in its luminosity.

surface mining   The process of harvesting useful stone and metals at above-ground sites, such as hillsides, and where drilling underground is not necessary or desirable.

swastika   A pattern resembling a cross with each arm bent at a right angle, an ancient Hindu symbol (also used by Buddhists and Jains); the term is derived from the Sanskrit word for "well-being."

swidden   An area cleared for temporary cultivation by cutting and burning the vegetation.

sykophantes   In the legal system of ancient Athens, a class of professional prosecutors.

syllabary   A written set of symbols that represent syllables.

sympathetic magic   Magic that looks to achieve its ends through imitation of the desired results.

symposium   A drinking party for Greek aristocrats featuring wine, games, poetry, and conversation.

synodic cycle   The lunar phase cycle of 29.5 days.

synoecism   In ancient Greece, the amalgamation of villages and towns into a larger unit.

synoikiai   In ancient Greece, blocks of apartment buildings.

syntax   The grammatical arrangement of words in a sentence.

syssitia   In ancient Greece, military-style messes or eating clubs to which every Spartan citizen belonged.

syumuu   In ancient Egypt, the dry season from March to July, literally meaning "the drought."

t'un-t'ien   Military colonies set up by the ancient Chinese.

tabby weave   A type of weave in which a single thread from the weft passes over and under one warp thread at a time.

tablinum   A "home office" for the head of household in a Roman home.

taboos Practices or objects that are forbidden or banned because of social custom or religious practices.

talent The largest unit of weight and money in the ancient world, variously defined as a man's weight in gold or the amount of gold one man could carry; in ancient Greece, a specific weight of metal equivalent to 60 minas, or 6,000 drachmas.

tallow Animal fat.

Talmud The Jewish book of law and scriptural commentary.

talud-tablero A system of construction generally associated first with the city of Teotihuacán in ancient Mesoamerica; facades are formed by vertical panels alternating with sloped and diagonal ones.

tang A narrow projection by which a tool, typically a knife, is attached to its handle.

tanning The process of drying, curing, and dyeing leather for use in clothing, armor, and shoes.

taper A slender candle.

taproot A primary root that sends out offshoots.

tarentine A thin, almost transparent white gown worn by the ancient Greeks.

taro A large-leaved plant that is typically cooked as a vegetable or ground into flour.

tartan A cloth woven in a plaid or checked pattern.

tebenna A short, semicircular woolen mantle worn by the Etruscans and which was the forerunner of the Roman toga.

techne Greek term meaning "art," "craft," or "expertise" and the root of such words as *technical* and *technology.*

tectonic plate One of seven major pieces of the earth's crust that moves slowly over the mantel

tell An ancient mound built up from the remains of earlier settlements.

templum Any sacred area (not necessarily a building) in which ancient Roman priests could conduct rituals of augury, or foretelling of the future.

teosinte The plant from which early Americans bred maize, or corn.

terra sigillata Ornate red pottery favored in and around the Roman Empire.

terrace A "step" cut into the slope of a hill, providing a flat place for farming or building.

terra-cotta A hard fired clay used in pottery, sculpture, and building decoration.

tessera (pl. tesserae) One of the small pieces of stone, ceramics, or glass used in making mosaics.

tetrachord The building block of Greek melodic theory, consisting of four notes, with the top and bottom note forming an interval of a fourth.

tetradrachm In ancient Greece, coin equal to four drachms, issued under several different weight standards.

tetrarchy Rule by four people.

thalassocracy Maritime dominance or supremacy.

thatch Roofing made of grasses or leaves.

theocracy A government or political system based on the rule or religious authority of a god or gods and their human representatives (such as kings and priests), as found in the ancient Near East.

theriac A medicine used by the ancient Romans as an antidote to poison and a cure-all or preventative against numerous diseases.

thermae Public bathhouses, found in all Roman cities.

thermoluminescence A process of measuring the age of an object, often used for ceramic objects between 10,000 and 300 years old to determine their authenticity.

thermopolium A shop in an ancient Roman city where people could buy hot wine and food.

tholia A high, pointed hat worn by ancient Greek women.

tholos A circular building used for religious purposes in ancient Greece.

thronos A solid, upright chair with armrests, usually found in ancient Greek temples or palaces.

throwing knife Multibladed weapon without a solid hilt and with one plain, flat side and one decorated or embossed side.

tidal bore A wave that travels from the ocean up a river.

tinfoil A thin sheet of tin used as a wrapping.

titulus crucis The *elogium* (headboard) attached to the cross above someone who has been crucified, stating the offense the person committed; specifically, the headboard above Jesus, with the inscription *Jesus of Nazareth, King of the Jews.*

toga The rounded, woolen mantle worn by Roman citizens.

Torah The Jewish book of scripture, generally referring to the first five books of the Old Testament.

torque Circular bar worn around the neck as jewelry by ancient Celts and Germans.

torsion catapult A launching device that derives its power from the twisting of ropes or wooden elements of the frame.

transhumant pastoralism A system in which some members of the community migrate with herds to distant pastures on a seasonal basis while most remain sedentary and focus on agricultural activities.

transliterate To reproduce in English letters the sound of a word's original pronunciation in another language.

transmigration The movement of a dead person's soul into the body of an already existing living person.

trapeza A four-legged table used by the ancient Greeks.

trappings Clothing, jewelry, and symbols of office.

trepanning An ancient European medical practice that consisted of sawing or drilling a hole in the skull to treat head or psychological disorders.

tribe Group of people related by lineage, kin, or clan with or without centralized leadership.

tribon A coarse, dark-colored wrap worn by the ancient Greeks.

tribulum A device to thresh grain, consisting of a heavy board with flints or small wheels on its underside.

tribunal The raised platform at one end of a basilica from where a judge or other magistrates presided over a hearing or tried legal cases.

tribune An elected representative of the plebeians of Rome.

tribute Goods, labor, or payment offered to the ruling classes, usually by obligation, in exchange for their rulership.

triclinium A Roman dining room containing three couches on which men reclined to eat.

trilithon A megalithic structure made of two large vertical stones supporting a horizontal stone laid across the top.

trireme An ancient ship with three rows of oars on each side.

trittys Political division in Athens consisting of several contiguous demes.

trypanosomiasis A disease caused by parasitic single-celled organisms generally transmitted by insect bites; the form popularly known as "sleeping sickness" is transmitted by tsetse flies.

tsetse fly A fly that spreads diseases among cattle and humans, including sleeping sickness.

tsunami A giant wave or series of waves created by earthquakes, volcanic eruptions, or other major impact to an ocean.

tubers Rounded roots, such as the potato, that grow underground.

tufa Soft volcanic rock that was frequently used as a filler or as facing stone in Roman buildings.

tumbaga An alloy of gold and copper used by the ancient Peruvians.

tumulus (pl. tumuli) An artificial mound built, in ancient Europe, usually over the remains of the dead; also called a *barrow*.

tundra A vast, cold, treeless plain characteristic of arctic and subarctic regions.

tunic A T-shaped garment with openings at the top for the head and arms.

turf Sod; a mat of grass and its roots.

tuyere Nozzle through which air is delivered into a furnace.

twill Fabric threads interwoven to give the cloth a parallel diagonal, diamond shape or herringbone ridges on the surface.

typhoon A hurricane occurring in the western Pacific region.

typology Within the discipline of historical linguistics, the characteristic of surface structural similarity.

tyrannos (pl. tyrannoi) In ancient Greece, sole ruler without hereditary claim to the throne; the word sometimes has negative connotations but less so than the English word *tyrant*.

Tyrian purple An ancient dye made from the secretions of marine snails and very highly valued throughout the ancient Mediterranean world.

Tzolkin Mayan sacred calendar based on a 260-day ritual cycle.

unguent A medicinal or cosmetic ointment.

univira A matron who had the honorable distinction of having married only once in her life and not having divorced.

untouchables People without caste in India, the lowest social group.

urbs Latin word for "city."

ushabtis In ancient Egypt, small figurines that were buried with the dead to accompany them into the underworld and work for them in the afterlife.

uttariya A scarf that covered the upper body, worn by ancient Indians.

vallus Ancient Roman reaping machine pulled by an animal and used to cut off the heads of wheat stalks and drop them in a container.

varna Associated with Hinduism; the name in India for the original social division of people into four main groups, which in turn contain thousands of subdivisions.

vassal A person, nation, or group that is dependent on or subordinate to another.

vault An arched brick or stone ceiling or roof.

Vedic laws Legal codes based on religious texts, such as the sacred writings of Hinduism.

vela A linen awning covering a Roman theater; sometimes called a *velarium.*

vellum A special kind of leather used to make sheets for writing. In general this was more prestigious and expensive than papyrus.

venatio Beast hunts that were conducted as a spectator sport in ancient Roman amphitheaters.

venator Hunter in a staged wild-animal hunt in the Roman arena.

veneer Thin strips of decorative wood applied to the surface of an object to hide a wood of less aesthetic value or to mask imperfections.

vestal virgins The priestesses of the Roman hearth goddess, Vesta, who were required to be virgins and entrusted with keeping a sacred flame burning in Vesta's temple.

vigesimal Referring to a number system based on 20.

vihara In Indian architecture, a small building consisting of cubicles arranged around a central courtyard, used by monks and visitors to meditate and do penance.

villa A self-sufficient community, including a residential building, gardens, workshops, and cultivated fields.

viticulture The science of growing grapes.

vivisection The cutting open of a living being for the investigational or diagnostic purposes.

vizier In ancient Egypt, the highest-ranking government official after the pharaoh.

volute A type of spiral scrollwork.

votive Given or done in fulfillment of a vow or pledge.

wabet The workshop in which bodies were embalmed before burial in ancient Egypt.

warp In weaving, the threads that run lengthwise.

warp-weighted loom A rectangular, upright loom with the warp hanging from the top crossbar and anchored by weights on the free ends.

wattle and daub A method of building construction that involves a wooden lattice structure covered with packed mud, clay, and other materials.

wedge To stamp on clay to remove air pockets and impurities.

weft In weaving, the threads that run crosswise.

weir trap A cone-shaped wicker basket with an internal funnel.

weld A plant used to make yellow dye.

well-field system During the Chinese Zhou Dynasty, the territory controlled by a duke and divided into nine equal portions arranged in a square; the commoners worked all the land, but the produce of the center square belonged to the duke.

were-jaguar An Olmec sculptural figure combining human and jaguar traits.

wet nurse A woman who nurses another woman's infant in exchange for wages.

whorl A pulley that helps to rotate a spindle.

wick A short length of cloth or fiber that draws fuel oil from a reservoir by capillary action and then can be burned to provide a steady light.

wickerwork shield A shield made from woven reeds or twigs supported by a wooden frame.

wisdom literature Ancient Egyptian texts that consist of either instructions or philosophical dialogue.

woad A plant used to make blue dye.

wuxing The five elements of ancient Chinese philosophy and science: fire, earth, water, wood, and metal.

xenia Greek word usually denoting the relationship between host and guest.

xenos Greek word meaning, variously, "foreigner," "stranger," or "guest-friend."

xoanon One of a set of wooden cult objects venerated in ancient Greece for the deities that they represented.

yakshi In India, a female supernatural being who guards the earth's mineral treasures.

yang In Chinese philosophy, the form of energy that supposedly is hard, bright, active, and "male."

yaws A bacterial skin infection marked by red skin eruptions and joint pain.

yin In Chinese philosophy, the form of energy that supposedly is soft, dark, receptive, and "female."

zaliths Members of an assembly who governed an Etruscan city-state.

zenith The point on the celestial sphere directly above the place on which the observer stands and opposite the zenith.

ziggurat In ancient Mesopotamia, a pyramid-shaped tower rising in stages of decreasing size to a shrine at the top.

zooarchaeology A field of science that has to do with uncovering, identifying, and interpreting animal remains in archaeological contexts.

zoomorphic Having animal attributes or an animal form.

zori A Japanese sandal that resembles modern flip-flops.

	AFRICA	THE MIDDLE EAST
prehistory – 10,000 B.C.E.	**Ca. 2 million years ago:** *Homo erectus* emerges and spreads to Asia and Europe **ca. 1 million–500,000 years ago:** *Homo erectus* gains the ability to make fire **ca. 200,000–100,000 years ago:** Homo sapiens emerges and spreads to Europe and Asia. **ca. 27,500–ca. 25,000 B.C.E.:** Date of the earliest-known rock art in Africa, found in eastern and southern Africa and produced by the San.	**ca. 10,000 B.C.E.:** Emergence of Natufian culture in the Middle East, to the west of the Euphrates River; establishment of the town of Abu Hureyra in present-day Syria; earliest firm evidence of domesticated dogs from a grave in Palestine. **ca. 11,000 B.C.E.:** As the glaciers retreat, fields of wild grain begin to appear in the Near East.
10,000 B.C.E. – 5000 B.C.E. (continues)	**ca. 11,000 B.C.E.:** Beginning of the African Humid Period, a period of warmer and wetter weather on the African continent. **ca. 9000 B.C.E.:** New Stone Age begins in Egypt. **ca. 8500 B.C.E.:** The harpoon is developed in present-day Sudan, allowing for the exploitation of deepwater fish. **ca. 7700 B.C.E.:** Nile Valley forms part of the Fertile Crescent. **ca. 7500 B.C.E.:** Egyptians first begin using reed boats; earliest-known African pottery is produced in the Sahara. **ca. 6000 B.C.E.:** Onset of dry conditions begins the desertification of the Sahara.	**ca. 10,000 B.C.E.:** Hunter-gatherers begin to domesticate the goat. **ca. 9000 B.C.E.:** The New Stone Age begins in Mesopotamia. **ca. 8000 B.C.E.:** Agriculture begins in the Near East; farmers use sticks to scratch up the earth to plant grains; thick beer ("drinkable bread") first brewed in Mesopotamia by the Sumerians; clay tokens first used for counting purposes in Mesopotamia. **ca. 7700 B.C.E.:** Milk from ewes (sheep) used widely as a food source in Near East. **ca. 7500 B.C.E.:** Reed boats come into use in Mesopotamia. **ca. 7000 B.C.E.:** Emmer wheat becomes a major food crop in portions of the Middle East.

Chronology by Region

ASIA AND THE PACIFIC

ca. 42,000 B.C.E.: The first seafaring colonists arrive in Australia from the Asian mainland.

ca. 28,500 B.C.E.: Seafaring colonists from Australia or the Asian mainland arrive in New Guinea.

ca. 27,000 B.C.E.: The first people arrive on the islands of Japan over land bridges or ice from the Asian mainland.

ca. 13,000–300 B.C.E.: Jōmon Period of Japan.

ca. 9000 B.C.E.: By this date people in Siberia and central Asia are using bones and skins from animals such as mammoths to build shelters.

ca. 7000 B.C.E.: Tropical horticulture begins in New Guinea.

ca. 6500 B.C.E.: Farming starts on the Indian subcontinent.

ca. 6400 B.C.E.: Pengtoushan in China is the oldest-known site of rice cultivation in Asia.

ca. 5500 B.C.E.: Beginning date for the earliest paintings in India, found on large stones and rock faces, mostly in central India.

ca. 5400–ca. 5200 B.C.E.: The Yellow River region in China provides the earliest evidence for the domestication of chickens in Asia.

EUROPE

ca. 1,000,000??–ca. 8,000 B.C.E.: Paleolithic Period.

ca. 34,000 B.C.E.: Beginning of the Aurignacian culture in the region of present-day Bulgaria, Hungary, and France.

ca. 25,000 B.C.E.: First human settlements in what is now Spain.

ca. 24,000 B.C.E.: First evidence of cold food storage and preservation, discovered in eastern Europe.

ca. 10,500 B.C.E.: Würm Glacial Age ends; ice withdraws so that humans can move into northern Europe.

ca. 9500 B.C.E.: Ice sheets start to melt in Europe.

ca. 8000–ca. 4000 B.C.E.: Mesolithic Period.

ca. 7200 B.C.E.: Sheep domesticated in the area of present-day Greece.

ca. 7000–ca. 2000 B.C.E.: Neolithic Period; emergence of agriculture, sometimes called the Neolithic Revolution.

ca. 6500 B.C.E.: Ancestor of cattle first domesticated in the region of present-day Yugoslavia.

THE AMERICAS

ca. 18,000–ca. 3,000 B.C.E.: The first Americans migrate from Siberia over the Bering Sea Land Bridge, now the Bering Strait, into present-day Alaska, though this date remains uncertain.

ca. 10,500 B.C.E.: Date assigned to early Clovis points (stone tools such as arrowheads, named after site in New Mexico where the first such points were found) at Monte Verde site in Chile.

ca. 10,200 B.C.E.: Dogs domesticated by earliest Americans.

ca. 9,500 B.C.E.: Date assigned to the first-discovered Clovis points in New Mexico; Clovis culture formed.

ca. 9200–ca. 8000 B.C.E.: Folsom tradition spreads across North America.

ca. 9000 B.C.E.: Bison herds cover the Great Plains of North America; first civilizations develop in the Arctic North.

ca. 8000 B.C.E.: First Americans arrive in South America; Archaic Age begins in North America, with dramatic changes in the landscape cause by receding of glaciers.

ca. 7000 B.C.E.: First cultivation of corn, or maize; agriculture begins to develop in the Americas.

AFRICA

10,000 B.C.E. – 5000 B.C.E.
(continued)

5000 B.C.E. – 4000 B.C.E.

ca. 5000 B.C.E.: Egyptians first build canals and dikes to irrigate crops.

ca. 4500 B.C.E.: Start of cattle herding in the Sahara.

ca. 4400 B.C.E.: First evidence of use of horizontal loom, depicted on Egyptian pottery.

4000 B.C.E. – 3000 B.C.E.

ca. 4000 B.C.E.: Beginning date for the cultivation of yam along the Niger River.

ca. 3600 B.C.E.: Beginning of Bronze Age in Egypt.

ca. 3500 B.C.E.: Egyptians develop complete number system.

ca. 3100 B.C.E.: Egyptian hieroglyphic writing emerges.

3000 B.C.E. – 2000 B.C.E.
(continues)

ca. 3000 B.C.E.: Egyptians begin to mine copper and develop the first crude paper, made of papyrus; Sahara Desert begins to form in North Africa.

Berbers arrive in North Africa.

ca. 2920 B.C.E.: The start of Egypt's First Dynasty, uniting Upper and Lower Egypt.

ca. 2650 B.C.E.: The first pyramid, the Step Pyramid, built by Imhotep in Egypt.

ca. 2575 B.C.E.: The Great Pyramid of Cheops is constructed.

ca. 2400–ca. 1500 B.C.E.: Kingdom of Karmah in Nubia.

THE MIDDLE EAST

ca. 6500 B.C.E.: A primitive plow called the *ard* is used in the Near East.

ca. 6000 B.C.E.: Production of wine begins in Mesopotamia and along the eastern shore of the Mediterranean Sea.

ca. 5000 B.C.E.: People in the valleys surrounding the Tigris and Euphrates rivers domesticate cattle and begin to build irrigation systems for crops.

ca. 4500 B.C.E.: Permanent settlement is established at Ur in Mesopotamia; clay tokens are first used for accounting purposes in Mesopotamia.

ca. 4300 B.C.E.: Turntable for pottery making is invented in Mesopotamia.

ca. 4200 B.C.E.: Copper mining begins in the area of modern-day Oman.

ca. 4000 B.C.E.: Earliest copper objects appear in the ancient Near East.

ca. 3500 B.C.E.: The Sumerians begin crafting tools out of bronze, a mixture of copper and tin, initiating the Bronze Age, which begins to reach its height in about 2000 B.C.E.; Sumerians also start to use wheeled vehicles pulled by animals.

ca. 3400 B.C.E.: Earliest form of cuneiform script is devised to record the language used by the ancient inhabitants of Uruk in southern Mesopotamia.

ca. 2800 B.C.E.: The sickle is invented by farmers in Sumer.

ca. 2750 B.C.E.: The Phoenician city of Tyre emerges as a great sea power.

ca. 2500 B.C.E.: Beginning of the Iron Age in the ancient Middle East.

ca. 2400 B.C.E.: The Babylonians first use the abacus for computation; Sumerians first use "positional notation," where numbers take their value depending on their position in a numerical group.

ca. 2350 B.C.E.: The Old Akkadian Empire begins rule of Mesopotamia.

ASIA AND THE PACIFIC

ca. 5000 B.C.E.: Longshan culture emerges in China.

ca. 4500 B.C.E.: China domesticates the water buffalo.

ca. 4000 B.C.E.: The people of the Indus Valley in India are cultivating a wide variety of crops, including dates, mangos, wheat, barley, and peas, using irrigation systems to water the crops.

ca. 3000 B.C.E.: People in the Indus Valley begin to weave fabric out of cotton; the Chinese begin to manufacture silk.

ca. 2900 B.C.E.: In China the mythical emperor Fu Xi develops the concept of yin and yang, fundamental to the practice of ancient Chinese medicine and the Chinese view of nature.

ca. 2700 B.C.E.: Mythical Chinese emperor Shennong develops the principles of acupuncture; tea is first used as a beverage in China.

ca. 2600 B.C.E.: Long-distance trade, particularly in luxury goods, develops among the nations of Southeast Asia; the major Indian cities of Harappa and Mohenjo Daro are founded.

ca. 2300 B.C.E.: Rice from the Indus Valley is introduced in northern China.

ca. 2296 B.C.E.: Chinese astronomers make the first recorded sighting of a comet.

EUROPE

ca. 5000 B.C.E.: Southeast European plains populated by agriculturalists.

ca. 5000–ca. 900 B.C.E.: Rock faces in Alps carved with figures of animals, warriors, and buildings.

ca. 4500–ca. 3500 B.C.E.: Europeans begin to use pottery with linear ornamentation.

ca. 4350 B.C.E.: Horses first domesticated in Europe and used for power.

ca. 3400–c. 1600 B.C.E.: Earliest evidence of wheeled vehicles in Europe (from a grave in Poland).

ca. 3200–c. 1600 B.C.E.: The "Iceman," equipped with a cast copper ax, dies while crossing the Alps near the present-day Italian-Austrian border.

ca. 3100–c. 1600 B.C.E.: Construction of Stonehenge megaliths in England.

ca. 3000 B.C.E.: The ox-drawn plow first used in Europe

ca. 2800 B.C.E.: Emergence of the Aegean Sea civilizations on Minoa and Crete, precursors of the Greeks.

ca. 2800 B.C.E.–ca. 700 B.C.E.: Bronze Age, marked by use of bronze tools.

ca. 2500 B.C.E.: Horses are introduced to Ireland.

ca. 2400 B.C.E.: People of the Beaker culture begin migration from Spain to France, Germany, and Britain.

THE AMERICAS

ca. 6000 B.C.E.: The Coahuiltecan culture forms in Texas; North American population groups become more settled, and cultural differences begin to emerge.

ca. 5000 B.C.E.: Cochise culture forms in Arizona and New Mexico.

ca. 4800 B.C.E.: Peoples from the Central American mainland become the first inhabitants of the Caribbean.

ca. 4300 B.C.E.: A variety of cotton is produced in the area of present-day Mexico.

ca. 4000 B.C.E.: First permanent shelters constructed in the North American Midwest; corn is domesticated in Mexico; llamas and alpacas are domesticated in the region of present-day Peru.

ca. 3000 B.C.E.: Early Alaskans begin to construct permanent villages; artwork produced by Native Americans begins to appear; Andes peoples of South America first cultivate potatoes; adobe pyramids built at Caral and El Aspero in modern-day Peru.

ca. 2600 B.C.E.: First temple mounds are constructed in Peru.

ca. 2500 B.C.E.: North Americans begin to make pottery; village cultures become predominant in the Americas.

ca. 2475 B.C.E.: Maize is domesticated and becomes a staple crop.

3000 B.C.E. – 2000 B.C.E.
(continued)

2000 B.C.E. – 1000 B.C.E.

1000 B.C.E. – 500 B.C.E.

AFRICA

ca. 2000 B.C.E.: Date assigned to the remains of cities in Mauritania, Africa's oldest cities.

ca. 2000–ca. 1000 B.C.E.: Emergence of Bantu language and its spread throughout much of Africa in what is called the Bantu Migration.

ca. 1700 B.C.E.: Date of the world's oldest mathematical document, on Egyptian papyrus.

ca. 1400 B.C.E.: Africa passes directly from the Stone Age to the Iron Age, skipping the Bronze Age important in other world cultures.

ca. 1380 B.C.E.: Egyptians complete construction of a canal linking the Nile River and the Red Sea.

ca. 1323 B.C.E.: Death of Egypt's King Tutankhamen.

ca. 1000–ca. 100 B.C.E.: The kingdom of Kush flourishes in Sudan.

ca. 800 B.C.E.: North African city of Carthage founded by the Phoenicians.

ca. 600 B.C.E.: The Sahel, south of the Sahara Desert, emerges as the site of numerous cities along an east–west trading route; Phoenician seafarers circumnavigate Africa.

ca. 580 B.C.E.: Africans first produce iron, in Meroë.

THE MIDDLE EAST

ca. 2000 B.C.E.: The Epic of Gilgamesh, written in cuneiform, is the world's oldest epic poem; its story of a great flood and an ark is believed to be the origin of the story of Noah's flood narrated in the biblical book of Genesis.

ca. 1800 B.C.E.: First taboos against eating pork develop in the Near East.

ca. 1850 B.C.E.: Judaism is founded by Abraham, a Mesopotamian prince.

ca. 1750 B.C.E.: Babylon's king Hammurabi dies.

ca. 1700 B.C.E.: Syria and Palestine develop the first alphabet; windmills first used by Babylonians.

ca. 1275 B.C.E.: Beginning of the 40-year-long Israelite migration from Egypt to the Near East, commonly called the Exodus and recorded in the Old Testament book of the same name.

ca. 1141 B.C.E.: The Jewish Ark of the Covenant is seized by the Philistines.

ca. 1124 B.C.E.: Nebuchadnezzar I becomes king of Babylon.

961 B.C.E.: The Great Temple of Jerusalem is constructed under the leadership of King Solomon.

ca. 800 B.C.E.: Babylonian astronomers discover how to predict lunar eclipses.

ca. 700 B.C.E.: Cities in the Near East build aqueducts to provide water to their populations.

ca. 689 B.C.E.: The Assyrians destroy the city of Babylon, but the city is rebuilt and in the next century is one of the great cities of the world.

ca. 600 B.C.E.: The religion Zoroastrianism found by Zoroaster in Persia.

ca. 587 B.C.E.: The Great Temple of Jerusalem is destroyed by Nebuchadnezzar; temple is rebuilt ca. 516 B.C.E.

ASIA AND THE PACIFIC

ca. 2205 B.C.E.: The Chinese become the first civilization to mill grain; sheep, oxen, dogs, pigs, and goats first domesticated in China.

ca. 2000 B.C.E.: Horses are first tamed by nomads on the Asian steppes.

ca. 1750 B.C.E.: In India two major historic cities, Harappa and Mohenjo Daro, collapse.

ca. 1500 B.C.E.: Aryan nomads arrive in India from the steppes of Eurasia, bringing with them cattle and sheep; Chinese begin to use vehicles drawn by horses.

ca. 1400 B.C.E.: China domesticates first poultry, the jungle fowl from Malaya.

ca. 1300 B.C.E.: Date assigned to the first evidence of Chinese writing.

ca. 1100 B.C.E.: The Chinese invent the crossbow and the kite and begin using ice for refrigeration.

ca. 1045 B.C.E.: Zhou Dynasty founded in China; the dynasty will last until approximately 256 B.C.E.

ca. 1000 B.C.E.: Polynesian expansion across the Pacific Ocean reaches Samoa and Tonga.

ca. 876 B.C.E.: The concept of zero first introduced in India.

ca. 700 B.C.E.: China introduces the concept of crop rotation.

ca. sixth century B.C.E.: Confucianism developed in China by philosopher Confucius (Kong Fuzi).

ca. 600 B.C.E.: The Upanishads, texts of Hinduism, are compiled in India.

ca. 565 B.C.E.: The Chinese philosopher Laozi founds the religious philosophy of Daoism.

ca. 528 B.C.E.: The religion of Buddhism wins its first adherents in India.

EUROPE

ca. 2000 B.C.E.: Seafarers from Crete and Phoenicia adopt sails and masts on ships.

ca. 1600 B.C.E.: Arrival of the Greeks in the Aegean region.

ca. 1500–ca. 1000 B.C.E.: Emergence of Celtic cultures in central Europe and the Balkans.

ca. 1470 B.C.E.: Minoan civilization in the Mediterranean Sea destroyed by volcanic eruption.

ca. 1200–ca. 800 B.C.E.: Hallstatt A and B cultures, of the Bronze Age, flourish in the region around present-day Austria.

ca. 1100 B.C.E.: Collapse of Mycenaean civilization; Iron Age begins in Europe, marked by the use of iron tools.

ca. 1100–ca. 750 B.C.E.: Greek Dark Ages.

ca. Eighth–seventh centuries B.C.E.: Homer writes/compiles Greek epics *The Iliad* and *The Odyssey*.

ca. 800–ca. 500 B.C.E.: Halstatt C and D cultures, of the Iron Age, arise in the region around present-day Austria.

ca. 776 B.C.E.: First ancient Olympic Games held in Greece.

ca. 753 B.C.E.: Traditional date of the founding of Rome, although archaeologists have found graves in Rome dating to at least a century earlier.

ca. 650–ca. 500 B.C.E.: Etruscan dominance of Rome, ending with Roman rebellion against Etruscans.

ca. 600 B.C.E.: Capitoline temple built in Rome.

ca. 525 B.C.E.: The Greek philosopher Pythagoras declares that the earth is round.

ca. 509 B.C.E.–ca. first century B.C.E.: Roman Republic.

ca. 508 B.C.E.: Beginning of democracy in Greece.

THE AMERICAS

ca. 2000 B.C.E.: Arctic ancestors of the Inuit begin to use small tools, especially the harpoon.

ca. 1800 B.C.E.: People in Peru first make pottery.

ca. 1600–ca. 1300 B.C.E.: Mounds constructed by peoples along the Mississippi River; best-known mound is Poverty Point.

ca. 1500–ca. 400 B.C.E.: Olmec civilization arises and flourishes in Mesoamerica.

ca. 1200 B.C.E.: The ancient ball game, the oldest-known game in the Americas, originates with the Olmec civilization.

ca. 1000 B.C.E.: Archaic Age ends in North America; cultivation of corn is introduced to North America from Mexico.

ca. 900–ca. 200 B.C.E.: The Chavín culture thrives in Peru.

ca. 800 B.C.E.: Pottery making emerges in Alaska; the temple center of Chavín de Huántar is established in Peru.

ca. 650 B.C.E.: The Maya begin using smoke to cure diseases.

	AFRICA	THE MIDDLE EAST
500 B.C.E. – 250 B.C.E.	**ca. 300 B.C.E.:** Carthaginians attain height of power and influence as traders and shipbuilders; date assigned to Namoratunga, a cluster of stone pillars in Kenya that may have served as a calendar; museum and Great Library are founded at Alexandria, Egypt. **ca. 280 B.C.E.:** Ptolemy II of Egypt completes a canal between the Mediterranean Sea and the Red Sea. **ca. 264 B.C.E.:** Beginning of the Punic Wars between Rome and Carthage.	**ca. 420 B.C.E.:** The Nabataeans establish a kingdom at Petra, in present-day Jordan. **ca. 311 B.C.E.:** The start of the Seleucid Empire, which rules Babylonia and Syria.
250 B.C.E. – 0	**ca. 250 B.C.E.:** Dromedaries are introduced into Egypt. **ca. 200 B.C.E.:** Formation of kingdom of Axum in northern Ethiopia. **ca. 146 B.C.E.:** Carthage falls to the Roman invaders, marking the end of the Third Punic War.	**ca. 66–ca. 73 B.C.E.:** The first great revolt of the Jews of Judea against the Romans, during which legions under Titus destroyed Jerusalem, looting and burning Herod's Temple. **37 B.C.E.:** Herod the Great is made king of Judea by the Romans. **7 B.C.E.:** Jesus of Nazareth born in Bethlehem; historians arrive at this date based on astronomical records.
0 – 250 C.E.	**ca. 100s C.E.:** The Bantu use iron utensils for cooking, iron spearheads for hunting, and iron hooks for fishing. **ca. 150 C.E.:** Kingdom of Meroë goes into decline from competition with the rival kingdom of Axum. **ca. 200 C.E.:** Kingdom of Ghana, a major gold producer, flourishes.	**33 C.E.:** Jesus Christ is condemned to death and crucified in Jerusalem; Christian religion founded. **ca. 50:** Farmers in Near East (and China) first begin using silos for grain storage. **67:** The apostle Paul, the leading member of the new Christian faith, is executed on June 29. **132–135:** The second (sometimes called the third) Jewish revolt against the Roman Empire; after this revolt the emperor Hadrian roots out Jews and Judaism from Judea and bars Jews from Jerusalem. **ca. 224:** Sassanian Dynasty begins in Persia and will rule until 651.

ASIA AND THE PACIFIC

ca. 475 B.C.E.: Beginning of the Iron Age in China.

ca. 400 B.C.E.: The Chinese become the first to use catapults in warfare.

ca. 301 B.C.E.: Nomadic tribes invade parts of northern China; Chinese construct a massive irrigation system to relieve flooding in river basins in Sichuan.

ca. 300 B.C.E.–ca. 300 C.E.: Yayoi Period in Japan; religion called Shinto may have originated during this period, though the matter is disputed.

ca. 221 B.C.E.: Qin Dynasty founded in China; country united.

ca. 202 B.C.E.: Han Dynasty begins in China.

ca. 101 B.C.E.: Using a compass for the first time, Chinese seafarers arrive on the eastern coast of India.

ca. 6 C.E.: People in China who want jobs as government officials have to take a civil service examination.

ca. 31: Earliest description of a Chinese horizontal waterwheel.

ca. 80: A massive migration of Asians moves westward with horses and cattle to join the Iranians and Mongols to become the Huns.

ca. 100: Japan imports rice for cultivation from China.

ca. 105: China develops the first paper made from fibers.

ca. 200: Japan invades and subdues Korea.

EUROPE

ca. 500 B.C.E.: Portions of Greece become the first to use coins.

ca. 480 B.C.E.–ca. 1 C.E.: La Tène culture, a Celtic Iron Age culture, emerges in the area of modern-day Switzerland, and the Celts expand through much of Europe.

ca. 457–ca. 429 B.C.E.: The "Golden Age" of Athens under the rule of Pericles.

ca. 450 B.C.E.: Celts arrive in the British Isles.

ca. 440 B.C.E.: The first textbook of geometry written by the Greek Hippocrates of Chios.

ca. 323–ca. 31 B.C.E.: Hellenistic Period of Greece.

ca. 312 B.C.E.: Construction on Roman Appian Way begins.

ca. 270 B.C.E.: Rome brings all of Italian Peninsula under its authority.

ca. 250 B.C.E.: Greek mathematician Archimedes calculates value of pi and develops the screw for pumping water.

ca. 170 B.C.E.: Rome builds the world's first paved streets.

58–51 B.C.E.: Julius Caesar subdues Gaul (France) in the name of the Roman Empire.

1st century B.C.E.–476 C.E.: Roman Empire.

55 B.C.E.–43 C.E.: Roman Empire invades Britain twice, and Roman domination and influence grow through trade and other interactions; city of London founded.

60s: First revolts against Roman rule by Germanic and Celtic tribes.

64: Great Fire destroys much of Rome; first persecutions of Christians.

75–77: Roman conquest of Britain is complete.

ca.138–ca. 192: Period of the so-called Antonine plague, a series of epidemics in the Roman world, including two notable outbreaks in 165 and 180.

167: The first Barbarian attacks on Rome.

THE AMERICAS

ca. 500 B.C.E.: Adena culture of the North American Midwest reaches its peak; date of the Maya story of creation, the Popol Vuh; the Cuspisnique build roads exclusively with walls.

ca. 400 B.C.E.: The Mayans begin using jugs with spouts.

ca. 400 B.C.E.–150 C.E.: Preclassic Period of Mayan civilization.

ca. 200 B.C.E.–ca. 600 B.C.E.: The Nazca create hundreds of earth drawings, or geoglyphs, that can been seen only from the air.

ca. 100 B.C.E.: Hopewell societies, especially in Illinois and Ohio, flourish; pottery from Peru and Ecuador shows the presence of facial ulceration, scarring, and malformation of the mucous membranes among the pre-Inca, an indication of epidemic *leishmaniasis*.

ca. 1 C.E.: Hohokam culture forms in U.S. Southwest; Toltec city of Teotihuacán founded.

ca. 50 C.E.: The city of Teotihuacán establishes control in the valley of Mexico; construction of the Pyramid of the Sun begins.

ca. 100–600: The Moche people flourish in northern Peru.

ca. 150–650: Classic Period of Mayan civilization.

250 c.e. – 500 c.e.

AFRICA

343 c.e.: King Ezana of Axum is converted to Christianity by Egyptian missionaries.

ca. 350: Kingdom of Axum defeats kingdom of Kush.

439 c.e.: Vandals capture the city of Carthage and establish a kingdom.

THE MIDDLE EAST

ca. 370: The Sassanian Dynasty attains the height of its power under the leadership of Shāpūr II.

ca. 460: Famine strikes the Sassanian Empire.

ASIA AND THE PACIFIC

ca. 280 c.e.: China is reunified under the Western Jin Dynasty.

ca. 300–ca. 538: Kofun Period in Japan.

ca. 320: Northern India unified by the Gupta Dynasty.

ca. 375 c.e.: Stirrups are invented in China.

ca. 450: The Chinese invent ink, made from lampblack.

EUROPE

313: Emperor Constantine I of Rome converts to Christianity and declares it the official religion of the empire.

330: Foundation of Constantinople by Emperor Constantine I of Rome.

ca. 360: Invasion of Europe by the Huns.

391: Roman emperor Theodosius I makes Christianity the sole legal religion of the Roman Empire.

410: Rome besieged by Visigoths under the command of Alaric.

ca. 430: Angles and Saxons from Denmark invade the eastern portion of Britain; the bubonic plague strikes Europe for the first time.

455: Vandals sack Rome.

476: The Roman Empire falls when the last of the Roman emperors in the West, Romulus Augustus, is deposed and not replaced.

THE AMERICAS

ca. 400 c.e.: The sacred site of Serpent Mound is created by the Hopewell culture in present-day Ohio.

General Bibliography

GENERAL

Adas, Michael, ed. *Agricultural and Pastoral Societies in Ancient and Classical History*. Philadelphia: Temple University Press, 2001.

Bahn, Paul G. *The Atlas of World Archaeology*. New York: Checkmark Books, 2000.

Bauer, Susan Wise. *The History of the Ancient World: From the Earliest Accounts to the Fall of Rome*. New York: W. W. Norton, 2007.

Bogucki, Peter. *The Origins of Human Society*. Malden, Mass., and Oxford, U.K.: Blackwell Publishers, 1999.

Clark, J. Desmond, and Steven A. Brandt, eds. *From Hunters to Farmers*. Berkeley: University of California Press, 1984.

Nagle, D. Brendan. *The Ancient World: A Social and Cultural History*, 6th ed. Upper Saddle River, N.J.: Prentice Hall, 2006.

Scarre, Christopher. *The Human Past: World Prehistory and the Development of Human Societies*. London: Thames and Hudson, 2005.

AFRICA

Boonzaier, Emile, ed. *Cape Herders: History of Khoikhoi of Southern Africa*. Athens: Ohio University Press, 1997.

Connah, Graham. *African Civilizations: An Archaeological Perspective*, 2nd edition. Cambridge, U.K.: Cambridge University Press, 2001.

Davis, R. Hunt Jr., ed. *Encyclopedia of African History and Culture*. Vol. 1: *Ancient Africa (Prehistory to 500 CE)*. New York: Facts On File, 2005.

Ehret, Christopher. *An African Classical Age: Eastern and Southern Africa in World History, 1000 B.C. to A.D. 400*. Charlottesville: University Press of Virginia, 1998.

Ehret, Christopher. *The Civilizations of Africa: A History to 1800*. Oxford, U.K.: James Currey, 2002.

Ehret, Christopher. *Sudanic Civilization*. Washington, D.C.: American Historical Association, 2003.

Hall, Martin. *Farmers, Kings, and Traders: The People of Southern Africa, 200–1860*. Chicago: University of Chicago Press, 1990.

Phillipson, David W. *African Archaeology*, 3rd edition. Cambridge, U.K.: Cambridge University Press, 2005.

Schoenbrun, David. *A Green Place, a Good Place: Agrarian Change, Gender, and Social Identity in the Great Lakes Region to the 15th Century*. Portsmouth, N.H.: Heinemann, 1998.

Strigner, Chris, and Robin McKie. *African Exodus: The Origins of Modern Humanity*. New York: Henry Holt, 1997.

Vansina, Jan. *How Societies Are Born: Governance in West Central Africa before 1600*. Charlottesville: University of Virginia Press, 2004.

Vansina, Jan. *Paths in the Rainforests: Toward a History of Political Tradition in Equatorial Africa*. Madison: University of Wisconsin Press, 1990.

Vogel, Joseph O., ed. *Encyclopedia of Precolonial Africa: Archaeology, History, Languages, Cultures, and Environments*. Walnut Creek, Calif.: AltaMira Press, 1997.

EGYPT

Baines, John, and Jaromir Malek. *Cultural Atlas of Ancient Egypt*. New York: Facts On File, 2000.

Bard, Kathryn, ed. *Encyclopedia of the Archaeology of Ancient Egypt*. London and New York: Routledge, 1999

Bunson, Margaret R. *Encyclopedia of Ancient Egypt*, rev. ed. New York: Facts On File, 2002.

David, Rosalie A. *Handbook to Life in Ancient Egypt*, rev. ed. New York: Facts On File, 2003.

Grimal, Nicolas-Christophe. *A History of Ancient Egypt*. Translated by Ian Shaw. Cambridge, Mass.: Blackwell, 1992.

Hornung, Erik. *History of Ancient Egypt: An Introduction*. Translated by David Lorton. Ithaca, N.Y.: Cornell University Press, 1999.

Hornung, Erik. *The Secret Lore of Egypt*. Translated by David Lorton. Ithaca, N.Y.: Cornell University Press, 2001.

Hornung, Erik, Rolf Krauss, and David A. Warburton. *Ancient Egyptian Chronology*. Leiden, Netherlands, and Boston: Brill, 2006.

Lichtheim, Miriam. *Ancient Egyptian Literature: A Book of Readings*. Berkeley: University of California Press, 2006.

Loprieno, Antonio. *Ancient Egyptian: A Linguistic Introduction*. New York: Cambridge University Press, 1995.

Manley, Bill. *The Penguin Historical Atlas of Ancient Egypt*. London and New York: Penguin Books, 1996.

Quirke, Stephen, and Jeffrey Spencer. *The British Museum Book of Ancient Egypt.* New York: Thames and Hudson, 1992.

Redford, Donald B., ed. *The Oxford Encyclopedia of Ancient Egypt.* Oxford and New York: Oxford University Press, 2000.

Shaw, Ian, ed. *The Oxford History of Ancient Egypt.* Oxford, U.K.: Oxford University Press, 2000.

Simpson, William Kelly, ed. *The Literature of Ancient Egypt: An Anthology of Stories, Instructions, and Poetry.* New Haven, Conn., and London: Yale University Press, 2003.

THE MIDDLE EAST

Aruz, Joan. *Art of the First Cities: The Third Millennium BC from the Mediterranean to the Indus.* New York: Metropolitan Museum of Art, 2003.

Bertman, Stephen. *Handbook to Life in Ancient Mesopotamia.* New York: Facts On File, 2003.

Bryce, Trevor. *The Kingdom of the Hittites.* Oxford, U.K.: Oxford University Press, 2005.

Due, Andrea, and M. Chesi. *The Atlas of the Bible Lands: History, Daily Life and Traditions.* New York: Peter Bedrick, 2001.

Frankfort, Henri. *The Art and Architecture of the Ancient Orient,* 5th ed. New Haven, Conn.: Yale University Press, 1996.

Kuhrt, Amelie. *The Ancient Near East, c. 3000–330 BC.* London: Routledge, 1995.

Leick, Gwendolyn. *Who's Who in the Ancient Near East.* London: Routledge, 2002.

Postgate, J. N. *Early Mesopotamia: Society and Economy at the Dawn of History.* London: Routledge, 1992.

Potts, D. T. *The Arabian Gulf in Antiquity.* Vol. 1: *From Prehistory to the Fall of the Achaemenid Empire.* Vol. 2: *From Alexander the Great to the Coming of Islam.* Oxford, U.K.: Clarendon Press, 1990.

Roaf, Michael. *Cultural Atlas of Mesopotamia and the Ancient Near East.* Oxford, U.K.: Equinox, 1990.

Snell, Daniel C. *Life in the Ancient Near East, 3100–332 BC.* New Haven: Yale University Press, 1998.

Wilkinson, T. J. *Archaeological Landscapes of the Near East.* Tucson: University of Arizona Press, 2003.

ASIA AND THE PACIFIC

Auboyer, Jeannine. *Daily Life in Ancient India: From 200 BC to 700 AD.* Translated by Simon Watson Taylor. London: Phoenix, 2002.

Chang, K.C. *Art, Myth, and Ritual: The Path to Political Authority in Ancient China.* Cambridge, Mass.: Harvard University Press, 1983.

Di Cosmo, Nicola. *Ancient China and Its Enemies: The Rise of Nomadic Power in East Asian History.* Cambridge, U.K.: Cambridge University Press, 2002.

Drège, Jean-Pierre, and Emil Bührer. *The Silk Road Saga.* New York: Facts On File, 1989.

Habu, Junko. *Ancient Jomon of Japan.* Cambridge, U.K.: Cambridge University Press, 2004.

Higham, Charles F. W. *The Bronze Age of Southeast Asia.* Cambridge, U.K.: Cambridge University Press, 1996.

Higham, Charles F. W. *Encyclopedia of Ancient Asian Civilizations.* New York: Facts On File, 2004.

Lewis, Mark Edward. *The Early Chinese Empires: Qin and Han.* Cambridge, Mass.: Harvard University Press, 2007.

Lilley, Ian, ed. *The Archaeology of Oceania: Australia and the Pacific Islands.* Malden, Mass.: Blackwell, 2006.

Loewe, Michael. *Everyday Life in Early Imperial China: During the Han Period, 202 BC–AD 200.* Indianapolis: Hackett, 2005.

Loewe, Michael, and Edward L. Shaughnessy, eds. *The Cambridge History of Ancient China: From the Origins of Civilization to 221 BC.* Cambridge, U.K.: Cambridge University Press, 1999.

Possehl, Gregory. *The Indus Civilization: A Contemporary Perspective.* Walnut Creek, Calif.: Altamira, 2002.

Sinor, Denis, ed. *The Cambridge History of Early Inner Asia.* Cambridge, U.K.: Cambridge University Press, 1990.

Thapar, Romila. *Early India: From the Origins to AD 1300.* Berkeley: University of California Press, 2002.

EUROPE

Aldhouse-Green, Miranda J. *Dying for the Gods: Human Sacrifice in Iron Age and Roman Europe.* Stroud, U.K.: Tempus, 2001.

Audouze, Françoise, and Olivier Buchsenschutz. *Towns, Villages, and Countryside of Celtic Europe: From the Beginning of the Second Millennium to the End of the First Century BC.* London: B. T. Batsford, 1992.

Bogucki, Peter, and Pam J. Crabtree. *Ancient Europe 8000 B.C.–A.D. 1000: An Encyclopedia of the Barbarian World.* New York: Charles Scribner's Sons, 2004.

Castleden, Rodney. *The Stonehenge People. An Exploration of Life in Neolithic Britain, 4700–2000 BC.* New York: Routledge, 1990.

Cunliffe, Barry W. *The Oxford Illustrated Prehistory of Europe.* Oxford, U.K. and New York: Oxford University Press, 1994.

Cunliffe, Barry W. *The Ancient Celts.* Oxford, U.K. and New York: Oxford University Press, 1997.

Fowler, Brenda. *Iceman: Uncovering the Life and Times of a Prehistoric Man Found in an Alpine Glacier.* New York: Random House, 2000.

Glob, P. V. *The Bog People: Iron Age Man Preserved.* Ithaca, N.Y.: Cornell University Press, 1969.

Harding, Anthony F. *European Societies in the Bronze Age.* Cambridge, U.K.: Cambridge University Press, 2000.

Hedeager, Lotte. *Iron-Age Societies: From Tribe to State in Northern Europe, 500 BC to AD 700.* Malden, Mass., and Oxford, U.K.: Blackwell, 1992.

James, Simon. *The World of the Celts.* London and New York: Thames and Hudson, 1993.

Laing, Lloyd Robert. *The Archaeology of Celtic Britain and Ireland, c. 400–1200 AD.* Cambridge, U.K.: Cambridge University Press, 2006.

Malone, Caroline. *Neolithic Britain and Ireland.* Stroud, U.K.: Tempus, 2001.

McIntosh, Jane. *Handbook to Life in Prehistoric Europe.* New York: Facts On File, 2006.

Moffat, Alistair. *Before Scotland: The Story of Scotland before History.* London: Thames and Hudson, 2005.

Piggott, Stuart. *Ancient Europe: From the Beginnings of Agriculture to Classical Antiquity: A Survey.* Edinburgh, U.K.: University Press, 1965.

Scarre, Christopher. *Exploring Prehistoric Europe.* New York: Oxford University Press, 1998.

Waldman, Carl, and Catherine Mason. *Encyclopedia of European Peoples.* New York: Facts On File, 2006.

Wells, Peter S. *The Barbarians Speak: How the Conquered Peoples Shaped Roman Europe.* Princeton, N.J.: Princeton University Press, 1999.

GREECE

Adkins, Lesley, and Roy Adkins. *Handbook to Life in Ancient Greece.* New York: Facts On File, 2005.

Camp, John. *The Archaeology of Athens.* New Haven, Conn.: Yale University Press, 2001.

Camp, John, and Elizabeth Fisher. *Exploring the World of the Ancient Greeks.* London: Thames and Hudson, 2002.

Cartledge, Paul. *The Cambridge Illustrated History of Ancient Greece.* New York: Cambridge University Press, 2002.

Finley, M. I. *The Ancient Greeks,* 2nd ed. New York: Penguin, 1991.

Garland, Robert. *Daily Life of the Ancient Greeks.* Westport, Conn.: Greenwood Press, 1998.

Green, Peter. *Ancient Greece: A Concise History,* 2nd ed. New York: Thames and Hudson, 1980.

Lassieur, Allison. *The Ancient Greeks.* New York: Franklin Watts, 2004.

Pedley, John G. *Greek Art and Archaeology,* 3rd ed. Upper Saddle River, N.J.: Prentice Hall, 2002.

Sacks, David. *Encyclopedia of the Ancient Greek World,* rev. ed. by Lisa R. Brody. New York: Facts On File, 2005.

Shuter, Jane. *Life in Ancient Athens.* Chicago: Heinemann Library, 2005.

Sparkes, Brian A., ed. *Greek Civilization: An Introduction.* Malden, Mass.: Blackwell Publishers, 1998.

Taylor, Pat. *The Ancient Greeks.* Chicago: Heinemann Library, 2007.

ROME

Adkins, Lesley, and Roy Adkins. *Handbook to Life in Ancient Rome.* New York: Facts On File, 2004.

Aldrete, Gregory S. *Daily Life in the Roman City: Rome, Pompeii, and Ostia.* Westport, Conn.: Greenwood Press, 2004.

Alston, Richard. *Aspects of Roman History, AD 14–117.* New York: Routledge, 1998.

Bunson, Matthew. *Encyclopedia of the Roman Empire,* rev. ed. New York: Facts On File, 2002.

Chrisp, Peter. *Ancient Rome.* New York: DK Publishing, 2007.

Coulston, Jon, and Hazel Dodge, eds. *Ancient Rome: The Archaeology of the Eternal City.* Oxford, U.K.: Oxford University School of Archaeology, 2000.

Hodge, Susie. *Ancient Roman Art.* Des Plaines, Ill.: Heinemann Library, 2006.

Jay, David. *Ancient Romans.* Brookfield, Conn.: Copper Beech Books, 2000.

Kleiner, Fred S. *A History of Roman Art.* Belmont, Calif.: Thomson Wadsworth, 2007.

Nardo, Don. *Ancient Rome.* San Diego: Kidhaven Press, 2002.

Ramage, Nancy, and Andrew Ramage. *Roman Art: Romulus to Constantine,* 4th ed. Upper Saddle River, N.J.: Pearson Prentice Hall, 2005.

Reece, Katherine. *The Romans.* Vero Beach, Fla.: Rourke Publishing, 2006.

Rees, Rosemary. *The Ancient Romans,* rev. ed. Chicago: Heinemann Library, 2006.

THE AMERICAS

Adams, Richard E. W., and Murdo J. MacLeod, eds. *The Cambridge History of the Native Peoples of the Americas.* Vol. 2: *Mesoamerica.* New York: Cambridge University Press, 2000.

Calloway, Colin G. *One Vast Winter Count: The Native American West before Lewis and Clark.* Lincoln: University of Nebraska Press, 2003.

Coe, Michael D., and Rex Koontz. *Mexico, From the Olmecs to the Aztecs,* 5th ed. New York: Thames and Hudson, 2002.

Evans, Susan Toby. *Ancient Mexico and Central America: Archaeology and Culture History.* New York: Thames and Hudson, 2004.

Foster, Lynn V. *Handbook to Life in the Ancient Maya World.* New York: Facts On File, 2002.

Josephy, Alvin M. Jr. *500 Nations: An Illustrated History of North American Indians.* New York: Grammercy, 2002.

Mann, Charles C. *1491: New Revelations of the Americas before Columbus.* New York: Knopf, 2005.

Moseley, Michael E. *The Incas and Their Ancestors: The Archaeology of Peru,* rev. ed. New York: Thames and Hudson, 2001.

Pohl, John M. D. *Exploring Mesoamerica.* New York: Oxford University Press, 1999.

Salomon, Frank, and Stuart B. Schwartz. *The Cambridge History of the Native Peoples of the Americas,* Vol. 3: *South America.* New York: Cambridge University Press, 1999.

Silverman, Helaine, ed. *Andean Archaeology.* Malden, Mass.: Blackwell Publishing, 2004.

Thomas, David Hurst. *Exploring Ancient Native America: An Archaeological Guide.* New York: Routledge, 1999.

Trigger, Bruce G., and Wilcomb E. Washburn, eds. *The Cambridge History of the Native Peoples of the Americas.* Vol. 1: *North America.* New York: Cambridge University Press, 1996.

von Hagen, Adriana, and Craig Morris. *The Cities of the Ancient Andes.* New York: Thames and Hudson, 1998.

Index